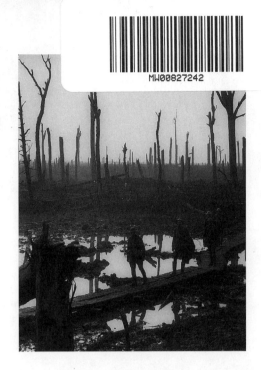

The Great War Reader

NUMBER FOUR
C. A. Brannen Series

The Great War Reader

Edited by James Hannah

FOREWORD BY FRANK E. VANDIVER

TEXAS A&M UNIVERSITY PRESS

College Station

The paper used in this book meets
the minimum requirements
of the American National Standard
for Permanence of Paper for
Printed Library Materials, z39.48-1984.
Binding materials have been chosen for durability.
♾

Frontispiece: A British padre praying over a dying German, near Ephey, Sept. 18, 1918. Photograph courtesy the Imperial War Museum, London, neg. Q.11,336.

Library of Congress Cataloging-in-Publication Data

The Great War Reader / edited by James Hannah ; foreword by Frank E. Vandiver.
    p. cm. — (C. A. Brannen series ; no. 4)
  Includes bibliographical references and index.
  ISBN 0-89096-908-6 (cloth); 0-89096-944-2 (pbk.)
  1. World War, 1914–1918 — United States.   I. Hannah, James, 1951–   II. C. A.
Brannen series ; 4.

D570.G74 2000
940.4'1273 — dc21   99-047316

For

THESE WOUNDED

William V. Henderson
Company I, 9th Infantry

Tom Hannah
Company B, 345 Machine Gun Battalion

THESE DEAD

William Hannah
Royal Scots Fusiliers

John D. Hannay
Canadians

Douglas R. M. Hannay
Royal Marines Light Infantry

and the other 37,500,000 casualties of war
lux perpetua luceat eis

The minstrel boy to the war is gone;
In the ranks of death you will find him.
His father's sword he has girded on
And his wild harp slung behind him.

"Land of song," said the Warrior Bard,
"Though all the world betrays thee.
One sword at least thy rights shall guard;
One faithful heart shall praise thee."
— *The Minstrel Boy,* a traditional song

Contents

Part Four: Poetry

Illustrations

Foreword

Anthologies come and go, a kind of ephemera on the edges of history and literature. They often serve well as refreshers, classroom additives, and appetizers, but they fade into their contents. James Hannah's *The Great War Reader* is different — it will persist as a solid contribution on its own.

Hannah has chosen a tough subject for anthology — the First World War, a.k.a. the Great War, the War to End All Wars, the Kaiser's War. Several things make this conflict difficult to anthologize: it is almost a forgotten war, especially in the United States, where it fell between the Civil War and the Second World War; its effects were so mammoth as to defy appreciation; its wages so awful in blood and treasure as to numb memory; its legacies so many as to overwhelm comprehension.

One of its legacies rose above carnage and catastrophe in efforts to hold them for the future, to remind humanity how low it could sink. That legacy was literature. All wars spawn an aftermath of works, but the Great War produced special recollection because it came at the height of hope to damn optimism and shame morality.

Many of the best words came from participants, a good many from men and women who never wrote before. Hannah offers a splendid sampling of soldiers' and nurses' memories — Edmund Blunden's fine *Undertones of War* is well sampled; Guy Chapman's often lyrical *A Passionate Prodigality* sets off May Wedderburn Cannan's "Rouen." The grinding bravery of the PBI (poor bloody infantry) glosses much of the memories, especially Frederic Manning's *The Middle Parts of Fortune,* Chapman's words, and Erich Maria Remarque's classic *All Quiet on the Western Front.* Terrors of the trenches wracked the best of men, and a new disease finally was recognized: shell shock. W. H. R. Rivers, a psychiatrist who served at Craiglockhart Hospital near Edinburgh, helped confirm the malady and saved many — including Siegfried Sassoon and Wilfred Owen, each of whom has an excerpt in this book.

After the fighting came novelists and historians, to trade on what had been remembered, to perspectivize it, and to make it into much it had not been. Against the travails of the common soldier, Alan Clark's *The Donkeys* ("Winter in the Trenches") parodies the generals, the staff, and officers. But a few participants remembered better of their leaders. And some historians cherished recollections from soldiers that were shaped into revelations—Lyn Macdonald's *Somme* ("Assault on High Wood") eloquently tells the story of how the war went in one of its great battles. Alistair Horne's *The Price of Glory* ("Fort Vaux") beckons reality as France suffers in the throes of a terrible winnowing of men. Marc Bloch, a pioneering interdisciplinary historian whose work changed the way of looking at history, served a highly decorated stint in the French infantry from 1914 to 1919. His *Memoirs of War, 1914—1915* gives graphic testimony to the dailiness of terror.

Out of such a cauldron of emotional chaos, surely poetry must have been quenched. Quite the opposite—poetry is one of the great strains in the war's literary legacy. From Rupert Brooke's patriotic "The Soldier," with the well-known opening "If I should die, think only this of me . . . " to Siegfried Sassoon's antiwar "Suicide in the Trenches," ending angrily with "Sneak home and pray you'll never know/The hell where youth and laughter go," poetic selections sparkle in Hannah's collection.

Broadly, boldly, inclusively conceived, James Hannah's *The Great War Reader* touches all sides and most places and concentrates the Great War's remembrance into a distillation of bravery, anger, squalor, disgust, madness, death, and humanity at once stunning and sobering.

Follow these pages into an experience to stay with you always.

—Frank E. Vandiver

There were many words that you could not
stand to hear and finally only the names of
places had dignity. . . . Abstract words such
as glory, honor, courage, or hallow were
obscene beside . . . the names of rivers, the
numbers of regiments and dates.

— Ernest Hemingway

Preface

The war at the beginning of the twentieth century indelibly marked all that came after it. Called by some an insanity, the collective suicide of Europe, the Great War established a very real boundary between the old ways of seeing institutions' and individuals' responsibilities to one another and a modernity best characterized by its attitudes of irony and skepticism.

The magnitude of the war measured in dead, wounded, and missing provided the twentieth century with its first collective sigh of despair. The old military tactics and antiquated generalship of nineteenth century cavalrymen married to the latest in research and development of the second wave of industrialization produced millions of tableaux in which the vulnerability of flesh yielded to the onslaught of iron, fire, and poison gas. Some modern historians argue that the most overused word in the literature of this war is *horror.* If that is so, then the blank created by its deletion from the vocabulary must come in conjunction with such words as *unspeakable* and *incomprehensible.* Better, then, to use a Victorian literary convention: When we speak of the war, we should insert a "———" to protect ourselves from taking offense.

After the seemingly miraculous way in which the Allies frustrated the Germans's inflexible Schlieffen Plan, which sought to bring a rapid end to the war in the west with a sweeping enveloping maneuver through Belgium and into Paris in just a few short weeks, the war on the western front settled into that essential anathema of modern generals: static, entrenched front lines. Men hunkered down in almost paralyzing fear along a virtually unbroken line extending nearly four hundred miles from the English Channel to

Switzerland as millions of artillery shells pounded them and the countryside into a sterile wasteland more surreal than any poet could ever have imagined.

Both sides went to great lengths in an effort to break the stalemate. The Germans introduced the concept of strategic bombing by sending Zeppelins and airplanes against English cities. Their scientists developed flamethrowers and introduced poison gas. Allied scientists countered every move. Chlorine gave way to phosgene and mustard gasses. The soldier's first protection was a urine-soaked handkerchief held over nose and mouth. By the war's end, respirators had become sophisticated enough to prevent most gas casualties. But the use of gas launched from cylinders or artillery shells became a fixed idea in the minds of a few future statesmen who saw it as a cheap way to murder the masses. If nuclear weapons had been available to the national leaders of 1917–18, they probably would have been used — anything to break the static front that ceaselessly consumed men and materiel.

All along the western front the armies tried to move without success. In 1915, the English orchestrated the world's first large-scale amphibious invasion on the Gallipoli Peninsula to bolster their faltering Russian ally and to draw off German troops from the western front. By the beginning of 1916, this too had failed miserably. Generals on both sides fantasized about achieving a massive breakthrough in which the enemy's front was punctured or his flanks rolled up, followed by a decisive dash to Paris or to the Rhine. In the English version of the dream, men on horseback, sabers glinting in the Flemish sunlight, push in after the infantry forces the gap. Cavalry dashing to victory. But no such breakthrough occurred until the very end, when the Allies launched a gigantic counterthrust after the failed German offensive of 1918. Even then there were no heroic mounted charges. Cavalry would hardly have been worth a moment's notice to field artillery and machine-gun platoons. Sometimes attackers managed to penetrate enemy lines and advance thousands of yards, even several miles. But the soldiers eventually outdistanced their support and supplies. More often than not, an offensive went nowhere. In 1915 and 1916, especially, men died for parcels of land no greater than their outstretched bodies.

Always for us there are the images in our minds' eyes — so much a part of distant memory that they have become rote and, most amazing of all, perversely romantic: Endless trench lines, barbed wire, machine guns, clouds of gas, and geysers of upheaved earth. Viewed from above, the zigzagging trench systems look appropriately like clumsy suturing on the blasted landscape. Yet it was a surgery that the rest of the century would prove had failed to resolve the international rivalries that caused the first of its great wars.

The Great War murdered romanticism, finishing off what the nineteenth century had begun. It proved a crippling blow to the remnants of the Enlightenment that had lasted for two centuries. If the world of men is perfectible, science and technology may not provide the means without the sharpened double-edged sword. The war provided the elements of existential alienation. A soldier couldn't trust his commanding officers. Field officers couldn't trust the general staff. No one could trust the prevaricating journalists or politicians. Faiths were lost: faith in a Christianity that put God on both sides, faith in nationalistic propaganda, and faith in an adequate definition of what mankind really was after men demonstrated what they were capable of doing to one another.

The British Empire began ailing at Lone Pine on the Gallipoli Peninsula and numerous other places where colonial troops felt themselves used up in a cause half a world away from their homes in Australia and New Zealand. The empire's expiration would be long and tedious, but July 1, 1916, the first day of the Somme offensive, produced the mortal ailment's first gut-wrenching pains. Woodrow Wilson's America rose up from the pulverized chalk of France and stepped onto the world stage. Despite Wilson's desire to enter as a peacemaker, the United States came in instead as the last, best hope of the Old World, tapping a seemingly endless supply of men and materiel.

The war provided some ugly lessons. The Germans saw how the Turks got away with genocide in Armenia while the rest of the world looked away. Some postwar military strategists believed the airplane and aerial bombardment, which had figured so little during World War I, would play a decisive role in future conflicts. Above all else, there was the realization that, given the scope of annihilation and the reluctance ever again to stagnate in despicable trenches, war would have to be swift and dynamic—full, in a way, of the terrible French idealism of élan vital. The German blitzkrieg a generation later was massive and swift, spearheaded by bombers and tanks with mobilized troop insertions by truck and parachute. Worst of all, civilians became legitimate targets of war. No longer was a front defined as a stationary zone where soldiers murdered themselves while civilians went about their lives. The Zeppelin bombardment of Liège, which killed mostly civilians, was only three decades removed from the London blitz, Dresden, and Hiroshima.

The Hall of Mirrors at Versailles becomes an appropriate emblem for the sleight-of-hand practiced on the world map that parceled out geographical dispensations with criminal carelessness. Some historians would agree that such rough handling of ethnic divisions—and the brandishing of blind hatreds that wished to undermine the enemies' futures economically in ways the war had not—sowed the seeds for another, even bigger world war. That war was simply a devastating continuation of the Great War, with but a brief respite for sons to obtain manhood and industries to be refurbished, retooled, and modernized.

Two diabolical systems of totalitarianism emerged from the First World War. In 1917, Russia's weak and insipid Nicholas II fell victim to his lineage's inability to adjust to modernity and the Bolsheviks seized control from more moderate factions supporting reform. In Germany, Adolf Hitler enraged himself with the idea that his beloved army and nation had been stabbed in the back by the military elite who, having never admitted their defeats to the public, unwittingly allowed their nationalistic propaganda to become the gassed Bavarian corporal's cue to step on stage.

Now, at century's end, it is wise to look back and calculate the costs. To attempt a consideration of the value and potential impact of the war's dead on the twentieth century is to form a conundrum that staggers the imagination. However, another way to calculate the war's impact is to consider what it meant to those who came after 1918. Paul Fussell says that we gained a sense of irony that helps us to recall events, an aid to memorialization, and thus provides a buffer between the cruelties of existence and the possibilities of living within those exigencies. But attendant to irony is cynicism and despair. When nothing is trusted beyond the frail self's interest, hardened by an ironic perspective, what is left of community but a gathering of skeptics willing to believe the worst of a situation? No wonder modern life is filled with conspiracy theories. When governments, the press, politicians, and religious leaders prove they can't be trusted, any humbug may be possible.

Heirs to the Great War's impact, we come to the end of the twentieth century full of irony and distrust. The Balkans remain a problem. However, the answer for some has been the continually shrugged shoulder. The instability of the former Soviet Union is reminiscent of the doddering czars and the declining Austro-Hungarian and Ottoman Empires of 1914. The heritage of colonial dilemmas haunts the world political stage, and the unsatisfactory partitioning of the Near East still threatens international stability. New leaders, unknowingly schooled by the Great War, have inherited a zeal for cheap weapons of mass destruction created from chemical and biological compounds.

The Great War and the subsequent reactions to it helped define the essentials of what *modern* means in terms of its impact on people, countries, and institutions. If sophistication is our legacy and skepticism our shibboleth, then perhaps one of the most worthwhile endeavors to emerge from the war is Wilson's League of Nations and its somewhat crude offspring, the United Nations. If modernity is also an ecumenical response to nations' problems, if what naturalist Aldo Leopold once said — that the most important discovery of the century is the complex linking of everything — is true, then perhaps violent excesses can be remedied by an amalgamation of skepticism with some belief in ourselves that transcends national chauvinism.

However, it would be a pity not to recall the painful lessons that got us through a century that began with so much promise so quickly obliterated. After the demise of a defensive strategy so macabre as to be called MAD

(Mutual Assured Destruction) and the cancellation of that most obscene of weapons, the neutron bomb, which would save buildings but murder their inhabitants, we owe all those who once stood firm in the face of impossible odds in memorialized and forgotten places a debt of respect. It is our duty to attempt to understand who they were, what they thought, and how they tried to survive in the Armageddon that shaped their lives and our world.

This book began twenty years ago, when, as a young writer, I was introduced to my spouse's uncle, Bill Henderson. I'm sure the family had listened to him before, grown used to his stories, and come to ignore them. I'm sure he had said enough often enough that he felt he should be quiet. He was infirm by the time I met him. He had taken to his bed, where he chain smoked Camels and snuffed them out on the pitted rubber edge of one of those miniature automobile tires enclosing an ashtray that had been used as a sales gimmick. I was young then, and my image of the Great War was one of men marching down avenues, captured forever on film in those jerky frames of faded black and white. They all looked the same, and none looked younger than thirty. They were shy men and women, unused to the hand-cranked camera. I wanted to write about their war, so I listened to his stories. He showed me the yellow swath the mustard gas had left, bright and unfaded, on his hairless old man's leg. Between pulls on his cigarette, he told me how he had learned to move up to the berm to escape the gas, which was made heavier than air so it would seek you out in the muddy trenches. He described fumbling in no-man's-land in the dark, where you could tell the French dead by the *pinard* you swallowed down from their canteens. He left East Texas to join Company M of the 5th Infantry Regiment. He was tall for his age, and thin, and serious. He was fifteen.

I sought a comprehensive anthology to serve my teaching of a graduate seminar in British literature of the Great War. There were many poetry anthologies and prose anthologies — sometimes both in one volume. But I could find none that combined memoirs, poetry, letters, diaries, fiction, and history. *The Great War Reader* is an attempt to remedy that dilemma. Like any other anthology, this is an idiosyncratic selection of the anthologist. A book just as good could be made numerous times over from selections I have not chosen. I have gathered material based on two working premises. First, I wanted to include works of the very highest literary caliber. Second, I wanted, where possible, to include longer rather than shorter excerpts. I readily concede that it is impossible to produce a single anthology that can cover all times and places where the war wrought its havoc.

Instead, I have created a mosaic, a selection of solos that, I believe, combine to generate a resonance that gives the modern reader some sense of what it was to be alive during those perilous and exhilarating times. The voices herein range the scale from the romantic patriotism of early writers such as Rupert Brooke to the bitter criticisms of Wilfred Owen, Siegfried Sassoon, and others who emerged as the hopes of a quick victory in 1914 gave way to interminable years of stalemate punctuated by bloody defeats and transitory victories.

Many of these works are out of print, some since the war ended. I have included a list of further suggested works that will direct the interested reader on a very fruitful course of study. One comes from such a study with a profoundly different idea of the modern world and its complex identity. These voices — of men and women; of Germans, Englishmen, and Italians; of the famous and the forgotten — help establish us more firmly in the present with all its dilemmas and delights than anything else I have read. These voices offer a threnody of equal parts grace and benevolence.

Acknowledgments

A cooperative enterprise from the onset, an anthology such as this only grows increasingly complex as the author searches across time and distance to incorporate works. It is quite impossible to show adequate appreciation for everyone involved. But, with that said, let me acknowledge several of the key participants, without whose help this book would have been incomplete. Out of the many gracious and helpful permissions controllers and representatives of literary societies, I would like to call to attention the endeavors of Catherine Trippett, of Random House, United Kingdom, and Jane Bishop, of the Society of Authors. I must also take this opportunity to thank J. Lawrence Mitchell for his understanding and camaraderie and the Department of English at Texas A&M University for its support. The staff at Texas A&M University Press have been outstanding, and I offer my deepest appreciation. This is not a brief book, and it has not been an easy book. I doubt I could have done half so well left to my own devices. But, as always, I single out Cecelia Hawkins, who, for half my life, has been unfailing in her encouragement and affection. Together we read the excerpts and relived a fraction of the pain, suffering, and triumph of all these many voices. For this, and for everything else over the years, I am deeply grateful.

Permission to reprint copyrighted material in this anthology is gratefully acknowledged. I have made every effort to locate copyright holders, and I offer my apologies to those I have been unable to find. The selections here appear as they did when published, including many elements of typography.

Aldington: *The Death of A Hero,* published 1929 by Chatto & Windus; reprint 1984 by Hogart Press. Copyright © Estate of Richard Aldington 1929, 1956. Reprinted by permission of Rosica Colin, Ltd.

Bloch: *Memoirs of War, 1914–1915,* translated by Carole Fink, published and copyrighted 1980 by Cornell University Press; reprint 1991 by Cambridge University Press. Reprinted with the permission of Cambridge University Press.

Blunden: *Undertones of War,* published 1928 by Richard Cobden-Sanderson. Reprinted by permission of The Peters Fraser and Dunlop Group Limited.

Brittain: *Testament of Youth: An Autobiographical Study of the Years 1900–1925,* published 1933 by Macmillan. The excerpts from *Testament of Youth* by Vera Brittain are reprinted with the permission of her literary executors.

Cannan: "Rouen," from *In War Time,* published 1917 by B. H. Blackwell. Reprinted by permission of James Slater.

Chapman: *A Passionate Prodigality: Fragments of an Autobiography,* published 1933 by Ivor Nicholson & Watson, Ltd. Reprinted by permission of Christopher Storm-Clark.

Clark: *The Donkeys,* published 1996 by Pimlico. Reprinted by permission of Random House, U.K.

Cole: "The Falling Leaves," from *Poems,* published 1918 by George Allen & Unwin, Ltd. Reprinted by permission of David Higham Associates.

Dyer: *The Missing of the Somme,* published 1995 by Penguin Books (Hamish Hamilton, 1994). Copyright © Geoff Dyer, 1994. Reprinted by permission of Toby Eady Associates, Ltd. Reprinted by permission of Penguin Books, Ltd.

Farjeon: "Easter Monday," from *First and Second Love,* published 1959 by Oxford University Press. Reprinted by permission of David Higham Associates.

Findley: *The Wars,* published 1977 by Clarke Irwin & Co., Ltd.; reprint 1978 by Penguin. Reprinted by permission of Timothy Findley and Pebble Productions, Inc.

Fussell: *The Great War and Modern Memory,* Copyright © 1975 by Oxford University Press, Inc. Used by permission of Oxford University Press, Inc.

Graves: *Good-bye to All That,* published 1985 by Doubleday. Reprinted by permission of Carcanet Press, Ltd.

Gurney: "De Profundis," "Ypres–Minsterworth," "First Time In," "Memory, Let All Slip," and "Laventie," from *Collected Poems of Ivor Gurney,* published 1982 by Oxford University Press. © Sole Trustee of the Gurney Estate, 1982. Reprinted from *Collected Poems of Ivor Gurney,* edited by P. J. Kavanagh (1982) by permission of Oxford University Press.

Horne: *The Price of Glory: Verdun 1916,* published 1963 by St. Martin's Press. Copyright © 1963 by Alistair Horne, first printed in *The Price of Glory.* Reprinted with the permission of The Wylie Agency, Inc.

Jünger: *The Storm of Steel: From the Diary of a German Storm-Troop Officer on the Western Front,* translated by Basil Creighton, published 1975 by Howard Fertig. First published by E. S. Mittler and Son. Reprinted by permission of Klett-Cotta, Stuttgart. Reprinted by permission of Dudley Steynor.

Lewis: *Sagittarius Rising,* published 1936 by Harcourt, Brace, and Co.; reprint 1963 by Stackpole. Reprinted by permission of Greenhill Books/Lionel Leventhal, Ltd.

Macdonald: *Somme,* published 1983 by Michael Joseph; reprint 1993 by Penguin. Copyright Lyn MacDonald, 1983. Reprinted by permission of Penguin Books, Ltd.

Manning: *The Middle Parts of Fortune,* published 1979 by New American Library. Reprinted by permission of C. P. Dickson.

Mew: "The Cenotaph," from *Collected Poems,* published 1953 by Gerald Duckworth & Co., Ltd. Reprinted by permission of Carcanet Press, Ltd.

Moorehead: *Gallipoli,* published 1956 by Harper & Brothers; reprint 1996 by Ballantine Books. Copyright Alan Moorehead, 1956. Copyright renewed by Alan Moorehead, 1984. Reprinted by permission of HarperCollins Publishers, Inc.

Mottram: *The Spanish Farm,* published 1927 by Dial Press. Reprinted by permission of Random House, U. K., Ltd., and by permission of executors of R. H. Mottram.

Moynihan: *A Place Called Armageddon: Letters from the Great War,* edited by Michael Moynihan, published 1975 by David & Charles. Copyright Sunday Times Newspapers, Ltd., 1975. Reprinted by permission of News International Syndication.

Owen: *The Poems of Wilfred Owen,* edited by Jon Stallworthy, published 1990 by Chatto & Windus. Reprinted by permission of the estate of Wilfred Owen, editor Jon Stallworthy, the Source, and Chatto & Windus as publishers.

Plowman: *A Subaltern on the Somme in 1916,* published 1928 by E. P. Dutton. Reprinted by permission of Greta Plowman.

Read: "The Raid," from *Ambush,* published 1974 by Haskell House Publishers, Ltd. Reprinted by permission of David Higham Associates.

Remarque: *All Quiet on the Western Front,* translated A. W. Wheen, published 1929 by Little, Brown & Co. *Im Westen Nichts Neues,* copyright 1928 by Ullstein A. G.; Copyright renewed by Erich Maria Remarque, 1956. *All Quiet on the Western Front,* copyright 1929, 1930 by Little, Brown and Co.; copyright renewed by Erich Maria Remarque, 1957, 1958. All rights reserved. Reprinted by permission.

Rivers: *Instinct and Unconscious,* published 1922 by Cambridge University Press. Reprinted by permission of Cambridge University Press.

Rosenberg: "From France," "Break of Day in the Trenches," "Louse Hunting," "Returning, We Hear the Larks," and "Dead Man's Dump," from *The Collected Works of Isaac Rosenberg,* edited by Ian Parsons, published 1979 by Chatto & Windus. Reprinted by permission of The Literary Executor and Copyright Holder of Isaac Rosenberg's Works.

Sassoon: "How to Die," "Lamentations," "Suicide in the Trenches," "Wirers," "The Road," "The Hero," "Counter-Attack," from *Collected Poems of Siegfried Sassoon* by Siegfried Sassoon. Copyright 1918, 1920 by E. P. Dutton. Copyright 1936, 1946, 1947, 1948 by Siegfried Sassoon. Used by permission of Viking Penguin, a division of Penguin Books USA, Inc. *The Memoirs of George Sherston,* published 1967 by Stackpole Books. Reprinted by permission of George Sassoon.

Seeger: "Rendezvous," from *Poems,* published 1917 by Charles Scribner's Sons. Reprinted with the permission of Scribner, a Division of Simon and Schuster from *Poems of Alan Seeger.* Copyright © 1916 by Charles Scribner's Sons, renewed 1944 by Elsie Adams Seeger.

Sitwell: "The Dancers," from *Clowns' Houses,* published 1918 by B. H. Blackwell. Reprinted by permission of David Higham Associates.

Sorley: "Two Sonnets," "When You See the Millions of the Mouthless Dead," and "All the Hills and Vales Along," from *The Collected Poems of Charles Hamilton Sorley,* edited by Jean Moorcroft Wilson, published 1985 by Cecil Woolf. Reprinted by permission of Cecil Woolf Publishers.

Stramm: "Stormtaking," "Battlefield," "Wounds," "In the Firing," "Grenades," and "War Grave," translated by Lucia Cordell Getsi. Copyright Lucia Cordell Getsi. Reprinted by permission of Lucia Cordell Getsi.

Sulzbach: *With the German Guns: Four Years on the Western Front,* translated by Richard Thonger, published 1998 by Leo Cooper, an imprint of Pen & Sword. Reprinted by permission of Pen & Sword.

Sutherland: *Six Weeks at the War,* published 1914 by *The Times.* Reprinted by permission of Elizabeth, Countess of Sutherland, and News International Syndication.

Tapert: *Despatches from the Heart: An Anthology of Letters from the Front during the First and Second World Wars,* edited by Annette Tapert, published 1984 by Hamish Hamilton. Letter of F. A. Holman reprinted by permission of Mr. Holman's literary executor. Letter of Ernest Foster reprinted by permission of Mr. D. N. Potter.

Trakl: "Lament," "In the East," "Grodek," translated by Lucia Cordell Getsi. Copyright Lucia Cordell Getsi. Reprinted by permission of Lucia Cordell Getsi.

Tuchman: *The Guns of August,* published 1962 by Macmillan Publishing Co. Copyright © 1962 by Barbara W. Tuchman. Copyright renewed in 1990 by Dr. Lester Tuchman. Reprinted by the permission of Russell & Volkening as agents for the author.

Ungaretti: "Watch," "Brothers," "The Rivers," and "Pilgrimage," from *Selected Poems of Giuseppe Ungaretti,* translated by Allen Mandelbaum, published 1975 by Cornell University Press. Copyright Allen Mandelbaum. Reprinted by permission of Allen Mandelbaum.

Vaughan: *Some Desperate Glory: The World War I Diary of a British Officer, 1917,* published 1981 by Henry Holt and Co. Reprinted by permission of Leo Cooper.

West: *The Diary of a Dead Officer: Being the Posthumous Papers of Arthur Graeme West,* published 1991 by the Imperial War Museum. Reprinted by permission of the Imperial War Museum.

Winter: *Death's Men: Soldiers of the Great War,* published 1978 by Allen Lane; reprint 1979 by Penguin. Copyright Denis Winter, 1978. Reprinted by permission of Penguin Books, Ltd.

Chronology

AUGUST, 1914

  1 Outbreak of World War I; German declaration of war on Russia

18 Wilson commands American neutrality

26 Battle of Tannenberg begins

SEPTEMBER, 1914

  5 First Battle of the Marne begins

  9 Germans begin retreat from the Marne

OCTOBER, 1914

  1 German siege of Antwerp begins

18 Battle of the Yser

19 First Battle of Ypres begins

NOVEMBER, 1914

  2 Action at Tanga, German East Africa

  8 British landings in Mesopotamia

16 Battle of Lodz begins

DECEMBER, 1914

16 German naval bombardment of Hartlepool, Whitby

20 First Battle of Champagne

JANUARY, 1915

18 Japan's Twenty-one Demands to China

19–20 First German zeppelin raid against Britain

24 Naval Battle of Dogger Bank

FEBRUARY, 1915

  4 Germany announces submarine blockade

19, 25 Allied naval bombardment of outer Dardanelles forts

MARCH, 1915

  1 American citizen dies in sinking of British passenger ship *Falaba*

10 Battle of Neuve Chapelle begins

11 Britain announces blockade of German ports

18 Allied naval attack on fortifications in the Dardanelles Narrows

APRIL, 1915

22 Second Battle of Ypres begins

25 British land at Cape Helles and Anzacs at Ari Burnu on the Gallipoli Peninsula

26 France, Russia, Italy, and Britain conclude secret Treaty of London

MAY, 1915

  2 Austro-German offensive in Galicia

  7 *Lusitania* sunk by German submarine off Irish coast

23 Italy declares war on Austria-Hungary

JUNE, 1915

23 First of twelve battles of the Isonzo begins on the Italian-Austrian front

JULY, 1915

12 British offensive at Cape Helles on Gallipoli Peninsula

21 President Wilson sends notes directing the beginning of a national defense program

AUGUST, 1915

6–8 British land at Suvla Bay on the Gallipoli Peninsula

21 *The Washington Post* reports that a million American soldiers may be sent overseas; U.S. government issues denial

25 Austro-German forces capture Brest Litovsk

SEPTEMBER, 1915

  2 Austro-German forces capture Grodno

25 Battle of Loos begins

28 Battle of Kut begins

OCTOBER, 1915

  5 Anglo-French force lands at Salonika, Greece

  6 Austro-German invasion of Serbia

NOVEMBER, 1915
     22 Battle of Ctesiphon begins

DECEMBER, 1915
      8 Allies begin evacuation of Gallipoli Peninsula
     18 Haig assumes command of the British Expeditionary Force

JANUARY, 1916
      9 Allies complete evacuation of Gallipoli Peninsula
     27 President Wilson begins nationwide whistle-stop campaign to generate support for war preparations

FEBRUARY, 1916
     21 Ten-month Battle of Verdun begins

MARCH, 1916
     24 Germans torpedo French passenger-liner *Sussex,* three Americans die

APRIL, 1916
     24 Irish Rebellion begins in Dublin on Easter Monday
  24–25 German naval bombardment of Lowestoft and Yarmouth
     27 Lord Kitchener asks for U.S. military participation in Europe
     29 Fall of Kut

MAY, 1916
      4 Germans announce Sussex Pledge, agree not to sink passenger ships without warning
     31 Naval Battle of Jutland begins

JUNE, 1916
      3 U.S. National Defense act expands army but limits size and authority of General Staff
      4 Brusilov Offensive against Austria-Hungary begins
      5 HMS *Hampshire* sinks; Lord Kitchener drowns
     13 Capture of Mecca by Arab Revolt

JULY, 1916
      1 Battle of the Somme begins; British suffer 60,000 casualties on first day
     30 Black Tom Island munitions plant destroyed; German sabotage suspected

AUGUST, 1916
6 Battle of Gorizia
18 Germans launch unsuccessful High Seas Fleet foray
28 Italy declares war on Germany

SEPTEMBER, 1916
15 British introduce tanks at Somme battle of Flers-Courcelette

OCTOBER, 1916
24 French launch offensive at Verdun

NOVEMBER, 1916
7 President Wilson reelected
28 First German daylight airplane raid on London

DECEMBER, 1916
5 English Prime Minister Asquith resigns; replaced by Lloyd George
12 Germans issue peace paper that suggests a compromise
18 President Wilson requests war objectives from belligerents in peace paper

JANUARY, 1917
10 Allies state war objectives in response to Wilson's demands
31 Germany resumes unrestricted submarine warfare

FEBRUARY, 1917
3 U.S. severs relations with Germany
13 British General Staff Chief Sir William Robertson expresses doubts about quality of American soldiers
24 Great Britain releases Zimmerman Note to U.S.
25 German naval bombardment of Margate and Broadstairs

MARCH, 1917
1 Zimmerman Note released to U.S. press
4 Senate filibuster of Armed Ship Bill
11 British capture Baghdad
13 President Wilson orders U.S. merchant ships armed
15 Czar Nicholas II abdicates
20 President Wilson's cabinet votes unanimously for war
29 U.S. Army War College Division issues report calling for up to a million American troops; Wilson calls for an army to be raised through conscription

APRIL, 1917

Heaviest German submarine damage of the war: 881,027 gross tons; 500,000 British

 2 President Wilson delivers war message to Congress
 6 U.S. declares war on Germany
10 Sir William Robertson says that getting some Americans killed would bring U.S. fully into war
16 Nivelle Offensive begins; Lenin arrives in Russia
17 French Army mutinies begin

MAY, 1917

18 President Wilson signs Selective Service Act
26 First U.S. troops arrive in France

JUNE, 1917

 7 U.S. proposes to send 120,000 soldiers per month to Europe; Battle of Messines begins
13 General Pershing lands in France
14 President Wilson says American Expeditionary Forces will be bolstered by troops to be trained abroad
15 U.S. Espionage Act passed

JULY, 1917

 6 General Pershing requests a million U.S. troops by 1918
11 General Pershing suggests U.S. war effort may take 3 million troops
31 Third Battle of Ypres (Passchendaele) begins

AUGUST, 1917

 6 Kerensky appointed Prime Minister of Russia

SEPTEMBER, 1917

 1 Pershing establishes headquarters at Chaumont
23 U. S. Tank Corps founded

OCTOBER, 1917

 3 War Revenue Act
24 Austro-German breakthrough at Caporetto

NOVEMBER, 1917

 8 Bolshevik Revolution
20 Battle of Cambrai begins; first massed tank attack
27 Allied Supreme War Council created

DECEMBER, 1917

  7 U.S. declares war on Austria

  9 British capture Jerusalem

15 Central Powers and Russians agree to armistice at Brest-Litovsk

JANUARY, 1918

  8 President Wilson makes Fourteen Points speech to joint session of Congress

20 Action at Dardanelles, *Goeben* beached, *Breslau* sunk

FEBRUARY, 1918

  1 Austrian naval mutiny, Cattaro

11 President Wilson makes Four Principles speech to joint session of Congress

21 British capture Jericho

MARCH, 1918

  3 Treaty of Brest-Litovsk ends war on the eastern front

21 Germans begin series of massive spring offensives with attack on British at the Somme

26 Marshal Foch given "coordinating authority" over Allied forces on the western front

APRIL, 1918

  9 German Lys offensive begins

14 Marshal Foch appointed commander-in-chief of Allied forces on the western front

22 British raid Zeebrugge and Ostend

MAY, 1918

16 U.S. Sedition Act passed

25 German submarines sighted in U.S. waters

27 German Aisne Offensive begins

28 U.S. 28th Infantry Regiment sees action at Cantigny

JUNE, 1918

  6 U.S. 2d Division captures Bouresches and southern part of Belleau Wood

  9 German Noyon-Montdidier Offensive

JULY, 1918

2 Allied Supreme War Council supports intervention in Siberia

6 Wilson agrees to American support in Siberia; Influenza reaches epidemic proportions in France

15 Second Battle of the Marne; nine U.S. divisions employed

AUGUST, 1918

3 Allied intervention begins at Vladivostok, Russia

4 British occupy Baku in the Caucasus

8 Amiens Offensive begins; General Ludendorff calls it "Black Day" for the German Army

26 Battles along the Hindenburg Line; Germans make ten-mile retreat

SEPTEMBER, 1918

4 American troops land at Archangel in northern Russia

12 Saint-Mihiel Offensive begins; first major U.S. operation

26 Meuse-Argonne Offensive begins; greatest offensive for U.S. soldiers

27 French and British armies storm the Hindenburg Line

28 Hindenburg and Ludendorff agree Germany must request an immediate armistice

OCTOBER, 1918

3 Germans and Austrians send notes to President Wilson requesting an armistice

20 Allies secure Belgian coast

21 Germany ceases unrestricted submarine warfare

29 German High Seas Fleet mutinies; war at sea ends

NOVEMBER, 1918

5 Republicans gain control of U.S. Congress

11 Armistice goes into effect at 11 A.M.

18 President Wilson announces he will attend peace conference

JANUARY, 1919

5 Communists revolt in Berlin

18 Peace negotiations begin in Paris

25 Peace conference accepts the principle of the League of Nations

FEBRUARY, 1919

14 Draft Covenant of League of Nations completed

MARCH, 1919
   4 Comintern established in Moscow
  13 Admiral Kolchak begins offensive against the Bolsheviks in Russian
       Civil War

APRIL, 1919
   7 Allies evacuate Odessa

MAY, 1919
   6 Peace conference disposes of Germany's colonies

JUNE, 1919
  21 German High Seas Fleet scuttled at Scapa Flow
  28 Treaty of Versailles signed

The Great War Reader

PART ONE

HISTORY

A French dugout in the Ravin de Souchez, October, 1915. Photograph courtesy the Imperial War Museum, London, neg. Q.49296.

Introduction

"Fifty years were spent in the process of making Europe. Five days were enough to detonate it." So begins one of the earliest and best histories of World War I by Capt. B. H. Liddell Hart. Since Liddell Hart's *The Real War, 1914–1918* was published seventy years ago, the Great War has proven to be fertile soil for historians. Indeed, some of the most insightful works further debates on strategy and tactics, the influences of national ambitions on policy, and the emergence of coalitions and consequences that would fuel future political and military adventures. No one disputes the impact of the war on the remainder of the twentieth century. In fact, historians now engaged in revising earlier interpretations and assessments of the conflict are helping revitalize our understanding of the war and all its attendant concerns. Many recent studies often eschew topics of panoramic sweep in favor of a tighter focus on such issues as soldiers' morale, the function of medicine, the experiences of the civilians, pacifism, propaganda, and art. However, despite this narrowing concentration, historians provide us with interpretations that would be perplexing to participants, be they privates or general staff officers. War historians always operate in a "present moment," after the confusion and turmoil of a conflict have given way to archival research. Battlefield necessities that demanded immediate reaction are antithetical to scholarly methodology. Instead, the historian can deliberately survey across time and place to ascertain causes and effects most likely utterly foreign to the participants. There is, therefore, more coherence — a comprehension of details both large and small — than the white-hot action of battle could ever yield to any single combatant. This book begins with history, allowing the reader to move from the more public view to perspectives more personal and imaginative.

One must be careful to qualify, however. A trip to any good bookstore will reveal, at most, a modest section on World War I. Interested readers will have to resort to libraries with more extensive archives or to interlibrary loan associations. Sandwiched between the seemingly innumerable books on the

Civil War and World War II, the modest array of Great War material is closer in size to works on the Korean War. The reason appears obvious. The neglect is not due to the war's historic distance but rather to the very nature of the war. Wars of movement — of dashing cavalry or the juggernaut of blitzkrieg — provide an inherent fascination that the stagnation of trench warfare and its passive victimization do not. Despite the so-called sideshows of World War I such as T. E. Lawrence's daring desert raids or the Australian Light Horse charge at Beersheba, the indelible image is of the trench and its accoutrements of barbed wire and machine guns. It is within this context that war historians must work to provide illumination of a war that more than ever defies the modern mind's understanding, for subsequent wars have, in large part, been attempts to avoid such martial impasses that draw in innumerable men and materiel for little visible gain.

The historians in this chapter represent a wide range of interests. Alan Clark, severely critical of the British General Staff, provides a detailed portrait of winter in Flanders among the "other ranks." Reacting to the war's legacy, Geoff Dyer writes of his visit to the war memorials and cemeteries of France, where he discovered a curious ongoing discourse on the Great War carried on in a visitors' guest book. From yet another vantage point, literature professor Paul Fussell considers the difficulties of writing about the incredible nature of the war in words that seemed unequal to the task.

In "Fort Vaux," Alistair Horne discusses the antique French notion of stationary forts under bombardment by modern artillery. Lyn Macdonald writes of the Battle of the Somme by using the recollections of the soldiers involved. This battle, along with Verdun, did much to weaken many citizens' beliefs in their politicians. Moving from major engagements to one of the sideshows, Alan Moorehead writes of the Allied attempt to alleviate some of the stress on the western front by landing forces on the Gallipoli Peninsula. A military failure, the engagement ended in a nearly bloodless Allied evacuation stunningly executed under the very noses of the Turkish defenders.

Barbara Tuchman provides some background to the continental debacle as she writes about the pomp and ceremony of Edward VII of England's funeral in 1910. The state occasion brought together the extended imbroglio of regal families of the old order that would, in four years, find themselves locked in a pernicious struggle which would not only destroy many of their subjects, but would alter the ideas of European statehood.

Finally, Denis Winter illuminates the strain of the soldiers' daily existence in the trenches. Shellshock or battle fatigue had long been present in warfare, but it was World War I that first provoked extended examinations of the causes and effects of those psychological aberrations. Winter records survival under situations of unprecedented dimensions.

Historians attempt to objectify the past, to provide illuminations of it through details of fact. With the best of them, this fortunately does not preclude writing that is vivid, fresh, and immensely engaging—in short, literature as compelling as any work of fiction.

*The region of the Lys basin and the plain of
Flanders consists entirely of low-lying
meadow. Throughout the winter months
the clayey subsoil holds the water
approximately two feet below the surface
and there is a tendency for any minor
declivity, whether natural or artificial, to
become water-logged.*
— Introductory note to *War Office
Manual,* 1913

Winter
in the Trenches

ALAN CLARK

No-Man's-Land was a grassy tufted waste, pockmarked with brown craters, with here and there the stumps of broken trees and little greyish mounds which, from their situation and contour, suggested human origin. At a distance—it varied from 80 to 200 yards—stood German emplacements. Through half-closed eyes, or when veiled by the damp mist that rose from the ground at dawn, the irregular line of grey and fawn hummocks that was enemy breastwork might have been a stretch of dunes on the seashore, with the dark bundles of wire straggling from their lower reaches like wild blackthorn.

Sometimes, at night, it was absolutely still for minutes at a time. The voices of the enemy could be heard and even the click of a sentry's heels at inspection. A subaltern in the Black Watch wrote in his diary:

'I could hear some Boche playing Schubert; it was "The Trout," that bit that goes up and down, on an old piano. They must have got it in a forward dug-out; even so it was incredible how clear the sound came across. But before he got to the end someone put a flare up over Auchy and the whole of No-Man's-Land went pale green. A nervous sentry fired a short M.G. burst and firing started up all along the line. It went on and off for about half an hour. I never heard the pianist again, although Corporal Duffy said he was performing on the following night. I often wondered whether he survived the War.'

As the November fighting died down the British troops had found themselves holding a 'line' of scattered trenches, the majority of them scratched hastily in the soil while the battles were at their height, unconnected with each other and without any proper system of communication and support to the rear. When these were linked up into one continuous strip by the engineers many weaknesses became apparent: the successive counter-attacks that had been made in the last days of November had recovered much of the ground lost but, owing to the exhaustion of the men and their depleted numbers, had been brought up short before any enemy positions of natural strength. The instructions from G.H.Q. that not an inch was to be yielded, and the terrible cost at which the ground had been re-won, alike made it difficult to alter the line where this might have meant giving up even a few hundred yards of territory. And so the British front, like the last few inches of a high tide, was everywhere indented by little areas of high ground, or groups of buildings at road junctions, or other sorts of positions that offered unusual advantages to the enemy.

In this way whole stretches were subject to crippling enfilade fire from the German positions, that gave rise to a constant drain of casualties in holding on to them; the digging of communication trenches was particularly dangerous in sectors such as these and in some cases had to be abandoned altogether, which in turn meant that long frontages were without proper connection to the support areas and were dependent for the supply of ammunition and other essentials, and for the evacuation of wounded, the provision of reliefs and so forth, on the hazardous and uncertain night traffic along the fire-trench itself.

The trenches themselves were pitiful affairs. The infantry 'showed considerable lethargy and a marked disinclination to dig,'[1] largely on account of the unfamiliarity of the medium and the G.H.Q. policy of switching units from sector to sector. This meant that the troops were seldom in a position long enough to effect any marked improvement, and there was a feeling that they were simply doing the work for those that came after, with the certainty that in the stretch where they themselves were next posted they would have to start all over again. This attitude persisted for many weeks, until it gradually became obvious that the condition of trench warfare was a permanent one. Certain regiments also, notably the Royal Scots and the Somerset, began to make it a point of prestige that 'no unit should ever have cause to complain when it takes over a stretch of line from us,'[2] and with the spreading of this practice the strength and habitability of the line began to increase. Even when the will was there, however, there was a painful shortage of means.

Picks and shovels were considered plentiful when there were as few as two or three per platoon and efforts to commandeer them from civilian sources met with little success, as the Flemish peasants used to bury them rather than part with the tools of their livelihood. There was also a serious shortage of actual construction material and particularly of sandbags and wattling for 'reveting' the sides of the trenches. The scarcity of sandbags was particularly serious in low-lying areas such as the Ypres salient and opposite Festubert, where the trenches were almost permanently waterlogged throughout the winter. In places such as these it was necessary for protection to construct a raised breastwork which, if it was adequately to protect against machine-gun fire, particularly at the very close ranges that separated the troops in many areas, had to be at least eight feet thick.

'Sergeant Doherty was killed by a sniper while supervising a building fatigue. This is the eighteenth casualty and the fourth N.C.O. we have lost in this way since we came into the line on Tuesday — it is a frustrating business. The Boche has got perfect observation of our lines from Frezenburg Ridge. The snipers pick the men off in the evening before they can get started. We slave away all night building a parapet of loose earth — I have hardly seen a sandbag since our arrival — then in the morning he calls over a few "crumps" and they blow the whole thing to blazes, usually burying some poor wretches alive at the same time as they unearth a lot of dead ones!'

Throughout these bleak months the German artillery dominated the situation, making life a misery for the British troops who were obliged to hold the line in greater strength either than the enemy or the French, owing to their own shortage of guns. For whereas their allies could afford to make their front positions little more than outposts that could call up an immense weight of artillery fire at the least sign of any suspicious activity on the part of the enemy, the British were dependent on rifle fire to cope with marauding patrols and local attacks. This was due to two things: in the first place the eighteen-pounders used for direct support were few in number,[3] and hesitated to expose themselves except in an emergency owing to the fact that the heavier guns needed to support them against German counter-battery fire were almost entirely absent. Secondly, they were so starved of ammunition as to make it futile to reveal their position for the sake of throwing the meagre daily 'ration' of shells at the enemy. In actual fact for the entire B.E.F there was in the field only about three-fifths of the regulation amount *calculated on the experience of the Boer War,* and really little more than a day's supply in modern battle.[4]

The fire-power of the men in the front line was also seriously diminished by the shortage — amounting in cases to non-existence — of trench-mortars and hand-grenades. Of the latter a number of extemporized missiles were tried out, the most notorious being the 'jam-pot,' the 'Battye bomb' and the 'hairbrush.' These were dangerous and difficult to construct, their ignition was chancy and impossible in wet weather, and in general it is likely that they caused as many casualties among the British as among the enemy. No 'Mills' hand-grenades were produced until the spring of 1915 — by March only forty-eight had been delivered. The trench-mortar, an ultra-short-range howitzer, more or less portable, with which the Germans were making great destruction, was even more rare in the Expeditionary Force. One officer, however, managed to do a private deal with the French, paying cash for a number of old Coehorn siege-mortars which were found to bear the cypher of Louis Philippe!

It was in these conditions, starved of the equipment in trench warfare, with little pretence even of support and seriously short of trained junior officers and N.C.O.s, that the British troops were crowded into the fire-trenches to suffer throughout the winter months extremes of physical privation.

It rained incessantly. From the 25th October until the 10th March there were only eighteen dry days, and on these the temperature was below freezing. The trenches themselves became little less than culverts, replacing in rudimentary fashion the drainage system of the countryside which had been dislocated by the artillery fire. It was impossible to dig deeper than eighteen inches without finding water, and along whole stretches of the line garrisons had to do their stint with the water waist-high, for the fire-step had crumbled away and there were not the materials to construct an adequate breastwork after the German fashion. Duck-boards were unknown and the wounded who collapsed into the slime would often drown, unnoticed in the heat of some local engagement, and concealed for days until their bodies, porous from decomposition, would rise once again to the surface. When the German guns opened fire the troops could only cower in the water because the dug-outs, built for protection during bombardment, were themselves awash to roof level and stank intolerably from the dead that floated there.

In an effort to alleviate these conditions, relieving the men every twelve hours was tried (the German rota was four days in the line, two in support and four at rest), but this led to great administrative confusion, particularly in the immediate rear and over the allotment of billets themselves 'filthy and inadequate,'[5] and to heavy casualties from sniping and shrapnel over the continuous traffic along the communication trenches.

It is thus not surprising that the 'wastage' from illness was very high — the more so in view of the fact that there were no proper facilities for drying clothing and the men frequently had to return to the line in the same soaking garments in which they had quitted it. 'De-lousing' stations were established, but the process consisted of no more than running a hot flat-iron over the troops' undergarments about once every ten days. Although the strictest criteria were applied before men were allowed to report sick, the returns for January 1915 show an average of about 4,500 a day, chiefly from pneumonia and blood-poisoning.

Wilson wrote that 'The water and mud increase and are getting horrible. The longer days will be very welcome when they come, especially to officers; the men do not mind so much.' But he gave no reasons to support this distinction of taste.

On Christmas Day, 1914, there had been no firing, and in many sectors the troops had climbed out of their trenches and, meeting in No-Man's-Land, had talked and exchanged gifts. But such a development met with the strongest disapproval at G.H.Q.[6] and the officers responsible were punished. It did not happen again.

G.H.Q. seems to have been slow in realizing that the unfortunate tactical siting of the line was making an important contribution to the 'wastage.'[7] Finally, when it was seen that the line must be altered, there never seems to have been any thought of achieving this by making local withdrawals and inviting the enemy to step forward into the 'bad ground.' Instead, a variety of small, but extravagant, attacks were authorized with the intention of straightening the line and eliminating some of the more tiresome German enfilade buttresses that dominated it.

It is hardly surprising, in view of the conditions under which they were ordered, that these were uniformly unsuccessful, in spite of being pressed with the utmost gallantry. Sometimes, very rarely, the infantry, or such small proportion of them as had survived the passage of No-Man's-Land, managed to evict the Germans; but by nightfall they were almost spent, ammunition was low, and they were under continuous fire from the German artillery. The reliefs, stumbling across a flare-lit waste where the sappers slaved to dig some pretence of a communication trench in the mud, some meagre channel that would afford protection in daylight, were as often as not cut down by the machine-guns before they got there. It became customary to 'send a company to relieve a platoon — only a platoon's strength will arrive.'

In the warmth and comfort of the Allied Headquarters, however, the mood was one of optimism. Charteris expressed the general view when he wrote home: '. . . don't believe Captain M. that the war will last another two years. Germany has shot her bolt here and failed. . . .' It was more prophetic, if also provoking a more ominous reaction, when:

> '. . . General Rice, our senior sapper, has made the most original forecast of all! He predicts that neither we nor the Germans will be able to break through a strongly defended and entrenched line, and that gradually the line will extend from the sea to Switzerland, and the war end in stalemate. *D.H. will not hear of it.* He thinks that we can push the Germans back to the frontier, and after that it will only be a matter of numbers.'[8]

Foch went even further, and thought that the time was already ripe. 'We are in a perfect condition, both morally and materially, for attacking,' he told Henry Wilson, whose diary also records:

> 'Long strategical talk [with Foch] in which we agreed that Germany still has one chance, and one only, namely, to shorten her front — and retire to the line Liège-Metz, or possibly even to the Rhine. Any middle course would be fatal to her.'[9]

In the closing weeks of the year preparations for a great winter offensive to accelerate this process were eagerly rushed forward; so eagerly, indeed, that a number of important considerations were overlooked, chief among these being the waterlogged state of the terrain and the dismal condition of the soldiers themselves. Then, at the last moment, Sir John French, who was to co-operate in the north, lost his nerve and 'impressed on every commander that he was not on any account to get ahead of his neighbours in the attack; everybody was to wait for the man on his left.' And in the event everybody did wait, including the left-hand man. Thus the offensive proved 'not merely a failure, but a fiasco. The only effect produced was on Franco-British relations.'[10]

This abortive operation also had deep and significant psychological after-effects. In the first place the security of Sir John French's position was further undermined, both in his own estimation and in reality. Wilson was sent to Foch to plead against any complaint that might be sent out from G.Q.G.

> 'I made the best case I could about advancing in echelon from the left, and he listened without saying a word. At the end he said, *"Mais mon cher Wilson, nous sommes militaires pas avocats."* That exactly expresses the straits I was pushed to. We discussed everything and he was as nice as

could be; but *"Père Joffre n'est pas commode,"* and it was clear that Sir John would be in a very difficult position if he did not put up some fight.'[11]

Wilson's mediation was of little use. Huguet noted that 'their [those of Joffre and French] relations which had never been trusting or cordial became colder and colder.' And there is no doubt that this made the Commander-in-Chief more jittery and indecisive than ever.

But more important, because more lasting, was the slur—as it was thought to be—left on the prowess of the Expeditionary Force. The French now openly declared that 'it might be helpful to hold the line and act defensively, but would be of little use in an attack.' Determination to redeem this and their own reputations was responsible for many of the worst excesses of stubborn leadership among the British commanders in the years to come.

Notes

From Alan Clark, *The Donkeys* (London: Pimlico, 1996), pp. 35–43.

1. O. H., 1915, I, 28.
2. Ewing, *The Royal Scots.*
3. The regulation number of batteries per division—not always achieved—was obtained by reducing the number of guns from six to four per battery (O.H., 1915, I, 9).
4. For example figures for the 17th November (2nd Corps) are 3rd Division, 363 rounds per field gun, 5th Division, 323. Reserve in park, 6, 28. 3rd Corps, 45,551 for all divisions—i.e. rather less than 300 per gun. *War Establishments,* Part I, p. 5 lays down minima of 528 and 280 for field-guns and howitzers, with a further 472 and 520 on lines of communication, in addition to the general reserve.
5. O. H., 1915, I, 28.
6. In *1914,* Sir John French wrote of '. . . individual unarmed men running from the German trenches across to ours holding Christmas trees above their heads. These overtures were in some places favourably received and fraternization of a limited kind took place during the day. It appeared that a little feasting went on and junior officers, N.C.O.s and men on either side conversed together in No-Man's-Land. When this was reported to me I issued immediate orders to prevent any recurrence of such conduct, and called the local commanders to strict account, which resulted in a good deal of trouble.'
7. O. H., 1915, I, 218.
8. Charteris, Brigadier-General, *G.H.Q.* The italics are mine.—A.C.
9. Wilson, *Memoirs,* p. 188.
10. Liddell Hart, *History of the World War, 1914–1918.*
11. Wilson, *Memoirs,* p. 192.

The Missing
of the Somme

GEOFF DYER

Despite the cold there were a handful of other visitors at the Memorial Park. The smaller cemeteries are deserted. Sometimes there are intervals of three or four weeks in the visitors' books. Often people come to visit one particular grave: a great uncle, a grandfather. They are always touching, these personal inscriptions in the book, especially when the pilgrimage is the fulfillment of a lifetime's ambition.

Most comments, though, are generic: 'RIP,' 'Remembering,' 'We Will Remember Them,' 'Lest We Forget,' 'Very Moving.' Sometimes there is a jaunty salute: 'All the best, lads,' 'Sleep well, boys.' As well as commenting on the cemetery itself — 'Peaceful,' 'Beautiful' — many people offer larger impressions of the war: 'Such a waste,' 'No more war,' 'Never again.' All those comments are heartfelt, even those like 'They died for freedom,' or 'For Civilization,' which, testifying to the enduring power of ignorance, end up meaning the opposite of what is intended: 'They died for nothing.' At the Connaught Cemetery for the massacred Ulster Division several visitors from Northern Ireland have written 'No surrender.' One entry, from Andy Keery, reads: 'No surrender. Proud to come from Ulster.' Beneath it his friend has written 'No surrender. I came with Andy.' Occasionally people quote a couple of lines of poetry. I add my own little couplet:

> *A lot of people have written 'no surrender.'*
> *That's how bigots remember.*

Sometimes people's comments are so idiosyncratic as scarcely to make sense: 'The bloke on the tractor spoiled it for me by his reckless driving.

16

Signed anon' — the unknown visitor. On 10 October 1992 at Tyne Cot Greg Dawson wrote, 'We really showed those fascists a thing or two!' Another person had drawn a Star of David and written, 'What about the 6 million Jews?' Beneath it someone else had written, 'Wrong war, mate.' This quickly becomes something of a catch phrase between the three of us: irrespective of its relevance, any remark elicits the droll rejoinder, 'Wrong war, mate.'

At the Sheffield Memorial a diligent student wrote a short essay pointing out, in closely reasoned detail, that blame for the Somme rested, ultimately, on Churchill's shoulders. He even added a footnote citing A. J. P. Taylor, complete with page reference, place and date of publication. Reluctant to get drawn into the minutiae of scholarly debate, another visitor had simply scrawled in the margin: 'Rubbish!'

Sometimes a dialogue does evolve, most obviously at one of the Redan Ridge cemeteries. The theme of the discussion here is exactly that announced by the anti-Taylorite at the Sheffield Memorial: rubbish.

There are three tiny, beautifully located cemeteries at Redan Ridge. Next to one of them is a stinking mound of farm rubbish. An entry from 10 July 1986 expresses the characteristic sentiments of most visitors: 'It's such a shame they must rest with a rubbish pit beside them.'[1] Several pages on, after numerous endorsements of these remarks, the first dissenting voice appears: 'If visitors fail to recognize the true pathos behind their visits here only to latch on to the presence of a rubbish dump, then *their* presence here disgusts me.'

This attempt to scotch the debate only inflames it. The characteristic tone becomes aggressively indignant: 'The rubbish is a thinly disguised insult to the memory of Pte. Tommy Atkins.' Adding injury to insult the next person to join in notes: 'It's quite apt: human waste next to more of it.' Comments like this mean that from now on the ire of those offended by the rubbish is directed not only against the farmer who dumped it but against those who implicitly condone him — and who, in turn, become steadily more aggressive in their responses: 'Sod the rubbish-tip — these men lived and died in it. Isn't rubbish a part of life?' That's a moot point, but for quite a few months now the rubbish has been playing a more important part in the visitors' book than the cemetery. Gradually the debate itself becomes the main subject of debate. The cemetery was ousted by the rubbish-tip; now both are only incidental to the real focus of attention: the visitors' book itself. You can imagine it being integrated into battlefield tours, becoming the main reason for people's visit. Conscious of this, someone has written: 'Quite frankly the wastage of human life is worthy of more comment than a ridiculous rubbish-tip saga.'

Every attempt to have the last word, however, demands a response and so the rubbish debate and the debate about the rubbish debate perpetuate themselves. It comes as something of a disappointment to read, on 9 September 1991: 'Glad the rubbish has finally gone.'

I note all this down on 9 November 1992. It is the second time I have been here and there is a strange pleasure in standing in exactly the same spot. I find the proof of my last visit, in my own handwriting, in the visitors' book. It was a different season then; now the sky sags like mud over the brown earth. The air is cold as iron. Rain is blowing horizontal. The smell of rotting farmyard waste pervades the scene. I write:

> *Returned here after my previous visit 5.9.91.*
> PS: *The rubbish has returned too.*

The pages of these visitors' books are clipped in a green ring-hooped binder. When there are no pages left, new ones are clipped in. What happens to the old ones? Burned? Filed away in archives? If the latter, then perhaps an academic will one day salvage all these pages and use this hoard of raw data as the basis of a comprehensive survey of attitudes to the war, the ways in which it is remembered and misremembered. There is certainly enough material to fill a book: people who come here are moved and want to record their feelings, explain themselves.

And *this* book, really, is just an extended entry, jotted on pages ripped from the visitors' book of a cemetery on the Somme.

Like the Newfoundland Memorial, the other major Canadian memorial, at Vimy Ridge, is located in an expanse of parkland in which the original trenches have been neatly maintained. A road winds up to the park through thick woods. Then, suddenly, the monument looms into view: two white pylons, each with a sculpted figure perched precariously near the top. Sunlight knifes through the clouds.

Twin white paths stretch across the grass. The steps to the monument are flanked by two figures, a naked man and a naked woman. The stone is dazzling white. It is difficult to estimate the height of the pylons. A hundred feet? Two hundred? Impossible to say: there is nothing around to stand comparison with the monument. It generates its own scale, dwarfing the idea of measurement. At its base, between the two pylons, is a group of figures thrusting a torch upwards towards the figures perched high above. The distance between them is measureless.

Carved on the walls are the names of Canada's missing: 11,285 men with no known graves. I walk round to the east side of the monument where a group of figures are breaking a sword. Far off, in the other corner, is another similar group whose details I cannot make out at this distance. Between them, brooding over a vast sea of grass, is the shrouded form of a woman, her stone robes flowing over the ground. The figure spans millennia of grieving women, from pietàs showing the weeping Virgin to photos of widowed peasant women wrapped in shawls against the cold. Below her, resting on a tomb, are a sword and steel helmet, the shadows of the twin pylons stretching out across the grass.

The Memorial took eleven years to construct. Unveiled, finally, in 1936, it was the last of the great war memorials to be completed. Walter Allward, the sculptor and designer, explained its symbolism in the following terms. The grieving woman represents Canada, a young nation mourning her dead; the figures to her left show the sympathy of Canada for the helpless; to her right the Defenders are breaking the sword of war. Between the pillars, Sacrifice throws the torch to his comrades; high up on the pylons are allegorical figures of Honour, Faith, Justice, Hope, Peace . . . This string of virtues recalls a speech made by Lloyd George in September 1914 in which he itemized

the great everlasting things that matter for a nation — the great peaks we had forgotten, of Honour, Duty, Patriotism and, clad in glittering white, the great pinnacle of Sacrifice pointing like a rugged finger to Heaven.

In its glittering whiteness Allward's monument seems the shorn embodiment of Lloyd George's words. Duty and Patriotism have fallen away; Honour takes its place alongside Hope and peace as allegorical decoration; Sacrifice remains undiminished: unmeasurable, sheer — but its meaning, too, has been transformed by the war. It is here confronted with the consequence of its meaning.

Discounting the allegorical 'Defenders' there are no military figures on the monument. The steel helmet on the tomb is the only clear symbolic link with the war it commemorates. The figures at the base of the pylons strain upward, straining to rise above their grief, to surmount it until, like the figures nestling in the sky above them, they can overcome it. This vertiginous transcendence is counterpoised by the earthward gaze of the woman. Mute with sorrow she makes no appeal to the heavens but fixes her eyes on the ground, making an accommodation with grief, residing in loss.

Owen, wrote C. Day Lewis, 'had no pity to spare for the suffering of bereaved women.' Vimy Ridge, by contrast, seems less a memorial to the dead, to the abstract ideal of Sacrifice, than to the reality of grief: a memorial not to the Unknown Soldier but to Unknown Mothers.

I remember reading of a soldier's visit to the mother of a dead friend: "'I've lost my only boy,'" was all she said, then became mute with grief.'

And then, as sometimes happens, this word 'grief' that I have used many times floats free of meaning and becomes a sound, an abstract arrangement of letters whose sense is suddenly lost. Grief, grief, grief. I say the word to myself until, gradually, it is reunited with the meaning it has always had.

Ruins, for the Romantics, fulfilled the useful function of being enduring monuments to transience: what faded as grandeur survived as ruins. As testaments to their own survival, ruins, typically, had the story of their own ruination inscribed within them. Wordsworth established an imaginative template with the stories of silent suffering read in the ruins of 'Michael' or 'The Ruined Cottage.' So pervasive was the cult of ruination that a ruin became a place where a certain set of responses lay perfectly intact.

The Great War ruined the idea of ruins. Instead of the slow patient work of ruination observed in Shelley's 'Ozymandias,' artillery brought about instant obliteration. Things survived only by accident or chance — like the cavalry at Ypres — or mistake. Destruction was the standard and the norm. Cottages and villages did not crumble and decay — they were swept away.

In France, researching his book on the Battle of the Somme in March 1917, John Masefield described the area around Serre as

skinned, gouged, flayed and slaughtered, and the villages smashed to powder, so that no man could ever say there had been a village there within the memory of man.

In Barbusse's *Under Fire* the squad are making their way to the village of Souchez when the narrator realizes they are already there:

In point of fact we have not left the plain, the vast plain, seared and barren — but we are in Souchez!
The village has disappeared . . . There is not even an end of wall, fence, or porch that remains standing.

Revisiting the scenes of battle near Passchendaele in 1920, Stephen Graham finds himself — or loses himself, more accurately — in what Barbusse calls a 'plain of lost landmarks':

The old church of Zandwoorde cannot now be identified by any ruins — one has to ask where it was. Even the bricks and the stones seem to have been swept away.

Considering the same area of land half a century later, Leon Wolff puts the scale of destruction in its historical context: 'In a later war, atomic bombs wrecked two Japanese cities; but Passchendaele was effaced from the earth.'

Shunning such emotive turns of phrase, Denis Winter emphasizes that the Somme presented a scene of devastation even more thorough than that observed in Belgium: 'Aerial photos of Passchendaele in its final stages show grass and even trees. By autumn 1916, on the other hand, there was no vestige of grass on the Somme.'

Passchendaele, Albert and other villages in the Somme were rebuilt, but to some of the villages around Verdun the inhabitants never returned. Fleury, Douaumont and Cumières vanished from the map forever.

Notes

1. The rubbish-tip controversy has obvious echoes with the fuss in 1981 over the then Labour leader Michael Foot turning up for the Remembrance Day Service at the Cenotaph wearing a donkey jacket. According to the *Daily Telegraph*, Foot laid his wreath 'with all the reverent dignity of a tramp bending down to inspect a cigarette end.'

The Romance Quest

PAUL FUSSELL

A distinguished critic of our time has specified the following as characteristic of a certain kind of narrative. The protagonist, first of all, moves forward through successive stages involving "miracles and dangers" towards a crucial test. Magical numbers are important, and so is ritual. The landscape is "enchanted," full of "secret murmurings and whispers." The setting in which "perilous encounters" and testing take place is "fixed and isolated," distinct from the settings of the normal world. The hero and those he confronts are adept at "antithetical reasonings." There are only two social strata: one is privileged and aloof, while the other, more numerous, is "colorful but more usually comic or grotesque." Social arrangements are designed to culminate in "pompous ceremonies." Training is all-important: when not engaged in confrontations with the enemy, whether men, giants, ogres, or dragons, the hero devotes himself to "constant and tireless practice and proving." Finally, those engaged in these hazardous, stylized pursuits become "a circle of solidarity," "a community of the elect." The critic defining this kind of narrative is Erich Auerbach, and he is talking not about war memoirs, of course, but about medieval romance, of the sort written in France by Chrétien de Troyes in the twelfth century and in England by Sir Thomas Malory in fifteenth.[1]

The experiences of a man going up the line to his destiny cannot help seeming to him like those of a hero of medieval romance if his imagination has been steeped in actual literary romances or their equivalent. For most who fought in the Great War, one highly popular equivalent was Victorian pseudo-medieval romance, like the versified redactions of Malory by Tennyson and the prose romances of William Morris. Morris's most popular romance was *The Well at the World's End,* published in 1896. There was hardly a literate man who fought between 1914 and 1918 who hadn't read it and been powerfully excited by it in his youth. For us it is rather boring, this protracted tale of 228,000 words about young Prince Ralph's adventures in search of the magic well at the end of the world, whose waters have the power to remove the scars of battle wounds. But for a generation to whom terms like *heroism* and *decency* and *nobility* conveyed meanings that were entirely secure, it was a heady read and an unforgettable source of images. The general familiarity with and the ease with which it could be applied to the events of the war can be gauged from this: in May, 1915, an illustrated weekly headed an account of a trench skirmish won by the British with a caption in the stylish poetic-prose of the period, which here goes all the way and turns into blank verse: "How Three Encountered Fifty and Prevailed."[2] The caption could easily stand as one of the chapter titles in *The Well at the World's End,* like "How Ralph Justed with the Aliens." An audience to whom such "chapter headings" appealed in journalism was one implicitly learned in Morris's matter and style, or one which could easily come to value them. C. S. Lewis was only sixteen when the war began, but by 1917 he was nineteen and ready to go in. Just before he left he did a vast amount of reading, discovering books for the first, ecstatic time. "My great author at this period," he writes, "was William Morris. . . . In [his friend] Arthur's bookcase, I found *The Well at the World's End.* I looked — I read chapter headings — I dipped — and next day I went off into town to buy a copy of my own."[3]

There were many who arrived at Mametz Wood and Trones Wood and High Wood primed by previous adventuring in Morris's Wood Debateable and Wood Perilous. Both the literal and the literary are versions of what Frye calls the "demonic vegetable world" often associated with romance quests, "a sinister forest like the ones we meet in *Comus* or the opening of the *Inferno,* or a heath, which from Shakespeare to Hardy has been associated with tragic destiny, or a wilderness like that of Browning's *Childe Roland* or Eliot's *Waste Land.*"[4] Morris's "end of the world" is a cliff overlooking a boundless sea, very unlike the world ending with the British front line. Yet in describing the landscape of the front Sassoon seems often to recall some of Morris's sinister settings as well echoing Morris's title. "On wet days," he says, "the trees a mile away were like ash-grey smoke rising from the naked ridges, and it felt very much as if we were at the end of the world. And so we were: for that enemy world . . . had no relation to the landscape of life."[5] Again, "The end-of-the-world along the horizon had some obscure hold over my mind which drew my eyes to it almost eagerly, for I could still think of trench warfare as an adventure. The horizon was quiet just now, as if the dragons which lived there were dozing."[6] At the front, he finds another time, "we had arrived at the edge of the world."[7] And so literary an imagination as Blunden's was of course not behindhand in recalling and applying Morris. Thiepval in the winter of 1916 we today would call something like *sheer hell:* he designates it as a "filthy, limb-strewn, and most lonely world's-end. . . ."[8]

The prevailing ghastliness of the line was often registered in images deriving from such romances as Morris's. The infamous white chalk Butte of Warlencourt whose machine guns dominated the Somme lines for miles was like a terrible enormous living thing. Carrington says of it: "That ghastly hill . . . became fabulous. It shone white in the night and seemed to leer at you like an ogre in a fairy tale. It loomed up unexpectedly, peering into trenches where you thought yourself safe: it haunted your dreams."[9] (As well it might: many said that it was not a natural terrain feature at all but a Gallic burial tumulus, an antique mass grave.) Guy Chapman experienced the same sense of being secretly observed, secretly followed, the sense that Eliot dramatized in the final section of *The Waste Land* (lines 360–66, and note). "There is a secret magic about these waste lands [i.e., environs of the derelict villages on the edge of the battlefields]. While you wander through the corrupted overgrown orchard, there is always someone at your back. You turn. It is nothing but the creak of a branch. . . ."[10]

Hugh Quigley was thoroughly familiar with Victorian literary and aesthetic texts, which he recalled constantly at the front to help him "see." He does this with Ruskin's *Modern Painters,* as we have seen, and he knows *The Well at the World's End* as intimately. To him the ghastly canal at Ypres, clotted with corpses, is "like" the poison pool under the Dry Tree in Morris, around which lay the bodies of men with "dead Leathery faces . . . drawn up in a grin, as though they had died in pain . . . (Book III, Chap. 18)."[11] One of Quigley's problems is how to remember. He seems to solve it by associating the thing to be remembered with an analog in a well-known literary text. This is what he does in recalling the bizarre look of the ruined Cloth Hall at Ypres in autumn, 1917. It was "so battered that not a single sculpture figure, or shadow of a figure, remained, except one gargoyle at the end, which leered down as jauntily as ever." He fixes this image by relating it to the Morris landscape, where similar figures leer: "When I come back, this incident will remain one of the treasured memories, something to recount time and again, as happening in a land of horror and dread whence few return, like that country Morris describes in *The Well at the World's End*."[12]

But there was one English "romance" even better known than Morris's. This was Bunyan's *Pilgrim's Progress*. Everybody had been raised on it. When in the *Daily Express* on November 12, 1918, the columnist "Orion" described his feeling upon hearing that peace had come, he wrote, "Like Christian, I felt a great burden slip from off my shoulders." The *Daily Express* was a "popular" paper, but "Orion" didn't have to say, "Like Christian in John Bunyan's *Pilgrim's Progress*." He knew he would be understood, not least by the troops, who had named one of the support trenches of the Hohenzollern Redoubt "Pilgrim's Progress." They would not fail to notice the similarity between a fully loaded soldier, marching to and from the line with haversack, ground-sheet, blanket, rifle, and ammunition, and the image of Christian at the out-set of his adventures: "I saw a man clothed in rags . . . and a great burden upon his back." Recalling a terrible night march in the mud, Quigley writes: "The spirit takes note of nothing, perception dies, and, like Christian, we carry our own burden [here, rifle and ammunition], thinking only of it."[13] Christian's burden drops away when he beholds the Cross; Private Anthony French's when his equipment is blown off by the shell that wounds him in the thigh: "I had ceased to be a soldier. Only my helmet remained. . . . I found myself without waterbottle, iron rations, gasmask. My watch had lost cover and glass. Then an enormous burden of responsibility seemed to roll away as if this were the end of a pilgrim's progress. There was no pain. I felt at rest."[14] R. H. Tawney's burden falls away when, attacking the first day on the Somme, he realizes — it is his first action — that he is not going to be a coward after all:

> I hadn't gone ten yards before I felt a load fall from me. There's a sen-tence at the end of *The Pilgrim's Progress* which has always struck me as one of the most awful things imagined by man: "Then I saw that there was a way to Hell, even from the Gates of Heaven, as well as from the City of Destruction." To have gone so far and be rejected at last! Yet undoubtedly man walks between precipices, and no one knows the rot-tenness in him till he cracks, and then it's too late. I had been worried by the thought: "Suppose one should lose one's head and get other men cut up! Suppose one's legs should take fright and refuse to move!" Now I knew it was all right. I shouldn't be frightened and I shouldn't lose my head. Imagine the joy of that discovery! I felt quite happy and self-possessed.[15]

Even when Gunner William Pressey chooses the word *great* instead of *large* to describe the burdens carried by the French civilians retreating before the German advance in spring, 1918 ("Some had carts, others great bundles on their back"[16]), we may suspect that *Pilgrim's Progress* is helping to determine his choice.

It is odd and wonderful that front-line experience should ape the pattern of the one book everybody knew. Or to put it perhaps more accurately, front-line experience seemed to become available for interpretation when it was seen how closely parts of it resembled the action of *Pilgrim's Progress*. Sassoon takes it for granted that his title *Sherston's Progress* will contribute significant shape to his episodic account of his passage through anxiety to arrive at his triumphant moment of relief as Rivers enters his hospital room. Like

Christian, he has been looking for something and going somewhere, and at the end he knows fully what his goal has been all the while. And allusion to Bunyan can work sardonically as well, as it does in Henry Williamson's *The Patriot's Progress* (1930), whose hero, John Bullock, enters the war with enthusiasm and endures it stoically, only to end in bitterness, one leg missing, patronized by uncomprehending civilians.

The problem for the writer trying to describe elements of the Great War was its utter incredibility, and thus its incommunicability in its own terms. As Bernard Bergonzi has said, "The literary records of the Great War can be seen as a series of attempts to evolve a response that would have some degree of adequacy to the unparalleled situation in which the writers were involved."[17] Unprecedented meaning thus had to find precedent motifs and images. It is a case illustrating E. D. Hirsch's theory of the way new meanings get proposed:

> No one would ever invent or understand a new type of meaning unless he were capable of perceiving analogies and making novel subsumptions under previously known types. . . . By an imaginative leap the unknown is assimilated to the known, and something genuinely new is realized.[18]

The "new type of meaning" is that of the new industrialized mass trench warfare. The "previously known types" are the motifs and images of popular romance. The "something genuinely new" is the significant memories of the war we have been focusing on, where *significant* means, in fact, *artistic*. Because Dante has never really been domesticated in Protestant England, when an English sensibility looks for traditional images of waste and horror and loss and fear, it turns not to the *Inferno* but to *Pilgrim's Progress*.

It would be impossible to count the number of times "the Slough of Despond" is invoked as the only adequate designation for churned-up mud morasses pummeled by icy rain and heavy shells. It becomes one of the inevitable clichés of memory. So does "the Valley of the Shadow of Death," where, in Bunyan, "lay blood, bones, ashes, and mangled bodies of men, even of Pilgrims that had gone this way formerly." Major Pilditch invokes that valley to help him describe the indescribable:

> The bare poles and brick heaps of Souchez looked perfectly weird and unnatural as the sun came out and threw it all up into a livid pink-hued distinctness. I knew I should never be able to describe its sinister appearance, but that I should never forget it. It reminded me of an old wood-cut in my grandfather's "Pilgrim's Progress," of the Valley of the Shadow of Death where Christian met Apollyon.[19]

When 2nd Lt. Alexander Gillespie was killed at Loos, on his body, we are told, was found a copy of *Pilgrim's Progress* with this passage marked: "Then I entered into the Valley of the Shadow of Death, and had no light for almost halfway through it. I thought I should have been killed there, and the sun rose, and I went through that which was behind with far more ease and quiet."[20] Apparently Gillespie had been using the passage as a sort of consolatory psalm, a version of Psalm 23:4 ("Yea, though I walk through the valley of the shadow of death, I will fear no evil") more appropriate for trench use because of its image of significant dawn.

Possessing so significant a first name, the artillery subaltern Christian Creswell Carver was in a special position to imagine himself re-enacting *Pilgrim's Progress*. Writing his brother in March, 1917, he describes a mounted ammunition detail at night on the Somme:

> To our right and below us is the river stretching across a vista of broken stumps, running water and shell pools, to the skeleton gleaming white of another village on the far bank. If only an artist could paint the grim scene now while the hand of war and death is still hovering over it. In our steel helmets and chain visors we somehow recall *Pilgrim's Progress,* armored figures passing through the valley of the shadow. On — for Apollyon's talons are ever near.[21]

And of course he signs this letter "Christian."

The road which Good Will advises Christian to follow to get from the City of Destruction to the Celestial City is specifically "straight and narrow." So was the infamous miry twelve-kilometer road that led from Poperinghe to Ypres; and it was while moving up into the Salient on this road in darkness that soldiers seem most often to have recalled Christian's journey, in order to confer some shape and meaning on their suffering. "Hundreds of thousands of men must remember the road from Poperinghe to Ypres," says Henry Williamson. "Its straitness begins between two long lines of houses. . . ."[22] Carrington finds *Pilgrim's Progress* applicable in an almost uncanny way. "To find the way in the dark" up this road, he remembers, "was a task worthy of Bunyan's pilgrim." He then quotes Bunyan's account of Christian's progress through the Valley of the Shadow of Death:

> The pathway was here also exceeding narrow, and therefore good Christian was the more put to it; for when he sought in the dark to shun the ditch on the one hand, he was ready to tip over into the mire on the other. Thus he went on, for the pathway was here so dark that oft-times, when he lifted his foot to set forward, he knew not where, nor upon what, he should set it next. And ever and anon the flame and

smoke would come out in . . . abundance, with sparks and hideous noises. . . . Thus he went on a great while; yet still the flames would be reaching towards him: Also he heard doleful voices and rushings to and fro, so that sometimes he thought he should be torn to pieces, or trodden down like mire in the streets.[23] .

Such scenes of hazardous journeying constitute the essence of *Pilgrim's Progress,* whose title page itself specifies "His Dangerous Journey" as one of the three stages of Christian's experience, the other two being "The Manner of His Setting Out" and "Safe Arrival at the Desired Country." If the title of Sherriff's *Journey's End* alludes overtly to Othello's famous speech of acquiescence and surrender (V, ii, 263–85), it points implicitly as well to such a world of literary romance as Bunyan's, where combat-as-journeying promises a meaning to be revealed at the end. Gordon Swaine's poem of the Second War, "A Journey Through a War," picks up the image of journeying, although by now the romance hero has attenuated to

> *A figure through the pages of a fable,*

and the allegorical meaning has clouded over:

> *Obscure the moral and the fancy feeble.*

It is the *Pilgrim's Progress* action of moving physically through some terrible topographical nightmare along a straight road that dominates Anthony French's memory, in 1972, of his whole war: "For me," he says, "and probably for all who served and survive, there runs through this panorama of memory, through the web of divergent, intersecting by-ways, from the last sunset of rational existence to the morning of armistice and reckoning, one road along which the continuity of those days is traced."[24]

   Although the delicate, sensitive batman Alfred M. Hale was never close to the line, he too interpreted his experience by calling *Pilgrim's Progress* to his assistance. If he had no occasion to advert to the Valley of the Shadow of Death, he did find a use for his memory of Christian's anxious care of his "roll with a seal upon it," his all-important "certificate" which admits him, finally, to the Celestial City. Christian loses this certificate once while asleep and spends an anxious time looking for it. Hale's "certificate" takes two forms. The first is the slip of paper marked C-2 attesting his status as a low-category man and constituting for a time his defense against his own Slough of Despond—i.e., "overseas": "This slip of paper I kept tight hold of and hugged to myself, as it were, until one day . . . it was suggested to me by a sarcastic N.C.O. that I really better keep it to myself, and not be so fond of trotting it out on all occasions." The second form Christian's "certificate" takes in Hale's agon is that of the magical Yellow Paper admitting the bearer to the Celestial City of demobilization and home.

The scene is the port at Dunkirk, March 4, 1919. Happy as bridegroom, Hale files with others marked for demobilization down "the cobbled roadway on our way at last for the sea and England." At the quay the Celestial City awaits: "Then I saw our steamer waiting for us in the mist and the rain." It is "the Big Ship"—the troops' mythological, pseudo-Arthurian term for the once only imaginable boat plying between France and Demobilization. In *Pilgrim's Progress* the Prophets, looking out over the gate of the City, are told: "These pilgrims are from the City of Destruction for the love that they bear to the King of this place." Then, Bunyan goes on, "The Pilgrims gave in unto them each man his certificate," whereupon the King "commanded to open the gate." Hale's welcome is less splendid but scarcely less gratifying: "The gangway was placed in position, and a very dirty looking individual in civilian garments stood on guard as we went one by one on board." Bunyan's account of Christian's salvation by certificate takes place in simple, passionate prose in which *then* is the principal connective, as in "Then the Pilgrims gave in unto them each man his certificate." Likewise Hale:

Then it was I both saw and knew, as I had not done before, the value of that yellow paper. For now we were bidden to show it, and I held tight to it in the rain and displayed it to view as I went on board. . . . as did everybody else with but one exception. My paper held so tightly was all limp and sodden and torn with much handling, but I had it safe and sound right enough, and that was all I cared for.

As Bunyan's Christian enters the gates and looks back, he sees Ignorance, "a very brisk lad," soliciting admission. "Asked for his certificate," Ignorance "fumbled in his bosom for one, and found none." Asked by the Prophets "Have you none?" Ignorance is silent. What follows is the same thing that stuck with R. H. Tawney:

The King . . . commanded the . . . Shining Ones . . . to go out and take Ignorance, and bind him hand and foot, and have him away. Then they took him up, and carried him through the air to the door that I saw in the side of the hill, and put him in there. Then I saw that there was a way to Hell, even from the gates of Heaven, as well as from the City of Destruction.

Hale's version of this is exquisite. Safe on the deck, ecstatic that his certificate has carried him to bliss everlasting, he looks back down to the quay one last time. "Not so the poor young devil pacing the quayside alone and forlorn. He had lost his paper; . . . I sincerely pitied him, . . . and have often wondered since what became of him."[25]

Bunyan's Celestial City is a fantasy of gold and jewels. It looks the way Dresden does when Vonnegut's Billy "Pilgrim," in *Slaughterhouse-Five*, sees it suddenly shining through the opened doors of a boxcar: "The doorways framed the loveliest city that most of the Americans had ever seen. The skyline was intricate and voluptuous and enchanted and absurd." Vonnegut's answer to the question "What did it look like?" suggests some of the continued capacity of *Pilgrim's Progress* to elicit the illusion of meaning from the wars of the twentieth century: "It looked like a Sunday school picture of Heaven to Billy Pilgrim."[26]

Notes

1. *Mimesis: The Representation of Reality in Western Literature,* trans. Willard Trask (Princeton, N.J., 1953; New York, 1957), pp. 107–24.
2. *Letters from the Front,* ed. John Laffin (1973), p. 12.
3. *Surprised by Joy,* p. 164.
4. *Anatomy,* p. 149.
5. *Memoirs of a Fox-Hunting Man,* pp. 372–73.
6. *Memoirs of an Infantry Officer,* p. 21.
7. *Sherston's Progress,* p. 41.
8. *Undertones of War,* p. 162.
9. *A Subaltern's War,* p. 117.
10. *A Passionate Prodigality,* p. 43.
11. *Passchendaele and the Somme,* p. 159.
12. *Passchendaele and the Somme,* pp. 128–129.
13. *Passchendaele and the Somme,* p. 77.
14. *Gone for a Soldier* (Kineton, Eng., 1972), p. 79.
15. *The Attack and Other Papers* (1953), pp. 13–14.
16. *People at War, 1914–1918,* ed. Michael Moynihan (1973), p. 148.
17. *Heroes' Twilight,* p. 41.
18. *Validity in Interpretation* (New Haven, Conn., 1967), p. 105.
19. IWM.
20. Laffin, ed., *Letters from the Front,* p. 15.
21. Housman, ed., *War Letters of the English Fallen,* p. 69.
22. *The Wet Flanders Plain,* p. 46.
23. *A Subaltern's War,* pp. 135–136.
24. *Gone for a Soldier,* p. ix.
25. IWM.
26. New York, 1969; 1971, p. 148.

Verdun has brought war back into honour,
the sort of war in which the individual man
and personal courage are given their full
chances of values.
— H. H. von Mellenthin,
The New York Times Monthly Magazine
(June 1916)

Fort Vaux

ALISTAIR HORNE

Fort Vaux was the smallest in the whole Verdun system, covering, less than one-quarter the area of Douaumont. It had no 155 mm. turret, only one bearing a single 75. But this had been completely destroyed when a German 420 detonated a three-quarters of a ton demolition charge laid there in the panic following the fall of Douaumont. As Vaux too had had all its flanking 75s removed by Joffre, by June 1916 it possessed no armament bigger than a machine gun. None of these was mounted in an armoured turret. Apart from the shattering of the 75 turret, one of the underground corridors had been opened by a shell, and was now blocked with sandbags; most of the outlying galleries had been damaged in some degree, and an enormous crack ran disquietingly along the length of the underground barracks. Otherwise the fort had withstood the bombardment well. Less satisfactory was the work carried out (or rather, not carried out) under Pétain's orders of February to rehabilitate the forts. No deep underground approach tunnel had been dug (as the Germans had done at Douaumont) to link the fort with the rear — so that it could easily be cut off. Worse still, nothing had been done to improve the water supply, despite grave warnings. Both these shortcomings were to have serious consequences.

In command of the fort was Major Sylvain-Eugène Raynal, a tough Colonial soldier from Bordeaux, aged forty-nine, to whom promotion had not been particularly kind. Badly wounded several times in the war already, he limped on a cane and should by rights have been invalided out of the army. He had however managed to persuade his seniors to send him back to the front, on fortress duty, which was considered less arduous than the trenches. On May 24th, the day the attempt to recapture Douaumont failed, Raynal reached his new post at Vaux. His first impression of the fort was of soldiers crowded together:

> in such numbers that it is extremely difficult to move, and I took a very long time to reach my command post. . . . If an attack materialised all the occupants would be captured before they could defend themselves.

Apart from its regular garrison, the fort was filled with stray stretcher-bearers, signallers and the debris of regiments that had lost contact with their units in the chaos of the German onslaught and had come to seek refuge. Raynal at once tried to chase these fugitives out, but still more arrived and soon it became impossible for troops to leave the fort. Thus when the siege began, instead of the maximum complement of 250 for which it was designed, Raynal found himself with over 600 troops in his charge, many of them wounded. In addition, Vaux's garrison numbered four carrier pigeons and a cocker-spaniel brought in by the survivors of a signal unit.

On June 1st, Raynal had watched helplessly through binoculars as the Germans advanced across the Bois de la Caillette a mile and a half away. If only he had had one 75 in the fort! Nevertheless, two machine guns set up on the superstructure, firing at extreme range, achieved miraculous results. Baffled by the mysterious, invisible weapon that was tearing holes in their ranks, the German Grenadiers kept on coming until Raynal could see a whole trench choked with grey bodies. Then the attackers disappeared out of sight into the valley.

To the northeast of Vaux, the land falls so rapidly towards the Woevre that the approaches right up to the fort wall lay in dead ground both to its guns and those of Delvert in R.1.[1] Now that the protective flank of La Caillette and Fumin had been lost, it was abundantly clear to Raynal that nothing could stop the Germans reaching Fort Vaux the following morning. The night was spent frantically erecting sandbag barricades, with loopholes for throwing grenades through, at nine breaches in various parts of the fort. Meanwhile the German bombardment rose in a tremendous crescendo; at one period, according to Raynal, shells were falling on the small area of the fort at a rate of 1,500 to 2,000 an hour. Just before dawn on the 2nd the barrage abruptly ceased. The moment had come.

Waiting in trenches less than 150 yards below the lip of the fort were two battalions of the German 50th Division, under the special direction of Major-

General Weber Pasha who had recently distinguished himself in organising the defence of the Turkish forts at Gallipoli. In a matter of seconds his men were swarming into the fort moat. At once, they came under heavy machine-gun fire from the two flanking galleries, similar to those that the Brandenburgers had found untenanted in Fort Douaumont, at the north-west and north-east corners. On these the initial fighting was focused. Crouching on the roof of the north-east gallery, German pioneers first tried unsuccessfully to knock it out by lowering bundles of hand-grenades and exploding them outside the loopholes.

The French machine-gunners continued to fire at the Germans attacking the other gallery. Then the pioneers heard below the unmistakable click followed by curses as the machine gun jammed. Quickly they hurled grenades into the gallery, dispatching the gun crew. Out leaped a courageous French officer, Raynal's second-in-command, Captain Tabourot. For a while, almost single-handed, he kept the attackers away from the entrance to the gallery by hurling hand-grenades, until—his abdomen ripped open by a German grenade—he crawled back into the interior to die. Shortly afterwards, the defenders, thirty-two men and an officer, surrendered the gallery; in it the Germans found two small cannon—minus their breech-blocks.

It was now 5 A.M., and the attackers had already taken one of Vaux's two main strongpoints. Things did not go quite so easily with the larger, double gallery at the north-west. Pioneers tried first to 'smoke out' its inmates by poking over the fort wall specially elongated tubes fitted to flamethrowers. In the initial surprise, the French machine guns stopped firing, and taking advantage of this Lieutenant Rackow of the 158th Paderborn Regiment managed to slip across the moat with about thirty men. They were the first Germans to reach the superstructure of the fort itself. But almost immediately the French machine guns were back in operation, and for several agonising hours Rackow and his small group sat isolated on the fort. In the terrible din of the Verdun bombardment their comrades only twenty yards away were unable to hear their shouts for support. The German pioneers, with considerable fortitude, now tried lowering sacks full of grenades on a rope outside the gallery, but did themselves more damage. All through the morning the struggle continued, until one after the other the French machine guns were silenced and some fifteen of the gallery's inhabitants had been wounded. Still it held out. Then at last the Germans on top of the fort discovered the sandbags with which Raynal had plugged a large breach in the corridor leading to the north-west gallery. They removed them, and began hurling grenades into the corridor. Realising what was happening, Raynal ordered the gallery to be abandoned immediately, before its defenders could be taken from the rear.

By about 4 P.M., Raynal had lost both his exterior defences, the superstructure was solidly occupied by the enemy, and the battle was about to move underground. A little like the children and the pirates in 'Peter Pan,' members of the fort garrison gazed helplessly through the slits of the observation cupolas at the young Germans sprawled out on the ground just above their heads, nonchalantly smoking pipes and occasionally making insulting gestures for their consumption. Meanwhile, during the contest for the galleries, Raynal had hastened to build sandbag barricades inside the corridors leading to them from the central fort.

As soon as both galleries had been occupied, Lieutenant Rackow, who had now assumed control of all operations on the fort, ordered a party under Lieutenant Ruberg of the Pioneers to break into the fort proper along the north-east corridor. Obediently Ruberg and a handful of men set off down a dark narrow passage, similar to the one that had confronted Sergeant Kunze in Douaumont three months earlier. A long flight of steps led down under the moat and then up again, and soon Ruberg came to a steel door barring his path. Behind it he could hear French voices whispering. Swiftly he prepared a charge out of hand-grenades (because of General von Deimling's acceleration of the attack on Vaux the Pioneers had had no time in which to prepare proper demolition charges), pulled the pin out of the last grenade and ran.

Behind the steel door was Raynal himself, inspecting a hastily erected barricade which was not entirely to his liking. From the noises made by Ruberg, he realised what was afoot and quickly ordered his men back. Just in time; for the barricade 'disintegrated in a powerful explosion.' On the other side of the door, the five-and-a-half-second grenade fuse had not given Ruberg time to get clear, and he was hurled backwards by the explosion, lacerated with splinters. The force of the blast and the wounding of their chief caused the Germans to hesitate before re-entering the deadly tunnel just long enough for Raynal to rebuild his barricade and site a machine gun behind it. For the time being the French remained masters of the corridor.

That night Raynal, with all his telephone lines to the rear already severed, sent off the first of his four pigeons bearing a report of the situation.

Early on the 3rd of June, German assault troops worked their way round to the south of the fort. Vaux was now completely cut off, even from R.1 which still maintained a tenuous link with the rest of the Second Army. The siege was on, and a curious stalemate was established with a German commander, Rackow, on top of the fort, and a French commander, Raynal, underground. All through the day the main battle continued ferociously in the two corridors leading to the heart of the fort. In each the French had built sandbag barricades several feet thick, defended by one brave grenadier. The German pioneers had meanwhile brought up more powerful explosives, so that it was only a matter of time before the French grenadier was knocked out, and his rampart demolished. But beyond was yet another barricade, from behind which a machine gun spewed death on the attackers at point-blank range, while the French were preparing yet a further series of obstacles to its rear. Yard by yard the Germans advanced, but at heavy cost.

Of all the horrors in the fighting at Verdun, it is difficult to imagine any much more appalling than the struggle that took place day after day in the underground corridors of Fort Vaux. Here the battle went on in pitch darkness, relieved only by the flash of exploding grenades, in a shaft for the most part no more than three feet wide and five feet high, in which no grown man could stand upright. Machine-gun bullets ricochetting from wall to wall inflicted wounds as terrible as any dum-dum, and in the confined space the concussion of the grenades was almost unendurable. Repeatedly men of both sides felt themselves asphyxiating in the air polluted by TNT fumes and cement dust stirred up by the explosions. Added to it was the ever-worsening stink of the dead, rapidly decomposing in the June heat, for whom there was no means of burial inside the fort.

The two attacking German battalions had already suffered grave losses. Before being silenced, Vaux's gallery machine guns had cut swathes in the attackers, and by the evening of June 2nd the battalion of the 53rd Regiment had only one officer left unwounded. Meanwhile, Rackow and his men on the roof of the fort were being exposed to an ever-increasing intensity of French gun-fire, to which the deadly 155 in nearby Fort Moulainville now added its voice. On the night of June 3rd both battalions had to be withdrawn exhausted. But for Raynal and his six hundred there was no relief.

Out at R.1 Delvert had meanwhile successfully repulsed two more German attacks, and spent the rest of the day under heavy bombardment. He noted in his diary that he had not slept for seventy-two hours. At 10 o'clock that night, Captain Delvert was overjoyed by the arrival of a subaltern, bringing a company of reinforcements. But the company numbered only eighteen men. An hour later, another subaltern appeared, claiming to have brought up a company.

'How many men have you?' asked Delvert.

'One hundred and seventy.'

Delvert counted them. There were twenty-five.

Back at Sector Headquarters, General Lebrun had received Raynal's pigeon message, and — under heavy pressure from Nivelle — prescribed an immediate counter-attack to regain the fort. Almost hysterically, Lebrun told the wretched general commanding the 124th Division that he was, if necessary, to lead the attack in person. At dawn on the 4th, the French went in in six dense waves, actually reaching the western extremity of the fort. But fresh replacements of Düsseldorf Fusiliers were already in position, and they drove off the attackers at bayonet point.

For Raynal, June 4th was to be the grimmest day so far. It nearly proved fatal. The previous night German Pioneers had managed, with a great effort, to bring up six flame-throwers on to the fort superstructure (four having been destroyed by artillery fire en route). They would smoke Vaux's heroic garrison out like rats. At a given moment, the Germans attacking below ground were withdrawn, and the nozzles of the infernal devices were inserted into apertures and breaches in the fort exterior. (Fortunately for the garrison a detachment of Germans trying to seal hermetically the fort by filling in one of the larger breaches was dispersed by the vigilant crew of the Moulainville 155.) The first warning Raynal had was a cry of 'Gas!' from all parts of the fort. Almost immediately an asphyxiating black smoke poured into the central gallery. Down the northwest corridor fled its defenders, faces blackened and burnt, their barricades abandoned. Flickers of flame began to appear in the main body of the fort, and for a moment mass panic threatened. Then the flame-throwers ceased. Reacting quickly, and with almost superhuman courage, Lieutenant Girard darted back into the smoke-filled north-west corridor. He reached the abandoned machine gun there a second before the Germans. Wounded several times in the ensuing action, he held on until the situation was re-established; then fell unconscious from the toxic effects of the smoke. Meanwhile, Raynal had ordered the opening of all possible vents to clear the smoke, and to minimise the recurrence of such an attack.

A similar German attempt to rush the defenders in the north-east corridor had also failed, while an attack on the bunker at the south-west corner of the fort had ended in a minor French triumph. All the German Pioneers had been killed, and their flame-throwers captured. With this acquisition the garrison were able to keep the southern moat of the fort clear of the enemy. The net result of the new German effort had been dreadful burns for some fifteen members of the French garrison and the capture of twenty-five yards of the north-west corridor, with one of Raynal's three observation cupolas.

Shortly before midday Raynal dispatched his last pigeon with the message:

We are still holding. But . . . relief is imperative. Communicate with us by Morse-blinker from Souville, which does not reply to our calls. This is my last pigeon.

Badly gassed in the recent attack, the wretched bird fluttered around half-heartedly, returning to settle on the loophole of Raynal's Command Post. After several more failures, it was finally coaxed into the air. It reached Verdun, was delivered of its message, then — like Pheidippides at Marathon — fell dead. (The only one of its species to be 'decorated' with the *Légion d'Honneur*, the noble emissary was stuffed and sits to this day in a Paris Museum.)

Reaction to the message brought by Raynal's last pigeon was speedy. Fort Souville, which suspected that Vaux had already succumbed and its signals were a German trick, now blinked out an encouraging message to Raynal, and the mounting of yet another relief attack was prepared.

Grave as had been the events of the morning, something far more menacing transpired in the fort that afternoon. Says Raynal:

A sergeant of the fort Quartermaster's Staff came to me, requesting a word in private, and said in a choking voice: *'Mon Commandant,* there is practically no water left in the cistern.'

I leaped up, I shook the sergeant, I made him repeat his words; 'But this is treachery!'

'Non, mon Commandant, we have distributed only the quantities you indicated, but the gauge was inaccurate.'

The agony began. I gave the order to preserve what little remained and to make no distribution today.[2]

The three-hundred odd supernumerary troops inside the fort had now become useless mouths that could endanger the whole garrison. Somehow, Raynal realised, it was imperative to evacuate them. But Vaux was encircled by the enemy. A desperate risk had to be taken. Summoning Officer Cadet Buffet, a nineteen-year-old brought up in an orphanage, he ordered him to scout a way out from the fort late that night. The bulk of the escaping troops would then follow in small, well-spaced packets.

While in the acrid darkness of the fort the garrison knew and cared little about the weather outside, Delvert in R.1 recorded that the 4th was a beautiful sunny Sunday. There were more German attacks, but in the June sunshine Delvert had time to comment lyrically on the essential beauty of the grenadiers poised to hurl their missiles, *'avec le beau geste du joueur de balle.'* Unfortunately, the day was later spoilt by a new prolonged bombardment from French guns, and by maddening thirst exacerbated by the heat. That night at 9.30, Delvert ordered his company to stand by to be relieved. The men were almost too tired to rejoice. An hour and a half later a runner arrived from regimental headquarters postponing the relief, 'because of circumstances.' Mercifully, there was rain the next day, and the company put out ground-sheets to catch the water. Meanwhile, in the German trenches opposite there were signs of unprecedented activity. Communication trenches were being widened, all of which could only mean a new all-out attack on R.1. Would relief come before the remnants of Delvert's heroic company were submerged?

After dark on the 5th, the awaited relief at last arrived. But the ordeal was not yet over. With no communication trench to provide cover, Delvert's company were silhouetted targets for the machine guns installed in R.2. Then followed a dreadfully accurate artillery barrage. When the company reached safety, it numbered only thirty-seven broken men; but—on German figures—it had inflicted over three hundred casualties. For another three days Delvert's successors continued the valiant defence; then R.1 fell to the Germans with 500 prisoners.

For Raynal and his men there could be neither relief nor rain-water to assuage their growing thirst. June 5th, the fourth day of the siege, had begun at dawn with a shattering explosion near the *Casemate de Bourges* on the south-west corner of the fort. A huge breach had been blown in the wall, and German Pioneers were on the spot at once with a flame-thrower. But a freak current of air blew the flame back in their faces. A grenade-thrower counter-sally, led by Lieutenant Girard, restored the situation. In the course of it, Girard was wounded again.

Through peepholes Raynal could now see the Germans, thwarted in their attacks up the corridors, digging fresh mineshafts under other parts of the fort from the outside.

It was not a pleasant sight. He flashed a message to Souville, requesting 'hit them quick with artillery.' The reply came with gratifying alacrity; there was a muffled thud, and the watching Raynal saw 'German bodies hurled into the moat. Work above us ceased at once.'

Outside the fort, the latest failure of the flame-throwers had flung the attackers into acute depression. The infernal machines, it was felt, were causing them more casualties than the besieged, and they were withdrawn. Little did the Germans realise how close the flame-throwers had come to breaking Vaux's resistance the day before; or that its water had run out. All they could see was the heavy toll exacted by the incessant French gunfire on the fort's superstructure, and the almost negligible progress being made along the underground corridors. The fort indeed seemed impregnable. Perhaps the men inside could hold out for another month, or a year. Finally, to make things worse, the Pioneers had received an insulting message from General von Deimling, declaring that the fort had been taken, but that a few isolated groups of French were still holding out in one or two cellars. These were to be 'mopped up' forthwith.

Later that same day, Raynal suffered two new reverses. A second after the blinker operator had completed a message to Souville a shell landed on the post, killing three men, and wounding several others, while destroying the signal equipment. In the course of the day's subterranean fighting along the north-east corridor, the enemy had taken the entrance to the last accessible latrine; an important morale factor in the already foully stinking fort. By now of the eight surviving officers under Raynal, one was gravely wounded; three had been wounded to a lesser extent (two of them at least twice), but stayed at their posts; a fourth had a bad case of fever, while Raynal himself was shivering with recurrent malaria. That evening he inspected his men,

> crushed with fatigue, silent and gloomy. If I were to ask one more effort of them, they would have been incapable. Therefore I decided to distribute to them the last drops of water. . . .

This amounted to less than a quarter of a pint per person, for men who had not had a drop the previous twenty-four hours — and it reeked vilely of corpses. There was no question of eating any of the highly salted 'singe' (of which there was a plentiful supply); Raynal noted that no food had passed his lips for two days. How much longer could the garrison keep up its strength? That night, rigging up an *ad hoc* blinker, Raynal signalled Fort Souville:

> Imperative be relieved and receive water tonight. I am reaching the end of my tether . . .

Suddenly, into this atmosphere of extreme dejection burst a mud-stained figure from another world. It was young Buffet, proudly wearing a bright new medal. The garrison crowded around him, fatigue and thirst temporarily forgotten.

He had achieved the impossible. It transpired that most of the escapers had been cut down by German machine guns, or taken prisoner, but Buffet and eight others had made it. Reaching the refuge of Fort Tavannes, he had been passed from the Brigadier to the Sector Commander, General Lebrun, and finally on to Nivelle himself, who had decorated him and told of an imminent counter-attack being prepared which would, this time, succeed. At once the nineteen-year-old Officer Cadet volunteered to creep through the German lines again to take the news back to the fort. The sergeant accompanying him was wounded and had to be abandoned on the way, but a second time Buffet got through.

Eagerly the garrison officers pressed Buffet for details of the promised relief attack. It was to begin at 2 A.M. the following morning, said Buffet, and a whole battalion would be taking part. 'I saw the faces of my officers darken,' recalls Raynal, 'and I guessed what was going on inside them, because I shared their thoughts; the operation, as conceived, seemed to be, *a priori*, inadequate.'

Shortly after midnight the fort defenders heard the characteristic scream of French 75 mm. shells. But not a single explosion. The 'softening-up' barrage was falling, quite harmlessly, well over the fort. At 2 A.M., the garrison took up positions to give support to the relief force. The barrage lifted, and anxiously the besieged searched the horizon for their deliverers. At 2.30, still no sign. Finally, towards 3 A.M., a message from the *Casemate de Bourges* reported sighting a small force, of about platoon strength, pinned down by German machine-gun fire a few yards from the fort. The observers watched in despair as the isolated French were picked off one by one and then rose from their shell-holes, hands above their heads. It was all Vaux saw of the relieving attack that Nivelle had promised Buffet. The relief force had done its best, and suffered terrible losses, with a sergeant-major taking over command of the battalion when every single officer was either killed or wounded.

Morale inside the fort fell to its lowest point. Under the strain, a young lieutenant went off his head and threatened to blow up the grenade depot. It would be impossible to hold out much longer. Raynal blinked out another message, pleading 'intervene before complete exhaustion . . . *Vive la France!'* But there was no longer any response from Souville, once again convinced that the fort must have succumbed. Later that day a huge shell landing on the fort caved in part of the vault of the central gallery, and now the threat of being buried alive was added to that of asphyxiation and thirst. Still the Germans could make no headway along the underground corridors. But by evening the suffering from thirst was indescribable. Over the past three June days each of the garrison had received a total of one half-glass of foul water. In their despair, men tried to lick the moisture and slime off the fort walls. As he inspected the fort, leaning heavily on his stick, Raynal found men fainting in the corridors, others retching violently — having drunk their own urine. Worst of all was the plight of the ninety-odd wounded, with no drop of water to assuage their raging fever, some atrociously burnt, and many lying in the dark, foul lazaret without proper attention since the beginning of June.

Fort Vaux had done its duty, Major Raynal decided. Shelled by Big Berthas, besieged, attacked by gas and fire, cut off from France, with nothing more imposing than machine guns for its defence, it had held off the weight of the Crown Prince's army for a week. Even after the Germans had actually penetrated the fort, they had been able to advance no more than thirty or forty yards underground in five days of fighting. Only thirst had conquered Vaux. What wonders could not mighty Douaumont have achieved had it been commanded by a Raynal!

Having made his decision, to Raynal late that night there came a last flicker of hope when once again the French guns flared up. Was Nivelle coming to save them after all? But by midnight a strangely eery silence fell over the whole battlefield. There would be no new relief attempt.

At 3.30 on the morning of June 7th, sleepy observers in Fort Souville picked up the corrupted fragment of a last blinker message from Vaux. '. . . *ne quittez pas* . . .' was all that could be deciphered. A few hours later the fort surrendered amid scenes of pre-twentieth century courtesy, an appropriate epilogue to what was one of the most heroic isolated actions of the war. From behind a barricade in the north-west corridor, Lieutenant Werner Müller of the German Machine Gun Corps saw a French officer and two men bearing a white flag. They handed over a formal letter addressed 'To The Commander of the German Forces Attacking Fort Vaux.' Barely able to conceal his joy, Müller fetched his captain and together they were led to Raynal past a guard of French soldiers, standing rigidly to attention, 'like recruits,' in the dimly-lit tunnel. The terms of surrender were formally signed, and then Raynal handed over to the Germans the highly ornamented bronze key of the Fort.

The evacuation of the captive garrison began. To one German war correspondent, its survivors presented 'the living image of desolation.' Nothing was more demanding of compassion than the spectacle of the captured, imitating Raynal's dog and crawling on their stomachs to drink frenetically of the putrid water from the very first shellhole. As they counted heads, the Germans were as surprised by the numbers of the garrison as they were by the sight of the cocker at Raynal's heels, bedraggled, battle-worn, but still alive. The garrison had suffered about a hundred casualties, including less than a score killed. To take Fort Vaux (which, but for thirst, could almost certainly have held out longer) the four German battalions (plus their Pioneers) directly concerned had alone expended 2,678 men and sixty-four officers. It was hardly surprising that French military thinkers would soon be making some far-reaching deductions about the value of underground forts.

Next day Raynal was taken to see the Crown Prince at Stenay. He was at once agreeably surprised to note that 'he is not the monkey our caricaturists have made him out to be . . . has none of that Prussian stiffness.' Speaking fluent French, the Crown Prince heaped praises on the French defenders, several times using the word 'admirable.' He congratulated Raynal on being decorated by Joffre with one of the highest degrees of the *Légion d'Honneur;* a piece of news that had not reached him in the fort. Finally, observing that Raynal had lost his own sword, as a supreme token of military esteem he presented him with the captured sword of another French officer.

Though Raynal and his men were on their way to two-and-a-half years in a prisoner-of-war camp, there remained one more tragic scene to be played out at Fort Vaux. Since June 2nd, Nivelle had ordered five separate attempts to be made to relieve the fort. Each, inadequate to the task, had foundered with bloody losses. Following the failure of the attack on June 6th that had broken the heart of Vaux's garrison, Nivelle had immediately ordered yet a sixth attack, this time to be carried out in brigade strength, by a special *Brigade de Marche* formed from crack units drawn from various parts of the Verdun front. It would be unleashed at dawn on June 8th. At a conference attended by some twenty of the generals under his command, vigorous protests were raised. Even Nivelle's evil genius, Major d'Alenson, seems to have been opposed to this new attempt. But Nivelle was adamant; his reputation was involved. When the German radio broadcast the news of the surrender of Fort Vaux the following day, he declared it to be a German hoax—just like the one in March.

The two regiments designated for the *'Brigade de Marche'* were the 2nd Zouaves and the *Régiment d'Infanterie Coloniale du Maroc;* both comprised of North African troops that were far from fresh. The commander, Colonel Savy, was told by Nivelle in person that they had been chosen.

> for the finest mission that any French unit can have, that of going to the aid of comrades in arms who are valiantly performing their duty under tragic circumstances.

Hastily the North Africans were pushed up to the front, under an avalanche of rain. Meanwhile, at the identical moment that they were to go in, the German 50th Division was about to capitalise on the capture of Vaux by thrusting out towards Fort Tavannes. The two attacks met head on.

Thirty-two-year-old Sergeant-Major César Méléra had been detailed—to his evident annoyance—to take up the rear of his battalion of the Régiment Colonial, and stop stragglers falling back. He describes tersely the ensuing action as viewed from the immediate rear. Leaving for the front, a man committed suicide, 'tired of the war which he neither understood nor saw.' On the approach march:

> The clay is so slippery and so difficult to climb that one marches as much on one's knees as one's feet. Arrived in a sweat at Souville Plateau where the Battalion is awaiting its rearguard. Lost the Machine-Gun Company. Found them again after half an hour. . . . Have to hold on to the coat of the man in front so as not to lose oneself. Fall into a hole. Arrive in a glade. Halt; the machine-gunners lost again. Three-quarters of an hour's pause.

At 4 A.M. Méléra reached Fort Tavannes, where he spent the day of the 8th. That night,

> runners bring news. The attack has miscarried . . . At the moment we were going to sortie, the Germans appeared at other points . . . the two infantries massacred by each other's artillery, obliged to return to their lines. 1st Battalion reaches Vaux. The Boche evacuate. Our own are forced to do the same. The Boche return. The 8th advances as far as the

wood on the right. The Boche evacuate. Ours are again forced to do the same. As for the Zouaves, situation similar. Nothing to be gained by attacking. The German infantry has again diminished in quality. A pile of mediocre men supported by a fantastic artillery. The Vaux garrison has capitulated. Nothing is left in the attacking battalions but debris.

The Zouaves, in fact, had never left their point of departure. Caught in an annihilating barrage of 210 mm. howitzers designed to clear the way for the Germans' own attack, the C.O. and all but one of the Zouave officers were killed. The survivor, a second lieutenant, led what remained of the battalion back to its starting position. The Moroccans alone attacked. Of the centre battalion, seven out of eight officers fell, and companies were reduced to an average of twenty-five men apiece. Inside Fort Vaux, which Colonel Savy's force had been told was still in French hands, the embrasures were tenanted by German machine-gunners. They waited until what remained of the attackers were within a few yards, then mowed them down at almost point-blank range.

In all the ten months' battle it would be difficult to find an action that was both more futile and bloody. That day Pétain, enraged at the slaughter, intervened in what was strictly his subordinate's prerogative, and ordered Nivelle to make no more attempts to retake Vaux.

Notes

1. Retranchment 1. *Ed.*
2. In fact, as a later inquiry showed, despite warnings as early as March about the inadequacy of Vaux's water supply, nothing had been done, and the cisterns appear to have been half-empty when Raynal assumed command. It was a piece of negligence on a par with the failure to garrison Fort Douaumont. — A. H.

Assault
on High Wood

LYN MACDONALD

Only two days ago, give or take the occasional spot where a stray shell had created havoc, the trees in High Wood had been in full leaf. But twenty-four hours of fighting and shelling had taken ghastly toll. The leaves were limp and yellowed by cordite. Branches hung splintered from lurching tree trunks. Whole trees had been uprooted and sent crashing into the trampled undergrowth, and the tangle of branches, now seeming to spring out of the ground, gave fine cover for snipers firing from behind them and, looming up fearful and grotesque in the light of the green star shells that rose and fell in the heart of the wood, barred the way to the infantry blundering forward.

It should have been a sylvan scene, the half-full moon riding high on a summer's night over the woods and valleys of the Somme. To observers in the British line, looking across the valley to the wood that swelled and sank in an inferno of flash and fire, the moon, the stars, the warmth seemed strangely incongruous.

Repeated reports had claimed that High Wood had been captured by the 7th Division, and Brigadier-General Baird, in command of a Brigade of the 33rd Division, had sent his men into it with orders to consolidate the line. 'Consolidate' meant 'dig,' and on a line running diagonally through the wood, they dug for half the night, cursing the undergrowth, cursing the tentacles of roots that entangled spades and entrenching tools, and cursing the fact that, for all their orders and all the reports and that the wood had been captured, machine-gun bullets were spraying them as they worked. In lulls between the bursts, they could hear voices very close in front of them shouting orders in a language that was unmistakably German. And, occasionally, the alien commands seemed to come from behind their backs.

It was a gruelling and frightful night of fear and crucifying labour. In the first light of the dawn, the weary men were ordered to filter back out of the wood, to abandon the new line, and to prepare the line outside High Wood for a fresh attack. The long night's digging had gone for nothing.

In spite of the insistence of Headquarters that High Wood had been captured — or nearly so — by the 7th Division, it was obvious to Brigadier-General Baird, from the experience of his own troops during the dreadful hours they had spent in it, that this was not the case. Furthermore, the new orders were that the whole division should pivot to face north and, with High Wood on its right, attack the trenchlines that lay between it and Martinpuich. The Glasgow Highlanders were to start out on this affray from the western corner of High Wood and, as no one knew better than the Glasgow Highlanders themselves, the western corner was still clenched in the hands of the Germans. Their orders were therefore inviting them, if not to turn their backs on the enemy, at least to launch into an attack which would bring them, in a matter of yards, within a hail of enfilade fire.

It was suicide to think of attempting it. In remarkably restrained but pungent terms, Brigadier Baird pointed out this fact to Divisional Headquarters and pointed out furthermore that, no matter how his troops were positioned, the attack could not hope to be successful unless the enemy had been cleared from High Wood. Judging by the experience of his troops in the night, this was palpably not the case. Divisional Headquarters was unperturbed. The troops had perhaps been edgy. It had been categorically claimed as long ago as ten o'clock the previous evening that High Wood had been captured, and the casualties which Baird's Brigade had unfortunately sustained, the difficulties they had encountered during the night, must have been due to isolated pockets of resistance — nothing that a little 'mopping up' would not put right. His opinion, they informed him in placatory tones, would be recorded. But the attack would go ahead.

In a lather of impotent fury, all that Brigadier Baird could do was to send a company of the King's Royal Rifle Corps up to the wood itself. When the main attack began they, with the remnants of three platoons of the Glasgow Highlanders, would attack through High Wood. At best they would clear the remaining 'pockets of resistance.' At worst they would divert the Germans' attention from the right flank of the 33rd Division as they pushed towards the north.

The attack was due to start at nine o'clock. The bombardment started at 8.30. It sounded loud and impressive. It had no particular effect.

Rifleman J. Brown, MM, No. 3 Platoon, A Coy., 16th King's Royal Rifle Corps (Church Lads Brigade)

We'd laid there all night in these little shelters what we'd dug and they were just bringing up the breakfast and the order came to march, so we never got no breakfast that morning. Cor' Blimey, I was frightened. Just thinking, 'Hope I'll get out of it.' But my legs worked, so I got up and walked out with the rest. We went across the valley and got up to High Wood and when we got along the side of the wood we lay down there and had a look down this valley what we'd come up. There was a Jock regiment marching up the road in fours and Jerry opened up on them and I remember two or three shells dropping right in among the column and they just closed ranks and came on — never faltered! Then our own bombardment started and, as usual, they was dropping short. They was falling in the fields behind us. Our own guns! I don't believe one of them went into High Wood and that's what they were supposed to be bombarding before *we* went in. They was too far away to hit us, because we was right up against the wood, and they certainly didn't hit the wood! I don't know what they was aiming at or whether they'd just had a good rum ration the night before! I reckon they were trying to ricochet off on to the target!

Corporal Jack Beament, MM, No. 1 Platoon, A Coy., 16th King's Royal Rifle Corps (Church Lads Brigade)

Just picture a lovely July sunny day. As we were waiting so many paces apart, I noticed there were hazel trees growing on the edge of the wood — hazel trees, with nuts on them. I was a stretcher-bearer in this attack and I was with George Illife who was my partner, the other stretcher-bearer. Then the Very light went up, which was the signal, and we had to go into the wood. Illife had got wounded while we were waiting and he cleared off, so I was there on my own.

Rifleman J. Brown, MM, No. 3 Platoon, A Coy., 16th King's Royal Rifle Corps (Church Lads Brigade)

The order come. Away we go! I remember Major Cooban — he was our Company Commander — going into High Wood bent forward, like, on the trot, with his revolver in his hand, and that's the last I see of him!

We follow on. There was some troops dug in about twenty yards inside High Wood, in little shell-holes, leaning forward on their arms, because the machine-gun bullets was whizzing about something awful. We went through past those chaps, but we didn't get much further. Me and another fellow got into a shell-hole, because there was no point just going on against these machine-guns and bullets spitting everywhere, so we had to sit there for a time and wait to see what was going to happen and if anyone in front was going to knock these machine-guns out so that we could get forward.

Corporal Jack Beament, MM, No. 1 Platoon, A Coy., 16th King's Royal Rifle Corps (Church Lads Brigade)

Major Cooban was a very, very brave man. He ought not to have been in that attack at all. He had lumbago so, technically, he was unfit, but he would insist on leading our Company. I never saw him after we got into the wood. It was an absolutely raging inferno. Shells and rifle fire, machine-gun fire, but, strangely enough, looking back on it, I don't think I felt all that frightened. You couldn't let fear get into your brain. You'd go berserk! All you could do was hope for the best and get on with the job. You hoped you wouldn't get killed though! I came across a chap who came from Cork, he was an Irishman and he was wounded in the head badly, but I got him into a shell-hole and bandaged him out and he managed to get out of the wood and cleared off. Then I went on a bit further, looking for more wounded but I had to take shelter, which is what all the boys were doing. I don't think that we really got twenty or thirty yards into the wood.

Rifleman J. Brown, MM, No. 3 Platoon, A Coy., 16th King's Royal Rifle Corps (Church Lads Brigade)

All of a sudden something hit me in the back. I thought it was the Jerries up behind me with a mallet! So I puts my hand round on my back and it was covered with blood. I thought to myself, 'I'm going to get out of this!' But when I tried to move my legs, they wouldn't go. I was all on my own in this shell-hole and — this is God's truth! — I lay down, put my arms under my head, laid my head on my arms and laid myself down to die. All I could think of was, 'Fancy training more than fifteen months for this!'

Corporal Jack Beament, MM, No. 1 Platoon, A Coy., 16th King's Royal Rifle Corps (Church Lads Brigade)

I got a bullet in the left shoulder, so I packed up. I started to crawl back where we'd come from and, while I was doing so, I came across a fellow from Redhill called Johnny Redman. He was wounded. He was a very tall, heavy man, but I got hold of him and I half-dragged him and half-carried him out of the wood. I got him somehow on to my shoulder and I remember wondering if the Germans had machine-guns up in the trees because, as we were getting back, I remember the bullets hitting the ground, just like heavy raindrops. They couldn't have been spent bullets from a distance, because they were so near and of course the Germans were shelling as well. There were explosions all over the place. It wasn't very pleasant. But I just had to struggle on as best I could and hope to God we would get back. What a shambles it was. I didn't get more than thirty yards, or forty yards at most. We just couldn't make any advance at all.

Rifleman J. Brown, MM, No. 3 Platoon, A Coy., 16th King's Royal Rifle Corps (Church Lads Brigade)

I was really resigned to dying and I just lay there quiet. After a while I said to myself, 'I'm a long time getting unconscious! I'll have another go.' So I had another go and my legs worked. They told me afterwards that the nerves in my spine must have been numbed with the bang of the bullet in my back, and they'd recovered a bit by then. It wasn't easy, but I chucked my equipment off and my rifle and left it in the shell-hole and when I looked at my haversack as I took it off (I'd got a primus stove in there, one of them little ones) and whatever it was that hit me had smashed that and it was full of petrol. It's a good job it never went up! So I started to crawl back out of the wood and, when I got clear of it, I was able to stand up a bit — but still creeping along like a half-shut knife because of this thing in my back.

Corporal Jack Beament, MM, No. 1 Platoon, A Coy., 16th King's Royal Rifle Corps (Church Lads Brigade)

It was a good struggle back over the open with this chap Redman over my shoulder — the one *I hadn't* got the bullet in! When I got out of the wood I was carrying him over open land. There were no trenches there, and I was going through the remains of this Cavalry. I remember a poor horse with no guts — guts all hanging out — and I had to pass that and get down somehow to the aid post. I passed Colonel Wyld on the way. I couldn't help feeling sorry for him. 'Lizzie Wyld' we called him. He became our CO when we got out to France and he used to ride round and, if he saw something he didn't like, he would bellow, 'I can see you all from my horse and I have the power to send you all home.' It was a joke in the Battalion; we made up a song, or a kind of a song and we used to sing it.

I can see you all from my horse
And I have the power
To send you a-a-all home!

Well! To see him then, I really felt sorry for him. There was a bank halfway across, just a low bank. He wasn't in the wood with us, because he was in charge of the four Companies and the other three were going in the other direction and only 'A' Company had gone into this part of the wood, to fix the Jerries on the right flank, you see. And so he had to stay outside to co-ordinate and give them the orders. He'd had to get messages somehow to each Company as to what action they could take. But things were going so badly against us that I suppose the poor devil didn't know what commands to give! And that look of anguish on his face! Poor old Lizzie! I suppose he must have been a bit shell-shocked. He was sent home after that.

Rifleman J. Brown, MM, No. 3 Platoon, A Coy., 16th King's Royal Rifle Corps (Church Lads Brigade)

There was a little doctor's shelter thing dug into the side of the hill, so I went in there and got bandaged up and that's where I did see Jack Beament. He'd just brought this chap Redman in and he'd got wounded and all. But the doctor said, 'Can you make it further back on your feet?' We both said we could, so we set off back together. What with the loss of blood, we was both feeling pretty queer by the time we got down to Happy Valley and there was a battery of guns firing there, just over the top of a steep bank. You wasn't supposed to go that near the guns but we was just plodding on. Anyhow they stopped firing and let us go by and then they started again when we'd got past. We get down to the dressing station eventually and then we was shipped off to the casualty clearing station in an old general service waggon. The Padre was at the dressing station asking us all when we came in if we'd seen anybody get killed and who they were. See anybody get killed! I should say we did!

Corporal Jack Beament, MM, No. 1 Platoon, A Coy., 16th King's Royal Rifle Corps (Church Lads Brigade)

It was a horrible, terrible massacre. We'd lost all the officers out of our company. We lost all the sergeants, all the full corporals and all the NCOs right down to Herbert King who was the senior Lance-Corporal. He was my pal and he brought 'A' Company out of the wood. He rallied them and brought them out. There were more than two hundred of us went in. And Herbert brought them out. Sixty-seven men. That was all.

It was 15 July. It would be exactly two months to the day, 15 September, before High Wood would be taken.

The trouble was the Switch Line, so long, so deep, so formidable, so heavily manned, so closely interlinked to the trenches that lay in front of it by a network of fortifications, that it was virtually impregnable. It ran from the village of Martinpuich along the valley, through the northeastern corner of High Wood and out beyond it, slicing across the open ground to pass behind Delville Wood and to form a bastion in front of the village of Flers. Switching direction as it went, with High Wood and Delville Wood beyond it, the Switch Line was an iron gateway, defending Flers and Martinpuich as a portcullis might once have defended the gateway of a castle against a besieging horde. So long as they held the Switch Line, the Germans would hold High Wood. From whatever direction they attacked — frontally or from the boundaries of the wood to the south or to the north — blundering through the thickets and briars or down the long rides that divided it, no matter how they scraped, dug, entrenched and consolidated, no matter how often successive lines of attack swept over the front line that stretched from the northwest to the south-east corner of the wood, no matter how they hacked and battled their way beyond it, again and again the troops came up against the deadly strong triangle that still held out at the corner of the wood. The cavalry who had galloped into the wood with pennants flying, the soldiers who had fought their way through it on 14 and 15 July were the vanguard of a whole host who were to fight in High Wood and to die in it.

At Delville Wood, just along the road, the story was even more appalling. Here they had pushed in the South African Brigade and, together with Scottish troops, they had taken the wood and had held it. But it had been held at a terrible cost. The South Africans had gone in three thousand strong. At roll call, when they eventually came out, seven hundred and sixty-eight men answered their names. The South Africans had suffered more than two thousand casualties — and, in this case, casualties meant dead. It was possibly the greatest sacrifice of the war.

In 'normal' battle conditions the proportion of casualties was reckoned to be, on average, four men wounded or taken prisoner for every man who was killed outright, or died within hours of his wounds. Even on the first black day of July, when the final casualty list had numbered more than fifty-seven thousand, appalling though the total was, roughly one man in every three casualties had been killed. Proportionately, the South Africans' losses had been far greater. Of the three thousand soldiers of the South African Brigade who went into Delville Wood, the handful of wounded were outnumbered, four to one, by the dead. None was taken prisoner.

Sunday, 15 July, dawned a fine morning in Winchester. The cathedral was packed and in the streets outside, the pavements were crowded with bystanders. Accustomed though they were, even in peacetime, to seeing soldiers about the city, the townspeople of Winchester still dearly loved a parade. So they lingered in the warm sun, feathered hats nodding, shoes polished to Sabbath brilliance, to enjoy the sight of the Reserve Battalions of The King's Royal Rifle Corps and The Rifle Brigade as they marched the short distance from the barracks to the cathedral. The soldiers had been roused at dawn and it had taken hours of preparation and spit and polish before their turn-out had achieved the standard of smartness necessary to satisfy the critical eyes of sergeant-majors and inspecting officers. It was no ordinary Church Parade. Even the King, although not actually present in person, would be represented at the head of the city's dignitaries by the venerable Field-Marshal, Lord Grenfell, and as many of its congregation as the cathedral would hold were admitted after the troops and official guests had filed into their places.

In spite of the glorious music and singing, it was a sombre service, dedicated to the memory of the soldiers who had a special bond with Winchester, the home of their Regimental Barracks. They were the officers and the men of The King's Royal Rifle Corps and of The Rifle Brigade who had fallen on the field of battle since the war had begun almost two years before. There were too many of them to enumerate. Besides, precise statistics might have been lowering to morale and might also, perhaps, have taken the edge off the note of ringing patriotism that crowned the solemnity of the service with a full-blooded rendering of the National Anthem.

As the second verse began and the verger swung open the big oak doors, the notes of the anthem spilled out of the cathedral into the streets. Passers-by froze where they stood; men removed their hats and most of them joined in:

O Lord our God, arise,
Scatter his enemies,
And make them fall;
Confound their politics;

Frustrate their knavish tricks;
On Thee our hopes we fix,
God save us all!

There were rather more of the fallen of The King's Royal Rifle Corps to honour than if the service had been held two days earlier. And a hundred and fifty miles away, on the scarred uplands of the Somme where the same morning sunlight shafted through the crippled trees of High Wood, more King's Royal Rifle Corps were dying, even as the patriotic notes swelled through the sunlit streets of Winchester.

The lucky ones, the boys who had been wounded and had dragged themselves or been carried away from the wood, were pressing towards the dressing station. By five in the evening, some one hundred and fifty of them had managed to reach it and had passed through it down the line.

Jack Brown ended up in the mortuary. Such was the chaos and disorganization, such was the flow of casualties pressing towards the second-stage dressing stations in the rear, where ambulances would take them to casualty clearing stations on the other side of Albert, that the walking wounded were literally queuing up for treatment. It was a long wait and, having just received an anti-tetanus injection, Jack was feeling distinctly queer. An orderly ducked out from a tent as the long line of men shuffled slowly past, and, through the flap, Jack glimpsed the still forms of wounded soldiers lying on stretchers inside. It did not occur to him that the soldiers lay very still indeed, only that there was one stretcher unoccupied. 'This'll do me!' he thought, as he slid discreetly from the throng of wounded into the dim half-light of the tent and painfully, gratefully lay down.

It was many hours before he awoke, and, even then, he only had the energy to open one eye, half-blinded by the swinging lantern in the hand of the orderly who bent over him. It was not until he heard the orderly yell as he ran out of the tent that Jack woke up fully and realized that something was wrong. The mistake was soon put right and, early in the morning, Jack was sent off in the first of the day's convoys to the casualty clearing station at Warloy on the first stage of his journey to a long convalescence at home. The unfortunate orderly, whom Jack had scared out of his wits, helped to load him into the ambulance. The parting glance he cast upon him was not a friendly one.

Jack Beament was already on his way to a base hospital at Rouen. His wound was not so serious as Brown's, and, in normal circumstances, his chances of getting home at all would have been slim, but the circumstances were far from normal. For, even two weeks after the disastrous first day of the battle, casualties who had been lying out from the first and later attacks were still being rescued and brought in and the seriously wounded men who had been rescued early from the battlefield, or who had been wounded in the line, were not yet fit to be moved by train, ship, and train again on the long haul back to Blighty. The situation had improved since the first calamitous forty-eight hours of the offensive, when the overflow of wounded arriving at casualty clearing stations was so great that even the vast reserves of spare stretchers were soon used up and, all around the big marquees, men were laid in patient rows on the bare earth, without even the benefit of a blanket to cover them.

It had been a miracle of organization that all had received emergency treatment and had been swiftly sent on to the superior comforts of base hospitals at Rouen or on the coast. But the base hospitals themselves were now packed far beyond their capacity. Beds were moved together, so close that there was barely room for the nurses to pass between them. When the beds ran out, stretchers were pressed into service, laid crossways at the foot and, in the largest marquees, in rows down the middle. And still more wounded were arriving all the time. It was the lightly wounded who came off best — the men who, otherwise, would have been treated for a week or so at the base hospitals, sent to convalescent camps for a few days and then returned to their units in the line. But there was no longer room for them. They, at least, could stand the journey and must be shipped off as quickly as possible to make room for the serious cases. Such fortunate soldiers found little to object to in this arrangement and simply thanked their lucky stars that they were out of it.

In the desperate aftermath of the big attack with every dressing station, casualty clearing station and hospital in France strained ten times beyond its limit, with every orderly, nurse and doctor working hollow-eyed around the clock, some men had not even passed through the base hospitals at all. The transport authorities, at their wits' end, had sent three train-loads of walking wounded straight from the front to the harbour at Boulogne, and, to the delight of their passengers, loaded them directly on to hospital ships bound for home. A few were 'accident cases,' suffering from nothing more serious than a sprained ankle, but, now that they had been packaged into the system, they could be sure of at least a few days' rest in a Home hospital, of a period of sick leave and then the blessed respite of a few weeks at their Regimental Base Camp before being drafted back to France and up the line.

Jack Beament, sent to hospital at Rouen, was not quite so fortunate in the short term, but he was nevertheless in for the greatest surprise of his life. It was also the greatest coincidence.

Corporal Jack Beament, MM, No. 1 Platoon, A Coy., 16th King's Royal Rifle Corps (Church Lads Brigade)

It was a hutment hospital on Rouen Racecourse and I was directed to Ward C.3. I could move under my own steam, because my legs were all right. When I got there, the nurse met me at the door and said to me, 'That's your bed over there on the right-hand side.' I thanked her and, as I was making for the bed, I heard a whistle and I looked round. On the other side of the ward, almost immediately opposite my bed, there was my brother Stanley! Just imagine! In all the scores and hundreds of hospitals in France, with all their scores and scores of wards in every hospital, I ended up in the same ward as my brother Stanley. And the even more amazing coincidence was that he had an almost identical wound to mine, only it was in the opposite shoulder. What a reunion that was! And how delighted the nurses were too! They simply couldn't get over it and they made a terrific fuss of us both.

Stanley Beament, in the 20th Battalion of Jack's own regiment, had joined up, on reaching military age, a year after Jack himself, and, as the 20th Battalion of The King's Royal Rifle Corps was a Pioneer Battalion, might have been expected to be immune from wounding by rifle fire. But, twenty-four hours before Jack had been wounded at High Wood, Stanley's company had been attached to the 8th Brigade of the Third Division where they stood in the line ready to launch the dawn attack in the early hours of 14 July. It was while they were consolidating the line between High Wood and Delville Wood, while the Pioneers were digging a new communication trench, that Stanley had been wounded. On his way back to the dressing station, he must have passed within yards of his brother Jack as the Church Lads, in their turn, marched up towards the line. Now, in the hospital at Rouen, the two brothers compared wounds, swapped experiences, gloated over their luck, and, in between painful dressings, thoroughly enjoyed being petted and fussed over and treated as minor celebrities. On 22 July they were bundled aboard a hospital ship and travelled home together.

On the same day, the most illustrious casualty of Bloody July met his death on the Somme. It was Major-General Ingouville-Williams, in command of the 34th Division. He died at Mametz Wood, killed by the explosion of an unlucky shell, as he moved up to reconnoitre the ground for the next stage of the hoped-for advance. It was a severe blow to the Army, for the Somme fighting had taken a heavy toll of colonels and brigadiers who had gone into the line with their troops and had been killed or wounded, and even a colonel or a brigadier was more easily replaced than an experienced major-general in command of a Division. The General's body was brought back and he was buried at Warloy with full military honours. Transport columns and gun batteries were scoured for black horses to draw the gun carriage bearing his coffin and two matching pairs were eventually found in 'C' Battery of the 152nd Brigade.

Sergeant Frank Spencer, No. 1113, 'C' Bty., 152nd Brigade, Royal Field Artillery

23 July: Good progress reported as a result of the strafe and batches of prisoners are continuously marched back to the rear but no definite news is obtainable. We now suffer a great loss by the death of our Officer Commanding our 34th Division — General Williams killed by a shell bursting last night. Our No. 2 black team is used for removal of the body. (Fritz leaves us alone, being evidently too preoccupied in dealing with infantry as great progress is made during the day.)

There had been another night attack on High Wood, and this time by the 51st Division.

Lance-Corporal David Watson, No. 3721, 9th Btn., Royal Scots, 51st Division

We were marched up through Fricourt, which was badly battered. That was the first real sign of war we had come through and, when we reached Mametz Wood, we cut through the wood across the valley and went into a trench behind the Bazentin le Petit wood. That was the assembly point for the 'do.' And the battle order was that, if the attack failed, we had to come back to this trench. When we reached the road at Bazentin village we turned left and moved up the road. We were in extended order right up that road and, oh, the German guns were knocking us down wholesale and the same with these machine-guns. We took up position along the wall and, at two minutes past twelve, we jumped the wall and ran down the hill to take, according to orders, a few minutes' rest in a valley. To me it was like a dried-up water course. A dip. Water would be there in the winter. And then we were to form up about fifty yards from High Wood to rush it. The Corporal and three of us, three privates, we reached the fifty yards spot but no order came to charge the wood. The Corporal decided to go and see what had happened but we saw him knocked down about fifty yards away from us. And he had given us an order, 'Don't move from where ye are until I get back.' But we couldn't move because we were pinned down with machine-gun fire. Bullets were flying all roads and men were dropping on each side. In fact, I saw Sergeant Thomson who was badly wounded being helped by a Lance-Corporal who had gone down on one knee and had the Sergeant sitting up against him, and a big shell splinter came across and sliced the Sergeant's head off. That poor Corporal, he was nearly demented. He was inches away from him.

We took up position ready to get into the wood. Nothing happened and our guns didn't seem to hit the wood at all because they should have been able to knock out these machine-gunners. They kept firing for a long time and there were only three of us left. One lad lost patience with the strain of waiting, just got up on to his feet and ran away and he went down. He was hit. You saw the flashes coming out of the machine-guns, pointing directly at us. They knew where we were but they hit everything bar the two of us. We could hear the bullets going into the ground in front, behind and at the side. Just never seemed to get us. We decided the best way was just to lie still because it was level ground and the bullets were whizzing over and hitting the earth all round about us. And it took us two hours before we got back to the assembly trench. After, it seemed to quieten down a bit, and it was obvious the thing had failed completely, and we gradually—just one at a time—moved back a little—we took just turn-about moving because, if one movement had been spotted, we would both get it. And we got down into this dip that was at the foot of this steep hill. There was a crucifix at the crossroads—and we got back down to the crucifix, down the road from Mametz Wood and then we climbed the hill behind the Bazentin Wood to get back into the trench. There were only eleven of us left. We were no good to anybody.

Sergeant Bill Hay, No. 1459, 9th Btn., Royal Scots, 51st Division

That was a stupid action, because we had to make a frontal attack on bristling German guns and there was no shelter at all. We were at the back, but C Company really got wiped out. We had a lot of casualties but they lost all their officers, all the NCOs, the lot—cleaned out! We knew it was pointless, even before we went over—crossing open ground like that. But, you had to go. You were between the devil and the deep blue sea. If you go forward, you'll likely be shot. If you go back, you'll be court-martialled and shot. So what the hell do you do? What can you do? You just go forward, because the only bloke you can get your knife into is the bloke you're facing.

There were dead bodies all over the place where previous battalions and regiments had taken part in previous attacks. What a bashing we got. There were heaps of men, everywhere— not one or two men, but heaps of men, all dead. Even before we went over, we knew this was death. We just couldn't take High Wood against machine-guns. It was ridiculous. There was no need for it. It was just absolute slaughter.

When it marched out of the line, the Battalion was a shadow of its former self. They passed through Fricourt in a straggling column, pathetically few in number, and a piper marched at their head. He belonged to the Battalion. He knew the terrible toll that High Wood had taken and, doubtless, his mind was on the bodies of the comrades they had left behind. Since the days of Culloden *The Flowers of the Forest* had been the traditional Highland lament. He chose to play it now. It seemed appropriate to the occasion.

As the Royal Scots marched away from the battle, the Australians were preparing to go into the attack. Their orders were, at all costs, to take Pozières.

The Evacuation
of the Gallipoli Peninsula

ALAN MOOREHEAD

Up to the end of November there was very little talk of evacuation. It was discussed in the trenches like any other possibility, but in a detached way, and few of the men really believed that it could happen. The physical presence of the Army, its air of permanence, was all around them; too much had been committed here, too many were dead, to make it possible for them to go away. And in any case there was at this stage no plan for withdrawing from Helles at all.

At the beginning of December, however, the men at Anzac and Suvla began to notice that something unusual was going on. Soldiers who reported sick with some minor ailment were not treated at the hospitals on the bridgehead but were at once sent off to the islands and were seen no more. In increasing numbers companies and battalions were taken off *en bloc*, and those who remained behind did not altogether believe the official explanation that this was part of the new 'winter policy of thinning out the bridgehead.' They thought for the most part that a new landing was to be made.

The problem was one of frightful complexity. There were some 83,000 men in the Suvla-Anzac bridgehead, and to these were added 5,000 animals, 2,000 vehicles, nearly 200 guns and vast quantities of stores. It was quite impractical to think of getting the whole of this army off in a single night, since there was neither room for them on the beaches nor sufficient boats to get them across to the islands. Equally a fighting withdrawal was out of the question: in a moment the enemy guns firing from the hills above would have wrecked all hope of embarkation.

The plan that was finally adopted was very largely the work of Colonel Aspinall, who was now serving as a brigadier-general on Birdwood's staff, and of Lieut.-Colonel White, an Australian at Anzac. They proposed a gradual and secret withdrawal which was to take place during successive nights until at last only a small garrison was left; and these last, the 'bravest and the steadiest men,' were then to take their chance on getting away before the Turks discovered what was happening. This meant that the operation would rise to an acute point of tension during the last hours — a rough sea would ruin all, a Turkish attack would expose them to slaughter — but still there seemed no other way.

There now began a period of intensive preparation. Once again a fleet of small boats was assembled in the islands. Twelve thousand hospital beds were got ready in Egypt, and fifty-six temporary hospital ships were ordered to stand ready to take the wounded off the beaches — the larger liners, the *Mauretania,* the *Aquitania* and the *Britannic,* to sail directly to England. Gangs of engineers put to work to repair the piers destroyed in the November storms,[1] and an elaborate time-table was worked out so that every man would know precisely what he had to do.

Clearly everything would depend on secrecy and the weather. Secrecy was even more vital now than it had been in the days before the landings, and it was a constant anxiety in Birdwood's headquarters that some soldier, wittingly or unwittingly, might give the plans away. A naval patrol sealed off the islands from Greek caiques trading with the mainland, and on Imbros a cordon was placed round the civilian village on the pretext that an outbreak of smallpox was suspected there.

In the midst of these arrangements Lord Milner and others chose to discuss openly the whole question of evacuation in the House of Lords in London. It was common knowledge, Lord Milner said, that General Monro had recommended evacuation. Had Kitchener gone out to the Dardanelles to give a second opinion? Or was Kitchener himself to command the operation? It was part of the old zany carelessness which had led people to address letters to 'The Constantinople Force' when Hamilton was first assembling the Army in Egypt, and on Imbros Birdwood's planning staff could do nothing but listen in despair. Fortunately, however, the Turks and the Germans simply could not bring themselves to believe that the British would give away their plans in this casual way; they revealed later that they regarded the debate in the House of Lords as propaganda.

Over the weather there could be even less control; the meteorologists said that it ought to hold until the end of the year, and one could only pray that they were right. One good southerly blow on the final night would wreck the whole adventure.

There remained one other imponderable, and that was the behaviour of the Army itself. On December 12 the soldiers at Suvla and Anzac were told for the first time that they were to be taken off, that this for them was the end of the campaign. There seems to have been a moment of stupefaction. Even those who had guessed that something of the sort was about to happen were astonished, and perhaps it was something more than astonishment, a dull awe, a feeling that this was a shaming and unnatural reversal of the order of things. Among the majority, no doubt, these thoughts were soon overtaken by a sense of relief, and they were content simply to accept instructions and to get away. Others, and there were very many of them, remained indignant. They, too, like Rupert Brooke, had seen a vision of Constantinople and had perhaps exclaimed, as he had, when they had first set out from Egypt only eight months before, 'Oh God! I've never been quite so happy before.' All this was now an embarrassment to remember, an absurd and childish excitement, and it was made more bitter by the endless disappointments, the death and the wastage that had intervened.

There was a simple and immediate reaction, and possibly it was a desire to remove the stigma of defeat, to create artificially a chance of heroism since the plan provided none: the men came to their officers in hundreds and asked to be the last to leave the shore. It was nothing more than a gesture, something for the pride to feed on, a kind of tribute to their friends who were already dead, but they were intensely serious about it. The veterans argued that they had earned this right, the newer arrivals insisted that they should be given this one last opportunity of distinguishing themselves. And so there was no need to call for volunteers to man the trenches at the end; it was a matter of selection.

But for the moment there was more need of cunning and discipline than heroism. In the second week of December the first stage of the evacuation began. Each evening after dusk flotillas of barges and small boats crept into Anzac Cove and Suvla Bay and there was a fever of activity all night as troops and animals and guns were got on board. The sick and wounded came first, the prisoners-of-war, and then, in increasing numbers, the infantry. The men walked silently down from the trenches, their boots wrapped in sacking, their footfall deadened by layers of blankets laid along the piers. In the morning the little fleet had vanished and all was normal again. Men and stores were being disembarked in the usual way, the same mule teams laden with boxes were toiling up to the front from the beaches, and there was no way for the Turks to know that the boxes on the mules were empty or that the disembarking men were a special group whose job was to go aboard the boats each night in the darkness and then return ostentatiously to the shore in the morning. Another deception was carried out with the guns. They ceased to fire soon after dark each night, so that the Turks should grow accustomed to silence and should not guess that anything was amiss on the final night when the last men were leaving the trenches. In the same way the infantry were ordered to hold back their rifle and machine-gun fire.

By the end of the second week of December these preliminary stages of the evacuation were well advanced. The weather held. The Turks apparently still suspected nothing and made no attempt to attack. But the British ranks were becoming very thin, and in order to keep up the deception it was necessary to march columns of men and animals like a stage army round and round the dusty tracks along the shore. No tents were struck, the gunners that remained fired twice as many rounds and kept moving their batteries from place to place; and thousands of extra cooking fires were lit in the morning and the evening. Throughout the daylight hours Allied aircraft flew along the coast in readiness to drive back any German aircraft that came out on reconnaissance.

On December 15 an acceleration of the programme began. All through the night channel steamers and barges shuttled back and forth between the islands and the coast, and even a battleship was called in to act as a transport. On the beaches huge piles of clothing, blankets, boots, water bottles, woollen gloves, tarpaulin sheets, motor cycles, tinned food and ammunition were made ready to be destroyed. Acid was poured over hundreds of unwanted sacks of flour, and, as a precaution against drunkenness, the commanders of units poured their stores of liquor into the sea.

By the morning of December 18 the beachmasters were able to report that half the force in the bridgehead, some 40,000 men, and most of their equipment had been taken off. Both Anzac and Suvla now were honeycombs of silent, half-deserted trenches, and the men that remained in them were utterly exposed to enemy attack. 'It's getting terribly lonely at night,' one of the English soldiers wrote in his diary. 'Not a soul about. Only the excitement keeps us from getting tired.'

All was now ready for the final stage. Twenty thousand men were to be taken off on the night of Saturday, December 19, and on Sunday — known as 'Z' night in the plan — the last 20,000 were to go. There was one thought in everybody's mind: 'If only the weather holds.' Through all this period the soldiers in the Cape Helles bridgehead, only thirteen miles away, knew nothing of what was going on.

Saturday morning broke with a mild breeze and a flat calm on the sea. There had been a short alarm at Anzac during the night when one of the storage dumps on the shore accidentally took fire, and everywhere the embarking men stood stock-still waiting to see if they were discovered at last. But nothing happened.

Through the long day the men went silently about their final preparations. A ton of high explosive was placed in a tunnel under the Turkish lines on the foothills of Chunuk Bair and made ready for detonation. Mines and booby traps were hidden in the soil, and to make certain that the troops avoided them on the final night long white lines of flour and salt and sugar were laid down from the trenches to the beach. The hard floor of the trenches themselves was dug up with picks to soften the noise of the final departure, and at places nearest the Turkish line torn blankets were laid on the ground.

Anzac posed a fantastic problem. At some places the British trenches were no more than ten yards from the Turks. Yet somehow the men had to be got out of them and down to the shore without the enemy knowing anything about it. They hit upon the device of the self-firing rifle. This was a contraption that involved the use of two kerosene tins. The upper tin was filled with water which dripped through a hole in the bottom into the empty tin below. Directly the lower tin became sufficiently weighted with water it overbalanced and fired a rifle by pulling a string attached to the trigger. There were several versions of this gadget: in place of water some men preferred to use fuses and candles that would burn through the string and release a weight on the rifle trigger, but the principle remained the same, and it was hoped that spasmodic shots would still be sounding along the line for half an hour or more after the last troops had gone. Thus it was believed that all might have at least a chance of getting away. Saturday went by in perfecting these arrangements. That night another 20,000 men crept down to the beaches at Suvla and Anzac and got away.

On Sunday morning the Turks shelled the coast rather more heavily than usual, and with new shells which evidently had been brought through Bulgaria from Germany. The Navy and such of the British guns as were left on shore replied. It was an intolerable strain, and the tension increased as the day went on. Now finally these last 20,000 men had returned to the conditions of the first landings in April. There was nothing more that the generals or the admirals could do to help them; as on the first day they were on their own in a limbo where no one knew what was going to happen, where only the individual will of the soldier could ruin or save them all. They waited very quietly. Many went for the last time to the graves of their friends and erected new crosses there; made little lines of stones and tidied up the ground; this apparently they minded more than anything, this leaving of their friends behind, and it was something better than sentimentality that made one soldier say to his officer, 'I hope *they* won't hear us going down to the beaches.'

On the shore the medical staff waited. They were to remain behind with the seriously wounded, and they had a letter written in French and addressed to the enemy commander-in-chief requesting that a British hospital ship be allowed to embark them on the following day. Still, no one could be sure how this would be received, or indeed be sure of anything. They were on their own.

In the afternoon some went down to the horse lines and cut the throats of the animals which they knew could not be got away. Others threw five million rounds of rifle ammunition into the sea, together with twenty thousand rations in wooden cases. Others again kept up the pretence that the Army was still there in its tens of thousands by driving about in carts, a last surrealist ride in a vacuum. Birdwood and Keyes came ashore for the last time and went away again. Up at the front the remaining men who held the line — at some places no more than ten against a thousand Turks — went from one loophole to another firing their rifles, filling up the kerosene tins with water, making as much of a show as they could. It amused some of them to lay out a meal in their dugouts in readiness for the Turks when they came. But most preferred to wreck the places which they had dug and furnished with so much care.

At last at five the day ended and a wet moon came up, misted over with clouds and drifting fog. There was a slight drizzle of rain. Except for the occasional crack of a rifle shot and the distant rumble of the guns at Helles an absolute silence fell along the front. The men on the flanks and in the rear were the first to go. Each as he left the trenches fixed his rifle for the last time, fell into line and marched in Indian file down the white lines to the beach. They came down from the hills in batches of four hundred and the boats were waiting. The last act of each man before he embarked was to take the two hand-grenades he was carrying and cast them silently into the sea.

Within an hour of nightfall both sectors at Anzac and Suvla were contracting rapidly towards their centres, and everywhere, from dozens of little gullies and ravines, like streams pouring softly down to join a river, men were moving to the shore. No one ran. Not smoking or talking, each group, when it reached the sea, stood quietly waiting for its turn to embark. At Anzac only 5,000 men were left at 8 P.M. At 10 P.M. the trenches at the front were manned by less than 1,500 men. This was the point of extreme danger; now, more than ever, every rifle shot seemed the beginning of an enemy attack. For several nights previously a destroyer had shone its searchlight across the southern end of the bridgehead to block the Turks' vision of the beach, and now again the light went on. Apart from this and the occasional gleam of the moon through the drifting clouds no other light was showing. Midnight passed and there was still no movement from the enemy. The handful of soldiers now left at the front moved quietly from loophole to loophole, occasionally firing their rifles, but more often simply standing and waiting until, with excruciating slowness, the moment came for them to go. The last men began to leave the trenches at 3 A.M. Fifteen minutes later Lone Pine was evacuated, and the men turned their backs on the Turks a dozen yards away. They had a mile or more to go before they reached the beach. As they went they drew cages of barbed wire across the paths behind them, and lit the fuses which an hour later would explode hidden mines beneath the ground. On the beach the hospital staff was told that, since there were no wounded, they too could leave. A private named Pollard who had gone to sleep at the front and had woken to find himself alone came stumbling nervously down to the shore and was gathered in.

They waited ten more minutes to make sure that none had been left behind. Then at 4 A.M., when the first faint streaks of dawn were beginning, they set fire to the dumps on the shore. On the hills above they could hear the automatic rifles going off and the noise of the Turks firing back spasmodically at the deserted trenches. At ten past four a sailor gave the final order, 'Let go all over — right away,' and the last boat put out to sea. At that instant the mine below Chunuk Bair went off with a tearing, cataclysmic roar, and a huge cloud, lit from beneath with a red glow, rolled upward over the peninsula. Immediately a hurricane of Turkish rifle fire swept the bay.

At Suvla a similar scene was going on, but it continued a little longer. It was not until ten past five that Commodore Unwin, of the *River Clyde,* pushed off in the last boat. A soldier fell over board as they were leaving, and the Commodore dived in and fished him out. 'You really must do something about Unwin,' General Byng said to Keyes, who was watching from his own ship off the shore. 'You should send him home; we want several little Unwins.'

And now a naval steamboat ran along the coast, an officer on board calling and calling to the shore for stragglers. But there were none. At Suvla every man and animal had been got off. At Anzac two soldiers were wounded during the night. There were no other casualties. Just before they vanished hull down over the horizon at 7 A.M. the soldiers in the last boats looked back towards the shore across the oily sea and saw the Turks come out of the foothills and run like madmen along the empty beach. At once the Navy opened fire on them, and a destroyer rushed in to ignite with its shells the unburnt piles of stores that had remained behind. On board the boats, where generals and privates were packed in together, a wild hilarity broke out, the men shaking one another's hands, shouting and crying. But before they reached the islands most of them had subsided to the deck and were asleep.

That night, sixteen hours after the last man had been taken off, a violent storm blew up with torrents of rain and washed away the piers.

Liman von Sanders says that he found great booty at Suvla and Anzac; five small steamers and sixty boats abandoned on the beaches, dumps of artillery and ammunition, railway lines and whole cities of standing tents, medicines and instruments of every kind, vast stacks of clothing, bully beef and flour, mountains of timber. And on the shore some hundreds of dead horses lay in rows. The ragged, hungry Turkish soldiers, who patched their uniforms with sacking and who subsisted on a daily handful of olives and a slice of bread, fell on this treasure like men who had lost their wits. Sentries were unable to hold them back; the soldiers rushed upon the food, and for weeks afterwards they were to be seen in the strangest uniforms, Australian hats, puttees wound round their stomachs, breeches cut from flags and tarpaulins, British trench boots of odd sizes on their feet. They carried in their knapsacks the most useless and futile things that they had picked up, but it was all glorious because it was loot, it was free and it was theirs. And they had won.

Liman von Sanders says too that he was planning a major attack on the Suvla and Anzac positions when he was forestalled by the evacuation, and he admits that right up to the early hours of Monday, December 20, he had no notion of what was happening at the front. Confusing reports came to him at his headquarters through the night, and these were made still more confusing by sea mist. At 4 A.M., however, he ordered a general alarm. Yet there were still delays. The Turkish soldiers advanced very gingerly into the foremost trenches where there had only been instant death for so many months before. After a little while they paused, fearing that some trick was being played, and an hour or more went by before their commanders, woken from their sleep, came up to the front and told them to go on again. Even the final advance to the beaches was very slow, because the troops were held up by barbed wire and booby traps; and on the shore itself they were shelled from the sea. And so an army slipped away.

Liman's first reaction was the obvious one: he immediately set about gathering up his best divisions — there were now twenty-one under his command — and marching them south for an assault on the last remaining British bridgehead at Cape Helles. 'It was thought possible,' he says, 'that the enemy might hang on there for some time. That could not be permitted.' While his preparations for the attack were going forward patrols were sent out into no-man's-land each night, and the Turkish commanders at the front were ordered to keep a constant watch on every movement in the British lines.

It was an impossible position for the British. They had four divisions in Cape Helles. If they stayed they knew it could not be long before the Turks mounted a major attack against them; if they attempted to go they were hardly likely to outwit the Turks a second time. Monro as ever was in no doubt at all as to what should be done. Directly the Anzac-Suvla evacuation was completed he sent a message to London urging that Helles should be given up as well; and this time he found an ally in Admiral Wemyss. Birdwood too was eager to be off. And eventually on December 27 the cabinet agreed.

There followed a rapid series of changes in the high command. On December 22 de Robeck came back from London to resume control of the Fleet and Wemyss was posted off to the East Indies. A few days later Monro himself was gone; a signal arrived appointing him to the command of the First Army in France, the place where in all the world he most wished to be. On New Year's Day he sailed for Egypt and Gallipoli saw him no more. Now everyone was averting their eyes from this graveyard of men and their reputations, and this last act seemed likely to be the most painful of all. It was left to Birdwood, de Robeck and Keyes, the three men who had been there from the beginning, to clean up the mess.

There was not much time. With every day the weather grew more threatening and the Turks more likely to attack; they were shelling now with terrible accuracy with their new German guns and ammunition. There were 35,000 men in the Helles bridgehead, nearly 4,000 animals and almost as many guns and stores as there had been at Suvla and Anzac. Once again it was decided that half the garrison should be evacuated secretly over a series of nights. General Davies, the corps commander, insisted that on January 9, the final night, he should be left with sufficient men to hold off the Turks for a week in case, at the last moment, he was cut off by foul weather. He fixed on the total of 17,000 as the minimum number of soldiers required for this rearguard, and this also happened to be the maximum number that the Navy could take off in a single night. By January 1, 1916, all was agreed and the movement began.

The French were the first to go, and they left such a yawning gap in the line that there was nothing for it but to bring back the British 29th Division, to take their places. There was not much left of the 29th. The division had been badly cut up in the August battles and when they were evacuated from Suvla they were down to less than half their strength. One thing however remained to them, and that was a reputation of great bravery and steadiness; so now, after a few brief days' respite in the islands, they found themselves landing again beside the *River Clyde* and marching back to the trenches which they had first occupied eight months before. Among so many anti-climaxes this, perhaps, was the hardest of all.

There was a constricting feeling in the British trenches at Cape Helles at this time. At first the soldiers had no idea that the bridgehead was to be evacuated — indeed they were given a printed order of the day specifically saying that they were to remain. They hated this prospect, and in particular they feared that they might become prisoners of war — a fear that was all the more lurid because a rumour got about that the Turks would castrate them.

About five days before the final night it became generally known that the bridgehead was to be evacuated, and then the period of real tension began. But still excitement was the drug and a fatalism intervened. Four divisions against twenty-one was a monstrosity even on such a narrow front as this, but there was nothing that anyone could do about it. And so they played football, they waited, they made a kind of security out of the accustomed routine in the trenches, and they saw no further than the day ahead. Night by night the battalions went away and no one questioned the order of withdrawal; one simply waited for the summons and it was absurdly like the atmosphere of a dentist's waiting room. 'You're next,' and another regiment vanished. The others, feeling neither lucky nor unlucky, but fixed simply in an unalterable succession of events, remained behind and waited as the last patients wait, amid vague smells of carbolic and grisly secret apprehensions, in the silence of an emptying room.

There were a number of alarms and misadventures. High winds blew up, and they had to throw in cases of bully beef and other stores to repair the breaches in the causeway at Sedd-el-Bahr. Once when a sailor flashed a torch on a lighter full of mules there was a stampede, and for a long time the animals were snorting and screaming in the sea. Another night the French battleship *Suffren* ran down a large transport and sent her to the bottom. The U-boat scare began again. Yet by January 7 they had got the garrison down to 19,000; and now at last, at this instant of greatest danger for the British, Liman von Sanders delivered his attack.

He had been much delayed. All had been ready forty-eight hours before, but Enver had chosen that moment to send a message from Constantinople ordering nine of the Gallipoli divisions to Thrace. It was Enver's last gesture in the campaign, and Liman countered it in the usual way; he sent in his resignation. In the usual way, too, Enver backed down. The order was countermanded and now, in the early afternoon on January 7, the Turks came in for the kill. They were equipped with wooden ramps to throw across the British trenches, and special squads carried inflammable materials with which they were to burn the British boats on the shore. This was to be the final coup.

The attack began with the heaviest artillery bombardment of the campaign, and it went on steadily for four and a half hours. There was a lull for a few minutes and then it recommenced. In the British trenches the soldiers waited for the inevitable rush that would follow the bombardment; and in the early evening it began. The Turkish infantry had a hundred yards or more to go before they reached the first British trenches, and they jumped up with their old cries of *Allah, Allah,* and *Voor, Voor* — strike, strike. Perhaps there was something of desperation in the answering fire of the British defence. It was so murderous, so concentrated and steady, that when only a few minutes had gone by the soldiers saw a thing which had scarcely ever happened before — the Turkish infantry were refusing to charge. Their officers could be seen shouting and striking at the men, urging them up and out into the open where so many were already dead. But the men would not move. By nightfall it was all over. Not a single enemy soldier had broken into the British lines.

Liman admits that this disastrous attack convinced him that the British were not going to evacuate Cape Helles after all, and nothing further was done to molest them all through that night and the following day.

There were now just 17,000 men left, and January 8 was another calm spring-like day. Once again as at Suvla and Anzac great piles of stores and ammunition were got ready for destruction. Landmines were laid, and the self-firing rifles set in position in the trenches. Once again the sad mules lay dead in rows.

During the day the wind shifted round to the south-west and freshened a little, but it was still calm when at dusk the long lines of boats and warships set out for the peninsula for the last time. From Clapham Junction, from the Vineyard and *Le Haricot,* and the other famous places which soon would not even be mentioned on the maps, the men came marching to the sea, a distance of three miles or so.

The thing that the soldiers afterwards remembered with particular vividness was the curious alternation of silence and of deafening noise that went on through the day. At Sedd-el-Bahr they crouched under the corner of the battered fort waiting their turn to embark, and in the overwhelming stillness of their private fear they heard nothing but the footfall of the men who had gone ahead; the clop, clop, clop of their boots as they ran across the pontoons to the *River Clyde* where lighters were waiting to embark them. Then, in an instant, all was dissolved in the shattering explosion of enemy shells erupting in the sea. Then again the clop, clop, clop of the boots as the line of running men took up its course again. To see safety so near and to know that with every second it might be lost — this was the hardest trial of all to bear, and it crushed the waiting soldier with nightmares of loneliness.

Apart from the spasmodic shelling there was no movement in the Turkish lines, and as the night advanced the Turks very largely ceased to count; it was the weather which engrossed everybody's mind. By 8 P.M. the glass was falling, and at nine when the waning moon went down the wind had risen to thirty-five miles an hour. The *River Clyde* held firmly enough — all through these nights the men had been passing under her lee to the boats — but the crazy piers in the bay strained and groaned as heavy seas came smashing up against them. Soon an alarm went up. Two lighters broke adrift and crashed through the flimsy timber. All further embarkation then was stopped while a gang of engineers, working in the black and icy sea, put things to rights again. Then when another 3,000 men had been got off the pier collapsed once more, and again there was another hour's delay.

By midnight when the last troops began to leave the trenches on their long walk to the shore the wind was rising with every minute that went by, and in the starlight there was nothing to be seen at sea but a waste of racing water. Two white rockets went up from the battleship *Prince George* — the signal that she was being attacked by a submarine. Two thousand men had just got aboard the ship, and de Robeck and Keyes in the *Chatham* rushed towards her. But it was nothing — the vessel had merely bumped some wreckage in the water.

Now everything depended upon the speed with which the last men could be got away. At 2 A.M. 3,200 still remained. Through the next hour most of them managed to reach the boats, and barely 200 were then waiting to be embarked. These, however, were in a critical situation. Under the charge of General Maude, the commander of the 13th Division who had insisted on being among the last to leave, they had made their way to Gully Beach, an isolated landing place on the west coast, only to find that the lighter which was to take them off had run aground. By now the trenches had been empty for two and a half hours, and it was apparent that they could not stay where they were. One hope remained: to march on another two miles to 'W' beach at the tip of the peninsula on the chance that they might still be in time to find another boat. They set off soon after 2 A.M. and had been on the road for some ten minutes when the General discovered with consternation that his valise had been left behind on the stranded lighter. Nothing, he announced, would induce him to leave without it, and so while the rest of the column went on he turned back with another officer to Gully Beach. Here they retrieved the lost valise, and placing it on a wheeled stretcher set off once more along the deserted shore. Meanwhile the others had reached 'W' beach, where the last barge was waiting to push off. They felt, however, that they could not leave until the General arrived — a decision which required some courage, for the storm had now risen to half a gale, and the main ammunition dump, the fuse of which had already been lighted, was due to explode in under half an hour.[2] After twenty minutes the commander of the boat announced that he could wait no more; in another five minutes all further embarkation would become impossible. It was at this moment that the General emerged from the darkness with his companion and came trundling his valise down the pier.

It was just a quarter to four in the morning when they pushed off, and ten minutes later the first of the ammunition dumps went up with a colossal roar. As the soldiers and sailors in the last boats looked back towards the shore they saw hundreds of red rockets going up from Achi Baba and the cliffs in Asia, and immediately afterwards Turkish shells began to burst and crash along the beach. The fire in the burning dumps of stores took a stronger hold, and presently all the sky to the north was reddened with a false dawn. Not a man had been left behind.

It had been a fantastic, an unbelievable success, a victory of a sort at a moment when hope itself had almost gone. Decorations were awarded to General Monro and his chief-of-staff who had so firmly insisted upon the evacuation.

No special medal, however, was given to the soldiers who fought in the Gallipoli campaign.

Notes

1. Several ships were sunk to form breakwaters at this time, and on Imbros Admiral Wemyss even proposed to use an old battleship in this way. Eventually, however, he requisitioned a collier which had just steamed in from England with 1,500 tons of coal on board. The captain protested but down the ship went to the bottom. The vessel was pumped out after the evacuation and sailed away apparently none the worse for her immersion.

2. The incident inspired the exasperated embarkation officer to compose the following lines:

   'Come into the lighter, Maude,
   For the fuse has long been lit.
   Hop into the lighter, Maude,
   And never mind your kit.'

   An alternative version runs:

   'Come into the lighter, Maude,
   For the night is nearly flown.
   Come into the lighter, Maude,
   And leave your bag alone.'

A Funeral

BARBARA TUCHMAN

So gorgeous was the spectacle on the May morning of 1910 when nine kings rode in the funeral of Edward VII of England that the crowd, waiting in hushed and black-clad awe, could not keep back gasps of admiration. In scarlet and blue and green and purple, three by three the sovereigns rode through the palace gates, with plumed helmets, gold braid, crimson sashes, and jeweled orders flashing in the sun. After them came five heirs apparent, forty more imperial or royal highnesses, seven queens — four dowager and three regnant — and a scattering of special ambassadors from uncrowned countries. Together they represented seventy nations in the greatest assemblage of royalty and rank ever gathered in one place and, of its kind, the last. The muffled tongue of Big Ben tolled nine by the clock as the cortege left the palace, but on history's clock it was sunset, and the sun of the old world was setting in a dying blaze of splendor never to be seen again.

In the center of the front row rode the new king, George V, flanked on his left by the Duke of Connaught, the late king's only surviving brother, and on his right by a personage to whom, acknowledged *The Times*, "belongs the first place among all the foreign mourners," who "even when relations are most strained has never lost his popularity amongst us" — William II, the German Emperor. Mounted on a gray horse, wearing the scarlet uniform of a British Field Marshal, carrying the baton of that rank, the Kaiser had composed his features behind the famous upturned mustache in an expression "grave even to severity." Of the several emotions churning his susceptible breast, some hints exist in his letters. "I am proud to call this place my home and to be a member of this royal family," he wrote home after spending the night in Windsor Castle in the former apartments of his mother. Sentiment and nostalgia induced by these melancholy occasions with his English relatives jostled with pride in his supremacy among the assembled potentates and with a fierce relish in the disappearance of his uncle from the European scene. He had come to bury Edward his bane; Edward the arch plotter, as William conceived it, of Germany's encirclement; Edward his mother's brother whom he could neither bully nor impress, whose fat figure cast a shadow between Germany and the sun. "He is Satan. You cannot imagine what a Satan he is!"

This verdict, announced by the Kaiser before a dinner of three hundred guests in Berlin in 1907, was occasioned by one of Edward's continental tours undertaken with clearly diabolical designs at encirclement. He had spent a provocative week in Paris, visited for no good reason the King of Spain (who had just married his niece), and finished with a visit to the King of Italy with obvious intent to seduce him from his Triple Alliance with Germany and Austria. The Kaiser, possessor of the least inhibited tongue in Europe, had worked himself into a frenzy ending in another of those comments that had periodically over the past twenty years of his reign shattered the nerves of diplomats.

Happily the Encircler was now dead and replaced by George who, the Kaiser told Theodore Roosevelt a few days before the funeral, was "a very nice boy" (of forty-five, six years younger than the Kaiser). "He is a thorough Englishman and hates all foreigners but I do not mind that as long as he does not hate Germans more than other foreigners." Alongside George, William now rode confidently, saluting as he passed the regimental colors of the 1st Royal Dragoons of which he was honorary colonel. Once he had distributed photographs of himself wearing their uniform with the Delphic inscription written above his signature, "I bide my time." Today his time had come; he was supreme in Europe.

Behind him rode the widowed Queen Alexandra's two brothers, King Frederick of Denmark and King George of the Hellenes; her nephew, King Haakon of Norway; and three kings who were to lose their thrones: Alfonso of Spain, Manuel of Portugal and, wearing a silk turban, King Ferdinand of Bulgaria who annoyed his fellow sovereigns by calling himself Czar and kept in a chest a Byzantine Emperor's full regalia, acquired from a theatrical costumer, against the day when he should reassemble the Byzantine dominions beneath his scepter.

Dazzled by these "splendidly mounted princes," as *The Times* called them, few observers had eyes for the ninth king, the only one among them who was to achieve greatness as a man. Despite his great height and perfect horsemanship, King Albert of the Belgians, who disliked the pomp of royal ceremony, contrived in that company to look both embarrassed and absentminded. He was then thirty-five and had been on the throne barely a year. In later years when his face became known to the world as a symbol of heroism and tragedy, it still always wore that abstracted look, as if his mind were on something else.

The future source of tragedy, tall, corpulent, and corseted, with green plumes waving from his helmet, Archduke Ferdinand of Austria, heir of the old Emperor Franz Josef, rode on Albert's right, and on his left another scion who would never reach his throne, Prince Yussuf, heir of the Sultan of Turkey. After the kings came the royal highnesses: Prince Fushimi, brother of the Emperor of Japan; Grand Duke Michael, brother of the Czar of Russia; the Duke of Aosta in bright blue with green plumes, brother of the King of Italy; Prince Carl, brother of the King of Sweden; Prince Henry, consort of the Queen of Holland; and the Crown Princes of Serbia, Rumania, and Montenegro. The last named, Prince Danilo, "an amiable, extremely handsome young man of delightful manners," resembled the Merry Widow's lover in more than name, for, to the consternation of British functionaries, he had arrived the night before accompanied by a "charming young lady of great personal attractions" whom he introduced as his wife's lady in waiting with the explanation that she had come to London to do some shopping.

A regiment of minor German royalty followed: rulers of Mecklenburg-Schwerin, Mecklenburg-Strelitz, Waldeck-Pyrmont, Saxe-Coburg Gotha, of Saxony, Hesse, Württemberg, Baden, and Bavaria, of whom the last, Crown Prince Rupprecht, was soon to lead a German army in battle. There were a Prince of Siam, a Prince of Persia, five princes of the former French royal house of Orléans, a brother of the Khedive of Egypt wearing a gold-tasseled fez, Prince Tsia-tao of China in an embroidered light-blue gown whose ancient dynasty had two more years to run, and the Kaiser's brother, Prince Henry of Prussia, representing the German Navy, of which he was Commander in Chief. Amid all this magnificence were three civilian-coated gentlemen, M. Gaston-Carlin of Switzerland, M. Pichon, Foreign Minister of France, and former President Theodore Roosevelt, special envoy of the United States.

Edward, the object of this unprecedented gathering of nations, was often called the "Uncle of Europe," a title which, insofar as Europe's ruling houses were meant, could be taken literally. He was the uncle not only of Kaiser Wilhelm but also, through his wife's sister, the Dowager Empress Marie of Russia, of Czar Nicolas II. His own niece Alix was the Czarina; his daughter Maud was Queen of Norway; another niece, Ena, was Queen of Spain; a third niece, Marie, was soon to be Queen of Rumania. The Danish family of his wife, besides occupying the throne of Denmark, had mothered the Czar of Russia and supplied kings to Greece and Norway. Other relatives, the progeny at various removes of Queen Victoria's nine sons and daughters, were scattered in abundance throughout the courts of Europe.

Yet not family feeling alone nor even the suddenness and shock of Edward's death—for to public knowledge he had been ill one day and dead the next—accounted for the unexpected flood of condolences at his passing. It was in fact a tribute to Edward's great gifts as a sociable king which had proved invaluable to his country. In the nine short years of his reign England's splendid isolation had given way, under pressure, to a series of "understandings" or attachments, but not quite alliances—for England dislikes the definitive—with two old enemies, France and Russia, and one promising new power, Japan. The resulting shift in balance registered itself around the world and affected every state's relations with every other. Though Edward neither initiated nor influenced his country's policy, his personal diplomacy helped to make the change possible.

Taken as a child to visit France, he had said to Napoleon III: "You have a nice country. I would like to be your son." This preference for things French, in contrast to or perhaps in protest against his mother's for the Germanic, lasted, and after her death was put to use. When England, growing edgy over the challenge implicit in Germany's Naval Program of 1900, decided to patch up old quarrels with France, Edward's talents as *Roi Charmeur* smoothed the way. In 1903 he went to Paris, disregarding advice that an official state visit would find a cold welcome. On his arrival the crowds were sullen and silent except for a few taunting cries of *"Vivent les Boers!"* and *"Vive Fashoda!"* which the King ignored. To a worried aide who muttered, "The French don't like us," he replied, "Why should they?" and continued bowing and smiling from his carriage.

For four days he made appearances, reviewed troops at Vincennes, attended the races at Longchamps, a gala at the Opéra, a state banquet at the Elysée, a luncheon at the Quai d'Orsay and, at the theater, transformed a chill into smiles by mingling with the audience in the entr'acte and paying gallant compliments in French to a famous actress in the lobby. Everywhere he made gracious and tactful speeches about his friendship and admiration for the French, their "glorious traditions," their "beautiful city," for which he confessed an attachment "fortified by many happy memories," his "sincere pleasure" in the visit, his belief that old misunderstandings are "happily over and forgotten," that the mutual prosperity of France and England was interdependent and their friendship his "constant preoccupation." When he left, the crowds now shouted, *"Vive notre roi!"* "Seldom has such a complete change of attitude been seen as that which has taken place in this country. He has won the hearts of all the French," a Belgian diplomat reported. The German ambassador thought the King's visit was "a most odd affair," and supposed that an Anglo-French rapprochement was the result of a "general aversion to Germany." Within a year, after hard work by ministers settling disputes, the rapprochement became the Anglo-French Entente, signed in April, 1904.

Germany might have had an English entente for herself had not her leaders, suspecting English motives, rebuffed the overtures of the Colonial Secretary, Joseph Chamberlain, in 1899 and again in 1901. Neither the shadowy Holstein who conducted Germany's foreign affairs from behind the scenes nor the elegant and erudite Chancellor, Prince Bülow, nor the Kaiser himself was quite sure what they suspected England of but they were certain it was something perfidious. The Kaiser always wanted an agreement with England if he could get one without seeming to want it. Once, affected by English surroundings and family sentiment at the funeral of Queen Victoria, he allowed himself to confess the wish to Edward. "Not a mouse could stir in Europe without our permission," was the way he visualized an Anglo-German alliance. But as soon as the English showed signs of willingness, he and his ministers veered off, suspecting some trick. Fearing to be taken advantage of at the conference table, they preferred to stay away altogether and depend upon an ever-growing navy to frighten the English into coming to terms.

Bismarck had warned Germany to be content with land power, but his successors were neither separately nor collectively Bismarcks. He had pursued clearly seen goals unswervingly; they groped for larger horizons with no clear idea of what they wanted. Holstein was a Machiavelli without a policy who operated on only one principle: suspect everyone. Bülow had no principles; he was so slippery, lamented his colleague Admiral Tirpitz, that compared to him an eel was a leech. The flashing, inconstant, always freshly inspired Kaiser had a different goal every hour, and practiced diplomacy as an exercise in perpetual motion.

None of them believed England would ever come to terms with France and all warnings of that event Holstein dismissed as "naïve," even a most explicit one from his envoy in London, Baron Eckhardstein. At a dinner at Marlborough House in 1902, Eckhardstein had watched Paul Cambon, the French ambassador, disappear into the billiard room with Joseph Chamberlain, where they engaged in "animated conversation" lasting twenty-eight minutes of which the only words he could overhear (the baron's memoirs do not say whether the door was open or he was listening at the keyhole) were "Egypt" and "Morocco." Later he was summoned to the King's study where Edward offered him an 1888 Uppmann cigar and told him England was going to reach a settlement with France over all disputed colonial questions.

When the Entente became a fact, William's wrath was tremendous. Beneath it, and even more galling, rankled Edward's triumph in Paris. The *reise-Kaiser*, as he was known from the frequency of his travels, derived balm from ceremonial entries into foreign capitals, and the one above all he wished to visit was Paris, the unattainable. He had been everywhere, even to Jerusalem, where the Jaffa Gate had to be cut to permit his entry on horseback; but Paris, the center of all that was beautiful, all that was desirable, all that Berlin was not, remained closed to him. He wanted to receive the acclaim of Parisians and be awarded the Grand Cordon of the Legion of Honor, and twice let the imperial wish be known to the French. No invitation ever came. He could enter Alsace and make speeches glorifying the victory of 1870; he could lead parades through Metz in Lorraine; but it is perhaps the saddest story of the fate of kings that the Kaiser lived to be eighty-two and died without seeing Paris.

Envy of the older nations gnawed at him. He complained to Theodore Roosevelt that the English nobility on continental tours never visited Berlin but always went to Paris. He felt unappreciated. "All the long years of my reign," he told the King of Italy, "my colleagues, the Monarchs of Europe, have paid no attention to what I have to say. Soon, with my great Navy to endorse my words, they will be more respectful." The same sentiments ran through his whole nation, which suffered, like their emperor, from a terrible need for recognition. Pulsing with energy and ambition, conscious of strength, fed upon Nietzsche and Treitschke, they felt entitled to rule, cheated that the world did not acknowledge their title. "We must," wrote Friedrich von Bernhardi, the spokesman of militarism, "secure to German nationality and German spirit throughout the globe that high esteem which is due them . . . and has hitherto been withheld from them." He frankly allowed only one method of attaining the goal; lesser Bernhardis from the Kaiser down sought to secure the esteem they craved by threats and show of power. They shook the "mailed fist," demanded their "place in the sun," and proclaimed the virtues of the sword in paeans to "blood and iron" and "shining armor." In German practice Mr. Roosevelt's current precept for getting on with your neighbors was Teutonized to, "Speak loudly and brandish a big gun." When they brandished it, when the Kaiser told his troops departing for China and the Boxer Rebellion to bear themselves as the Huns of Attila (the choice of Huns as German prototypes was his own), when Pan-German Societies and Navy Leagues multiplied and met in congresses to demand that other nations recognize their "legitimate aims" toward expansion, the other nations answered with alliances, and when they did, Germany screamed *Einkreisung!* — Encirclement! The refrain *Deutschland ganzlich einzukreisen* grated over the decade.

Edward's foreign visits continued — Rome, Vienna, Lisbon, Madrid — and not to royalty only. Every year he took the cure at Marienbad where he would exchange views with the Tiger of France, born in the same year as himself, who was premier for four of the years that Edward was king. Edward, whose two passions in life were correct clothes and unorthodox company, over-looked the former, and admired M. Clemenceau. The Tiger shared Napoleon's opinion that Prussia "was hatched from a cannon ball," and saw the cannon ball coming in his direction. He worked, he planned, maneuvered in the shadow of one dominant idea: "the German lust for power . . . has fixed as its policy the extermination of France." He told Edward that when the time came when France needed help, England's power would not be enough, and reminded him that Napoleon was beaten at Waterloo, not Trafalgar.

In 1908, to the distaste of his subjects, Edward paid a state visit to the Czar aboard the imperial yacht at Reval. English imperialists regarded Russia as the ancient foe of the Crimea and more recently as the menace looming over India, while to the Liberals and Laborites Russia was the land of the knout, the pogrom, and the massacred revolutionaries of 1905, and the Czar, according to Mr. Ramsay MacDonald, "a common murderer." The distaste was reciprocated. Russia detested England's alliance with Japan and resented her as the power that frustrated Russia's historic yearning for Constantinople and the Straits. Nicholas II once combined two favorite prejudices in the simple statement, "An Englishman is a *zhid* (Jew)."

But old antagonisms were not so strong as new pressures, and under the urging of the French, who were anxious to have their two allies come to terms, an Anglo-Russian Convention was signed in 1907. A personal touch of royal friendliness was felt to be required to clear away any lingering mistrust, and Edward embarked for Reval. He had long talks with the Russian Foreign Minister, Isvolsky, and danced the Merry Widow waltz with the Czarina with such effect as to make her laugh, the first man to accomplish this feat since the unhappy woman put on the crown of the Romanovs. Nor was it such a frivolous achievement as might appear, for though it could hardly be said that the Czar governed Russia in a working sense, he ruled as an autocrat and was in turn ruled by his strong-willed if weak-witted wife. Beautiful, hysterical, and morbidly suspicious, she hated everyone but her immediate family and a series of fanatic or lunatic charlatans who offered comfort to her desperate soul. The Czar, neither well endowed mentally nor very well educated, was, in the Kaiser's opinion, "only fit to live in a country house and grow turnips."

The Kaiser regarded the Czar as his own sphere of influence and tried by clever schemes to woo him out of his French alliance which had been the consequence of William's own folly. Bismarck's maxim "Keep friends with Russia" and the Reinsurance Treaty that implemented it, William had dropped, along with Bismarck, in the first, and worst, blunder of his reign. Alexander III, the tall, stern Czar of that day, had promptly turned around in 1892 and entered into alliance with republican France, even at the cost of standing at attention to "The Marseillaise." Besides, he snubbed William, whom he considered *"un garçon mal élevé,"* and would only talk to him over his shoulder. Ever since Nicholas acceded to the throne, William had been trying to repair his blunder by writing the young Czar long letters (in English) of advice, gossip, and political harangue addressed to "Dearest Nicky" and signed "Your affectionate friend, Willy." An irreligious republic stained by the blood of monarchs was no fit company for him, he told the Czar. "Nicky, take my word for it, the curse of God has stricken that people forever." Nicky's true interests, Willy told him, were with a *Drei-Kaiser Bund,* a league of the three emperors of Russia, Austria, and Germany. Yet, remembering the old Czar's snubs, he could not help patronizing his son. He would tap Nicholas on the shoulder, and say, "My advice to you is more speeches and more parades, more speeches, more parades," and he offered to send German troops to protect Nicholas from his rebellious subjects, a suggestion which infuriated the Czarina, who hated William more after every exchange of visits.

When he failed, under the circumstances, to wean Russia away from France, the Kaiser drew up an ingenious treaty engaging Russia and Germany to aid each other in case of attack, which the Czar, after signing, was to communicate to the French and invite them to join. After Russia's disasters in her war with Japan (which the Kaiser had strenuously urged her into) and the revolutionary risings that followed, when the regime was at its lowest ebb, he invited the Czar to a secret rendezvous, without attendant ministers, at Björkö in the Gulf of Finland. William knew well enough that Russia could not accede to his treaty without breaking faith with the French, but he thought that sovereigns' signatures were all that was needed to erase the difficulty. Nicholas signed.

William was in ecstasy. He had made good the fatal lapse, secured Germany's back door, and broken the encirclement. "Bright tears stood in my eyes," he wrote to Bülow, and he was sure Grandpapa (William I, who had died muttering about a war on two fronts) was looking down on him. He felt his treaty to be the master coup of German diplomacy, as indeed it was, or would have been, but for a flaw in the title. When the Czar brought the treaty home, his ministers, after one horrified look, pointed out that by engaging to join Germany in a possible war he had repudiated his alliance with France, a detail which "no doubt escaped His Majesty in the flood of the Emperor William's eloquence." The Treaty of Björkö lived its brief shimmering day, and expired.

Now came Edward hobnobbing with the Czar at Reval. Reading the ambassador's report of the meeting which suggested that Edward really desired peace, the Kaiser scribbled furiously in the margin, "Lies. He wants war. But I have to start it so he does not have the odium."

The year closed with the most explosive faux pas of the Kaiser's career, an interview given to the *Daily Telegraph* expressing his ideas of the day on who should fight whom, which this time unnerved not only his neighbors but his countrymen. Public disapproval was so outspoken that the Kaiser took to his bed, was ill for three weeks, and remained comparatively reticent for some time thereafter.

Since then no new excitements had erupted. The last two years of the decade while Europe enjoyed a rich fat afternoon, were the quietest. Nineteen-ten was peaceful and prosperous, with the second round of Moroccan crises and Balkan wars still to come. A new book, *The Great Illusion* by Norman Angell, had just been published, which proved that war had become vain. By impressive examples and incontrovertible argument Angell showed that in the present financial and economic interdependence of nations, the victor would suffer equally with the vanquished; therefore war had become unprofitable; therefore no nation would be so foolish as to start one. Already translated into eleven languages, *The Great Illusion* had become a cult. At the universities, in Manchester, Glasgow, and other industrial cities, more than forty study groups of true believers had formed, devoted to propagating its dogma. Angell's most earnest disciple was a man of great influence on military policy, the King's friend and adviser, Viscount Esher, chairman of the War Committee assigned to remaking the British Army after the shock of its performance in the Boer War. Lord Esher delivered lectures on the lesson of *The Great Illusion* at Cambridge and the Sorbonne wherein he showed how "new economic factors clearly prove the inanity of aggressive wars." A twentieth century war would be on such a scale, he said, that its inevitable consequences of "commercial disaster, financial ruin and individual suffering" would be "so pregnant with restraining influences" as to make war unthinkable. He told an audience of officers at the United Service Club, with the Chief of General Staff, Sir John French, in the chair, that because of the interlacing of nations war "becomes every day more difficult and improbable."

Germany, Lord Esher felt sure, "is as receptive as Great Britain to the doctrine of Norman Angell." How receptive were the Kaiser and the Crown Prince to whom he gave, or caused to be given, copies of *The Great Illusion* is not reported. There is no evidence that he gave one to General von Bernhardi, who was engaged in 1910 in writing a book called *Germany and the Next War*, published in the following year, which was to be as influential as Angell's but from the opposite point of view. Three of its chapter titles, "The Right to Make War," "The Duty to Make War," and "World Power or Downfall" sum up its thesis.

As a twenty-one-year-old cavalry officer in 1870, Bernhardi had been the first German to ride through the Arc de Triomphe when the Germans entered Paris. Since then flags and glory interested him less than the theory, philosophy, and science of war as applied to "Germany's Historic Mission," another of his chapter titles. He had served as chief of the Military History section of the General Staff, was one of the intellectual elite of that hard-thinking, hard-working body, and author of a classic on cavalry before he assembled a lifetime's studies of Clausewitz, Treitschke, and Darwin, and poured them into the book that was to make his name a synonym for Mars.

War, he stated, "is a biological necessity"; it is the carrying out among humankind of "the natural law, upon which all the laws of Nature rest, the law of the struggle for existence." Nations, he said, must progress or decay; "there can be no standing still," and Germany must choose "world power or downfall." Among the nations Germany "is in social-political respects at the head of all progress in culture" but is "compressed into narrow, unnatural limits." She cannot attain her "great moral ends" without increased political power, an enlarged sphere of influence, and new territory. This increase in power, "befitting our importance," and "which we are entitled to claim," is a "political necessity" and "the first and foremost duty of the State." In his own italics Bernhardi announced, "What we now wish to attain must be *fought for*," and from here he galloped home to the finish line: "Conquest thus becomes a law of necessity."

Having proved the "necessity" (the favorite word of German military thinkers), Bernhardi proceeded to method. Once the duty to make war is recognized, the secondary duty, to make it successfully, follows. To be successful a state must begin war at the "most favorable moment" of its own choosing; it has "the acknowledged right . . . to secure the proud initiative." Offensive war thus becomes another "necessity" and a second conclusion inescapable: "It is incumbent on us . . . to act on the offensive and strike the first blow." Bernhardi did not share the Kaiser's concern about the "odium" that attached to an aggressor. Nor was he reluctant to tell where the blow would fall. It was "unthinkable," he wrote, that Germany and France could ever negotiate their problems. "France must be so completely crushed that she can never cross our path again"; she "must be annihilated once and for all as a great power."

King Edward did not live to read Bernhardi. In January, 1910, he sent the Kaiser his annual birthday greetings and the gift of a walking stick before departing for Marienbad and Biarritz. A few months later he was dead.

"We have lost the mainstay of our foreign policy," said Isvolsky when he heard the news. This was hyperbole, for Edward was merely the instrument, not the architect, of the new alignments. In France the king's death created "profound emotion" and "real consternation," according to *Le Figaro*. Paris, it said, felt the loss of its "great friend" as deeply as London. Lampposts and shop windows in the Rue de la Paix wore the same black as Piccadilly; cab drivers tied crepe bows on their whips; black-draped portraits of the late king appeared even in the provincial towns as at the death of a great French citizen. In Tokyo, in tribute to the Anglo-Japanese alliance, houses bore the crossed flags of England and Japan with the staves draped in black. In Germany, whatever the feelings, correct procedures were observed. All officers of the army and navy were ordered to wear mourning for eight days, and the fleet in home waters fired a salute and flew its flags at half-mast. The Reichstag rose to its feet to hear a message of sympathy read by its President, and the Kaiser called in person upon the British ambassador in a visit that lasted an hour and a half.

In London the following week the royal family was kept busy meeting royal arrivals at Victoria Station. The Kaiser came over on his yacht the *Hohenzollern,* escorted by four British destroyers. He anchored in the Thames Estuary and came the rest of the way to London by train, arriving at Victoria Station like the common royalty. A purple carpet was rolled out on the platform, and purple-covered steps placed where his carriage would stop. As his train drew in on the stroke of noon, the familiar figure of the German emperor stepped down to be greeted by his cousin, King George, whom he kissed on both checks. After lunch they went together to Westminster Hall where the body of Edward lay in state. A thunderstorm the night before and drenching rains all morning had not deterred the quiet, patient line of Edward's subjects waiting to pass through the hall. On this day, Thursday, May 19, the line stretched back for five miles. It was the day the earth was due to pass through the tail of Halley's comet, whose appearance called forth reminders that it was traditionally the prophet of disaster — had it not heralded the Norman Conquest? — and inspired journals with literary editors to print the lines from *Julius Caesar:*

> *When beggars die there are no comets seen;*
> *The heavens themselves blaze forth the death of princes.*

Inside the vast hall the bier lay in somber majesty, surmounted by crown, orb, and scepter and guarded at its four corners by four officers, each from different regiments of the empire, who stood in the traditional attitude of mourning with bowed heads and white gloved hands crossed over sword hilts. The Kaiser eyed all the customs of an imperial Lying-in-State with professional interest. He was deeply impressed, and years later could recall every detail of the scene in its "marvelous medieval setting." He saw the sun's rays filtered through the narrow Gothic windows lighting up the jewels of the crown; he watched the changing of the guards at the bier as the four new guards marched forward with swords at the carry-up and turned them point down as they reached their places, while the guards they relieved glided away in slow motion to disappear through some unseen exit in the shadows. Laying his wreath of purple and white flowers on the coffin, he knelt with King George in silent prayer and on rising grasped his cousin's hand in a manly and sympathetic handshake. The gesture, widely reported, caused much favorable comment.

Publicly his performance was perfect; privately he could not resist the opportunity for fresh scheming. At a dinner given by the King that night at Buckingham Palace for the seventy royal mourners and special ambassadors, he buttonholed M. Pichon of France and proposed to him that in the event Germany should find herself opposed to England in a conflict, France should side with Germany. In view of the occasion and the place, this latest imperial brainstorm caused the same fuss, that had once moved Sir Edward Grey, England's harassed Foreign Secretary, to remark wistfully, "The other sovereigns are so much quieter." The Kaiser later denied he had ever said anything of the kind; he had merely discussed Morocco and "some other political matters." M. Pichon could only be got to say discreetly that the Kaiser's language had been "amiable and pacific."

Next morning, in the procession, where for once he could not talk, William's behavior was exemplary. He kept his horse reined in, a head behind King George's, and, to Conan Doyle, special correspondent for the occasion, looked so "noble that England has lost something of her old kindliness if she does not take him back into her heart today." When the procession reached Westminster Hall he was the first to dismount and, as Queen Alexandra's carriage drew up, "he ran to the door with such alacrity that he reached it before the royal servants," only to find that the Queen was about to descend on the other side. William scampered nimbly around, still ahead of the servants, reached the door first, handed out the widow, and kissed her with the affection of a bereaved nephew. Fortunately, King George came up at this moment to rescue his mother and escort her himself, for she loathed the Kaiser both personally and for the sake of Schleswig-Holstein. Though he had been but eight years old when Germany seized the duchies from Denmark, she had never forgiven him or his country. When her son on a visit to Berlin in 1890 was made honorary colonel of a Prussian regiment, she wrote to him: "And so my Georgie boy has become a real live filthy blue-coated Pickelhaube German soldier!!! Well, I never thought to have lived to see that! But never mind, . . . it was your misfortune and not your fault."

A roll of muffled drums and the wail of bagpipes sounded as the coffin wrapped in the Royal Standard was borne from the Hall by a score of bluejackets in straw hats. A sudden shiver of sabers glittered in the sun as the cavalry came to attention. At a signal of four sharp whistles the sailors hoisted the coffin on to the gun carriage draped in purple, red, and white. The cortege moved on between motionless lines of grenadiers like red walls that hemmed in the packed black masses of perfectly silent people. London was never so crowded, never so still. Alongside and behind the gun carriage, drawn by the Royal Horse Artillery, walked His late Majesty's sixty-three aides-de-camp, all colonels or naval captains and all peers, among them five dukes, four marquises, and thirteen earls. England's three Field Marshals, Lord Kitchener, Lord Roberts, and Sir Evelyn Wood, rode together. Six Admirals of the Fleet followed, and after them, walking all alone, Edward's great friend, Sir John Fisher, the stormy, eccentric former First Sea Lord with his queer un-English mandarin's face. Detachments from all the famous regiments, the Coldstreams, the Gordon Highlanders, the household cavalry and cavalry of the line, the Horse Guards and Lancers and Royal Fusiliers, brilliant Hussars and Dragoons of the German, Russian, Austrian, and other foreign cavalry units of which Edward had been honorary officer, admirals of the German Navy—almost, it seemed to some disapproving observers, too great a military show in the funeral of a man called the "Peacemaker."

His horse with empty saddle and boots reversed in the stirrups led by two grooms and, trotting along behind, his wire-haired terrier, Caesar, added a pang of personal sentiment. On came the pomp of England: Pour-suivants of Arms in emblazoned medieval tabards, Silver Stick in Waiting, White Staves, equerries, archers of Scotland, judges in wigs and black robes, and the Lord Chief Justice in scarlet, bishops in ecclesiastical purple, Yeomen of the Guard in black velvet hats and frilled Elizabethan collars, an escort of trumpeters, and then the parade of kings, followed by a glass coach bearing the widowed Queen and her sister, the Dowager Empress of Russia, and twelve other coaches of queens, ladies, and Oriental potentates.

Along Whitehall, the Mall, Piccadilly, and the Park to Paddington Station, where the body was to go by train to Windsor for burial, the long procession moved. The Royal Horse Guards' band played the "Dead March" from *Saul*. People felt a finality in the slow tread of the marchers and in the solemn music. Lord Esher wrote in his diary after the funeral: "There never was such a break-up. All the old buoys which have marked the channel of our lives seem to have been swept away."

The Strain
of Trench Warfare

DENIS WINTER

Writing in the *British Medical Journal* during November 1914, Dr Albert Wilson gave his opinion that 'I do not think that the psychologists will get many cases.' Any wear and tear would soon be rectified by alcohol, he added. As a source of quickly absorbed calories, alcohol might be poison to the office worker but was, in Wilson's professional opinion, manna to the hill gillies who grew so old in Scotland. What, after all, was the soldier but another type of peasant plying his trade in the open air.

Visitors to the front line may well have agreed with the *BMJ*. The matter-of-fact response of soldiers to the dangers round about them was most striking. A strict convention laid down that all reference to fear was to be avoided except perhaps obliquely and in jest: 'Cheer up, cockie. It's your turn next'; 'three to a loaf tomorrow lads.' Such wounded men as would be encountered were still in a state of initial shock and appeared to accept their condition stoically. Moran described a typical case: 'Just now a man was brought to my dugout on a stretcher. Half his hand was gone and his leg below the knee was crushed and broken. While his wounds were being dressed he smoked, lighting each cigarette from the stump of the old one. His eyes were as steady as a child's. Only his lips were white. Afterwards he was carried away, with the men looking on in silence. But, when the groundsheet flapped down again over the entrance, my servant grinned. 'You always know the old 'uns,' he said. The casual visitor might therefore conclude that the Kitchener soldier fitted into the same quietly heroic mould of which he had read so much in his Henty or Kipling or *Boy's Own* magazine.

This proved not to be the case. Though De Lisle always insisted that there was no fear in the 29th Division, and that his cure for men who showed the first symptoms was to tie them to front-line barbed wire for thirty seconds 'with most effective results,' no amount of bravado could cover the facts. In 1914, 1,906 cases of behaviour disorder without physical cause were admitted to hospital. In 1915 the number grew to 20,327 or 9 per cent of battle casualties. Often the men had good war records — heroes like Owen or Sassoon — so the blanket tag of 'cowardice' could not be applied. By the end of the war 30,000 mental cases had been evacuated to England, and in 1922 some 50,000 men had been awarded war pensions on mental grounds alone. Though these figures were never publicized and are often forgotten today, the government acknowledged them discreetly. When planning for war in 1938, the authorities laid it down that in the next war mental to physical casualties would probably be in the ratio of three to one, while four million hospital beds should be laid aside for psychiatric cases during the first six months when Britain would be bombed from the air.

Just what the soldiers classified as mental cases were suffering from baffled most people at the time. Though shell bursts apparently triggered off most of the patients, only 3 per cent of those classified officially as 'shellshock' cases had actual brain lesions. In February 1915 the *Lancet* could only suggest molecular commotion in the brain as a result of high-frequency vibration. *John Bull*, Bottomley's sensational magazine widely read by the troops, advertised Dr Muller's Nerve Nutrient (guaranteed not German). 'The primary trouble in all phases of nerve exhaustion,' ran the advertisement, 'is the semi-starvation of the nerve cells, the reason being that the sufferer fails to extract from his daily food the precious, concentrated nutrient that nerve cells live and thrive on.' As an opinion, it was no farther from the truth than official medical pronouncements of the time.

Today we understand better how severe physical symptoms may be generated by mental anxiety and we know in addition that, given the way Kitchener's armies were recruited, casualties of the mind were bound to be numerous. In the 1940s, the US army examined eighteen million men and rejected 29 per cent out of hand, one-third of these on mental grounds. Nevertheless one in seven became ineffective for mental reasons alone. In 1914 all men were swept into our army — the alcoholic, the subnormal, the mentally unbalanced. Very soon after the start the army's psychological consultant, Myers, submitted a written memorandum to Haig, stating his belief that such men would be better employed in the Pioneer corps; where with tact, firmness and understanding they could survive in a relatively low-stress environment. Having invited the memorandum, Haig turned it down, and these men were then bound to become a greater disability than the diseased, supplying a high proportion of the discontented, the inefficient, the absentees.

Even for those perfectly A1 in health and mental balance, the Great War posed a greater test than any previous war. It was not just that a civilian had been taken from his family and friends and fitted into the Procrustean, disciplined army, where he found his individual will hamstrung, his diet and sleep subverted, his hands taught to kill and mutilate in a way which conflicted with his basic civilian standards; it was rather that he was hardly ever out of danger. In earlier wars battles had gone on for a day, and then with little noise and over so small an area that a general on horseback could control operations by eye and voice. High-explosive missiles in the Great War changed all this.

In France no man was safe. My father saw a man shot in the stomach miles from the front when a bullet ignited in the heat of a brazier burning waste material. Dearden observed a man whose stomach had been blown away while he was cutting down a tree. The axe had missed the tree and hit a buried grenade. Death could hit men in the same way in the relative safety of the reserve line. Few shells could reach at that distance, but Moran described an unnerving exception. 'The medical officer of the Durhams, who had been through the battle of Hooge in autumn 1915 without a scratch, was walking in the woods around Poperinghe. His head was taken off by a stray shell, the only one that dropped in those woods in our time.' Men expected heavy casualties in a battle or trench raid; what they could never adapt to was the constant haemorrhage in the front line. Plowman wrote of a mother's petition after two of her three sons had been killed. Colonel Rowley promised that the remaining son would be sent into the back area the next time out of the line. The man involved, Private Stream, was the only company fatality in that particular tour of duty. Another case concerned Hann of the 7th Somerset light infantry. He had come from the yeomanry and went up to the front wearing a bullet-proof waistcoat sent by his parents. He was shot through the forehead the first time up in the line.

Death on such a scale and in such unexpected places worried most men. Maze recaptures the unspoken fear beautifully in a story of two days before the attack of 3rd Ypres.

> I rode slowly along the marching battalions. I heard the regular sound of an engine and saw puffs of smoke shooting up from a house on the road. A steam saw was cutting rhythmically through wood, working at high pressure with a tearing sound. Seeing the yard in front of the house piled high with wooden crosses and thinking to spare the men, I hurried in to have them removed. The Belgians engaged in the work threw up their hands in despair and pointed through the window to the back of the house and an ever bigger pile. Nothing could be done.

I watched the men as they passed by. Some smiled, others passed a joke, some wouldn't look. But I knew that they all saw and understood.

The chief trigger of this deepest of all fears seems to have been the sight of a corpse. Seldom could front-line soldiers get away from these reminders of mortality for any length of time. Confronted with so many visible witnesses, the mind tried to defend itself by a steadfast refusal to think beyond the concrete and immediate. 'There is no man so totally absorbed by the present as a soldier,' wrote Allen. 'It claims all his attention and he lives from moment to moment in time of danger with animal keenness that absorbs him utterly. This is a happy and saving thing.' Boy soldier Hope recaptured well the stock defence of the front line man attempting to distance himself from uncomfortable thoughts and pretend that death had no relation to himself. 'Death lies about in all its forms. A limbless body here, the tunic fitting the swollen body like a glove. He may have wanted a tunic to fit him like that all his life—he gets it in death. A body without a head like a rumjar without a label. A form fast turning green, lying in a pool of grey-green gas vomit. Death in a thousand different masks. A youngster not much older than myself is bringing his inside up. Poor blighter. It's a pity. Heaven knows when our next rations will arrive.'

Nevertheless always at the back of the mind was the knowledge that the corpse was once a living man like oneself, in the same situation and therefore initially no more likely to meet death than oneself. Here Manning describes the deepest feelings of the fearful eye-witness:

The dead are quiet. Nothing in the world is more still than a dead man. One sees men living, living desperately and then suddenly emptied of life. A man dies and stiffens into something like a wooden dummy at which one glances for a second with furtive curiosity. One sees such things and one suffers vicariously the inalienable sympathy of man for man. One forgets quickly. The mind is averted as well as the eyes. It reassures itself after the first despairing cry: 'It is I—not it is not I. I shall be like that.' And one moves on, leaving the mauled and bloody thing, gambling on the implicit assurance each one has in his own immortality.

Corpses newly dead or in a lifelike position broke right through morale no matter who the observer. Gladden wrote:

The dead man lay amidst earth and broken timber. It seemed like a sacrilege to step over him but there was no evading the issue. Never before had I seen a man who had just been killed. A glance was enough.

His face and body were terribly gashed as though some terrific force had pressed him down, and blood flowed from a dozen fearful wounds. The smell of blood mixed with the fumes of the shell filled me with nausea. Only a great effort saved my limbs from giving way beneath me. I could see from the sick grey faces of the file that these feelings were generally shared. A voice seemed to whisper with unchallengeable logic, 'Why shouldn't you be the next?'

There are references without number to the depths of fear soldiers felt when confronted with death in its most tangible form. Ewart after Loos saw a whole company, one by one, turn to look at a dead man who seemed almost to be asleep. They did not find the clue they were looking for. Reid once emptied three Lewis gun drums into a German platoon 'with fierce satisfaction at doing frightful execution' at Morval, but afterwards he and his whole section stood for a few moments silently watching a heavily bandaged, dead German holding a rosary in his sole remaining hand. Reid thought that most of the men were visibly shaken. They had not expected an enemy to die like themselves.

The effects of these thoughts and the situations which triggered them was cumulative, reinforced by shellbursts, illness, lice, mud and constant uncertainty. Perceptive men saw that at the time. Sassoon observed that the effect of war could be traced in weeks and months, though differences of age and rank affected the precise timing. Graves pinned the thing down more precisely. He thought three weeks sufficient to learn the rules of safety and degrees of danger, with peak efficiency reached in three months. Thereafter there would be rapid decline. Aldington concluded that after six months most line troops were off their heads, horribly afraid of seeming afraid. It is interesting that Second World War studies agreed with these subjective opinions and timings.

Rest could not save a man. Indeed the constant stop-start pattern of the war routine might add to the problem. Priestley found himself more apprehensive every time he went up the line. Burrage once remarked that the longer he was away from the trenches, the more he disliked going in. Some recent animal experiments support this in a curious way by suggesting that development of stomach ulcers is related not to the degree of stress nor to its intensity but to its repetition at unpredictable intervals.

At the time little was known of the physical nature of fear or of the stresses which progressively wore a man out, though acute observers plotted clearly the physical symptoms — as the sharpest of them, Lord Moran, put it: 'men wear out in battle like their clothes. In battle the soldier's senses are dulled but, even if he comes out unscathed, the ordeal will shorten his life in the line . . . it is the long-drawn-out exercise of control which is three parts of courage that causes wear and tear.' Most men did not realize what was happening, but in their diaries many plotted the stages of the decline. Private Wear joined the RAMC at the age of seventeen. His diary reads progressively:

> . . . a story book come true . . . extraordinary luck . . . not dismayed by the sick or wounded applied for a commission since I felt the war eluding me . . . one evening, just after supper, a 4.2-inch shell came through the wall into the room, bursting at once. We were thrown to the ground but marvellously no one was hurt. It was from this time that I began to experience what fear was. This sudden shock (I trembled for an hour afterwards) gave me a completely new outlook on life, life and war being of course synonymous terms . . . found myself on quiet nights in the trenches shivering with horror at what might happen . . . changed mentally and morally by leave on 31 December 1917 . . . going up the line a horrible necessity . . . no sustaining feeling of the slaughter leading anywhere . . . nightmares even now . . . bitterly unwilling to go back . . . prompt rations and whisky the only concern . . . depression increased by new drafts . . . feeling that I had outlived my time . . . trying to grow young ever since.

The unpublished letters of the Eton schoolmaster, Christie, who founded the Glyndebourne opera are as moving. Despite bad eyesight and crippled limbs, he had volunteered. By October he was writing back to Eton: 'Yes. I should not refuse a job at home. Should like a home battalion to train. Think I could do this rather well. Doubt whether I can pull this before I am wounded. Might develop rheumatism in my ankle.'

The most vulnerable men could stand very little extra stress. Enid Bagnold describes a typical case of a man who in civilian life and in a well-protected job might have been able to cope but broke under the greater demands of Flanders, demands in his case which did not even reach the test of high explosive.

> 'Me 'ead's that queer, nurse. It seems to get queerer every day. I can't 'elp worrying. I keep thinking of them 'orses.' I said to the charge nurse, 'Is number twenty-four really ill?' 'There's a chance of him being mental,' she replied. 'He is being watched.' Was he mental before the war took him, before the sergeant used to whip the horses as they got to the jumps, before the sergeant cried out, 'Cross the stirrups'? There are strong and feeble men. A dairyman's job is a gentle job. He could have scraped through life alright. Now he sleeps in the afternoons and murmurs, 'Drop the reins. Them 'orses, sergeant. I'm coming, sergeant.

Don't touch 'im this time,' and then he shouts in a shriller voice, 'Don't touch 'im,' and he wakes. He nods and smiles every time one looks at him, frantic to please. He will sit in a chair for hours, raising and lowering his eyebrows and fitting imaginary gloves to his fingers. An inspecting general, pausing at his bed this morning, said, 'A dairyman are you? Afraid of horses are you? Then what do you do about cows?' He was pleased with his own joke and the dairyman smiled too, his eyebrows shooting up and down like swallow's wings. Such jokes meant nothing to him. He is where no jokes but his own will ever please him any more.

More often men reached the front line, stood it for a period, then cracked suddenly. Moran described such a case.

At Armentières there was a big curly-headed sergeant with a red face and an open smile, who appeared quite indifferent to the war. He really commanded the company in those days. He was so imperturbable on patrol that men liked to go out with him. He was deaf and could not hear the bullets or any of those sounds which set men's brains working to their undoing. Then at Vimy something happened all at once. It was not the shelling—only mortars which made a big crater but did little harm. The sergeant got into the habit of watching them. He seemed fascinated by them. Soon I discovered to my astonishment that they were doing him no good. As he stood with his eyes glued to the little dark objects still high in the air, he began to think. It occurred to him that he had been a long time with the battalion. He began to go over in his mind what had happened to those who had come over with him. A fortnight after we left Vimy, he came to me to report sick. He got back to England.

When men did crack, they often showed the most diverse responses to identical pressures. Myers noted one incident in which a shell had hit a dugout. Only two men survived. One wandered in the open with his clothes off, believing that he was going to bed. After just four days at a field ambulance station he was back in service. The other man was in a coma for a fortnight with rigid limbs. On the seventeenth day he sat up and said, 'Did you see that one, Jim?' then relapsed, remaining deaf and mute. In a final hysterical seizure he shouted battlefield orders, then came round to his normal condition. Another man who came under Myers was a soldier who had seen his closest friend killed at his side. He went into a tearful semi-stupor, showed no reflexes and took no notice of pinpricks. After two days, however, he got out of bed and talked to his orderly quietly about his old civilian life but retained no memory whatsoever of anything in his war hitherto.

For all the varied nature of their symptoms and their probable background — a sample of shellshocked men between November 1916 and May 1917 found that 80 per cent had a previous psychiatric record — the prognosis for such men was good. Indeed 87 per cent would be back again in front-line service within a month of being incapacitated. This was due to the prompt response of the Army Council. Myers, made 'specialist in nerve shock' in May 1915, had by the end of 1916 created four special centres with forward sorting centres. The four centres provided a picturesque view, the expectation of recovery and a reassuring medical officer, who made no examination, so suggesting that the original diagnosis was infallible. On the other hand, just fifteen miles from the front line, the guns could be heard. The soldier could not be under the impression that he had escaped while PE was regular and men were marched about by patients who were NCOs. Malingerers were picked out fast. The 'deaf' were caught by lip reading: the 'blind' by having their heads plunged into water; the 'severe headaches' by lumbar punctures and the 'blackouts' by sodium amytal injections. With so bracing and 'normal' a regime, sedation and rest and the avoidance of the words 'shellshock' and 'neurasthenia,' most men were reparable. After all, to an old hand like Myers, shellshock symptoms were not new. They were just like the symptoms shown by the survivors of industrial accidents or natural disasters.

Many soldiers under such severe stress staved off the breakdown of 'shellshock,' though very few could do so easily. Trembling eyelids or reflex shivering under shellfire showed with what effort soldierly bearing was maintained. 'The men usually cast off a bad day as they would have dismissed a nightmare,' wrote Partridge. 'Human nature's elasticity and power of recovery is never more helpful than in wartime. Yet there always remains a residue of impaired courage, destroyed enthusiasm. The driving force had gone. For instance, the shelling of brigade HQ in August 1917 when the men had been out of the line for two months brought back the old haunted look and restless hands.' The drain of reserves could suddenly show itself when there was no immediate trigger, in one of those panics so well known to our men of the two world wars.

Carrington recalled:

We were well below the skyline and a mile from the nearest section of front when we encountered a large party of men from a strange division without an officer. They were carrying water up the line unarmed. A stretcher party converged on us and fifty yards of trench was jammed with about a hundred men going different ways. Suddenly shelling broke out about a furlong from us. It was near enough for some over-strained stretcher bearer. In a hysterical voice he suddenly shouted, 'Look. They're coming over the top.' In a flash of time the whole trench was in confusion. My little party of stalwarts was swept away. The whole hundred men vanished in all directions. Looking back, to my joy, I saw Yates and my other men lying on the parapet loading their rifles and looking for an aim at imaginary foes.

For men who did not crack suddenly but slowly wound down, there was little official help that could be given. The men could only shelter behind such supports as could be found.

The chief prop was mates. Moran explained why. 'There is no answer to fear. It shakes the foundations of the mind. Physical contact is the one thing that helps.' Proximity allowed the dispersal of free-floating fear in conversation, while songs expressed indirectly all the shared fears. Private Kenway trembled during working parties in no-man's-land throughout his three years' service but never if he was out with the imperturbable Bob Lawrence, a slow and easy-going butcher in civilian life with his hairless body part disguised with a ginger wig. Lucy's nerve broke and he wept profusely on the death of his closest friend, Ryan. Lucy's colonel, thought to be a ferocious killer, confided to Lucy that he had never been the same since the death of his inseparable friend, Collins. His hand shook every night at dinner so that he had to lead every night patrol just to reassure himself.

Responsibility provided another prop. If a man felt the need to uphold the reputation of a crack regiment, had a special job to do like running a message or being the senior soldier of a section, then he would go on longer. The officer in particular, looking after the comfort of his men, strolling round the trenches rather than stuck on sentry, spreading a feeling of purpose, was kept going by the awareness that in a tight corner men looked to the officer for guidance and example. Macmillan remarked once how much easier it was to lead his men into battle, since custom laid down the role; how lost he was when alone and wounded in a shellhole, reading his own pocket edition of Aeschylus. At the end of the day officers were just half as likely to break down as their men.

Other props might be more durable, but these were more personal. Highly neurotic men seem to have survived best and even gone on fighting to the end. Failure to adapt to a changing environment could be beneficial in war as it had been a handicap in civilian life. In an environment where danger was so constant that it could not be predicted and where no regular pattern of behaviour fitted, those who responded in only a limited or mal-adaptive way to the present were fortunate.

Moran gives us a beautiful picture of such a man.

He was a soldier of the old style because his father had been in the service and his grandfather. His mental processes were not easily followed. When a man came before him on a charge, he was convicted *pour encourager les autres*. A trench to him was but another billet to be inspected for empty tins and stray equipment. In his mind it stirred no tactical problems. That was the problem he could deal with. For him, the people who emptied tea leaves in odd corners were the real problem. Maps were his pet aversion, especially trench maps. They conveyed very little to him. He loathed all paper. One morning a gunner came into the mess and asked the colonel if he would mind marking the line which the battalion held. He stood gazing at the map, his broad, flat face a little sulky and quite without intelligence. Presently he placed his fat, hairy paw with mere stumps for fingers where it covered the greater part of north France then with a rude and impatient gesture he moved away and rapidly began to describe the ground as he must often have seen it in his travels overland, for he had the horseman's eye for the country. No man could ever remember that he was sick or sorry. When anyone fell ill, the colonel plainly could not understand it, though at bottom he was good-natured. He got up before anyone else to turn out the servants. He got into his trench kit and set off alone by some overland track that he had discovered was mostly dead ground. He had an old balaclava drawn over his head. Across his shoulders he threw an old waterproof sheet, which he secured below his chin with a bit of string, and in his hand he carried a long pole. When he came to a particularly exposed place, he stopped and pulled out a knife to remove great lumps of mud from his shoes, which he wore with stockings in all weathers, holding that gumboots made him slow. The men grinned as he jumped into the trench, though he had never been known to praise anyone and mostly went about finding fault. After dinner he spread out the *Morning Post,* which made up his literature.

Better even than the neurotic were the schizoid, men cold, aloof, unable to express hostility or fear, men noted as eccentric or secluded introverts in civilian life. Preoccupied with an inner reality, these men could not sustain personal relationships and tended to face all complex situations with a withdrawal response. In the Second World War such men were more likely to join the air force, where there was little interpersonal contact in combat; during the first war, of necessity, most stayed on the ground. With their quixotic judgement and unpredictable behaviour, they won a disproportionate number of decorations. The Cheyenne Indians had called them 'the contraries,' the Crow Indians 'crazy dogs wishing to die.' General Seeley noted with surprise how the most lasting and violent soldiers, as during the Boer war in his experience, 'were in every instance the quiet, gently, dreamy type' — in other words, men outside the group, detached, driven by an inner daemon in a dangerous situation.

Some endured, more broke entirely, the majority ceased to fight except in a shadow-boxing way after a few months in the front line. This seems the gist of stress pressure in the Great War. The fact of the taboo on expressing fear, in France and later, cannot eliminate the 65,000 soldiers in mental hospitals when pensions were finalized in 1929. These were the tip of a vast iceberg. Each week I see in Leavesden mental hospital, the largest in England, a man whose memory is perfect, within the limits of his great age, to 1917. Thereafter he can remember nothing. An explosion had wiped the recording mechanism from his life and hospitalized him from that day to this. Nor can the taboo eliminate those broken men whose lives were needlessly taken. If a man accused and convicted of cowardice or desertion pleaded shellshock, he was kept under observation. Dr Macpherson checked about seventy such men, observed them for about four weeks, talked with them twice daily and examined their dossiers three or four times. These men were therefore only shot after some scrutiny. The official figures stated that 11 per cent of court-martial death-sentences were carried out. Macpherson thought the proportion about right from his own experience. Nevertheless it is hard to believe that mistakes were not made — or from the sample of memoirs that I have taken that the official figures are correct. Most fighting soldiers would have backed Evans at the time:

> A man was shot for cowardice. The volley failed to kill. The officer in charge lost his nerve, turned to the assistant provost-marshal and said, 'Do your own bloody work, I cannot.' We understood that the sequel was that he was arrested. Officially this butchery has to be applauded but I have changed my ideas. There are no two ways. A man either can or cannot stand up to his environment. With some, the limit for breaking is reached sooner. The human frame can only stand so much. Surely, when a man becomes afflicted, it is more a case for the medicals than the APM. How easy for the generals living in luxury well back in their châteaux to enforce the death penalty and with the stroke of a pen sign some poor wretch's death warrant. Maybe of some poor, half-witted farm yokel, who once came forward of his own free will without being fetched. It makes one sick.

PART TWO

LETTERS AND DIARIES

Dead and wounded Australian and German soldiers in the railway cutting on Broodseinde Ridge, Belgium, October 12, 1917. From the Australian War Memorial, neg. E03864.

Introduction

"Somewhere in France," the letters and diaries would be titled. The heavily censored passages read like an alphabet soup of initials for villages, regions, fellow soldiers.

"Yes this is my third birthday away from home . . ."

"How is the Boy getting on with his schooling, . . ."

"[His death] was by no means a lingering painful one nor was he disfigured in any way."

"Imagine the scene — here in the moonlight, close to the enemy, these foolhardy devils running round with no cover, while bullets were whistling all about them, shying for pears."

"Dear Madam, I am very sorry to have to tell you . . ."

In the letters, the impressions of the war are captured in the most personal and intimate of terms for the expected readers were wives, lovers, or friends. With many of the diaries, the conversation was deeper still — a strictly inner discourse reflecting the constant worries and transitory joys of the soldier's life under fire or in rest billets close behind the firing lines. Describing a battlefield after the close of a heavy engagement, an observer is surprised by the number of fluttering pages of paper emerging from torn jackets and smashed pocketbooks. The wind whips it in eddies; the pages collect against the web of wire, the berms of trenches.

Officers heavily censored the letters of the "other ranks." The officers' letters, in turn, were supposedly reviewed higher up the chain of command — something that may or may not have happened. Keeping a diary was strictly forbidden because such a document in enemy hands might give away valuable intelligence. Fortunately for us, few, it seems, obeyed the command. There are perhaps thousands of diaries still bound shut, lying in boxes in the Imperial War Museum.

And who knows how many letters there are in trunks in attics. Every so often some emerge to find their way into print in single collections or in anthologies — voices from the Great War anxious to be heard, requesting our attention again.

They are often profound in their calmness and solitude amidst the very antithesis of serenity. The men worry about their children's schooling. Husbands remind wives of things that need tending. Soldiers yearn for home and the small events of daily living that passed unnoticed before the hostilities began. They speak of their current duties and responsibilities to each other and to their officers. Some admit their loss of faith; others renew it.

Midshipman George Leslie Drewry tells his father in great detail of the day at Gallipoli when he won the Victoria Cross. Medical Officer Ian Martin, besieged by the Turks at Kut in Mesopotamia, writes his mother about their menus of "potted horse" and variations of desserts with dates.

Corporal Forster tries to console the parents of a dead friend. Immediately after the war's end, Frederick Holman tells his wife of the grandiose spectacle of the German fleet escorted to Scapa Flow to be scuttled. Private Bruckshaw, who served at Gallipoli and, later, on the western front, writes of his quiet, almost leisurely detail near Salonika. He records recipes of crushed biscuit, bacon grease, water, and sugar. His routine is one of delousing, humping ammunition, and felling trees for trench supports.

An Orientalist and linguist, Aubrey Herbert served at Gallipoli. There he practiced a crude form of psychological operations by using a megaphone, attempting, in Turkish, to convince the enemy to surrender. His net gain, much to the chagrin of the soldiers in the nearby trenches, was a flurry of hand grenades. In quieter moments, Herbert describes the beauty of the peninsula, recalling that just across the Dardenelles is Troy, another place made famous by war.

Herbert Sulzbach, a German artillery officer, writes in 1918 when everywhere the war is turning against the Central Powers. Most of his friends are dead. When he returns to a French village where he was billeted in 1915, he finds unexpected peace and comfort.

The reader encounters a desperate attack on the western front with Edwin Vaughan and comes to see how precarious the struggle is when the smallest circumstance separates victory from tragedy. At the end, Vaughan writes, "out of our happy band of 90 men, only 15 remained."

Arthur West's diary, one of the earliest made public, was artfully reconstituted by a friend to show a growing bitterness toward the war. But despite that, West's words provide an insight into the relations between the "other ranks" and the officers who commanded them. "I shall always remember," West writes, "sitting at the head of this little narrow trench smoking a cigarette and trying to soothe the men simply by being quiet."

These are intimate viewpoints and personal assessments of the war. At times, confused by the events; at other times, meditative. Hard actions give way to probing reflection and create an amazing kaleidoscopic view. If one wonders what these men of the Great War were like, the answer is to be found in such accounts.

A young German hopes that "After the war, there will be a deepening of religious feeling and people will be simpler and more devout."

"It is a sunny day," a British officer reflects, "and against the walls and in sheltered places the heat is pleasant. Out on the E . . . Road the whole of F . . . lies before us; a mist is gathering over it from the surrounding hills and from the chimneys of the jute factory. Little girls pass and repass through the crowd of officers with quiet happy eyes. I am very happy. I love all the men, and simply rejoice to see them going on day by day their own jolly selves, building up such a wall of jocundity around me."

Voices from somewhere in France, on Gallipoli, in Galicia, Italy, Mesopotamia.

A Place Called Armageddon

Sergeant Bert James Fielder, Royal Marines. Killed near Albert, October, 1916

June 26. I am now in billets in a farmhouse in a village called Dieval near Lens about 25 miles from the firing-line, but rest assured that I am quite safe as the battalion is a new one and is to have about three months training as soon as we get more to join it, which will be some time yet. You will notice I have gone back to sgt but I am expecting to get made company sgt in two or three days. That is what the Colonel has promised me if I suit him. I am the only Marine in the btn and the Colonel is Mr Asquith the eldest son of Mr Asquith the Prime Minister, so if I can settle in this btn I shall be in luck once more . . .

'I am pretty busy at present as I have taken over company sgt-major, of a brand new coy, and you can bet there is some hard work to do until I can get it into some shape. I wonder what news you are getting in England. I think something is doing here as I lay awake last night listening to those big guns of ours going off around Lens, I think the Germans are at last getting a strafing.'

'*27 July.* I've been doing night work, I have to go to a place some miles from here each evening and don't get back until sometimes 4 in the morning, of course I don't walk it but the riding in the night air does not improve my cold. One good thing is we have had the last six days without rain, it is quite a change to be choked with dust from the road instead of the usual coating of mud, but I suppose all the troubles will come to an end "Après la guerre" as the French people say. Don't keep the Boy from school more than you can possibly help, if he once gets in the habit of staying away you will have a rare job to get him to go again . . .'

'*26 September.* Yes this is my third birthday away from home and I am having a day off on the strength of it, or rather it has happened by chance. Yesterday while returning from Field Exercise I jumped down a bank a bit awkward and sprained my right ankle, the result is I'm struck off all duties for the day by order of the doc, but quite expect to be fit tomorrow. What a strange thing that it is exactly eight years ago this month I was in the hospital with the same injury only caused through playing football.

'We got the news here yesterday about the Zep raid, surely it is about time "Kaiser Bill" found out that that game is not worth the candle . . . Yes, the leave has commenced, but only very small numbers are going at a time, you see the people that have been on the peninsula the whole time are going first, and it won't be my turn for a long time yet.'

'*12 October*. What sort of weather are you getting, it is very windy here today, some more rain about I expect which means sticking to the tent all day, but we've got a gramophone to while away the time and plenty of books to read, so you see we don't do so bad. How is the Boy getting on with his schooling, ask him from me when he is going to write Daddy that letter. I think this is all I've got to say at present, shall be very glad when I can write you a long letter, but still we must be patient and wait a little longer.'

'*26 October*. Your letter of the 15th received yesterday noon and those of 16th and 18th last night. It is a pity that you did not let me know of Mother's illness by sending a wire as I have been informed by the OC Coy that I could have had a special leave.

Am sorry I have not been able to write this last week but we've been in a terrible muddle, not been able to settle anywhere, have had a short stay in the trenches and am now back again for a short rest, and a very much needed clean up, for I can tell you there is *some* mud here at present. Am glad you are both keeping well, am in the pink myself except for a cold which of course is not to be wondered at whilst this wet weather lasts. Hoping this will find you still in the best of health, I must conclude with lots of love from your loving Husband, Bert. XXXXXX.'

'*30 October*. Dear Madam, I am very sorry to have to tell you that Sergeant Fielder, B. J., 15388 RMLI, died in No 11 Casualty Clearing Station last night. He was admitted during the day severely wounded in thigh and foot and from the first there was almost no hope of his recovery. He was unconscious till the evening when he gave us your address, but that was practically all we could get out of him. It was found necessary to operate in the afternoon and his right leg had to be taken off. He had every care and attention possible but in spite of everything he gradually sank and passed quietly away during the night. His wounds were so numerous and at the same time so serious that it was almost hopeless from the first. With *deepest* sympathy in your bereavement, Yours faithfully, Sister-in-Charge.'

'*All Saints' Day*. Just a line to express my deepest sympathy with you in your great loss. Your husband was only in this hospital a short time and was unconscious so that I was unable to have any conversation with him. All Saints' Day brings a ray of comfort to the bereaved, leading our thoughts to the time when we hope one day to meet those loved ones who have gone before. I am sure he was a fine fellow and it must be some comfort to feel that he gave up his life for his country. I buried him with the same old service that we use at home in a little cemetery for English soldiers. Excuse more as I am very busy. Very sincerely yours, H. L. Connor, Chaplain

'PTO. A little cross marks the grave where he was buried and it is registered so that you will be able to find it after the war.'

Midshipman George Leslie Drewry, VC, Royal Naval Division. Born 1895. Awarded the Victoria Cross for his actions during the landing of the River Clyde *at Gallipoli. Died in 1918 in an accident at sea.*

HMS *River Clyde*
Sedd-el-Bahr
Turkey
12 May 1915

'Dearest Father, I'm awfully afraid I've made you anxious by missing the last two mails, I did write a letter on the 21st of April but tore it up again. In my last letter I think I told you that two RN midshipmen were joining the *Hussar* to help me. Well they came, and we worked in three watches for two days until I got tired of doing nothing so asked the Captain [Unwin] for more work, well I got it with a vengeance.

'He took me on board this ship and gave me thirty Greeks and told me to clean her. Well she was the dirtiest ship I've seen. She was in ballast and had just brought French mules up from Algiers, they had built boxes and floors in the tween-decks and carried the mules there without worrying about sanitary arrangements.

'We knocked the boxes up and cleaned her up for troops, painted the starboard side P & O colour. A large square port was cut on each side of each hatch in the tween-decks and from the No 2 ports I rigged stages right round the bow. A party of the armoured car people came on board and rigged small huts of plates and sandbags and put maxims in them, 11 altogether. After two days' delay on account of weather we put to sea on the 23rd April at 1 PM towing three lighters and a steamboat alongside (port) and a steam hopper on the starboard side. As soon as we cleared the shipping we dropped the lighters astern.

'Now I will tell you of our crew. Capt: Comdr. Unwin, RN (retired supplementary), 1st Lieut: Mid. Drewry, RNR and Warrant Eng. Horend, RNR, nine seamen and nine stokers, one carpenter's mate, the original ship's steward and the Captain's servant. [The two VC seamen were Williams and Samson, mentioned later.] Can you imagine how proud I felt as we steamed down the line, I on the fo'c's'le-head. The flagship (no longer *Hussar*) wished us luck as we passed. As soon as the tow was dropped I took the bridge until the Capt had lunch then I had mine and carried on with the work for there were many things to be done. At dusk we anchored off Tenedos and that night we had pheasant for dinner, a present from the captain of the *Soudan*.

'Next morning things looked bad, a nasty breeze made us afraid our show would not come off, but it died quickly. About 6 AM a signal came to us telling us we were in someone's berth so we had to weigh and for an hour we wandered among the ships with our long tail just scraping along ships' sides and across their bows. We were nobody's dog, nobody loved us. Finally we tied up to the stern of the *Fawcette* and we put the last touches to the staging on the bow. About 4 PM the sweepers came alongside with the troops. At 11:30 PM all was ready and the Capt told me to snatch some sleep. At midnight we proceeded in this fashion [sketch of ship with vessels in tow].

'At 2 AM or thereabouts the Capt turned over to me, and I found myself on the bridge very sleepy with only the helmsman, steering towards the Turkish searchlights on a calm night, just making headway against the current, shadowy forms of destroyers and battleships slipping past me. Visions of mines and submarines rose before me as I thought of the 21 thousand men in the holds and I felt very young. Between 3 and 4 AM the Capt took over again and I went to sleep again being called at 5 AM, "Captain says you are to take over the hopper." So I climbed over the side across the lighters into the hopper.

'Then came an anxious time, we steered straight toward Cape Helles and in a few minutes the bombardment commenced, Dad it was glorious! Dozens of ships, battleships, cruisers, destroyers and transports. The morning mist lay on the land, which seemed to be a mass of fire and smoke as the ships raked it with their 12 inch, the noise was awful and the air full of powder. Shells began to fall round us thick but did not hit us. We were half a mile from the beach and we were told not yet, so we took a turn round two ships, at last we had the signal at 6 AM and in we dashed, Unwin on the bridge and I at the helm of the hopper with my crew of six Greeks and one sailor Samson.

'At 6:10 the ship struck, very easily she brought up, and I shot ahead and grounded on her port bow. Then the fun began, picket boats towed lifeboats full of soldiers inshore and slipped them as the water shoaled and they rowed the rest of the way, the soldiers jumped out as the boats beached and they died, almost all of them wiped out with the boats' crews. We had a line from the stern of the hopper to the lighters and this we tried to haul in, the hardest haul I've ever tried. Then the Capt appeared on the lighters and the steam pinnace took hold of the lighters and plucked them in until she could go no closer. Instead of joining up to the hopper the Capt decided to make the connection with a spit of rock on the other bow.

'Seeing this we let go our rope and Samson and I tried to put a brow out over the bow, the Greeks had run below and two of us could not do it, so I told him also to get out of the rain of bullets, and I jumped over the bow and waded ashore, meeting a soldier wounded in the water. I and another soldier from a boat tried to carry him ashore but he was again shot in our arms, his neck in two pieces nearly, so we left him and I ran along the beach towards the spit. I threw away my revolver, coat and hat and waded out to the Captain, he was in the water with a man named Williams wading and towing the lighters towards the spit. I gave a pull for a few minutes and then climbed aboard the lighters and got the brows lowered onto the lighter. The Capt still in the water sang out for more rope, so I went onboard and brought a rope down with the help of a man called Ellard. As we reached the end of the lighters the Capt was wading towards us carrying Williams. We pulled him onto the lighters and Ellard carried him onboard the ship on his shoulders, but he spoilt the act by not coming down again. Williams was dead however.

'I got a rope from the lighter to the spit and then with difficulty I hauled the Capt onto the lighter, he was nearly done and I was alone. He went inboard and the doctor had rather a job with him. All the time shells were falling all round us and into the ship one hitting the casing of one boiler but doing no further damage. Several men were killed in No 4 hold. I stayed on the lighters and tried to keep the men going ashore but it was murder and soon the first lighter was covered with dead and wounded and the spit was awful, the sea round it for some yards was red. When they got ashore they were little better off for they were picked off many of them before they could dig themselves in.

'They stopped coming and I ran onboard into No 1 hold and saw an awful sight, dead and dying lay around the ports where their curiosity had led them. I went up to the saloon and saw the Capt being rubbed down, he murmured something about the third lighter so I went down again and in a few minutes a picket boat came along the starboard side and gave the reserve lighter a push that sent it as far as the hopper (the lighters had drifted away from the spit) with Lieut Morse and myself on it. Just as we hit the hopper a piece of shrapnel hit me on the head knocking me down for a second or two and covering me with blood. However we made the lighter fast to the hopper and then I went below in the hopper and a Tommy put my scarf round my head and I went up again.

'Now we wanted a connection to the other lighters so I took a rope and swam towards the other lighters but the rope was not long enough and I was stuck in the middle. I sang out to Mid Malleson [the other Midshipman VC] who had arrived with Morse in the picket boat, to throw me a line but he had no line except the one that had originally kept the lighters to the spit, he stood up and hauled this line in (almost half a coil) and then, as I had drifted away, he swam towards the lighter I had left and made it alright. Then I made for home but had a job climbing up the lighters for I was rather played out.

'When I got onboard the doctor dressed my head and rubbed me down, I was awfully cold. He would not let me get up and I had to lay down and listen to the din. Then I heard a cheer and looking out of the port I saw the Capt standing on the hopper in white clothes, a line had carried away and by himself he had fixed it. Then I went to sleep and woke at 3 PM to find the hopper's bow had swung round and there was no connection with the shore. I got up and found that nothing was going to be done until dark. At dusk the firing seemed to cease, and the connection was made to the spit again.

'During the time I was asleep the Captain and one or two volunteers had taken seven loads of wounded from the lighters to No 4 hold by the starboard side. A great feat which everyone is talking about. About 8 PM the troops commenced to land again and things went well as far as firing goes. While the troops were going out I had a party getting wounded from the hopper and lighters and putting them onboard a trawler lying under our quarter. An awful job, they had not been dressed at all and some of the poor devils were in an awful state, I never knew blood smelt so strong before.

'About 11:30 PM the trawler had left and almost all the troops were ashore and the Turks gave us an awful doing, shell, shrapnel and every other nasty thing, but everyone lay low and little harm was done. They finished about 2 AM. All through the night the village was burning and gave us too much light to be pleasant.

'Next day was not pleasant, early in the morning our people worked up the right and took the fort and then worked slowly into the village and took it house by house. Then Col Doughty Wylie led a charge up the ridge and was killed just as he led his men into the old fort on top of the ridge. All this we saw plainly from the ship. I had a run ashore across the spit and took a photo from the beach but the bullets began to fly so I ran back. It was not until the next day that all the snipers were cleared from the ridge and village.

'Samson my hopper man did very well on the Sunday afternoon, two or three times he took wounded from the beach to the hopper. On the second day he was severely wounded while sniping from the fore deck. Nothing much happened that night except that a dog frightened one Tommy, he fired at it and so did the rest for nearly an hour.

'I won't follow up the soldiers or the censor would tear this up, ten minutes walk and I can see the men in the trenches, in the straits I can see the enemy's shells falling round our ships and always the roar of guns goes on. We have been bombarded by aeroplanes but no damage done. I've seen a German chased by two of our planes.

'My Capt has just left us for another job and soon I expect to be back to the *Hussar* again. By next mail I hope to send you some photos taken here, some of them I believe will be of interest and I'm wondering if you could send them to the papers for me.

'The Admiral sent for me on the 28th and gave me a shift of clean clothes and the use of his bath, some luck.

'There is lots yet I could tell you but I must not so will send my love and close.

Best of health,
Your affectionate Son,
George

'NB Have just received yours of the 15th and 22nd, glad you are keeping so well.'

Captain J. S. S. (Ian) Martin, Medical Officer. Born 1889. Martin was among the British and Indian soldiers besieged by the Turks in Kut-al-Amara for five months. The Turks captured the city on April 29, 1916. Major General Martin died in 1974.

'The enemy have snipers on the other bank who practice shooting down all the streets running at right angles to the river. It is pitiful to see the poor Arab women rushing down at nightfall to fill their waterjugs. One or two of them are always brought to hospital wounded. We have become the favourite hospital for the Arabs. I had some success in digging out bullets from various inaccessible places: and our fame has spread abroad. Moreover, we put "Medicine" on their wounds: other ambulances not so — they put the dressing on straight away. They come all ages and sexes — pretty little girls with bullets in the groin to hoary old sinners with shrapnel in the belly. They do make marvellous recoveries — and as a result we try rather marvellous operations on them — so far invariably successfully. So that our street is full of Arab seekers-after-health every day.

'Though we have had but few patients injured by bombardment it is very different with the General Hospitals. They are nearer the river front, and so to our heavy guns, which attract the enemy's fire. They cover an enormous area of the town. Every day fifteen to twenty shells hit them somewhere: the marvel, is not that they have casualties, but that any survive. I myself one day saw a shell land on the roadway and kill two and wound one sepoy about 20 yards away. I was able to give first aid—luckily as the man was bleeding very freely. But it's not what you expect in a hospital. And just about five yards away Barber, the OC of the hospital, was calmly sewing away inside a bullet-smitten abdomen, with two doctors assisting him.

'Another day, looking in at the Stationary Hospital operating theatre, King, of our service, was cutting off the remnants of a leg. "Hullo," I said, "who's that you're amusing yourself with?" "Oh, only one of my sub-assistant surgeons" was his answer. "He got his leg blown off and two order-lies were killed just in the office about twenty minutes ago!"

'As the enemy trenches have closed in, so the wounds from our front-line trenches have become more severe. They are often inflicted at point-blank range and the wound is consequently "explosive"—ie a comparatively small wound is seen where the bullet has entered but the exit is a great bulging mass of torn muscles, tendons and crushed up splinters of bone. All you can do is to give an anaesthetic and cut away the protruding mass and clean up things as best you can, hoping that it won't go too awfully septic. Of course in trench warfare a very large number of the total wounds are through the head: these only come into the ambulance to die: one can do absolutely nothing for them: they are already unconscious and need no anodyne.

'For myself I got laid up with influenza on the 24th and it certainly doesn't tend to bring your temperature down to have these beastly shells banging and screaming about: especially when people are killed not five yards from where you are lying in bed and practically in front of your eyes. However, Xmas day by some unspoken contract was kept in absolute peace and rest. Not a single shot was fired the whole twenty-four hours: even the snipers ceased. They say it was partly due to the German advisers of the Turkish C-in-C. The Turks also wished to collect and bury their dead at the Fort—which I understand they were permitted to do. [. . .]

'Now if we go over the advantages of Kut in a siege the chief is that it is normally a great trading centre for the surrounding agricultural country, and a favourite trade route from the Persian highlands. The whole of the export trade of corn was stopped by order of the Governor of Kut early in November. So great stores of wheat and barley—mostly the latter—had accumulated here when our retreating division arrived. Now you will see the reason for the grain-crushing engines, and the saving of the paraffin. Very soon the entire stock of ordinary flour ran out and we became dependent on the three oil engines we were lucky enough to find installed here. A mixture of about one part wheat to four parts barley flour now is used in making our bread, and is issued to the Indians to make chupatties. This makes the most delicious bread you ever tasted: one knows it is made direct from the pure grain: nothing is wasted—it is dark brown and delightfully flavoured . . .

'Sugar gave out almost at once, also molasses for the Indians. Milk—well, we stuck to our cows as long as we could: but one cow and her calf soon succumbed to the necessity for a meat ration. We were on bully beef for quite a while: then they began to slaughter the draught oxen of the heavy 5″ guns. Luckily we had about 120 of these, the finest bullocks in India and such beef! As the Indians weren't getting any they did us quite a long time.

'About three weeks ago (early February) the first horse fell under the butcher's knife. Since then they have been slain daily, about 20 at a time. About 2,000 mules and 3,000 horses and ponies have been cooped up along with us: we kept them as long as we might but as they each eat daily about ten men's grain ration you can see that they are a considerable burden on the community. So we began on them as soon as we could, before the bully beef or the bullocks were quite finished. For a long time officers' messes generally got a bit of beef if they wished but now are reconciled to daily horse. We have him in steak and kidney pie, horse olives, horse mince, horse rissoles, potted horse, horse soup, stuffed horse heart, horse liver etc ad nauseum.

'The other staple in our ration is the date. I expect you have by this time received the dates I sent you before Xmas. Well do you know, I have many a time in this siege been selfish enough to wish I had kept that case for myself! It must be the weather, or the brown bread, or the muchness of work that does it, but I have never been so consistently and chronically hungry in all my life before. I had quite a good lunch at 1 PM and already am longing for four o'clock tea though I have an hour to wait. To return to dates — he turns up every day in our ration — 2 oz each — and we have him for pudding at dinner in various disguises. He is excellent by himself with a dash of ginger and lime juice, and a little boiled rice to tone him down served with him. He makes an excellent and savoury mush stewed with a few dried apricots: dates charlotte is delicious: date dumpling is a dream: and he is an excellent ingredient of suet puddings. [. . .]

'Today completes the 120th day of the siege. This brings us level with Ladysmith . . . The only ration now is — British 1 lb bread, 1 lb horsemeat: Indian 10 oz barley flour (of the crudest description, largely chaff) only. They [the men] wish the siege ended and care not which way so they get their bellies filled. It is difficult for us officers to realise their hunger and weakness — we have all the time had at any rate a sufficiency of palatable food and enough Mess stores to give a change of diet when needed.

'I am now going to bring this letter to a close. I hope I have succeeded in interesting you and helping you to realise this rather marvellous siege. I am afraid that as my interest in events declined, so failed my descriptive powers. Possibly I have provided but a dull ending.

'I don't think I have yet told you how the discovery of the siege was some toffee you got some lady to send me from England. Peppermint. I had one tin left which I had forgotten. The discovery was historic. It was at the end of February, when none of us had tasted sugar for two months. By jove how good it was!

'Then one eventful day I opened, at long last, my box of shirts. I had been saving them up for just such an emergency as we are now in. The wounded were without any available change of clothing — they came in soaking wet and chilled to the bone from the trenches. Now the shirts weren't very warm, but they were clean and white and with blankets and hot bottles were really delicious to the wounded. They are really beautifully made — I feel as if I should love to wear them myself!

'If relief should come, I hope to write to let you know all about it but this letter will at any rate let you know that it has come. I may find myself too busy to write at any length, as there will be all the sick and wounded to evacuate. Even should the worst happen, and we fall into the enemy's hands, I hope to plead the Geneva convention and to get away before the end of the war. The Turks have certainly so far tried, I think, to observe the convention, and certainly have shown themselves (as our Intelligence proves) humane and considerate in their treatment of such prisoners as they have captured . . .

'Goodbye then, darling mother. I have been longing for news of you and also specially of Jim, the family soldier . . . Au revoir — your loving devoted son, Ian.'

Despatches
from the Heart

*Corporal E. Foster, 62nd Brigade, Royal Field Artillery. He writes
the parents of his friend killed in December, 1917.*

Mr. and Mrs Fairhead,
Please allow me to express, on behalf of myself and chums, the deep and very
real sympathy we feel for you in your bereavement. I want to write the kind
of letter that is calculated to cheer you a little and if I am too clumsy please
remember that is my intention and forgive me. First let me assure you that
Fred's death was by no means a lingering painful one nor was he disfigured
in any way. And secondly let me tell you that he died as I knew he would;
like a real Englishman. He was struck in the chest and simply said "I'm done
boys" and passed quietly away. We brought him down and at 6 PM on the
10th buried him decently in a little English cemetery close by here. Today
some of the boys got away for a little while and brought back some nice little
rose trees and other plants so tomorrow if his cross is finished we shall go up
and do our little best for one whose cheerful presence is missed by a good
many. Possibly you have heard of me through Fred. He and I chummed up
about twelve months ago when he joined C. Battery and have been good
friends in good times and in bad times ever since. Since the advance we have
worked together most of the time and I think I may say, have had some
tough jobs to handle but whatever the job or whatever the conditions Fred
Fairhead was never a shirker nor was he ever anything but cheerful. I for one,
shall miss him in a good many ways and having known him so well can
understand fully what a big trial his loss will be to you. I am by no means a
good Christian but last night I said just a little prayer which I shall repeat
tonight. That you may be given the strength to bear your affliction and every

possible consolation. And now I will close hoping I have accomplished what I set out to do, and with my very best wishes to all of you believe me to be yours very sincerely.

Ernest Foster.

P.S. When next you write to Frank will you please tell him I shall be pleased to see him or hear from him at any time.

Frederick Holman, aboard the HMS Versatile, *writes his wife about the surrender of the German High Seas Fleet on November 24, 1918.*

My own dear Edie,

DORA[1] is now dead and letters will no longer be censored. cheers. loud and prolonged cheers. Well, in the first place I will tell you where we are or try to. We are miles from anywhere. Water! Water everywhere, we lost sight of land about 4 o'clock this afternoon. It is now getting on for 7 o'clock so we are about 60 miles from Scapa Flow. We are on our way back to the Firth of Forth having left Inchkeith yesterday morning with 20 German destroyers which we escorted safely to Scapa where they are interned. Well darling, as you have not had many letters lately I will try and give you a detailed account of what we have been doing, on that evening of Nov. 20th we found our-selves with other destroyers anchored almost under the shadow of Inchkeith Rock awaiting orders which we guessed would be to go out and bring the pick of the German Navy in. I turned in as usual and was called at 3:45 AM as I had to go on watch at 4 o'clock, we had been under way about an hour and were just passing May Island. I was on watch in the Wheel House from which a good view can be obtained, and at about 7:45 we sighted them through the morning haze. Their Battleships, Battle Cruisers, Light Cruisers, and destroyers in one long line, stretching right out of sight, 74 ships, the pick of the German Navy. We were in four long lines, 125 destroyers, what we had behind the destroyers I do not know, the end being out of sight. We steamed to meet them and two of our lines went down one side of the Huns and two lines down the other side so our four lines were going in one direc-tion and the Huns line down the middle of us in the opposite direction we steamed for three quarters of an hour at 12 knots, the Huns steaming at about the same speed. By this time the whole five lines were level. The signal was run up and as it was pulled down all the British Destroyers turned inwards in a half circle and now all five lines were going in the same direction, all in perfect order. It was a wonderful sight I can assure you. I don't suppose I shall see the like again, all this time all guns, torpedo tubes etc. were manned in case they should try their usual tricks, but nothing happened and we reached Inchkeith safely. In the afternoon our Captain, officers, and some of the crew went aboard one of the German boats to see if all shells, explosives etc had been removed, all of them were treated in this way and found correct. Our chaps said the place was dirty, the crews were dressed anyhow, the bread they saw was black, one man was having his dinner which consisted of swedes and potatoes, the destroyers (ours) were complimented on the smartness in maneouvering and the way all our 125 destroyers dropped anchor the whole 125 anchors going splash together. The Commodore of the Flotilas being very pleased.

I always said they would never come out but when I saw that long line of armed might, the mighty ships of war of the second Naval Power in the world, I and every man aboard was amazed that such a powerful evil should have given in without striking a blow. I think all the world wondered.

If they had sent their whole fleet out the battle would have been awful. I don't think for one moment that they would have won, but they would have given us a terrible smashing and the loss of life would have been terrible, but they did not. Why! Goodness knows they must have had a horror of the British Navy, or else they must have had a fearful hammering at the Battle of Jutland, perhaps some day we shall know. For myself I am not sorry they saw fit to stay in harbour. Most of the German destroyers are now at Scapa. I was able to see the German crews quite near, they did not look starved, but nearly all of them were busy fishing to help the black bread down I suppose. . . .

Please keep this letter safe. I see the papers give a somewhat different account. They say we sighted the Germans at 9 o'clock for one thing which is quite wrong. They might have done so but we sighted them at 7:45. They were already sighted by scouts at 7.7. You can show this to anyone that you may think would like to read it but please keep it clean.

Love,
Fred

Notes

1. DORA: Defence of the Realm Act

German Students'
War Letters

FRIEDRICH (FIDUS) SOHNREY, *Student of Political Economy, Berlin*

Born December 21st, 1887, at Möllenden.
Killed November 8th, 1914, near Clamecy.
In the Trenches near Clamecy, October 24th, 1914.
I go every day into the village here to see a family with six children. The father is in the war. The woman says that he is a Reserve Dragoon. She innocently believes that he has not yet been under fire, but she has had no news for two months. She sheds tears when she tells me that and hears that we get letters from home every day. I get hot water there so as to have a good wash after four days' interval, but I can't stop too long, as suspicious scratchings on the part of the children indicate undesirable house-mates.

One does feel sorry for these poor people, who have hardly a stitch of underclothing to change into, not to speak of anything to eat — nothing left but potatoes, and the woman is always tearfully asking me how much longer she and her children will have to go on living like that. She is always lamenting over the war: 'C'est triste pour nous et pour vous.' She lays the blame for it on the English and curses them. It makes her very unhappy when I tell her that we are making preparations for the winter and shall probably spend Christmas in the village. She just sobs helplessly. By way of thanks I leave her some bread and army biscuit, which the children fall upon with shouts of delight. The youngest is five months old. It is true that one cow has been left in the village, by order of the Area-Commandant, to supply milk for the babies, but even so that is little enough. On the second day I gave each of the children two sous. The woman was very much pleased and touched by my sympathy. She followed me to the door and assured me that her house was always 'à votre disposition.'

We all pity these poor people, who are clinging to the last remnants of their former happy existence, though in constant danger of seeing all their possessions burnt and smashed up by their own artillery, and I hardly think that a single one of our soldiers would treat them with anything but friendliness. Many of the men habitually give them some of their bread. The inhabitants of the place gather round our field-kitchens regularly to collect their tribute. So we are seeing to it that our enemies' belongings do not starve. Kindliness is probably that part of the German character from which it derives its greatness. 'It is the German soul, that makes a sick world whole' — and no doubt that means the German heart.

WERNER LIEBERT, *Student of Law, Leipzig*

Born June 14th, 1892, at Dresden.
Killed May 10th, 1915, near Givenchy.
Morning of December 4th, 1914.
MY DEAR, DEAR PARENTS, —

Your letter of the 26th brought me the sad certainty that my dear brother had died a hero's death for Germany's victory. The post came early this morning.

My pain is inexpressible. I am not to be comforted. I can't yet realize that I shall not see Hans or hear his voice again. The thought that the dear fellow, who went off so full of joy and hope, will never again see that home and those dear ones for whom he was no doubt longing just as I am, is intolerable. Of you and your sorrow I cannot think without tears. Only one thing comforts me a little: since I have known that my dear brother is no more, a wonderful change has taken place in me. I suddenly believe in immortality and in a meeting again in the other world. Those conceptions were empty words to me before. Since the day before yesterday they are objects of firm faith. For it cannot be that death should part one for ever from those one loves. What would be the use of all love and affection, which are the most beautiful flowers in human life, if they were to be destroyed for ever in an instant? This is certainly but a small consolation for the fact that the poor fellow has been deprived of all his life's happiness. How beautiful life is one only realizes out here, where one has constantly to risk losing it.

ALBIN MÜLLER, *Student of Theology, Bamberg Lyceum*

Born December 16th, 1892, at Tiefenstockheim, Unterfranken.
Died March 28th, 1915, in the Military Hospital at Tourcoing.

Comines, January 19th, 1915.

Here with us it pours with rain every day. You can't possibly imagine how filthy we get, wet to the skin. To-day we had to lie down in such filth that at first it made me shudder. But then I said to myself: 'Into it, in the name of God!' And while the others were cursing I thought of the story of our Holy Father St. Francis, how he said to one of the Brothers: 'When we get home, soaked with rain and besmirched with mud as we are, and knock at the door of the Convent, and the porter strikes us and calls us thieves and rogues, therein is perfect joy.'

LOTHAR DIETZ, *Student of Philosophy, Leipzig*

Born December 12th, 1889, in Pegau.
Killed April 15th, 1915, near Ypres.
November, 1914. Dug-out in the Trenches on Hill 59; 3 km. south-east of Ypres.
You at home can't have the faintest idea of what it means to us when in the newspaper it simply and blandly says 'In Flanders to-day again only artillery activity.' Far better go over the top in the most foolhardy attack, cost what it may, than stick it out all day long under shell-fire, wondering all the time whether the next one will maim one or blow one to bits. For the last three hours a corporal has been lying groaning on my right, here in the dug-out, with one arm and both legs shattered by a shell. The boyau runs down so steeply that it is impossible to carry him that way on a ground-sheet, and the other communication trench is under water. So 'good advice is dear.' Anyone who is badly wounded generally dies while he is being got out of here. To-day has cost us four killed, two dangerously and three slightly wounded.

Only 60 yards away from us are the English, and they are very much on the alert as they would be only too glad to get back our hill. We have a fairly decent trench up here, because we drain all the water into the English trenches lower down, but our neighbours on the left, the 143rd, have to keep two electric pumps going night and day, otherwise they couldn't escape the wet.

Six hundred yards behind here is our reserve position, a little wooded valley in which the most frightful hand-to-hand fighting has taken place. Trees and bushes are torn to pieces by shells and larded with rifle-bullets. All about in the shell-holes are still lying bodies, though we have already buried many. Any number of dud shells of every calibre have burrowed into the ground in the wood.

There is a quantity of French equipment lying about. In the slope on one side of the valley we have constructed our dug-outs: holes in the earth, with plank floors, ceilings of tarred felt, and provided with small stoves which are certainly not enough to heat the place, but at least serve for warming up food, and even for cooking.

As one can't possibly feel happy in a place where all nature has been devasted, we have done our best to improve things. First we built quite a neat causeway of logs, with a railing to it, along the bottom of the valley. Then from a pinewood close by, which had also been destroyed by shells, we dragged all the best tree-tops and stuck them upright in the ground; certainly they have no roots, but we don't expect to be here more than a month and they are sure to stay green that long. Out of the gardens of the ruined chateaux of Hollebecke and Camp we fetched rhododendrons, box, snowdrops and primroses and made quite nice little flower-beds. We have cleaned out the little brook which flows through the valley, and some clever comrades have built little dams and constructed pretty little water-mills, so called 'parole-clocks,' which, by their revolutions, are supposed to count how many minutes the war is going to last. We have planted bushes of willow and hazel with pretty catkins on them and little firs *with* their roots, so that a melancholy desert is transformed into an idyllic grove. Every dug-out has its board carved with a name suited to the situation: 'Villa Woodland-Peace,' 'Heart of the Rhine,' 'Eagle's Nest,' etc. Luckily there is no lack of birds, especially thrushes, which have now got used to the whistling of bullets and falling of shells, and wake us in the morning with their cheerful twittering.

Zwickau, November 13th, 1914.

Nine hundred men are just off from here to reinforce 105 at the Front, with bands playing and church-bells ringing, and the tears are running down my face because I have to sit here doing nothing while my comrades out there are fighting so gallantly. I should be in absolute despair if I were not sure of being back in the line in a few weeks' time. I have been persuading the doctor to pronounce me fit for active service as soon as it is anyway possible. He is quite pleased with the way my wound is healing. It is discharging a lot now, but that is a good thing as it gets rid of the poison. As clinical treatment is not necessary, I am entered as an out-patient, which means I only have to go to the hospital every day to have the wound dressed.

I was wounded in the attack on that louse's-nest Gheluveld, which had been fortified and was defended by 18,000 picked English troops, after we had captured two lines of trenches protected by the most awful barbed-wire entanglements and contact-mines. Out of the seventeen Deputy Officers who went to the Front with me, five have been killed and seven wounded.

WILHELM WOLTER, *Student of Philosophy, Munich*

Born May 28th, 1895, at Kladow, Mecklenburg.
Killed April 16th, 1915, near Vouziers.
Near Vouziers, April, 1915.
Outside the rifle-fire has been rattling all night; from what we have observed, they seem to be getting ready for another attack. I have been long since prepared for anything that may happen. People are always saying that it is easier for the young men to face death than for the older ones, the fathers of families and others. I hardly think so, for such a man knows — at least, if he has been conscious of any mission in life — that he has at any rate partially fulfilled it, and that he will survive in his works, of whatever kind they are, and in his children. It can't be so hard for *him* to die in a just cause. But I too feel that I have a mission in life. I believe that I have a message to deliver and I long to give back to mankind some of that rich treasure which God has put into my heart and before which I have sometimes trembled with joy. But I have not yet had time for any harvest; and am I to be allowed no reaping? Forgive such words. It will not be so, and even if it were, God in His goodness will always provide some compensation, some means of perfecting and fulfilling one's desires, and it must be one's consolation that such sublime beauty is certainly eternal, a foretaste of immortality which gives a faint presage of the reality and cannot end with death.

PAUL ROHWEDER, *Student of Theology, Kiel*

Born December 18th, 1890, at Zarpen (Holstein).
Killed April 23rd, 1915, near Het Sas.
October 29th, 1914.
Under a golden poplar lies a dead comrade. In the peasants' farmyards lie dead cattle. The windows are broken by shell-fire. Not a bird is to be seen. All nature holds its breath with fear. The air is heavy with the reek of gunpowder. The sun is setting, blood-red. Yet I cannot say that things are going ill with me. A man feels himself really free and independent only when he has learned to be ready to give up his life at any moment.

I have already fired many a shot and the bullets may have gone home. I can now only think with disgust of the battle-pictures which one sees in books. They show a repulsive levity. One never takes a real battle lightly. When one is in the midst of it and fully conscious of its reality, one can speak of it only in the most deeply earnest spirit. How many a quite young married man have I seen lying dead! One must not attempt to sweeten or beautify such a thing as that.

I dream so often of you. Then I see our house in the moonlight. In the sitting-room a light is burning. Round the table I see your dear heads: Uncle Lau is reading; Mum is knitting stockings; Dad is smoking his long pipe and holding forth about the war. I know that you are all thinking of me.

If only our warfare achieves the right kind of success; if it brings blessing upon the Fatherland and eventually on the whole of mankind; if we were sure of that, we should bear our sufferings and privations gladly. How I thank God that I am naturally endowed with such powers of endurance! I never felt so strong as I do now.

WALTER ROY, *Student of Medicine, Jena*

Born June 1st, 1894, at Hamburg.
Killed April 24th, 1915, in the attack on the Heights of Combres, near Les Eparges.
Döberitz, November 14th, 1914.
. . . Oh how suddenly everything has changed! First the free, sunshiny, en-chanting summer, golden happiness, a life of liberty, enthusiasm for Nature, poetry, music, brightness and joy, all the effervescence of youth: oh, what a lovely summer it was! And now cold, cruel, bitter earnest, stormy winter, death and misery! And everything vanished so suddenly. How I lived and loved is now like a dream, a passing mood, the sweet remembrance of a passing mood. Only one thing is real now — the war! And the only thing that now inspires and uplifts one is love for the German Fatherland and the desire to fight and risk all for Emperor and Empire. All else is thrust into the back-ground and is like a dream, like a distant rosy cloud in the evening sky.

When, on the march, I observed the autumn beauties of Nature, then indeed I thought sadly and yearningly: I should like to dream about you, to love you, to sing of you, to be rapt and meditative, but I have no time for you now: I am entirely occupied with thoughts of war and suffering and with enthusiasm for our holiest duty. Lenau, Goethe, Eichendorff, Schwind and Feuerbach, Beethoven, Wagner, Puccini, and Mozart — how I long for them! But I could not really enjoy them now, I could not live in their spirit. Thoughts press in upon me so many, so urgent, but I can't think them. I lack the needful repose and quiet.

I sometimes think that I have become rather strange. But when at last, at long last, I get to the Front — it should be about December — then if only I might give my life for our Germany, for my Kaiser, for my Fatherland! I have had a life, short indeed, but so beautiful, so golden, so full of light and warmth, that I should be happy to die if I had only myself to consider. And this life full of light and sunshine I owe to the dear people whose thoughts accompany me and of whom you too are one.

Before the attack on April 24th, 1915.

YOU, MY DEAR ONES, —

I hope that a trusty comrade will not have to send this letter to you, for it is a farewell letter. If it comes into your hands, you will know that I have died for my Kaiser, for my Fatherland and for you all.

There is going to be a terrible battle and it is radiant, enchanting spring-time!

I have nothing more to tell you, for I have had no secrets. You know how I thank you all three for all your goodness to me, how I thank you for all the sunshine and happiness in my life. If I am to die, I shall do so joyfully, grate-fully and happily! This is just another message of purest love to you all and to all who love me. I shall carry this last greeting with me till the last. Then it will be sent to you by my faithful comrades and I shall be with you in spirit. May the greatest and gracious God protect and bless you and my German Fatherland!

In tenderest love,
Your devoted
Walter.

WALTER HORWITZ, *Student of Philosophy, Heidelberg*

Born October 20th, 1893, at Hamburg.
Died May 1st, 1915, in the Military Hospital at Roulers, of wounds received April 24th, near Kerselaere.

Poelcapelle Station, January 12th, 1915.

At last I can find time and self-command to thank you for the brave letter in which you told me the very sad news of the death of our dear Hans.

I had already heard it, just before Christmas, from Gotthilf, when we were in billets at Westroosebeke. He came in, looking very much upset, and whis-pered to me that he had had bad news from home, and then out it came: 'Hans is killed.' We went outside and I tried in vain to find words to comfort him; it was impossible for me to express my own sympathy with him either: I felt too plainly how much he, you, and I and all of us have lost. And so too to-day I don't know what to say to you when at last I at least try to tell you how much I grieve with you for the loss of this splendid comrade. Only one text comes into my mind, the one I quoted to my own family, telling them to comfort themselves with it if God should also call me — it must and will help us in the death and loss of our dear ones: 'Death is swallowed up in victory! O death, where is thy sting? O grave, where is thy victory?' When Brahms wrote his glorious 'German Requiem' to comfort himself for the death of his beloved mother, he made this Bible text its climax, because it seemed to him to comprise all that was necessary for the acceptance of the inevitable. In the same way in which I quoted it to my family, so I now send it to you, dear friend, although I know that your brave German heart possesses in itself enough strength to support this heavy loss. It will comfort you, all the same, when you see that all the people who stood nearest to your fallen hero understand and share your suffering.

Dear friend, we are all looking death in the face almost daily, and that makes the soul quite calm in the presence of eternity. All the best of us are ready to tread the same path along which Hans has gone before as a shining example. We are ready with our whole hearts, because we are ripe for the great harvest and will greet the reaper worthily and willingly when he reaches out his sickle towards us.

GEORG STILLER, *Commercial High School, Berlin*

Born September 20th, 1895.
Killed May 29th, 1915, near the Heights of Combres.
Sunday, May 16th, 1915.
To-day I am sitting in the worst position on the Hill of Combres. It is Sunday; elsewhere there is rest and peace; here the murdering goes on — everlasting shells, shrapnel and rifle-fire. Nature wears its most beautiful spring dress, the sun laughs from the blue tent of heaven, but through blossoming, green-growing Nature fly the shells, destroying trees and fresh bushes, tearing deep holes in the earth, and annihilating young, blossoming human lives.

I have performed my Sunday devotions to-day, a thing I very seldom did in time of peace. One learns to pray again here and to cling to one's dear God. Here one first discovers what a support in time of need and danger is a real, fervent faith, and how comforting and soothing a hymn or a psalm can be. If the good God spares my life, if He brings me safely through the war, then I will always be His faithful, devoted disciple. It is a strange thing about the human heart — when danger is nearest, God is greatest — which I should express less bluntly by saying that when so long as all goes well with a man he does not think of asking God to guide his actions and ways, but if he is in danger he suddenly remembers that he has a support to which he can cling. I don't want to make myself out better than I am but that is how it has been with me. Since leaving school I had arranged a religion for myself, just what happened to suit me, without reference to my conscience or my deepest convictions. Danger has brought me near to my God again. I believe that this has been the experience of many others who also had thoughtlessly forgotten God and their religion, but who now, through death and danger, have regained their faith. And this will be not least among the advantages gained through the gigantic World War — it has deprived us of so much that we held dear, but it will also be productive of much good. After the war there will be a deepening of religious feeling and people will be simpler and more devout.

PETER FRENZEL, *Student of Law, Berlin*

Born May 11th, 1892, at Rössel, East Prussia.
Killed August 13th, 1915, near Luniew.
When we were on our way from Kielce to the Front, it seemed to me that the world ended at the railhead — far away lay the war, but the space was empty. The same pictures kept recurring. Simple wooden crosses beside the road and shell-shattered, still smouldering dwellings. One tragic feature was strikingly repeated: the tall, lonely chimney, standing beside the hearth, like a pathetic forsaken member of the family, patiently awaiting the return of his dear ones.

Every evening there is a repetition of another scene. In their flight the Russians set fire to villages, and especially the bridges. After sunset the glare lights up the sky in two or three different places, and the most remarkable cloud-formations drift across the heavens. For instance, a few days ago I saw a maiden rising out of the smoke lifting imploring hands towards the setting sun. Another time I saw a picture from an old French tapestry — a husband and wife in flight, carrying a gaily shouting child.

It is very extraordinary how I seem to have ceased to feel anything here; only my imagination is more lively and full of fantasy than ever, and the longing for home, for quiet tranquil work and mature enjoyment of life, grows daily greater.

GOTTHOLD von ROHDEN, *Student of Theology, Marburg*

Born February 4th, 1895, at Bielefeld.
Killed September 26th, 1915, in Champagne.
Beaurains, before Arras, December 26th, 1914.
. . . On Christmas Eve we were more than usually on the alert, as it seemed likely that the French would attack. The half-moon was shining in full glory — most unsuitable weather for going on patrol! Six War-Volunteers put themselves under my guidance and soon after it got dark we crawled out, the enemy being barely 400 yards away.

A slight natural hollow in the ground ran down towards the enemy, and in its shelter we managed to get fairly close. While you were sitting happily round the glittering Christmas tree and the children were excitedly awaiting the removal of the snow-white coverings from the present-tables, after which every one had adequately to admire the wonderful things which the others had received; and while, later on, you were perhaps sitting cosily and contentedly side by side, enjoying the mere being together, I was creeping, step by step, with every nerve strained to the utmost in order to detect the slightest rustle or sign of a dark form, towards the enemy's trench.

At last I got so far that I thought only one more 'lap' would be necessary, but meanwhile the Frenchies had at last become conscious of our approach, and the sound of the first sharp shots rang through the 'Holy Night.' We four mannikins—I had already left two behind for fear of our being cut off—crouched behind a small bit of cover. I had at once made up my mind what to do: to defend ourselves would certainly be fatal, for they were advancing upon us from the right and from straight in front, so that we could not prevent ourselves from being surrounded—we must get back. I had seen and observed quite enough.

Thirty yards behind us was another little bit of cover, but before we could reach it, one of the many bullets brought down my comrade K. W. One of the other men, who had one bullet through the sleeve of his tunic and overcoat, and another through his coat between his legs, wanted to stay with me, and only when I sternly ordered him to go did he make his escape into the darkness. The fourth man had lost his head, rushed back and upset the whole Company, including the Captain, by informing them that W. and I had been taken prisoner.

The French came nearer, and my fate seemed sealed: Adieu, you over there and you at home. If the French have any humanity we may meet again after the war! In any case I couldn't, of course, leave W. alone. Every second I expected to see the French come round the edge of my cover, but God had other designs for us: at the very spot where we had been just before they paused and stood audibly talking, evidently discussing this nocturnal disturbance. So there I lay with the wounded man; made a pillow for his head; whispered words of comfort and encouragement to him; tried to bind up his wound, which was in the upper part of the thigh; and thought about Christmas—and about many other things.

And no doubt it was just the fact of its being Christmas that saved us, for the Frenchies had evidently been seeking to celebrate the Feast with alcohol and were now loudly singing the Marseillaise, 'God save the King,' a Christmas hymn, and soldier-songs. One bellowed across: 'You want come to Paris; you not come!'

Our own men sang Christmas hymns in parts and the songs of the

Fatherland. When one gave a solo those opposite clapped in applause. The Frenchmen kept as quiet as mice while they listened to the Christmas hymns which no doubt you were singing at the same time.

The enemy close in front of us has moved away, and does not trouble to send out a patrol to see whether any thing is happening in 'no-man's-land.' Only once does he take any notice of the wounded man's movements and groans, and then the bullets pass over us.

When I saw how much blood W. was losing I did think of giving myself up, lest he should bleed to death. The Captain laughed at me when I told him that, and said I was indeed a sweet innocent if I imagined that the enemy would be magnanimous enough to bother about a wounded German! Luckily W. himself quickly dissuaded me: 'Anything rather than be taken prisoner!' he whispered; then he added, more loudly: 'Won't they ever come and fetch us!'

As I gradually became convinced that the French would not discover us for the present, I began to think about how we could escape, though that had seemed so hopeless at first. With impatient longing I watched the shadow of the bank lengthen as the moon sank. It would be impossible for me to relate in a few sentences all that I thought and felt during those two hours before it really grew darker and a plucky stretcher-bearer did manage to crawl out to us, although he did not know where we were lying, how far away we might be, or even whether we were still there, and might well have turned back ten yards sooner. One thing only I must tell you — I was perfectly calm and never felt a moment's fear of what might happen, knowing myself to be in a Higher Hand. Also just the consciousness of being the only hope and protection of another is in itself a help and support.

Boiry, February 19th, 1915.

A few days ago I came upon a bit of trench which was decorated in a highly original manner: the bays and breastwork were adorned with pots of flowers, the most noticeable being some Howitzer cartridge-cases full of snowdrops, the first flowers of the coming spring. Their frail delicacy seems particularly out of keeping with the surrounding shambles. No careful hand will tend them. Shells will tear up the ground, and crush and smother them. When I saw the first I picked and kept them. It wasn't easy to get them, I had to crawl out on my tummy, for the Frenchie keeps a good look-out!

One part of the trench runs through the middle of a beautiful park. When the trees are green it must be an idyllic spot, in striking contrast to the shattered dwellings. It is miserable to clamber over the ruins and see that not a single house has been spared. Even the church has been shot to bits by the French; against the exposed wall leans a whitewashed pedestal on which is a gaily painted, bare-headed saint, letting the rain pour down on him and the sun dry him, while he gazes down from morning till night on the devastation

at his feet, with only a look of silent reproach visible in his eyes. In the churchyard the crosses and tombstones are broken; even the dead have no rest beneath the earth, for the shells plunge deep into the ground and blow up the graves; at such spots one realizes to the full the misery of war.
Salency, July 8th, 1915.

. . . I can quite understand your wishing us to tell you as much as possible, but I can't myself place as much value on the written word as you do — I mean on the use of writing at all — I only do it to please you. It seems to me as if we who are face to face with the enemy are loosed from every bond that used to hold us; we stand quite detached, so that death may not find any ties to cut painfully through. All our thoughts and feelings are transformed, and if I were not afraid of being misunderstood I might almost say that we are *alienated* from all the people and things connected with our former life.

From your 'neutral' standpoint you reproach me for being *too* ready to sacrifice myself. Oh, you dear things Harald is quite right when he speaks enthusiastically of the work we shall have to do after the war. I should be surprised if it were otherwise. But we who are in the war — and compared with those of others my experiences are almost nothing — feel that we are confronting powers and influences where every normal, sensible, logical force, or what is generally considered as such, is utterly useless. The mind is no longer capable of Harald's 'right way of thinking.' We can only say, 'Death, here you have me!' feeling at the same time, 'but you shall not take me lying down, or too easily!' One man regains his balance more quickly, thanks to a naturally optimistic temperament; another is hampered by his tendency to be always seeking after truth, and owing to his more thoughtful nature, takes a darker view. But such waverings aren't of much account.

All attempts, however, to put such things into words seem banal and almost sacrilegious; such immense effects cannot be compressed into the tiny compass of human understanding. I have had to live through the experience of seeing my old regiment fight and die, and I cannot talk about it. All we can do is to be silent and hold up our heads. 'After the war' expresses an idea which seems miles away from us.
July 23rd, 1915.

Many thanks for your letter of July 16th. I return the Casualty List at once. I hadn't seen any details before about what happened to the 2nd Battalion of the 26th or the 2nd and 3rd Companies, and that interests me particularly. Now I know all about what occurred during the battle. The 3rd and 4th Companies were wiped out — *one* patrol only fought its way through. They were surrounded and attempts on the part of the 2nd and 3rd Battalion to rescue them failed, the 3rd being blown up, while the 4th, under their heroic wounded Commander, held out for six days without succour, until they had fired their last cartridge. One of the Platoon-Commanders — the 17-year-old youngest Lieutenant in the regiment—was killed, and his elder brother, commanding the 9th Company of the 26th, was wounded. Four officers were taken prisoner—we have had good news of them; my Fähnrich comrade H. H. is said by an eye-witness to have been killed. Only three Regular officers of the old regiment are left. The Machine-gun Corps had few casualties.

These are mere bald statements of events, but what terrible memories do they not hold for the human soul! All the books in the world could not contain them! It is enough to haunt a man for the rest of his life to have seen one man die; the soldier is doomed to appear unfeeling, hard and brutal. And during an attack? you ask. 'Then a man is no longer a man,' as once said a Jaeger officer who had been in the Argonne since September and taken part in storm after storm, including the last. Each of these experiences stands alone, incomprehensible, inexplicable, irrational.

Many a fine poem, enthusiastically composed perhaps in a snug sitting-room, about the hero's end and the glory of such a death, will now be read with a bitter smile.

August 2nd, 1915.

. . . Your question, the old, old question about the Redemption, has found a strange answer here. Even those who call themselves Christians, Christians of the old believing kind, have, in moments of the most intense physical, and perhaps also spiritual, suffering, found themselves unable to accept the idea of Redemption through the death of Christ; others have gone to their death with a consciousness of the sacred call of duty, content to leave all question of a life after death to a Higher Power, for one's own ego, with its realization of sin and despair, steps quite into the background. I myself cast all care with regard to my physical and spiritual well-being upon the Power above me, and leave it at that!

That is all very well during the war. Afterwards? Well, then your questions will again become more and more important, weightier, and more pressing.

MAX BÄSSLER, *Student of Administration and History, Leipzig*

Born February 19th, 1895, at Leipzig.
Killed September 12th, 1916, on the Somme.
Near Ypres, middle of May, 1915.
. . . The Lieutenant came and told me to see that our dead had proper funerals. They had already been temporarily buried by other hands, but we knew the places.

On the way back to Nuns' Copse, I noticed a field-postcard stuck up on the right of the trench, and on it was written: Rifleman Kurt Limke. A little farther on was a short post bearing the names of Beer and Lichtenberger.

I made the necessary arrangements at Polygon Wood the same evening, and got a day's leave from the regiment.

The work had to be done under the cloak of night, and before 3 A.M. Guck's rough voice called to me from outside the dug-out. In the opaque darkness stood the working-party with spades and picks. Silently we went our way. Outside the trench we divided up into small groups and I went with one to fetch Beer's body. We had to dig deeper than we expected. A horrible, sickly-sweet smell rose from the earth and we dared not smoke because of the enemy. First we found an infantryman who had been buried as a third in the same grave. Then we lifted poor Beer out. I helped carry him, four men remaining behind to dig out Lichtenberger.

We wrapped the body in a ground-sheet, and fixed poles at the sides to carry it by. Slowly the day dawned, palely red. It reminded me of Hauff's song. A dead man on such a primitive bier is rather heavy to carry, but on the edge of Nuns' Copse a wagon was waiting. Knoblauch and Hunger were already lying on it. The former, with his beautiful long dark beard, looked like a suffering Christ. Then they brought Lichtenberger, the only one who looked at all as he did when alive, and Zietzschmann, whose face was covered with blood. Lemke had not been found; his grave was empty.

At our camp in Polygon Wood we had a short rest. Then we went on, by way of the old position and the old relief road, to Becelaere. There the Drivers were working at the graves, in the little Military Cemetery beside the church. We fetched some large glazed tiles from the roof of a summerhouse to put round the graves, and picked some lilac-blossom and branches of red and yellow leaves to decorate them. Then we made the graves as much deeper as was necessary.

Meanwhile all who wished to take part in this last act of respect had assembled. We lowered the comrades into the earth. A Driver of the 248th, a Brother of the Rauhen-House in Hamburg, said a few moving words. The lilac gave out its lovely scent and the coloured leaves glowed on the fresh sods, but the earth crumbled as it were impatiently. Two big tears stood in old Böhne's eyes. Then we scattered the flowers and leaves over the dead, and began to shovel in the earth. The last service I was able to render my dear Rudolf was to brush a little blue butterfly from his cold check. When I saw him dead I almost envied him his unconscious state, but now, as I watched the worms and other creatures being shovelled in with the earth, and the last bit of ground-sheet disappearing, I was glad after all, that for me the May sun still shone bright and that for me the lilac still bloomed and perfumed the air.

KURT ROHRBACH, *Student of Theology*

Born August 21st, 1893, at Stettin.
Killed October 6th, 1916, on the Somme.

Flanders, August 26th, 1915.

Last night, towards 11 o'clock, my men and I were sent off as usual 'pumping'—that is to say, we had to go right up, in order to pump out the tiresome filthy water which is always trickling back into the communication-trench leading to the front line.

Armed with the heavy hand-pump we started. It was a lovely night. The full-moon shone in the sky and lit up the way, which on a dark night is hard to find owing to the many trenches and wire entanglements. The Frenchies were keeping comparatively quiet, and only now and then there was the report of a rifle and a bullet whizzed by, or a missile struck a tree, ricocheted and flew on with a melancholy note. Also as it was bright moonlight very few flares went up. Far away on the left, probably near Ypres, the thunder of guns growled. Otherwise all was still.

Soundlessly we proceeded over the duck-boards along the narrow trench. When we reached the wet place the work began. My men took hold valiantly, and as there had been but little rain during the previous few days, the trench was soon pumped dry.

Suddenly one of the men said: 'Hallo, there's the pear-tree which the stretcher-bearers said was chock full of ripe pears!' And before I could stop them, the chaps had jumped out of the trench and begun—only 120 yards from the enemy—to pelt the tree with bits of stick and lumps of clay! Imagine the scene—here in the moonlight, close to the enemy, these foolhardy devils running round with no cover, while bullets were whistling all about them, shying at pears! Certainly they were screened from observation by a fine white mist which was lying over the land. In a few minutes they had got every single pear off the tree, and, loaded with fruit, we started back.

Then as we were crossing a bit of open ground we heard a strange swishing, rustling noise, and as we got nearer we discovered some of our men mowing corn. Swung by powerful arms, the scythes were swishing through the ripe stalks. So much corn had sowed itself during the last harvest that, thanks to the rich soil and fine weather, there was quite a good crop. One must own that it contained a good many weeds, not only in the shape of thorns and thistles, but also of barbed wire, bits of entanglement-frame, and telegraph wire, and now and then the scythe got caught in one or other of these or struck the case of a shell, with a sharp, rasping noise. In spite of that, many a fine sheaf of corn was bound and so saved from rotting by German thrift and love of order. I don't suppose you ever heard before of such a harvest, garnered by moonlight and to the accompaniment of the weird music of elves, dancing their fairy measures in the form of 'blue beans [bullets]'!

WALTER SCHMIDT, *Student of Natural History, Tübingen*

Born October 12th, 1892, at Tuttlingen.
Killed April 16th, 1917, near Laon.
Temessag, near Temesvar, September 27th, 1915.

'Stradom, De-lousing Station!' — It was just beginning to get light as we climbed sleepily out of the train, dragging all our belongings with us, and stood shivering at the frost-covered barrier till the horses had been got into the other train.

The train which had brought us steamed off, back to the still lousy Front, while we, after having been *de-loused,* were transferred into a new, disinfected train.

As we stepped firmly towards the mysterious buildings, we could see in the morning light the distant tower of the Abbey Church of Czenstochau. There are six to eight *Lausoleums* on the Frontier, each of which cost a million marks, but they are obviously necessary for, according to some Professor's calculation, each Russian prisoner harbours some 9,000 lice on his person.

We officers went into one shed, the men into another. There were separate buildings for engines, disinfecting apparatus, bathrooms, sick-wards, and drying-rooms. We had to strip stark naked, give up uniforms and underclothing at a counter, also sleeping-bag and boots, lock up valuables, and then — in one's 'birthday-suit' — stand for half an hour under a hot shower-bath, rubbing oneself with liquid soap, to get rid of body-parasites which might be adhering to the skin. Then one dried oneself, put on a dressing-gown and went into a warm room, where, in classic simplicity of attire, we all sat round, from the General — who was cursing like anything because his under-clothes were so long in coming — to the youngest 'deputy' from the Light-Column.

At last uniforms and under-garments emerged from the formalin vapour with which they had been treated, still damp and so reeking with disinfectant that one's eyes watered and a universal chorus of lamentation went up from the much-tried men, which, however, changed to laughter when one of them couldn't find his trousers, which had unfortunately got left behind in the boiler.

A good solid breakfast in the very nicely arranged canteen followed. After that we drove out to Czenstochau — about 20 minutes away — to do a a lot shopping, and there we once more came in contact with civilization.

A pretty boulevard planted with lime-trees, very badly paved, runs right through the town to the Abbey. Unluckily it was a Jewish holiday and none of the Jewish shops were open, so we drove up to the Abbey to see the Black Virgin. The imposing baroque building crowns a gentle slope and with its moat and surrounding walls looks almost like a fortress. The fourteen Stations-of-the-Cross are represented in immense groups of statuary all around. Passing through several courtyards we reached the church, the interior of which is being restored. But, hark! through a side door we hear the muffled voices of a fine male choir. We walk towards the sound, which rings louder and louder through the aisles — the Latin chant of monks. Before the open door of a chapel our footsteps with their clink of spurs pause — there in the darkness is a kneeling throng and beyond, blazing in the light of a thousand candles, shines the golden altar with the Miraculous Image behind it. The chant is hushed; the priest proceeds with the Mass, and at the Sanctus the choir breaks out again in a triumphant strain to the accompaniment of a burst of organ music. Truly one of the most impressive scenes witnessed during the war! Here in the Heart of the Mother of God the suffering find comfort and succour and the afflicted a refuge! Even we rough, matter-of-fact men, driven hither and thither by the winds of war, whose sole aim for a whole year has been the defeat and annihilation of the enemy, were wonderfully moved by the thought that there were still people who have nothing to do with all that, whose kingdom is not of this world.

HANS OLUF ESSER, *Student of Natural History, Freiburg i.B.*

Born August 30th, 1894, at Elberfeld.
Killed April 17th, 1917, near Corbény, Chemin-des-Dames.
July 6th, 1916.
. . . Oh, you chaps, what sport I have had to-day! I was supposed to have breakfast at 5, but I overslept and didn't wake till half-past 6, so that I should have had to be off at once, but luckily it was too misty.

At 8 I drove my machine out and waited to start till there was something happening. At 8.25 two dots suddenly appeared in the sky, and somebody called out: 'There come two!' Off I started and just at the last moment someone shouted that eight enemy planes were approaching. Sure enough, hardly was I over Vouziers, when I saw high above me — at about 11,000 ft. — I myself being only 1,600 ft. up — a number of machines: first six, then eight, then ten — more and more — all flying towards the north.

I at once set off in pursuit, losing sight of them several times, but keeping to the north. Then suddenly I discovered the whole seventeen over Charleville — a fine sight! I was about on a level with the lowest–1,000 ft. At that moment they swooped down like birds of prey, leaving only a few above as cover. There were twelve duplex-engine Caudron bi-planes and five enemy one-seater Nieuport fighting-bi-planes. I try to attack one Caudron while they are all circling round in order to drop their bombs, but I have scarcely begun firing when I am driven off by the Nieuports. Finally they flew off again towards the south, while I followed them closely in case one should drop behind.

And that's just what happens. A Caudron, rather below me, hangs back, guarded, unfortunately, by a Nieuport. Seizing an opportunity when the Nieuport is a little in advance, I dive down, but the Nieuport is already back again. A vigorous fight ensues — most daring stunts on both sides. I am astonished how well I can do it, but the Frenchman can do it better still! He rolls, flies on his back for six seconds, shooting all the while; loops the loop — it's marvellous! However, he accomplishes his object only partially — he doesn't shoot me down, but I have lost touch with the squadron. After ten minutes he decamps, and I follow, thinking that he will try to rejoin his squadron.

Over Attigny, a little to the north of our aerodrome, I am again under the squadron, having unluckily dropped too low during the fight. Drawing to one side, I try to fire at them from below, and so I twice got quite close to a Caudron. Now came the crucial moment. Suddenly, from the Front, a Fokker comes dashing in between us, in pursuit of a Caudron. Two more Caudrons and two Nieuports swoop down from above upon the Fokker, while I rush to help him. I attack the hunted Caudron, which comes at me to within 30 yards, as if it wanted to ram me, but I slip through underneath. Then I find myself face to face with a Nieuport, and fire at him. He banks, makes a steep spiral and drops from 8,000 to 2,500 ft., finds me close behind him and tries to escape straight ahead. But I am in front of him and fire. Another nose-dive, another attempt to escape, then another dive, and so on, till I lose him. He was very well camouflaged.

Suddenly I see a shadow skimming along the ground, so I know that he can't be more than 325 ft. up. I immediately fire down, and already he is preparing to land, seeing that it is all up with him. I fly round him several times, waving my handkerchief, and he also shows a white flag. I then make a beautiful landing beside him, just in time to stop him setting fire to his machine.

He came up to me and said in German, 'You are surely no N.C.O.?' and then introduced himself, 'Lieutenant Jean Raby.' I did the same, and we shook hands. He and his machine were quite uninjured, he had only had an attack of nerves and at the same moment his machine-gun jammed. He expressed his gratitude to me for his being alive, and said I flew very well. In the afternoon we were both invited to coffee with the Flight, and smoked the pipe of peace. A very pleasant young man, from Saubnes, near Longwy, studying engineering in Paris, and very intelligent.

So now I have got my first, and I am very glad to have brought him down quite safe and sound.

RUDOLF KRÜGER, *Medical Student, Berlin*

Born May 9th, 1898, in Berlin.
Killed May 3rd, 1917, near Rheims.
April 23rd, 1917, near Rheims.
Yesterday, that is to say on April 22nd, I received my baptism of fire from enemy Artillery. We had to occupy a Reserve Position again, but this time we had to go up over open ground. It was not long before the enemy guns spotted us and scattered some very heavy crumbs for our benefit! Just at this spot four of our Company were killed by direct hits. I did not wink an eyelash and was not in the least uneasy or upset, though the beastly things often landed quite close to me, but all the same I thanked God in the evening when we were out of it.

Here we are living in an absolutely uncivilized fashion—no houses or beds, and no means of washing or shaving, and look like wild men of the woods. My own sweet face is adorned with a yellowish-red beard, the color of pickled-cabbage, a yard long! In the morning one cleans one's eyes with 'spit' and then spits on one's handkerchief to do the rest of one's 'washing.' The whole business is beautifully simple and accomplished in a few movements of the hand. And yet how I long to get back to decent conditions, where one could also get the rags off one's body and a proper night's rest oftener than once a week!

A mail has just come in after a long interval, and I have got letters. I am glad to hear that you have seen the *Evangelimann* at the Opera. I once took part in it as a supernumerary, and ran from left to right across the stage carrying a long pole as a fireman during the burning of the church. I still remember distinctly how beautifully the rising of the moon was represented. Oh, what a glorious *motif* that is: 'Blessed are they who are persecuted for righteousness' sake.'

What wouldn't I give to be able to do a theatre once again, or—what would be simply ideal—to spend a few days with you! I simply long to make my 'cello sing for joy during a trio-evening. But brace up! All will yet be well! Besides, Papa has taken immense trouble in copying out a whole lot of beautiful well-known musical themes for me. By that means one can listen, if only with one's mind's ear, to the glorious old melodies which have so often thrilled us.

KARL SCHENKEL, *Theological Candidate, Marburg*

Born June 18th, 1892, at Murr.
Killed May 5th, 1917, near Douai.
On the Arras Front, April 20th, 1917.

You know that the situation here was anything but rosy when we arrived. The English had broken through to a distance of 5 miles in one push. There was a thin line of infantry in front of us, and the English were just where our heavy guns used to be. All that had been saved in the rear of our section was five heavy howitzers and a few field-guns. This was the state of things when we took hold. The enemy had tanks, cavalry, and thick swarms of infantry, while we were entirely dependent on rifles and machine-guns; but we were perfectly cool from the start. 'If those chaps were worth anything at all—if they were Germans—they'd have broken through long ago!' we all thought. Day and night, with a calmness and determination which is characteristic only of Germans, our reinforcements arrived. After two or three days we had collected such a lot of guns that no English attack had any success.

Wonderful to relate our morale remained perfectly good in spite the intense bombardment and its ensuing casualties. That ought to be a cause of deep gratitude to you at home, not gratitude to us—we do our duty and are not responsible for our morale—but to God.

You must realize that the time now approaching must and will require that we should shed rivers of blood—he who would gain so great an object must throw his all into the balance. Who knows how soon the last hour may strike for us or for someone we love! What then? One thing I do earnestly beg of you: do not be anxious about me. And if the supreme sacrifice should be demanded of us, then do not give way, do not indulge in vain lamentations, for it is just at such moments that war is the test of our faith. Sorrowful we must indeed be—that we cannot help—but two things are still possible to us: we can transform our suffering into a blessing and we can set an example to others.

KURT BERGTER, *Electrical Student, High School, Darmstadt*

Born February 6th, 1893.
Killed June 20th, 1917, near Het Sas.
You must know that we are waging three different wars here: one against the lousy Russian; one against the Russian louse (which is now attacking me with greater violence); and — one for the 'thick' in the camp-kettle! Living in the open of course one gets a tremendous appetite, and when there is pea-soup all the dear comrades fight for the honor of being the one to fetch rations for every eight men. Do you think that is out of Christian charity? Not much! It is the same thing with peas as with people: the empty heads are superficial; those with something in them go deep into the matter, which in the peas' case is the kettle! My partner comes back and sadly announces that he got nothing but 'thin,' and to prove it lets me just look into the can but *not stir it*. Then, very carefully, 'so as not to spill any,' he pours the soup into my mess-tin; but I make a quick dive into it and spoon out my share of the 'thick,' amid a torrent of abuse from him: 'Greedy pig! No sense of comradeship!' etc. This battle, which is all the fiercer because so far we have only got rations at night, is fought daily, and the same comedy is played everywhere. I, as a young recruit and one who is accustomed to simple student's fare, don't think anything of it; but I wonder how men accustomed to grand table-d'hôte meals in a restaurant feel when they have to join in the battle for 'the thick in the kettle'!

HANS FINK, *Student of Law, Marburg*

Born May 10th, 1893, at Hünfeld.
Killed August 31st, 1917, in Flanders.
May 27th, 1917.
On account of our continual losses the Company-Commander has the difficult, unceasing task of fitting reinforcements into the Company. There are no old, experienced men left — nothing but Deputy-Reservists and re-cruits. The officer has himself to create an efficient body of N.C.O.'s. And what soldier nowadays has any self-reliance? All impetus must come from the officer, whose influence is more important than it ever was. Although I am no longer in command of the Company I do believe that my influence had a good effect, and that Prometheus feeling is the finest thing about being in command. It is quite a novel sensation to find that just with one glance one can make chaps advance under the fiercest fire.

GERHARD GÜRTLER, *Student of Theology, Breslau*

Born December 21st, 1895, at Breslau.
Killed August 14th, 1917, in Flanders.
At the Front, August 10th, 1917.

We spent the whole of the 30th of July moving up to the wagon-lines, and that night, at 2:30 A.M., we went straight on to the gun-line — in pouring rain and under continuous shell-fire; along stony roads, over fallen trees, shell-holes, dead horses; through the heavy clay of the sodden fields; over torn-up hills; through valleys furrowed with trenches and craters. Sometimes it was as light as day, sometimes pitch-dark. Thus we arrived in the line.

Our battery is the farthest forward, close behind the infantry, so that we can see the English position on the left. Our position is a perfectly level spot in the orchard of a peasant's ruined farm. In the square of trees, on each side of the road which runs through the middle, stand two houses. One is a mere blackened heap of bricks; the other has three shattered red walls still standing. The whole place is in the middle of arable fields reduced to a sea of mud, churned up to a depth of 15 feet or more by the daily barrage of the English 6- to 8- and 11-inch shells, one crater touching another. To this the never-ceasing rain adds a finishing touch! Nothing can be seen far and wide but water and mud. From the position the hill gradually rises to the front line. In order to have some cover our two guns stand under a tree to which extra green boughs have been added. We can't have a proper dug-out because the ground is so soft and wet, only a sort of rather superior wooden hut, covered with tarred felt, sand and leafy branches, so that when it rains, as it generally does, we simply have to lie in the water.

Then the work began, for there has to be something behind the trails to prevent the gun from running back too far, so we had to dig, bale out water, and drag tree-trunks into position. That went on all day and all the next night.

> 'We joyfully marched full of hope to the war,
> Our companion was ardour, his banner we bore,
> And gay youthful voices sing out as they roam:
> "Little birds in the forest, we'll soon be at home!"'

But we new arrivals were disappointed at first, all the same.

Towards the afternoon the fire increased noticeably until it developed into a regular barrage. And then came what is the worst thing of all in our life here — the lugging up of shells. In themselves the baskets aren't particularly heavy — 70 to 80 lb. — but when you have a hundred, a hundred and fifty or two hundred of them, it's no joke. The ammunition-columns usually arrive at night, so that one has to be as quick as possible, because of the English fire and one's anxiety about the horses, and what with the darkness and the slippery ground it isn't easy.

At last we thought we were going to have a rest—and then the great Flanders battle started! Nothing is so trying as a continuous, terrific barrage such as we experienced in this battle, especially the intense English fire during my second night at the Front—dragging shells and dragging shells, and then the actual artillery duel in the rain and filth.

Darkness alternates with light as bright as day. The earth trembles and shakes like a jelly. Flares illumine the darkness with their white, yellow, green and red lights and cause the tall stumps of the poplars to throw weird shadows. And we crouch between mountains of ammunition (some of us up to our knees in water) and fire and fire, while all around us shells upon shells plunge into the mire, shatter our emplacement, root up trees, flatten the house behind us to the level of the ground, and scatter wet dirt all over us so that we look as if we had come out of a mud-bath. We sweat like stokers on a ship; the barrel is red-hot; the cases are still burning hot when we take them out of the breech; and still the one and only order is, 'Fire! Fire! Fire!'— until one is quite dazed.

And now came the most dangerous time for me. It was just getting dark when suddenly our bolt jammed: 'Gürtler, you must go to the other Section and fetch the battery-artificer.' Through the darkness, through the enemy barrage of 6- and 8-inch shells, to No. 2 Section. That was the night of the great Flanders battle. I leapt from shell-hole to shell-hole while fresh shells fell to right and left of me, in front and behind. The nearest one burst only three yards away, but I escaped the splinters as I was lying deep in the mud of a crater. The mud I naturally did not escape! Thus I proceeded for half an hour into the void—not knowing the way, not knowing the position, but only the direction. In one crater I found a wounded infantryman, and crouched beside him for quite half an hour. It is not pleasant to await the arrival of an 8-inch in the slimy yellow water of a shell-hole! Will it get you, or will it not?

Then on again. Sometimes I thought I should get stuck. Once when I dragged my foot out of the mud, my high boot remained behind! At last I reached the Battery, delivered my message, and then came the journey back! And once more the bringing up of fresh ammunition, hauling shells, making up and collecting cartridges, removing empty cases, until the artificer arrived and we could go on firing till the end of the English attack. Then the gun emplacement had to be cleaned up and aeroplane camouflage procured— that is to say, grass mown and branches cut.

Half the morning had already passed, and now came the sequel which follows every battle—and the battle of Flanders not least: a long file of laden stretcher-bearers wanting to get to the chief dressing station; large and small parties of slightly wounded with their field-service dressings — some crying and groaning so that the sound rings in one's ears all day and takes away one's appetite, others dumb and apathetic, trudging silently along the soft, muddy road in their low, heavy boots, which look like nothing but lumps of mud; others again quite cheery, knowing that they are in for a fairly long rest: 'For at home, for at home, we shall meet our friends again!' Their thoughts wander back into their past lives like stray birds that do not know the way. Some figure appears before their mind's eye: perhaps a little old mother, holding a tattered letter close before her eyes — a fresh young girl stroking the narrow gold ring on her finger — a boisterous small boy 'presenting arms' with a stick.

And those men who are still in the front line hear nothing but the drumfire, the groaning of wounded comrades, the screaming of fallen horses, the wild beating of their own hearts, hour after hour, night after night. Even during the short respite granted them their exhausted brains are haunted in the weird stillness by recollections of unlimited suffering. They have no way of escape, nothing is left them but ghastly memories and resigned anticipation. . . .

My gun is the only one which has had no casualties. 'Haven't you got a bullet for me, Comrades?' cried a Corporal who had one leg torn off and one arm shattered by a shell — and we could do nothing for him. Of us new ones from Jüterbog, two have already been killed — a one-year man and a bombardier — not to mention sick and wounded. And we have no news of the other batteries, all communication being cut off. . . .

The battle-field is really nothing but one vast cemetery. Besides shell-holes, groups of shattered trees and smashed-up farms, one sees little white crosses scattered all over the ground — in front of us, behind us, to right and left. 'Here lies a brave English man' or 'Bombardier——,6.52.' They lie thus, side by side, friend beside friend, foe beside foe. In the newspapers you read: 'Peacefully they rest on the spot where they have bled and suffered; where they have striven; under the eyes of the dear comrades with whom they marched to war; while the guns roar over their graves, taking vengeance for their heroic death, day after day, night after night.' And it doesn't occur to anybody that the enemy is also firing; that the shells plunge into the hero's grave; that his bones are mingled with the filth which they scatter to the four winds; and that after a few weeks the morass closes over the last resting-place of the dead soldier, and only a little, crooked, white cross marks the spot where once he lay. . . .

JOHANNES PHILIPPSEN, *Student of Philosophy, Kiel*

Born April 19th, 1893 at Dollerup (Angeln).
Killed September 20th, 1917, near Poelkapelle.
Saarlouis, July 22nd, 1917.
The time of waiting is over. I received my marching orders today and am off tomorrow. How different this departure is from the last! and how different, again, from the first in December, 1914! Things have become more and more serious, and, in spite of all our victories, the burden presses more and more heavily upon our country. And that impatient longing to fight, the wild joy at the idea of being on the spot when the enemy got his *coup de grace,* that cannot be expected from anybody who knows what life in the trenches is like and who has experienced in his own body the full gravity of the situation. I am delighted when I see such feelings exhibited by our boys, and I should think it an outrage to try and quench them by cold-blooded sarcasm; but we, who have seen the dark side, must substitute for that enthusiasm a deep-seated determination to stand by the Fatherland whatever happens as long as it has need of us. We know that death is not the worst thing that we have to face. Thoroughly to realize everything and yet to go back, not under compulsion but willingly, is not easy. To try and deceive oneself by working oneself up into a state of excitement is, I hold, unworthy. Only genuine self-command is any use to me.

I know that I have been permitted by a benign fate to drink deeply of the clear spring of the German nation's courageous attitude towards life in itself. On wonderful journeys my eyes have been gladdened with the sight of Germany's beauty, and I have a home that I can truly love. This shows me where I belong when it is a case of defending that land. That was how I felt when I went to the Front for the first time, and it is just the same now.

A new chapter of life is beginning, and I must learn afresh to face the end with calm. One must not omit to examine oneself as to one's merits and deserts in the past. We do not practice auricular confession, but one must honorably clear these things up in one's own mind. One thing I must say to you, anyhow: I shall most certainly be fully conscious of all the kindness and comfort and friendly sympathy which I have met with even where I did not deserve it. For your large share in this I thank you from the bottom of my heart. Don't grieve because I have to go out again. My place is at the Front. That you must recognize.

HERMANN LABUDE, *Student of Philosophy*

Born February 12th, 1894, at Bredau.
Killed March 29th, 1918, near Beaufort, before Montdidier.

Before Dünaburg, December 8th, 1917.

At the moment we are having an armistice, from December 7th to the 17th, here. In my Division it started on the 2nd. The first rumors began to circulate on December 1st. On the 2nd I was occupying an observation post which is exceptionally near the railway, in order to make a sketch from there. I saw that the telegraph-wires along the railway embankment were being mended. That told a tale, and I was further enlightened by the arrival in the 2nd line of several motor-cars.

At 4 P.M. there appeared upon the railway-line which runs between the Russian trenches the white smoke of a locomotive, and through the storm-gaps in the barbed-wire entanglements came the Russian delegation. There were about 32 people — officers in uniform, civilians, and — prepare for a shock — one female! A thaw was in progress, and in their elegant clothes they hopped valiantly through the deep mud and in and out of the shell-holes which were brim-full of water.

Behind our front line they were joined by our Excellencies. Farther back they traveled a little way in our light-railway until they and their dispatch-cases were received by a pullman-car which was awaiting them. In one of the big H. Q. towns they met our Bavarians and the Austrians.

During the past years we have often, as a joke, asked anybody who came in from a forward observation post: 'Well, Comrade, did you see Peace passing by?' Now, on this Sunday, I really did see her, and this is what she looked like: telegraph-wires, dispatch-cases, and a special train!

A Quiet Front

HORACE BRUCKSHAW

Monday Feb 21st, 1916

Very heavy rain this morning. Received orders to move at 1.15 P.M. but this was postponed until 2.45 P.M. We made our way to the pier through the slush staggering along under the weighty loads which a Light Infantryman is called upon to bear nowadays. Lighters then took us aboard the packet *Princess Alberta*. Here we're packed like herrings my own billet being in a narrow and very draughty passage. What a prospect, dossing here on a pile of gear. We set sail about 5.30 P.M. and soon after managed to get some hot water to brew some tea. It was bitterly cold and the wind seemed to beset my passage from all sides. After dark all lights on the ship were extinguished and I piped down, completely covering myself with a waterproof sheet.

Tuesday Feb 22nd, 1916

Woke up early, stiff and numb with cold and very glad we were when we got hold of some warm tea. We arrived at Stavros about 8 A.M. and landed immediately.

Stavros is about 40 miles from Salonica I believe. We made our way to our bivouac and proceeded to make our little huts with waterproofs and make ourselves at home. An enemy aeroplane paid us a visit this morning and was fired on by a monitor lying off the beach. Piped down about 8 P.M. and very soon fell asleep.

Wednesday Feb 23rd, 1916

Got out about 7 A.M. and got some breakfast after which we went to fetch some horses from a transport. This fatigue we finished by dinner time when we returned to camp. The old aeroplane paid us another visit this morning. The monitor fired on her but did not hit.

The country here is very mountainous. In the distance they are snow capped and make you feel cold to look at them. Those close to us are covered with bushes, mostly a small variety of holly. It is a real picture for scenery and should be lovely during the summer.

Thursday Feb 24th, 1916

Up at daybreak. Packed up to move forward. We are to do our outpost scheme as the enemy are expected sooner or later to retire this way. Was told off for working party to go with transports. Moved up valley at 8 A.M. and unloaded at foot of a gully where headquarters are to be. Here I developed into section cook for the time being and got dixie under weigh for some tea etc. It looks rather like rain just now.

We set off to join our platoon about 3.30 P.M. Our route lay along the valley for some distance. Wooded mountains towered above us on either side and a pretty stream wound its way in the bottom. About two miles up this valley we started to the right, up one of the mountains. Here we dropped on the 2nd Batt. of the Shropshire Lt. Inf. We had a long weary climb to reach our comrades who were bivouacked at the top. Arrived, we had some tea and pitched our new house, waterproofs rigged up on timber. We piped down early being about fagged out. Our slumbers were somewhat disturbed by the constant howling of jackals with which these hills seem to be infested and a dismal wail they make.

Friday Feb 25th, 1916

We spent the morning in the mist, or I should say amongst the clouds, improving our hut. In the afternoon we made a trip down the mountain for some water. It is a devil of a climb. We went on guard on the trench and entanglements. It is a most eerie job especially when your companions are jackals. I pity the Bulgarians or Germans if they try to get over our defences for they are superb. Our duty is to see that they are not tampered with during the night.

Saturday Feb 26th, 1916

The night passed uneventfully but I feel very sleepy. Had a nap during the morning. It is very wet today. Disguised our house with bushes in the afternoon. Got some bread today, hurray! Rations seem very scarce. Received Xmas parcel from Cis. Full of good things.

Sunday Feb 27th, 1916

Rained heavily during night. Found my boots half full of water this morning. Weather promises better this morning. After breakfast went gathering stones and built an incinerator. Now that the clouds are dispersing a bit we can see rather a large lake in front of us. I suppose that the stream in the gorge takes its source here. The country is extremely pretty but makes everything into damned hard work. Rigged up a mud oven this morning. Baked some cakes for tea. Recipe. Crushed biscuits, bacon fat and water, added a little sugar, all we had. Mixed well and baked until brown. Enjoyed them much better than hard biscuits. Had Café au Lait for supper thanks to Cis' Xmas parcel. There is a very cold wind blowing tonight.

Monday Feb 28th, 1916

Nice morning but rather windy. Hung on in bed too long and got shoved in the rattle for not having rifle cleaned. Fell to work improving trenches, dig ammunition pits etc until 11.45 A.M. when alarm sounded and we had to man the trenches. White flags were hoisted at the extremes of the trenches so we could locate the positions of the other platoons. We dispersed again at 12 o'clock. Went on guard at 6 P.M. The jackals are rather lively tonight. Capt. Tetley having returned from home leave paid the guard a visit about 9 o'clock. A very cold dark night it has been and we were not sorry when the twelve hours were over.

Tuesday Feb 29th, 1916

Came off guard at 6.15 A.M. and got breakfast under weigh. Had odd jobs to do during the morning. After dinner we fell in to improve the trenches. Real waste of time for they are as good as they can be. We had what we call a 'wet' sergeant or in other words 'daft' sergeant in charge and there was a bit of a scrap which might have ended with serious consequences if it had not been checked. The sergeant struck a lad a blow in the face when he could not defend himself. We prevented any retaliation so I do not know if anything more will be heard of the affair or not.

Wednesday March 1st, 1916

Fell in for work digging a new trench and relaying some wire. Rained in the afternoon. We were standing by for it to cease.

Thursday March 2nd, 1916

Raining and cold all day. Working all day on the new entrenchments. Told off for guard tonight. From 4 P.M. onwards it simply poured with rain. We mounted guard at 6 P.M. It was pitch dark, wet and cold. The most miserable night I have spent for some long time.

Friday March 3rd, 1916

Came off guard at 6 A.M. Cooked some breakfast to warm us up. It is beautifully warm and sunny today. An aeroplane came over us today and was fired on by our guns. We are duty section doing all sorts of odd jobs about the camp.

Saturday March 4th, 1916

A lovely morning again. Felt much more lively after a good night's sleep. Working in the entrenchments again today. An enemy aeroplane paid us a visit and was fired on by our guns. Am on guard again tonight.

Sunday March 5th, 1916

Came off guard at 6 A.M. and prepared breakfast. Rifle inspection at 9 o'clock after which I had a bath. It is a lovely sunny and warm day. In the afternoon I had a short nap.

Monday March 6th, 1916

Have now turned into a woodman. Spent the morning clearing trees and undergrowth from front of the new trench. Arrived at bivouac for dinner to find that our home had been pulled down and remodelled lean-to design. It is a great improvement on the original. At 8 P.M. Chapman, Taylor and myself went up to Batt. Headquarters on patrol. The idea was to use ourselves to moving in the dark. It is a devil of a job finding your way amongst the trees in the inky darkness. We found our way alright arriving there in seventeen minutes, returning in rather less than that time. I turned in as soon as we got back.

Tuesday March 7th, 1916

Working at the tree clearing process again today. Received 10/- pay at dinner time. Am to go on guard tonight. The guard passed off pleasantly enough but it was rather cold. The jackals gave us rather a noisy concert.

Wednesday March 8th, 1916

Came off guard at daybreak and got some breakfast ready. Had some digging to do during the morning. Settled for some canteen gear which we got yesterday afternoon. The Greeks here fairly see us off. One and fourpence for a loaf of inferior quality. Figs 10d per string. Chocolate 6d per small packet which is only 3d in England. These are only a few of the frauds others are even worse. In the afternoon I had a snooze and had some tea. We have had a cigarette issue tonight thank goodness for during the past few days there has been a famine in that line. I shall be all on my own tonight as the two chaps in my caboosh are to go on guard.

Thursday March 9th, 1916

We fell in at the usual time but as rain came on we were dismissed for the time being. I commenced to write a letter but was soon stopped by the falling in whistle going again. We went to start work about 9:45 A.M. but soon had to pack up again. It poured with rain all day long and things were most uncomfortable for water streamed into our bivouac from the top and from underneath as well. We all got wet through trying to drain the water away, but we were only partially successful. The rain kept up all night. We put our blankets down and slept in the quagmire with the result that I woke with a stiff neck and toothache and one of the other chaps with the earache and I think all three of us had the heartache for the nice feather bed at home.

Friday March 10th, 1916

Got up wet and stiff and got some breakfast after which we proceeded to make a new galley. The old one and the cooks had been completely washed away during the night. The cooks' bivouac fell in on top of him and they were messing about until daylight minus trousers and tunics. We had not fared the worst by any means. The gully below the galley which up to now had been perfectly dry is now like Niagara Falls on a small scale. Our rifles were like old scrap iron. We spent the day in making our bivouac a bit more weatherproof and in cleaning up generally. There are a good many nights which stand out prominently in my memory during the past twelve months and last night is certainly one of them.

Sixteen Platoon have just returned from the Isolation Camp at Mudros, 5 P.M. They are being split up amongst the other platoons I think. I am looking forward to a pleasanter night tonight than we had last night. It is quite fine at present if it will only keep so. Made some porridge for supper and then turned in.

Saturday March 11th, 1916

It is a lovely morning. It became daylight at 5 A.M. We turned out at 6.30 A.M. and made some porridge and then cooked some bacon. During the breakfast a fleet of our own aeroplanes came over from the direction of the lake. There were 20 in number. I fancy that there must have been a raid somewhere during the night. They returned about 11 A.M. We were all navvying in the new trench. Just as we were leaving work at 4 P.M., we had to commence dismantling the trench again. I believe it all has to come down, why I cannot say. We always seem to do a lot of work needlessly, and we have spent a week or two on that particular trench. It has been sheer waste of time and energy.

Sunday March 12th, 1916

Fell in for rifle inspection at 9 A.M. after which I did my little bit of washing. After dinner I had a snooze and then proceeded to mix some batter for some pancakes, with flour, water and fat and a smell at a Nestle's milk tin. We do live and no mistake. Told off for guard tonight. It is a lovely moonlight night so that it should pass pleasantly enough.

Monday March 13th, 1916

Came off guard just after daylight came, made a fire and prepared some porridge and bacon for breakfast. It looks rather like rain this morning. Am duty section today. Unloaded pack mules in the morning. After dinner we had to hump some boxes of ammunition to a new dump. It is a very heavy job and my shoulder fairly aches. We had a beano for tea, salmon and bread and butter as well as some cake sent by Cis about November last and which has only just arrived. Having secured some flour we rendered down some fat bacon and made some flour, fat and water pancakes for supper, and a small gift having arrived from the people of Plymouth containing some Bivouac cocoa we were enabled to have a real good feed again at supper time. This diary will soon develop into a regular Mrs Beeton. If things keep up like this we shall soon get fat.

Tuesday March 14th, 1916

Got up rather late this morning and had to hurry a bit to get on parade at the proper time. We were all working on the trenches all the morning and afternoon, remodelling same. Got back to camp tired and quite ready to make a hole in our bread ration.

Wednesday March 15th, 1916

Rather rainy this morning. Went to work on the trench at the usual times. Nothing of importance occurred all day.

Thursday March 16th, 1916

Digging again all day. Nothing moving at all just now.

Friday March 17th, 1916

Still very busy on the new trench. There is plenty of work to last some little time if the enemy give us time to carry out all the ideas which seem to crowd upon our officers. I think we shall just about complete the scheme and then peace will be declared. Flights were made during the afternoon by two of our seaplanes. They circled above our heads at an enormous height.

Although we see them so often our interest does not diminish a bit and we never tire of watching their evolutions. This afternoon I felt as if I would have given anything to be up aloft with the pilot. It is as safe nowadays as taking a trip in a motor car.

Saturday March 18th, 1916

Got up late this morning and had to do a double shuffle. We did manage to get on parade in time however. We spent all day on the new trenches. Some of the chaps have been busy all the afternoon cutting down trees to build a good fire on the site of the old galley, tonight, where there is to be a company concert. I expect the accompaniment will be given by the jackals. I think it is about time we had another mail up. There has been a parcel on the way from Cis for about five weeks now with cakes in and must say I am beginning to feel hungry. We made some cocoa for supper after which we went to the open-air-concert hall. A big fire was lit in the centre and we grouped our-selves all round on the slope of the gully. There were some very good turns indeed. One was an exhibition of club swinging by a chap who had carved the clubs himself. Capt. Tetley, our Commanding Officer, sang us 'Tavistock Goosey Fair,' an old West Country song, and gave us a few tales in the west country dialect which were very amusing. We spent a very enjoyable little time and then turned in.

Sunday March 19th, 1916

Parade at 9 o'clock. Had a washing day. Boiled down some of the lice in my shirt. I wish we had some way of getting rid of those damned things. After dinner we had a short nap. After tea Thorpe and Rend went down the hill for some canteen gear. We managed to obtain some tinned plums, Quaker oats and some chocolate. We made some oatmeal for supper.

Monday March 20th, 1916

Went down to the new trenches as usual. They have a new hobby on with us now giving us a certain amount of digging to do for the day's work. They do not forget to pile on the agony either. Nothing important occurred today.

Tuesday March 21st, 1916

Another set task today. Mr Wooley says we have to get out 96 cu. ft. of earth today. I commenced arguing that this was too much in the hard ground and the awkward position that we were working in. He fairly chewed me up and kept us at work like a lot of lunatics. Officers are all very well but some of them are fair nigger drivers. I feel fairly tired out tonight, and feel fed up with everything. Wrote a few letters in the evening and then turned in.

Wednesday March 22nd, 1916

Got up late this morning and had to rush about a bit. Went working as usual and went on to task work again. This system of working is neither more nor less than slave driving. However, we stand no chance of saying anything and have to put up with it. I am detailed for guard tonight. I managed to lose the toss for the first and last watches, so I was on sentry from 10 P.M. until 2 A.M. It was a beautifully moonlight night but a bit cold. A thick mist came on just as I was going off watch. Two or three jackals were constantly scrambling about in the bushes about two yards from me all the time I was on sentry.

Thursday March 23rd, 1916

Came off guard at daybreak. Prepared breakfast and then paraded. We had to take some tools to No. 13 Platoon first thing and a devil of a climb we had coming back. A Taube flew over us at a great height when we were returning. It came over us again about 10.30 A.M. and was fired on by our batteries. The shots were very close but they did not hit. I had a nap in the afternoon to make up for lost time last night. Our supply of drinking water up the gully is nearly done now we are getting a bit of dry weather, worse luck. About 8 P.M. some Veras lights we observed being sent up somewhere near the K.L.S.I.s lines. Cpl. Thorpe, Rendell and myself were sent to 15 Platoon with a message for the officer to investigate the matter. It was pitch dark and a very rough path. I only fell three times on the way down the hill, but we landed back without any further mishap.

Friday March 24th, 1916

It is a lovely morning again and promises to be quite hot. After the usual parade we made our way to our workshop down the hill. I have been carrying sandbags all day for the revetment of the new trenches. I have as much sand down my back almost as there is in the bags. When we finished at tea time I had to change my shirt and have a good rub down. It is a good job I did some washing last Sunday. It has been a very hot day today, almost like mid-summer. It has been a great day for the flying men. Aeroplanes have been up practically all day. A Taube came over once or twice and we were able to witness some very pretty shooting by one of our hill batteries. They were very close indeed and made the enemy machine hop it at a good speed.

Saturday March 25th, 1916

Another lovely day. Work as usual. I have been cutting sods all day. Quite a nice soft job after digging trenches. There was to have been a medical inspection this evening at 5 P.M. but something prevented the doctor from turning up and it was swung. About 8.30 P.M. a wire came through to say that some activity had been notified on the part of the Germans. We are now standing by to man the trenches at any moment. This will not disturb my dreams however for they have a long way to come before they reach our positions. I only hope that our officers do not get what the marines call 'Dizzy' and turn us out on a dummy run during the night.

Sunday March 26th, 1916

Had a champion night's rest in spite of the 'German Activity' and did not wake until breakfast was called this morning. We were even too late to cook the bacon and made our morning meal off marmalade. Last evening we fetched a biscuit tin of washing water from the gully ready for a splash in the morning. We are plagued with rats in our bivouac and they are extremely fond of pinching our biscuits etc. One must have thought that our washing tin was full of them for this morning we found a rat inside it, drowned. May they all meet with the same death. We are all standing by and no one is allowed to leave the camp until further orders. About 11 A.M. another wire came through telling us to carry on as usual, everything being normal in front. Last nights 'dizzy' turn was evidently a spasm. After doing my weekly bit of washing we proceeded to make a pudding for dinner. We only had a small quantity of flour and so made up the required amount with crushed biscuits. We had no suet but found an excellent substitute in bacon fat. We regaled ourselves at dinner time on a most excellent jam 'duff.' The afternoon was spent in the 'Land of Nod.'

Monday March 27th, 1916

I was awakened at daybreak by hearing a heavy bombardment somewhere over the direction of the lake. It lasted until after 6 A.M. and then gradually died down. My two comrades who had just come off guard said that before it got absolutely daylight they could see the shells bursting in the air. It must have been a great distance away and we shall probably hear some particulars later on. We went down to work as usual. Was carrying barbed wire down the hill all the morning. Some little rain fell. We could hear gunfire intermittently all morning. At 2 P.M. we had the deferred medical inspection for which we must be very thankful for it got us half a day stand off. Went up the rocks for some water this evening. The supply seems to have nearly winked out. We have since heard that the guns firing this morning were our own guns in the front registering. I thought that the enemy must be nearer than I had any idea of for us to hear any bombardment so plainly. Capt. Tetley has just told us (7 P.M.) that there was an air raid, rather a big affair, on Salonica this morning and that we could probably hear gun fire from there 40 miles away.

Tuesday March 28th, 1916

Work as usual. Digging all morning. In the afternoon the Company went to the Q.M. Stores near the beach for barbed wire. When we had tramped down I should imagine it to be about three miles, the mules were all loaded up with the wire ready to bring it up the hills. The QM actually had the neck to unload again and allow us to hump it one roll per man. It was nearly 5 o'clock when we got back to the bivouac. At night I was on guard.

Wednesday March 29th, 1916

The night passed uneventfully. After breakfast we, as duty section, took tools down to the new trenches. During the morning a Taube flew over us and of course was promptly fired on. There was some excellent shooting. I am certain she was hit with one shot for she wobbled and nearly turned turtle and we all made sure she was coming down. She righted herself however and made off. In the afternoon the Platoon went down to the beach for a bath. Being one of the duty section I did not go. We had another trip down to the new trench to fetch tools up during the afternoon.

Thursday March 30th, 1916

Spent all the morning in carrying turf to cover the parapet in front of the new trenches. For a change in the afternoon I cut the turf instead of carried. Just as we were having tea a couple of men from 15 Platoon escorted a Greek or at any rate we thought he was a Greek, who had been observed getting through the barbed wire entanglement. He was interviewed or rather questioned by one of our officers and then escorted up to our headquarters. He looked to me to have been a sort of a tramp and had lost his way on the hills or something of that sort, for he had a bundle on his back, was ragged and had sacks on his feet in place of boots. Of course one has to be careful with anyone coming from your front at a time like this.

Friday March 31st, 1916

Went to work, turf carrying this morning. After dinner we had to go to the 1st Field Ambulance for a hot bath. I should imagine it to be about 4 miles good. We did it in a boiling sun and really had a good bath before we eventually arrived there. The return journey was even worse for we had the rotten bit of hill climbing to do to reach our bivouacs. Today the names of the landing party have been taken for home leave. I hear that fifty are to go from the Battalion this time and that in turn we are to go each month. I am hoping to have my turn before long. I am put back a long way by my having been in hospital for three months. It is counted almost a crime to go sick or get wounded by the look of things. However everything comes to him who waits. In the course of conversation today the subject of rations was raised. I asked a comrade what he thought the most useful thing that was served out to us. He said bacon, because we were able to fry it, boil it, use it in lieu of suet in puddings etc., fry other eatables in it, use it instead of butter, as a boot lubricant, it was a splendid substitute for rifle oil and useful for keeping rust from our accoutrements and when our candle supply ran out we were able to utilize it in an old tobacco tin and with a strip of flannelette as a wick, make an excellent lamp for the caboosh. There was an amusing yet very annoying incident which occurred last night or rather during the night time and which had almost slipped my memory. One of the fellows in 15 Platoon by name, Green and rather green by nature, nicknamed 'Ginger,' was sent on patrol at 8 P.M. last night and somehow or other managed to lose himself. At 11 P.M. he had not returned. About seven patrols were sent out from his platoon, each consisting of three men with rifles and ammunition to find the wanderer. These patrols followed the trail until past two this morning. They shouted 'Ginger' until they were hoarse and had wakened every sleepy warrior within miles. A big bonfire was set alight to guide Ginger home but he was not found until nearly half past two this morning. They found him amongst a dense growth of bushes that would have puzzled an acrobat to get in in the daylight and when asked what he was doing there he said 'Only lost.' This episode was remarkable for the fact that it caused a fair amount of rather unparliamentary language. 'Ginger' has called down the vengeance of all the Marine speaking inhabitants of the hills around Stavros.

Saturday April 1st, 1916

Rather stormy looking this morning. After inspection this morning we had to hump boxes of ammunition down to headquarters in the gully. It was a terrible ordeal. We then went to the Q.M.'s stores near the beach and carried some iron stanchions back to the top of the hills, three per man. We were about done up by the time we reached 'home.' After dinner we proceeded to the new trench where we were turf laying. It came on to rain rather heavily and we had the order to pack up. Just as we were ready for shoving off however it gave over and we had to return to our task and finish the afternoon out. I hear that we are once again moving our quarters in the course of a day or two and that the Servians are taking over this part of the front. Of course this latter may simply be rumour but I fancy it is as likely to be correct as not. Today we have had a full ration of bread i.e. half a loaf per man. This is the first time since coming to Stavros. Just after dark, a big bon-fire was lit on the old gully site and we were able to sit on the banks round and enjoy a very decent concert the items of course being provided by men and officers of the Company.

Sunday April 2nd, 1916

After inspection this morning we had to take all tools down to the Q.M.'s stores near the beach. We are expecting to move from here tomorrow at any rate as far as the beach. I believe that we are to move to Mudros for re-fitting and to reorganize, after which no-one seems to know what is in store for us. Sufficient unto the day is the evil thereof. We are fairly content to do as Asquith once said 'Wait and see.' It has been a lovely day today and we are really sorry to leave Stavros just as hard work is promising to get less and less.

Kaba Tepé
and Anzac

AUBREY HERBERT

Diary. Wednesday, April 28th. I got up at 4 A.M. this morning, after a fine, quiet night, and examined a Greek deserter from the Turkish Army. He said many would desert if they did not fear for their lives. The New Zealanders spare their prisoners.

Last night, while he was talking to me, Colonel C. was hit by a bit of shell on his hat. He stood quite still while a man might count three, wondering if he was hurt. He then stooped down and picked it up. At 8 P.M. last night there was furious shelling in the gully. Many men and mules hit. General Godley was in the Signalling Office, on the telephone, fairly under cover. I was outside with Pinwell, and got grazed, just avoiding the last burst. Their range is better. Before this they have been bursting the shrapnel too high. It was after 4 P.M. their range improved so much. My dugout was shot through five minutes before I went there. So was Shaw's. . . .

Colonel Chaytor was knocked down by shrapnel, but not hurt. The same happened to Colonel Manders. We heard that the Indian troops were to come to-night. Twenty-three out of twenty-seven Auckland officers killed and wounded.

11 A.M. All firing except from Helles has ceased. Things look better. The most the men can do is to hang on. General Godley has been very fine. The men know it.

4.30 P.M. Turks suddenly reported to have mounted huge howitzer on our left flank, two or three miles away. We rushed all the ammunition off the beach, men working like ants, complete silence and furious work. We were absolutely enfiladed, and they could have pounded us, mules and machinery, to pulp, or driven us into the gully and up the hill, cutting us off from our water and at the same time attacking us with shrapnel. The ships came up and fired on the new gun, and proved either that it was a dummy or had moved, or had been knocked out. It was a cold, wet night.

The material which General Birdwood and General Godley had to work upon was very fine. The Australians and the New Zealanders were born fighters and natural soldiers, and learnt quickly on Active Service what it would have taken months of training to have taught them. But like many another side-show, Anzac was casual in many ways, as the following excerpt from this diary will show: —

Diary. Thursday, April 29th. Kaba Tepé. I was woken at 2.30 A.M., when the New Zealanders stood to arms. It was wet and cold, and a wind blew which felt as if it came through snowy gorges. The alarm had been given, and the Turks were supposed to be about to rush the beach from the left flank in force. Colonel Chaytor was sent to hold the point. He told me to collect stragglers and form them up. It was very dark, and the stragglers were very straggly. I found an Australian, Quinn, and told him to fetch his men along to the gun emplacement, beyond the graves, on the point where Chaytor was. Every one lost every one.

I found Colonel Chaytor with an Australian officer. He said to him: "Go out along the flank and find out where the Canterbury Battalion is, and how strong. On the extreme left there is a field ambulance. They must be told to lie down, so that the Turks will not shoot them." I said I would look after them. We started. I heard the Australian, after we had gone some hundreds of yards, ordering the Canterburys in support to retire. I said: "But are your orders to that effect? A support is there to support. The Canterburys will be routed or destroyed if you take this support away." He said: "Well, that's a bright idea." He went back, and I heard him say, in the darkness: "This officer thinks you had better stay where you are." I don't know if he was a Colonel, or what he was, and he did not know what I was.

I found the field ambulance, a long way off, and went on to the outposts. The field ambulance were touchingly grateful for nothing, and I had some tea and yarned with them till morning, walking back after dawn along the beach by the graves. No one fired at me.

When I got back I heard the news of Doughty's[1] death, which grieved me a great deal. . . . He seems to have saved the situation. The description of Helles is ghastly, of the men looking down into the red sea, and the dying drowned in a foot of water. That is what might have, and really ought to have happened to us.

One hears the praise of politicians in all men's mouths. . . .

A beautiful night, last night, and a fair amount of shrapnel. Every evening now they send over a limited number of howitzers from the great guns in the Dardanelles, aimed at our ships. That happens also in the early morning, as this morning. To-night an aeroplane is to locate these guns, and when they let fly to-morrow we are to give them an immense broadside from all our ships.

At this time the weather had improved, but we were living in a good deal of discomfort. We were not yet properly supplied with stores, the water was brackish, occasionally one had to shave in salt water, and all one's ablutions had to be done on the beach, with the permission of the Turkish artillery.

The beach produced a profound impression on almost all of us, and has in some cases made the seaside distasteful for the rest of our lives. It was, when we first landed, I suppose, about 30 yards broad, and covered with shingle. Upon this narrow strip depended all our communications: landing and putting off, food and water, all came and went upon the beach—and the Turkish guns had got the exact range. Later, shelters were put up, but life was still precarious, and the openness of the beach gave men a greater feeling of insecurity than they had in the trenches.

Diary. Our hair and eyes and mouths are full of dust and sand, and our nostrils of the smell of dead mules.

There were also colonies of ants that kept in close touch with us, and our cigarettes gave out. Besides these trials, we had no news of the war or of the outer world.

Diary. Tahu and I repacked the provisions this morning. While we did so one man was shot on the right and another on the left. We have been expecting howitzers all the time, and speculating as to whether there would be any panic if they really get on to us. The Turks have got their indirect, or rather enfilading, fire on us, and hit our mules. One just hit a few yards away. . . . Imbros and Samothrace are clear and delicate between the blue sea and the hot sky. The riband of beach is crowded with transport, and Jews, Greeks, Armenians, New Zealanders, Australians, scallywag officers, and officers that still manage to keep a shadow of dandyism between their disreputable selves and immaculate past. And there's the perpetual ripple of the waves that is sometimes loud enough to be mistaken for the swish of shrapnel, which is also perpetual, splashing in the sea or rattling on the beach. There is very little noise on the beach in the way of talk and laughter. The men never expected to be up against this. When we left Lemnos we saw one boat with an arrow, and in front of it "TO CONSTANTINOPLE AND THE HAREM." Precious few of those poor fellows will ever see Constantinople, let alone the Harem.

May 1st. A beautiful dawn, but defiled by a real hymn of hate from the Turks. Last night the *Torgut Reiss* sent us some shells. This morning it was supposed to be the *Goeben* that was firing. I woke to hear the howitzers that everybody had been talking of here droning over us, and watched them lifting great columns of water where they hit the sea. Then there came the sigh and the snarl of shrapnel, but that to the other is like the rustle of a lady's fan to the rumble of a brewer's dray. This hymn of hate went on for an unusually long time this morning from the big stuff. A lot of men were hit all round, and it has been difficult to wash in the sea. All the loading, unloading, etc., is done at night. The picket-boats are fairly well protected. The middies are the most splendid boys. We are all very cramped and the mules add to the congestion. We shall have a plague of flies before we are done, if we don't have a worse plague than that. The New Zealanders are all right. . . .

Colonel White, Rickes, and Murphy, all hit at breakfast this morning, but not hurt. One of the Greek donkey-boys says he is a barber. This would be a great advantage if he wasn't so nervous and did not start so much whenever there is a burst.

There is a fleet of boats in front of us, and even more at Helles; the Turks must feel uncomfortable, but another landing, between us, would be pretty risky. They are fighting splendidly. Opinions are divided as to what would happen if we fought our way to Maidos. Many think we could be shelled out again by the *Goeben*. This expedition needed at least three times the number of men. The Indians have not come, and the Territorials cannot come for a long time.

General Godley wants to change Headquarters for us. Colonel Artillery Johnston's battery is on our right, facing the Turks, and only a few yards away. The Turks spend a lot of time shooting at it, missing it, and hitting us. Another man killed just now. Shrapnel, heaps of it, is coming both ways on us. Nobody speaks on the beach. We have two tables on the top of the dug-out. One is safe, and the other can be hit. The punctual people get the safe table.

B. has lunched. He says that Rupert Brooke died at Lemnos. I am very sorry; he was a good fellow, and a poet with a great future. B. was blown up by a shell yesterday. He has to go back to-night. While we lunched a man had his head blown off, 20 yards away. . . .

Orders have come that we are to entrench impregnably. We are practically besieged, for we can't re-embark without sacrificing our rearguard, and if the howitzers come up we shall be cut off from the beach and our water. A lot more men have been killed on the beach. . . .

Sunday, May 2nd. 6 A.M. Shrapnel all round as I washed. Beach opinion is if this siege lasts they must be able to get up their heavy guns. The Indians have gone to Helles, and the Naval Division is being taken away from us. New Turkish Divisions are coming against us. There are no chaplains here for burial or for anything else.

Waite took a dozen prisoners this morning—gendarmes, nice fellows. They hadn't much to tell us. One of them complained that he had been shot through a mistake after he had surrendered. There ought to be an interpreter on these occasions. . . .

It is a fiery hot day, without a ripple on the clear sea, and all still but for the thunder coming from Helles. I bathed and got clean. The beach looks like a mule fair of mutes, for it is very silent. We are to attack to-night at seven. We have now been here a week, and advanced a hundred yards farther than the first rush carried us. There is a great bombardment going on, a roaring ring of fire, and the Turks are being shelled and shelled.

At night the battleships throw out two lines of searchlights, and behind them there gleam the fires of Samothrace and Imbros. Up and down the cliffs here, outside the dugouts, small fires burn. The rifle fire comes over the hill, echoing in the valleys and back from the ships. Sometimes it is difficult to tell whether it is the sound of ripples on the beach or firing.

Monday, May 3rd. I was called up at 3 A.M. to examine three prisoners. Our attack has failed, and we have many casualties, probably not less than 1000. The wounded have been crying on the beach horribly. A wounded Arab reported that our naval gun fire did much damage.

The complaint is old and bitter now. We insist that the Turks are Hottentots. We give them notice before we attack them. We tell them what we are going to do with their Capital. We attack them with an inadequate force of irregular troops, without adequate ammunition (we had one gun in our landing) in the most impregnable part of their Empire. We ask for trouble all over the East by risking disaster here.

The *Goeben* is shelling the fleet, and (11.30) has just struck a transport. The sea is gay, and a fresh wind is blowing, and the beach is crowded, but there is not a voice upon it, except for an occasional order. . . .

The Turks are now expected to attack us. We suppose people realize what is happening here in London, though it isn't easy to see how troops and reinforcements can be sent us in time — that is, before the Turks have turned all this into a fortification. A good many men hit on the beach to-day. The mules cry like lost souls.

Tuesday, May 4th. The sea like a looking-glass, not a cloud in the sky, and Samothrace looking very clear and close. The moon is like a faint shadow of light in the clear sky over the smoke of the guns. Heavy fighting between us and Helles. A landing is being attempted. Pessimists say it is our men being taken off because their position is impossible. The boats coming back seem full of wounded. It may have been an attempt at a landing and entrenching, or simply a repetition of what we did the other day at Falcon Hill or Nebronesi, or whatever the place is.

The attack has failed this morning. Perfect peace here, except for rifles crackling on the hill. Ian Smith and I wandered off up a valley through

smilax, thyme, heath and myrtle, to a high ridge. We went through the Indians and found a couple of very jolly officers, one of them since killed. There
are a good many bodies unburied. Not many men hit. We helped to carry
one wounded man back. The stretcher-bearers are splendid fellows, good to
friend and enemy. At one place we saw a beastly muddy little pond with a
man standing in it in trousers, shovelling out mud. But the water in a tin was
clear and cool and very good. . . .

General Godley and Tahu Rhodes got up to the Turkish trenches, quite
close to them. The Turks attacked, threw hand-grenades, and our supports
broke. The General rallied the men, but a good many were killed, amongst
them the General's orderly, a gentleman ranker and a first-rate fellow.

Wednesday, May 5th. Kaba Tepé. The other day, when our attack below
failed, the Turks allowed us to bring off our wounded. This was after that
unfortunate landing.

Went on board the *Lutzow* to-day, and got some of my things off. Coming
back the tow-rope parted, and we thought that we should drift into captivity.
It was rough and unpleasant.

Thursday, May 6th. Very cold night. The dead are unburied and the
wounded crying for water between the trenches. Talked to General Birdwood
about the possibility of an armistice for burying the dead and bringing in the
wounded. He thinks that the Germans would not allow the Turks to accept.

Colonel Esson[2] landed this morning. He brought the rumor that 8000
Turks had been killed lower down on the Peninsula. We attacked Achi Baba
at 10 A.M. There was an intermittent fire all night.

This morning I went up to the trenches with General Godley by Walker's
Ridge. The view was magnificent. The plain was covered with friendly olives. . . . General Birdwood and General Mercer, commanding the Naval Brigade, were also there. The trenches have become a perfect maze. As we went
along the snipers followed us, seeing Onslow's helmet above the parapet, and
stinging us with dirt. Many dead. I saw no wounded between the lines. On
the beach the shrapnel has opened from a new direction. The Turks were
supposed to be making light railways to bring up their howitzers and then
rub us off this part of the Peninsula. This last shell that has just struck the
beach has killed and wounded several men and a good many mules. . . .

Friday, May 7th. A bitter night and morning. . . . This morning a shell
burst overhead, when I heard maniac peals of laughter and found the cook
flying up, hit in the boot and his kitchen upset; he was laughing like a mad-
man. It's a nuisance one has to sit in the shade in our dining-place and not
in the sun. They have got our exact range, and are pounding in one shell
after another. A shell has just burst over our heads, and hit a lighter and set
her on fire.

The mules, most admirable animals, had now begun to give a good deal of trouble, alive and dead. There were hundreds of them on the beach and in the gullies. Alive, they bit precisely and kicked accurately; dead, they were towed out to sea, but returned to us faithfully on the beach, making bathing unpleasant and cleanliness difficult. The dead mule was not only offensive to the Army; he became a source of supreme irritation to the Navy, as he floated on his back, with his legs sticking stiffly up in the air. These legs were constantly mistaken for periscopes of submarines, causing excitement, exhaustive naval manoeuvres and sometimes recriminations.

My special duties now began to take an unusual form. Every one was naturally anxious for Turkish troops to surrender, in order to get information, and also that we might have fewer men to fight. Those Turks who had been captured had said that the general belief was that we took no prisoners, but killed all who fell into our hands, ruthlessly. I said that I believed that this impression, which did us much harm, could be corrected. The problem was how to disabuse the Turks of this belief. I was ordered to make speeches to them from those of our trenches which were closest to theirs, to explain to them that they would be well treated and that our quarrel lay with the Germans, and not with them.

Diary. Friday, May 7th. At 1.30 I went up Monash Valley, which the men now call the "Valley of Death," passing a stream of haggard men, wounded and unwounded, coming down in the brilliant sunlight. I saw Colonel Monash[3] at his headquarters, and General Godley with him, and received instructions. The shelling overhead was terrific, but did no damage, as the shells threw forward, but the smoke made a shadow between us and the sun. It was like the continuous crashing of a train going over the sleepers of a railway bridge.

Monash, whom I had last seen at the review in the desert, said: "We laugh at this shrapnel." He tried to speak on the telephone to say I was coming, but it was difficult, and the noise made it impossible. Finally I went up the slope to Quinn's Post, with an escort, running and taking cover, and panting up the very steep hill. It felt as if bullets rained, but the fact is that they came from three sides and have each got about five echoes. There's a *décolleté* place in the hill that they pass over. I got into the trench and found Quinn, tall and open-faced, swearing like a trooper, much respected by his men. The trenches in Quinn's Post were narrow and low, full of exhausted men sleeping. I crawled over them and through tiny holes. There was the smell of death everywhere. I spoke in three places.

In conversations with the Turks across the trenches I generally said the same thing: that we took prisoners and treated them well; that the essential quarrel was between us and the Germans and not between England and the Turks; that the Turks had been our friends in the Crimea; and I ended by quoting the Turkish proverb: "Eski dost dushman olmaz" ("An old friend cannot be an enemy"). These speeches probably caused more excitement amongst our men than in the ranks of the Turks, though the Constantinople Press declared that a low attempt to copy the *muezzin's* call to prayer had been made from our lines. There were many pictures drawn of the speech-maker and the shower of hand-grenades that answered his kindly words. It must be admitted that there was some reason for these caricatures. Upon this first occasion nothing very much happened — to me, at any rate. Our lines were very close to the Turkish lines, and I was able to speak clearly with and without a megaphone, and the Turks were good enough to show some interest and in that neighbourhood to keep quiet for a time. I got through my business quickly, and went back to the beach. It was then that the consequences of these blandishments developed, for the places from which I had spoken were made the object of a very heavy strafe, of which I had been the innocent cause, and for which others suffered. When I returned two days later to make another effort at exhortation, I heard a groan go up from the trench. "Oh, Lord, here he comes again. Now for the bally bombs." On the first occasion, when not much had happened, it had been: "Law, I'd like to be able to do that meself."

Diary. Friday, May 7th. On getting back here we had a very heavy fire, which broke up our dinner party, wounded Jack Anderson, stung Jack (my servant), hit me. Jack is sick. . . . Here are three unpleasant possibilities:

1. Any strong attack on the height. The Navy could not help then. We should be too mixed in the fighting.

2. The expected blessed big guns to lollop over howitzers.

3. Disease. The Turks have dysentery already.

There is an uncanny whistling overhead. It must come from the bullets and machine guns or Maxims a long way off. It sounds eldritch. T. very sick after seeing some wounded on the beach, and yet his nerves are very good. Eastwood told me that he was sure to get through. I told him not to say such things. He had three bullets through his tunic the other day. I went on the *Lutzow* to get the rest of my stuff off, and found Colonel Ryan ("Turkish Charlie")[4] full of awful descriptions of operations. Many wounded on the boat, all very quiet. . . . Had a drink with a sailor, the gloomiest man that ever I met. He comes from Southampton, and thinks we cannot possibly win the war. It's become very cold.

Most of the diary of May 9th is too indiscreet for publication, but here are some incidents of the day:

Worsley[5] says it's very hard to get work done on the beach; in fact it's almost impossible. It was said that the gun which had been enfilading us was knocked out, but it is enfilading us now, and it looks as if we shall have a pretty heavy bill to pay to-day. The beach is holding its breath, and between the sound of the shrapnel and the hiss there is only the noise of the waves and a few low voices. . . . Harrison, who was slightly wounded a few days ago, was yesterday resting in his dugout when he was blown out of it by a shell. To-day he was sent to the *Lutzow,* and we watched him being shelled the whole way, his boat wriggling. It seems as if the shells know and love him. I am glad he won't be dining with us any more; a magnet like that is a bore, though he is a very good fellow. The land between us and the 29th is reported to be full of barbed wire entanglements.

Monday, May 10th. Raining and cold. Jack better.

Colonel Braithwaite woke me last night with the news of the sinking of the *Lusitania.* Last night we took three trenches, but lost them again this morning. S. B. came last night; I was glad to see him.

S. B. had been a great friend of mine in Egypt and brought me and others letters, of which we were badly in need, and stores, which were very welcome. We met upon the beach and decided to celebrate the occasion in the Intelligence dugout, for my friend had actually got some soda and a bottle of whisky, two very rare luxuries on the beach.

Diary. We went into the Intelligence dugout and sat there. Then a shell hit the top of the dugout. The next one buzzed a lot of bullets in through the door. The third ricochetted all over the place and one bullet grazed my head. I then said: "We'd better put up a blanket to save us from the ricochets." At the same time J. was shot next door and Onslow's war diary was destroyed. A pot of jam was shot in General Cunliffe Owen's hand, which made him very angry. V., the beachmaster, dashed into our Intelligence dugout gasping while we held blankets in front of him. Two days ago a man was killed in his dugout next door, and another man again yesterday. Now two fuses had come straight through his roof and spun like a whipping-top on the floor, dancing a sort of sarabande before the hypnotized eyes of the sailors. . . .

Also S. B.'s whisky was destroyed in the luncheon basket. He broke into furious swearing in Arabic.

Wednesday, May 12th. Rain, mud, grease, temper all night, but we shall long for this coolness when it really gets hot. No bombardment this morning, but the Greek cook, Christopher of the Black Lamp, came and gave two hours' notice, with the rain and tears running down his face. I am not surprised at his giving notice, but why he should be meticulous about the time I can't think. Conversation about the shelling is getting very boring.

Had a picturesque walk through the dark last night, past Greeks, Indians, Australians, across a rain-swept, wind-swept, bullet-swept hill-side. Many of the Colonels here are business men, who never in their wildest dreams contemplated being in such a position, and they have risen to the occasion finely.

The Generals have at last been prevailed upon not to walk about the beach in the daytime. . . . Two German and one Austrian submarines expected here. The transports have been ordered to Mudros.

Thursday, May 13th. Very calm morning, the echoes of rifle fire on the sea. I went with C. to take General Russell[6] up from Reserve Gully to Walker's Ridge. It was a beautiful morning, with the sky flaming softly, not a cloud anywhere, and the sea perfectly still. The scrub was full of wildflowers; not even the dead mules could spoil it. Guns thundered far off . . . After breakfast examined an intelligent Greek prisoner, Nikolas, the miller from Ali Keni. Then I was telephoned for by Colonel Monash in great haste, and went off up his valley with a megaphone as quickly as possible. In the valley the men were in a state of nerves along the road because of the snipers. The Turks had put up a white flag above their trenches opposite Quinn's Post. I think this was an artillery flag and that they hoped to avoid the fire of the fleet by this means. . . . The people at Helles aren't making headway, and it seems unlikely, except at tremendous cost, and probably not then, that they will. We are pretty well hung up except on our left; why not try there? The Turks are not yet entrenched or dug in there as in other places. . . . I had to bully Yanni of Ayo Strati till he sobbed on the cliff. I then threatened to dismiss him after which he grew cheerful, for it was what he wanted. . . .

The Turks have again got white flags out. Have been ordered to go up at dawn.

Friday, May 14th. Walked up the valley. The crickets were singing in the bushes at the opening of the valley and the place was cool with the faint light of coming dawn. Then a line of stretcher-bearers with the wounded, some quiet, some groaning. Then came the dawn and the smell of death that infects one's hands and clothes and haunts one.

They weren't over-pleased to see me at first, as after my speech the other day they had had an awful time from hand-grenades, and their faces fell when I appeared. I spoke from the same place. Then I went to another, and lastly to a trench that communicated with the Turkish trench. The Greek who had surrendered last night came down this trench and the Turks were said to be five to ten yards off. It was partly roofed, and there were some sandbags, between two and three feet high, that separated us from them. Leading into this was a big circular dugout, open to heaven. I got the men cleared out of this before speaking. In the small trench there were two men facing the Turks and lying on the ground with revolvers pointed at the Turks. I moved one man back out of the way and lay on the other — there wasn't anything else to be done — and spoke for five minutes with some intervals. Once a couple of hand-grenades fell outside and the ground quivered, but that was all. I then got the guard changed. . . .

The loss of the *Goliath* is confirmed and the fleet has gone, leaving a considerable blank on the horizon and a depression on the sunlit beach. Four interpreters were arrested to-day and handed over to me.

I put them on to dig me a new dugout, round which a colony of interpreters is growing: Kyriakidis, who is a fine man and a gentleman; Ashjian, a young Armenian boy, aristocratic-looking, but very soft, whom I want to send away as soon as possible; and others. My dugout is in the middle of wildflowers, with the sea splashing round. Since the ships have all gone we are, as a consequence, short of water. . . . The Turks have been shelling our barges hard for an hour. We are to make an attack to-night and destroy their trenches.

Saturday, May 15th. The attack has failed. There are many of our wounded outside our lines. Have been told to go out with a white flag. Was sent for by Skeen[7] to see General Birdwood in half an hour. While Colonel Skeen and I were talking a shell hit one man in the lungs and knocked Colonel Knox on the back without hurting him. General Birdwood was hit yesterday in the head, but won't lie up, General Trottman the day before. While we talked water arrived. A message came from Colonel Chauvel to say there was only two wounded lying out. . . . In a few minutes a telephone message arrived from the doctor in the trenches that the two wounded had died. . . . I came back to Headquarters, and heard General Bridges[8] asking the General if he might go up Monash Valley. In a few minutes we heard that he was shot in the thigh. The snipers are getting many of our men. If the Germans were running this show they would have had 200,000 men for it.

Last night Kyriakidis heard a nightingale. I notice that the cuckoo has changed his note, worried by the shrapnel. I don't blame the bird. My new dugout is built. It has a corridor and a patio, and is sort of Louis Quinze. The food is good, but we are always hungry.

Went out with Colonel N. He is a very great man for his luxuries, and looks on cover as the first of these. He is very funny about shelling, and is huffy, like a man who has received an insult, if he gets hit by a spent bullet or covered with earth. They have got the range of our new Headquarters beautifully — two shells before lunch, one on either side of the kitchen range. The men and the mess table covered with dust and stones. The fact is our ships have gone; they can now do pretty much as they like.

Most people here agree that the position is hopeless, unless we drive the Turks back on our left and get reinforcements from Helles, where they could quite well spare them.

Sunday, May 16th. A day fit for Trojan heroes to fight on. As a matter of fact, there is a good deal of Trojan friction. Went into the Intelligence dugout, as five men were hit below it. They have just hit another interpreter, and are pounding away at us again. I was warned to go out with a flag of truce and a bugler this afternoon.

•

Monday, May 17th. I walked out to the left with S. B., and bathed in a warm, quiet sea. Many men bathing too, and occasionally shrapnel also. There was a scent of thyme, and also the other smell from the graves on the beach, which are very shallow. I got a touch of the sun, and had to lie down. When I got back I heard that Villiers Stuart had been killed this morning, instantaneously. He was a very good fellow, and very good to me.

Tuesday, May 18th. Last night Villiers Stuart was buried. The funeral was to have been at sunset, but at that time we were savagely shelled and had to wait. We formed up in as decent a kit as we could muster, and after the sun had set in a storm of red, while the young moon was rising, the procession started. We stumbled over boulders, and met stretcher-bearers with dead and wounded, we passed Indians driving mules, and shadowy Australians standing at attention, till we came to the graves by the sea. The prayers were very short and good, interrupted by the boom of our guns and the whining of Turkish bullets overhead. His salute was fired above his head from both the trenches. . . .

We shelled the village of Anafarta yesterday, which I don't much care about. A good many here want to destroy the minaret of the mosque. I can see no difference in principle between this and the destruction of Rheims Cathedral. Kyriakidis told me a Greek cure for sunstroke. You fill the ears of the afflicted one with salt water; it makes a noise like thunder in his head, but the sunstroke passes. Christo thereupon got me salt water in a jug without telling me, and several thirsty people tried to drink it. . . .

A German submarine seen here. . . . A day of almost perfect peace; rifle fire ceased sometimes for several minutes together, but 8-inch shells were fired into the trenches. . . . Men are singing on the beach for the first time, and there is something cheerful in the air. The enfilading gun has been, as usual, reported to be knocked out, but gunners are great optimists. No news from Helles. . . . Turkish reinforcements just coming up. Attack expected at 3 A.M. We stand to arms here.

Wednesday, May 19th. Work under heavy shell fire. This grew worse about 6.30. Several heavy shells hit within a few yards of this dugout and the neighbouring ones, but did not burst. A little farther off they did explode, or striking the sea, raised tall columns and high fountains of white water. Colonel Chaytor badly wounded in the shoulder. A great loss to us. He talked very cheerfully. I have got leave to send away Ashjian. . . . This, after all, is a quarrel for those directly concerned. The Germans have brought up about twelve more field guns and four or five Jack Johnsons, and the shelling is very heavy. Saw a horrid sight: a barge full of wounded was being towed out to the hospital ship. Two great Jack Johnsons came, one just in front of them; then when they turned with a wriggle, one just behind them, sending up towers of water, and leaving two great white roses in the sea that turned muddy as the stuff from the bottom rose. They had shells round them again, and a miraculous escape. It's cruel hard on the nerves of wounded men, but of course that was bad luck, not wicked intentions, because the enemy couldn't see them.

If the Turks had attacked us fiercely on the top and shelled us as badly down here earlier, they might have had us out. Now we ought to be all right, and they can hardly go on using ammunition like this. Their losses are said to be very great. New Turkish reinforcements said to be at Helles. They have done what we ought to have done. Now they are throwing 11-inch at us. It's too bad. . . . I saw Colonel Skeen. He said to me: "You had better be ready to go out this afternoon. We have just shot a Turk with a white flag. That will give us an excuse for apologizing"; quite so: it will also give the Turk an excuse for retaliating. A Turkish officer just brought in says that the real attack is to be this afternoon, now at 1.30. I spent an hour in the hospital, interpreting for the Turkish wounded. The Australians are very good to them. On returning I found the General's dugout hit hard. Nothing to be done but to dig deeper in.

From the third week of May to the third week in June was the kernel of our time in Anzac. We had grown accustomed to think of the place as home, and of the conditions of our life as natural and permanent. The monotony of the details of shelling and the worry of the flies are of interest only to those who endured them, and have been eliminated, here and there, from this diary.

During this month we were not greatly troubled. The men continued to make the trenches impregnable, and were contented. It was in some ways a curiously happy time.

The New Zealanders and the Australians were generally clothed by the sunlight, which fitted them, better than any tailor, with a red-brown skin, and only on ceremonial occasions did they wear their belts and accoutrements.

Our sport was bathing, and the Brotherhood of the Bath was rudely democratic. There was at Anzac a singularly benevolent officer, but for all his geniality a strong disciplinarian, devoted to military observances. He was kind to all the world, not forgetting himself, and he had developed a kindly figure. No insect could resist his contours. Fleas and bugs made passionate love to him, inlaying his white skin with a wonderful red mosaic. One day he undressed and, leaving nothing of his dignity with his uniform, he mingled superbly with the crowd of bathers. Instantly he received a hearty blow upon his tender, red and white shoulder, and a cordial greeting from some democrat of Sydney or of Wellington: "Old man, you've been amongst the biscuits!" He drew himself up to rebuke this presumption, then dived for the sea, for, as he said, "What's the good of telling one naked man to salute another naked man, especially when neither have got their caps?"

This month was marked by a feature that is rare in modern warfare. We had an armistice for the burial of the dead, which is described in the diary.

On the Peninsula we were extremely anxious for an armistice for many reasons. We wished, on all occasions, to be able to get our wounded in after a fight, and we believed, or at least the writer was confident, that an arrangement could be come to. We were also very anxious to bury the dead. Rightly or wrongly, we thought that G.H.Q., living on its perfumed island, did not consider how great was the abomination of life upon the cramped and stinking battlefield that was our encampment, though this was not a charge that any man would have dreamed of bringing against Sir Ian Hamilton.

Notes

1. Colonel Doughty Wylie, V.C.
2. Colonel Esson was Q.M.G. of the New Zealand Division.
3. Now Lieut.-General Sir John Monash, commanding the Australian Forces.
4. Because he had been through the siege of Plevna and was covered with Turkish decorations.
5. Supply officer of the New Zealand Division.
6. Now Lieut.-General Sir A. H. Russell, K.C.M.G., K.C.B.
7. Now Chief of Staff in India.
8. Commanding Australian Division.

1918: *The Assault on the Chemin des Dames*

HERBERT SULZBACH

1 June: The day begins with a heavy rumble from both sides. The fighting sways to and fro. We have two casualties right at the start, Captain von Mutius of the infantry being wounded, and his adjutant with him; he was the man who took Montdidier on 27 March. I am with our Brigade Commander, Colonel Zechlin, who is as courageous as he is good-natured. I have to attend tactical discussions now, to deal with problems which arise in the course of the fighting.

I have to add here that yesterday 2/Lt May of No. 5 had to put his guns out of action when the French counter-attacked; and today he took his men out and brought the guns back again, unluckily losing his courageous Sergeant Faller, who was killed in action.

We have been supplied with two messenger-dogs, who arrived with four dog-handlers — the two dog-leaders and their opposite numbers.

Meanwhile we have got as filthy and unshaven as we were in 1914, but in the mad rush of duties to perform we completely forget about this lack of personal neatness.

Paris has been shelled once again by our famous long-distance gun, the French having reported it as having been destroyed some time ago! The official military communiqué for 29 May writes once more of the 'tirelessly advancing infantry and artillery.' A further official report, under the headline 'Fame achieved by the German Artillery,' describes the brilliant performance achieved by every single Battery Commander since 27 May.

The day closes without our having been able to advance any further, but also without the French being able to record the slightest advantage obtained from their counter-attacks.

2 June: Heavy attack by our neighbouring division. Chaudun, which is not in our hands yet, is riddled with machine-gun nests. The French put on an attack; and in the afternoon, with some hard fighting, our infantry at last take Chaudun. The supply columns are operating fantastically, e.g. when my No. 5 Battery obtained replacements, three new guns for three of theirs which had been knocked out, within a few hours. I really feel I must correct the remarks which are so often made against Staff people: I can see it here myself; even General Weber, who is commanding a Division, is very frequently up here with us, and during the attack the Brigade staff are up with the regimental and battalion staffs, in some places in advance of the batteries.

Chaudun has fallen into our hands through the singlehanded daring of one corporal and five men. Prisoners were being taken back to the rear, and as one of our men saw these young Frenchmen, in the pink of condition, he said to one of his mates, 'All they need is our officers, and they'd be the best soldiers you could want!' The day closed without any substantial gains having been achieved.

3 June: Missy is in our hands. It seems that the attack — or the whole offensive — has achieved its objective, and that we are not moving any further forward for the moment. We march back to Ploisy and pass through the ruins of Bercy. It all looks really dreadful here, worst of all up on the road to Chaudun. Seasoned fighting men that we are, we can't help being shaken at the sight of all these bodies which have been torn to pieces, and then cut up over and over again; friend and foe, white and black, all jumbled together. It is also very hot, and the stink of corpses is more than one can bear, but we have no time to bury the dead now. There has been very heavy fighting round Ploisy — this place where I am sitting and writing was once a splendid château. From up here you get a view into a pleasant valley, with steep slopes and hilly meadows — it reminds me of the Black Forest; and overhead, the bluest of blue summer skies, and birds singing away; the most lively picture of Nature, and just beside it all, death, decay and destruction! The château itself has been honeycombed with direct hits, and even though the outer walls are still standing, the whole interior is just a dreadful mess, and the whole building is as good as a ruin; but fresh red roses are blooming in the garden.

We, the 9th I.D., are at last being withdrawn to the second line after seven of the heaviest days in the first wave. There are a lot of prisoners coming through Ploisy again, including arabs and negroes from Martinique — black as coal those chaps are. I shouldn't like to be taken prisoner by them!

4 June: So our Division is going to rest stations, we are being billeted at the rear in Billy; the casualties among our horses have been very great indeed.

5 June: In Billy. Marvellous day. In the evening I go with 2/Lt von Seebach and visit some gentlemen at Brigade, and we sit with them until 2.30 in the morning in a fabulous garden, talk about the last few days, and have rather more to say about the days ahead.

New flying stars have appeared in the Flying Corps sky: Udet has got to his 26th, Menckhoff to his 31st, and Löwenhardt to his 27th.

The dream of going to rest stations has now been dreamed, and on 7 June we are moving away from our pleasant quarters in Billy to go back to the front with the whole 2nd Battalion; we are being brought into action for fresh preparatory fire and a new attack. We stay another night at Ploisy and reconnoitre the positions east of Missy.

8 June: We move to a command post to the north of Chaudun, in a narrow sunken track. For the moment I am alone with Seebach. The telephone lines are laid at once, the batteries move into their positions, and we set up house here with our runners. We dig a large hole in one bank of the sunken track: this is our quarters. The battlefield up at the top is a dreadful sight: the knocked-out tanks stand about barren and deserted, and there are more corpses lying about than you can count; a truly blood-soaked landscape. It looks as though there is going to be some large-scale action here once again. The infantry belonging to our Division has been withdrawn, and ahead of us we have other infantry regiments; or else we belong temporarily to another Division.

Our regimental Adjutant, Lt Stürken, has pneumonia and is going to hospital — the whole Regimental staff is gradually breaking up. Our officer casualties since 21 March, 1918, have been 28.

The general morale among the troops, including the new chaps whom we shall be fighting with here, is quite exceptional. Evening is falling, and the columns are bringing ammunition up to the front very quietly; there are a few fresh graves around us; in spite of the hurry and the fact that we are right near the front, they have been laid out with loving care.

9 and 10 June pass in our sunken track; we spend the time waiting, with a few minor artillery skirmishes on both sides. Hope it's going to start again at last!

Our next-door unit but one is stationed outside Compiègne. At 10 P.M., as it is very quiet, I walk out of our sunken track with Seebach, and we walk to and fro up forward as though there were no front. It is one of these marvellous summer nights. The columns are moving along further to the rear on the high ground, and the silhouettes of men and horses stand out beautifully against the night sky. Men and beasts, trotting along on the everlasting iron path of duty, taking it all for granted; somewhere someone presses a button, and the whole thing begins to operate. A High Command — or the Supreme Command — gives an order, and it filters down through a thousand lower commands to the units and columns. It's pleasant chatting this evening, and Seebach and I have become good friends; we never disagree, either on tactics, or about our duties, or in our private lives.

I must note here that another new type of plane is flying over our sector: a Fokker biplane. In spite of the enemy's superiority in numbers, our tactical superiority in the air is simply overwhelming; the engineers and technicians at home are working away all the time, improving and improving — to say nothing of the perfection achieved in chemical research and development! Our new Yellow Cross gas[1] is a nasty one; we fire it sometimes in shells, and it holds out in the ground for weeks. Incidentally, we are under orders to fill the great forest of Villers-Cotterets with gas, and then to skirt round it.

11 June: I have to go down twice to Ploisy, the adjutants having been ordered to attend a discussion there. Stürken's successor on the Regimental staff is 2/Lt Strelocke. Everything has been worked out for a new attack, preparation fire for 90 minutes, creeping barrage and start of the infantry assault at 5 A.M. In fact, only three or four divisions are going to take part in the attack.

12 June: The fireworks start at 3.30 A.M. — and it's still 86 batteries, or 350 guns in round figures. It bangs and thunders away, as is our custom in our repeated offensives; but it isn't the same as it was on 21 March or 27 May. Not even 'quite a small' event compared with those two.

But the infantry regiments don't get off the ground after the creeping barrage; they don't seem to be regiments like ours were in the 9th Infantry Division. All we take is the village of Doumiers, and the fighting sways to and fro, but our men don't get into a proper fighting mood. The French have concentrated a lot of troops here to frustrate any further offensive. It is evening before Saint Pierre Aigle gets taken — now we do seem to be moving forward at last! A plane circles over us, a German plane; he comes down close, just above us, circles again, and throws down a huge bundle of newspapers right near us — a marvellous present!

Late in the evening a Würtemberg infantry regiment comes past our sunken track. They are reinforcements, and I mention it here because I was able to take a good look at every one of these splendid chaps as they moved past: strong, youthful, healthy and cheerful! What a picture, to see them moving into battle, one behind the other, with their steel helmets, their heavy packs on their backs, and their light machine-guns — once again the same inspiring scene, and every one of them the incarnation of the highest devotion to duty. I watch them walking past their comrades' graves and the dead still unburied, and see some of them look at each other, and they look serious . . .

At 9.30 P.M. we receive orders that we are moving to the rear after all.

So, after these laborious weeks, we are going back for a well-earned rest.

We do a night march to Chivres through Noyant and Billy. It's a beautiful warm summer night, with large-scale activity in the air, as might be expected; you can hear our bombs going off in the French rear area and heavy fire from the French ack-ack batteries. We march in the direction of 1st Army's rear echelon.

13 June: We spend the day in wooden huts at Chivres, and on *14 June* move on through Billy and Fismes, on the splendid Route Nationale between Soissons and Rheims, to Courlandon. We move into quarters on a small country estate belonging to a French senator who must be highly devoted to art, and so has a splendid library of the best French, English and German works. Among writings of a high intellectual level, however, this well-educated man has placed scurrilous works of the meanest sort, published in the pre-war years to attack Germany and the person of our Emperor, so base and filthy that one simply cannot reproduce them. When we see this, any sorrow or sympathy we might have felt for the destruction of enemy civilian property soon evaporates, and we feel that the only proper attitude to have is a ruthless determination to win. We find crate after crate of these inflammatory pamphlets, and also leaflets appealing to our soldiers — which have in the meantime been dropped by French planes — and forged Reklam paper-backs.[2] Our men will never fall for these crude forgeries; I'd like to have the job showing these pamphlets to the troops — and then every single man whom I showed them to would demonstrate his unshakeable German attitude in the clearest possible way.

15 June: We move on, marching and riding, to Varennes, on a road completely churned up by traffic. A huge amount of motor traffic, one column of lorries behind the other. We move into quarters at Guyencourt, in the local school. In the evening the band of the 351st puts on a concert; they give a most sensitive and artistic performance; I talk to the bandmaster, who in civilian life is a conductor at the Chemnitz City Theatre. Our old area of 1917, from Juvincourt to Corbeny, is quite near here, except that we are now stationed in the area which we were then shelling.

16 June: Rest day. I go off on a very pleasant walk to Roucy, where I get a lovely view over 'Winter Hill,' once so hotly fought for. I think back to my times in the Juvincourt area a year ago with my No. 2 Battery and my three mates, of whom 2/Lt Zimmer and *Pieselmax* have now been killed in action, and Lt Knauer, my battery commander, is in hospital — why ever am *I* still here?

17 June: We move further back into the rear area, through Cormicy and the whole desert representing the static war along the Aillette, between Juvincourt and Berry-au-Bac. It's miserable to look at, everything churned up and shot to pieces, like the whole French theatre of war. We approach the desolate

Champagne area, north of Rheims, and take up quarters in a hutted camp which has been extended a bit, with block-houses for men and horses. It is known as Hindenburg Camp, and has been got ready for troops in reserve or those in need of rest. It has been fitted up in the latest style; one hut has been turned into a reading-room, with a piano and a canteen.

We hear that the Austrians have made another attack on the River Piave.

18 June: We move on to the place called Pilnitz Camp, near Neuville.

There is an epidemic on, what they call Spanish 'flu, so that even leave has been stopped. We are quite near now to Pont Faverger, of happy memory: spent Christmas here in 1914. Back then, I went for walks with Kurt, there, and we talked about war and peace, but we didn't think of death.

In a written message of thanks from Wichura Group, our Division is picked out for quite exceptional recognition, not only for its brilliant infantry attack but also for its heroic defense after 30 May; the artillery is then mentioned in the following words:

> The support batteries showed tireless energy in overcoming the exceptional difficulty of the terrain and keeping level with the front-line infantry.

We are not all that far now from my well-beloved Les Petites Armoises, where I was stationed for several weeks after the battle of the Champagne country in 1915, billeted on those nice French people.

The Austrians have in fact crossed the Piave.

19 June: I'm sitting in — Les Petites Armoises! And Mademoiselle Valentine is milking the cows, as she did over three years ago. Les Petites Armoises! The village with the mild, sweet, peaceful atmosphere — how often I've longed to be back there! Today I made it come true and rode 80 kilometres out of my way to see the village and my French friends again. I rode alone through Machault and Vouziers, and there I visited Sister Agnes Braunfels, who is in Vouziers now, and whom I visited before at St Quentin — a most joyful reunion. I then rode on along the old road through Quatre Bas and Chatillon and then, there is Les Petites Armoises spread out in front of me! With my heart beating with anticipation at the joy of reunion, I trot into the little village and stop by the Vesserons' house. Valentine and old Mother Pauline rush out, crying:

> *'Erbère! Non, c'est impossible, mon Dieu, mon Dieu!'*
> ("Erbert! No, it can't be — my God, my God!')

It is impossible to express the joy felt by these good people at seeing me alive again after all these years; I had not been able to send any kind of message. They asked about all my comrades of the old days, especially about Kurt, and they were overwhelmed by the news of his death. I have really never known joy like this. My horse and I were as lavishly entertained as if it were peacetime; then they dragged me round to the other local families, especially to the Mayor, Monsieur Bertholet, who nearly collapsed with surprise. All of a sudden the good old chap nipped up a ladder, groped on a shelf, and produced a tobacco-tin; it was the one I had brought back for him from Frankfurt in May, 1915, after I had been on leave, and I had completely forgotten about it. I strolled on through the broad, clean village streets, and then went for a walk with Valentine to the old mill. Back then, Valentine had been sixteen and I had been twenty. Today she is prettier still, frank and jolly, with coal-black hair and big brown eyes, a real village beauty. We strolled along, chatting arm in arm, and walked back to the village, where we met someone else, the old deaf and dumb man from the old days, and he recognized me and made signs to explain just where my artillery limber horses used to be kept. By great good fortune, war and its real horrors have not yet visited this village and its people, for all that they live anxiously, laden with cares. Valentine gets the little room ready which I had in the old days; it still has the names chalked on the door: Bombardier R. [Kurt Reinhardt], D. [Duden],[3] W. [unidentified] and S. [Sulzbach]. Late in the evening I look out of the window, but nothing has changed, it's the same peaceful, unsuspecting outdoor scene. I think back to those practical jokes we played — that time we put hundreds of cockchafers into old Mother Millet's bed.

20 June: I rode off at 4 in the morning after tearful good-byes; Mère Pauline and Valentine had been so excited that they hadn't slept a wink.

Five hours later I reached Mesmont, our rest station, where our regiment had arrived in the meanwhile.

Here we received the sad news that Lt W., who by the irony of fate had been run over by a gun-carriage during the advance, had died of his injuries; a day before he had been awarded the Hohenzollern House Order; he had once been Adjutant of the 2nd Battalion too. We spend some restful days at Mesmont, and I make another trip from this rest station to Les Petites Armoises — just as pleasant and harmonious as the first.

The Austrians have relinquished their position on the banks of the Piave.

Notes

1. Yellow Cross gas shells contained Dichlorethylsulphide, known as Mustard Gas.
2. The firm Reklam published then, as now, a huge range of well-printed books in very cheap paper-back editions. — R.T.

3. The brother of Lilo Milchsack (*neé* Duden) who founded the *Deutsch-Englische Gesellschaft,* the Anglo-German society based in the Rhineland in 1950, a year before the foundation of the British-based Anglo-German Association of which both the author and the translator are members. Frau Milchsack was created a D.C.M.G. by the Queen in 1972.

Assault
on 'Springfield'

EDWIN CAMPION VAUGHAN

August 24. I received details for the attack this afternoon. It is to be a tremendous push. Our battalion is to be the second wave of an attack over our late sector with our right boundary on the cemetery, our left on Springfield. The 7th Warwicks attacks first and captures the enemy front line, from Winnipeg to Triangle Farm, then we go through and capture the top of Langemarck Ridge from Arbre to Genoa Farm. Then the 4th Berks will take the final objective along the line of Von Tirpitz and Hubner farms.

In our attack, 'A', 'B' and 'D' Companies will be the leading wave, and I will bring up 'C' Company in support. On the night of the 26th, the whole of the leading battalion will form up in the area which I had been holding, and I have been detailed to take 'C' Company up tomorrow and work each night on improving the shell-holes to receive them. All the work we carry out is to be camouflaged before dawn so that the enemy will not know that preparations are afoot.

August 25. Having dressed in my Tommy's uniform and made personal preparations for the attack, I led 'C' Company out at dusk to bridge 2A which we crossed at 8 P.M. We had a very nerve-racking journey, for Jerry was shelling the track and as the men were carrying shovels and the track was badly battered I had to walk very slowly. Buffs Road was a pandemonium of shelling, with bodies of men and horses everywhere; the misty rain kept the reek of shells and decay hanging about the ground. I had only one officer in the Company—a quiet fellow named Wood. We had several casualties along this stretch.

At Admiral's Crossroads there was nothing but a churned area of shell-holes where limbers and tanks were shattered and abandoned. The battery of

60-pounders which Ewing and I had visited two days earlier had been blown up and now there remained only the yawning holes, with burst guns, twisted ironwork and bodies. It was in sickly terror that I led the Company off to the left towards St Julien.

Through an avenue of shell-bursts we reached the 'village' and striking across the mud to the left came to the concrete blockhouse which was to be our shelter. It was a very long pillbox in which a corridor opened into about eight baby-elephant cubicles. The 5th Warwicks were holding the line, and Major Bloomer and his staff had one of these cubicles; the next one was filled with German flares and Very lights; the next I took for Wood and myself. Into the remainder I crammed three platoons. Then I led the remaining platoon forward across the Steenbeck to the Boilerhouse, where they were to stay until called upon during the advance.

Then I went back and reported myself to Major Bloomer. He was a ripping fellow, so chummy and utterly unruffled that it was difficult to believe that he had been sitting under Ypres conditions for four days. I sent Sergeant Woodright with a couple of other fellows on to the road to intercept the limbers bringing camouflage, and then I went out into the open to look round. This was a foolish move, for as I gazed into the inky darkness, rain pouring off my tin hat, shells crashing on to the road and screaming overhead to the batteries, with the filthy stench of bodies fouling the air, an absolute panic seized me. There was nothing but death and terror, and the fitful flicker of guns and bright flashes of bursting shells filled the night with maddening menace.

I found myself staggering from hole to hole towards the Boilerhouse. As I dragged myself through the mud of the Steenbeck, I saw dimly the figure of a corpse which terrified me. I could just see the outline with a startlingly white chest on to which the rain beat, and a horror seized me of being hit and falling across it. I simply hurled myself away from it, and reached the Boilerhouse in a fever heat. There, in comparative safety, I calmed down. A couple of candles were burning and I smoked a cigarette as I explained to the men the scheme of attack and the digging job we had to carry out. When I left them I was too terrified of the white corpse to go straight back, but chose the shell-swept road. In St Julien I found Sergeant Woodwright and one of his companions, gibbering like monkeys. They had been blown up and shell-shocked. I sent them back to the aid post and returning to the pillbox I despatched another party to await the camouflage.

I had just settled down in my cubicle with Wood when shells began to fall about us; the fourth one hit the wall outside our door with a mighty crash. Our candle went out and chips of concrete flew across the room. Then there came a strange spitting and crackling and the darkness flared into horrid red and green flame. We dashed out into the corridor and followed the escaping troops, for the dump of pyrotechnics in the next room had caught fire. For 20 minutes we cowered from the shelling amongst the dead bodies in lee of the pillbox, before we could return to our rooms. Even then the woodwork was blazing and the place was filled with pungent fumes.

Wood, who had appeared to me all along to be very windy, was now absolutely helpless; he could not walk or even talk but lay shuddering on a wire bed. I gave him whacking doses of rum until he went to sleep. Then I went in to Major Bloomer and taught him how to play patience at a franc a card. We played until 2 A.M., when he paid me 30 francs, I told him to keep it and play it off after the attack, but he replied grimly that it would be better to settle up then. At 2 A.M. I had some food from my small supply.

August 26. Sunday. The limber did not arrive at all, so no preparations were made for the incoming troops; I did not get any sleep. It rained heavily all night and when I went out at dawn I found the shell-holes filled to the brims with water. The ground about the blockhouse was a most ghastly sight. Dozens of English and German bodies were strewn about the entrances and dotted between us and the Boilerhouse. Wire, broken ironwork, timber and equipment were littered all over the mud. Jerry stopped shelling as the dull day broke and I returned to my room to sleep. As I lay down a runner brought me a message to say that the limbers had been hit by shells and that the camouflage would be sent up at dusk.

I slept fairly well throughout the day and at dusk was much more cheerful. The nearness of the attack was rather appalling, but the necessity for a certain amount of intelligence tended to suppress my fear. The 7th Warwicks moved in at 9 P.M. and took over the line, so Bloomer left me in full possession of the pillbox. At 10.30 P.M. our battalion rolled up and was led off to their forming-up position near some old gunpits. There was still no sign of the camouflage, and in any case the heavy rain had turned the ground into a huge swamp upon which it would have been impossible to do any work. There was a terrific congestion of traffic on the road, including tanks, shell-waggons, cookers and limbers. From midnight on our machine guns kept up a constant fire to drown the noise of the tanks crawling up into position.

August 27. In the rations came a gift from General Fanshawe which consisted of a special meat and vegetable meal in a self-heating tin called 'Auto bouillant.' They were remarkably good and the troops blessed Fanny for a hot meal. There were also a lot of cold cooked rabbits in the rations! I said to Dunham jokingly. 'You hang on to my rabbit, I'm going to eat that on Langemarck Ridge.'

Just after midnight I made my way over to the Boilerhouse where Pepper now had his HQ. He was in a fairly cheerful mood but ridiculed the idea of attempting the attack. The rain had stopped for the time being, but the ground was utterly impassable being covered with water for 30 yards at a stretch in some parts, and everywhere shell-holes full of water. He showed me the final orders which detailed zero hour for 1.55 P.M. — a midday attack! My instructions were that at zero minus 10 (i.e. 1.45) I was to move my troops forward to the line of the Steenbeck. Then as the barrage opened Wood was to rush forward with three platoons to the gunpits while I reported to Colonel Hanson in the pillbox next to the Boilerhouse.

While we were talking a message arrived from Brigade: 'There is a nice drying wind. The attack will take place. Render any final indents for materials forthwith.'

Pepper read this out to me in a tone which implied 'This is the end of *us!*' Then he scribbled a few words on a message pad and tossed it across saying, 'Shall I send that?' He had indented for '96 pairs Waterwings. Mark III.' I laughed and bade him 'cheerio.' As I went out, I met the CO moving up to his HQ. He stopped for a moment while I explained why I had done no work. Then I said 'It doesn't look very promising for the attack, Sir.' 'No,' he said, seriously, 'but it's too late to put it off now.' Then we parted and I returned to my blockhouse.

Wood was still lying on his bed in a fuddled state with eyes staring out of his head, and as I turned in I thought to myself bitterly, 'What chance have we got of putting up a show tomorrow! My only officer out of action already and me commanding a company in which I don't know a single man and only about two NCOs by sight. Thank God Merrick is a sergeant major I can hang my shirt on!'

At 8 A.M. I woke to find the air quite silent. Not a gun was firing anywhere along the front and bright sunlight was flooding across the mud and water. Dunham had prepared breakfast which I ate with Wood who, although a little brighter, was still singularly lifeless and very nervous. Then at 10 o'clock I went up to HQ to see if there were any new instructions. I took with me an old oilsheet with which to cover that distressing body at Steenbeck. My impression that his chest was white had been erroneous, for he is coal black but had dragged his tunic open to try to staunch his wound, and now a more or less white vest was exposed. I covered him up because I was frightened of his unnerving me when I passed him for the last time at zero hour.

I found the CO and Mortimore sitting in the open on the lee side of their little ruin of a pillbox, and I sat down beside them. They had no further orders to give me, and after we had talked casually about affairs in general for a few minutes, realizing that they would have plenty to occupy their time, I saluted and returned to my HQ. I tried unsuccessfully to get a little life into Wood and then as noon came on I had some more food. As the hands of my watch whirled round I busied myself with totally unnecessary enquiries and admonitions amongst the troops in order to keep my mind free from fear. Then from my wrist in lines of fire flashed 1.45, and feeling icy cold from head to foot I took my troops out and through the ominous silence of the bright midday we advanced in line to the Steenbeck Stream.

My position in the centre of the Company brought me right into my oil-sheeted friend; I had grimly appreciated this when an 18-pounder spoke with a hollow, metallic 'Bong'; then came three more deliberate rounds: 'Bong! Bong! Bong!' An instant later, with one mighty crash, every gun spoke, dozens of machine guns burst into action and the barrage was laid. Instantaneously the enemy barrage crashed upon us, and even as I rose, signalling my men to advance, I realized that the Germans must have known of our attack and waited at their guns.

Shells were pouring on to the St Julien–Triangle Road as we advanced, and through the clouds of smoke and fountains of water I saw ahead the lines of figures struggling forward through the mud. It only took us five minutes to reach the Boilerhouse, but during that time I saw, with a sinking heart, that the lines had wavered, broken, and almost disappeared. Over our heads there poured a ceaseless stream of bullets from 16 machine guns behind, and all around us spat the terrifying crackle of enemy fire.

At the Boilerhouse I sent Wood on to the gunpits with three platoons, while I grouped my HQ staff under shelter of the concrete wall before reporting to the CO. I found him peering round the corner of the pillbox watching the attack and I stood beside him. With a laboured groaning and clanking, four tanks churned past us to the Triangle. I was dazed, and straining my eyes through the murk of the battle I tried to distinguish our fellows, but only here and there was a figure moving. In the foreground I saw some of Wood's men reach the gunpits, but the bullets were cracking past my head, sending chips of concrete flying from the wall; the CO pulled me back under cover and I heard him muttering 'What's happened? What's happened?'

Then, standing on the road in front with drums of ammunition in each hand, I saw Lynch shaking and helpless with fear. I ran out and told him to go forward. 'Oh, I can't, Sir, I can't,' he moaned. 'Don't be a fool,' I said, 'you will be safer in the gunpits than you are here — right in the barrage.' 'Oh, I can't walk,' he cried, and I shook him. 'You know what your duty is,' I told him. 'Are you going to let Rogers and Osborne and the rest go forward while you stay here?'

'No, Sir!' he said, and ran across the road. Before he had gone three yards he fell dead.

Then I returned to the CO and we waited on and on; the shells continued to crash around us, the sky clouded and rain began to fall. Time after time he sent out runners to find out what the position was, but none returned. Two of the tanks were stranded on the road just beyond Hillock Farm, and in front, save for occasional movement near the gunpits, there was no sign of life. The hours crept on; our barrage had lifted from the German line and now was falling on Langemarck Ridge. At last, when sick with the uncertainty and apprehension the CO, Mortimore, Coleridge and I were huddled in the tiny cubicle of HQ, a runner arrived with a report from Taylor that the attack was completely held up: 'casualties very heavy.'

It was then 6.30 P.M. With grey face the CO turned to me saying, 'Go up to the gunpits, Vaughan, and see if you can do anything. Take your instructions from Taylor.' As I saluted, backing out of the low doorway, he added forlornly: 'Good luck.' I called up my HQ staff and told them that we were making for the gunpits, warning them to creep and dodge the whole way. Then I ran across the road and dived into the welter of mud and water, followed by Dunham and — at intervals — by the eight signallers and runners.

Immediately there came the crackle of bullets and mud was spattered about me as I ran, crawled and dived into shell-holes, over bodies, sometimes up to the armpits in water, sometimes crawling on my face along a ridge of slimy mud around some crater. Dunham was close behind me with a sandbag slung over his back. As I neared the gunpits I saw a head rise above a shell-hole, a mouth opened to call something to me, but the tin hat was sent flying and the face fell forward into the mud. Then another head came up and instantly was struck by a bullet. This time the fellow was only grazed and, relieved at receiving a blighty, he jumped out, shaking off a hand that tried to detain him. He ran back a few yards, then I saw him hit in the leg; he fell and started to crawl, but a third bullet got him and he lay still.

I had almost reached the gunpits when I saw Wood looking at me, and actually laughing at my grotesque capers. Exhausted by my efforts, I paused a moment in a shell-hole; in a few seconds I felt myself sinking, and struggle as I might I was sucked down until I was firmly gripped round the waist and still being dragged in. The leg of a corpse was sticking out of the side, and frantically I grabbed it; it wrenched off, and casting it down I pulled in a couple of rifles and yelled to the troops in the gunpit to throw me more. Laying them flat I wriggled over them and dropped, half dead, into the wrecked gun position.

Here I reported to Taylor and was filled with admiration at the calm way in which he stood, eyeglass firmly fixed in his ashen face, while bullets chipped splinters from the beam beside his head. He told me that the attack had not even reached the enemy front line, and that it was impossible to advance across the mud. Then he ordered me to take my company up the hard road to the Triangle and to attack Springfield. He gave his instructions in such a matter-of-fact way that I did not feel alarmed, but commenced forthwith to collect 'C' Company men from the neighbouring shell-holes. Of all my HQ staff, only Dunham was left — the others had been picked off, and were lying with the numerous corpses that strewed the ground behind us. I sent Dunham all the way back to the Boilerhouse to lead the platoon from there up to the stranded tanks.

So many of our men had been killed, and the rest had gone to ground so well, that Wood and I could only collect a very few. The noise of the firing made shouting useless. I came across some of 'C' Company and amongst them MacFarlane and Sergeant Wilkes. I said to MacFarlane, 'We're going to try to take Springfield, will you come?'

'No fear!' he replied. 'We've done our job.'

'What about you, Wilkes?'

'No, Sir. I'm staying here.'

Finally Wood and I led 15 men over to the tanks. The fire was still heavy, but now, in the dusk and heavy rain, the shots were going wide. As we reached the tanks, however, the Boche hailed shrapnel upon us and we commenced rapidly to have casualties. The awful spitting 'coalboxes' terrified the troops and only by cursing and driving could my wonderful Sergeant Major Merrick and myself urge them out of the shelter of the tanks.

Up the road we staggered, shells bursting around us. A man stopped dead in front of me, and exasperated I cursed him and butted him with my knee. Very gently he said 'I'm blind, Sir,' and turned to show me his eyes and nose torn away by a piece of shell. 'Oh God! I'm sorry, sonny,' I said. 'Keep going on the hard part,' and left him staggering back in his darkness. At the Triangle the shelling was lighter and the rifle fire far above our heads. Around us were numerous dead, and in shell-holes where they had crawled to safety were wounded men. Many others, too weak to move, were lying where they had fallen and they cheered us faintly as we passed: 'Go on boys! Give 'em hell!' Several wounded men of the 8th Worcesters and 7th Warwicks jumped out of their shell-holes and joined us.

A tank had churned its way slowly round behind Springfield and opened fire; a moment later I looked and nothing remained of it but a crumpled heap of iron; it had been hit by a large shell. It was now almost dark and there was no firing from the enemy; ploughing across the final stretch of mud, I saw grenades bursting around the pillbox and a party of British rushed in from the other side. As we all closed in, the Boche garrison ran out with their hands up; in the confused party I recognized Reynolds of the 7th Battalion, who had been working forward all the afternoon. We sent the 16 prisoners back across the open but they had only gone a hundred yards when a German machine gun mowed them down.

Reynolds and I held a rapid conference and decided that the cemetery and Spot Farm were far too strongly held for us to attack, especially as it was then quite dark; so we formed a line with my party on the left in touch with the Worcesters, who had advanced some 300 yards further than we, and

Reynolds formed a flank guard back to the line where our attack had broken. I entered Springfield, which was to be my HQ.

It was a strongly-built pillbox, almost undamaged; the three defence walls were about ten feet thick, each with a machine gun position, while the fourth wall, which faced our new line, had one small doorway — about three feet square. Crawling through this I found the interior in a horrible condition; water in which floated indescribable filth reached our knees; two dead Boche sprawled face downwards and another lay across a wire bed. Everywhere was dirt and rubbish and the stench was nauseating.

On one of the machine gun niches lay an unconscious German officer, wearing two black and white medal ribbons; his left leg was torn away, the bone shattered and only a few shreds of flesh and muscle held it on. A tourniquet had been applied, but had slipped and the blood was pouring out. I commenced at once to readjust this and had just stopped the bleeding when he came round and gazed in bewilderment at my British uniform. He tried to struggle up, but was unable to do so and, reassuring him, I made him comfortable, arranging a pillow out of a Boche pack. He asked me faintly what had happened, and in troops' German I told him 'Drei caput — others Kamerad,' at which he dropped back his head with a pitiful air of resignation. I offered him my waterbottle, but when he smelled the rum he would not touch it, nor would he take whisky from my flask, but when one of my troops gave him water he gulped it greedily.

Then he became restless, twisting and turning so that his leg kept rolling off the platform and dragging from his hip; I took it on to my knees and moved it gently with him until at last he lay quiet. On one of the beds was a German flash lamp and I sent a fellow out to signal to our lines '8th Warwick in Springfield.' Time after time he sent it, but there was no acknowledgement. All was quiet around us now, but the Germans were still shelling the St Julien road. Suddenly I heard a commotion at the doorway and two fellows crawled in dragging a stretcher which they hoisted on to the wire bed in front of me. It was an officer of the 8th Worcester who greeted me cheerily.

'Where are you hit?' I asked.

'In the back near the spine. Could you shift my gas helmet from under me?'

I cut away the satchel and dragged it out; then he asked for a cigarette. Dunham produced one and he put it between his lips; I struck a match and held it across, but the cigarette had fallen on to his chest and he was dead.

I picked up a German automatic from the bed and in examining it, loosed off a shot which hit the concrete near the Boche's head; he gave a great start and turned towards me, smiling faintly when he saw that it was accidental. Then he commenced to struggle to reach his tunic pocket; I felt in it for him and produced three pieces of sugar. Taking them in his trembling hand, he let one fall into the water, gazing regretfully after it; another he handed to me. It was crumbling and saturated with blood so I slipped it into my pocket whilst pretending to eat it. I now produced some bread and meat; he would not have any, but I ate heartily sitting on the wire bed with my feet in the water and my hands covered in mud and blood. Dunham was sitting near me and pointing to the shapeless mass of mud-soaked sandbag I asked, 'What the hell are you carrying in there Dunham?'

'Your rabbit, Sir!' he replied stoutly. 'You said you would eat it on Lange-marck Ridge.'

But when he had peeled off the sacking, we decided to consign the filthy contents to the watery grave below.

Now with a shrieking and crashing, shells began to descend upon us from our own guns, while simultaneously German guns began to shell their own lines. In my haversack all this time I had been carrying a treasure which I now produced—a box of 100 Abdulla Egyptians. I had just opened the box when there was a rattle of rifles outside and a voice yelled 'Germans coming over, Sir!' Cigarettes went flying into the water as I hurled myself through the doorway and ran forward into the darkness where my men were firing. I almost ran into a group of Germans and at once shouted 'Ceasefire!' for they were unarmed and were 'doing Kamerad.'

The poor devils were terrified; suspicious of a ruse I stared into the darkness while I motioned them back against the wall with my revolver. They thought I was going to shoot them and one little fellow fell on his knees babbling about his wife and 'Zwei kindern.' Going forward I found that several of the party were dead and another died as I dragged him in. The prisoners clustered round me, bedraggled and heartbroken, telling me of the terrible time they had been having, 'Nichts essen,' 'Nichts trinken,' always shells, shells, shells! They said that all of their company would willingly come over. I could not spare a man to take them back, so I put them into shell-holes with my men who made great fuss of them, sharing their scanty rations with them.

Re-entering the pillbox I found the Boche officer quite talkative. He told me how he had kept his garrison fighting on, and would never have allowed them to surrender. He had seen us advancing and was getting his guns on to us when a shell from the tank behind had come through the doorway, killed two men and blown his leg off. His voice trailed away and he relapsed into a stupor. So I went out again into the open and walked along our line; a few heavies were still pounding about us, but a more terrible sound now reached my ears.

From the darkness on all sides came the groans and wails of wounded men; faint, long, sobbing moans of agony, and despairing shrieks. It was too horribly obvious that dozens of men with serious wounds must have crawled for safety into new shell-holes, and now the water was rising about them and, powerless to move, they were slowly drowning. Horrible visions came to me with those cries — of Woods and Kent, Edge and Taylor, lying maimed out there trusting that their pals would find them, and now dying terribly, alone amongst the dead in the inky darkness. And we could do nothing to help them; Dunham was crying quietly beside me, and all the men were affected by the piteous cries.

How long, I wondered, could this situation last. No message had reached me from HQ and at any moment the Boche might launch a counter-attack to recover Springfield. My pitiful defences would be slaughtered in a few minutes, and behind us, as far as I knew, was no second line, though somewhere in rear was the 4th Berks Battalion in reserve. We had no Very lights and only the ammunition that we carried in our pouches. In desperation I returned to the pillbox and commenced to flash messages back to HQ — knowing all the time that they could not be read through the rain and mist.

Suddenly, at 11.15, there came the squelching sound of many bodies ploughing through the mud behind. Wildly wondering whether the Boche had worked round behind us, I dashed back yelling a challenge; I was answered by Coleridge who had brought up a company of 4th Berks. 'To reinforce us?' I asked.

'No. To relieve you' — and my heart leapt. 'We are going back to Reigersburg.'

He — and the whole of HQ — had not known that we had got Springfield, and he had reached me by spotting my lamp flashing. I told Wood to carry out the relief of the line and march the troops back to Reigersburg Château. Then I handed over to the company commander — a calm, brave fellow who, after sitting under the barrage at the back all day, had now to take over this precarious position for four or five days, with a much depleted company. When we had walked round the line, I picked up Coleridge, and the one runner whom I had told to wait, and started back.

The cries of the wounded had much diminished now, and as we staggered down the road, the reason was only too apparent, for the water was right over the tops of the shell-holes. From survivors there still came faint cries and loud curses. When we reached the line where the attack had broken we were surrounded by the men who earlier had cheered us on. Now they lay groaning and blaspheming, and often we stopped to drag them up on to the ridges of earth. We lied to them all that the stretcher-bearers were coming, and most resigned themselves to a further agony of waiting. Some cursed us for leaving them, and one poor fellow clutched my leg, and screaming 'Leave me, would you? You Bastard!' he dragged me down into the mud. His legs were shattered and when Coleridge pulled his arms apart, he rolled towards his rifle, swearing he would shoot us. We took his rifle away and then continued to drag fellows out as we slowly proceeded towards HQ. Our runner was dead beat and we had to carry him the last part of the way.

I hardly recognized the Boilerhouse, for it had been hit by shell after shell and at its entrance was a long mound of bodies. Crowds of Berks had run there for cover and had been wiped out by shrapnel. I had to climb over them to enter HQ, and as I did so, a hand stretched out and clung to my equipment. Horrified I dragged a living man from amongst the corpses. The shallow passageways and ruined cubicles were filled with wounded, amongst whom the medical staff were at work.

I crawled into the HQ cubicle where Colonel Hanson and Mortimore were sitting; the CO looked years older. My face was a mask of mud and I had to tell them who I was, and that we had got Springfield. As I talked to them, my eyes were fixed above Mortimore's head on a huge block of concrete which at every shell burst moved half an inch inwards. It was only a matter of time before the pillbox would collapse. I asked the CO if there was anything I could do there, but wearily he told me that there was nothing except that I should report the situation to the Brigadier at Cheddar Villa. Mortimore also asked me to have some stretcher-bearers sent up from Brigade.

Then I went out and walked with Coleridge down the shell-swept road to St Julien, where, at the crossroads, a regular hail of shells was keeping most of the traffic out of the mud. But we were past caring, and walked through them unscathed. Before we reached Cheddar Villa our runner was killed and we dragged him out into a hole.

Brigade HQ was an elaborate concrete blockhouse with many rooms; I found Beart (the Brigadier Major) and Walker (Intelligence Officer) interrogating a German major. Beart greeted me cheerily and told me to go through to the Brigadier, so raising the blanket of an inner door I entered a small room lit by numerous candles. At a table covered by a clean cloth and bearing the remains of a meal sat Sladden, our Brigadier, and Watts, General commanding 145 Brigade. Sladden peered up at me, asking 'Who's that?' 'Vaughan of the Eighth, Sir,' I replied, and he cordially bade me sit down while he poured me a whisky. He was very bucked to learn that we had come from Springfield and he asked me numerous questions about the intensity and accuracy of the barrage and the present dispositions of the enemy.

When I went out I asked Beart to send up stretcher-bearers, which he promised to do, remarking that he had already sent up eight parties which had all been knocked out. We left the building just as the Boche major was being taken out by two Tommies. He was very sulky because they were hanging on to his arms, and when they jollied him, he made no reply. I called out some remarks to him and he took no notice until one of his escort said ''Ere! that's an orficer be'ind.' Whereupon he halted and, by an authoritative look, made his escort involuntarily release him; then he walked beside me.

Assault on 'Springfield' 183

August 28. With ironical politeness I apologized in French for the condition of the roads and he replied in all seriousness that we had made a greater mess of theirs. Thinking he might be interested, I told him that Springfield had fallen, and he immediately asked me what had happened to the officer. He was very distressed when I told him for, he said, they had been at school together and also served together in the army. Close to Irish Farm he was taken off to the prisoner of war cage, while we continued on to Reigersburg. Not one word did we speak of the attack, and in the camp we separated in silence. I found that I was alone in my tent, which I entered soaked in mud and blood from head to foot. It was brightly lighted by candles and Martin had laid out my valise and pyjamas. As I dragged off my clothes he entered and filled my canvas bath with hot water.

Doggedly driving all thoughts out of my head I bathed, crawled into bed and ate a large plateful of stew. Then I laid my utterly vacuous head upon the pillow and slept.

At about 9 A.M. I dragged myself wearily out to take a muster parade on which my worst fears were realized. Standing near the cookers were four small groups of bedraggled, unshaven men from whom the quartermaster sergeants were gathering information concerning any of their pals they had seen killed or wounded. It was a terrible list. Poor old Pepper had gone — hit in the back by a chunk of shell; twice buried as he lay dying in a hole, his dead body blown up and lost after Willis had carried it back to Vanheule Farm. Ewing hit by machine gun bullets had lain beside him for a while and taken messages for his girl at home.

Chalk, our little treasure, had been seen to fall riddled with bullets; then he too had been hit by a shell. Sergeant Wheeldon, DCM and bar, MM and bar, was killed and Foster. Also Corporals Harrison, Oldham, Mucklow and the imperturbable McKay. My black sheep — Dawson and Taylor — had died together, and out of our happy little band of 90 men, only 15 remained.

I thanked God that Harding was safe, but he had not been in the show; he had been transferred some days ago to the School of Musketry. The only officers who are left are Berry, Bridge, Coleridge, Samuel and MacFarlane, in addition to the CO and Mortimore.

So this was the end of 'D' Company. Feeling sick and lonely I returned to my tent to write out my casualty report; but instead I sat on the floor and drank whisky after whisky as I gazed into a black and empty future.

The Diary
of a Dead Officer

ARTHUR GRAEME WEST

In the Trenches

Sunday, Sept. 17th, 1916.

A tedious morning in the trenches prompts me to write down experiences and trivial little events which ordinarily I would not value enough to record, simply to pass the time. The trenches I am in are near G. . . . ., were originally German, and have been recently captured by the British. I have not been really in the trenches for a long time, and find the renewal of the experience particularly trying.

We got up here about 2.20 A.M. Sunday morning — a terribly long relief, for we started out for this line from G. . . . . Ridge at 8.30 P.M. Saturday night. The men were dog-tired when they got here, and though ordered to dig, complied very unwillingly, and were allowed to sit about or lean on their spades, or even to stand up and fall asleep against the side of the trench. It was a smelly trench. A dead German — a big man — lay on his stomach as if he were crawling over the parades down into the trench; he had lain there some days, and that corner of trench reeked even when someone took him by the legs and pulled him away out of sight, though not out of smell, into a shell-hole. We sat down and fell into a comatose state, so tired we were. On our right lay a large man covered with a waterproof, his face hidden by a sand-bag, whom we took to be a dead Prussian Guardsman, but the light of dawn showed him to be an Englishman by his uniform. From where I sit I can see his doubled-up knees.

The men lay about torpidly until 4.30 A.M., when B. . . . . ordered a stand-to. We tried to keep awake merely for form's sake while the light very slowly grew. Stand down went at 5.30, and B. . . . . made us tea, and added rum for the others; the very smell of rum makes me sick, because it is connected with the trenches last winter.

One always feels better with daylight—of this kind of life alone is the psalmist's saying true—in ordinary modern life, where unhappiness consists so much in *mental* agitation, it is startlingly false.

We joke over the tea and biscuits, go into the next bay and talk to the men about the German things they have found and are determined to get home somehow—a rifle, a belt-buckle with "Gott mit uns" on it, a bayonet, and so on.

We try and make out where we are on the map, and find we are at least 1,000 yards away.

Then we resolve that as we had practically no sleep last night nor the night before, and I had little even the night before that, we will try and get some. We lie . . .

Wednesday, Sept. 20th, 1916.

So far I had written when it became evident that our quiet Sunday was to be of the usual kind and we were to be bombarded. H.E. shells, about 6-inch ones, came over with a tremendous black smoke, making an explosion and sending up a column of earth about thirty feet high. The first intimation I had was when I went round the corner to the next bay to see where one had fallen, and found a man with a little ferrety nose and inadequate yellow moustache, in a very long great-coat, sitting muttering away on the firing-step like a nervous rabbit and making vague gestures with his hands and head. He would return no answer to questions, and I was told two men had just been buried in a dug-out near by. I went round and found two more pale men, rather earthy. I talked to them and did my best to comfort them. A few more shells came over, unpleasantly near, but it was not yet certain whether they were definitely after us.

Soon this was clear. They worked down a winding trench, and blew in the walls; we lost six men by burying and ten others wounded or suffering from shell-shock. It was horrible. A whistle would be heard, nearer and nearer, ceasing for a mere fraction of a second when the shell was falling and about to explode. Where was it coming?

Men cowered and trembled. It exploded, and a cloud of black reek went up—in the communication trench again. You went down it; two men were buried, perhaps more you were told, certainly two. The trench was a mere undulation of newly-turned earth, under it somewhere lay two men or more. You dug furiously. No sign. Perhaps you were standing on a couple of men now, pressing the life out of them, on their faces or chests. A boot, a steel helmet—and you dig and scratch and uncover a grey, dirty face, pitifully drab and ugly, the eyes closed, the whole thing limp and mean-looking: this is the devil of it, that a man is not only killed, but made to look so vile and filthy in death, so futile and meaningless that you hate the sight of him.

Perhaps the man is alive and kicks feebly or frantically as you unbury him: anyhow, here is the first, and God knows how many are not beneath him. At last you get them out, three dead, grey, muddy masses, and one more jabbering live one.

Then another shell falls and more are buried.

We tried to make them stand up.

It is noticeable that only one man was wounded; six were buried alive.

I shall always remember sitting at the head of this little narrow trench, smoking a cigarette and trying to soothe the men simply by being quiet. Five or six little funk-holes dug into the side of the trench served to take the body of a man in a very huddled and uncomfortable position, with no room to move, simply to cower into the little hole. There they sit like animals for market, like hens in cages, one facing one way, one another. One simply looks at his hands clasped on his knees, dully and lifelessly, shivering a little as a shell draws near; another taps the side of his hole with his fingernails, rhythmically; another hides himself in his great-coat and passes into a kind of torpor. Of course, when a shell falls on to the parapet and bores down into the earth and explodes, they are covered over like so many potatoes. It is with the greatest difficulty that we can shift the men into another bit of trench and make them stand up.

I found myself cool and useful enough, though after we had been shelled for about two and a half hours on end my nerves were shaky and I could have cried for fright as each shell drew near, and longed for nothing so much as to rush down a deep cellar. I did not betray any kind of weak feeling.

It was merely consideration of the simple fact that a shell, if it did hit me, would either wound me or kill me, both of which were good inasmuch as they would put a pause to this existence — that kept me up to my standard of unconcern. And the more I experience it, the more fear seems a thing quite apart from possible consequences, which may occur in a person even when he assents fully to the proposition I have noted above.

I feel afraid at the moment. I write in a trench that was once German, and shells keep dropping near the dug-out. There is a shivery fear that one may fall into it or blow it in.

Yet *what* do I fear? I mind being killed because I am fond of the other life, but I know I should not miss it in annihilation. It is not that I fear.

I don't definitely feel able to say I *fear* the annihilation of pain or wound. I cannot bind the fear down to anything definite. I think it resolves itself simply into the realisation of the fact that being hit by a shell will produce a new set of circumstances so strange that one does not know how one will find oneself in them. It is the knowledge that something may happen with which one will not be able to cope, or that one's old resolutions of courage, &c., will fail one in this new set of experiences. Something unknown there is. How will one act when it happens? One may be called upon to bear or perform something to which one will find oneself inadequate.

The shelling went on — on this Sunday, I mean — for about five hours, and we had a few biscuits and a tot of whisky about 1 o'clock. By then the whole of the little communication trench had been battered by successive shells, and we had left off going down it after each one, as the Germans had turned machine-gun fire on to the levelled portion of trench. We stood, B. . . . . , G. . . . . , Bl. . . . . , and I, in the only undamaged bay, eating and drinking, and watching the huge columns of earth and smoke as the work of destruction went on. They had worked rather off this particular trench, and the men still stood all about it, but I believed for certain that they would return towards the end and smash in the only bay to which they would naturally have hoped to have driven us. I had had enough whisky to enable me to view this prospect with nothing but interested excitement, and really did not flinch as the shells fell, seemingly groping their way towards their mark.

Just as they drew near, a runner from the X. . . . .'s came down to say the Germans had broken through on their left and were attacking, would we look after the third line and the flank? This news woke us all up from this rather unreal alertness of impending destruction and we rushed off with rifles, bayonets, and all manner of weapons to man the trench. No foe appeared, but it cheered us, and they did not shell very much more that night. The strain of the whole thing was very much worse than anything we had ever had at the B. . . . . section.

Living for the Moment

Tuesday, Nov. 23rd, 1916.

A grey, warmer day. The sun looked through only for a minute or two in the afternoon. We went in the evening to an estaminet on the left. After that Cl. . . . . and I walked down the road under the moon, and talking to him then I grew more convinced of the brutalising process that was going on: how impossible it was to read, even when we had leisure, how supremely one was occupied with food and drink. Cl. . . . . himself said he had found the same on his first campaign; it took him three weeks to get back to a state where he could read, and so it is. All my dreams of the days after the war centre round bright fires, arm-chairs, good beds, and abundant meals.

In and Out of the Trenches

Monday, Sept. 25th, 1916.

A better village than we have been in yet, on the A. . . . . River. Poplar lanes and water-meadows, and red sunsets, calm and chilling.

Moved to The C. . . . . , in a valley with a camp in it about seven miles this side of M. . . . . A comfortable night there.

Tuesday, Sept. 26th, 1916.

Moved at 8.30 towards the Front. Everybody rather fed up and tired. Reached a shell-torn ridge just near G. . . . . about noon, and stayed there till 6 P.M. eating, drinking, and sleeping; then moved up to occupy trenches near M. . . . . A quiet enough night, but not much sleep.

Wednesday, Sept. 27th, 1916.

The French came up behind us in large numbers, very active and talkative. Daylight showed a fearful lot of dead Germans round the trench and an appalling shambles in the dug-outs.

A fairly quiet day, sunny. The French moved about all over the valley regardless of anything. We had two good meals. We were relieved at night by the French.

Thursday, Sept. 28th, 1916.

Left trenches at about 4.30 A.M. Fearfully tiring march back to C. . . . . where we lived in a kind of manhole in the trench. B. . . . . , Bl. . . . . , and I had one to ourselves, and our valises with us. Slept and fed. Read "Scholar Gipsy" and "Thyrsis" and talked about Oxford together at night. These two are the only valuable men among the officers of the Company.

Friday, Sept. 29th, 1916.

Rainy and depressing. Up to trenches again by T. . . . . Wood. Seven men killed by a shell as soon as we got in the trench; beastly sight! I went up to find the way at G. . . . . at night. I got back to find a Buszard's cake — jolly evening. Slept on the floor of a dug-out. Stomach troubles.

Points of View: Atheism

Saturday, Sept. 30th, 1916.

Walked through D. . . . . Wood with B. . . . . Wood in an unspeakable mess. The fields are all over dandelion and vetch here; the sun, of course is in the April-May position again.

Wrote to M. . . . . , C. . . . . , and N. . . . . We moved back a few hundred yards to B. . . . . Wood and slept in a rough bivouac. I was very warm and comfortable. It is notable that to-night we discussed ever so slightly the problems of atheism. I had pronounced a few days ago that I was an atheist, and after a few of the usual jabs at Balliol the thing passed off. To-night I said something about my being a respectable atheist, to which it was promptly answered that there could be no such thing: and people said "You aren't really an atheist, are you?" Thus we see how men cannot get out of their minds "the horrid atheist" idea — the idea that intellectual convictions of this sort must of necessity imply some fearful moral laxity.

The most religious men are really the extreme Christians or mystics, and the atheists — nobody can understand this. These two classes have really occupied their minds with religion.

Utterances of a German Prince

Sunday, Oct. 1st, 1916.

A fine morning; wrote to C. . . . . We built a kind of shelter during the day, and had a pleasant day altogether; good meals, but never quite enough. Peace came near to-night in several ways and filled us with a happy contentment as we went to bed in our shelter with plenty of candles. Warmth, and a misty autumn night; fairly quiet, too, for the Front!

I received to-day a memorandum about Bertrand Russell telling of a course of lectures he would give, and containing a statement by himself of what the W.O. had recently done to him. It showed the strength of the conscientious objector and pacifist movement, even in this welter of brute force. Then I read of an article by a German, A Prince H. . . . . , on the necessity of at once stopping the war, making the usual and obvious points very well; it was good to find a German and a prince speaking so wisely.

S. . . . . , an officer here from Oxford, Nonconformist and, I think, religious, came back from a machine-gun course and remarked, half-ashamedly, that he had really come to the conclusion since he had been away that the war was really very silly, and we all ought to go home.

Nobody took any notice of what he said, or else treated it laughingly; but I saw he meant it, and really had seen something new. It had come to him as a definite vision and he was a bit disquieted. This is as it should be, and I must get talking to him.

In and Out of the Trenches Again

Monday, Oct. 2nd, 1916.

Rain. Read "Tristram Shandy" with much pleasure. *New Age* came. We sang jollily in our bivouac at night, B. . . . . , G. . . . . , and I. We slept well.

S. . . . . took a carrying party, which didn't return till 5.30 A.M. C. . . . . came back and brought a bottle of whisky with him.

Tuesday, Oct. 3rd, 1916.

Rain! Went in search of a canteen with G. . . . . , and failed to find one. Started at 3.30 in the afternoon to go up in support. Didn't arrive at our right trench till 2.30 next morning; misty and cold; very tired.

Wednesday, Oct. 4th, 1916.

Rain all morning. We sat and sang. Went out at night; very fatigued! G. . . . . came in with a working-party at 7 A.M. on Thursday morning. We were in bivouac at T. . . . . Wood. He had great trouble with the men.

The Common View

Thursday, Oct. 5th, 1916.

Dull. I observed several more features in the common opinions concerning the war. G. . . . . said: "Fancy all this trouble being brought on us by the Germans." Universal assent.

Then B. . . . . , the captain, remarked that it was really very silly to throw pieces of lead at one another, and from this someone developed the idea that our civilisation was only a surface thing, and we were savages beneath the slightest scratch.

What no one seems to see is that our country may be at any rate partially responsible, or that those who, like conscientious objectors, refuse to debase themselves to the level of savages are worthy of any respect, intellectually, if not morally.

One observes again the "It had to be!" attitude, which Hardy notes about the D'Urberville family.

So it is. People will not really move a finger to mould even their own lives outside the rules of the majority or public opinion. No one sits down to consider the rightness of his every action, and his judgments on political action he takes from the papers.

Independent judgment in private or public affairs is the rarest thing in the world.

We did nothing all day but rest. I read "Tristram Shandy" and wrote letters. S.O.S. signals came through at night, just at dinner, and perturbed us somewhat. They were soon cancelled.

Friday, Oct. 6th, 1916.

Fair! Arrangements made for an attack to-morrow. I was left out. I was very glad to go. Reached the transport lines about 7 P.M. and had a good dinner and sleep.

Went off to C. . . . . by lorry. Saw B. . . . . walking along the road near T. . . . . and had lunch with him and his ambulance.

C. . . . . is a delightful town, quite small, but compact and efficient. I bought butter and cheese and fruit, and had tea at an excellent small pâtisserie. A kind of large paved hall in the fashion of the Dutch pictures gave off from behind the shop, and one fed at tables round it. There were cages of canaries there that sang lustily, and a few great dogs. These sounds, combined with laughter, quick talk and the song of girls echoing in the spacious area, were the most pleasant thing that I had heard. I left C. . . . . about 4.30 and got back about 7. Battalion attacked.

After the Attack

Sunday, Oct. 8th, 1916.

News came through on this day of heavy rain and wind of our losses in the attack. Very heavy. B. . . . ., L. . . . ., and Bl. . . . ., all killed. Bl. . . . . a good blighty; G. . . . ., dangerously wounded. I never felt more utterly sick and miserable than to-day. We moved up at midnight to B. . . . . Wood to await the Battalion's return from the trenches. They were very glorious when they came, but arrived at the sand-pits near M. . . . . a very tired crowd, about 1.30 P.M.

Sunday, Oct. 15th, 1916.

Moved from M. . . . . It was very pleasant there in some ways: dinner was good with O. . . . ., the doctor, and parson; not bad arguments, and a good deal of freedom. I, being the only man outside headquarters who has any idea of logical abstract argument, was in the more favour.

The parson I like. He has wit and a pleasing frankness. The doctor is feline, almost Jewish and strokeable.

Friday, Nov. 3rd, 1916.

I sit on a high bank above a road at H. . . . . By my side stands a quarter of a bottle of red wine at 1.50 francs the bottle. The remaining three-quarters are in my veins. I am perfectly happy physically: so much so that only my physical being asserts itself. From my toes to the very hair of my head I am a close compact unit of pleasurable sensations. Now, indeed, it is good to live; a new power, a new sensibility to physical pleasure in all my members. The whistle blows for "Fall in!" I lift the remnant of the wine to my lips and drain the dregs. All the length of the march it lasts me, and the keenness, the compactness, the intensity of perpetual well-being doesn't even leave my remotest finger-tips.

The silver veil of gossamer webs are round my hair, the juice of the autumn grape gladdening all my veins. I am the child of Nature. I wish always to be so.

Special Course of Training in France

Saturday, Feb. 10th, 1916.

The course at F. . . . . which I entered on at the beginning of January is now over. About twenty of us in one mess, at an inn in the rue de Th. . . . . , were my principal companions. They were of all regiments, three or four Australians, two Scotchmen, two Guardsmen, and the rest mainly North Country. Here, as usual, is the same lesson to be learnt about men in the lump. They were all very nice, and couldn't understand me. They thought I was a pro-German, a Socialist, and a Poet. Anyone who isn't at once intelligible is put down at any rate as the first of these. They are all full of petty narrow loyalties to regiment or county. I think North Country people are more intensely narrow and venomous in this way. They are all rather against America, or were when Wilson was beginning his negotiations, and talk of Yanks and yellow races. I don't think they give much thought to anything. They argue by assertions proclaimed louder than their opponents. A gramophone has occurred during the last day, and they play "The Bing Boys." But how I love them all. It is 5 o'clock and the light has just been turned on. R. . . . . and I have spent the day since 9 A.M. waiting for 'buses up at the back gate of the White Château. 'Bus after 'bus, with lorries too, has come up, some with officers and men for the following course, all covered with white dust, but very happy to have got here. Their kits are wheeled off in barrows by their servants into the billets where we have been sleeping for five weeks. We stand about and talk to other officers, go for slow walks out on the E. . . . . or A. . . . . Road: we talk of ourselves, of our natures and moods, of what we would do if we were home: we tell one another what we were doing before the war; of our friends. R. . . . . tells me about his wife. We confide our dreams to one another; we talk of the other people in the mess and of the men in our own battalions. It is a sunny day, and against the walls and in sheltered places the heat is pleasant. Out on the E. . . . . Road the whole of F. . . . . lies before us; a mist is gathering over it from the surrounding hills and from the chimneys of the jute factory. Little girls pass and repass through the crowd of officers with quiet happy eyes. I am very happy. I love all the men, and simply rejoice to see them going on day by day their own jolly selves, building up such a wall of jocundity around me.

NOTICE.

We regret to announce that an insidious disease is affecting the Division, and the result is a hurricane of poetry. Subalterns have been seen with a notebook in one hand, and bombs in the other absently walking near the wire in deep communion with the muse. Even Quartermasters with books, note, one, and pencil, copying, break into song while arguing the point re boots. gum, thigh. The Editor would be obliged if a few of the poets would break into prose as a paper cannot live by "poems" alone.

The Wipers Times, Mar. 20, 1916.

The Wipers Times (The "New Church" Times), Apr. 17, 1916.

THE NEUVE EGLISE HIPPODROME

GRAND NEW REVIEW, ENTITLED:

"SHELL IN"

POSITIVELY THE GREATEST SPECTACULAR PERFORMANCE EVER STAGED.

BRINGING BEFORE THE PUBLIC AT ONE AND THE SAME TIME THE FOLLOWING HIGHLY-PAID STARS:

THE CRUMPS.
LITTLE PIP-SQUEAK
DUDDY WHIZZ-BANG.
HURLA SHELLOG, etc., etc.

THRILLING OPENING CHORUS ARRANGED BY LEWIS VICKERS.

Exciting! Hair-raising!! Awe-inspiring!!!

SEE WHAT THE PAPERS SAY.   BOOK EARLY.   PRICES DOUBLE THIS WEEK.

TO HARASSED SUBALTERNS.

—o—o—o—o—

IS YOUR LIFE MISERABLE? ARE YOU UNHAPPY?

DO YOU HATE YOUR COMPANY COMMANDER?

—o—o—o—o—

YES! THEN BUY HIM ONE OF

OUR NEW PATENT TIP DUCK BOARDS

YOU GET HIM ON THE END—THE DUCK BOARD DOES THE REST

—o—o—o—o—

Made in three sizes, and every time a "Blighty."

—o—o—o—o—

" It once he steps on to the end,
'Twill take a month his face to mend "

—o—o— o—o—

WRITE AT ONCE & ENSURE HAPPINESS

THE NOVELTY SYNDICATE, R.E. HOUSE   Tel.: " Dump '

The Wipers Times (The "New Church" Times), May 8, 1916.

The Wipers Times (The Kemmel Times), July 3, 1916.

ARE YOU A VICTIM TO
OPTIMISM?

—o—o—o—o—

YOU DON'T KNOW?

—o—o—o—o—

THEN ASK YOURSELF THE FOLLOWING QUESTIONS.

—o—o—o—o—

1.—DO YOU SUFFER FROM CHEERFULNESS?
2.—DO YOU WAKE UP IN A MORNING FEELING THAT ALL IS GOING WELL FOR THE ALLIES?
3.—DO YOU SOMETIMES THINK THAT THE WAR WILL END WITHIN THE NEXT TWELVE MONTHS?
4.—DO YOU BELIEVE GOOD NEWS IN PREFERENCE TO BAD?
5.—DO YOU CONSIDER OUR LEADERS ARE COMPETENT TO CONDUCT THE WAR TO A SUCCESSFUL ISSUE?

IF YOUR ANSWER IS "YES" TO ANYONE OF THESE QUESTIONS THEN YOU ARE IN THE CLUTCHES OF THAT DREAD DISEASE.

WE CAN CURE YOU.

TWO DAYS SPENT AT OUR ESTABLISHMENT WILL EFFECTUALLY ERADICATE ALL TRACES OF IT FROM YOUR SYSTEM.
DO NOT HESITATE—APPLY FOR TERMS AT ONCE TO:—

Messrs. Walthorpe, Foxley, Nelmes and Co.

TELEPHONE 72, "GRUMBLESTONES."   TELEGRAMS: "GROUSE."

The Wipers Times (The Somme-Times), July 31, 1916.

Intelligence Summary.

—o—o—o—

X REGIMENT.

—o—o—

For the 24 hours ending in the Early Morning. (?)

7 a.m.—Bosche seen at K.42.b.9.7, wearing a pair of boots. (Normal.)

3˙45 a.m.—Hun aeroplane pursued one of our carrier pigeons over our lines. After a burst of M.G fire, our pigeon was seen to crumple up and crash to the ground.

9˙30 a.m.—One of our machines in retaliation dropped a 200 ton bomb on a German at H.69.b.2 3. Good results were observed. Our machine returned safely.

11˙5 a.m.—Enemy fired 10 Pomegranates and one Pumpkin into our sap at H.62.c.7.8.

Noon —.A bombardment by our Stokes's guns was followed by shrieks and groans from the enemy trenches.

12˙50 p.m.—Enemy fired 80 Minnies. Seventy of these exploded in our front line. No damage was done. Our heavy artillery at once replied by bombarding our own support line for two hours. At the finish of the bombardment our support line was completely obliterated. This proves the superiority of our ammunition.

3 p.m.—Sniper located at H.Z.0.5, dispersed by the fire of our heavy artillery.

4.10 p.m.—Four sandbags in our front line damaged by T.M. fire. A Court of Inquiry will be held to fix the responsibility for placing them there.

6.50 p.m.—A Very light fired by a Bosche burst into puce and yellow stars. These were thought to be crescent shaped. Nothing unusual followed.

9.50 p.m.—Strange noise heard near, sounded like an ostritch in the Bosche trenches munching glass. or a train.

12 m.n.—Flight of 20 Zeppelins seen by officer on duty, who failed to report on the proper form, and no action was taken.

2.50 a.m.—One of our patrols brought in a pink garter, whereby an important identification has been established.

4˙10 a.m.—Bosche heard playing a barrel-organ in No Man's Land. Organ located at H 22 c.3.4. After a heavy concentration of fire the music ceased. The organ had disappeared by daylight.

The Wipers Times (The B.E.F. Times), Dec. 26, 1916.

CAN YOU SKETCH?

Some of you may be able to draw corks.
Very few of you can draw any more money.
Probably some of you can draw sketches.

Here is a letter I have just received from a pupil at the front :—

"The other day by mischance I was left out in No Man's Land. I rapidly drew a picture with a piece of chalk of a tank going into action, and while the Huns were firing at this I succeeded in returning to the trenches unobserved "

COULD YOU HAVE DONE THIS?

—o—o—o—o—

SEND A COPY OF THE FOLLOWING ON A CHEQUE :—

Francs 500 - -

AND BY RETURN I WILL SEND YOU A HELPFUL CRITICISM AND MY FOURTEEN PROSPECTUSES.

PLEASE SIGN YOUR NAME IN THE BOTTOM RIGHT-HAND CORNER TO PREVENT MISTAKES.

CORPS CHRISTMAS CARD COMPANY.

The Wipers Times (The B.E.F. Times), Aug. 15, 1917.

TO-DAY'S GOSSIP.

BADGES OF RANK.—When an officer wears a trench coat it is impossible to tell what his rank is. However, I am told that a useful new regulation provides for the wearing of rank badges on the garment.—THE RAMBLER in the "Daily Mirror."

A FRIEND of mine, a Staff Officer of considerable rank, informs me that many misunderstandings arise through the difficulty of distinguishing between officers of G and Q Branches of the Staff during the dark hours of night. Some genius of the War Office has, however, introduced a new order whereby members of G side will in future wear bright red pyjamas and those of Q bright green ones, thus overcoming a really serious difficulty.

AN unpaid lance-corporal, in one of our famous Shetland regiments at the front, writes to me as follows :— "I was nearly court-martialed the other day for failing to salute an officer I met in the trenches one dark and foggy night." On making enquiries I am happy to inform my readers that a new regulation is being framed by the "powers that be," whereby officers in the forward area will in future have their rank stars illuminated by powerful electric lamps, the battery for same being carried in the pocket. Stars will be distinguished by white lamps, crowns by red lamps, and Generals and above will be known by a combination light green and dark ginger.

MUCH correspondence has reached me asking me to explain the meaning of the patches of many colours, shapes and sizes worn on the arms and backs of our brave lads home on leave from the front. I am told by "one who knows" that an illustrated guide book is shortly to be issued at the small figure of five shillings whereby Londoners and others will be able to understand and distinguish these mystic signs.

THE BABBLER.

The Wipers Times (The B.E.F. Times), Nov. 1, 1917.

LATE NEWS FROM THE RATION DUMP.

—o—o—o—

Three submarines have been mined on the Menin Road. Crew of one captured.

—o—o—o—

The Swedes have declared war. Hence the shortage of turnips. Serious rumours that the Jamaicans are preparing for war and will cut off the rum issue.

—o—o—o—

The Germans have only 14 shells left.

—o—o—o—

Three flying pigs reached the Hun trenches. (This is probably an optimist rumour.)

—o—o—o—

The pay for men at the base is going to be doubled owing to the increased cost of living, and halved for those in the line as they are not in a position to spend it.

—o—o—o—

12 Zeppelins have been forced to descend, as we have discovered a new method of extracting gas from any distance.

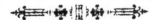

The Wipers Times (The B.E.F. Times), Nov. 1, 1917.

WHY??? LET THE HUNS WIN THE WAR AFTER THE WAR?

THEY ARE PREPARING BY MEANS OF A TRENCH UNIVERSITY. ALL RANKS CAN TAKE POST-GRADUATE COURSES, AND KEEP THEIR BRAINS ACTIVE, IN FACT,

THEY Are acquiring useful knowledge while, **YOU** are only studying C.R.O., and similar periodicals. WHAT YOU WANT—and must have—is your own series of lectures.

—o—o—o—o—

TO THIS END———US.

—o—o—o—o—

MARCH 3rd.—" SHELLS. What they are. Their uses. How to find them. Having found them, how to use the field dressing, etc , etc."
By Professor W. I. Z. BANGS, R.A., etc.

MARCH 10th.—" ALCOHOL AND ITS TERRIBLE RAVAGES. With particular reference to the wicked issue of rum to the troops "
By Professor T. T. BILGE, H 2 O.
(THIS IS EXPECTED TO BE A VERY POPULAR LECTURE, AND TO AVOID DISAPPOINTMENT YOU SHOULD BOOK EARLY,)

MARCH 17th.—" THE GREAT WAR ; and how we won it every year until the Germans had no more reserves left."
By Professor HILLARY BULLOCK.

MARCH 24th.—" THE GERMAN AT HOME. His culture. Kindly Nature. Chivalry. Is he one of Nature's gentlemen ? Etc., etc."
By Professor RAMESES SNOWDEN.

—o—o—o—o—

THE ANGLO-AMERICAN UNIVERSITY EXTENSION LECTURE SYNDICATE, ACTIVE SERVICE BRANCH.

Secretary : **S.** U. M. NUTT.   Telegrams : " WATAHOPE, B.E.F."

DO NOT READ THIS!!!
UNLESS YOU HAVE A GIRL AT HOME.

—o—o—o—o—

If you have, of course. you want to send her a souvenir. WE can supply just the tasty little thing you want   Thousands to choose from :—

GERMAN SHOULDER STRAPS : 1/- each   —   —   10/- a dozen
DITTO, BLOODSTAINED : 1/6 each   —   —   15/ a dozen
SHELL HOLES, COMPLETE : 50/- each
DUCKBOARDS—ENGLISH : 5/- each
DITTO GERMAN : 10/- each
IRON CROSSES : 6d. a gross.

OUR SPECIALITY : BULLETS CAREFULLY FIXED IN BIBLES (FOR MAIDEN AUNTS) PHOTOGRAPHS (FOR FIANCEES.)

—o—o—o—o—

" To please your best girl, it is clear,
You must procure a souvenir."

—o—o—o—o—

SOUVENIR MANUFACTURING COMPANY, CAMBRAI.

The Wipers Times (The B.E.F. Times), Feb. 26, 1918.

PART THREE

MEMOIRS

Baroness T'Serclaes and Miss Mairi Chisholm; the two "Women of Pervyse" outside their sandbagged third "poste," Pervyse, July 30, 1917. Photograph courtesy the Imperial War Museum, London, neg. Q.2663.

Introduction

Almost all of them have fallen silent. In a few more years, none will remain to reminisce. Already, in filmed interviews, those left struggle to recollect. Their faces wince in concentration; their eyes look beyond the interviewers, seeking memories on some more distant horizon — in the sunlight or dark of a day eight decades gone. And, if they do recall, if whatever out there to be apprehended by concentration does come back, then often the words fail. After all, it has been eighty years since the war and most of the twentieth century has transpired. If they survived Mons, Vimy Ridge, Suvla Bay, the Somme, the Marne, Ypres, and subsequent illnesses and wars, they have lived an entire lifetime beyond the world of endless boggy trenches, the pineapple scent of gas, the pandemonium of casualty clearing stations.

Yet, when the last participants pass away, fortunately they will be survived by myriad volumes of memoirs — some better known than others; many now difficult to obtain. This section provides a sampling of some of these accounts. But this is not to say that the section is in the least comprehensive. It does not pretend to capture the whole of the Great War, where sustained action could give way, in certain sectors, to months of remorseless inactivity. But it does try to capture the rhythms of that exceptional existence. I have attempted to bring together neglected as well as celebrated memoirs from men and women, from British, French, and Germans who fought and nursed in Belgium, France, and East Africa. The manifold nature of their worlds — their own personal reactions recollected and organized after the event — provides us with some sense of how they defined themselves in relationship to such abstractions as courage, despair, and duty.

Millicent, Duchess of Sutherland, and Vera Brittain served as nurses. Millicent Sutherland crossed the Channel with one of the first ambulance sections sent to Belgium in August of 1914. During her six weeks there, she recorded the trampling underfoot of that small country as the German invaders crossed into France for what everyone, on both sides, believed would be a war finished by Christmas. Vera Brittain, without doubt the most famous woman memoirist of the war, served as a Voluntary Aid Detachment (V.A.D.) nurse in hospitals in England and France. Her accounts of the wounded and her own misery at losing both a fiancé and a brother powerfully reveal the degree of sacrifice demanded from noncombatants.

Although selections from some of the most famous frontline memoirs are included here, the less celebrated works are every bit as well crafted and insightful. Historian Marc Bloch writes movingly about his life as a poilu, an ordinary French soldier. Francis Brett Young evokes the far-flung aspects of the war as he describes his adventures as a medical officer with General Smuts, whose colonial forces chased Germans across East Africa. Ernst Jünger offers the perspective of an ardent storm-troop officer wounded twenty times in his almost four years at the front. Much less well known are Guy Chapman and Max Plowman. Both bring an intensity of observation and literary acumen to their works. Chapman's *A Passionate Prodigality* has been rightly called one of the masterpieces of the war.

Finally, there are the classic English memoirs of the war. Robert Graves, certainly the most famous, details his officer's life in controlled understatement, the irony of "stiff upperlipmanship" his chosen vehicle for his portrait of trench existence. Edmund Blunden's *Undertones of War* harks back to an earlier literary tradition. His juxtaposition of the pastoral wonders of the French countryside with the mechanized destruction of the front line epitomizes the shock of the technological obliterating the traditional. In Siegfried Sassoon, one can chart the growing despair after 1915. Always the brave soldier — perhaps to the point of foolhardiness — Sassoon nevertheless issued a public proclamation denouncing the war and then, later, returned to the front because of the allegiance he felt he owed his men. I have also included a glimpse of the aviators' war with an excerpt from Cecil Lewis's *Sagittarius Rising*, which chronicles the young pilot's first reconnaissance flight over the Somme in preparation for the battle — a compelling mixture of fear and feverish labor.

For years afterward, no one wanted to talk about the war. In truth, people would have liked to have forgotten it. However, as the eminent physician W. H. R. Rivers well knew, such repression is death to the soul. In treating Siegfried Sassoon, Wilfred Owen, and numerous other shell shock victims, Rivers attempted to facilitate the patients' articulation of their experiences. Remembering, he believed, was the shortest path to healing. When, in the late 1920s the books did begin to emerge, many readers thought them too critical and cynical. Some writer-soldiers reacted by extolling the virtues of camaraderie, undaunted courage, and national character. In truth, all of the better memoirs balance these concerns.

The war could not be left in silence. It had played havoc with too much and too many. It had altered the face of everything. The works that follow speak to us about the very best and worst in human beings. Memoirs are always narrowed by single perspectives, but, at their best, they recount unflinchingly what the mind's eye would like best to blink away.

Memoirs of War, 1914–1915

MARC BLOCH

I had the honor of taking part in the first five months of the campaign of 1914–15. Now on sick leave in Paris, I am gradually recovering from a severe case of typhoid fever, which on January 5, 1915, forced me to leave the front. I intend to use this respite to fix my recollections before their still fresh and vibrant colors fade. I shall not record everything; oblivion must have its share. Yet I do not want to abandon the five astonishing months through which I have just lived to the vagaries of my memory, which has tended in the past to make an injudicious selection, burdening itself with dull details while allowing entire scenes, any part of which would be precious, to disappear. The choice it has exercised so poorly I intend this time to control myself.

I

August 1914! I still see myself standing in the corridor of the train that was bringing my brother and me back from Vevey, where we had learned on July 31 of Germany's declaration of a state of war.[1] I watched the sun rise in a beautiful, cloudy sky, and I repeated under my breath these rather trivial words, which nevertheless seemed laden with a terrible and hidden meaning: "Behold the dawn of the month of August 1914!" On arriving at the Gare de Lyon in Paris, we learned from the newspapers that Jean Jaurès had been assassinated. To our grief was added a painful doubt. War seemed inevitable. Would riots sully its first moments? Today, everyone knows how groundless these concerns were. Jaurès was gone. The influence of his noble spirit did survive, however, as the reaction of the socialist party demonstrated to the nations of the world.

One of the most beautiful memories the war has given me was the sight of Paris during the first days of mobilization. The city was quiet and somewhat solemn. The drop in traffic, the absence of buses, and the shortage of taxis made the streets almost silent. The sadness that was buried in our hearts showed only in the red and swollen eyes of many women. Out of the specter of war, the nation's armies created a surge of democratic fervor. In Paris there remained only "those who were leaving" — the nobility — and those who were not leaving, who seemed at that moment to recognize no obligation other than to pamper the soldiers of tomorrow. On the streets, in the stores and streetcars, strangers chatted freely; the unanimous goodwill, though often expressed in naive or awkward words and gestures, was nonetheless moving. The men for the most part were not hearty; they were resolute, and that was better.

Very early on the morning of August 4, I left for Amiens.[2] I went part of the long way between the avenue d'Orléans and the Gare de la Chapelle in a market gardener's wagon that a police constable had requisitioned for my use. Because I sat in the back, wedged between baskets of vegetables, the fresh and slightly acrid odor of cabbage and carrots will always bring back the emotions of that early-morning departure: my enthusiasm and the constriction that gripped my heart. At the Gare de la Chapelle, an aged, white-haired father made heroic but unavailing efforts to hold back his tears as he embraced an artillery officer. At Amiens I found an extraordinarily animated city, its streets predictably teeming with soldiers; yet I have never understood why there were so many pharmacist officers among them.

On August 10, at 1:30 A.M., the 272d regiment, to which I had been assigned as sergeant (18th company, 4th platoon), left Amiens. Marching through suburban streets in the nocturnal silence, we reached the Longueau station, where we entrained for a long, exhausting journey in oppressive dog-day heat. At Sedan we received an official communiqué announcing the capture of Mulhouse. Happy to speak of a victory at the site of a great defeat, I read it to my men while we were still on the train. At Stenay we disembarked.

From August 11 to 21 the regiment remained in the region of the Meuse, first in the valley itself, where we guarded the bridges, and then on the right bank, close to the border. To be sure, I have not retained a very precise memory of this period. Beautiful days, very calm but a bit monotonous, were filled with the petty details of camp duties. The sun, the rustic pleasures — fishing, swimming in the river, and dozing on the grass — in addition to the prospect of an unknown countryside that, although lacking color and sparkle, was not devoid of charm, all would have been agreeable enough had they not been permeated by our feverish anticipation.

During the night of the 20th to the 21st, the platoon to which I belonged was quartered in the town hall in Quincy, a village in the northern part of the Woëvre forest. In the middle of the night an officer from staff headquarters appeared in the schoolroom in which we slept. Rudely awakened, our platoon leader jumped into his slippers and went to take the orders of the intruder, who wanted to be conducted to the colonel. The regiment left an hour later. We marched toward the front. In the open country, at the foot of the citadel of Montmédy, whose ancient bastions rose above a grassy escarpment, we first heard the cannon that the troops called "the brute"; and it was on the next day, during a halt, that we saw our first shrapnel as distant white wreaths in an azure sky. On the night of the 21st, we took up quarters in a tiny village next to Montmédy, called Iré-les-Prés; in the morning we left as escort to the supply train of our army corps. We had been told we were about to enter Belgium. I shall never forget the men's joy at this news. On the way a counterorder arrived, and a very long and very hard march brought my company to Velosnes, a village right next to the Belgian border. It was occupied by troops of the fourth regiment, some of whom had just returned from combat. In a house on the small square where the washhouse was located we could see three German prisoners through the window. We slept huddled together in a cold barn. As for me, stretched out on a pile of twigs, it was not too bad a night.

On the 23rd we encountered the first wounded I had seen during the campaign. Our company was assigned to dig trenches in front of Thonne-la-Long, a village as near to the border as Velosnes, though farther west. It was there, in those trenches we occupied until the morning of the 25th, that I spent my first two nights in the open. I find these words in my journal for August 23: "First day the impression is truly serious. . . . Many wounded on the roads. We could see beside the road (which was perpendicular to the trenches we were guarding) the remnants of two battalions of the 87th regiment. In sum, the rear of a great battle and, I believe, a great victory. Since the 21st, however, I have known that the Germans are in Brussels."

On the morning of the 25th we beat a retreat, and I realized that the hope expressed in the lines I have just quoted was misplaced. This immensely bitter disappointment, the stifling heat, the difficulties of marching along a road encumbered by artillery and convoys, and finally, the dysentery with which I was stricken the night before make the 25th of August live in my memory as one of the most painful days I have known. Shall I ever forget the two cups of hot coffee that a peasant woman gave me in a village near Han-les-Juvigny, where we happened to stop that day? For obvious reasons, I had had nothing to drink since morning. As long as I live, no liquid will ever give me greater pleasure than those two cups of foul "juice."

We spent the night in a forest. In summer, when the weather is fine, there is no nicer site for a bivouac, or, I believe, any more agreeable place to sleep. The leafy branches of the shelter filter any raw edge from the night air, and their barely perceptible fragrance lightly perfumes the fresh breezes that occasionally caress the sleeper's face. These slumbers "under the stars," this unencumbered sleep in which the lungs breathe easily, and from which one never awakes with a heavy head, though not deep, still provides pleasures unknown to those who sleep indoors. While we were relishing these charms, the enemy approached.

Owing to a delay in our order to move out, we were almost caught. Our rude awakening was followed by a forced march. On the way, we saw people abandoning their village in haste. Men, women, children, furniture, bundles of linen (and often the most disparate objects!) were piled on their wagons. These French peasants fleeing before an enemy against whom we could not protect them left a bitter impression, possibly the most maddening that the war has inflicted on us. We were to see them often during the retreat, poor refugees crowding the roads and village squares with their wagons. Wrenched from their homes, disoriented, dazed, and bullied by the gendarmes, they were troublesome but pathetic figures. At Baricourt, on the night of the 26th, while we slept in a sort of stable, they slept outside with their carts in the rain, the women holding their babies in their arms. The next morning, while held in reserve on a plateau that dominated the left bank of the Meuse, we watched the smoke from burning villages rise into a shrapnel-speckled sky.

The retreat lasted until September 5, interrupted by a three-day rest in the Grandpré hollow, first at Ternes, then at Grandpré itself, followed by four days of very hard marching. It left me with a vague but generally painful feeling similar to the ache that follows a bad night. The dusty roads along which the company was all too often strung out, the suffocating heat, especially while crossing woods whose meager growth provided little shade yet impeded the rare breaths of fresh air, the extremely late stops for the night and too-early departures, the uncomfortable accommodations, and the monotony of each day, all these would have been minor had we not had our backs constantly turned to the border, continually retreating without fighting. What was happening? We knew absolutely nothing. I suffered acutely from this ignorance. I stand bad news better than uncertainty, and nothing irritates me more than the suspicion that I am being deceived. Oh, what bitter days of retreat, of weariness, boredom, and anxiety!

On September 6 we saw the first wounded of the great battle that was then under way and which would become known to history as the Battle of the Marne. We were in front of the Château du Plessis, near Orconte in Champagne. Some wounded from colonial units passed us on the road, and we gave them something to drink. We were then deployed in a firing line behind a ditch. We thought we were about to go into action. Tired of doing nothing, the men were pleased but also solemn. This, however, proved a false alarm. On the morning of the 7th we moved to Larzicourt, a village of white rock on the right bank of the Marne; there the orchards were laden with delicious plums. We rested for three days, staying in the village only at night. By day we occupied the trenches we had dug in the wheat fields to the north. The weather was warm and beautiful. In front of us a forest hid the horizon. To the left, on the side of Vitry-le-François, in a sky that seemed immense above this flat countryside, we could see shells bursting incessantly in the distance.

On the evening of the 9th, just as my platoon had bedded down in our hayloft, we were awakened by an alert. Our regiment joined a long infantry column, and an interminable nocturnal march began. On leaving Larzicourt, we crossed the Marne. I believed our trenches were intended to cover, if necessary, a retreat beyond the river, and were therefore to be held at all costs and abandoned only after a total defeat. Hadn't we read at Larzicourt Joffre's order "to die on the spot rather than yield"? But now it seemed the great retreat had begun, since we were crossing the bridge we had been ordered to defend. Once more we resumed the long, dreary movement to the rear which had taken us from the border of Belgian Luxembourg to the Marne. So many times we had hoped to see it end: at the Meuse, at Grandpré, at almost all the villages in which we had billeted for a night, and finally, in the trenches of Larzicourt. Now once again we moved on. I believed all was lost. Had I only known! That night I sadly made my way along a tortuously winding road beside which clusters of trees took on a ghostly air against the dark sky; with anger in my heart, feeling the weight of the rifle I had never fired, and hearing the faltering footsteps of our half-sleeping men echo on the ground, I could only consider myself one more among the inglorious vanquished who had never shed their blood in combat. Yet back in Paris, at General Staff headquarters, they recognized, or at least suspected, victory. At Larzicourt, however, we knew nothing. On that march I suffered through long, painful hours.

Eventually, however, despite our endless detours, I realized that we were no longer heading southwest. I began to suspect that we were participating not in a retreat but in one of those troop movements that occur so frequently on arrival at a field of battle. This was true. As dawn approached, a heavy, chilling rain began to fall. We continued to march, despite our extreme fatigue and empty stomachs. One man found a German helmet, and we all tried it on in turn to relieve our boredom. At a crossroads we were met by an automobile. An officer from headquarters got out, spoke with our colonel for a few minutes, and then dashed off. We left the road through some high, soaked grasses on the right and climbed a steep slope. Abandoning our normal formation (in column), we shifted to one of platoons, four lines abreast, which regulations prescribe for troops approaching the line of fire under the threat of enemy artillery. Before reaching the crest, the regiment halted, and we were ordered to kneel. Day was breaking. The air was fresh. The rain had just stopped. Our damp capes were heavy. I was no longer sleepy. Our lieutenant left to see the captain or the battalion commander, I no longer remember which, and when he returned said, "You are about to fight. You have wanted this for a long time."

Resuming our march, we crossed the ridge and dropped into a valley that followed a road. We stopped again along its edge. On the left we could see the buildings of a farm, called, I believe, the Grand Perthes. The halt lasted a good while, perhaps an hour. The men were calm and a little pale. Our old captain, more shaken than ever, lit a pipe with the remark that it might well be his last. A lieutenant protested politely. I opened a can of cherry jam that the company's cyclist had picked up in some village the night before and passed it around. The first large shells arrived with a whistle. They fell a few hundred meters away, giving off heavy black smoke. A cow was killed and a man nearby. Then we began to move forward again, leaving the road and climbing the slope opposite the one by which we had come. We then passed a line of trenches occupied by another regiment, the 100th, I believe.

It is likely that as long as I live, at least if I do not become senile in my last days, I shall never forget the 10th of September, 1914. Even so, my recollections of that day are not altogether precise. Above all they are poorly articulated, a discontinuous series of images, vivid in themselves but badly arranged like a reel of movie film that showed here and there large gaps and the unintended reversal of certain scenes. On that day, under extremely violent fire from heavy artillery and machine guns, we advanced a few kilometers—at least three or four—from ten in the morning until six at night. Our losses were severe; my company alone, which was certainly not the worst hit, suffered almost one-third casualties. If my memory is correct, the time did not seem long; indeed, those dreadful hours must have passed fairly quickly. We advanced on an undulating field, at first dotted with clumps of trees, then completely bare. I recall that while crossing a hedge, I sharply questioned a man who had stopped. He answered, "I've been wounded." In fact, though he had not actually been hit, he had been stunned by the blast of a shell. He was the first to be hurt. Farther on I noticed the first body, a corporal who did not belong to our regiment. He lay on a slope all rigid with his face down, while around him were scattered some potatoes that had escaped from his camp kettle, which had opened as he fell. Machine gun bullets rustled through the branches like swarms of wasps. The heavy detonations of the shells shook the air, followed by the chorus of bursts that accompanied each explosion. The shrapnel shell, in particular, vibrates gently while tumbling through the air, only to stop abruptly at the end of its fall. How many of those murderous melodies did I hear on that day! I hunched my head between my shoulders, awaiting the silence and perhaps the fatal blow.

Behind one of the small woods I lost my platoon, but I found it again farther on. The men were lying face down on the yellow earth. Behind us the colonel had been knocked over by a large shell, but he got up and rejoined us unhurt. Next to me a corporal had been wounded in the arm and knee. The other platoon leader and I began bandaging his wounds, but were both hit: my colleague fairly seriously in the thigh, I only slightly in the right arm. The bullet, after piercing my sleeve, had the decency to exit immediately, merely burning my skin. Since the pain was severe, I first thought I was seriously injured, but then quickly realized that it was nothing. At about the same time, a sudden panic gripped our platoon, caused, as far as I can remember, by some machine gunners' horses. Someone had stupidly brought the guns up there to establish a battery, which was quite impossible under such a hail of fire. The animals stampeded and spread confusion among the rest of us. I still see myself running, upright, trying to get away from two horses that for some inexplicable reason seem prodigiously large in my memory. I also recall shouting, "Don't panic. Above all, don't panic, or we're lost." Then, on our lieutenant's order, we all rushed toward the right to reach a ridge behind which the next platoons had already taken cover. Quartermaster S. was settled there, half seated, half reclining against the slope. As I passed at top speed, he shouted at me to dive into the ditch in front of him, and I followed his excellent advice.

How long did we stay in that fold in the earth? How many minutes, or how many hours, I am not sure. We were crowded against each other and piled one on top of another. Since the enemy artillery had us under fire on the right flank, the slope in front offered us illusory protection at best. Many men were killed or wounded. For some time I had on my right our chief sergeant major, a big blond fellow with an open manner and a peasant's speech. He had been hit on the hand; a blood-soaked rag reddened his fingers. The wound was light. The poor man was killed toward the end of the day, but by then I had lost track of him. I was half lying on my neighbor to the left. I think I have never detested anyone so much as that individual, whom I had never seen before that day, never met again, and doubtless would not recognize if I ever should meet him in the future. He had cramps in his legs, on which I was lying, and he insisted that to relieve him I should raise myself, although this would have needlessly exposed me to death. I am still glad I refused, and I hope the self-centered clod suffers often from rheumatism. In front of me, next to S., my company's adjutant was seated with his back against the slope; although he had placed his haversack on his head for added protection, he trembled each time a shell whistled by. The wounded cried out. One of them begged the colonel alternately first to help him, then to finish him off. I believe I was quite calm. The spirit of curiosity, which rarely deserts me, had not disappeared. I remember first noting that the smoke from time shells was an ochre color, as distinguished from the black fumes of the percussion shells. I nevertheless found war an ugly business, the faces of men awaiting and dreading death not beautiful to behold, and I vaguely recalled some pages from Tolstoy.

The colonel was on my left together with his adjutant. With one knee on the ground, he was attempting to see over the ridge. He was pale and seemed undecided. Finally he ordered an advance. A few of our regiment had pushed on ahead of us and we had to catch up with them. I said "ordered," but "beseeched" would be more accurate. "Let's go, boys, we must move forward. Your comrades are out there in front. They're firing. You can't leave them alone. Noncoms, lead the way!" It was hard to leave our slope. I have already explained why it gave only meager protection, but we nonetheless had felt ourselves more secure than we really were. We had confidence in this chance cover, poor as it was, and we were filled with a quite understandable reluctance to launch ourselves upright into open space. I remember thinking very clearly at that moment, "Since the colonel wants it, we must get up and go forward. But it's all over, there's no use hoping. I will be killed." Then we rose and ran. I shouted, "Forward, Eighteenth!" We reached a path that followed a slight rise in the ground. There, finding a small group of soldiers, we stopped. Beyond the irregularly tufted grass that covered the crest of the slope, we could see a wide landscape. With good eyesight, apparently, it was possible to make out the enemy's positions. The officers ordered us to open fire. My arm being too painful to manage my rifle, I simply transmitted the orders. In any case, firing over such a long distance at objects so difficult to see was undoubtedly ineffective. Some men near me were wounded. The day was nearly over. We prayed for the arrival of complete darkness, which would end the fighting. The German bombardment gradually slowed. At the same time, our guns picked up the pace. What joy to hear not German but French shells whistling above us and aimed at the enemy! As evening fell, I risked leaving the shelter of the slope to go to one of our corporals who lay seriously wounded a few meters behind. I could not do much for him. At nightfall I ordered two of his men to carry him to an ambulance; but unable to get through, they finally had to abandon him along the way. In the deepening dusk the regiment fell back to the embankment where our last advance had begun.

It was there that we spent the night. From time to time a few bullets whistled by. About 10 P.M., I believe, the German machine guns resumed firing without doing us any harm. They soon fell silent. We were famished. I had a can of sardines; I opened it, ate a few, and shared the rest. It was cold. During the summer campaign we had never before experienced such chill. The wounded screamed or groaned. Many asked for something to drink. We organized a fatigue party to get water, but despite a long search it found nothing. Its return caused an alarm and, I suspect, drew some rifle fire. Later during the night we had several anxious moments. I recall getting myself up to order the men, who had been more or less assembled, to fix their bayonets, though after a sleepless night followed by a rough day they would probably have offered feeble resistance to any attack. The smell of blood permeated the air. Yet despite this stale odor, despite the cries and the groans, despite our fears, I slept for a few hours, stretched out in a furrow.

Shortly before daybreak, the order came for us to return to the rear. We reached the valley where we had spent the evening before going into combat. The colonel commanding our brigade passed on horseback. He congratulated us, shouting, "Vive le 272!" and informed us that the Germans had retreated. Since we had nothing to eat, he ordered the lieutenant who was acting as commander of the company in place of our wounded captain to kill one cow and one sheep from the flocks that were wandering scattered and bewildered, with no shepherds, on the hill behind us. These innocent victims were put to death with revolver shots. During the morning I went to visit the field hospital, where one of the wounded had asked for me. There I saw injuries and faces in agony. The men did not cry out, as they had done the day before on the battlefield. They barely moaned, and their faces spoke more of weariness than of suffering.

Despite so many painful sights, it does not seem to me that I was sad on that morning of September 11. Needless to say, I did not feel like laughing. I was serious, but my solemnity was without melancholy, as befitted a satisfied soul; and I believe that my comrades felt the same. I recall their faces, grave yet content. Content with what? Well, first content to be alive. It was not without a secret pleasure that I contemplated the large gash in my canteen, the three holes in my coat made by bullets that had not injured me, and my painful arm, which, on inspection, was still intact. On days after great carnage, except for particularly painful personal grief, life appears sweet. Let those who will condemn this self-centered pleasure. Such feelings are all the more solidly rooted in individuals who are ordinarily only half aware of their existence. But our good humor had another, more noble source. The victory that the colonel had announced to us so briefly as he trotted by had elated me. Perhaps if I had thought about it, I might have felt some doubts. The Germans had retreated before us, but how did I know they had not advanced elsewhere? Happily, my thoughts were vague. The lack of sleep, the exertions of the march and combat, and the strain of my emotions had tired my brain; but my sensations were vivid. I had little comprehension of the battle. It was the victory of the Marne, but I would not have known what to call it. What matter, it was victory. The bad luck that had weighed us down since the beginning of the campaign had been lifted. My heart beat with joy that morning in our small, dry, devastated valley in Champagne. [. . .]

The nights left even more vivid memories than the days. We were becoming better adapted. I now rarely ordered any firing. Nevertheless, I hardly slept. I spent long hours listening to the sounds of the forest. There was always a man on guard in the trench, ordered to inform me of the slightest alert. When he was not in his place beside me, the information he wished to give me was transmitted in a low voice from mouth to mouth. If the lookout was a bit nervous, the communications I received were occasionally bizarre. Some were weirdly precise, such as: "Sergeant, *they* are at twelve meters," when in reality *they* had not budged from their holes. On the other hand, some were terribly vague: "Sergeant, we heard a noise." When I asked, "What noise? Where?" I received no answer.

The nights were very dark. Our eyes were of no use. To avoid being surprised, we could count only on our ears. I learned to distinguish the sounds that comprise the great nocturnal murmur: the tap-tap of the raindrops on the foliage, so like the rhythm of distant footsteps, the somewhat metallic scraping sound of very dry leaves falling on the leaf-strewn forest floor (which our men so often mistook for the click of an automatic loader introduced into a German rifle breech). I could not contemplate my odd occupation there without laughing, and it was with astonishment that I realized I was matching the heroes of James Fenimore Cooper: the subtle Mohicans, or the keen trappers whom I had so admired as a child.

Things began to happen on October 17. I have mentioned that our left was covered by a trench, manned by some of the 20th company. I had visited it while establishing liaison with our neighbors. It was a pretty poor job, too shallow and much too wide. Its occupants were at fault for not working to improve it. Having frequently been fired at by artillery, rifles, and trench mortars, they finally abandoned the position on the morning of the 19th. I realized that something serious was taking place when some panic-stricken soldiers rushed into my trench crying, "Here we are! Here we are!" I had trouble understanding what they wanted. They were men of the 20th, apparently attached to a reserve unit, who had been sent to reinforce their comrades. Having lost their way in the woods, they threw themselves into the first trench they saw. I sent them along in the right direction.

Then there was the arrival of our reserve platoon, the third, commanded at the time by Adjutant Mathon. It took up a position on our left, deployed in a skirmish line. We feared that the Germans, taking advantage of the withdrawal of the 20th, would try to disrupt our line. We had to prevent my trench from being outflanked. I helped Mathon place his men. With a single shot, Mathon, one of the best marksmen in the regiment, killed a German who, having crept stealthily through the trees, had suddenly appeared a short distance in front of us. Accompanied by a sergeant and two soldiers, Mathon went to retrieve the body. Those were our orders: staff headquarters relied heavily on the papers that we sometimes found in the enemy's pockets. Of the four-man patrol, only Mathon returned uninjured, but without the body. One soldier was killed, and the sergeant and the second soldier were both seriously wounded. Our enemies protected themselves well.

That afternoon our third platoon was replaced by one from the 24th company, sent to strengthen our battalion. A group of our new companions established themselves in the woods to the left. The rest came to reinforce us in our own trenches. Normally their leader, an adjutant, should have taken over the command that I had held up to then. By tacit agreement, however, not only the men of my own squad but all the others in the trench remained under my orders. The adjutant spent the entire time seated at the bottom of a hole, his saber between his legs and his head bowed. He lacked authority. When the commander of a trench orders a volley, presumably his chief concern is to make his men aim with care. To aim is to look, and to look is to offer one's head to enemy fire. To aim is thus dangerous. But I know only one way to persuade others to take risks, and that is to take the same risk yourself. Elementary as this truth may seem, the adjutant to whom I have referred apparently did not understand it. During the first days my men aimed too high, which was inevitable because they did not dare to raise their bodies, and too quickly, because their main purpose was to expose themselves for the least possible time. I remember having landed with all my might on one of my neighbors who, cowering in the trench with only his hand above the parapet, was brandishing his gun backward with the trigger in the air. Needless to say, I used such forceful arguments only in exceptional cases. Ordinarily I reasoned with the men, I shamed them, and with each command to fire I repeated, "Aim low!" Above all, at every volley I set the example by not hesitating to raise my own head. In this way my men rapidly acquired the habit of courage. The precision of their shooting saved us, as we shall see.

The night of the 17th to 18th was not bad: a few alerts, a few volleys, and that was all. Toward eight o'clock on the morning of the 18th, the Germans began to shower us furiously with big grenades from their trench mortars. They fell with a thud and did not explode until a few seconds after impact. As a result, we had to develop skills to avoid them. Our observers were trained to distinguish the noise they made on landing and to shout, "Bomb on the right!" or "Bomb on the left!" We would throw ourselves down, shielding our heads with a knapsack or duffel on the side from which the threat came. But on that particular morning we were still inexperienced, and so in spite of everything, it was one of those situations in which all precautions were without effect. I was on the extreme right of the trench. I had placed myself there because I had hoped—unrealistically, as it proved—to be able to maintain voice communication with the corporal of the 13th squad, who, while nominally under my orders, commanded the neighboring trench. On my left was a miner, G., from the Pas-de-Calais, a fine lad, intelligent and calm, who I knew could be counted on in any crisis. I was genuinely fond of him, as he was of me. I had stationed him beside me, first because his conversation amused me, but even more because his acute vision reinforced my own weak eyes. At the beginning of that appalling bombardment he had said, "This is going to be another bad day for the 272d." I answered, "Of course not, not at all!" We were each crouched in our own corner, with our knapsack, haversack, and canteen set up around our heads like so many shields. It seemed to me that we had been in that position for some time, with the shells raining all around without hitting anyone. Then one burst with a roar on the parapet about three meters to my left. I heard G. groan and felt his body slump heavily on my shoulder. I could not turn around without fully exposing myself, so I muttered some words of encouragement of the sort that instinctively comes to mind on such occasions: "Courage, old man. It's nothing. Don't be afraid." Finally, taking advantage of a lull, I looked at him. When I saw his face, I stopped talking. A few minutes later he was dead. His poor body had been pierced by a fragment coming my way which had been stopped by his flesh, unquestionably saving my life. Our neighbors thought that it was I who was *in extremis.* A man of the 24th was wounded by the same blast, and gathering all his energy he attempted to leave the trench and get his wounds bound up. I tried to stop him but without success. At last the bombardment ended. I rose quickly and ordered the men to fire, fearing an attack that did not materialize. I was able to summon some men from the rear to come and get G.'s body. I helped them leave the trench. For the very first time, my arms strained under the weight of human flesh from which life had departed. Also, for the first time in this campaign, I mourned a true friend. The 24th also had a fatality. Until the morning of the 19th, he remained unburied on the rear parapet where he had been carried, his face turned toward the sun.

Through the following night we waited in vain for the attack. The day of the 19th passed without any serious incidents, though not without shrapnel and bombs. One man of the 24th suffered a slight wound in his hand when he ventured outside the trench. During the afternoon we noticed that the Germans, who were some thirty meters from us, were building a yellowish ramp. They were working lying down or on their knees; their hands were exposed for only an instant while they threw the dirt from their shovels. I ordered the men to fire, but we neither hit nor frightened them. M.,[3] who had taken charge of the fourth platoon, replacing the sick lieutenant, sent word that our commanding officers were expecting an attack.

At dusk, about 5 P.M., we were hit by a sudden volley of bullets. Through the clatter of rifle fire I immediately recognized the characteristic sound of those machine guns that our men had aptly named "coffee mills." One of them was extremely close. If we gave it time, it would demolish our parapet. Then its fire would force us to cower in the bottom of the trench, so that the Germans could pounce on us without warning. We had to silence it. Alas, if we had only had the weapons then that we were issued later, especially those marvelous melanite grenades! But we had only our rifles. To rid ourselves of the machine gun, we had to fire at its gunners. That was possible during the intervals in its firing, which was not continuous. But how to hit it, if we did not know its exact location? I raised myself up while it was firing and saw its flame: a big flash, redder than that of ordinary rifles. It stood there under a tree, precisely where, during the day, we had seen the yellow ramp, which I suddenly understood had been built specifically to protect this formidable weapon. The machine gun stopped. I ordered a volley, directing the fire by pointing at the target. The men aimed admirably. The machine gun resumed its spraying of our trench; and we ceased firing. Once more it stopped, and we resumed our volleys. And so on. After a little time, the Germans repositioned their gun, and the same old game continued. How long, altogether, did it last? I do not know; but I do know that the machine gun was finally silenced. We no longer heard it; and at almost the same moment, the German rifles fell silent. M. sent us his congratulations as well as those of the captain.

The Germans had not, however, given up hope of wiping out our position. During the night they attacked us three times. What a racket! They left their trenches; we heard them coming, but we never saw them. Our shots stopped them each time. I directed the fire standing up, scanning the woods to judge its effect. I had rolled up my blanket around my chin as a sort of protective collar. Only my eyes showed from under my kepi; and I folded a scarf over my face in the no doubt mistaken hope that it would diminish the force of any hit. I had placed myself near the middle of the trench. My two neighbors, a corporal of the 24th company, very brave and self-possessed, and a soldier from my platoon, both pulled my cloak to force me back down. I said, "You're very kind, but leave me alone!" The third attack found me asleep, having succumbed to my fatigue in spite of myself. Someone woke me with "Sergeant, sergeant!" and I rose just in time to shout, "Fire at will at the brush in front. Fire hard! Fire hard!"

In the morning we were finally relieved under a hail of bullets. One man lost his way in the woods. We never saw him again. What a relief, when we were finally out of La Gruerie, to see the sun shining on the meadows of La Harazée! I learned that there were three wounded in the third squad and two in the second half platoon. We returned, exhausted, parched, and light-hearted, to La Neuville-au-Pont. During a halt on the side of the road where it turns off from Vienne-le-Château, the captain came and congratulated me, telling my men that they could follow me under fire with confidence, and added that I was a real *poilu*. I answered that my beard, now full grown and wholly unkempt, justified the epithet.

Notes

1. Proclaimed that afternoon by Wilhelm II. On August 1 Germany ordered mobilization and declared war on France's ally, Russia.
2. On August 3 Germany had declared war on France and invaded Belgium.
3. Mathon.

Undertones
of War

EDMUND BLUNDEN

III

THE CHERRY ORCHARD

We returned to the front line, and after some nights there Penruddock told me that we were going out to rest billets; I was to go ahead with some non-commissioned officers to take over the accommodation. Other representatives from the other companies would join me next morning early in the Old British Line opposite our former headquarters. I therefore took my party there that night, and gave them word about reappearing at the proper hour; then, entering our little dugout now held by another company's officers, I asked someone's leave to sleep on a bench there. My warm-coat was not adequate, and I was irritably awake in the early day when from his more comfortable lair in the recess the company commander, yawning and stretching, looked over to me and charitably asked, "What's that thing?" I sat up quickly and told him; he stayed with the battalion long enough for me to be equally uncharitable to him, but at that luxurious period there was a wonderful superiority about some of the original officers of the battalion. It made life difficult. When the billeting party was assembled, this haughtiness was again discernible. Man is a splendid animal, wherever possible.

The joyful path away from the line, on that glittering summer morning, was full of pictures for my infant war-mind. History and nature were beginning to harmonize in the quiet of that sector. In the orchard through which we passed immediately, waggons had been dragged together once with casks and firm gear to form barricades; I felt that they should never be disturbed again, and the memorial raised near them to the dead of 1915 implied a closed chapter. The empty farmhouses were not yet effigies of agony or mounds of punished, atomized material; they could still shelter, and they did. Their hearths could still boil the pot. Acres of self-sown wheat glistened and sighed as we wound our way between, where rough scattered pits recorded a hurried firing-line of long ago. Life, life abundant sang here and smiled; the lizard ran warless in the warm dust; and the ditches were trembling quick with odd tiny fish, in worlds as remote as Saturn.

Presently we came to a shrine on a paved road, and near by the houses were still confidently held by their usual families. Their front windows, between the blue shutters, one and all exhibited silk postcards, with excessively loving messages and flags ("The Flags of Civilization") and flowers on them, neighboured by "Venus" pencils, red herrings in tumblers, and chocolate bouchées in silver paper. Innocency of life! how it carried one back, so that the long hot walk to Hinges, our due resting-place, was like the flight of a bird. And yet, when war seemed for the time being left behind, belts of barbed wire again appeared, crossing the beetfields, and wicker-lined trenches curved along waterways and embankments. And yet — so I thought! not having cleared up the point that the defence of a country must be miles in depth.

Had our leaders cleared it up? This may be lightly touched upon as I proceed.

Hinges was a village on the canal from Béthune to Aire, a place of orchards "hidden from day's garish eye," of mud barns, of columned pollards and level flourishing fields. That part of it which we were to inhabit was called Hingettes, and adjoined the canal. I found the company commander from whom I was to take over sitting pleasantly in the tall open parlour window of a big farmhouse, just as Shelley would have been sitting; he received me as a sort of fellow-collegian, and my business was made easy for me. Such characters and occasions were the charm of the B.E.F. There was a grace that war never overcast. If you except the great refuse reservoir in the middle of the farmyard, this place was in itself one of the happiest to which my lamented battalion ever went. But the men had hardly exchanged nods with sleep, next morning, when a training programme was put into force. One of the few advantages which I had fancied we should have in coming to France was a relaxation from the artificial parts of army life — "eyewash," in the term then universal. But here, after two or three weeks in the line, was a battalion undergoing the same old treatment, which uselessly reduced its chances of rest. Uselessly? I believe so: these men were volunteers of the first months of the war, most willing but most intelligent, and the only effect that petty militarism and worrying restlessness had on them was to set them grumbling. About now, the signallers revealed the general feeling by sending in to the colonel a round robin protesting against field punishment awarded one of them. This beautiful but unregimental act was the cause of a parade, when the colonel spoke with surprise and anger; yet I believe he knew what was really annoying his subjects, without being able to change the orders from above.

The training programme did not last long. About five one afternoon, when the greener light began to cool the senses, and many a letter was being written and many a pack of cards starting to run, all officers were called to battalion headquarters. Mystery: theory: premonition. "I told you so, Limbery," muttered Charlwood, with a doleful smile. "I knew we should be tooling up the road again in a couple of nights." What exactly was amiss at the line the adjutant, speaking in his dry, deliberate way, did not announce: there was something in the air, he admitted, and the battalion was to take over trenches south of the Canal. Another doleful smile from Charlwood to Limbery-Buse. The conference scattered to the various billets with no delay, and the companies prepared for the new trench tour. Floors were swept clean, stores of bully beef and bombs examined and found correct, and all else attended to. But I, to my surprise, was not to go up at once to the trenches; an elementary gas course, lasting three days, was prescribed for me. I nevertheless watched the company depart down the muddy by-road past the ovens and tents in a depressed mood, nor was I alone in regret. The smelly little farmyard dog, who had been taken off his chain in the night by our humanitarians, and walked out into a liberty which he could scarcely remember since his puppy days, also gazed, and hung a mournful head.

It must have been during this brief encampment at Hinges that Kapp ceased to philosophize, scandalize, harmonize and anatomize among us, and departed for that mysterious Press Bureau where it was supposed his remarkable faculty for languages would be needed; and, while we lost him, we gained another artist of quality. This was Neville Lytton. Tall, of a fine carriage, his outward and physical appearance expressing an intellect rather than a body, he at once attracted me. He was outspoken in his loathing of war, he did not rely on his rank to cover all points of argument or action, and his gallantry in going through the dirtiness, the abnegations of service, the attack upon all his refinement, was great. It naturally remained unrecognized by the crasser part of the officers and men. He commanded the company with thoroughness and caution, and sat at our mess, piously endeavouring to keep up his vegetarian habits, and to keep alive a spirit of artistic insight without refusing military method.

So the company has gone down the road, and doesn't know quite where it is bound for; and here, with my batman Shearing, lately a gardener, I am free for an hour to play *Il Penseroso* round the cherry orchard and between the orderly thrifty root-crops. I will stay in this farmhouse while the gas course lasts — the school is only a few miles away, at Essars — and get the old peasant in the evenings to recite more *La Fontaine* to me, in the Béthune dialect! and read — Bless me, Kapp has gone away with my *John Clare!*

He has the book yet, for all I know; has he the memory of Hinges?

On the next morning, that had risen in calm glories as though there were no war, I took my way along the canal bank towards Essars, swinging my stick, and noticing the "twined flowers," the yellowhammer and the wagtail. The water was clear, and glittering roach buoyed themselves in the light, or young jack shooting into deeper water flicked up the mud in the shallows. A Red Cross barge steamed in state along the channel. Presently I turned across the fields, and the spire of Essars came in view among the rich mantles of trees, which canopied the road from Béthune to Neuve Chapelle. The gas school was a little cluster of huts in this busily traversed yet unruined village; and here a number of us went through gas chambers and took spasmodic notes of lectures. It was all very leisurely, alarming and useful. A slight asthma caused me to be exempt from running with the flannel bag over my head. The flannel mask was respected, for (as I had already noticed in the line) it kept your ears warm! It smelt odd and breathing in it became sugary, while the goggles seemed to be inevitably veiled with moisture, highly beneficial in a crisis to one's opponent.

At lunch-time I vanished into the fields, and under one knotty willow by a dyke, ate my ration, still, as an angler of sorts, studying the waters. But one of my constant instinctive terrors in early life had been the sudden sight of great fish lurking; and I remember the start with which I became aware, in this little dyke, under a thick hanging branch, of a ponderous and ugly carp. He set eyes on me almost as soon, and dived. I mention this, to show what tenacity the fancy had in days of "grim reality." One lunch hour I spent less irrationally with two officers of the Gloucester Pioneer Battalion, which had an enviable reputation as a gathering of good fellows altogether; my friends were Hillard and Crockford, whom I see yet in the *al fresco* spirit of that leafy corner; but Hillard was killed soon afterwards. There was poetry about these two, nor was I afraid to speak of poetry to them, and so long as the war allowed a country-rectory quietude and lawny coolness three kilometres from the line, and summer had even greater liberty than usual to multiply his convolvulus, his linnets and butterflies, while life was nevertheless threatened continually with the last sharp turnings into the unknown, an inestimable sweetness of feeling beyond Corot or Marvell made itself felt through all routine and enforcement; an unexampled simplicity of desire awoke in the imagination and rejoiced like Ariel in a cowslip-bell. It was for a short time, but even that fact heightened the measure.

IX

The Storm

Marching west from Béthune, we had nothing to trouble us except our packs and the General, who never exhibited his talent for being in all places at once more terrifically. My own place was alongside my friends C. and R., who, with the prospect of a court-martial, were at first rather quiet, but presently began to be themselves. They rejoiced at least that their equipment was carried on the transport. Mine was not, and every halt was welcome. Our road showed us noble woods, and gentle streams turning water-wheels, and cleanly green and white villages. The battalion was billeted at Auchel, a considerable mining town, for one night; I remember that well because, when we got in at eleven or so, the advance party had not made all their arrangements, and I set out to find shelter for my servant and myself. Seeing a young woman at an upper window, looking out in some wonder at the sudden incursion in the streets, I addressed her with the most persuasive French I could find, and she (note it, recording Angel, or spirit of Sterne, if you did not then) hastened down to give us food and lodging, and next day piano practice and *L'Illustration*. Emerging from the slag-heaps of Auchel, the battalion moved deviously, but now definitely southward, and came without unusual event to the flimsy outlandish village of Monchy-Breton (known, of course, as Monkey Britain), near St. Pol. The weather was heavy and musty, the usual weather of British operations.

Near this place was an extent of open country (chiefly under wheat) which in its ups and downs and occasional thick woodlands resembled the Somme battlefield; here, therefore, we were trained for several days. The Colonel told us that the ground was held to be an excellent facsimile of the scene of our "show." Hardly a man knew so much as the name of the southern village from which we were to attack; but we saw with mixed feelings from our practice that the jumping off position was one side of a valley, the position to be captured the other side, and all began to be proficient in moving to the particular "strong point" or other objective plotted out for them. Gas was loosed over us; we crouched down in trenches while the roaring heat of the flammenwerfer curled up in black smoke above; a Scottish expert, accompanied by well-fed, wool-clad gymnastic demonstrators, preached to us the beauty of the bayonet, though I fear he seemed to most of us more disgusting than inspiring in that peacefully ripening farmland. In the intervals we bought chocolate from the village women who had tramped out far enough to reach us; and so we passed the time. Our manoeuvres and marches were quite hard work, and in the evenings the calm of Monchy-Breton and its mud huts under their heavy verdure was not much insulted.

At battalion headquarters conferences were held over attack. "Jake" Lin-tott, the clever assistant-adjutant who had been with the Canadians at Ypres, had drawn a fine bold map of the destined ground and trenches on the reverse of our waterproof table-cloth. When conferences began, the table-cloth was turned over, and the map used. One sunny evening after we had been talking out the problems and proceedings of the coming battle, and making all clear, with the map, it was felt that something was wrong, and some one turning noted a face at a window. We hurried out to catch a spy, but missed him, if he was one; certainly he was a stranger.

Nothing else distinguished our Monchy-Breton period; after a fine night or two sleeping under the stars, we left its chicken-runs and muddy little cart-tracks about the middle of August, and were entrained at Ligny St. Flochel, between Arras and St. Pol. A German aeroplane hovered above the act, and we sat waiting for the train to start, in a familiar attitude, with trying apprehensions. We travelled with the gravity due to hot summer weather, and found the process better than marching. But the Somme was growing nearer! Leaving the railway, we were billeted one night in a village called Le Souich. The occasion was marked at battalion headquarters by a roast goose, which the old farmer whose house we had invaded had shot at shortest range with the air of a mighty hunter *("Je le tire à l'oeil!")*; and I joyfully remember how Millward, that famed cricketer, gave us an hour's catching practice in the orchard with apples instead of cricket-balls or bombs.

Thence the battalion took the road, in great glare and heat and dust, kilometre after kilometre. The changeful scenery of hills and woods was indeed dramatic and captivating after our long session in the flat country, but as the march wore on most of us were too used up to comment on it. Many men fell out, and officers and non-commissioned officers for the most part were carrying two or three rifles to keep others in their place. At Thievres there was a long halt, and a demand for water; some thrifty inhabitants produced it at so much a bucket, thus giving occasion for a critical pun on the name of the place. The villagers' device for dismantling wells and pumps, and their inquisitive probing for information, disturbed our men's philosophy a little. Eventually the battalion encamped in a solemnly glorious evening at the edge of a great wood called Bois du Warnimont, with the divisional artillery alongside; the stragglers came in, and were sternly told their fault at "orderly room" next day—we blush to think how many there were, but our experience of marching had recently been meagre.

Warnimont Wood, verdant and unmolested, was six or seven miles west of the terrible Beaumont Hamel, but we hardly realized that yet. A reconnoitring party was soon sent up to the line, and I remember thinking (according to previous experience) that I should be able to buy a pencil in the village of Englebelmer, on the way; but when we got there its civilians had all been withdrawn. Therein lay the most conspicuous difference between this district and our old one with the cottagers and débitants continuing their affairs almost in view of the front trench. The majority of the reconnoitring party went on horseback, I on a bicycle; and the weather had turned rainy, and the quality of Somme mud began to assert itself. My heavy machine went slower and slower, and stopped dead; I was thrown off. The brake was clogged with most tenacious mud, typifying future miseries. Presently we reached an empty village called Mesnil, which, although it stood yet in the plausible shape of farmhouses and outbuildings, not shattered into heaps, instantly aroused unpleasant suspicions. These suspicions were quickly embodied in the savage rush of heavy shrapnel shells, uncoiling their clingy green masses of smoke downwards while their white-hot darts scoured the acre below. On the west side, a muddy sunken lane with thickets of nettles on one bank and some precarious dugouts in the other led past the small brick station, and we turned out of it by two steps up into a communication trench chopped in discoloured chalk. It smelt ominous, and there was a grey powder here and there thrown by shellbursts, with some of those horrible conical holes in the trench sides, blackened and fused, which meant "direct hits" and by big stuff. If ever there was a vile, unnerving, and desperate place in the battle zone, it was the Mesnil end of Jacob's Ladder, among the heavy battery positions, and under enemy observation.

Jacob's Ladder was a long trench, good in parts, stretching from Mesnil with many angles down to Hamel on the River Ancre, requiring flights of stairs at one or two steep places. Leafy bushes and great green and yellow weeds looked into it as it dipped sharply into the green valley by Hamel, and hereabouts the aspect of peace and innocence was as yet prevailing. A cow with a crumpled horn, a harvest cart should have been visible here and there. The trenches ahead were curious, and not so pastoral. Ruined houses with rafters sticking out, with half-sloughed plaster and crazy window-frames, perched on a hillside, bleak and piteous that cloudy morning; derelict trenches crept along below them by upheaved gardens, telling the story of savage bombardment. Further on was a small chalk cliff facing the river, with a rambling but remarkable dugout in it called Kentish Caves. The front line lay over this brow, and descended to the wooded marshes of the Ancre in winding and gluey irregularity. Running through it towards the German line went the narrow Beaucourt road, and the railway to Miraumont and Bapaume; in the railway bank was a look-out post called the Crow's Nest, with a large periscope. South of the Ancre was massive high ground, and on that a black vapour of smoke and naked tree trunks or charcoal, which I found was called Thiepval Wood. The Somme indeed!

The foolish persistence of ruins that ought to have fallen but stood grimacing, and the dark day, chilled my spirit. Let us stop this war, and walk along to Beaucourt before the leaves fall. I smell autumn again. The Colonel who was showing Harrison the lie of the land betrayed no such apprehension. He walked about, with indicatory stick, speaking calmly of the night's shelling, the hard work necessary to keep the trenches open, and the enemy's advantage of observation, much as if showing off his rockery at home; and this confidence fortunately began to grow in me, so that I afterwards regarded the sector as nothing too bad. As we went along the slippery chalk cuttings and past large but thin-roofed and mouldy dugouts, it was my duty to choose positions for forward dumps of bombs, ammunition, water and many other needs, against the approaching battle. When we had made our round, we went back across the village to the colonel's exemplary underground headquarters in Pottage Trench, a clean and quiet little alley under the whispering shadow of aspen trees in a row; and thence, not unwillingly, back further, up Jacob's Ladder to Mesnil, which now smelt stronger still of high explosive, and away.

The battalion moved up to a straggling wood called from its map reference P. 18, near the little town of Mailly-Maillet. Here, three miles from the enemy's guns, it was thought sufficient to billet us in tents (and those, to round off my posthumous discontent, used specimens). Mailly-Maillet was reported to have been until recently a delightful and flourishing little place, but it was in the sere and yellow; its long château wall was broken by the fall of shell-struck trees; its church, piously protected against shrapnel by straw mats, had been hit. On the road to the town, we had remarked on almost every cornfield gate the advertisement of "Druon-Lagniez, Quincaillier à Mally-Maillet"; but, seeking out his celebrated shop, one found it already strangely ventilated, and its dingy remnants of cheap watches or brass fittings on the floor somehow disappointing to the expectation. In a garden solitude of this little town there rose a small domed building, as yet but a trifle disfigured, with plaster and glass shaken down to the mosaic floor, in the middle of which stood the marble tomb of a great lady, a princess, if I do not forget, of a better century. There the pigeons fluttered and alighted; and the light through the high pale-tinted panes seemed to rest with inviolable grace on holy ground.

Work at Hamel immediately called for me, with a party of good warriors, duly paraded and commanded by my invincible friend Sergeant Worley. The first night that we reached the village, wild with warfare, rain was rushing down, and we willingly waited for dawn in a musty cellar, wet through, yet not anxious on that account. I had already chosen the nooks and corners in the front line where I would make up in readiness for our battle small reserves of rations, rifle ammunition, grenades, reels of barbed wire, planks, screw pickets, wire netting, sandbags; my party therefore took up their burdens from the central stores in Hamel, and followed me to the different points.

The chief dump in Hamel lay between a new but not weather-proof residence (its back door opening on Thiepval), and a tall hedge with brambles straying over our stacks of planks and boxes, making a scene passably like the country builder's yard. A soldiers' cemetery was open at all hours just behind this kind illusion. I may say that we worked hard, up and down, and even felt a little proud as the forward stores grew to useful size. When the Brigade bombing officer, suddenly pouncing upon me in a lonely trench, told me that my boxes of bombs at one place would all be ruined by exposure to the weather, and that he should report me to the General, I damned him and wept. My critic (an old adversary) had just arrived from England. But I was afraid of the General. Apart from that, there was no great trouble; once carelessly stacking some bombs above the parados in sight of some enemy post, we returned with the next consignment to find nothing but new shellholes there. All day long that valley was echoing with bombardment, but for the most part it was on Thiepval Wood that the fury thundered; and we, at mealtimes, sat freely like navvies in some ruin and put away considerable quantities of bread, bully, and cheese. And how well we knew our Hamel! The "Café du Centre" was as real to us as the Ritz, though now it was only some leaning walls and a silly signboard. The insurance agent's house, with its gold bee sign still inviting custom (not in our line!); the stuffed pheasant by his glass dome, drooping a melancholy beak and dishonoured plumage, opposite our duckboard and wire repository; the superior hip bath lying on the roadside towards the line; the spring of beautiful clear drink there; the level-crossing keeper's red house, with its cellars full of petrol-tins of water, in the direction of Thiepval—these and every other lineament of poor Hamel photographed themselves in us. The ridiculously fat tom-cat which had refused to run wild knew us well. We humped our boxes of deadly metal past the agricultural exhibition of innocent metal on the wayside; what were ploughs and drags and harrows to Hamel now? What rural economist had collected them there?

The date of the attack was suddenly postponed. A runner discovered me, with this news. We went back to the wood in which the battalion, not too well pleased with its surroundings, had dug short protective lengths of trench. These, however, could not protect us from a plague of wasps, and the engineers had to add to their varied service that of clearing some monstrous nests with gun-cotton. After an agreeable evening passed in exploring the rambling streets of Mailly, and in watching a huge howitzer in action, fed with shells by means of a pulley, and those shells large enough to be seen plainly mounting up to the sky before they disappeared in annihilating descent upon "Thiepval Crucifix," we turned in. I was as bold as Harrison and others, and put on my pyjamas; but at midnight the shriek of shells began, meant for our camp, and we slipped shivering into the nearest slit of trench.

There were gas shells, and high explosive, and samples of both missed our trench by yards; the doctor, who was huddling next to me with his monkey in his arms, was suddenly affected by the gas, and his pet also swallowed some. They were both "sent down the line"; but I was unharmed. When the hate was over, it seemed perhaps difficult to sleep again, warm as the blankets might be, and it was one more case of waiting for daylight.

Expecting that I should not again see that wood, I went up next night with some heavy materials for the dump in Hamel, carried on the limbers. The transport officer, Maycock, was with us, which is saying we talked all the way. At Mesnil church, a cracked and toppling obelisk, there were great craters in the road, and when one of the limbers fell in, it was necessary to unload it before it could be got out. While this delay lasted, in such a deadly place, my flesh crept, but luck was ours and no fresh shells came over to that church before we were away. The journey into Hamel that evening was unforgettable. One still sees in rapid gunlights the surviving fingerpost at the fork in the unknown road. It helped us. As we plodded down the dark hill, the blackness over by Thiepval Wood leapt alive with tossing flares, which made it seem a monstrous height, and with echo after echo in stammering mad pursuit the guns threshed that area; uncounted shells passed over with savage whipcracks, and travelled meteor-like with lines of flame through the brooding sultry air. One scarcely seemed to be alive and touching earth, but soon the voices of other beings sounded, at Hamel Dump, like business— "Back in 'ere, lad," "Any more?" The following day I had an opportunity to improve my small forward dumps, and to choose with Sergeant Rhodes, the master-cook, a "retired spot" where he might prepare the rum and coffee, to be served to the attacking troops. This matter introduced an incident. All day, on and off, our guns were battering the German trenches, and one saw almost without a thought our salvoes bursting every few minutes on such tender points as trench junctions, clearly marked in that sector of chalk parapets and downland. The German guns answered this brilliant provocation unexpectedly. Thus, as the thin and long cook-sergeant and I were walking comfortably in Roberts Trench, the air about us suddenly became ferocious with whizzbangs, the parapets before and behind sprang up in clods and roarings; there seemed no way out. They were hitting the trench. Rhodes stared at me, I at him for a suggestion; his lean face presented the wildest despair, and no doubt mine was the same; we ran, we slipped and crouched one way and the other, but it was like a cataract both ways. And then, sudden quiet; more to come? Nothing; a reprieve.

Another postponement took me dustily back to the battalion in the wood watched by so many German observation-balloons in the morning sun. The wood, shelled deliberately because of its camps and accidentally because of some conspicuous horse-lines and silhouetted movements on the hill to the west, had frayed the men's keenness; there had been casualties; and then the anticlimax twice repeated had spoiled their first energetic eagerness for a battle. Yet, still, they were a sound and capable battalion, deserving far better treatment than they were now getting, and a battle, not a massacre, when they left their wretched encampment. On the evening of September 2, the battalion moved cautiously from Mailly-Maillet by cross-country tracks, through pretty Englebelmer, with ghostly Angelus on the green and dewy light, over the downs to Mesnil, and assembled in the Hamel trenches to attack the Beaucourt ridge next morning. The night all round was drowsily quiet. I stood at the junction of four forward trenches, directing the several companies into them as had been planned. Not one man in thirty had seen the line by daylight—and it was a maze even when seen so, map in hand. Even getting out of the narrow steep trenches with weighty equipment, and crossing others, threatened to disorder the assault. Every man remembered the practice attacks at Monchy-Breton, and was ready, if conditions were equal, to act his part; among other things, the "waves" had to form up and carry out a "right incline" in No Man's Land—a change of direction almost impossible in the dark, in broken and entangled ground, and under concentrated gunfire. When the rum and coffee were duly on the way to these men, I went off to my other duty. A carrying-party was to meet me in Hamel, and for a time the officer and I, having nothing to do but wait, sat in a trench along the village street considering the stars in their courses. An unusual yet known voice jubilantly interrupted this unnaturally calm conversation; it was a sergeant-major, a fine soldier who had lost his rank for drunkenness, won it again, and was now going over in charge of a party carrying trench mortar ammunition. A merry man, a strong man; when we had met before, he had gained my friendliest feelings by his freedom from any feeling against a schoolboy officer. Some N.C.O.'s took care to let their superior training and general wisdom weigh on my shyness: not so C. He referred to the attack as one might speak of catching a train, and in it a few hours later he showed such wonderful Saint Christopher spirit that he was awarded a posthumous Victoria Cross. Meanwhile, all waited.

The cold disturbing air and the scent of the river mist marked the approach of the morning. I got my fellow-officer to move his men nearer to my main supply of bombs, which were ready in canvas buckets; and time slipped by, until scarcely five preliminary minutes remained. My friend then took his men into cellars not far away, there to shelter while the bombardment opened; for their orders were to carry bombs to our bombing officer, young French, who was ordered to clear the suspected German dugouts under the railway bank, a short time after the attacking waves had crossed. As for me, I took off my equipment and began to set out the bomb buckets in a side trench so that the carriers could at the right moment pick them up two at a time; and while I was doing this, and the east began to unveil, a stranger in a soft cap and a trench coat approached, and asked me the way to the German lines. This visitor was white-faced as a ghost, and I liked neither his soft cap nor the mackintosh nor the right hand concealed under his coat. I, too, felt myself grow pale, and I thought it as well to show him the communication trench, Devial Alley, then deserted; he scanned me, and quickly went on. Who he was, I have never explained to myself; but in two minutes the barrage opened, and his chances of doing us harm (I thought he must be a spy) were all gone.

The British barrage opened. The air gushed in hot surges along that river valley, and uproar never imagined by me swung from ridge to ridge. The east was scarlet with dawn and the flickering gunflashes; I thanked God I was not in the assault, and joined the subdued carriers nervously lighting cigarettes in one of the cellars, sitting there on the steps, studying my watch. The ruins of Hamel were crashing chaotically with shells, and jags of iron and broken wood and brick whizzed past the cellar mouth. When I gave the word to move, it was obeyed with no pretence of enthusiasm. I was forced to shout and swear, and the carrying party, some with shoulders hunched, as if in a snowstorm, dully picked up their bomb buckets and went ahead. The wreckage around seemed leaping with flame. Never had we smelt high explosive so thick and foul, and there was no distinguishing one shell-burst from another, save by the black or tawny smoke that suddenly appeared in the general miasma. We walked along the river road, passed the sandbag dressing-station that had been built only a night or two earlier where the front line crossed the road, and had already been battered in; we entered No Man's Land but we could make very little sense of ourselves or the battle. There were wounded Highlanders trailing down the road. They had been in the marshes of the Ancre, trying to take a machine-gun post called Summer House. Ahead, the German front line could not be clearly seen, the water-mist and the smoke veiling it; and this was lucky for the carrying party. Halfway between the trenches, I wished them good luck, and pointing out the place where they should, according to plan, hand over the bombs, I left them in charge of their own officer, returning myself, as my orders were, to my colonel. I passed good men of ours, in our front line, staring like men in a trance across No Man's Land, their powers of action apparently suspended.

"What's happening over there?" asked Harrison, with a face all doubt and stress, when I crawled into the candled, overcrowded frowsiness of Kentish Caves. I could not say. "What's happening the other side of the river?" All was in ominous discommunication. A runner called Gosden presently came in, with bleeding breast, bearing a message written an hour or more earlier. It did not promise well, and, as the hours passed, all that could be made out was that our attacking companies were "hanging on," some of them in the

German third trench, where they could not at all be reached by the others, dug in between the first and the second. Lintott wrote message after message, trying to share information north, east and west. Harrison, the sweat standing on his forehead, thought out what to do in this deadlock, and repeatedly telephoned to the guns and the general. Wounded men and messengers began to crowd the scanty passages of the Caves, and curt roars of explosion just outside announced that these dugouts, shared by ourselves and the Black Watch, were now to be dealt with. Death soon arrived there, among the group at the clumsy entrance. Harrison meanwhile called for his runner, fastened the chin-strap of his steel helmet, and pushed his way out into the top trenches to see what he could; returned presently, with that kind of severe laugh which tells the tale of a man who has incredibly escaped from the barrage. The day was hot outside, glaring mercilessly upon the burned, choked chalk trenches. I came in again to the squeaking field telephones and obscure candlelight. Presently Harrison, a message in his hand, said: "Rabbit, they're short of ammunition. Get round and collect all the fellows you can and take them over — and stay over there and do what you can." I felt my heart thud at this; went out, naming my men among headquarters "odds and ends" wherever I could find them squatted under the chalk banks, noting with pleasure that my nearest dump had not been blown up and would answer our requirements; I served out bombs and ammunition, then thrust my head in again to report that I was starting, when he delayed, and presently cancelled, the enterprise. The shells on our breathless neighbourhood seemed to fall more thickly, and the dreadful spirit of waste and impotence sank into us, when a sudden report from an artillery observer warned us that there were Germans in our front trench. In that case Kentish Caves was a death-trap, a hole in which bombs would be bursting within a moment; yet here at last was something definite, and we all seemed to come to life, and prepared with our revolvers to try our luck.

The artillery observer must have made some mistake. Time passed without bombs among us or other surprise, and the collapse of the attack was wearily obvious. The bronze noon was more quiet but not less deadly than the morning. I went round the scarcely passable hillside trenches, but they were amazingly lonely: suddenly a sergeant-major and half a dozen men bounded superhumanly, gasping and excited, over the parapets. They had been lying in No Man's Land, and at last had decided to "chance their arm" and dodge the machine-guns which had been perseveringly trying to get them. They drank pints of water, of which I had luckily a little store in a dugout there, now wrecked and gaping. I left them sitting wordless in that store. The singular part of the battle was that no one, not even these, could say what had happened, or what was happening. One vaguely understood that the waves had found their manoeuvre in No Man's Land too complicated; that the

Germans' supposed derelict forward trench near the railway was joined by tunnels to their main defence, and enabled them to come up behind our men's backs; that they had used the bayonet where challenged, with the boldest readiness; "used the whole dam lot, minnies, snipers, rifle-grenades, artillery"; that machine-guns from the Thiepval ridge south of the river were flaying all the crossings of No Man's Land. "Don't seem as if the 49th Div. got any further." But the general effect was the disappearance of the attack into mystery.

Orders for withdrawal were sent out to our little groups in the German lines towards the end of the afternoon. How the runners got there, they alone could explain, if any survived. The remaining few of the battalion in our own positions were collected in the trench along Hamel village street, and a sad gathering it was. Some who had been in the waves contrived to rejoin us now. How much more fortunate we seemed than those who were still in the German labyrinth awaiting the cover of darkness for their small chance of life! And yet, as we filed out, up Jacob's Ladder, we were warned by low-bursting shrapnel not to anticipate. Mesnil was its vile self, but we passed at length. Not much was said, then or afterwards, about those who would never again pass that hated target; among the killed were my old company commanders Penruddock and Northcote (after a great display of coolness and endurance) — laughing French, quiet Hood, and many more. The Cheshires took over the front line, which the enemy might at one moment have occupied without difficulty; but neither they nor our own patrols succeeded in bringing in more than two or three of the wounded; and, the weather turning damp, the Germans increased their difficulty in the darkness and distorted battlefield with a rain of gas shells.

Testament
of Youth

VERA BRITTAIN

I have not seen Uppingham since 1914, and probably should not recognise to-day the five-mile road winding up to the village from Manton, nor the grey school buildings and the tiny cramped rooms of the Waterworks Cottage where we stayed. But for ever in my mind's eye remains a scene which in fact no longer exists, since its background vanished when Edward's House was pulled down to make room for the Uppingham War Memorial.

It is late evening on a hot July day. My mother has gone to talk to the housemaster, and Edward and I are standing in a dark quadrangle outside the lighted windows of the prefects' studies. "There are boys about in various stages of undress, so we can't go inside with you here," Edward informs me.

I am waiting, as I admit afterwards in my diary, "to get a glimpse of the person on whose account, even more than on Edward's, I must confess I have come" — and whose Uppingham nickname, I have already gathered, is "the Lord" or, alternatively, "Monseigneur." But naturally, when his shy, eager face appears at the open window, I give no indication of my anxiety to see him; I just laugh, and mock and tease him for having broken the Uppingham record for prizes.

"I shall look out for every atom of conceit when you get them tomorrow," I tell him, "and as soon as I see the least symptom, I mean to squash it flat."

He caps my criticism without hesitation.

"Well," he replies, "you won't be so very original, after all. One of the housemaster's wives was asked the other day what she thought of the boy who was taking so many prizes, and she said she knew nothing about him except that he was the biggest mass of conceit in the whole of Uppingham.

I wanted to tell her," he adds, "that I perfectly agreed with her, only I didn't ask her to say it out loud in front of so many people."

When, however, I saw Roland—who like Edward was in the Officers' Training Corps—wearing his colour-sergeant's uniform at the corps review on the Middle Field next morning, I did not feel inclined to tease him any more. On his mother's side he had military ancestors, and took the O.T.C. very seriously. He and Edward and their mutual friend Victor, the third member of the devoted trio whom Roland's mother had christened "the Three Musketeers," were going into camp together near Aldershot for a fortnight after the end of the term.

Some of the masters, perhaps, were more prescient, but I do not believe that any of the gaily clad visitors who watched the corps carrying out its manoeuvres and afterwards marching so impressively into the Chapel for the Speech Day service, in the least realised how close at hand was the fate for which it had prepared itself, or how many of those deep and strangely thrilling boys' voices were to be silent in death before another Speech Day. Looking back upon those three radiant days of July 1914, it seems to me that an ominous stillness, an atmosphere of brooding expectation, must surely have hung about the sunlit flower gardens and the shining green fields. But actually I noticed nothing more serious than the deliberate solemnity of the headmaster's speech at the prize-giving after the service.

At that time the Headmaster of Uppingham was habitually referred to by the boys as "the Man." A stern and intimidating figure, he had a wide reputation for tact with parents both male and female, and whenever he met my mother—who went to Uppingham much oftener than my father—he never failed to recognise her or to make some discreet comment on Edward's progress. In this respect he was wiser and more modern-minded than some of his scholastic and clerical contemporaries, who tended to regard women as "irrelevant," and even to-day occasionally combine to write letters to the Press on family life without the collaboration of those who are responsible for the family's continuation. At least one famous pre-war headmaster, who afterwards became a bishop, was widely regarded as a woman-hater—a reputation hardly guaranteed to inculcate respect for their mothers and their future wives in the impressionable adolescents who came under his influence.

Since the noblest and profoundest emotions that men experience—the emotions of love, of marriage, of fatherhood—come to them, and can come to them, only through women, it seems curious and not a little disturbing that so many schoolmasters appear to regard contempt for the female sex as a necessary part of their educational equipment. I often wonder how many male homosexuals, active and potential, owe their hatred and fear of women to the warped minds of the men who taught them at school.

At Uppingham Speech Day, however, I had no personal grounds for deploring the attitude of the older boys towards their feminine contemporaries. As the Headmaster strode, berobed and majestic, on to the platform of the School Hall, I was in the midst of examining with appreciation my Speech Day programme, and especially the page headed "Prizemen, July, 1914," of which the first seven items ran as follows:

Nettleship Prize for English Essay	R. A. Leighton
Holden Prize for Latin Prose	1st, R. A. Leighton
	2nd, C. R. B. Wrenford
Greek Prose Composition	R. A. Leighton
Latin Hexameters	R. A. Leighton
Greek Iambics	R. P. Garrod
Greek Epigram — "γνῶθι σεαυτόν"	R. A. Leighton
Captain in Classics	R. A. Leighton

But, still automatically responsive to school discipline, I hastily put down the programme as the Headmaster began, with enormous dignity, to address the audience.

I do not recall much of the speech, which ended with a list of the precepts laid down for boys by a famous Japanese general — a monument of civilisation whose name I forget, but whose qualities were evidently considered entirely suitable for emulation by young English gentlemen. I shall always, however, remember the final prophetic precept, and the breathless silence which followed the Headmaster's slow, religious emphasis upon the words:

"If a man cannot be useful to his country, he is better dead."

For a moment their solemnity disturbed with a queer, indescribable foreboding the complacent mood in which I watched Roland, pale but composed, go up to receive his prizes.

As Roland had no relatives there of his own — his mother was finishing a book, and in any case took her son's triumphs for granted with a serenity which seemed to my own inconspicuous family almost reprehensible — he sat with me after luncheon at the school concert. This function gave Edward, who had as usual been second or third in every subject, the opportunity to atone for his lack of prizes by playing a violin solo, Dvořák's "Ballade." Apart from his performance, I was less interested in the music than in the various contemporaries of Edward and himself whom Roland pointed out to me in the choir and orchestra.

Of these I recall only one, Ivan Dyer, son of the general of Amritzar notoriety, but I missed an acquaintance of Edward's whom I had seen at the Old Boys' cricket match the previous summer, and Roland told me that this boy, Henry Maxwell Andrews — now the husband of Rebecca West — had left Uppingham in 1913. Henry Andrews, a slim, serious, very tall boy with dark, spectacled eyes, reappeared in my life ten years afterwards as a friend and New College contemporary of my husband. He seemed to me then to have altered very little since I saw him at Uppingham, and four years in Ruhleben — he had gone to Germany for the 1914 summer vacation, and was interned when war broke out — had developed in him a measure of kindness and tolerant wisdom considerably beyond the unexacting standards of the average Englishman.

The afternoon was so hot, and our desire for conversation so great, that Roland and I were relieved when the concert ended, and we could lose ourselves in the crowd at the Headmaster's garden-party. I remember to-day how perfectly my dress — a frilled pink ninon with a tiny pattern, worn beneath a rose-trimmed lace hat — seemed to have been made for our chosen corner of the garden, where roses with velvet petals softly shading from orange through pink to crimson foamed exuberantly over the lattice-work of an old wooden trellis. But even if I had forgotten, I should still have Roland's verses, "In the Rose-Garden," to renew the fading colours of a far-away dream.

We were not long left in peace to resume our perpetual discussion of Olive Schreiner and immortality. Roland was deeply engrossed in explaining to me Immanuel Kant's theory of survival, when our seclusion was suddenly invaded by his and Edward's housemaster, who remarked, with the peculiar smile reserved by the middle-aged for very young couples who are obviously growing interested in one another, "Ha! I *thought* I should find you here," and bore us off triumphantly to tea. But we continued the conversation next day both before and after Sunday chapel, and leaving Edward and my mother to entertain each other, walked up and down a wooded park known as Fairfield Gardens in spite of long intervals of slow, quiet rain.

Two years afterwards Victor, a handsome, reticent boy even taller than Edward, who was alternatively known to him and to Roland as "Tah" and "the Father Confessor," spoke to me of this day.

"I can't of course remember," he told me in effect, "exactly what he said to me on that Sunday. It's difficult to summarise the intangible. Do you remember the two Karg-Elert pieces that Sterndale Bennett played at the beginning of the service that afternoon? One of them, *'Clair de Lune,'* seemed to move him deeply. He said it reminded him of you in its coldness and the sense of aloofness from the world. He said that after talking with you in Fairfield it seemed very strange to go and mix with the others in the chapel. . . . I told him that he loved you then. He said he didn't, but I could see that that was merely a conventional answer. I said, 'Very well, we'll meet here again on Speech Day 1924 and see who is right.' I think he agreed to this."

If Victor reported the conversation correctly, Roland at that time was certainly more courageously self-analytical and more articulate than I — though the latter quality may merely have been due to the fortunate possession of a friend with whom articulateness was easy. Not having any such confidant — since Edward was already too much depressed at the prospect of separation from Roland, who was going to another Oxford college, and from Victor, who had qualified for Cambridge, to be further burdened by a sister's emotions which would then have seemed to him absurdly premature — I was thrust back as usual upon an inner turmoil for which there seemed no prospect of relief.

After bidding good-bye to Roland at the lodge gates that evening, I was conscious of nothing more definite than intense exasperation, which lasted without intermission for several days. All through the journey back to Buxton next morning I was indescribably cross; I answered my mother's conversational efforts in surly monosyllables, and couldn't find a polite word to say.

Chapter V

I

After the solid, old-fashioned comfort of the Buxton house, it seemed strange to be the quarter-possessor of a bare-boarded room divided into cubicles by much-washed curtains of no recognisable colour, with only a bed, a washstand and a tiny chest of drawers to represent one's earthly possessions. There was not, I noticed with dismay, so much as a shelf or a mantelpiece capable of holding two or three books; the few that I had brought with me would have to be inaccessibly stored in my big military trunk.

As soon as I had unpacked in the cold, comfortless cubicle, I sat down on my bed and wrote a short letter to Roland on an old box-lid.

"I feel a mixture of strangeness and independence and depression and apprehension and a few other things to-night. Though I am really nearer to you, you somehow feel farther away. Write to me soon," I implored him. "London — darkest London — sends you its love too, and wishes — oh! ever so much! — that it may soon see you again."

Now two insignificant units at the 1st London General Hospital, Camberwell — the military extension of St. Bartholomew's Hospital — Betty and I had reported to the Matron that afternoon. We were among the youngest members of the staff, we learnt later, only two of the other V.A.D.s being "under age." The nucleus of the hospital, a large college, red, gabled, creeper-covered, is still one of the few dignified buildings in the dismal, dreary, dirty wilderness of south-east London, with its paper-strewn pavements, its little mean streets, and its old, ugly houses tumbling into squalid decay.

Formerly — and now again — a training centre for teachers, it was commandeered for use as a hospital early in the War, together with some adjacent elementary schools, the open park-space opposite, and its satellite hostel nearly two miles away on Champion Hill.

To this hostel, as soon as we had reported ourselves, Betty and I were dispatched with our belongings. Our taxicab, driving through Camberwell Green over Denmark Hill and turning off the summit of Champion Hill into a pleasant, tree-shaded by-road, deposited us before a square, solid building of dirty grey stone, with gaping uncurtained windows. Closely surrounded by elms and chestnuts, tall, ancient and sooty, it looked gloomy and smelt rather dank; we should not be surprised, we thought, to find old tombstones in the garden.

At that stage of the War the military and civilian professional nurses who had joined Queen Alexandra's Imperial Military Nursing Service or the Territorial Force Reserve were still suspicious of the young semi-trained amateurs upon whose assistance, they were beginning to realise with dismay, they would be obliged to depend for the duration of the War. Only about a dozen V.A.D.s had preceded the batch with which I was sent, and the arrangements made for our reception were typical of the spirit in which, as a nation, we muddled our way through to "victory."

It still seems to me incredible that medical men and women, of all people, should not have realised how much the efficiency of over-worked and under-trained young women would have been increased by the elimination of avoidable fatigue, and that, having contemplated the addition of V.A.D.s to the staff for at least six months before engaging them, they did not make the hostel completely ready for them before they arrived instead of waiting till they got there. But in those days we had no Institute of Industrial Psychology to suggest ideal standards to professional organisations, and a large proportion of our military arrangements were permeated with a similar unimaginativeness. On a small scale it undermined the health and even cost the lives of young women in hospitals; on a large scale it meant the lack of ammunition, the attempt to hold positions with insufficient numbers, and the annihilation of our infantry with our own high-explosive shells.

Each morning at 7 A.M. we were due at the hospital, where we breakfasted, and went on duty at 7.30. Theoretically we travelled down by the workmen's trams which ran over Champion Hill from Dulwich, but in practice these trams were so full that we were seldom able to use them, and were obliged to walk, frequently in pouring rain and carrying suitcases containing clean aprons and changes of shoes and stockings, the mile and a half from the hostel to the hospital. As the trams were equally full in the evenings, the journey on foot had often to be repeated at the end of the day.

Whatever the weather, we were expected to appear punctually on duty looking clean, tidy and cheerful. As the V.A.D. cloak-room was then on the top floor of the college, up four flights of stone steps, we had to allow quarter of an hour for changing, in addition to the half hour's walk, in order to be in time for breakfast. This meant leaving the hostel at 6.15, after getting up about 5.45 and washing in icy water in the dreary gloom of the ill-lit, dawn-cold cubicle. After a few grumbles from the two eldest of the room's five occupants, we accepted our unnecessary discomforts with mute, philosophical resignation. When the rain poured in torrents as we struggled up or down Denmark Hill in the blustering darkness all through that wet autumn, Betty and I encouraged each other with the thought that we were at last beginning to understand just a little what winter meant to the men in the trenches.

Many chills and other small illnesses resulted from the damp, breakfastless walk undertaken so early in the morning by tired girls not yet broken in to a life of hardship. After I left I heard that a V.A.D. living at the hostel had died of pneumonia and had thus been responsible for the establishment of morning and evening ambulances, but until then no form of transport was provided or even suggested. Neither, apparently, did it occur to the authorities who so cheerfully billeted us in a distant, ill-equipped old house, that young untried women who were continually in contact with septic wounds and sputum cups and bed-pans, and whose constantly wet feet became cumulatively sorer from the perpetual walks added to the unaccustomed hours of standing, required at least a daily bath if they were to keep in good health.

At the hostel, to meet the needs of about twenty young women, was one cold bathroom equipped with an ancient and unreliable geyser. This apparatus took about twenty minutes to half fill the bath with lukewarm water, and as supper at the hospital was not over till nearly nine o'clock, and lights at the hostel had to be out soon after ten, there was seldom time after the journey up Denmark Hill for more than two persons per evening to occupy the bathroom. So temperamental was the geyser that the old housekeeper at the hostel refused to allow anyone but herself to manipulate it. While the tepid water trickled slowly into the bath she would sit anxiously perched beside the antique cylinder, apparently under the impression that if she took her eye off it for a moment it was bound to explode.

Any gas company could probably have installed an up-to-date water-heater in half a day, but it had not occurred to anybody to order this to be done. As several Sisters also slept in the hostel the V.A.D.s had seldom much luck in appropriating the bath, so in the bitter November cold we did our shivering best to remove the odours and contacts of the day with tiny jugfuls of lukewarm water. Later a second bathroom was installed, a process which, as I told Roland a few weeks afterwards, "for some reason or other requires the cutting off of the entire hot water supply. . . . It is rather an amusing state of affairs for the middle of London." Never, except when travelling, had I to put up with so much avoidable discomfort throughout my two subsequent years of foreign service as I endured in the centre of the civilised world in the year of enlightenment 1915.

Much subsequent reflection has never enabled me to decide who was really responsible for our cheerless reception. Probably, in the unfamiliar situation, responsibility was never formally allocated to anyone by anybody, and, human nature being incurably optimistic and fundamentally hostile to assuming any work not established as its own by long tradition, each person who might have shouldered the task of organisation hopefully supposed it to have been performed by one of the others.

Organisation and regulation of another sort existed in plenty; it was evidently felt that, without the detailed regimentation of their daily conduct, amateur intruders would never fit into the rigid framework of hospital discipline. We went on duty at 7.30 A.M., and came off at 8 P.M., our hours, including three hours' off-time and a weekly half day—all of which we gave up willingly enough whenever a convoy came in or the ward was full of unusually bad cases—thus amounted to a daily twelve and a half. We were never allowed to sit down in the wards, and our off-duty time was seldom allocated before the actual day. Night duty, from 8 P.M. to 8 A.M. over a period of two months, involved a twelve-hour stretch without off-time, though one night's break was usually allowed in the middle. For this work we received the magnificent sum of £20 a year, plus a tiny uniform allowance and the cost of our laundry. Extra mess allowance was given only on foreign service, but at Camberwell the food, though monotonous, was always sufficient.

Those of us whose careers survived the Denmark Hill conditions gradually came, through the breaking-in process of sheer routine, to find the life tolerable enough. We all acquired puffy hands, chapped face, chilblains and swollen ankles, but we seldom actually went sick, somehow managing to remain on duty with colds, bilious attacks, neuralgia, septic fingers and incipient influenza. It never then occurred to us that we should have been happier, healthier, and altogether more competent if the hours of work had been shorter, the hostel life more private and comfortable, the daily walks between hostel and hospital eliminated, the rule against sitting down in the wards relaxed, and off-duty time known in advance when the work was normal. Far from criticising our Olympian superiors, we tackled our daily duties with a devotional enthusiasm now rare amongst young women, since a more cynical post-war generation, knowing how easily its predecessors were hoodwinked through their naïve idealism, naturally tends to regard this quality with amusement and scorn.

Every task, from the dressing of a dangerous wound to the scrubbing of a bed-mackintosh, had for us in those early days a sacred glamour which redeemed it equally from tedium and disgust. Our one fear was to be found wanting in the smallest respect; no conceivable fate seemed more humiliating than that of being returned to Devonshire House as "unsuitable" after a month's probation. The temptation to exploit our young wartime enthusiasm must have been immense—and was not fiercely resisted by the military authorities.

2

Most of the patients at Camberwell were privates and N.C.O.s, but the existence of a small officers' section made me dream of fascinating though improbable coincidences.

"I wonder," I wrote to Roland, "if some fine morning I shall come on duty and hear indirectly from a friendly V.A.D. that a certain Lieutenant L. of the 7th Worcestershires came in with the convoy last night. . . . But it's too good to think of. It is the kind of thing that only happens in sensational novels."

My first ward was a long Tommies' hut in the open park, containing sixty beds of acute surgical cases. The knowledge of masculine invalid psychology that I gradually acquired in my various hospitals stopped short at the rank of quartermaster-sergeant, for throughout the War I was never posted to a British officers' ward for longer than a few hours at a time. Apparently my youth and childish chocolate-box prettiness gave every Matron under whom I served the impression that if I were sent to nurse officers I should improve the occasion in ways not officially recognised by the military authorities.

When I began to work in the long hut, my duties consisted chiefly in preparing dressing-trays and supporting limbs—a task which the orderlies seldom undertook because they were so quickly upset by the butcher's-shop appearance of the uncovered wounds. Soon after I arrived I saw one of them, who was holding a basin, faint right on the top of the patient.

"Many of the patients can't bear to see their own wounds, and I don't wonder," I recorded.

Although the first dressing at which I assisted—a gangrenous leg wound, slimy and green and scarlet, with the bone laid bare—turned me sick and faint for a moment that I afterwards remembered with humiliation, I minded what I described to Roland as "the general atmosphere of inhumanness" far more than the grotesque mutilations of bodies and limbs and faces. The sight of the "Bart's" Sisters, calm, balanced, efficient, moving up and down the wards self-protected by that bright immunity from pity which the highly trained nurse seems so often to possess, filled me with a deep fear of merging my own individuality in the impersonal routine of the organisation.

"There is no provision," I told Roland in one of my earliest letters from Camberwell, "for any interests besides one's supposed interest in one's work.

Of course I hate it. There is something so starved and dry about hospital nurses — as if they had to force all the warmth out of themselves before they could be really good nurses. But personally I would rather suffer ever so much in my work than become indifferent to pain. I don't mind anything really so long as I don't lose my personality — or even have it temporarily extinguished. And I don't think I can do that when I have You."

It was perhaps fortunate that I did not know how inexorably the months in which I should have to do what I hated would pile themselves up into years, nor foresee how long before the end I too, from overwork and excessive experience, should become intolerant of suffering in my patients. Even without the bitterness of that knowledge I felt very desolate, and as much cut off from what philosophers call "the like-minded group" as if I had been imprisoned in one of the less "highbrow" circles of Dante's *Purgatorio*. My first experience of convoys — the "Fall in" followed by long, slowly moving lines of ambulances and the sudden crowding of the surgical wards with cruelly wounded men came as a relief because it deprived me of the opportunity for thought.

"I had no time to wonder whether I was going to do things right or not," I noted; "they simply *had* to be done right."

But afterwards the baffling contrast between the ideal of service and its practical expressions — a contrast that grew less as our ideals diminished with the years while our burden of remorseless activities increased — drove me to write a puzzled letter to Roland.

"It is always so strange that when you are working you never think of all the inspiring thoughts that made you take up the work in the first instance. Before I was in hospital at all I thought that because I suffered myself I should feel it a grand thing to relieve the sufferings of other people. But now, when I am actually doing something which I know relieves someone's pain, it is nothing but a matter of business. I may think lofty thoughts about the whole thing before or after but never at the time. At least, almost never. Sometimes some quite little thing makes me stop short all of a sudden and I feel a fierce desire to cry in the middle of whatever it is I am doing."

As the wet, dreary autumn drifted on into grey winter, my letters to him became shorter and a little forlorn, though my constant awareness of his far greater discomforts made me write of mine as though they possessed a humour of which I was too seldom conscious. The week-ends seemed especially tiring, for on Saturdays and Sundays even the workmen's trams ceased to function, and the homeward evening walk through the purlieus of Camberwell was apt to become more adventurous than usual.

"I picture to myself," I told Roland, "Mother's absolute horror if she could have seen me at 9.15 the other night dashing about and dodging the traffic in the slums of Camberwell Green, in the pitch dark of course, incidentally getting mixed up with remnants of a recruiting meeting, munition workers and individuals drifting in and out of public houses. It is quite thrilling to be an unprotected female and feel that no one in your immediate surroundings is particularly concerned with what happens to you so long as you don't give them any bother."

After twenty years of sheltered gentility I certainly did feel that whatever the disadvantages of my present occupation, I was at least seeing life. My parents also evidently felt that I was seeing it, and too much of it, for a letter still exists in which I replied with youthful superiority to an anxious endeavour that my father must have made to persuade me to abandon the rigours of Army hospitals and return to Buxton.

"Thank you very much for your letter, the answer to which really did not require much thinking over," I began uncompromisingly, and continued with more determination than tact: *"Nothing —* beyond sheer necessity — would induce me to stop doing what I am doing now, and I should never respect myself again if I allowed a few slight physical hardships to make me give up what is the finest work any girl can do now. I honestly did not take it up because I thought you did not want me or could not afford to give me a comfortable home, but because I wanted to prove I could more or less keep myself by working, and partly because, not being a man and able to go to the front, I wanted to do the next best thing. I do not agree that my place is at home doing nothing or practically nothing, for I consider that the place now of anyone who is young and strong and capable is where the work that is needed is to be done. And really the work is not too hard — even if I were a little girl, which I no longer am, for I sometimes feel quite ninety nowadays."

Fortunately most of my letters home were more human, not to say schoolgirlish, in content. Their insistent suggestions that my family should keep me supplied with sweets and biscuits, or should come up to London and take me out to tea, are reminders of the immense part played by meals in the meditations of ardent young patriots during the War.

3

Apart from all these novel experiences, my first month at Camberwell was distinguished by the one and only real quarrel that I ever had with Roland. It was purely an epistolary quarrel, but its bitterness was none the less for that, and the inevitable delay between posts prolonged and greatly added to its emotional repercussions.

On October 18th, Roland had sent a letter to Buxton excusing himself, none too gracefully, for the terseness of recent communications, and explaining how much absorbed he had become by the small intensities of life at the front. As soon as the letter was forwarded to Camberwell, I replied rather ruefully.

"Don't get *too* absorbed in your little world over there — even if it makes things easier. . . . After all the War *cannot* last for ever, and when it is over we shall be glad to be what we were born again — if we can only live till then. Life — oh! life. Isn't it strange how much we used to demand of the universe, and now we ask only for what we took as a matter of course before — just to be allowed to live, to go on being."

By November 8th no answer had come from him — not even a comment on what seemed to me the tremendous event of my transfer from Buxton into a real military hospital. The War, I began to feel, was dividing us as I had so long feared that it would, making real values seem unreal, and causing the qualities which mattered most to appear unimportant. Was it, I wondered, because Roland had lost interest in me that this anguish of drifting apart had begun — or was the explanation to be found in that terrible barrier of knowledge by which War cut off the men who possessed it from the women who, in spite of the love that they gave and received, remained in ignorance?

It is one of the many things that I shall never know.

Lonely as I was, and rather bewildered, I found the cold dignity of reciprocal silence impossible to maintain. So I tried to explain that I, too, understood just a little the inevitable barrier — the almost physical barrier of horror and dreadful experience — which had grown up between us.

"With you," I told him, "I can never be *quite* angry. For the more chill and depressed I feel myself in these dreary November days, the more sorry I feel for you beginning to face the acute misery of the winter after the long strain of these many months. When at six in the morning the rain is beating pitilessly against the windows and I have to go out into it to begin a day which promises nothing pleasant, I feel that after all I should not mind very much if only the thought of you right in it out there didn't haunt me all day. . . . I have only one wish in life now and that is for the ending of the War. I wonder how much really all you have seen and done has changed you. Personally, after seeing some of the dreadful things I have to see here, I feel I shall never be the same person again, and wonder if, when the War does end, I shall have forgotten how to laugh. The other day I did involuntarily laugh at something and it felt quite strange. Some of the things in our ward are so horrible that it seems as if no merciful dispensation of the Universe could allow them and one's consciousness to exist at the same time. One day last week I came away from a really terrible amputation dressing I had been assisting at — it was the first after the operation — with my hands covered with blood and my mind full of a passionate fury at the wickedness of war, and I wished I had never been born."

No sudden gift of second sight showed me the future months in which I should not only contemplate and hold, but dress unaided and without emotion, the quivering stump of a newly amputated limb—than which a more pitiable spectacle hardly exists on this side of death. Nor did Roland—who by this time had doubtless grown accustomed to seeing limbs amputated less scientifically but more expeditiously by methods quite other than those of modern surgery—give any indication of understanding either my revulsion or my anger. In fact he never answered this particular communication at all, for the next day I received from him the long-awaited letter, which provoked me to a more passionate expression of apprehensive wrath than anything that he had so far said or done.

"I can scarcely realise that you are there," he wrote, after telling me with obvious pride that he had been made acting adjutant to his battalion, "there in a world of long wards and silent-footed nurses and bitter, clean smells and an appalling whiteness in everything. I wonder if your metamorphosis has been as complete as my own. I feel a barbarian, a wild man of the woods, stiff, narrowed, practical, an incipient martinet perhaps—not at all the kind of person who would be associated with prizes on Speech Day, or poetry, or dilettante classicism. I wonder what the dons of Merton would say to me now, or if I could ever waste my time on Demosthenes again. One should go to Oxford first and see the world afterwards; when one has looked from the mountain-top it is hard to stay contentedly in the valley. . . ."

"Do I seem very much of a phantom in the void to you?" another letter inquired a day or two later. "I must. You seem to me rather like a character in a book or someone whom one has dreamt of and never seen. I suppose there is such a place as Lowestoft, and that there was once a person called Vera Brittain who came down there with me."

After weeks of waiting for some sign of interested sympathy, this evidence of war's dividing influence moved me to irrational fury against what I thought a too-easy capitulation to the spiritually destructive preoccupations of military service. I had not yet realised—as I was later to realise through my own mental surrender—that only a process of complete adaptation, blotting out tastes and talents and even memories, made life sufferable for someone face to face with war at its worst. I was not to discover for another year how completely the War possessed one's personality the moment that one crossed the sea, making England and all the uninitiated marooned within its narrow shores seem remote and insignificant. So I decided with angry pride that—however tolerant Roland's mother, who by his own confession had also gone letterless for longer than usual, might choose to be—I was not going to sit down meekly under contempt or neglect. The agony of love and fear with which the recollection of his constant danger always filled me quenched the first explosion of my wrath, but it was still a sore and unreasonable pen that wrote the reply to his letter.

"Most estimable, practical, unexceptional adjutant, I suppose I ought to thank you for your letter, since apparently one has to be grateful nowadays for being allowed to know you are alive. But all the same, my first impulse was to tear that letter into small shreds, since it appeared to me very much like an epistolary expression of the Quiet Voice, only with indications or an even greater sense of personal infallibility than the Quiet Voice used to contain. My second impulse was to write an answer with a sting in it which would have touched even R. L. (modern style). But I can't do that. One cannot be angry with people at the front—a fact which I sometimes think they take advantage of—and so when I read "We go back in" to the trenches tomorrow I literally dare not write you the kind of letter you perhaps deserve, for thinking that the world might end for you on that discordant note.

"No, my metamorphosis has not been as complete as yours—in fact I doubt if it has occurred at all. Perhaps it would be better if it had, for it must be very pleasant to be perfectly satisfied both with yourself and life in general. But I cannot. . . . Certainly I am as practical and outwardly as narrow as even you could desire. But although in this life I render material services and get definite and usually immediate results which presumably ought therefore to be satisfying, I cannot yet feel as near to Light and Truth as I did when I was "wasting my time" on Plato and Homer. Perhaps one day when it is over I shall see that there was Light and Truth behind all, but just now, although I suppose I should be said to be "seeing the world," I can't help feeling that the despised classics taught me the finest parts of it better. And I shan't complain about being in the valley if only I can call myself a student again some day, instead of a "nurse." By the way, are you *quite* sure that you are on "the mountain-top?" You admit yourself that you are "stiff, narrowed, practical, an incipient martinet," and these characteristics hardly seem to involve the summit of ambition of the real you. But the War kills other things besides physical life, and I sometimes feel that little by little the Individuality of You is being as surely buried as the bodies are of those who lie beneath the trenches of Flanders and France. But I won't write more on this subject. In any case it is no use, and I shall probably cry if I do, which must never be done, for there is so much both personal and impersonal to cry for here that one might weep for ever and yet not shed enough tears to wash away the pitiableness of it all."

To this unmerited outburst, though I received other letters from him, I did not get an answer for quite a long time. Just before I wrote it he was transferred to the Somerset Light Infantry for temporary duty, and could get his letters only by riding over some miles of water-logged country to the 7th Worcesters' headquarters at Hebuterne, which was not, in winter, a tempting afternoon's occupation. But when, at the end of November, the reply did come, it melted away my fear of his indifference into tears of relief, and made me, as I confessed to my diary, "nearly mad with longing for him, I wanted him so."

"Dearest, I do deserve it, every word of it and every sting of it," he wrote in a red-hot surge of impetuous remorse. "'Most estimable, practicable, unexceptional adjutant.' . . . Oh, damn! I have been a perfect beast, a conceited, selfish, self-satisfied beast just because I can claim to live half my time in a trench (in very slight, temporary and much exaggerated discomfort) and might possibly get hit by something in the process, I have felt myself justified in forgetting everything and everybody except my own Infallible Majesty. . . . And instead of calling it selfishness pure and simple I call it 'a metamorphosis,' and expect, in consequence, consideration and letters which can go unanswered."

He didn't deserve, he concluded, to get my letters at all, but only to be ignored as completely as he had ignored me and his family. Apparently he had found my unhappy little tirade as soon as he arrived at Hebuterne that afternoon; it made him, he told me, so furious with himself that he left the rest of his correspondence lying on the table and rode straight back.

"I don't think I have ever been so angry or despised myself so much. I feel as if I hardly dare write to you at all. And to make it worse I have given up my chance of getting any leave before Christmas in order to be with this battalion a month instead of only a week. Oh, damn!"

For the time being, at any rate, these young, inflammatory emotions had burned down whatever barrier might have existed, and once more his letters became alive and warm with all the sympathy that I could desire for the unæsthetic bleakness of days and nights in hospital. But I, too, had by then something more to write about than the grey duties of Camberwell, for in the interval between my angry letter and his repentant response I had been down again — and for the last time — to Lowestoft. [. . .]

7

Certainly the stage seemed perfectly set for his leave. Now that my parents had at last migrated temporarily to the Grand Hotel at Brighton, our two families were so near; the Matron had promised yet again that my own week's holiday should coincide with his, and even Edward wrote cheerfully for once to say that as soon as the actual date was known, he and Victor would both be able to get leave at the same time.

"Very wet and muddy and many of the communication trenches are quite impassable," ran a letter from Roland written on December 9th. "Three men were killed the other day by a dug-out falling in on top of them and one man was drowned in a sump hole. The whole of one's world, at least of one's visible and palpable world, is mud in various stages of solidity or stickiness. . . . I can be perfectly certain about the date of my leave by to-morrow morning and will let you know."

And, when the final information did come, hurriedly written in pencil on a thin slip of paper torn from his Field Service note-books, it brought the enchanted day still nearer than I had dared to hope.

"Shall be home on leave from 24th Dec. — 31st. Land Christmas Day. R."

Even to the unusual concession of a leave which began on Christmas morning after night-duty the Matron proved amenable, and in the encouraging quietness of the winter's war, with no Loos in prospect, no great push in the west even possible, I dared to glorify my days — or rather my nights — by looking forward. In the pleasant peace of Ward 23, where all the patients, now well on the road to health, slept soundly, the sympathetic Scottish Sister teased me a little for my irrepressible excitement.

"I suppose you won't be thinking of going off and getting married? A couple of babies like you!"

It was a new and breath-taking thought, a flame to which Roland's mother — who approved of early marriages and believed that ways and means could be left to look after themselves far better than the average materialistic parent supposed — added fuel when she hinted mysteriously, on a day off which I spent in Brighton, that *this* time Roland might not be content to leave things as they were. . . . Suppose, I meditated, kneeling in the darkness beside the comforting glow of the stove in the silent ward, that during this leave we did marry as suddenly, as, in the last one, we became "officially" engaged? Of course it would be what the world would call — or did call before the War — a "foolish" marriage. But now that the War seemed likely to be endless, and the chance of making a "wise" marriage had become, for most people, so very remote, the world was growing more tolerant. No one — not even my family now, I thought — would hold out against us, even though we hadn't a penny beyond our pay. What if, after all, we did marry thus foolishly? When the War was over we could still go back to Oxford, and learn to be writers — or even lecturers; if we were determined enough about it we could return there, even though — oh, devastating, sweet speculation! — I might have had a baby.

I had never much cared for babies or had anything to do with them; before that time I had always been too ambitious, too much interested in too many projects, to become acutely conscious of a maternal instinct. But on those quiet evenings of night-duty as Christmas approached, I would come, half asleep, as near to praying as I had been at any time, even when Roland first went to France or in the days following Loos.

"Oh, God!" my half-articulate thoughts would run, "do let us get married and let me have a baby — something that is Roland's very own, something of himself to remember him by if he goes. . . . It shan't be a burden to his people or mine for a moment longer than I can help, I promise. I'll go on doing war-work and give it all my pay during the War — and as soon as ever the War's over I'll go back to Oxford and take my Finals so that I can get a job and support it. So *do* let me have a baby, dear God!"

The night before Christmas Eve, I found my ward transformed into the gay semblance of a sixpenny bazaar with Union Jacks, paper streamers, crinkled tissue lampshades and Christmas texts and greetings, all carried out in staggering shades of orange and vivid scarlet and brilliant green. In the cheerful construction of red paper bags, which I filled with crackers and sweets for the men's Christmas stockings, I found that the hours passed quickly enough. Clipping, and sewing, and opening packets, I imagined him reading the letter that I had written him a few days earlier, making various suggestions for meeting him, if he could only write or wire me beforehand, when the Folkestone train arrived at Victoria, and travelling down with him to Sussex.

"And shall I really see you again, and so soon?" it had concluded. "And it will be the anniversary of the week which contained another New Year's Eve — and *David Copperfield,* and two unreal and wonderful days, and you standing alone in Trafalgar Square, and thinking — of — well, what *were* you thinking of? When we were really both children still, and my connection with any hospital on earth was unthought-of, and your departure for the front merely the adventurous dream of some vaguely distant future date. And life was lived, at any rate for two days, in the Omar Khay-yámesque spirit of

> *Unborn to-morrow and dead yesterday —*
> *Why fret about them if To-day be sweet?*

But we are going to better that — even that — this time. Au revoir."

When I went to her office for my railway-warrant in the morning, the Matron smiled kindly at my bubbling impatience, and reminded me how lucky I was to get leave for Christmas. At Victoria I inquired what boat trains arrived on Christmas Day, and learnt that there was only one, at 7.30 in the evening. The risk, I decided, of missing him in the winter blackness of a wartime terminus was too great to be worth taking: instead, I would go straight to Brighton next morning and wait for him there.

As Christmas Eve slipped into Christmas Day, I finished tying up the paper bags, and with the Sister filled the men's stockings by the exiguous light of an electric torch. Already I could count, perhaps even on my fingers, the hours that must pass before I should see him. In spite of its tremulous eagerness of anticipation, the night again seemed short; some of the convalescent men wanted to go to early services, and that meant beginning temperatures and pulses at 3 A.M. As I took them I listened to the rain pounding on the tin roof, and wondered whether, since his leave ran from Christmas Eve, he was already on the sea in that wild, stormy darkness. When the men awoke and reached for their stockings, my whole being glowed with exultant benevolence; I delighted in their pleasure over their childish home-made presents because my own mounting joy made me feel in harmony with all creation.

At eight o'clock, as the passages were lengthy and many of the men were lame, I went along to help them to the communion service in the chapel of the college. It was two or three years since I had been to such a service, but it seemed appropriate that I should be there, for I felt, wrought up as I was to a high pitch of nervous emotion, that I ought to thank whatever God might exist for the supreme gift of Roland and the love that had arisen so swiftly between us. The music of the organ was so sweet, the sight of the wounded men who knelt and stood with such difficulty so moving, the conflict of joy and gratitude, pity and sorrow in my mind so poignant, that tears sprang to my eyes, dimming the chapel walls and the words that encircled them: "I am the Resurrection and the Life: he that believeth in Me, though he were dead, yet shall he live: and whosoever liveth and believeth in Me shall never die."

Directly after breakfast, sent on my way by exuberant good wishes from Betty and Marjorie and many of the others, I went down to Brighton. All day I waited there for a telephone message or a telegram, sitting drowsily in the lounge of the Grand Hotel, or walking up and down the promenade, watching the grey sea tossing rough with white surf-crested waves, and wondering still what kind of crossing he had had or was having.

When, by ten o'clock at night, no news had come, I concluded that the complications of telegraph and telephone on a combined Sunday and Christmas Day had made communication impossible. So, unable to fight sleep any longer after a night and a day of wakefulness, I went to bed a little disappointed, but still unperturbed. Roland's family, at their Keymer cottage, kept an even longer vigil; they sat up till nearly midnight over their Christmas dinner in the hope that he would join them, and, in their dramatic, impulsive fashion, they drank a toast to the Dead.

The next morning I had just finished dressing, and was putting the final touches to the pastel-blue crêpe-de-Chine blouse, when the expected message came to say that I was wanted on the telephone. Believing that I was at last to hear the voice for which I had waited for twenty-four hours, I dashed joyously into the corridor. But the message was not from Roland but from Clare; it was not to say that he had arrived home that morning, but to tell me that he had died of wounds at a Casualty Clearing Station on December 23rd.

*'... mere militia ... which are to be
looked upon only as temporary excrescences
bred out of the distemper of the State.'*
— Blackstone's Commentaries

A Passionate Prodigality

GUY CHAPMAN

I

For a long time I used to think of myself as part of a battalion, and not as an individual. During all that time the war, the forms and colours of that experience, possessed a part of my senses. My life was involved with the lives of other men, a few living, some dead.

It is only now that I can separate myself from them. For that and other reasons this is more strictly the account of a company and begins in July, 1915, when a battalion of the New Army set out for France.

I was loath to go. I had no romantic illusions. I was not eager, or even resigned to self-sacrifice, and my heart gave back no answering throb to the thought of England. In fact, I was very much afraid; and again, afraid of being afraid, anxious lest I should show it. Nevertheless, I concluded that it was easiest to meet a fate already beginning to overawe, as an integral figure in the battalion I had been born into.

As yet it had little but familiarity to commend it. When (after three months in the Inns of Court and a strenuous course at the Staff College) I joined it on the eve of 1915, I was shocked by my first contact with the New Army. It was not so much the circumstances; the dull little south coast watering-place in winter; the derelict palazzo, the headquarters, facing on one side the tumbling grey sea and on the other an unkempt field; it was not the men in shabby blue clothes and forage caps with their equipment girt about them with bits of string: it was the obvious incapacity and amateurishness of the whole outfit which depressed. The 13th had been broken off from a swarm of men at the depot some three months earlier, and from then left almost completely to its own devices. It never had more than three regular officers, and those very senior and very retired, two from the Indian Army and not one from the regiment. In consequence it learned nothing of the traditions of its name — few could have told you anything of Alma or Albuera — knew nothing of its four regular battalions. Below these seniors lay a heterogeneous mass of majors, captains and subalterns from every walk of life; colonial policemen, solicitors, ex-irregulars, planters, ex-rankers, and in three cases pure *chevaliers' d'industrie*. Many displayed only too patently their intention of getting through the war as quietly, comfortably, and as profitably as they could manage. They effectively discouraged the juniors from demonstrations of excessive zeal, and by sheer negation tried to stifle our hunger for information. They failed, but nevertheless, the miasma of petty jealousy, bickering and foolish intrigue, which surrounded them, was the cause of much melancholy and profanity in us juniors. In the ranks there were a few time-expired N.C.O.s, among whom one was found giving the fire-commands of forty years before, 'Ready — present — fire.' The ten months' training, which the battalion went through before it reached France, was therefore a compound of enthusiasm and empiricism on the part of the junior subalterns and the other ranks. Even now I am amazed at the zeal which induced some of us after dinner to push matches representing platoons about the table, uttering words of command in hoarse whispers, or on Sunday mornings climb the frosty, wind-cropped downs to practise map-reading and marching by the compass. We had one to explain things to us. We had to get our textbooks by heart before we could impart a crumb of information to our platoons. We seized on and devoured every fragment of practical experience which came our way, gobbled whole the advice contained in those little buff pamphlets entitled *Notes from the Front,* advice, alas! out of date before it was published. We listened hopefully to the lectures of general officers who seemed happier talking of Jubbulpore than of Ypres. We pondered the jargon of experts, each convinced that his peculiar weapon, machine gun, rifle, bayonet, or bomb, was the one designed to bring the war to a satisfactory conclusion. We were inclined to resist their pedantry, suspecting that in truth they knew little more than ourselves; and we — we knew nothing. We were in fact amateurs, and though we should stoutly have denied it, in our hearts amateurs we knew ourselves to be, pathetically anxious to achieve the status of the professional. The testing of the results of all these pains and ardours now lay elsewhere.

The bugle blew the 'Fall in,' and the companies clustered on the edge of the camp poured themselves into the mould of a battalion. I told off my sections and stood at ease, noticing with an uneasy eye that the sergeant of the platoon in front was hiccoughing gently and swaying on his feet. The colonel gave the word and the battalion moved off. The band played *The British Grenadiers.* The sun shone its bravest. A group of ladies in summer frocks waved handkerchiefs. We had started for France.

The train carried us slowly through the south of England, hopeful by following branch lines to be inconspicuous. But the men hung their newly shaved heads out of windows, waved, roared, shrieked, yelled, sang, and defeated official precaution. In the corner of my compartment, an elderly major slept. He knew all about departures, and was thankful for the opportunity of a few hours' peace. The rest of us chattered away about our anticipations. We were all very young and girded impatiently at the slowness of the train. At one point I saw the house of an elderly friend and hoped I might survive to drink his port again. The train seemed abominably dilatory. Our first juvenile excitement waned as we began to suffer that other juvenile softness, hunger. Darkness came down. We had now been six hours on our way and fell to debating whether after all we were to embark. Then a quiet voice said, 'Folkestone.'

The boat lay at the lower pier. We clattered down the iron steps and thrust our way on board. In spite of protests, the junior subaltern — myself — was detailed for duty somewhere in the bottom of the ship. I seated myself on a flight of steps and trusted that I should not be sick. The men lay tightly pressed together, rows of green cigars, and a great odour of sweaty, dusty humanity clotted between the decks. A jerky movement was imposed upon our smooth passage. I began to feel qualms. There was a bar in this part of the ship, much frequented by a party of Highlanders returning from leave. As they came down the stairs, each man jolted against me, and at each jolt, my nausea increased. At last, I rose and kicked out the subaltern who was due to relieve me. I climbed wretchedly into the bows. Two destroyers flirted playfully round and about us, making signals at intervals. Someone began to talk of submarines. I didn't care. I looked down into the sea and was very ill.

In my misery, I hardly noticed our entrance into harbour, and was nearly the last to leave the boat. As I staggered on to the quay, burdened with a pack weighing 53 lbs., a rifle, a revolver, field-glasses, a prismatic compass, 120 rounds of rifle ammunition and 24 of revolver, my newly nailed boots shot from under me and I clattered on the pavé. 'Nah then,' roared a voice from the darkness. 'Come on you — always late, blast yer!' I was far too shattered to answer the R.S.M. I tottered up and ran painfully down the quay.

So on the 31st July, 1915, we landed in France. It was one o'clock of the morning. As we swung over the bridge, the band broke into the Marseillaise. Windows were flung up and night-capped heads thrust forth. They were very angry. A stray dog or so joined us; and a small boy attached himself to me, offering the services of his sister—jig-a-jig. I cuffed his head. We began to climb a hill, which rapidly became the side of a house. The band gasped and broke down. A man fainted and was dragged to the side of the road. The pace dwindled to a crawl. As we reached the top, panting, the column of the Grande Armée, rising darkly against the sky, sneered at us from its veteran experience. At the camp, the men tumbled gladly into their tents, and we, after a rapid inspection of our own, elected for the open air. In ten minutes, we were asleep.

We woke in broad sunlight. Women were walking between our prostrate bodies, offering apples. I bought some; they were very sour. Below us, Boulogne preened itself, and the sea was all golden dimples. As soon as I had finished breakfast, the adjutant seized me and bade me go in search of a station called Pont de Briques. I was inclined to grumble until I heard the Colonel declaring that it was a fair day for a route march round Boulogne. I fled thankfully. Chestnut avenues shaded me, and at Pont de Briques I found not only a station but commendable beer. During the afternoon subalterns were permitted one hour in Boulogne in batches of four. We bathed, and later sought the bar of the Folkestone, where we gazed round-eyed at the resplendent figures, rich as Spanish galleons, of the Base Commandant's staff. One specimen, an A.D.C. clad in golden breeches and golden puttees, carrying in his arms a Pekinese, particularly took my fancy. 'See what comes of being good,' I murmured to myself.

Night was falling as we marched down the hill. We waited an hour at Pont de Briques, and then, as if by a miracle, a train clattered in bearing our transport, which had come by way of Havre, the second-in-command, and the quartermaster. We made our first acquaintance with HOMMES 40, CHEVAUX-EN-LONG 8. 'Where are we going?' we asked; but no one could answer us. Captain Burns, the T.O. (a Cockney Fluellen, if ever such existed, a solemn man with a very private sense of humour; on occasions it permitted him to grin and twinkle below and above his heavy cavalry moustache) reproved our excited conjectures. 'You'll find out quite soon enough,' he muttered, 'too soon, may be.'

At length, it may have been some three hours later—those hours spent in sauntering along French railways contract with the space of years—our train came to a considered halt. We fell in on the platform. A damp board, spelled out by torchlight from end to end, proclaimed this place as Watten—empty information since we had no maps. I was given a bicycle and told to follow the brigade billeting officer. We rode in silence down silent roads, colourless, wreathed in mist. At last at the entrance to a village, he dismounted. 'This is Nortleulinghem. You've got the whole village. Put your men where you like; — and don't wake the *maire*': a supererogatory piece of advice. I should not dare to wake anything so august. Too shy to question him as to where Nortleulinghem might be by the map, I saluted and he faded into the mist.

I walked to the crossroads and in the waking dawn looked up and down. Everywhere there was silence; not even a cock. Faint misgivings as to whether I was or was not in the war zone beset me. It was better to be on the safe side. Unbuttoning my holster and loosening my revolver, I strode into Nort-leulinghem and began to explore. A charming village with well-built houses and barns. Trees heavy with fruit bowed over walls. A field of corn on the hillside looked almost ripe for cutting. A lean cat came out, yawned and was friendly. A dog woke into passionate yelps. I chalked signs and numbers on doors. Still not a gun fired, not a rifle. Where was this fabled war?

At last there was the sound of marching feet and the battalion came in sight. I reported to the adjutant, and then asked diffidently, 'Where exactly is Nortleulinghem, sir?' 'Where?' he echoed. 'Oh, about ten minutes behind St. Omer.' I withdrew confusedly.

Four days passed rapidly in Nortleulinghem, days on which we drew odd-ments of equipment, learned to put on our gas-masks, started to censor let-ters. The battle atmosphere began to pervade us. Captain Burns stalked the village, upbraiding subalterns he found wanting. ''Ere,' he would say, 'where's your revolver? Suppose a body of Oolans was to come down that hill, where'ud you be? Don't answer me back. Go and put it on.'

On the fifth morning we resumed our march. I had carefully mislaid my rifle. [. . .]

Still there was leisure to explore Hannescamps, a deserted skeleton through whose ribs coarse weeds and grass were already pushing their way. Here one discovered the eternal difference between the French and English. The Frenchman will take infinite pains and spare no labour to make himself safe and comfortable; the English prefer indolent discomfort and to chance their arm. Hannescamps had been badly battered. Perhaps two roofs of the thirty-odd houses still pretended to offer a shelter from the wind and rain. Of those nearest to the line only a few broken walls stood. Rank grasses were pursuing their march over what had been brick floors. On this side of the main street the French had built from the stone debris a high wall some five hundred yards in length, perhaps ten feet high, to protect passersby from stealthy as-sassination by the bullets which came flying over the ridge half a mile away and, helped by the fall of the ground, whined through the orchards like evil insects. It was a wise precaution, but such was our perversity, that before we left this Arcadia, we had torn down most of it for other purposes; and the rest had lapsed into ruin.

The British had already begun to take over the village. The crossroads were placarded as Piccadilly Circus (we were a completely London brigade), and the ruins of the large farm at the corner naturally became Leicester Square. The machine gunners with prompt wit had named their dark hovel 'The Two Inch Tap.'[1] Exploration led one into the wilderness of a civilization overcome. Here behind Leicester Square lay a secluded garden. The lawn was draggled and mossy, but pink roses nodded and scented the air, while the peacock, so cunningly carved from a box bush, still flaunted a defiant shell-burnt tail. He at least had no doubts of the outcome of the war; but when I passed that way in the spring of 1918, nature, a kindlier wrecker, had sprouted him to a mere shrub.

As one pushed deeper into the outlying parts of this tangled maze, there was always something to arrest the eye: a stentorian Michelin advertisement, miraculously preserved, a grey rat creeping under a fallen log, a bird shouting nonsense from a dilapidated apple-tree, slugs fat and horribly red. On the plaster of this broken wall is drawn in pencil with supreme genius a mêlée of legs and buttocks, a pornographic satire; yet with so much spirit has the pattern been wrought that we catch our breath in admiration for this un-known, perhaps dead, Gavarni.

There is a secret magic about these waste lands. While you wander through the corrupted overgrown orchard, there is always someone at your back. You turn. It is nothing but the creak of a branch, broken with the same wanton merriment with which a shell breaks a human limb and leaves it hanging by the frail tension of the skin. In all these destroyed places at the fringe of the line, places to be manned only in case of attack, such as the keeps on the road from Pont Fixe to Chocolate Menier Corner, the suburbs of Arras, Voormezeele, Calonne and this place Hannescamps, there is always the apprehension of ghosts; not those of the men who have died there, but of something older, something less perishable, the spirit of the place itself which watches the inquisitive idler with eyes half fearful, as if to ask, 'Will you too profane me?' But if you turn to surprise the watcher, there is nothing except the fog filtering between the trees and the smell of rank vegetation. You stand still, half hoping to surprise the wounded guardian, but while you wait — your involuntary summons about to be answered — the spell is shattered. An internal woodpecker, the machine gun in the distance, taps; bullets slap against the crumbling wall; and the spirit which you hoped to incarnate has shrivelled and is gone.

We took what shelter we could find. The accommodation was scanty, but most of the cellars had been converted into living rooms; and here and there a recess hollowed in a bank had been fashioned into an *abri* with plank sides and a timbered and clodded roof, warm and pleasant, but infested with rats, which ran across one in the dark and plucked boldly at one's blankets.

If I dwell too long among these forgotten ruins, I crave forgiveness. This broken village and its defences was the school where this battalion grew to manhood, and though we passed through many worse as well as easier periods, it is by Hannescamps that the originals swear. To have been at Hannescamps made you free of the battalion. A late comer, however gallant, however loved, had to earn his right to that primitive integrity before he was admitted to the brotherhood. Years later when I was asked to do something, I forget what, and shyly protested my unworthiness in the face of better men, I was reproached with, 'Ah! but you was at Hannescamps.' And for those words, I summon as powerfully as my poor words will command, the ghost of that devastated hamlet once more to fill a skyline.

There was a concert held at Bully-Grenay, one of the unforgettable nights. The small hall was crowded. Beer and rum punch — one wondered whether the quartermaster distilled the spirit, or merely pinched it — were sufficient. We applauded the sentimental tenor and sang the chorus with a wealth of feeling which we should deny in the morning. We cheered Sergeant Hyams of the Lewis Guns in *0-0-0, I'm an Eskimo*, a song of suitable simplicity. Fairburn sang *Mandalay,* and later, under pressure, *Little Pigs make the best of pork,* with vehement gesticulation. But these only led up to our adjutant. He will never again have such an audience. *Winters' Nights* is a ragtime melody, the words negligible; but it will make an exile dream. Cuthbertson sang it so quietly that the dreams were undisturbed. In the end we were crooning the tune, would have sung it until we rocked asleep. In a moment's pause Boche shells could be heard tearing the night outside and dropping with subdued crashes in the square. But no small strafe could have disturbed us: we lay back and sang.

Autumn was coming in, and we stood-to at dawn in white mists which peeled slowly away and kept us waiting. From the south came the earliest stories of the hush-hush cars, in the attacks of the 15th September. They were well-garnished newspaper tales and we began to expect the advertised breakthrough. Yet there was a churlish expectation that the reports would prove to be highly coloured. The war was not going to end quite so easily, we felt. Within a few weeks our refusal of the G.H.Q. illusionist's tricks was confirmed by the arrival of a Canadian reconnoitring party. The 15th September had not been the jam with which these parental authorities tried to disguise the powder. The Canuck captain who took over from me lumped the tanks and the French Canadian battalions in one almighty explosive sentence. It was a long sentence, about a minute in duration and of a blasting searing quality. Otherwise he was efficient, cheerful, monosyllabic and thirsty.

This relief was unexpected. We had looked to stay in these quiet pastures for another month. But we had grazed long enough, and as Smith put it, we were fat enough for the slaughter. Rain clouds, heavy with expectant Walküre, blackened the evening sky as we marched from Bully-Grenay to Hersin. We passed a sinister platoon of the recently cursed French Canadians. A pullet swinging from a rifle muzzle and the wolvish faces of the men recalled Callot's *reiter*. They stared blankly and refused our greeting; but several broke from their ranks to accost in their clipped dialect some women who were standing beside the road.

Next day we were watching. It was the 18th October and the smell of autumn lay heavy on the air; a chill colourless morning, but the sun broke through as we passed a lonely sentry before a lonely handsome château near Ranchicourt, an army or corps headquarters; at least, something too august for our acquaintance. Our trench-cramped limbs were already growing aware of their novel freedom. We stepped lighter and with a rhythmical swing. That night we came to Magnicourt-en-Comté, and there we lay two days.

When we moved out, there was a nip in the air. The first frosts had come. Beeches showered us with copper and yellow coin. Briars shaken by our tread flung us the crystals from their sprays. The way was lined with brave colours; streamers of travellers' joy waved in the faint breeze and hawberries shook their crimson heads at the tramp of our boots. As we passed under a tunnel of dark trees, the band broke into its thunderous jollity. Blow, fife; rattle, drum. On this morning the clatter of *Brian Boru* is better than all Beethoven's nine symphonies. Even the immortal Ninth pales before the chorus: *And we'll buy a pair of laces orfer pore — old — Mike.* The battalion is moving as one man; very strong, very steady, with a sway in the shoulders and a lilt in the feet: We have regained our youth; we have recovered the innocence with which we came to France, an innocence not now of ignorance but of knowledge. We have forgotten whither we are marching: we do not greatly care what billets we find tonight. We are content to live in the moment, to feel the warm sun, to enjoy the strength of our bodies, and to be lulled by the rhythmical momentum with which we march. We are no longer individuals but a united body. The morning, the sun, the keen air, and the rhythm of our feet compound a draught more heady than doctored *vin blanc,* than the forgotten kisses of the girl in the billet. Few had forebodings of their destiny. At the halts they lay in the long wet grass and gossiped, enormously at ease. The whistle blew. They jumped for their equipment. The little grey figure of the colonel far ahead waved its stick. Hump your pack and get a move on. The next hour, man, will bring you three miles nearer to your death. Your life and your death are nothing to these fields — nothing, no more than it is to the man planning the next attack at G.H.Q. You are not even a pawn. Your death will not prevent future wars, will not make the world safe for your children. Your death means no more than if you had died in your bed, full of years and respectability, having begotten a tribe of young. Yet by your courage in tribulation, by your cheerfulness before the dirty devices of this world, you have won the love of those who have watched you. All we remember is your living face, and that we loved you for being of our clay and our spirit.

So, marching, we came to Magnicourt-sur-Canche, on a hill-side with the grey water of the Canche rippling against wooded banks. There were trout below the bridge. I wondered if they would rise to a Ministerial Deevil, the fly the last trout I hooked had fallen to. But these thoughts should be banished in October. Let me, instead, recall the proud four-poster bed under whose lace curtains I smothered, and the tessellated pavement on which it stood. 'Fit for Sir Douglas himself,' commented my herculean batman, Johns, as he produced a mug of tea in the morning.

The battalion threw the eighteen miles to Gézaincourt over their shoulder as easily as apple rind. Some of us explored the Bon Air that evening. Uncle cut jests in evil French with the villainous old dame.

The next day was painful marching. The weather had changed. Out of a dull sky a chill wind blew with a hint of showers in it. Four miles from Puchevillers, it turned to rain in good earnest. We reached the camp wet through.

What a camp it was! It had been the temporary accommodation for troops for 1st July. No doubt a pleasant enough place in midsummer, this six-acre orchard with tents under germinating apple-trees. Since then it had been used by every arm of the service. There was no grass. The ground, churned and stamped by hoofs and boots, was six inches deep in mud and horse droppings and smelled stale. The trees were plastered with mud, lacerated with ropes, and the bark torn with the teeth of mules. The men sheltered in threadbare tents; the officers in two leaking canvas huts. And it rained. It rained remorselessly: it was neither heavy nor light; just rain; it never altered its tempo; it never changed its tone. In the rare hours it ceased, its irritation was supplied by heavy drops slapping on the canvas. It was cold, too. We crouched miserably over braziers filled with wet green wood. The smoke filled the barracks, and flavoured our food and our tobacco. Our clothes were sodden, our kits damp. There were no means of amusing the men, no place to see them. Our spirits fell to the bottom of the scale.

We were waiting for Z day. Z day was postponed, and then postponed again. On a raw grey afternoon, the colonel rode out, accompanied by Smith, four company commanders, the adjutant, and Archbold, the intelligence officer. The horses after long days of idleness were fresh. They bolted down the road to Toutencourt, Archbold and Cuthbertson leading, our frail little colonel with difficulty holding in his pony, and Uncle, no centaur, bumping ferociously and growling between his teeth: 'Whoa — Whoa — you beggar — oh — oh — oh — stop, you brute, and let me get my giglamps straight.' We passed through unenchanting villages where the walls were splashed to the eaves with oily mud by the lorries grumbling to and fro. Pools of dark fluid covered with iridescent scum lay across the road. Labour battalions and Boche prisoners were struggling vainly against the advancing tide. These villages, Varennes and Hedauville, were packed with troops resting, pale drab men who walked listlessly. Beyond there was the unsteady tossing of the gunfire round the Thiepval ridge. At last we moved into open country and surveyed a long grey hill whose top was vanishing in the drizzle. 'This is our rendezvous,' said the colonel. 'Can you find your way here again?' We surveyed the dismal ground. The tall elms of Englebelmer seemed at peace; but every now and then the mist reddened as a heavy coughed its shell into the air. The rumbling and tossing of gun-fire was growing stronger, pulsing into an uneasy rhythm. Yes, we nodded. 'All right, go home.'

The ponies needed no urging. In a minute we had scattered over the turf. The mist had turned to rain again, and night was falling. Harding, a grim colonist, and I galloped ahead and by hard riding reached our melancholy camp by five o'clock. The others gradually came in until only Uncle was missing. We clustered round the smoky brazier and speculated on his fate. Seven, eight o' clock passed: and then about nine, through the hum of rain and the splash of drippings from the trees, we heard the sock-sock-sock of weary hoofs picking their way through mud, and the voice of Uncle raised in melancholy song, 'Be it never so 'umble, there's no-o place like 'ome.' He had been left at the start. He had reached the Hedauville crossroads, and ignorant of his direction, turned down the road to Albert. Discovering his error after four or five miles, he turned back. Reaching Hedauville a second time he once more failed to discern his right road and rode due northwards to Acheux. It was now dark and the rain on his spectacles made his difficulties even greater. He passed through Acheux about 6.30 on our reckoning. Somewhere north of here he dismounted from his horse to examine a signpost; and then cramped and soaking was unable to mount again. He plodded along a dark muddy road. The few wayfarers he met were quite ignorant of the existence of Puchevillers. At last he found a military policeman who had not only heard of the place but was able to hoist our poor friend into the saddle and put him on the right road. At a conservative estimate we reckoned that Uncle had covered about thirty miles in his Odyssey. Happily we were not short of whisky.

The next morning we heard that Z day was once more postponed and that afternoon an order was handed to me: 'You will report, at 63rd Bde.

H.Q. at Terramesnil this evening for a course of instruction in G staff duties.'
It was the intervention of a kindly fate: and I resented it. I knew we were on
the eve of a serious engagement. But for the weather we should have been
in it a week ago. I had no illusions — those cheerful staff illusions — of what
was encouragingly termed a walk-over; and I disliked being shelled as much
as anyone has ever disliked it. But I did not want to leave the battalion or the
company. It was flagrant desertion to leave at this point. Afterwards would
be another matter, but at the moment I had no relish for the wary and pious
discretion commended by Sir Thomas Browne. I sought out the colonel and
had a short passionate interview under the streaming trees.

'May I stay till we come out, sir?'

'No. You've go to go. It's an order. My dear boy, don't be an ass. You've
got to obey.'

'Couldn't you ask Brigade, sir?'

'No. I don't see how I can. It's an order. No. No. No.'

He wandered off into the rain and I flung away angrily. I said good-bye
to a few friends in the hut who looked at me enviously, to the C.S.M., whose
eyes I could scarcely meet, to the company pony. Johns rolled up my kit and
we bundled it on to the mess cart. The six miles to Terramesnil were some
of the most wretched I have ever driven. I was worn with misery as we drew
up at the red lamp of the Brigade H.Q. A light shone from an open door
and beyond there was a dry clean room with a blazing fire.

Notes

1. Before the war, a machine gunner was trained to tap the butt of his gun with
   sufficient strength to move it two inches, which deflected the muzzle so that
   at, I think, 200 yards, there was an unbroken arc of fire.

Good-bye
to All That

ROBERT GRAVES

By the end of August 1915, particulars of the coming offensive against La
Bassée were beginning to leak through the young staff officers. The French
civilians knew about it; and so, naturally, did the Germans. Every night now
new batteries and lorry-trains of shells came rumbling up the Béthune–La
Bassée road. Other signs of movement included sapping forward at Ver-
melles and Cambrin, where the lines lay too far apart for a quick rush across,
and the joining up of the sap-heads to make a new front line. Also, orders
for evacuation of hospitals; the appearance of cavalry and New Army divisions; issue of new types of weapons. Then Royal Engineer officers super-
vised the digging of pits at intervals along the front line. They were sworn
not to reveal what these would hold, but we knew that it would be gas-
cylinders. Ladders for climbing quickly out of trenches were brought up by
the lorry-load and dumped at Cambrin village. As early as September 3rd, I
had a bet with Robertson that our Division would attack from the Cambrin-
Cuinchy line. When I went home on leave six days later, the sense of impending events had become so strong that I almost hated to go.

Leave came round for officers about every six or eight months in ordinary
times; heavy casualties shortened the period, general offensives cut leave altogether. Only one officer in France ever refused to go on leave when his turn
came — Colonel Cross of the Fifty-second Light Infantry (the Second Battalion of the Oxford and Bucks Light Infantry, which insisted on its original
style as jealously as we kept our 'c' in Welch). Cross is alleged to have refused
leave on the following grounds: 'My father fought with the Regiment in the
South African War, and had no leave; my grandfather fought in the Crimea
with the Regiment, and had no leave. I do not regard it in the Regimental

tradition to take home-leave when on active service.' Cross, a professional survivor, was commanding the Battalion in 1917 when I last heard of him.

London seemed unreally itself. Despite the number of uniforms in the streets, the general indifference to, and ignorance about, the War surprised me. Enlistment still remained voluntary. The universal catch-word was 'Business as usual.' My family were living in London now, at the house formerly occupied by my uncle, Robert von Ranke, the German consul-general. He had been forced to leave in a hurry on August 4th, 1914, and my mother undertook to look after the house for him while the War lasted. So when Edward Marsh rang me up from the Prime Minister's office at 10 Downing Street to arrange a meal someone intervened and cut him off — the telephone of the German consul-general's sister was, of course, closely watched by the anti-espionage section of Scotland Yard. The Zeppelin scare had just begun. Some friends of the family came in one night, and began telling me of the Zeppelin air-raids, of bombs dropped only three streets off.

'Well, do you know,' I said, 'the other day I was asleep in a house and in the early morning a bomb dropped next door and killed three soldiers who were billeted there, a woman and a child.'

'Good gracious,' they cried, 'what did you do then?'

'It was at a place called Beuvry, about four miles behind the trenches,' I explained, 'and I was tired out, so I went to sleep again.'

'Oh,' they said, 'but that happened in France!' and the look of interest faded from their faces as though I had taken them in with a stupid catch.

'Yes,' I agreed, 'and it was only an aeroplane that dropped the bomb.'

I went up to Harlech for the rest of my leave, and walked about on the hills in an old shirt and a pair of shorts. When I got back to France, 'The Actor,' a regular officer in 'A' Company, asked me: 'Had a good time on leave?'

'Yes.'

'Go to many dances?'

'Not one.'

'What shows did you go to?'

'I didn't go to any shows.'

'Hunt?'

'No.'

'Sleep with any nice girls?'

'No, I didn't. Sorry to disappoint you.'

'What the hell *did* you do, then?'

'Oh, I just walked about on some hills.'

'Good God,' he said, 'chaps like you don't deserve leave.'

On September 19th we relieved the Middlesex Regiment at Cambrin, and were told that these would be the trenches from which we attacked. The preliminary bombardment had already started, a week in advance. As I led my platoon into the line, I recognized with some disgust the same machine-gun shelter where I had seen the suicide on my first night in trenches. It seemed ominous. This was by far the heaviest bombardment from our own guns we had yet seen. The trenches shook properly, and a great cloud of drifting shell-smoke obscured the German line. Shells went over our heads in a steady stream; we had to shout to make our neighbours hear. Dying down a little at night, the racket began again every morning at dawn, a little louder each time. 'Damn it: we said, 'there can't be a living soul left in those trenches.' But still it went on. The Germans retaliated, though not very vigorously. Most of their heavy artillery had been withdrawn from this sector, we were told, and sent across to the Russian front. More casualties came from our own shorts and blow-backs than from German shells. Much of the ammunition that our batteries were using was made in the United States and contained a high percentage of duds; the driving bands were always coming off. We had fifty casualties in the ranks and three officer casualties, including Buzz Off—badly wounded in the head. This happened before steel helmets were issued; we would not have lost nearly so many with those. I got two insignificant wounds on the hand, which I took as an omen of the right sort.

On the morning of the 23rd, Thomas came back from Battalion Headquarters carrying a note-book and six maps, one for each of us company officers. 'Listen,' he said, 'and copy out all this skite on the back of your maps. You'll have to explain it to your platoons this afternoon. Tomorrow morning we go back to dump our blankets, packs and greatcoats in Béthune. The next day, that's Saturday the 25th, we attack.' This being the first definitive news we had been given, we looked up half startled, half relieved. I still have the map, and these are the orders as I copied them down: —

'FIRST OBJECTIVE — *Les Briques Farm* — The big house plainly visible to our front, surrounded by trees. To reach this it is necessary to cross three lines of enemy trenches. The first is three hundred yards distant, the second four hundred, and the third about six hundred. We then cross two railways. Behind the second railway line is a German trench called the Brick Trench. Then comes the Farm, a strong place with moat and cellars and a kitchen garden strongly staked and wired.

'SECOND OBJECTIVE — *The Town of Auchy* — This is also plainly visible from our trenches. It is four hundred yards beyond the Farm and defended by a first line of trench half-way across, and a second line immediately in front of the town. When we have occupied the first line our direction is half-right, with the left of the Battalion directed on Tall Chimney.

'THIRD OBJECTIVE — *Village of Haisnes* — Conspicuous by high-spired church. Our eventual line will be taken up on the railway behind this village, where we will dig in and await reinforcements.'

When Thomas had reached this point, The Actor's shoulders were shaking with laughter.

'What's up?' asked Thomas irritably.

The Actor giggled: 'Who in God's name is responsible for this little effort?'

'Don't know,' Thomas said. 'Probably Paul the Pimp, or someone like that.' (Paul the Pimp was a captain on the Divisional Staff, young, inexperienced and much disliked. He 'wore red tabs upon his chest, And even on his undervest.') 'Between the six of us, but you youngsters must be careful not to let the men know, this is what they call a "subsidiary attack." There will be no troops in support. We've just got to go over and keep the enemy busy while the folk on our right do the real work. You notice that the bombardment is much heavier over there. They've knocked the Hohenzollern Redoubt to bits. Personally, I don't give a damn either way. We'll get killed whatever happens.'

We all laughed.

'All right, laugh now, but by God, on Saturday we've got to carry out this funny scheme.' I had never heard Thomas so talkative before.

'Sorry,' The Actor apologized, 'carry on with the dictation.'

Thomas went on:

'The attack will be preceded by forty minutes' discharge of the accessory,[1] which will clear the path for a thousand yards, so that the two railway lines will be occupied without difficulty. Our advance will follow closely behind the accessory. Behind us are three fresh divisions and the Cavalry Corps. It is expected we shall have no difficulty in breaking through. All men will parade with their platoons; pioneers, servants, etc., to be warned. All platoons to be properly told off under N.C.O.'s. Every N.C.O. is to know exactly what is expected of him, and when to take over command in case of casualties. Men who lose touch must join up with the nearest company or regiment and push on. Owing to the strength of the accessory, men should be warned against remaining too long in captured trenches where the accessory is likely to collect; but to keep to the open and above all to push on. It is important that if smoke-helmets have to be pulled down they must be tucked in under the shirt.'

The Actor interrupted again. 'Tell me, Thomas, do you believe in this funny accessory?'

Thomas said: 'It's damnable. It's not soldiering to use stuff like that, even though the Germans did start it. We're sure to bungle it. Look at those new gas-companies — sorry, excuse me this once, I mean accessory-companies — their very look makes me tremble. Chemistry-dons from London University, a few lads straight from school, one or two N.C.O's of the old-soldier type, trained together for three weeks, then given a job as responsible as this. Of course they'll bungle it. How could they do anything else? But let's be merry. I'm going on again:

'Men of company: what they are to carry:

Two hundred rounds of ammunition (bomb-throwers fifty, and signallers one hundred and fifty rounds).

Heavy tools carried in sling by the strongest men.

Waterproof sheet in belt.

Sandbag in right tunic-pocket.

Field-dressing and iodine.

Emergency ration, including biscuit.

One tube-helmet, to be worn when we advance, rolled, up on the head.
   It must be quite secure and the top part turned down. If possible
   each man will be provided with an elastic band.

One smoke-helmet, old pattern, to be carried for preference behind the
   back, where it is least likely to be damaged by stray bullets, etc.

Wire-cutters, as many as possible, by wiring party and others; hedging
   gloves by wire party.

Platoon screens, for artillery observation, to be carried by a man in each
   platoon who is not carrying a tool.

Packs, capes, greatcoats, blankets will be dumped, not carried.

No one is to carry sketches of our position or anything to be likely of
   service to the enemy.

'That's all. I believe we're going over first with the Middlesex in support. If we get through the German wire I'll be satisfied. Our guns don't seem to be cutting it. Perhaps they're putting that off until the intense bombardment. Any questions?'

That afternoon I repeated the whole rigmarole to the platoon, and told them of the inevitable success attending our assault. They seemed to believe it. All except Sergeant Townsend. 'Do you say, Sir, that we have three divisions and the Cavalry Corps behind us?' he asked.

'Yes,' I answered.

'Well, excuse me, Sir, I'm thinking it's only those chaps on the right that'll get reinforcements. If we get half a platoon of Mons Angels,[2] that's about all we will get.'

'Sergeant Townsend,' I said, 'you're a well-known pessimist. This is going to be a really good show.'

We spent the night repairing damaged trenches.

When morning came we were relieved by the Middlesex, and marched back to Béthune, where we dumped our spare kit at the Montmorency barracks. The Battalion officers messed together in the château near by. This billet was claimed at the same time by the staff of a New Army division, due to take part in the fighting next day. The argument ended amicably with the Division and Battalion messing together. It was, someone pointed out, like a brutal caricature of The Last Supper in duplicate. In the middle of the long table sat the two pseudo-Christs, our Colonel and the Divisional General. Everybody was drinking a lot; the subalterns, allowed whiskey for a treat, grew rowdy. They raised their glasses with: 'Cheerio, we will be messing together tomorrow night in La Bassée!' Only the company commanders were looking worried. I remember 'C' Company Commander especially, Captain A. L. Samson, biting his thumb and refusing to join in the excitement. I think it was Childe-Freeman of 'B' Company who said that night: 'The last time the Regiment visited these parts we were under decent leadership. Old Marlborough had more sense than to attack the La Bassée lines; he masked them and went around.'

The G.S.O. 1 of the New Army division, a staff-colonel, knew the Adjutant well. They had played polo together in India. I happened to be sitting opposite them. The G.S.O. 1 said, rather drunkenly: 'Charley, see that silly old woman over there? Calls himself General Commanding! Doesn't know where he is; doesn't know where his division is; can't even read a map properly. He's marched the poor sods off their feet and left his supplies behind, God knows how far back. They've had to use their iron rations and what they could pick up in the villages. And tomorrow he's going to fight a battle. Doesn't know anything about battles; the men have never been in trenches before, and tomorrow's going to be a glorious balls-up, and the day after tomorrow he'll be sent home.' Then he ended, quite seriously: 'Really, Charley, it's just as I say, no exaggeration. You mark my words!'

That night we marched back again to Cambrin. The men were singing. Being mostly from the Midlands, they sang comic songs rather than Welsh hymns: 'Slippery Sam,' 'When We've Wound up the Watch on the Rhine,' and 'Do Like a S'nice S'mince Pie,' to concertina accompaniment. The tune of the 'S'nice S'mince Pie' ran in my head all next day, and for the week following I could not get rid of it. The Second Welsh would never have sung a song like 'When We've Wound up the Watch on the Rhine.' Their only songs about the War were defeatist:

I want to go home,
I want to go home.
The coal-box and shrapnel they whistle and roar,
I don't want to go to the trenches no more,
I want to go over the sea
Where the Kayser can't shot bombs at me.
Oh, I
Don't want to die,
I want to go home.

There were several more verses in the same strain. Hewitt, the Welsh machine-gun officer, had written one in a more offensive spirit:

I want to go home,
I want to go home.
One day at Givenchy the week before last
The Allmands attacked and they nearly got past.
They pushed their way up to the Keep,
Through our maxim-gun sights we did peep,
Oh, my!
They let out a cry,
They never got home.

But the men would not sing it, though they all admired Hewitt.

The Béthune–La Bassée road was choked with troops, guns and transport, and we had to march miles north out of our way to circle round to Cambrin. Even so, we were held up two or three times by massed cavalry. Everything radiated confusion. A casualty clearing-station had been planted astride one of the principal cross-roads, and was already being shelled. By the time we reached Cambrin, the Battalion had marched about twenty miles that day. Then we heard that the Middlesex would go over first, with us in support; and to their left the Second Argyll and Sutherland Highlanders, with the Cameronians in support. The junior Royal Welch officers complained loudly at our not being given the honour of leading the attack. As the senior regiment, they protested, we were entitled to the 'Right of the Line.' An hour or so past midnight we moved into trench sidings just in front of the village. Half a mile of communication trench, known as 'Maison Rouge Alley,' separated us from the firing line. At half-past five the gas would be discharged. We were cold, tired, sick, and not at all in the mood for a battle, but tried to snatch an hour or two of sleep squatting in the trench. It had been raining for some time.

A grey, watery dawn broke at last behind the German lines; the bombardment, surprisingly slack all night, brisked up a little. 'Why the devil don't they send them over quicker?' The Actor complained. 'This isn't my idea of a bombardment. We're getting nothing opposite us. What little there seems to be is going into the Hohenzollern.'

'Shell shortage. Expected it,' was Thomas's laconic reply.

We were told afterwards that on the 23rd a German aeroplane had bombed the Army Reserve shell-dump and sent it up. The bombardment on the 24th, and on the day of the battle itself, compared very poorly with that of the previous days. Thomas looked strained and ill. 'It's time they were sending that damned accessory off. I wonder what's doing.'

The events of the next few minutes are difficult for me now to sort out. I found it more difficult still at the time. All we heard back there in the sidings was a distant cheer, confused crackle of rifle-fire, yells, heavy shelling on our front line, more shouts and yells, and a continuous rattle of machine-guns. After a few minutes, lightly wounded men of the Middlesex came stumbling down Maison Rouge Alley to the dressing-station. I stood at the junction of the siding and the Alley.

'What's happened? What's happened?' I asked.

'Bloody balls-up,' was the most detailed answer I could get.

Among the wounded were a number of men yellow-faced and choking, their buttons tarnished green — gas cases. Then came the badly wounded. Maison Rouge Alley being narrow, the stretchers had difficulty in getting down. The Germans started shelling it with five-point-nines.

Thomas went back to Battalion Headquarters through the shelling to ask for orders. It was the same place that I had visited on my first night in the trenches. This cluster of dug-outs in the reserve line showed very plainly from the air as Battalion Headquarters, and should never have been occupied during a battle. Just before Thomas arrived, the Germans put five shells into it. The Adjutant jumped one way, the Colonel another, the R.S.M. a third. One shell went into the signals dug-out, killed some signallers and destroyed the telephone. The Colonel, slightly cut on the hand, joined the stream of wounded and was carried back as far as the base with it. The Adjutant took command.

Meanwhile 'A' Company had been waiting in the siding for the rum to arrive; the tradition of every attack being a double tot of rum beforehand. All the other companies got theirs. The Actor began cursing: 'Where the bloody hell's that storeman gone?' We fixed bayonets in readiness to go up and attack as soon as Captain Thomas returned with orders. Hundreds of wounded streamed by. At last Thomas's orderly appeared. 'Captain's orders, Sir: 'A' Company to move up to the front line.' At that moment the storeman arrived, without rifle or equipment, hugging the rum-bottle, red-faced and retching. He staggered up to The Actor and said: 'There you are, Sir!', then fell on his face in the thick mud of a sump-pit at the junction of the trench and the siding. The stopper of the bottle flew out and what remained of the three gallons bubbled on the ground. The Actor made no reply. This was a crime that deserved the death penalty. He put one foot on the storeman's neck, the other in the small of his back, and trod him into the mud. Then he gave the order 'Company forward!' The Company advanced with a clatter of steel, and this was the last I ever heard of the storeman.

It seems that at half-past four an R. E. captain commanding the gas-company in the front line phoned through to Divisional Headquarters: 'Dead calm. Impossible discharge accessory.' The answer he got was: 'Accessory to be discharged at all costs.' Thomas had not over-estimated the gas-company's efficiency. The spanners for unscrewing the cocks of the cylinders proved, with two or three exceptions, to be misfits. The gas-men rushed about shouting for the loan of an adjustable spanner. They managed to discharge one or two cylinders; the gas went whistling out, formed a thick cloud a few yards off in No Man's Land, and then gradually spread back into our trenches. The Germans, who had been expecting gas, immediately put on their gas-helmets: semi-rigid ones, better than ours. Bundles of oily cotton-waste were strewn along the German parapet and set alight as a barrier to the gas. Then their batteries opened on our lines. The confusion in the front trench must have been horrible; direct hits broke several of the gas-cylinders, the trench filled with gas, the gas-company stampeded.

No orders could come through because the shell in the signals dug-out at Battalion Headquarters had cut communication not only between companies and Battalion, but between Battalion and Division. The officers in the trench had to decide on immediate action; so two companies of the Middlesex, instead of waiting for the intense bombardment which would follow the advertised forty minutes of gas, charged at once and got held up by the wire — which our artillery had not yet cut. So far it had only been treated with shrapnel, which made no effect on it; barbed wire needed high-explosive, and plenty of it. The Germans shot the Middlesex men down. One platoon is said to have found a gap and got into the German trench. But there were no survivors of the platoon to confirm this. Argyll and Sutherland Highlanders went over, too, on the Middlesex left; but two companies, instead of charging at once, rushed back out of the gas-filled assault trench to the support line, and attacked from there. It will be recalled that the trench system had been pushed forward nearer the enemy in preparation for the battle. These companies were therefore attacking from the old front line, but the barbed-wire entanglements protecting it had not been removed, so that the Highlanders got caught and machine-gunned between their own assault and support lines. The other two companies were equally unsuccessful. When the attack started, the German N.C.O's had jumped up on the parapet to encourage their men. These were Jägers, famous for their musketry.

The survivors of the two leading Middlesex companies now lay in shell-craters close to the German wire, sniping and making the Germans keep their heads down. They had bombs to throw, but these were nearly all of a new type issued for the battle. The fuses were lighted on the match-box principle, and the rain had made them useless. The other two companies of the Middlesex soon followed in support. Machine-gun fire stopped them half-way. Only one German machine-gun remained in action, the others having been knocked out by rifle- or trench-mortar fire. Why the single gun survived is a story in itself.

It starts with the privilege granted British colonial governors and high-commissioners of nominating one or two officers from their countries for attachment in wartime to the Regular Army. Under this scheme, the officers began as full lieutenants. The Captain-General of Jamaica (if that is his correct style) nominated the eighteen-year-old son of a rich planter, who went straight from Kingston to the First Middlesex. He was good-hearted enough, but of little use in the trenches, having never been out of the island in his life or, except for a short service with the West India militia, seen any soldiering. His company commander took a fatherly interest in 'Young Jamaica,' and tried to teach him duties. This Company Commander was known as 'The Boy.' He had twenty years' service with the Middlesex, and the unusual boast of having held every rank from 'boy' to captain in the same company. His father, I believe, had been the regimental sergeant-major. But 'Jamaica,' as a full lieutenant, ranked senior to the other experienced subalterns in the company, who were only second-lieutenants.

The Middlesex Colonel decided to shift Jamaica off on some course of extra-regimental appointment at the earliest opportunity. Somewhere about May or June, when instructed to supply an officer for the brigade trench-mortar company, he had sent Jamaica. Trench-mortars, being both dangerous and ineffective, the appointment seemed suitable. At the same time, the Royal Welch had also been asked to detail an officer, and the Colonel had sent Tiley, an ex-planter from Malaya, and what is called a 'fine natural soldier.' Tiley was chosen because, when attached to us from a Lancashire regiment, he had showed his resentment at the manner of his welcome somewhat too plainly. But, by September, mortars had improved in design and become an important infantry arm; so Jamaica, being senior to Tiley, held the responsible position of Brigade Mortar Officer.

When the Middlesex charged, The Boy fell mortally wounded as he climbed over the parapet. He tumbled back and began crawling down the trench to the stretcher-bearers' dugout, past Jamaica's trench-mortar emplacement. Jamaica had lost his gun-team, and was boldly serving the trench-mortars himself. On seeing The Boy, however, he deserted his post and ran off to fetch a stretcher-party. Tiley, meanwhile, on the other flank opposite Mine Point, had knocked out all the machine-guns within range. He went on until his mortar burst. Only one machine-gun in the Pope's Nose, a small salient facing Jamaica, remained active.

At this point the Royal Welch Fusiliers came up Maison Rouge Alley. The Germans were shelling it with five-nines (called 'Jack Johnsons' because of their black smoke) and lachrymatory shells. This caused a continual scramble backwards and forwards, to cries of: 'Come on!' 'Get back, you bastards!' 'Gas turning on us!' 'Keep your heads, you men!' 'Back like hell, boys!' 'Whose orders?' 'What's happening?' 'Gas!' 'Back!' 'Come on!' 'Gas!' 'Back!' Wounded men and stretcher-bearers kept trying to squeeze past. We were alternately putting on and taking off our gas-helmets, which made things worse. In many places the trench had caved in, obliging us to scramble over the top. Childe-Freeman reached the front line with only fifty men of 'B' Company; the rest had lost their way in some abandoned trenches half-way up.

The Adjutant met him in the support line. 'Ready to go over, Freeman?' he asked.

Freeman had to admit that most of his company were missing. He felt this disgrace keenly; it was the first time that he had commanded a company in battle. Deciding to go over with his fifty men in support of the Middlesex, he blew his whistle and the company charged. They were stopped by machine-gun fire before they had got through our own entanglements. Freeman himself died — oddly enough, of heart-failure — as he stood on the parapet.

A few minutes later, Captain Samson, with 'C' Company and the remainder of 'B,' reached our front line. Finding the gas-cylinders still whistling and the trench full of dying men, he decided to go over too — he could not have it said that the Royal Welch had let down the Middlesex. A strong, comradely feeling bound the Middlesex and the Royal Welch, intensified by the accident that the other three battalions in the Brigade were Scottish, and that our Scottish Brigadier was, unjustly no doubt, accused of favouring them. Our Adjutant voiced the extreme non-Scottish view: 'The jocks are all the same; both the trousered kind and the bare-arsed kind: they're dirty in trenches, they skite too much, and they charge like hell — both ways.' The First Middlesex, who were the original 'Diehards,' had more than once, with the Royal Welch, considered themselves let down by the jocks. So Samson charged with 'C' and the remainder of 'B' Company.

One of the 'C' officers told me later what happened. It had been agreed to advance by platoon rushes with supporting fire. When his platoon had gone about twenty yards, he signalled them to lie down and open covering fire. The din was tremendous. He saw the platoon on his left flopping down too, so he whistled the advance again. Nobody seemed to hear. He jumped up from his shell-hole, waved and signalled 'Forward!'

Nobody stirred.

He shouted: 'You bloody cowards, are you leaving me to go on alone?'

His platoon-sergeant, groaning with a broken shoulder, gasped: 'Not cowards, Sir. Willing enough. But they're all f—ing dead.' The Pope's Nose machine-gun, traversing, had caught them as they rose to the whistle.

'A' Company, too, had become separated by the shelling. I was with the leading platoon. The Surrey-man got a touch of gas and went coughing back. The Actor accused him of skrimshanking. This I thought unfair; the Surrey-man looked properly sick. I don't know what happened to him, but I heard that the gas-poisoning was not serious and that he managed, a few months later, to get back to his own regiment in France. I found myself with The Actor in a narrow communication trench between the front and support lines. This trench had not been built wide enough for a stretcher to pass the bends. We came on The Boy lying on his stretcher, wounded in the lungs and stomach. Jamaica was standing over him in tears, blubbering: 'Poor old Boy, poor old Boy, he's going to die; I'm sure he is. He's the only one who treated me decently.'

The Actor, finding that we could not get by, said to Jamaica: 'Take that poor sod out of the way, will you? I've got to get my company up. Put him into a dug-out, or somewhere.'

Jamaica made no answer; he seemed paralyzed by the horror of the occasion and could only repeat: 'Poor old Boy, poor old Boy!'

'Look here,' said The Actor, 'if you can't shift him into a dug-out we'll have to lift him on top of the trench. He can't live now, and we're late getting up.'

'No, no,' Jamaica shouted wildly.

The Actor lost his temper and shook Jamaica roughly by the shoulders. 'You're the bloody trench-mortar wallah aren't you?' he shouted.

Jamaica nodded miserably.

'Well, your battery is a hundred yards from here. Why the hell aren't you using your gas-pipes to some purpose? Buzz off back to them!' And he kicked him down the trench. Then he called over his shoulder: 'Sergeant Rose and Corporal Jennings! Lift this stretcher up across the top of the trench. We've got to pass.'

Jamaica leaned against a traverse. 'I do think you're the most heartless beast I've ever met,' he said weakly.

We went up to the corpse-strewn front line. The captain of the gas-company, who was keeping his head, and wore a special oxygen respirator, had by now turned off the gas-cocks. Vermorel-sprayers had cleared out most of the gas, but we were still warned to wear our masks. We climbed up and crouched on the fire-step, where the gas was not so thick—gas, being heavy stuff, kept low. Then Thomas arrived with the remainder of 'A' Company and with 'D,' we waited for the whistle to follow the other two companies over. Fortunately at this moment the Adjutant appeared. He was now left in command of the Battalion, and told Thomas that he didn't care a damn about orders; he was going to cut his losses and not send 'A' and 'D' over to their deaths until he got definite orders from Brigade. He had sent a runner back, and we must wait.

Meanwhile, the intense bombardment that was to follow the forty minutes' discharge of gas began. It concentrated on the German front trench and wire. A good many shells fell short, and we had further casualties from them. In No Man's Land, the survivors of the Middlesex and of our 'B' and 'C' Companies suffered heavily.

My mouth was dry, my eyes out of focus, and my legs quaking under me. I found a water-bottle full of rum and drank about half a pint; it quieted me, and my head remained clear. Samson lay groaning about twenty yards beyond the front trench. Several attempts were made to rescue him. He had been very badly hit. Three men got killed in these attempts; two officers and two men, wounded. In the end his own orderly managed to crawl out to him. Samson sent him back, saying that he was riddled through and not worth rescuing; he sent his apologies to the Company for making such a noise.

We waited a couple of hours for the order to charge. The men were silent and depressed; only Sergeant Townsend was making feeble, bitter jokes about the good old British Army muddling through, and how he thanked God we still had a Navy. I shared the rest of my rum with him, and he cheered up a little. Finally a runner arrived with a message that the attack had been postponed.

Rumours came down the trench of a disaster similar to our own in the brick-stack sector, where the Fifth Brigade had gone over; and again at Givenchy, where men of the Sixth Brigade at the Duck's Bill salient had fought their way into the enemy trenches, but been repulsed, their supply of bombs failing. It was said, however, that things were better on the right, where there had been a slight wind to take the gas over. According to one rumour, the First, Seventh and Forty-seventh Divisions had broken through.

My memory of that day is hazy. We spent it getting the wounded down to the dressing-station, spraying the trenches and dug-outs to get rid of the gas, and clearing away the earth where trenches were blocked. The trenches stank with a gas-blood-lyddite-latrine smell. Late in the afternoon we watched through our field-glasses the advance of reserves under heavy shell-fire towards Loos and Hill 70; it looked like a real break-through. They were troops of the New Army division whose staff we had messed with the night before. Immediately to the right of us we had the Highland Division. Ian Hay has celebrated their exploits on that day in *The First Hundred Thousand;* I suppose that we were 'the flat caps on the left' who 'let down' his comrades-in-arms.

At dusk, we all went out to rescue the wounded, leaving only sentries in the line. The first dead body I came upon was Samson's, hit in seventeen places. I found that he had forced his knuckles into his mouth to stop himself crying out and attracting any more men to their death. Major Swainson, the Second-in-command of the Middlesex, came crawling along from the German wire. He seemed to be wounded in lungs, stomach, and one leg. Choate, a Middlesex second-lieutenant, walked back unhurt; together we bandaged Swainson and got him into the trench and on a stretcher. He begged me to loosen his belt; I cut it with a bowie-knife I had bought at Béthune for use during the battle. He said: 'I'm about done for.'[3] We spent all that night getting in the wounded of the Royal Welch, the Middlesex and those Argyll and Sutherland Highlanders who had attacked from the front trench. The Germans behaved generously. I do not remember hearing a shot fired that night, though we kept on until it was nearly dawn and we could see plainly; then they fired a few warning shots, and we gave it up. By this time we had recovered all the wounded, and most of the Royal Welch dead. I was surprised at some of the attitudes in which the dead had stiffened — bandaging friends' wounds, crawling, cutting wire. The Argyll and Sutherland had seven hundred casualties, including fourteen officers killed out of the sixteen who went over; the Middlesex, five hundred and fifty casualties, including eleven officers killed. Two other Middlesex officers besides Choate came back unwounded; their names were Henry and Hill, recently commissioned second-lieutenants, who had been lying out in shell-holes all day under the rain, sniping and being sniped at. Henry, according to Hill, had dragged five wounded men into a shell-hole and thrown up a sort of parapet with his hands and the bowie-knife which he carried. Hill had his platoon-sergeant there, screaming with a stomach wound, begging for morphia; he was done for, so Hill gave him five pellets. We always took morphia in our pockets for emergencies like that.

Choate, Henry and Hill, returning to the trenches with a few stragglers, reported at the Middlesex Headquarters. Hill told me the story. The Colonel and the Adjutant were sitting down to a meat pie when he and Henry arrived. Henry said: 'Come to report, Sir. Ourselves and about ninety men of all companies. Mr Choate is back, unwounded too.'

They looked up dully. 'So you've survived, have you?' the Colonel said. 'Well, all the rest are dead. I suppose Mr Choate had better command what's left of 'A' Company; the Bombing Officer will command what's left of 'B' (the Bombing Officer had not gone over, but remained with Headquarters); Mr Henry goes to 'C' Company. Mr Hill to 'D.' The Royal Welch are holding the front line. We are here in support. Let me know where to find you if you're needed. Good night.'

Not having been offered a piece of meat pie or a drink of whiskey, they saluted and went miserably out.

The Adjutant called them back. 'Mr Hill! Mr Henry!'

'Sir?'

Hill said that he expected a change of mind as to the propriety with which hospitality could be offered by a regular colonel and adjutant to temporary second-lieutenants in distress. But it was only: 'Mr Hill, Mr Henry, I saw some men in the trench just now with their shoulder-straps unbuttoned and their equipment fastened anyhow. See that this does not occur in future. That's all.'

Henry heard the Colonel from his bunk complaining that he had only two blankets and that it was a deucedly cold night.

Choate, a newspaper reporter in peacetime, arrived a few minutes later; the others had told him of their reception. After having saluted and reported that Major Swainson, hitherto thought killed, was wounded and on the way down to the dressing-station, he boldly leaned over the table, cut a large piece of meat pie and began eating it. This caused such surprise that no further conversation took place. Choate finished his meat pie and drank a glass of whiskey; saluted, and joined the others.

Meanwhile, I took command of what remained of 'B' Company. Only six company officers survived in the Royal Welch. Next day we were down to five. Thomas was killed by a sniper while despondently watching through field-glasses the return of the New Army troops on the right. Pushed blindly into the gap made by the advance of Seventh and Forty-seventh Divisions on the previous afternoon, they did not know where they were or what they were supposed to do. Their ration supply broke down, they flocked back, not in panic, but stupidly, like a crowd returning from a cup final, with shrapnel bursting above them. We could scarcely believe our eyes, it was so odd.

Thomas need not have been killed; but everything had gone so wrong that he seemed not to care one way or the other. The Actor took command of 'A' Company. We lumped 'A' and 'B' Companies together after a couple days, for the sake of relieving each other on night watch and getting some sleep. I agreed to take the first watch waking him up at midnight. When the time came, I shook him, shouted in his ear, poured water over him, banged his head against the side of the bed. Finally I threw him on the floor. I was desperate for a lie-down myself, but he had attained a depth of sleep from which nothing could rouse him; so I heaved him back on the bunk, and had to finish the night without relief. Even 'Stand-to!' failed to wake him. In the end I got him out of bed at nine o'clock in the morning, and he was furious with me for not having called him at midnight.

We had spent the day after the attack carrying the dead down for burial and cleaning the trench up as best we could. That night the Middlesex held the line, while the Royal Welch carried all the unbroken gas-cylinders along to a position on the left flank of the Brigade, where they were to be used on the following night, September 27th.

This was worse than carrying the dead; the cylinders were cast-iron, heavy and hateful. The men cursed and sulked. The officers alone knew of the proposed attack; the men must not be told until just beforehand. I felt like screaming. Rain was still pouring down, harder than ever. We knew definitely, this time, that ours would be only a diversion to help a division on our right make the real attack.

The scheme was the same as before: at 4 P.M. gas would be discharged for forty minutes, and after a quarter of an hour's bombardment we should attack. I broke the news to the men about three o'clock. They took it well. The relations of officers and men, and of senior and junior officers, had been very different in the excitement of battle. There had been no insubordination, but a greater freedom of speech, as though we were all drunk together. I found myself calling the Adjutant 'Charley' on one occasion; he appeared not to mind in the least. For the next ten days my relations with my men were like those I had in the Welsh Regiment; later, discipline reasserted itself, and it was only occasionally that I found them intimate.

At 4 P.M., then, the gas went off again with a strong wind; the gas-men had brought enough spanners this time. The Germans stayed absolutely silent. Flares went up from the reserve lines, and it looked as though all the men in the front trench were dead. The Brigadier decided not to take too much for granted; after the bombardment he sent out a Cameronian officer and twenty-five men as a feeling-patrol. The patrol reached the German wire; there came a burst of machine-gun and rifle-fire, and only two wounded men regained the trench.

We waited on the fire-step from four to nine o'clock, with fixed bayonets, for the order to go over. My mind was a blank, except for the recurrence of ' 'S'nice 'S'mince Spie, 'S'nice 'S'mince Spie . . . I don't like ham, lamb or jam, and I don't like roly-poly . . .'

The men laughed at my singing. The acting C.S.M. said: 'It's murder, Sir.'

'Of course, it's murder, you bloody fool,' I agreed. 'And there's nothing else for it, is there?' It was still raining. 'But when I sees a s'nice s'mince spie, I asks for a helping twice . . .'

At nine o'clock Brigade called off the attack; we were told to hold ourselves in readiness to go over at dawn.

No new order came at dawn, and no more attacks were promised us after this. From the morning of September 24th to the night of October 3rd, I had in all eight hours of sleep. I kept myself awake and alive by drinking about a bottle of whiskey a day. I had never drunk it before, and have seldom drunk it since; it certainly helped me then. We had no blankets, greatcoats, or waterproof sheets, nor any time or material to build new shelters. The rain continued. Every night we went out to fetch in the dead of the other battalions. The Germans continued indulgent and we had very few casualties. After the first day or two the corpses swelled and stank. I vomited more than once while superintending the carrying. Those we could not get in from the German wire continued to swell until the wall of the stomach collapsed, either naturally or when punctured by a bullet; a disgusting smell would float across. The colour of the dead faces changed from white to yellow-grey, to red, to purple, to green, to black, to slimy.

On the morning of the 27th a cry arose from No Man's Land. A wounded soldier of the Middlesex had recovered consciousness after two days. He lay close to the German wire. Our men heard it and looked at each other. We had a tender-hearted lance-corporal named Baxter. He was the man to boil up a special dixie for the sentries of his section when they came off duty. As soon as he heard the wounded man's cries, he ran along the trench calling for a volunteer to help him fetch him in. Of course, no one would go; it was death to put one's head over the parapet. When he came running to ask me, I excused myself as being the only officer in the Company. I would come out with him at dusk, I said — not now. So he went alone. He jumped quickly over the parapet, then strolled across No Man's Land, waving a handkerchief; the Germans fired to frighten him, but since he persisted they let him come up close. Baxter continued towards them and, when he got to the Middlesex man, stopped and pointed to show the Germans what he was at. Then he dressed the man's wounds, gave him a drink of rum and some biscuit that he had with him, and promised to be back again at nightfall. He did come back, with a stretcher-party, and the man eventually recovered. I recommended Baxter for the Victoria Cross, being the only officer who had witnessed the action, but the authorities thought it worth no more than a Distinguished Conduct Medal.

The Actor and I had decided to get in touch with the battalion on our right. It was the Tenth Highland Light Infantry. I went down their trench sometime in the morning of the 27th and walked nearly a quarter of a mile without seeing either a sentry or an officer. There were dead men, sleeping men, wounded men, gassed men, all lying anyhow. The trench had been used as a latrine. Finally I met a Royal Engineer officer who said: 'If the Boche knew what an easy job he had, he'd just walk over and take the position.'

So I reported to the Actor that we might find our flank in the air at any moment. We converted the communication trench which made the boundary between the two battalions into a fire-trench facing right; and mounted a machine-gun to put up a barrage in case the Highlanders ran. On the night of the 27th they mistook some of our men, who were out in No Man's Land getting in the dead, for the enemy, and began firing wildly. The Germans retaliated. Our men caught the infection, but were at once ordered to cease fire. 'Cease fire!' went along the trench until it reached the H.L.I., who misheard it as 'Retire!' A panic seized them and they went rushing away, fortunately down the trench, instead of over the top. They were stopped by Sergeant McDonald of the Fifth Scottish Rifles, a pretty reliable territorial battalion now in support to ourselves and the Middlesex. He chased them back at the point of the bayonet; and was decorated for this feat.

On the 3rd of October we were relieved by a composite battalion consisting of about a hundred men of the Second Warwickshire Regiment and about seventy Royal Welch Fusiliers — all that was left of our own First Battalion. Homer Jones and Frank Jones-Bateman were both seriously wounded. Frank had his thigh broken with a rifle bullet while stripping the equipment off a wounded man in No Man's Land; the cartridges in the man's pouches had been set on fire by a shot and were exploding.[4] We went back to Sailly la Bourse for a couple of days, where the Colonel rejoined us with his bandaged hand; and then farther back to Annezin, a little village near Béthune, where I lodged in a two-roomed cottage with a withered old woman called Adelphine Heu.

Notes

1. The gas-cylinders had by this time been put into position on the front line. A special order came round imposing severe penalties on anyone who used any word but 'accessory' in speaking of the gas. This was to keep it secret, but the French civilians knew all about the scheme long before this.
2. According to the newspapers, a vision of angels had been seen by the British Army at Mons; but it was not vouchsafed to Sergeant Townsend, who had been there, with most of 'A' Company.
3. Major Swainson recovered and was at the Middlesex Depôt again after a few weeks. On the other hand, Lawrie, a Royal Welch quartermaster-sergeant back at Cambrin, was hit in the neck that day by a spent machine-gun bullet which just pierced the skin, and died of shock a few hours later.
4. He was recommended for a Victoria Cross, but got nothing because no officer evidence, which is a condition of award, was available.

The Storm
of Steel

ERNST JÜNGER

We detrained in Staden to the distant thunder of guns and marched through the unfamiliar landscape to our camp. On either side of the dead-straight road were green and fruitful fields, raised up in plots like flower-beds, and luscious, well-watered meadows surrounded by hedges. There were clean farmhouses scattered here and there, with low thatched or tiled roofs, and on the walls bundles of tobacco-plants hung out to dry. The countryfolk on the roads were of German type, and their rough speech had a pleasant, homely sound. We spent the afternoon in the farm gardens to avoid being seen from the air. Now and then the shells of heavy naval guns could be heard rushing hoarsely overhead from far back and then exploding not far from us. A number of men of the 91st Regiment who were bathing in one of the numerous little streams were killed.

Towards evening I had to go with an advance detachment to the front line to prepare for the relief, and we went through Houthulst Forest and the village of Koekuit to the reserve battalion. On the way we had to 'break step' once or twice on account of some heavy shells. In the darkness I heard the voice of a recruit: 'The officer never lies down!'

'He knows what he is about,' an older soldier informed him. 'Wait till a proper one comes, and he'll be the first to lie down!'

The man had noticed the principle I always followed: 'Only take cover when it is necessary, and then do it quickly.'

It is true that only the experienced can judge of the necessity, and feel the end of the shell's trajectory before the recruit has even recognized the light warning whisper in the air.

Our guides, who did not seem to be quite sure of themselves, took us along an endless box-trench. Such is the name for trenches that are not dug in the ground, because the water would stand in them at once, but built up above its level with sandbags and fascines. Then we went along the side of a terribly dishevelled wood, from which a few days before, according to our guides, a regimental staff had been driven by the small matter of one thousand 24-centimetre shells. 'Things seem to be done on a large scale here,' I thought to myself.

After we had wandered backwards and forwards through thick undergrowth, we came to a halt in a piece of ground overgrown with weeds and fringed by a marshy swamp in whose black pools the moonlight was reflected. Our guide had abandoned us, and all the while shells were falling somewhere and slinging up the mud that splashed back again into the water. At last the miserable guide returned to receive the full volley of our wrath and to announce that he had found the way. Nevertheless, he again led us astray till we came at last to a dressing-station over which shrapnel shells were bursting in couples at short and regular intervals. The bullets and empty cases rattled through the branches. The M.O. on duty gave us a sensible fellow, who took us on to the Mäuseburg, the headquarters of the reserve line.

From there I went straight on to the company of the 225th Regiment that our 2nd Company was to relieve. It took me a long search in the shell-pitted country before I found a few ruinous houses that were fortified inside by reinforced concrete. One had been smashed in the day before by a shell and the occupants squashed like mice beneath the falling roof-plate.

I spent the rest of the night in the company commander's overcrowded concrete block-house. He was an honest front-line swine who, with his orderlies, was passing the time over a bottle of schnaps and a good chunk of pork, with frequent intervals during which he listened to the steadily increasing shell-fire and shook his head. Then he would fall to bemoaning the good old days on the Russian front, and cursing the way his regiment had been pumped out. At last I fell asleep.

My sleep was heavy and oppressed. The H.E. shells falling all round the house in the pitch darkness evoked a sense of indescribable loneliness and forlornness from the murdered landscape. Involuntarily I nestled up to a man who shared the same bunk. Once I was scared by a heavy thump. My men made a light and looked to see if the wall had been penetrated. It was found that a light shell had exploded against the outer wall.

I spent the next afternoon with the commanding officer of the battalion at the Mäuseburg, as there were still some important points on which I had to be informed. All the time 15-centimetre shells were falling round headquarters, while the captain, with his adjutant and the orderly officer, played an endless game of Skat over a sodawater bottle full of raw spirits. Sometimes he put his cards down to send off a report, or to discuss very seriously whether our concrete shelter was bomb-proof. We convinced him, in spite of the warmth with which he argued the contrary (the wish being clearly the father to the thought), that we were not fitted to sustain a direct hit from the air.

In the evening the customary artillery fire rose to frantic intensity, and in the front line there was an unceasing display of coloured lights. Dust-covered despatch-carriers brought in reports that the enemy was attacking. After weeks of drum-fire the infantry battle had begun.

I went back to company headquarters, and waited there for the arrival of the 2nd Company. It appeared at four in the morning during a very lively burst of shell-fire. I took command of my platoon at once and led it to a position covered with the fragments of a shell-destroyed house, a spot most unspeakably forlorn in the midst of an immense and dreary waste of shell-holes.

At six in the morning the Flanders mist lifted and gave us a glimpse of our ghastly surroundings. At once a swarm of low-flying enemy machines appeared, scrutinizing the battered ground and sounding sirens. Any scattered detachments of infantry that were above ground instantly endeavoured to hide themselves in shell-holes.

Half an hour later a terrific artillery fire set in. It raged round our refuge like a typhoon-scourged sea round an island. The hail of shells thickened to a throbbing wall of fire. We crouched together, expecting each second the crashing hit that would sweep us up with our concrete blocks and make our position indistinguishable from the desert of craters all round.

The whole day passed in bursts of heavy shell-fire like this, with pauses during which we prepared ourselves for the next bout.

In the evening an exhausted orderly turned up and handed me an order. From this I learned that the 1st, 3rd, and 4th Companies were to counter-attack at 10.30, and that the 2nd Company after being relieved was to swarm into the front line. In order to get a little strength to face the hours ahead, I lay down, never dreaming that my brother Fritz, whom I supposed to be still in Hanover, was in a section of the 3rd Company, and passing close to my hut in a hurricane of fire on his way to the attack.

My sleep was disturbed for a long while by the pitiful cries of a wounded man whom two Saxons had brought in. They had lost their way, and were utterly done up and had fallen asleep. When they woke in the morning, their comrade was dead. They carried him to the nearest shell-hole, and after covering him with a few shovelfuls of earth they went on their way, leaving one more to be added to the countless lonely and unknown graves of the war.

I woke at eleven out of a heavy sleep. I washed in my helmet, and sent for orders to the company commander. To my astonishment, he had already gone, without letting me or Kius or our platoons know anything of it.

This showed the consequence of putting officers of another arm of the service in command of front-line troops, only because of seniority, and though they did not know even how to handle a rifle. Let such fetishes be followed when human lives are not at stake.

While I still sat cursing on my bunk and considered what to do, an orderly appeared from battalion headquarters with the order to take immediate command of the 8th Company.

I learnt that the counter-attack of the 1st Battalion on the previous night had been repulsed with heavy loss, and that what was left had taken up a defensive position in a small wood called Dobschütz wood, and to right and left of it. The 8th Company had been given the task of swarming into the wood in support. It had, however, run into a barrage in the intervening ground and suffered heavy losses. As the company Commander, Lieutenant Büdingen, was among the fallen, I was to lead the company on in a fresh advance.

After I had taken leave of my orphaned platoon, I made my way with the orderly across country. The desolation lay under a rain of shrapnel, and as we went along half-bent we were checked by a despairing voice. In the distance we could see a figure with bleeding arm-stumps raising itself from a shell-hole. We pointed to the hut we had just left, and hastened on.

I found the 8th Company crouching behind a row of concrete positions: an utterly dispirited little mob.

'Platoon commanders!'

Three N.C.O.s came forward and declared that a further advance towards Dobschütz wood was out of the question. It was indeed the fact that the shells were bursting on our front like a wall of fire. Next I had the platoons assembled behind three concrete positions. Each was about fifteen to twenty men strong. At this moment the fire lifted and came on to us. The scene was indescribable. At the concrete position on the left a whole section was blown into the air; the right got a direct hit and buried Lieutenant Büdingen, who was still lying there wounded, beneath its tons of masonry. We were in a mortar and beaten down by incessant concussions. Faces as white as death stared at one another, and the cries of those who were hit never ceased.

It was all the same now whether we stayed where we were, or went on or back. So I gave the command to follow me, and sprang out into the fire. After a few steps I was covered with earth and flung into a shell-hole by a shell which fortunately exploded straight upwards. I observed soon after, however, that the fire was not so heavy further on. When I had worked my way forward another two hundred metres, I looked about me. There was not a soul in sight.

Finally, two men emerged from the clouds of dust and smoke. Then one more. Then another two. With these five men I safely arrived at my goal.

I found Lieutenant Sandvoss, commander of the 3rd Company, and little Schultz seated in a half-smashed-up concrete pill-box with three heavy machine-guns. I was greeted with a loud 'Hullo!' and a sip of cognac; and then the situation, by no means a pleasant one, was explained to me. The English were close in front of us, and both our flanks were in the air. We cordially agreed that this was a corner too tight for any but old veterans who had grown grey in the smoke of battle.

Without a word of warning Sandvoss asked me if I had heard anything of my brother. My feelings can be imagined when I heard that he had been in yesterday's attack and was missing. A moment later a man came and told me that my brother was lying wounded in a shelter close by, and pointed out to me a desolate blockhouse covered with uprooted trees. I hurried across a clearing which was covered by rifle-fire, and went in. What a meeting! My brother lay among a crowd of groaning stretcher-cases in a place that stank of death. He was in a sad plight. He had been hit by two shrapnel bullets in the attack, one of which had pierced the lung and the other his right shoulder. Fever shone in his eyes; it was only with difficulty that he could move or speak or breathe. He returned the pressure of my hand, and we began to talk.

It was clear to me that I could not leave him there, for at any moment the English might attack, or a shell put an end to the already damaged concrete shelter. It was a brother's duty to get him sent back at once. In spite of Sandvoss, who would not hear of any weakening of our strength, I ordered the five men who had come with me to get my brother back to the Kolumbusei dressing-station, and from there to bring back with them men to rescue the other wounded also. We tied him in a ground-sheet, and stuck a long pole through it, which rested on two of the men's shoulders. I squeezed his hand again, and the sad procession started on its way.

From the edge of the wood I watched the swaying load on its way through another wood, among towering shell-bursts. As each one struck, I caught myself together, though the place where I was was no safer. It is odd that another's danger makes a stronger impression than one's own. This may be explained partly by the confidence in his own luck that every one has. The belief that nothing can happen to himself makes each man underestimate the danger. It is only in another's case that one sees how overwhelming it is and how defenceless its victim.

After I had skirmished a little from the shell-holes on the forward edge of the wood with the English, who were coming on very slowly, I spent the night with my men and a machine-gun section among the ruins of the concrete pill-box. H.E. shells of quite extraordinary ferocity were going up all the time close by us. In the evening I was within an ace of being killed by one of them. The machine-gun began rattling off towards morning, when some figures approached in the darkness. It was a patrol of the 76th

Regiment, come to get into touch with us. One of them was killed. There were many such mistakes during these days, but it was of no use to dwell on them.

At six in the morning we were relieved by a detachment from the 9th Company. They brought me orders to occupy the Rattenburg with my men. I had a casualty on the way, a Fahnenjunker wounded by a shrapnel bullet.

We found the Rattenburg to be a shell-shot house walled up with concrete slabs. It stood close by the marshy bed of the Steenbeek, which no doubt well deserved its name.

Somewhat done up, we entered into possession and flung ourselves down on the straw-covered bed boards. After a good feed and a pipe of tobacco we felt more ourselves again.

In the early hours of the afternoon we were heavily shelled with shells up to the heaviest calibres. Between six and eight one explosion overlapped another, and the building often trembled at the sickening thump of a dud and threatened to collapse. When the fire ebbed later on, I went cautiously over a hill that was covered in a close and whirring mesh of shrapnel to the Kolumbusei dressing-station, and asked for news of my brother. The doctor, who was examining the terribly mangled legs of a dying man, told me to my joy that he had been sent back in a fairly promising state.

Later in the night my ration-party turned up and brought the company, now reduced to twenty men, warm food, bully-beef, coffee, and bread, tobacco and schnaps. We ate heartily, circulating the bottle of '98 per cent' without any irksome distinctions of rank. Then we turned in; but our rest, owing to the swarms of gnats that rose from the marshy banks of the stream, the shells, and the gas that was shot over occasionally, was not exactly undisturbed.

The result was that I was so fast asleep the next morning that after a heavy bombardment had gone on for hours my men had to rouse me. They told me that men were coming back all the time, saying that the front line had been evacuated and that the enemy were coming on.

I first followed the old soldier's maxim, 'A good breakfast holds body and soul together,' and then, after lighting a pipe, went outside to see what was happening.

I could not see a great deal, as the surroundings were veiled in a thick haze. The artillery fire was increasing from moment to moment, and soon reached that pitch of intensity which the nerves, incapable of further shock, accept with an almost happy indifference. Showers of earth clattered incessantly on the roof, and the house itself was hit twice. Incendiary shells threw up heavy milk-white clouds, out of which fiery drops rained on the ground. A piece of this burning stuff came smack on a stone at my feet, and went on burning for a good minute. We were told later that men hit with it had rolled on the ground without being able to put it out. Shells with delay-action fuses burrowed into the ground, rumbling and pushing out flat disks of soil. Swathes of gas and mist crept over the battlefield, hugging the ground. Immediately in front we heard rifle and machine-gun fire, a sign that the enemy must have advanced already.

Below, beside the stream, I saw some men walking through a constantly changing scenery of mud fountains shooting high into the air. I recognized the commanding officer, Captain von Brixen, supported by two stretcher-bearers, and with an arm bound up. I hastened towards him; he called out that the enemy was advancing, and warned me not to delay in getting under cover.

Soon the first bullets smacked in the shell-holes near by or were shivered against the broken masonry. More and more fleeing figures disappeared to our rear, while in front a storm of rifle-fire testified to the embittered defence put up by those who were holding on.

It was time to act. I decided to defend the Rattenburg, and made it plain to the men, among whom at this there were some rueful faces, that I had not the remotest thought of retiring. I posted the men at loopholes, and our one machine-gun was mounted on a window-sill. A shell-hole was chosen and a stretcher-bearer, who soon had plenty to do, was installed there. I, too, took a rifle I found lying about, and hung a belt of cartridges round my neck.

As my crowd was very small I tried to get reinforcements from the numbers of men who were passing by in disorder. Most of them obeyed my call willingly, glad to join up, while others whose nerve had gone hurried past after a hasty pause to see that there was nothing to be got by staying with us. In such cases a tender consideration has no place.

'Fire!' I called to the men who stood in front of me in the cover of the house, and a few shots rang out. Overcome by the eloquence of the rifle-muzzle, the shirkers, of whom in every battle there must always be some, came slowly nearer, though it was plain from their faces how little eager they were to give us their company. A canteen orderly whom I knew well made all kinds of excuses to get away. But I would not let go of him.

'But I have no rifle!'

'Then wait till there's a man shot.'

During a final crisis of artillery fire, in the course of which the ruins of the house were hit several times and the fragments of bricks pattered down on our helmets from high in the air, I was thrown down to the ground in the flash of a terrific burst. To the astonishment of the men, I got up again unhurt.

After this wild whirligig of shells it became calmer. The fire lifted over us and rested on the Langemarck-Bixschoote road. But we were none the better off in mind, for so far we had not seen the wood for trees; the danger had been so overwhelming that we had had no time or power to think of it. Now that the storm had swept on past us, every one had time to get ready for what was inevitably coming nearer. And it came.

The rifles in front were silent. The opposition had been overcome. Out of the haze emerged a thick advancing line. My men fired crouching behind the wreckage. The machine-gun tacked out. As though they had been wiped away, the attacking line vanished into shell-holes and opened fire on us. Strong detachments went on to the left and right. We were soon surrounded by a ring of fire.

The position was pointless, and there was no object in sacrificing the men. I gave the order to retire. Now that they had started, it was difficult to make the men give up the fight.

Making use of a low-lying cloud of smoke, we got away unobserved, partly by wading above the hips along the stream. I was the last to leave the little fort. Lieutenant Höhlemann, whom I helped along, was bleeding from a severe head-wound, though he joked and made light of it as we went.

As we crossed the road we ran into the 2nd Company, who had been sent up in support. After a brief consultation we decided to stay where we were and await the enemy. Here, too, we had to compel troops of other units, who wished to carry out retirements on their own, to remain. Stern measures were necessary to persuade artillerymen, and signallers, and so on, that even they in circumstances like these had to take hold of a rifle and get into the firing-line. With the help of Kius and a few quiet folk I soon got matters into order by means of entreaties, commands, and blows with the butt-end.

Then we sat ourselves in a half-dug trench and had breakfast. Kius pulled out his inevitable camera and took photographs. On our left there was some movement on the outskirts of Langemarck. The men began shooting at some figures that were running here and there, until I told them to stop. Immediately after a N.C.O. came up and reported that a company of the Fusilier Guards were taking up a position on the road, and that our fire had inflicted losses.

I gave the order thereupon to advance and occupy the highest part of the road. There was lively rifle-fire, some of the men fell, and Lieutenant Bartmer of the 2nd Company was severely wounded. Kius remained at my side and finished his piece of bread-and-butter as we went. When we occupied the line of the road, whence the ground fell away to the Steenbeek, we saw that the English had been on the point of doing the same. The first khaki uniforms were already within twenty metres of it. As far as the eye could see, the ground to our front was full of troops in line and column. They were swarming round the Rattenburg too.

We made full use of the surprise of our sudden appearance and at once opened a steady fire on them. Along the Steenbeek a whole column broke up. One man had a coil of wire on his back of which he was unrolling one end. Others jumped like hares this way and that while our bullets raised clouds of dust among them. A sturdy corporal of the 8th Company rested his rifle with the greatest calm on a shattered tree-stump and shot four of the enemy one after the other. The remainder crept into shell-holes and lay concealed there till nightfall. We had made a good clearance.

At about 11 o'clock aeroplanes tied with streamers came diving down on us and were driven off by a lively fire, which they replied to from above. In the midst of the wild clatter I could not help smiling when a man reported to me and desired to have it placed on record that he had shot down a machine in flames with his rifle.

Immediately after occupying the road I had made a report to regimental headquarters and asked for reinforcements. At mid-day detachments of infantry, engineers, and machine-guns came up in support. According to the time-honoured tactics of Old Fritz all of them were crammed into the already crowded front-line. Here and there the English laid out a few of the men who incautiously crossed the road.

About 4 o'clock a very unpleasant bombardment with shrapnel started. The volleys got the road to a T. It was clear to me that the aeroplanes had ascertained the line on which we were making a stand, and that there were worse times ahead.

And, in fact, we were soon being heavily shelled with shells of all sizes. We lay close to one another in the narrow and crowded ditch of the road. Fire danced before our eyes; twigs and clods whistled about our ears. Close to me on my left a flash flared out, leaving a white suffocating vapour behind it. I crept on all-fours to the man next me. He moved no more. The blood trickled from many wounds caused by small jagged splinters. On my right, too, there were many hit.

After half an hour it was quiet and we set to digging out the shallow trough of the ditch so as to have at least protection from splinters in case of a second bombardment. Our entrenching tools came against rifles, equipment, and cartridge-cases of 1914, showing that this soil was not drinking blood for the first time.

As dark came on we were given another thorough good do. I crouched beside Kius in a little hole that had cost us some blisters. The ground rocked like a ship's deck under hit after hit at the least possible distances. We were ready for the end.

I chewed my pipe, my helmet pressed on to my forehead, and stared at the pavé whose stones showered sparks under the bursting lumps of metal; and I succeeded in philosophizing myself into courage. The most remarkable thoughts shot through my head. I took a trashy French novel, *Le Vautour de la Sierra,* that I had picked up at Cambrai, into lively consideration. I repeated several times to myself a saying of Ariosto, 'A great heart cares nothing for death when it comes, so long as it be glorious.' It may seem extraordinary, but it helped me to keep control over myself. When the shells gave our ears a little peace, I heard fragments of the beautiful song from *The Black Whale of Askelon* close beside me, and I thought that my friend Kius must have had a drop too much. Every one has his own manner of calming his nerves.

At the end of it a large splinter struck my hand. Kius took out a torch. We found only a scratch.

Hours such as these were without doubt the most awful of the whole war.

You cower in a heap alone in a hole and feel yourself the victim of a pitiless thirst for destruction. With horror you feel that all your intelligence, your capacities, your bodily and spiritual characteristics, have become utterly meaningless and absurd. While you think it, the lump of metal that will crush you to a shapeless nothing may have started on its course. Your discomfort is concentrated in your ear, that tries to distinguish amid the uproar the swirl of your own death rushing near. It is dark, too; and you must find in yourself alone all the strength for holding out. You can't get up and with a *blasé* laugh light a cigarette in the wondering sight of your companions. Nor can you be encouraged by the sight of your friend clipping a monocle into his eye to observe a hit on the traverse close beside you. You know that not even a cock will crow when you are hit.

Well, why don't you jump up and rush into the night till you collapse in safety behind a bush like an exhausted animal? Why do you hang on there all the time, you and your braves? There are no superior officers to see you.

Yet some one watches you. Unknown perhaps to yourself, there is some one within you who keeps you to your post by the power of two mighty spells: Duty and Honour. You know that this is your place in the battle, and that a whole people relies on you to do your job. You feel, 'If I leave my post, I am a coward in my own eyes, a wretch who will ever after blush at every word of praise.' You clench your teeth and stay.

All of us held on that evening, all who lay along that dark Flanders road. Officers and men alike showed what they were made of. Duty and Honour must be the corner-stones of every army. And a heightened sense of duty and honour must be inculcated in the officer who fights in the forefront of the battle. For that, suitable material and a fixed mould are required. The truth of this is fully known only in war. . . .

It began to drizzle after midnight; patrols of a regiment which had come up meanwhile in support went forward as far as the Steenbeek and found nothing but mud-filled shell-holes. The enemy had withdrawn beyond the stream.

Worn out by the fatigues of this tremendous day, we got down into our holes, with the exception of the men on guard. I pulled the cloak of my dead neighbour over my head and fell into a restless sleep. As it grew light I was awakened by a curiously cold feeling and discovered that I was in a sad way. It was raining in torrents and the drainage of the road was pouring into the hole where I was sitting. I built a small dam and bailed out my resting-place with a saucepan-lid. In consequence of the ever-increasing volume of water I had to add one course after another to my earthwork, till at last faulty construction yielded to growing weight and a muddy stream gurgled in and filled my refuge to the brim. While I was busy fishing out my revolver and helmet, tobacco and rations were borne away along the ditch, whose other occupants were faring just as I was. We stood shivering with cold and without a dry stitch on our bodies, knowing that when next we were shelled we had no protection whatever. It was a cheerful situation. And here I permit myself the observation that even artillery fire does not break the resistance of troops so surely as wet and cold.

The steady downpour was nevertheless a true blessing in its effects upon the further course of the battle; for the English offensive was just in its first and most critical days. The enemy had to bring up his artillery over a morass of water-logged shell-holes, while we had undamaged roads for the transport of all we needed.

At 11 in the morning, when we were already desperate, an angel appeared in the person of a despatch-rider who brought the order for the regiment to assemble in Koekuit.

We saw on the way how difficult communications must have been on the day of the attack. The roads were packed with men and horses. Twelve horribly mutilated horses lay in one heap near some limbers whose wreckage was scarcely recognizable.

What was left of the regiment assembled in a rain-soaked meadow over which single bursts of shrapnel opened their white balls. It was a shock to see what was left — a body of about the strength of a company with a small group of officers in the midst. What losses! Of two battalions, nearly all the officers and men! The survivors stood in pouring rain with gloomy faces till quarters were assigned. Then we dried ourselves in a wooden hut, crowding round a glowing stove, and got fresh courage from a hearty meal. Human nature is indeed indestructible.

Towards evening shells fell in the village. One of the huts was hit and several men of the 3rd Company killed. In spite of the shelling we soon lay down to sleep, only hoping that we should not have to counterattack in the rain or be flung without warning into some gap in the line.

At 3 in the morning orders came that we were definitely to be taken out of the line. We marched along the pavé to Staden. It was strewn all the way with dead bodies and smashed-up transport. Twelve dead lay round the crater of one gigantic burst alone. Staden, that had been so full of life on our arrival, now had many houses shelled; the deserted market-place heaped up with household goods hurriedly taken out of the houses. One family was leaving the town at the same time as we were. It led a cow as its only possession. The man had a wooden leg, and the woman led the crying children by the hand. The confused din behind added to the sadness of the picture.

The remains of the 2nd Battalion were quartered in a lonely farm, concealed behind tall hedges in the midst of luxuriant fields. There I was given command of the 7th Company. Till the end of the war its fortune and mine were one.

In the evening we sat before an old tiled hearth and refreshed ourselves with a stiff grog while we listened to the thunder of battle breaking out afresh. A sentence from the army *communiqué* suddenly met my eyes in a recent newspaper: 'We succeeded in holding up the attack on the Steenbeek.'

It was odd to feel that our apparently confused doings in the depth of night had won a place in history. The enemy offensive, launched with such tremendous force, had been brought to a standstill, and we had had a large share in that result.

Soon we turned in in the hayloft. In spite of the profound sleep in which they were sunk, most of the sleepers tossed to and fro in their dreams, as though they had to fight their Flanders battle over again.

On the 3rd of August we set off on the march to the station of the neighbouring town of Gits. We took much of the cattle and produce of the now deserted neighbourhood with us. The whole battalion, in fine spirits again, shrunken though it was, had coffee in the station restaurant. Two buxom Flemish waitresses added to its flavour and to the general contentment by their bold speeches. The men were particularly delighted when they addressed every one, officers included, as 'thou,' as it is the local custom to do.

Sagittarius Rising

CECIL LEWIS

After ten hours of this came my first real job—to photograph the enemy second-line trenches. The lines, from the air, had none of the significance they had from the ground, mainly because all contours were non-existent. The local undulations, valleys, ravines, ditches, hillsides, which gave advantage to one side or the other, were flattened out. All you saw was two more or less parallel sets of trenches, clearer in some places than in others according to the color of the earth thrown up in making them. These faced each other across the barren strip of No-Man's-Land, and behind them started a complicated network of communication trenches, second-line trenches, more communication trenches, and then the third-line trenches. The network was more complex at the important positions along the line; but everywhere it was irregular, following the lie of the ground, opening up to a wide mesh at one place, closing up, compact and formidable, at another. As positions were consolidated more trenches were dug, and later, when I came to know my own section of the line as well as the palm of my hand, I could tell at a glance what fresh digging had been done since my last patrol.

The surveying of the German line was difficult from the ground. You couldn't very well walk about with a theodolite and a chain in full view of the enemy, so the making of maps was largely a matter of aerial photography. In the spring of 1916 with the big offensive on the Somme preparing, the accuracy of these maps was of the greatest importance. So our job that day was to go over the front line at 7500 feet and fly all along the enemy second-line trenches from Montauban, round the Fricourt salient and up to Boisselle, photographing as we went.

If there was ever an aeroplane unsuited for active service, it was the BE 2c. The pilot sat slightly aft of the main planes and had a fair view above and below, except where the lower main plane obscured the ground forward; but the observer, who sat in front of him, could see practically nothing, for he was wedged under the small center section, with a plane above, another below, and bracing wires all round. He carried a gun for defense purposes; but he could not fire it forward, because of the propeller. Backwards, the center-section struts, wires, and the tail plane cramped his style. In all modern machines the positions are reversed; the pilot sits in front, leaving the observer a good field of fire aft and using his own guns, which can be fired through the propeller, forward. But in 1916 the synchronized gear enabling a machine gun to be fired through the whirling propeller and still miss the blades had not been perfected.

The observer could not operate the camera from his seat because of the plane directly below him, so it was clamped on outside the fuselage, beside the pilot; a big, square, shiny mahogany box with a handle on top to change the plates (yes, plates!). To make an exposure you pulled a ring on the end of a cord. To sight it, you leaned over the side and looked through a ball and cross-wire finder. The pilot, then, had to fly the machine with his left hand, get over the spot on the ground he wanted to photograph — not so easy as you might think — put his arm out into the seventy-mile-an-hour wind, and push the camera handle back and forward to change the plates, pulling the string between each operation. Photography in 1916 was somewhat amateurish.

So I set out on that sunny afternoon, with a sergeant-gunner in the front seat, and climbed up towards the lines. As I approached them, I made out the place where we were to start on the ground, comparing it with the map. Two miles the other side of the front line didn't look far on paper; but it seemed a devil of a way when you had to fly vertically over the spot. The sergeant knelt on his seat, placed a drum on the Lewis gun, and faced round over the tail, keeping a wary eye open for Fokkers. But the sky was deserted, the line quiet. Jerry was having a day off. I turned the machine round to start on my steady course above the trenches, when two little puffs of gray smoke appeared a hundred feet below us, on the left. The sergeant pointed and smiled: "Archie!" Then three others appeared closer, at our own height. It was funny the way the balls of smoke appeared magically in the empty air, and were followed a moment later by a little flat report. If they didn't range us any better than that they were not very formidable, I thought, and began to operate the camera handle.

There are times in life when the faculties seem to be keyed up to super-human tension. You are not necessarily doing anything; but you are in a state of awareness, of tremendous alertness, ready to act instantaneously should the need arise. Outwardly, that day, I was calm, busy keeping the trenches in the camera sight, manipulating the handle, pulling the string; but inside my heart was pounding and my nerves straining, waiting for something, I did not know what, to happen. It was my first job. I was under fire for the first time. Would Archie get the range? Would the dreaded Fokker appear? Would the engine give out? It was the fear of the unforeseen, the inescapable, the imminent hand of death which might, from moment to moment, be ruthlessly laid upon me. I realized, not then, but later, why pilots cracked up, why they lost their nerve and had to go home. Nobody could stand the strain indefinitely, ultimately it reduced you to a dithering state, near to imbecility. For always you had to fight it down, you had to go out and do the job, you could never admit it, never say frankly: "I am afraid. I can't face it any more." For cowardice, because, I suppose, it is the most common human emotion, is the most despised. And you did gain victories over yourself. You won and won and won again, and always there was another to be won on the morrow. They sent you home to rest, and you put it in the background of your mind; but it was not like a bodily fatigue from which you could completely recover, it was a sort of damage to the essential tissue of your being. You might have a greater will-power, greater stamina to fight down your failing; but a thoroughbred that has been lashed will rear at the sight of the whip, and never, once you had been through it, could you be quite the same again.

I went on pulling the string and changing the plates when, out of the corner of my eye, I saw something black ahead of the machine. I looked up quickly: there was nothing there. I blinked. Surely, if my eyes were worth anything, there had been something . . . Yes! There it was again! This time I focused. It was a howitzer shell, one of our own shells, slowing up as it reached the top of its trajectory, turning slowly over and over, like an ambling porpoise, and then plunging down to burst. Guns fire shells in a flat trajectory; howitzers fling them high, like a lobbed tennis ball. It follows that, if you happen to be at the right height, you catch the shell just as it hovers at its peak point. If you are quick-sighted you can then follow its course down to the ground. I watched the thing fascinated. Damn it, they weren't missing the machine by much, I thought; but I was left little time to consider it, for suddenly there was a sharp tearing sound like a close crack of thunder, and the machine was flung upwards by the force of the explosion of an Archie burst right underneath us. A split second later, and it would have been a direct hit. A long tear appeared in the fabric of the plane where a piece of shrapnel had gone through. There was a momentary smell of acrid smoke. "Ess! Ess!" shouted the sergeant. "They've ranged us!" I flung the machine over and flew west, then turned again, and again, and again. . . . The Archie bursts were distant now. We had thrown them off.

"How many more?" shouted the sergeant, with a jerk of his head to the camera box.

"Two."

Flying on a steady course is the surest way to get caught by Archie, and we had been, right enough. If we were quick we might snatch the other two photos and get away before he ranged us again. I turned back over the spot, pulled the string and flew on to make the last exposure, when the sergeant suddenly stiffened in his seat, cocked his gun, and pointed: "Fokker!"

I turned in my seat and saw the thin line of the monoplane coming down on our tail. He had seen the Archie bursts, no doubt, had a look round to see if we were escorted, and, finding it all clear, was coming down for a sitter.

I got the last photo as he opened fire. The distant chatter of his gun was hardly audible above the engine roar. It didn't seem to be directed at us. He was, I know now, an inexperienced pilot, he should have held his fire. We replied with a chatter that deafened me, the muzzle of the Lewis gun right above my head. The Fokker hesitated, pulled over for a moment, and then turned at us again. The sergeant pulled his trigger. Nothing happened. "Jammed! Jammed!" he shouted. He pulled frantically at the gun, while the stuttering Fokker came up. I put the old 2c right over to turn under him. As I did so, there was a sharp crack, and the little wind-screen a foot in front of my face showed a hole with a spider's web in the glass round it.

It was Triplex: no splinters; but another foot behind would have put that bullet through my head—which was not Triplex. A narrow shave. Instinctively I stood the machine on its head and dived for home. At that moment, as if to cap it all, the engine set up a fearful racket. The whole machine felt as if it would fall to pieces.

"Switch off! Switch off!" yelled the sergeant. "The engine's hit."

I obeyed, still diving, turning sharply as I did so to offer a more difficult target to the Fokker. But, luckily for us, he decided not to pursue. In those days the Huns did not adventure much beyond their own side of the lines, and now we were back over ours.

We saw him zoom away again. He had us at his mercy, had he known. There was a moment of wonderful relief. We laughed. It had all happened in much less time than it takes to tell, and we were still alive, safe!

"Make for the advance landing-ground," shouted the sergeant. He was furious with the gun jamming, jumpy at our narrow shave, and, anyway, didn't relish his job with inexperienced pilots like me, just out from home.

I spotted the advance landing-ground—thank Heaven I had been down on it previously—and circled to make my landing. It would have been a fine thing, I thought, if that had happened a few miles farther over and I had been forced down in Hunland on my first patrol. I skimmed over the telegraph poles, got down without mishap, and jumped out to examine the machine.

The sergeant was apostrophizing the gun: "These bloody double drums!" he said. "Always jamming! He had us sitting, God dammit!"

I pulled over the prop. There was a hollow rattle from the inside. Something serious, a big end gone, or a smashed connecting-rod, probably. Anyway, they would have to send out another engine. . . . But we were down! Here was the ground under my feet; the sky above, serene, impersonal; the machine solid beneath my touch, swaying slightly in the wind. All that remained to bear witness of our escape was the rattle of the engine, the tear in the plane, the smashed wind-screen, and the tiny perforations of the bullet holes in the body, two down behind my seat, more in the tail. The sergeant came up.

"Are you all right, sir?"

"Fine! And you?"

"Quite, thank you, sir. I thought he'd got us with that second burst. Always turn, sir, as soon as a machine attacks. It can't get its sights on you so easy. And it has to allow for the traverse. . . . If you'll phone the squadron, sir, and order out a tender and a repair squad, I'll dismount the camera and get a guard put over the machine. You got all the photos, didn't you, sir?"

"Yes. Twenty-two in all."

"The Corps will be pleased. They wanted them badly."

Well, we'd got away with it! We'd done the job! If you'd heard me phoning the squadron ten minutes later, you might have imagined from my casual manner I'd been through that sort of thing every day for a month.

A Subaltern
on the Somme

MAX PLOWMAN

July 1916

Charing Cross Station: A sombre, sunless place, crowded with khaki figures thinly interspersed with civilians, mostly women, dressed in sombre colours. The figures in plain khaki are listless, but those decorated with ribbons, and still more those with red or blue tabs, look animated with the bustle of busy self-importance. To-day the heavy lugubrious atmosphere that often seems to pervade a London terminus is lightning-charged, so that the air vibrates with repressed emotions, felt all the more intensely because no one gives them relief. The hopes and fears of all are the same; but they are not shared: each one bears his own.

Beyond the barrier lie the trains: long black sleeping snakes. We disregard them, as if they were not. They are public servants that have become our masters. We turn away from them because we know that in this scene they are the chief instruments of destiny.

I am hideously self-conscious. One half of me is tunic, belt, puttees, badges, revolver — a figure hoping it presents an approved appearance in the public eye and faintly flattered by the sense of voluntary heroism; the other is a mind seething. This mind has become like a cloud brooding above my body, so full of violence and revolt that constant effort is required to keep it suppressed. Its impulses suggest the maddest actions. Now, as my young wife and I weave an outwardly nonchalant way through the crowd (she does not touch my arm: we know the etiquette), I am on the point of proposing that we walk straight out of the station, get into a taxi and drive and drive and drive till the car breaks down. Even the thought brings a sense of relief, for it opens a vista upon a garden of old enchantment. I draw a shutter across it violently. We go upstairs and drink coffee in the gloomy buffet.

One glance round to see there are no officers of one's own regiment here, then heart's ease for a moment. We can smile to one another. We do not speak. There is nothing to say now. Twenty-two months ago we saw this hour. We were reading *The Globe* after a little dinner at a place near the Marble Arch. We looked up, and as our eyes met we saw this day. That was a lifetime ago; but from that hour every step has been towards this chasm. Then, the rumble of earthquake bringing foreknowledge as clearly as if the red printed page had announced it: now the event, so many times lived in imagination it is difficult to realise it as fact. We look in each other's eyes to reassure one another. The look implies: "You are you. I am I. Nothing else matters."

For all the months of grace between then and now we are not ungrateful. We have reason to give thanks. Love's embodiment now lives. I listened to the flutter of his heart as he lay on my arm last night. Kind was the fate that had kept me from going sooner; for had it been otherwise one victory over death might have been lost. We are free from double dread. For that my heart sings a song often to be sung again in strange places.

We must go. Back through the khaki whirlpool: up the long platform. Ah! There's Brunning the South African, and Zenu the bright, blond beauty, and Leonard the weed, and some more.

Brunning has a full-dress introduction. He is that timely relief, a natural humorist. Besides, he has served in German West Africa, where he lost his right ear. We see in him sound proof that war is not all death. Fat and smiling—Brunning, you're our man for to-day. We'll keep pace with you, though we ride Rosinante.

There is something like a dozen of us in this odd saloon-car with its large, broad windows. We take our places like guests at a conference.

Now the last fierce moment comes. "Step inside, please." Your hand. "Good-bye. Might be back in a fortnight: you never know. Good-bye. Never good-bye." The train moving: a girlish figure running beyond the end of the platform waving, all sadness gone, still waving. . . . Snap! The cord is broken. Back through the window, and here's this collection sitting round like the figures in the poem, "all silent and all . . ." Well, you never know. Some will come back: some won't.

Already I am away in my mind. I know it clearly enough; but the sickly Leonard is sitting beside me starting a whispered confidential burble. It appears he also has an affair of the heart and therefore presumes we must feel alike. He has a grievance, too. It is that younger men than either of us are still at the training-camp. "They've no such ties as we have, and Roberts has been fairly crawling round the old colonel to be kept on as adjutant. Roberts is a perfect swine. He has been chortling about the number of fellows he sent out who were killed on the first of July. When he signed Leonard's papers he sniggered over "another death warrant." The whole bloody war was rotten. Of course, it didn't matter to fellows who had no ties. But even if they did get back, who could say what might happen in the meantime with all these crowds of slackers about? The damned Huns! They ought to chuck taking prisoners — that'd soon end it. How long did I think it would last? It couldn't last much longer. Had I been on the musketry course at Catterick? He ought to have gone — ought to be there now — would have been, but for Roberts. It would be good if we got in the same company, wouldn't it? So few fellows understood."

Feeling much dislike for Leonard and his comparisons, I respond in monosyllables. Yet I am sorry for him, and when at last he stops, I find that his hang-dog misery and petty resentments have been good for nerves stretched, five minutes ago, almost to breaking-point. At least there shall be no grovelling. Well enough I know that I shall never be the real soldier. He lives on pinnacles of indifference I have long decided I shall never reach; but at least one can die decently: at least I've resolution enough for that. Whether I have sufficient to look a man in the face and then blow out his brains with this revolver remains to be seen. What I shall experience at the sight of a bayonet entering my own vitals also remains, possibly, to be known. Now there is no knowing — only possibilities to be faced. Yet a thousand less ghastly things might happen: honours, wounds, hospital, leave, peace. God! Peace itself will come one day. Fancy living to see it! One might.

There is peace outside, there in the fields of Kent. Nature here knows nothing of the war. Through the window I see the fruit-trees dancing in the sunlight. Now they are changed for the rich ranks of hops, bobbing as we pass; and now again the clustering apple-trees. That green and lovely world is at peace; and though the very sunlight seems at times an insult, one would not have Nature lose her loveliness. The mere knowledge that beauty somewhere still persists is relief.

THE CHANNEL

> *Oh ye! who have your eye-balls vex'd and tir'd,*
> *Feast them upon the wideness of the sea.*

It is in its happiest, most bewitching humour. There is just enough movement to show the sea has a life of its own. The sun shines down, master of the dance. I have not seen the sea for nearly two years. This might be a summer holiday, except that astern there's a deadly-looking little destroyer: our escort, I suppose. Mines, torpedoes — the sea is full of man's filth: there is enough to provide a remote possibility we might never reach France. Well, the sea looks bewitching.

A man comes up by my side at the rail. He is a captain in a line regiment, and looks elderly for his rank. His large, mobile features do not suggest the army. He is certainly not of the regular army, for captains in the regular army do not begin conversations with subalterns. He devoutly hopes he is not for the Front this time: he has done his share of fighting in Gallipoli. He believes there's a good chance of his being appointed Director of Entertainment Parties for troops just out of the line: close up, of course, but not actually under fire.

I wonder at his frankness. Somebody's got to do the fighting. Is everyone in France quite as ready to leave it to somebody else? He explains that he is over forty, and after Gallipoli rather thought they might give him a job at home. He is an actor and went to enlist straight from a London theatre on the day war broke out. Oh yes! Of course; now I remember him. I am pleased and flattered by his geniality, for in the theatre he is a person of importance. Who'd have thought, that day when I sat in the pit, I should next see him here? He talks to me now, I suppose, because most men become sociable in time of misfortune.

BOULOGNE

What a change has come over Boulogne since August 1st, 1914! It has been converted from a guest-house into a workshop. As we steamed up the harbour on the day of France's mobilisation nearly two years ago, cheers greeted us from the pier, blue figures on the quay waved their flags and a band played. Boulogne was French, and full of French excitement and cordiality. To-day, as we silently drifted in like cargo, and like cargo lay waiting I know not what formalities before we could land, I felt that Boulogne had been Anglicised. Now, after lunching at the British Officers' Club, as I drift about the town waiting for the train that is to take us to Étaples, it seems as if the French element had retired to its fastness before an invader. The place wears a big British mask, and the mask shows the broad commercial features of John Bull. Boulogne is busier than it has ever been; but it has lost its character in the exigencies of war.

That the war is not very far away I am made conscious as I enter the station. An ambulance train has just come in and suddenly "walking cases" appear, their heads or arms swathed in bandages. They look like men let out of prison, so much bustle and vigour they have: so much anxiety to get along. The blood still stains their dressings and shocks by its gross reality. The hours of idling in Boulogne made an anti-climax in our journey: we seemed to have missed our way to the Front. Now these blood-stained heads come as a sharp reminder of our destination. Quite surely we are bound for the places these men have left.

ÉTAPLES

Dusk is falling as we detrain at Étaples. We have been a long time making the short journey, and are glad to shake our limbs after being wedged tight in those uncomfortable wooden carriages. We drop out by the side of the rails and scuttle up a sandy slope, where we report and receive details of our quarters for the night. We wander through a sea of canvas, our valises following, and now by the light of a candle unroll them on the wooden floor of a bell-tent. Zenu, Hill and two others share this tent with me. They are soon asleep. Even the longest day comes to an end at last. A gramophone at a Y.M.C.A. hut some way down on the side of this sandy hill is playing tunes from *The Maid of the Mountains*. It stops. Through the door-flap of the tent I can see the stars. Hill snores loudly as I get into my bag. What a release to feel alone and free from military busyness! Passionately I try to send waves of something deeper than thought across the estranging miles, and in the effort fall asleep.

"THE BULL RING"

It is nine o'clock on a day that promises heat. We are on our way to the Bull Ring: two hundred of us, officers who have not been to the Front and are therefore due for a course of intensive training till some battalion of our regiments shall require us. Here we are, slogging along under the command of a captain, back in the ranks again, carrying rifles. This appears to be an indignity to some of these fellows; but it does not trouble me, for I have no gift for the assertion of authority, and find it easier to obey army orders than to give them. The responsibility of command is an effort which diverts thought from what are much more natural, if useless, channels.

These huts to our right and left are hospitals. And what is that, looking like an ungrown hop-yield? A British cemetery, Lord! How many have died already! The ground is smothered with wooden crosses. We march on in the heat till we come to a great open sandy arena. Out on to this plain we file, and now we are put through physical jerks by officers who have risen from the regular ranks; and now are drilled by sergeant-majors who have been chosen for this duty presumably by virtue of the harshness of their voices and the austerity of their manners. It is hot work, and there is a fierce, vindictive atmosphere about this place, which makes its name of "Bull Ring" intelligible. Later we climb up among the sand dunes on the other side of the road, and there practise firing rifle grenades and throwing those small egg-shaped cast-iron missiles known as Mills' bombs. Here too we learn more of the methods of gas attack and defence, and practise the art of shoving our heads quickly into the clammy flannel bags that are dignified by the name of P. H. helmets. We finish the morning's work by running obstacle races over a prepared course back on the arena.

In other times, all signs of our activity banished, these sand dunes must make a place of delightful holiday. Even to-day one's eyes wandered instinctively toward the blue estuary that lay below us, where the tiny white sail of a yacht moved slowly up-stream.

GRAMOPHONES

The tents in this camp are uncountable. All the way down this sandy slope, up the next hillock and down over the other side, beyond, away and on all sides they stretch, interspersed here and there with more solid buildings: canteens, army ordnance depots and Y.M.C.A. huts. It is a city of canvas whose inhabitants are always changing. Men and officers, they are here to-day and gone to-morrow. We are all waiting. A batch of Somersets arrived last night. To-day they belong to the Black Watch and have gone up the line in kilts. The casualties since July 1st have been too heavy to allow every draft to go to its own regiment.

Off parade there is little to do. We write letters: eat and drink in the mess: talk or play cards in the hut. And whether we like it or not, we listen to the eternal gramophone. At every hour of the day, and half the night, some gramophone is going. Up the slope the pitiful wail is carried on the breeze:

If you were the only girl in the world
And I were the only boy.

A pathetic hymn before battle. Yet it serves as a reminder that, under many layers of treacly sentiment, the human heart still beats: even this war cannot remove that organ. Nero did well to play the fiddle: the gramophone is our best substitute. Add that pathetic tune, who knows but its terrible popularity is due to the subconscious craving in every one of us here for his own suspended individual life? [...]

PRISONERS' CAGES

While we are forming up outside Méricourt station I see for the first time a prisoners' "cage." Surely this is the foulest insult to mankind the war has begotten. The cage is like a poultry-run, only laced in disordered strands with wire that is "barbed" after the pattern of the crown of thorns.

A sentry stands at the gate with fixed bayonet, and his smart and soldierly appearance stands out in terrible contrast with that of the creatures who loll about or sit on the bare ground within, hatless, ragged and lousy.

A viler invention than barbed wire was never conceived: it is the perfect symbol of cruelty. The man who first devised it must have received a peerage in hell. And here it is used to provide a place of rest and habitation for the lords of creation. These "lords" have sunk below the status given to the monkeys at the Zoo; and certainly, in their decrepitude and dejection, the inmates of this cage cannot compare with the nimble beasts whose cages have no barbs. I cannot get by without a shudder. This is the bottom of degradation. Call them Huns if you like: there remains a limit to the indignity judges may impose upon criminals without grave moral damage to the judges. These cages pass that limit. We should show more natural feeling if we lined these poor devils up in a row and shot them. That at least would acknowledge their manhood.

I should like to be allowed to go inside and apologise, explaining that the beastly necessities of the times have driven us to means we abhor.

DERNANCOURT

We are bivouacking on the side of a chalk hill about a mile west of Dernancourt. The wide valley of the Ancre stretches out before us, the sluggish river itself running where those pollard willows stand, two hundred yards from the road that passes at the foot of this hill. Albert lies hidden about a couple of miles north-east, and the battle-line is now somewhere beyond those hills on our left.

The boom of the guns is continuous. We are not far from our destination, for we can see the absurd sausage-balloons that are let up on their cords into the sky and slowly drawn to earth again when observation is over. Aeroplanes, too, are busy, usually flying singly; the red, white and blue rings of the Allied planes just distinguishable in the sky. Occasionally two or three German machines will penetrate our line as far as this, and then there is a clatter of anti-aircraft guns and puffs of white smoke form little clouds around the hawk-like objects in the blue that have the white Maltese crosses on their breasts. The "archies" make it too hot for them to come far, though we never see a hit.

The road below is a highway to the battle. Day and night a continuous stream of traffic trundles by; guns, limbers, wagons, lorries, they flow along. Destruction has a big appetite and feeds incessantly.

On the hillside, kits are set out in rows just as the men were halted, and there they sleep in the open, for the weather is gloriously fine. We officers of C Company prefer the open to a tent and have planted ourselves under a bank near the crest of the hill. Now it is afternoon and the men have gathered in circles to play a game, new to me, known as "House." It seems to be a strange game, for it is accompanied by a lot of shouting on the part of one who presumably acts in the capacity of "bookie," counting and shouting all the time.

Other men sit on their ground-sheets addressing those highly coloured silk-sewn cards that will one day adorn many an English cottage mantel-shelf. These cards, with their bright hues, sentimental messages and French character, are very popular: they supply a compendious want. They also save platoon-officers from the business of censoring, which tends to become irksome whenever the men have much time on their hands. Censoring letters is an unpleasant, impertinent duty, to be hurried over and treated as formally as possible. By constant repetition it becomes a deadly bore. Occasionally there is a patch of rich unconscious humour, but the formula is almost unvaried. The writer is in the pink, in spite of everything: a condition he hopes is mutual. He believes there's a war on, so we must keep smiling. Hopes and fears for leave are always expressed, and promises of battle-souvenirs are usually remembered. There is the inevitable P.S.: "The cakes were all right, but a bit smashed, and I'd like some Woodbines: the fags they serve out here are rotten."

UGLY PUNISHMENTS

There is a boy from D Company doing Field Punishment No. 1 down by the road this afternoon. His outstretched arms are tied to the wheel of a travelling field-kitchen. The regimental-sergeant-major has just told me that the boy is there for falling out on the march. He defended himself before the C.O. by saying that he had splinters of glass in his feet; but the M.O. decided against him. Quite possibly the boy is a liar; but wouldn't the army do well to avoid punishments which remind men of the Crucifixion?

And these two men being marched up and down in the blazing heat, under the raucous voice of the provost-sergeant, they disturb all peace of mind. I do not know from what offences they are doing "pack-drill," but it is depressing to see them loaded with rifles and full packs, going to and fro over a piece of ground not more than twenty yards long, moving like automata under that awful voice.

Volunteers going shortly into battle! It is not a pleasant picture. It calls to mind too vividly those propagandist posters of the "bonny boys." Besides, surely this war wants all our energy. The most fearfully arduous task, if it served some purpose, would be preferable to these senseless evolutions, designed merely to fatigue. Volunteers going into battle! I think with almost physical sickness of the legends that sustain our armchair patriots at home. [. . .]

THE OLD FRONT LINE

Hardy and I are off to Pommiers Redoubt, Mametz, where we are to report that the battalion will arrive this evening. We descend the long hill leading to Fricourt, dodging about the stream of traffic that stirs the dust of the road to a thick haze. Near the bottom of the hill we come upon the old front line of July 1st. The country here is stricken waste: the trees that formed an avenue to the road are now torn and broken stumps, some still holding unexploded shells in their shattered trunks, others looped about with useless telegraph-wire. The earth on both sides of the road is churned up into a crumbling mass, and so tossed and scarred is the ground that the actual line of the front trenches is hardly distinguishable. On the far side, in the face of a steep rise, we see the remains of what were deep German dug-outs, but everything needs pointing out, for the general impression is of a wilderness without verdure or growth of any kind. To our right we notice a ruined cemetery. It looks as if it might have heard the Last Trump. Graves are opened and monuments of stone and beaded wire lie smashed and piled in heaps.

Now, as we near Mametz, we come upon guns hidden under the banks of the roadside and camouflaged above by netting. The road through Mametz is still under enemy observation; so we turn sharply to the right to go round the back of the rising ground that faces us. All that remains of the village of Fricourt is a pile of bricks; there appear to be just about enough to build one house; and Mametz Wood is nothing more than a small collection of thin tree-trunks standing as if a forest fire had just swept over them. On the right of the sunken road we have now taken is a mound of sinking freshly-turned earth. It marks the grave of the Devons who died in the capture of Montauban. A little farther on we come upon all that remains of a German field cemetery: two or three painted triangular wooden crosses; the other graves will now go unmarked for ever. Here we leave the road and begin to climb over the forsaken trenches. Barbed wire, bombs, bully-beef tins, broken rifles, rounds of ammunition, unexploded shells, mess-tins, bits of leather and webbing equipment, British and German battered steel helmets, iron stakes, and all the refuse of a battlefield, still litter the mazy ground. I come across a skull, white and clean as if it had lain in the desert.

We can only move slowly over this confusion of forsaken trenches running in every direction, but at last we are clear of them and mount the hill which is our objective. It broadens out to a wide plateau. Little holes are cut in the ground just big enough to shelter one or two men and presumably give them cover from observation. The large old German dug-outs are not at first visible. We report at one of them and return along the hot road by the way we came.

TRENCHES ON THE SOMME

We are going to the trenches. That little knot of men two hundred yards ahead, just disappearing over the barren crest of the rise, is Hill's platoon. Two hundred yards behind us is Smalley's. This afternoon the sun glares down on earth that has lost its nature, for, pitted everywhere with shell-holes, it crumbles and cracks as though it has indeed been subject to earthquake. Up here we can be seen by the enemy; but there is no hurrying, for we have to keep distance between platoons. Hill has halted: we must halt, too. The men behind me swear with nervous irritation and mutter about being stuck out here to be fired at, I turn to look at them. Standing loaded up with boxes of bombs and sandbags of rations, how utterly unlike the red-coats of romance they appear.

We are off again, now traversing the slope that leads to the valley of Longueval. "Death Valley," it is nicknamed, and it has earned its title, for everywhere there are signs of death: an inverted bottle with a bit of paper in it: a forage-cap hung on a stick: a rough wooden cross bearing the pencilled inscription, "To an Unknown British Soldier." These signs recur: pathetic, temporary memorials; will they outlast the war? In the bottom of the valley lie broken trucks and the shattered rails of a tramway. As we come to the end of the tram-line we have to pass the body of a dead horse, foul and distended, poisoning the air. Suddenly, like a rat, a human figure comes out of the earth. Who would have thought there were dug-outs here? As quickly it disappears and we pass on. We march in silence, broken occasionally by a jest that fails to catch on, or by an irritable rebuke from one jogged by his companion. There is no singing now; 'tis as if we moved under an invisible cloud.

We halt for a moment in a chalk-pit where the M.O. has his dug-out, and then follow the narrowing sunken road that leads up St. George's Hill. By the time we have reached the top we are moving in single file round the horseshoe bend of the trench we are to occupy, pushing by the troops that wait for us to relieve them.

This is an old German trench that has been reversed and now forms part of our second line facing High Wood, just distinguishable as such, about five hundred yards away on the hill opposite. We have hardly entered the trench before we come on a stretcher lying on the ground. It bears the body of a boy: the face quite black. He has just been killed. It appears there was an old German latrine close to the parapet of the trench; two boys had gone to it when a shell came over and killed them both. As we push along I find that this particular sector falls to my platoon. The shell has made a big breach. To-night we shall have to repair it and clean up the mess which is beyond description.

The men are posted and the relieved troops scuttle out. In this narrow gap between two deep walls of clay we shall spend the next four days. The air is tainted with the sickly-sweet odour of decaying bodies. At certain corners this odour intensified by the heat, becomes a stench so foul the bay cannot be occupied. Just now I tripped over a lump in the floor of the trench. It was necessary to get a shovel and quickly cover the spot. Literally we are the living among the dead.

Shelling is incessant. There is not a moment when something is not passing overhead; but the fire is not upon this trench, it is meant for the batteries now crammed up close behind on the rearward slope of the hill. Our batteries are replying, shell for shell. Somewhere very close to my sector a French seventy-five barks deafeningly.

I look for a place to lay my ground-sheet and rations, and find a hole burrowed in the side of the parapet and a new German saxe-blue coat lying on the floor. This hole will give cover from shrapnel and serve to deaden the noise if there's any chance of sleep; but it would prove an ugly death-trap if a shell dropped near. I lay my things in the hole and turn to see Rowley and the company-sergeant-major coming along to inspect. We go round together till we come to a spot in a traverse behind my sector where the smell of decay is so strong they are convinced there is a body lying out. Sure enough, just behind the parados, the dead body of a gunner lies on a stretcher evidently left in haste. Both shin-bones are broken, but otherwise the poor fellow looks unhurt. We have the corpse carried out along the narrow trench: a difficult, awkward business.

I see Jackson considering the gap in our parapet and speak to him about it. He has the whole thing sized up, and without any fuss makes himself responsible for a particularly filthy job, telling me just what he proposes to do as soon as it is dark. He seems more at his ease in the trenches. I shall like this man.

Wondering how Hill fares I go down the trench to see him, and we decide we shall have to spread out our platoons, that are much under strength if we are to keep in touch. I am just returning along the unoccupied gap between us when rapid rifle-fire suddenly starts in the valley below. What does it mean? I get up on a firestep and peer over. There's nothing to see, but the firing continues, causing a cloud of smoke that begins to fill the air. Are they coming over? If they do — well, I've this bit of the line to myself. I pull out my revolver, load it and wait, wondering ironically what anyone would give for my chances. If they come as soon as this, it will have been quick work. The firing continues so that the smoke obscures all view. Then to my relief the sergeant-major comes along. He too is wondering what is going to happen and we wait together silently. Gradually the firing dies down. It ceases. We go back to my platoon and beyond to see Smalley on the right. He has put his men into their P. H. helmets, mistaking the smoke for a gas attack. "All's well that ends well." But we do not fail to chaff Smalley about his precaution. [. . .]

SHELLING IN TRENCHES

I've a prescription for anyone who wants to know what being shelled in trenches is like. Here it is.

Dig a hole in the garden fairly close to the house, a few yards long, six feet deep and about four feet wide. At night go armed with a pop-gun and stand in this hole. Then persuade the members of your family to throw into the hole from the upper windows of the house every utensil and article of furniture they can lay hands on: crockery, fire-irons, coal, chairs, tables, beds, let them heave the lot at you, not forgetting the grand piano, just to give you an idea of a nine-inch shell. You must not leave the hole, but while the bombardment is going on you are quite at liberty to march up and down, eat, sleep, remove the debris that doesn't hit you, and generally to pretend that nothing unpleasant is happening. Remain there for a few days or you will evade the trench-dweller's worst enemy, boredom; and if you want to be realistic, add heat, shortage of water, stench, shortage of sleep, and give yourself the actual possibility of being killed every moment.

It would give some idea. Of course you would miss the noise. But you would know the sense of futility which being shelled in a trench produces. At the end of your "tour" I think you would understand how sage a comment on the experience was that made by a poor scared fellow I met on Pommiers Redoubt. He had just come out of trenches where most of his companions had been killed by shelling and, looking at me with wide, staring eyes, he said, "Why, this isn't war at all. It's bloody murder."

"A SOFT TIME"

We seem to have been here for weeks: actually we have been here three days. It has been what is called "a soft time," too, for the only casualties in the battalion have occurred in the company behind us, and there they have only had about half a dozen killed and wounded. We hear the batteries have suffered heavily, and small wonder, for so far the shelling has never stopped.

This afternoon, frayed out with the incessant noise, I went to see Rowley in his miserable little dug-out for the sole purpose of asking him whether shelling ever did stop. He smiled and inquired what I expected, adding that it was "a bit steep," but we ought to be thinking ourselves damned lucky we weren't getting it. I was immensely grateful to him, for he was friendly and not in the least superior. I shall owe him something for that kindness as long as we are together.

The Memoirs
of George Sherston

SIEGFRIED SASSOON

At a midnight halt the hill still loomed in front of us; the guides confessed that they had lost their way, and Leake decided to sit down and wait for daylight. (There were few things more uncomfortable in the life of an officer than to be walking in front of a party of men all of whom knew that he was leading them in the wrong direction.) With Leake's permission I blundered experimentally into the gloom, fully expecting to lose both myself and the Company. By a lucky accident, I soon fell headlong into a sunken road and found myself among a small party of Sappers who could tell me where I was. It was a case of "Please, can you tell me the way to the Hindenburg Trench?" Congratulating myself on my cleverness I took one of the Sappers back to poor benighted B Company, and we were led to our Battalion rendezvous.

The rendezvous took some finding, since wrong map references had been issued by the Brigade Staff, but at last, after many delays, the Companies filed along to their ordained (and otherwise anathematized) positions.

We were at the end of a journey which had begun twelve days before, when we started from Camp 13. Stage by stage, we had marched to the life-denying region which from far away had threatened us with the blink and growl of its bombardments. Now we were groping and stumbling along a deep ditch to the place appointed for us in the zone of inhuman havoc. There must have been some hazy moonlight, for I remember the figures of men huddled against the sides of communication trenches; seeing them in some sort of ghastly glimmer (was it, perhaps, the diffused whiteness of a sinking flare beyond the ridge?) I was doubtful whether they were asleep or dead, for the attitudes of many were like death, grotesque and distorted. But this is nothing new to write about, you will say; just a weary company, squeezing past dead or drowsing men while it sloshes and stumbles to a front-line trench. Nevertheless that night relief had its significance for me, though in human experience it had been multiplied a millionfold. I, a single human being with my little stock of earthly experience in my head, was entering once again the veritable gloom and disaster of the thing called Armageddon. And I saw it then, as I see it now—a dreadful place, a place of horror and desolation which no imagination could have invented. Also it was a place where a man of strong spirit might know himself utterly powerless against death and destruction, and yet stand up and defy gross darkness and stupefying shell-fire, discovering in himself the invincible resistance of an animal or an insect, and an endurance which he might, in after days, forget or disbelieve.

Anyhow, there I was, leading that little procession of Flintshire Fusiliers many of whom had never seen a front-line trench before. At that juncture they asked no compensation for their efforts except a mug of hot tea. The tea would have been a miracle, and we didn't get it till next morning, but there was some comfort in the fact that it wasn't raining.

It was nearly four o'clock when we found ourselves in the Hindenburg Main Trench. After telling me to post the sentries, Leake disappeared down some stairs to the Tunnel (which will be described later on). The Company we were relieving had already departed, so there was no one to give me any information. At first I didn't even know for certain that we were in the Front Line. The trench was a sort of gully, deep, wide, and unfinished looking. The sentries had to clamber up a bank of loose earth before they could see over the top. Our Company was only about eighty strong and its sector was fully 600 yards. The distance between the sentry-posts made me aware of our inadequacy in that wilderness. I had no right to feel homeless, but I did; and if I had needed to be reminded of my forlorn situation as a living creature I could have done it merely by thinking of a Field Cashier. Fifty franc notes were comfortable things, but they were no earthly use up here, and the words "Field Cashier" would have epitomized my remoteness from snugness and security, and from all assurance that I should be alive and kicking the week after next. But it would soon be Sunday morning; such ideas weren't wholesome, and there was a certain haggard curiosity attached to the proceedings; combined with the self-dramatizing desperation which enabled a good many of us to worry our way through much worse emergencies than mine.

When I had posted the exhausted sentries, with as much cheeriness as I could muster, I went along to look for the Company on our left. Rather expecting to find one of our own companies, I came round a corner to a place where the trench was unusually wide. There I found myself among a sort of panic party which I was able to identify as a platoon (thirty or forty strong). They were jostling one another in their haste to get through a cavernous doorway, and as I stood astonished one of them breathlessly told me that "the Germans were coming over." Two officers were shepherding them downstairs and before I'd had time to think the whole lot had vanished. The Battalion they belonged to was one of those amateur ones which were at such a disadvantage owing to lack of discipline and the absence of trained N.C.O.s. Anyhow, their behaviour seemed to indicate that the Tunnel in the Hindenburg Trench was having a lowering effect on their *morale*.

Out in no-man's-land there was no sign of any German activity. The only remarkable thing was the unbroken silence. I was in a sort of twilight, for there was a moony glimmer in the low-clouded sky; but the unknown territory in front was dark, and I stared out at it like a man looking from the side of a ship. Returning to my own sector I met a runner with a verbal message from Battalion H.Q. B Company's front was to be thoroughly patrolled at once. Realizing the futility of sending any of my few spare men out on patrol (they'd been walking about for seven hours and were dead beat) I lost my temper, quietly and inwardly. Shirley and Rees were nowhere to be seen and it wouldn't have been fair to send them out, inexperienced as they were. So I stumped along to our right-flank post, told them to pass it along that a patrol was going out from right to left, and then started sulkily out for a solitary stroll in no-man's-land. I felt more annoyed with Battalion Headquarters than with the enemy. There was no wire in front of the trench, which was, of course, constructed for people facing the other way. I counted my steps; 200 steps straight ahead; then I began to walk the presumptive 600 steps to the left. But it isn't easy to count your steps in the dark among shell-holes, and after a problematic 400 I lost confidence in my automatic pistol, which I was grasping in my right-hand breeches pocket. Here I am, I thought, alone out in this god-forsaken bit of ground, with quite a good chance of bumping into a Boche strong-post. Apparently there was only one reassuring action which I could perform; so I expressed my opinion of the War by relieving myself (for it must be remembered that there are other reliefs beside Battalion reliefs). I insured my sense of direction by placing my pistol on the ground with its muzzle pointing the way I was going. Feeling less lonely and afraid, I finished my patrol without having met so much as a dead body, and regained the trench exactly opposite our left-hand post, after being huskily challenged by an irresolute sentry, who, as I realized at the time, was the greatest danger I had encountered. It was now just beginning to be more daylight than darkness, and when I stumbled down a shaft to the underground trench I left the sentries shivering under a red and rainy-looking sky.

There were fifty steps down the shaft; the earthy smell of that triumph of Teutonic military engineering was strongly suggestive of appearing in the Roll of Honour and being buried until the Day of Judgment. Dry-mouthed and chilled to the bone, I lay in a wire-netting bunk and listened to the dismal snorings of my companions. Along the Tunnel the air blew deathly cold and seasoned with mephitic odours. In vain I envied the snorers; but I was getting accustomed to lack of sleep, and three hours later I was gulping some peculiar tea with morose enjoyment. Owing to the scarcity of water (which had to be brought up by the Transport who were eight miles back, at Blairville) washing wasn't possible; but I contrived a refreshing shave, using the dregs of my tea.

By ten o'clock I was above ground again, in charge of a fatigue party. We went half-way back to St. Martin, to an ammunition dump, whence we carried up boxes of trench mortar bombs. I carried a box myself, as the conditions were vile and it seemed the only method of convincing the men that it had to be done. We were out nearly seven hours; it rained all day and the trenches were a morass of glue-like mud. The unmitigated misery of that carrying party was a typical infantry experience of discomfort without actual danger. Even if the ground had been dry the boxes would have been too heavy for most of the men; but we were lucky in one way; the wet weather was causing the artillery to spend an inactive Sunday. It was a yellow corpse-like day, more like November than April, and the landscape was desolate and treeless. What we were doing was quite unexceptional; millions of soldiers endured the same sort of thing and got badly shelled into the bargain. Nevertheless I can believe that my party, staggering and floundering under its loads, would have made an impressive picture of "Despair." The background, too, was appropriate. We were among the débris of the intense bombardment of ten days before, for we were passing along and across the Hindenburg Outpost Trench, with its belt of wire (fifty yards deep in places); here and there these rusty jungles had been flattened by tanks. The Outpost Trench was about 200 yards from the Main Trench, which was now our front line. It had been solidly made, ten feet deep, with timbered fire-steps, splayed sides, and timbered steps at intervals to front and rear and to machine-gun emplacements. Now it was wrecked as though by earthquake and eruption. Concrete strong-posts were smashed and tilted sideways; everywhere the chalky soil was pocked and pitted with huge shell-holes; and wherever we looked the mangled effigies of the dead were our *memento mori*. Shell-twisted and dismembered, the Germans maintained the violent attitudes in which they had died. The British had mostly been killed by bullets or bombs, so they looked more resigned. But I can remember a pair of hands (nationality unknown) which protruded from the soaked ashen soil like the roots of a tree turned upside down; one hand seemed to be pointing at the sky with an accusing gesture. Each time I passed that place the protest of those fingers became more expressive of an appeal to God in defiance of those who made the War. Who made the War? I laughed hysterically as the thought passed through my mud-stained mind. But I only laughed mentally, for my box of Stokes gun ammunition left me no breath to spare for an angry guffaw. And the dead were the dead; this was no time to be pitying them or asking silly questions about their outraged lives. Such sights must be taken for granted, I thought, as I gasped and slithered and stumbled with my disconsolate crew. Floating on the surface of the flooded trench was the mask of a human face which had detached itself from the skull. [. . .]

The first few days were like lying in a boat. Drifting, drifting, I watched the high sunlit windows or the firelight that flickered and glowed on the ceiling when the ward was falling asleep. Outside the hospital a late spring was invading the home-service world. Trees were misty green and sometimes I could hear a blackbird singing. Even the screech and rumble of electric trams was a friendly sound; trams meant safety; the troops in the trenches thought about trams with affection. With an exquisite sense of languor and release I lifted my hand to touch the narcissi by my bed. They were symbols of an immaculate spirit — creatures whose faces knew nothing of War's demented language.

For a week, perhaps, I could dream that for me the War was over, because I'd got a neat hole through me and the nurse with her spongings forbade me to have a bath. But I soon emerged from my mental immunity; I began to think; and my thoughts warned me that my second time out in France had altered my outlook (if such a confused condition of mind could be called an outlook). I began to feel that it was my privilege to be bitter about my war experiences; and my attitude toward civilians implied that they couldn't understand and that it was no earthly use trying to explain things to them. Visitors were, of course, benevolent and respectful; my wound was adequate evidence that I'd "been in the thick of it," and I allowed myself to hint at heroism and its attendant horrors. But as might have been expected my behaviour varied with my various visitors; or rather it would have done so had my visitors been more various. My inconsistencies might become tedious if tabulated collectively, so I will confine myself to the following imaginary instances.

Some Senior Officer under whom I'd served: Modest, politely subordinate strongly imbued with the "spirit of the Regiment" and quite ready to go out again. "Awfully nice of you to come and see me, Sir." Feeling that I ought to jump out of bed and salute, and that it would be appropriate and pleasant to introduce him to "some of my people" (preferably of impeccable social status). Willingness to discuss active service technicalities and revive memories of shared front-line experience.

Middle-aged or elderly Male Civilian: Tendency (in response to sympathetic gratitude for services rendered to King and Country) to assume haggard facial aspect of one who had "been through hell." Inclination to wish that my wound was a bit worse than it actually was, and have nurses hovering round with discreet reminders that my strength mustn't be overtaxed. Inability to reveal anything crudely horrifying to civilian sensibilities. "Oh yes, I'll be out there again by the autumn." (Grimly wan reply to suggestions that I was now honourably qualified for a home-service job.) Secret antagonism to all uncomplimentary references to the German Army.

Charming Sister of Brother Officer: Jocular, talkative, debonair, and diffidently heroic. Wishful to be wearing all possible medal-ribbons on pajama jacket. Able to furnish a bright account of her brother (if still at the front) and suppressing all unpalatable facts about the War. "Jolly decent of you to blow in and see me."

Hunting Friend (a few years above Military Service Age): Deprecatory about sufferings endured at the front. Tersely desirous of hearing all about last season's sport. "By Jingo, that must have been a nailing good gallop!" Jokes about the Germans, as if throwing bombs at them was a tolerable substitute for fox-hunting. A good deal of guffawing (mitigated by remembrance that I'd got a bullet hole through my lung). Optimistic anticipations of next season's Opening Meet and an early termination of hostilities on all fronts.

Nevertheless my supposed reactions to any one of these hypothetical visitors could only be temporary. When alone with my fellow patients I was mainly disposed toward self-pitying estrangement from everyone except the troops in the Front Line. (Casualties didn't count as tragic unless dead or badly maimed.)

When Aunt Evelyn came up to London to see me I felt properly touched by her reticent emotion; embitterment against civilians couldn't be applied to her. But after she had gone I resented her gentle assumption that I had done enough and could now accept a safe job. I wasn't going to be messed about like that, I told myself. Yet I knew that the War was unescapable. Sooner or later I should be sent back to the Front Line, which was the only place where I could be any use. A cushy wound wasn't enough to keep me out of it.

I couldn't be free from the War; even this hospital ward was full of it, and every day the oppression increased. Outwardly it was a pleasant place to be lazy in. Morning sunshine slanted through the tall windows, brightening the grey-green walls and the forty beds. Daffodils and tulips made spots of colour under three red-draped lamps which hung from the ceiling. Some officers lay humped in bed, smoking and reading newspapers; others loafed about in dressing-gowns, going to and from the washing room where they scraped the bristles from their contented faces. A raucous gramophone continually ground out popular tunes. In the morning it was rag-time — *Everybody's Doing it* and *At the Fox-Trot Ball. (Somewhere a Voice is calling, God send you back to me,* and such-like sentimental songs were reserved for the evening hours.) Before midday no one had enough energy to begin talking war shop, but after that I could always hear scraps of conversation from around the two fireplaces. My eyes were reading one of Lamb's Essays, but my mind was continually distracted by such phrases as "Barrage lifted at the first objective," "shelled us with heavy stuff," "couldn't raise enough decent N.C.O.s," "first wave got held up by machine-guns," and "bombed them out of a sap."

There were no serious cases in the ward, only flesh wounds and sick. These were the lucky ones, already washed clean of squalor and misery and strain. They were lifting their faces to the sunlight, warming their legs by the fire; but there wasn't much to talk about except the War.

In the evenings they played cards at a table opposite my bed; the blinds were drawn, the electric light was on, and a huge fire glowed on walls and ceiling. Glancing irritably up from my book I criticized the faces of the card-players and those who stood watching the game. There was a lean airman in a grey dressing-gown, his narrow whimsical face puffing a cigarette below a turban-like bandage; he'd been brought down by the Germans behind Arras and had spent three days in a bombarded dug-out with Prussians, until our men drove them back and rescued him. The Prussians hadn't treated him badly, he said. His partner was a swarthy Canadian with a low beetling fore-head, sneering wide-set eyes, fleshy cheeks, and a loose heavy mouth. I couldn't like that man, especially when he was boasting how he "did in some prisoners." Along the ward they were still talking about "counterattacked from the redoubt," "permanent rank of captain," "never drew any allowances for six weeks," "failed to get through their wire." . . . I was beginning to feel the need for escape from such reminders. My brain was screwed up tight, and when people came to see me I answered their questions excitedly and said things I hadn't intended to say.

From the munition factory across the road, machinery throbbed and droned and crashed like the treading of giants; the noise got on my nerves. I was being worried by bad dreams. More than once I wasn't sure whether I was awake or asleep; the ward was half shadow and half sinking firelight, and the beds were quiet with huddled sleepers. Shapes of mutilated soldiers came crawling across the floor; the floor seemed to be littered with fragments of mangled flesh. Faces glared upward; hands clutched at neck or belly; a livid grinning face with bristly moustache peered at me above the edge of my bed; his hands clawed at the sheets. Some were like the dummy figures used to deceive snipers; others were alive and looked at me reproachfully, as though envying me the warm safety of life which they'd longed for when they shivered in the gloomy dawn, waiting for the whistles to blow and the bombardment to lift. . . . A young English private in battle equipment pulled himself painfully toward me and fumbled in his tunic for a letter; as he reached forward to give it to me his head lolled sideways and he collapsed; there was a hole in his jaw and the blood spread across his white face like ink spilt on blotting paper. . . .

Violently awake, I saw the ward without its phantoms. The sleepers were snoring and a nurse in grey and scarlet was coming silently along to make up the fire. [. . .]

Sunshade in one hand and prayer-book in the other, Aunt Evelyn was just starting for morning service at Butley. "I really must ask Captain Huxtable to tea before you go away. He looked a little hurt when he inquired after you last Sunday," she remarked. So it was settled that she would ask him to tea when they came out of church. "I really can't think why you haven't been over to see him," she added, dropping her gloves and then deciding not to wear them after all, for the weather was hot and since she had given up the pony cart she always walked to church. She put up her pink sunshade and I walked with her to the front gate. The two cats accompanied us, and were even willing to follow her up the road, though they'd been warned over and over again that the road was dangerous. Aunt Evelyn was still inclined to regard all motorists as reckless and obnoxious intruders. The roads were barely safe for human beings, let alone cats, she exclaimed as she hurried away. The church bells could already be heard across the fields, and very peaceful they sounded.

July was now a week old. I had overstayed my leave several days and was waiting until I heard from the Depot. My mental condition was a mixture of procrastination and suspense, but the suspense was beginning to get the upper hand of the procrastination, since it was just possible that the Adjutant at Clitherland was assuming that I'd gone straight to Cambridge.

Next morning the conundrum was solved by a telegram, *Report how situated*. There was nothing for it but to obey the terse instructions, so I composed a letter (brief, courteous, and regretful) to the Colonel, enclosing a typewritten copy of my statement, apologizing for the trouble I was causing him, and promising to return as soon as I heard from him. I also sent a copy to Dottrell, with a letter in which I hoped that my action would not be entirely disapproved of by the First Battalion. Who else was there, I wondered, feeling rather rattled and confused. There was Durley, of course, and Cromlech also — fancy my forgetting him! I could rely on Durley to be sensible and sympathetic; and David was in a convalescent hospital in the Isle of Wight, so there was no likelihood of his exerting himself with efforts to dissuade me. I didn't want anyone to begin interfering on my behalf. At least I hoped that I didn't; though there were weak moments later on when I wished they would. I read my statement through once more (though I could have recited it only too easily) in a desperate effort to calculate its effect on the Colonel.

"*I am making this statement as an act of willful defiance of military authority, because I believe that the War is being deliberately prolonged by those who have the power to end it. I am a soldier, convinced that I am acting on behalf of soldiers. I believe that this War, upon which I entered as a war of defence and liberation, has now become a war of aggression and conquest. I believe that the purposes for which I and my fellow soldiers entered upon this War should have been so clearly stated as to have made it impossible to change them, and that, had this been done, the objects which actuated us would now be attainable by negotiation. I have seen and endured the sufferings of the troops, and I can no longer be a party to prolong these sufferings for ends which I believe to be evil and unjust. I am not protesting against the conduct of the War, but against the political errors and insincerities for which the fighting men are being sacrificed. On behalf of those who are suffering now I make this protest against the deception which is being practised on them; also I believe that I may help to destroy the callous complacency with which the majority of those at home regard the continuance of agonies which they do not share, and which they have not sufficient imagination to realize.*" It certainly sounds a bit pompous, I thought, and God only knows what the Colonel will think of it.

Thus ended a most miserable morning's work. After lunch I walked down the hill to the pillar-box and posted my letters with a feeling of stupefied finality. I then realized that I had a headache and Captain Huxtable was coming to tea. Lying on my bed with the window curtains drawn, I compared the prospect of being in a prison cell with the prosy serenity of this buzzing summer afternoon. I could hear the cooing of the white pigeons and the soft clatter of their wings as they fluttered down to the little bird-bath on the lawn. My sense of the life-learned house and garden enveloped me as though all the summers I had ever known were returning in a single thought. I had felt the same a year ago, but going back to the War next day hadn't been as bad as this. [. . .]

It would be an exaggeration if I were to describe Slateford as a depressing place by daylight. The doctors did everything possible to counteract gloom, and the wrecked faces were outnumbered by those who were emerging from their nervous disorders. But the War Office had wasted no money on interior decoration; consequently the place had the melancholy atmosphere of a decayed hydro, redeemed only by its healthy situation and pleasant view of the Pentland Hills. By daylight the doctors dealt successfully with these disadvantages, and Slateford, so to speak, "made cheerful conversation."

But by night they lost control and the hospital became sepulchral and oppressive with saturations of war experience. One lay awake and listened to feet padding along passages which smelt of stale cigarette-smoke; for the nurses couldn't prevent insomnia-ridden officers from smoking half the night in their bedrooms, though the locks had been removed from all doors. One became conscious that the place was full of men whose slumbers were morbid and terrifying — men muttering uneasily or suddenly calling out in their sleep. Around me was that underworld of dreams haunted by submerged memories of warfare and its intolerable shocks and self-lacerating failures to achieve the impossible. By daylight each mind was a sort of aquarium for the psychopath to study. In the daytime, sitting in a sunny room, a man could discuss his psycho-neurotic symptoms with his doctor, who could diagnose phobias and conflicts and formulate them in scientific terminology. Significant dreams could be noted down, and Rivers could try to remove repressions. But by night each man was back in his doomed sector of a horror-stricken Front Line, where the panic and stampede of some ghastly experience was reenacted among the livid faces of the dead. No doctor could save him then, when he became the lonely victim of his dream disasters and delusions.

Shell-shock. How many a brief bombardment had its long-delayed after-effect in the minds of these survivors, many of whom had looked at their companions and laughed while inferno did its best to destroy them. Not then was their evil hour, but now; now, in the sweating suffocation of nightmare, in paralysis of limbs, in the stammering of dislocated speech. Worst of all, in the disintegration of those qualities through which they had been so gallant and selfless and uncomplaining — this, in the finer types of men, was the unspeakable tragedy of shell-shock; it was in this that their humanity had been outraged by those explosives which were sanctioned and glorified by the Churches; it was thus that their self-sacrifice was mocked and maltreated — they, who in the name of righteousness had been sent out to maim and slaughter their fellow-men. In the name of civilization these soldiers had been martyred, and it remained for civilization to prove that their martyrdom wasn't a dirty swindle.

Six Weeks
at the War

MILLICENT SUTHERLAND

Here is an extract from my diary of August 23: —

"Namur.

"Never shall I forget the afternoon of August 22. The shelling of the past hours having suddenly ceased, I went to my dormitory. I had had practically no rest for two nights, and after the emotions of the morning I was falling asleep when Sister Kirby rushed into my room, calling out, 'Sister Millicent! the wounded!'

"I rushed down the stone stairs. The wounded. indeed! Six motorcars and as many waggons were at the door, and they were carrying in those unhappy fellows. Some were on stretchers, others were supported by willing Red Cross men. One or two of the stragglers fell up the steps from fatigue and lay there. Many of these men had been for three days without food or sleep in the trenches.

"In less than 20 minutes we had 45 wounded on our hands. A number had been wounded by shrapnel, a few by bullet wounds, but luckily some were only wounded by pieces of shell. These inflict awful gashes, but if they are taken in time the wounds rarely prove mortal.

"The wounded were all Belgian — Flemish and Walloon — or French. Many were Reservists. Our young surgeon, Mr. Morgan, was perfectly cool and so were our nurses. What I thought would be for me an impossible task became absolutely natural: to wash wounds, to drag off rags and clothing soaked in blood, to hold basins equally full of blood, to soothe a soldier's groans, to raise a wounded man while he was receiving extreme unction, hemmed in by nuns and a priest, so near he seemed to death; these actions seemed suddenly to become an insistent duty, perfectly easy to carry out.

"All the evening the wounded and the worn out were being rushed in. If they had come in tens one would not have minded, but the pressure of cases to attend to was exhausting. One could not refuse to take them for they said there were 700 in the military hospital already, while all the smaller Red Cross ambulances were full.

"So many of the men were in a state of prostration bordering almost on dementia, that I seemed instantly enveloped in the blight of war. I felt stunned — as if I were passing through an endless nightmare. Cut off as we were from all communication with the outer world, I realized what a blessing our ambulance was to Namur. I do not know what the nuns would have done without our nurses at such a moment. No one, until these awful things happen, can conceive the untold value of fully-trained and disciplined British nurses. The nuns were of great use to us, for they helped in every possible tender way, and provided food for the patients. The men had been lying in the trenches outside the forts. Hundreds of wounded, we believed, were still waiting to be brought in, and owing to the German cannonading it was impossible to get near them. I kept on thinking and hoping that the allied armies must be coming to the rescue of Namur."

"Later.

"The guns never cease. They say the heavy French artillery arrived last night, and have taken up the work of the Marchevolette fort, which is reported to be out of action, but one of our wounded tells us that this artillery came 24 hours too late and that the French force on the Meuse is not sufficient. The Belgian Gendarmerie have just been in and collected all arms and ammunition. I have been seeking for the rosaries the patients carry in their purses. They want to hold them in their hands or have them slung round their necks. On the floor there is a confusion of uniforms, képis, and underclothing, which the nuns are trying to sort. It looks a hopeless occupation. Our surgeon is busy in the operating theatre, cutting off a man's fingers; he was the first to be brought in and had his right hand shattered."

"Sunday, August 23.

"There is a dreadful bombardment going on. Some of our wounded who can walk wrap themselves in blankets and go to the cellars. Nothing that I could say would stop them. They are fresh from the trenches. Luckily we are in a new fire-proof building, and I must stay with my sick men who cannot move. The shells sing over the convent from the deep booming German guns — a long singing scream and then an explosion which seems only a stone's throw away. The man who received extreme unction the night before is mad with terror. I do not believe that he is after all so badly wounded. He has a bullet in his shoulder, and it is not serious. He has lost all power of speech, but I believe that he is an example of what I have read of and what I had never seen — a man dying of sheer fright.

"The nurses and one or two of the nuns are most courageous and refuse to take shelter in the cellars, which are full of the novices and schoolchildren. The electric and gas supplies have been cut off. The only lights we have to use are a few hand lanterns and nightlights. Quite late in the afternoon we heard a tremendous explosion. The Belgians had blown up the new railway bridge, but unfortunately there are others by which the Germans can cross, and presently we hear that they are in the town. There is some rapid fusillading through the streets and two frightened old Belgian officers run into the convent and ask for Red Cross bands, throwing down their arms and maps. In a few minutes, however, they regained self control and went out in the streets without the Red Cross bands. Heaven knows what happened to them.

"Now the German troops are fairly marching in. I hear them singing as they march. They sing wonderfully — in parts as if well trained for this singing. It seems almost cowardly to write this, but for a few minutes there was relief to see them coming and to feel that this awful firing would soon cease. On they march! Fine well-set-up men with grey uniforms. They have stopped shooting now. I see them streaming into the market-place. A lot of stampeding artillery horses gallop by with Belgian guns. On one of the limbers still lay all that was left of a man. It is too terrible. What can these brave little people do against this mighty force? Some of the Germans have fallen out and are talking to the people in the streets. These are so utterly relieved at the cessation of the bombardment that in their fear they are actually welcoming the Germans. I saw some women press forward and wave their handkerchiefs.

"Suddenly upon this scene the most fearful shelling begins again. It seemed almost as if the guns were in the garden. Mr. Morgan, Mr. Winser, and I were standing there. I had just buried my revolver under an apple tree when the bombardment began once more. The church bells were clanging for vespers. Then whizz! bang! come the shells over our heads again. Picric acid and splinters fall at our very feet. We rush back into the convent, and there are fifteen minutes' intense and fearful excitement while the shells are crashing into the market-place. We see German soldiers running for dear life. Can it be the French artillery that is driving them out? There is clang-clanging at the convent bell. Women half fainting, and wounded, old men and boys are struggling in. Their screams are dreadful. They had all gone into the Grande Place to watch the German soldiers marching, and were caught in this sudden firing. A civilian wounded by a shell in the stomach was brought into the Ambulance. He died in 20 minutes. We can only gather incoherent accounts from these people as to what had happened. The Germans sounded the retreat and the shelling seemed to stop. At last it leaks out that the German troops on the other side of the town did not know that their own troops had crossed the Meuse on the opposite side. They were firing on the Citadel, an antiquated fort of no value. The shells fell short, and before the Germans discovered their mistake they had killed many of their own soldiers and Belgian civilians who had rushed up to see the German troops. It seems a horrible story, but absolutely true.

"Now it is quiet again, save for the sighs of the suffering. All night long we hear the tramp, tramp, tramp, of German infantry in the streets, their words of command, their perpetual deep-throated songs. They are full of swagger, and they are very anxious to make an impression upon the Belgians — to cow them in fact — these Belgians so used to peaceful country-sides and simple useful employments. Our wounded are doing well, and one must remember that, if their nerves have gone to pieces, to lie in trenches with this awful artillery fire bursting over them, knowing that even if they lifted their heads a few inches it might be blown off, must be an appalling sensation. The Germans hate hand to hand encounters, but they love to manipulate cannon that can blow you to pieces at a distance of six miles. If one believes the Belgian soldiers, apart from artillery work the Germans shoot badly and in a very odd position with their rifles resting on their hips and their heads protected by one arm as they lie on the ground; their firing must be very wild. A Belgian soldier told me that the Germans have a second line behind the first line, called "watchers," who do not fire on the enemy at all, but simply watch the men in front to see that they are doing their duty properly and never let a man fall out.

"The Doctor and I went up into the tower in the dark. The bombardment had ceased, but everywhere on the horizon there were blazing fires, villages and country mansions flaring in the darkness. Motorcars dashed past. Instead of Belgian, one sees now only German motors filled with German officers. Where are the English and the big French troops? That is what I am wondering. And what is the end to be?"

In my diary on August 23, 1914, I have written what I considered the most awful experience of my life, but last night, August 24, there was another climax, and I hope I shall never live through such a night again.

The day was peaceful enough after the previous soul-stirring hours. The man who had lost his voice was beginning to whisper. All be could say was, "J'ai peur, j'ai peur." These words seem ordinary words from a child or a woman, but they were terrible coming perpetually from a strong man under such circumstances. One gathered from them an idea of the horrors he must have seen and heard. The wounded gave me terrible accounts of the new German siege guns. When the shell explodes it bursts everything to smithereens inside the forts. The men who are not killed and wounded become utterly demoralized and hysterical, even mad, in awful apprehension of the next shot. They say the Namur forts were jerry-built and absolutely unreliable. The Germans declare that they destroyed one fort at Liège with a single shot of this siege cannon. They have a range of at least 16 kilometres (ten miles). The Germans say 24 (15 miles), but then they are boastful.

Early in the afternoon a German Count with a Red Cross on his arm came and inspected our ambulance at the convent. He was perfectly civil, and one had to be civil in return. He drank the beer which the nuns tremblingly pressed upon him, and took a note of the sacks of flour which the nuns were keeping in the cellars.

"Pour l'autorité militaire Belge?" they said.

"Allemande," the young Count replied significantly.

Inwardly I made a mental note to get possession of that flour, for the German troops were rapidly depleting Namur of all its food, and refugees were streaming into the town. We had not seen butter, milk, or eggs for days. Now the nuns came to me and said there was no yeast for the bread, and they were trying various recipes to make bread without yeast. It sounded indigestible.

The German Count adopted a sort of "gnädigste Frau" (charming woman) manner to me, and paid compliments to English women; he seemed thoroughly pleased with himself. He said, "Now the Germans are in possession of Namur all will be quiet and well arranged. There will be no trouble unless the civilians are treacherous and fire on the soldiers. If they do that we shall set fire to the town." Having said this he clattered out. The Namuriens had suffered so much and had seemed so utterly broken down, it did not strike me that the civilians would venture to fire on these thousands of troops that were filling their streets, their barracks, and their shops. All I kept on thinking was, "Where are the English and the French?"

L'Ami de l'Ordre, the Namur paper, had been promptly secured by the Germans and only gave us exactly what the Germans told them to write. Some of the lightly wounded prisoners wanted the blood of the editor, and wrote frantic letters, which I had to confiscate, expressing their indignation at the new tone of their precious Press.

It was a hot, still summer night. We had begun to laugh again. We were so interested in our wounded. "Silly Billy," "Bonny Boy," "Baby boy" — they had all their nick-names — and we were so relieved at the cessation of firing save of one distant cannon which would not stop and was evidently attacking the last fort. It was 10 o'clock and I decided to go to bed and was nearly undressed when a few rifle shots rang out in the street near the convent. A pause, and then came a perfect fusillade of rifle shots. It was dreadful while it lasted. Had the Belgians disregarded the warning of the Town Council, of *L'Ami de l'Ordre,* and of the German "swankers," and refused to take their defeat lying down? Of course, if the civilians were firing, it was mad rashness. My door burst open and Mr. Winser, our stretcher-bearer, rushed in, calling out, "My God, Duchess, they have fired the town."

It is almost impossible to describe the scene that followed. The Hôtel de Ville was on fire, the market place was on fire, they said that the Arsenal was on fire, but I found that the powder magazine had been emptied long ago. Then came the message that the town was fired at the four corners. One of the buildings of the convent was absolutely fire-proof and in this portion the worn-out wounded were very quiet. We had about a hundred in a dormitory in an older building. The flames simply shot up beside this and the sparks were falling about the roof. Fortunately the convent was all surrounded by a garden and the wind was blowing the flames away from us. The whole sky was illuminated; we came to the conclusion that there was nothing to do but to wait and watch the fire, and leave the patients alone until we saw the flames *must* reach us. It was a terrible hour. The nurses courageously re-assured the wounded and persuaded most of them to remain in bed.

My mind became a perfect blank. We had gone through so much that it was perfectly impossible to think of what was going to happen or of what had happened. I was wondering if we should have to leave the burning building and go out into the street, whether I had better dress again or keep on my pyjamas and pull my top boots over them — into such a silly condition does one's brain degenerate.

The Padre came in at last and said that the flames would not reach us. While we were all talking and wondering what would happen next, there was a violent ringing at the convent bell, then a banging at the door and a German voice ordering loudly, "Oeffnen! Oeffnen!" I persuaded one of the nuns to undo the latch and I and one or two of the nurses went out with Dr. Morgan. While we were struggling with the lock I felt as if I were actually *living* some book of adventure, such as I had read in my youth. The flames shooting into the sky, the smoke pouring over the convent, and, though the rifle firing had ceased, the distant booms of the cannon — And here were the Germans rattling at the door!

Outside was a smart motor-car full of soldiers armed to the teeth protecting a young German officer who was so like the Crown Prince that he might have been his brother. He was very cross and very nervous. He said he wanted to know the way to the Citadel. A nun whom I called out, said that the only way to the Citadel was past the Hôtel de Ville. He said he did not wish to go that way, for it was burning to a cinder. He looked at me and asked me to go with him and show him another way. But I stood my ground, and said I was a stranger and an Englishwoman and had never been to the Citadel in my life. So he spared me that unpleasant experience. He told me that some of the civilian inhabitants had been shooting at the soldiers from dark windows. He said that the whole town would be burnt. He seemed in a towering rage, and in a good fear, too. He said that, of course, all Red

Cross people were safe and "always women." Then he drove away with his soldiers, perhaps to his death.

We were very fortunate at being on the Meuse side of the town. Though the fire had started there, the soldiers' barracks were in our direction and they certainly would put the flames out before they reached their quarters. Even now the Tocsin was ringing. It rang all night. When the danger of the fire became less we snatched a little sleep. I was very tired. When I awoke I heard that the Commander-General von Below had given an order to blow up houses to prevent the spread of the fire and the Fire Brigade was out with the hose.

In the afternoon we ventured into the smoky street. It was like walking through a dense fog. All the buildings were smouldering. The whole of the market-place and the Hôtel de Ville had been burnt and the dear little café where we went for our meals before the bombardment. All the shutters were up on the shops that had not been burnt and one could hardly walk for the number of German troops massed in the streets bivouacking with their rifles stacked before them. The streets were practically impassable, but infantry battalions forced a way through artillery batteries, and hundreds and hundreds of motor transport waggons.

The Germans seemed to be doing the whole of this campaign on gasolene — that is to say, they use motor transport throughout, and they may, therefore, find themselves in difficulty when the roads are cut up and the rains come. Their transport is very perfect, but is too heavy and their supply of gasolene may fail them.

The doctor and I thought we had better visit the Commander, General von Below. The Germans were perfectly civil to us. Some of them spoke to us and said that they were marching on to Maubeuge in a few days, and that they had already invested Brussels. They seemed so absolutely sure of themselves that they still treated the English with politeness and were for the moment only terrorizing and bullying the Belgians. I have never yet been able to probe the mystery of the rapid fall of the Namur forts — I had been told they would hold out a month — I do not understand why the Belgian General Staff should have left the town 12 hours before the fall leaving the soldiers without any officers, but I had heard too much of the words "trahison" and "espionage," and I suppose the whole thing was wise strategy. I think it was a good thing that Namur was a Clerical centre because later the Commander took up his residence with the Bishop, and probably the Bishop restrained him from enforcing too harsh measures against the population. This, however, is only my surmise.

Herr General von Below and his smartly-uniformed officers received my card with great courtesy, and I began to see that it would be necessary to keep up this courtesy by a fixed determination on my part to get all I wanted.

The Headquarters Staff was established at the Hôtel de Hollande. The Germans were being importuned by residents asking various favours and questions. One Belgian lady asked if she might follow her husband, who was a prisoner, to Germany. "You may follow him if you like, madame," was the reply, "but you cannot accompany him." The lady looked very sorrowful.

General von Below apologized for receiving me in his bedroom, so terribly overflowing were all the other rooms with officers. Feld-Marschall von der Goltz, who arrived *en route* to take up his duties in Brussels, was kept waiting while the General spoke to me. I was merely introduced to this elderly gentleman of Turkish fame. He was buttoned up to his nose in an overcoat. Above the collar gleamed a pair of enormous glasses. He was covered with orders. He shook me by the hand, and went out.

I did not discuss the situation with General von Below. I took him for granted. He said he was sure he had met me at Homburg, and that he would arrange with one of the diplomats to get a telegram through to Berlin, which he trusted would be copied in the London papers, announcing the safety of our Ambulance.

"Accept my admiration for your work, Duchess," he said. He spoke perfect English. To accept the favours of my country's foe was a bad moment for me, but the Germans were in possession of Namur and I had to consider my hospital from every point of view. Also those who are of the Red Cross and who care for suffering humanity and for the relief of pain and sickness should strive to remember nothing but the heartache of the world and the pity of it.

General von Below "did me the honour" to call the next morning at our Ambulance. He was accompanied by Baron Kessler, his aide-de-camp, who composed the scenario of *La Légende de Josephe*. He had been much connected with Russian opera in London during the past season. It was exceedingly odd to meet him under such circumstances, after having so often discussed "art" with him in London.

I was able, with the assistance of Mr. Winser, our stretcher-bearer, whose sister had married a German, to obtain an order that the flour in the cellars might be kept for the use of our Ambulance. I left the order with the nuns; and I trust that all those sacks will be for the benefit of the poor of Namur and surrounding districts during the terrible trying winter which is before them. Our nurses continued to tend the patients and dress their wounds as if nothing had ever happened and they were in a hospital in London! How grateful those French and Belgians were to them! The Flemish were most amusing in their efforts to make us understand their language.

The women wounded patients gave us the most trouble. They cried and screamed all the time. The Germans had brought us in two more Belgian wounded soldiers; one very badly shot in the arm.

I went into the convent garden, so tired I was of the grey German troops, their songs, and their invasion of the streets. I was feeling horribly sad. Had the English and French been beaten? Why were there no English soldiers amongst our wounded? Was it really true that none of them had come into Belgium at all? I felt utterly cut off from the outside world. The Germans seemed so overwhelming, at the first glance, so numerically appalling. There is an old legend that Namur never suffers too much injury from disaster owing to the special protection of the Virgin. Flowers bloom around her statue. Perhaps these beliefs are comforting. I suppose that it must have been under the influence of St. Julienne de Cornillon that I went to Namur. *She* said, "Let us go to Namur. It is the usual refuge of exiles!" If it were not for our wounded how quickly, if it were possible, would I escape!

At 3 o'clock on the afternoon of September 9 our train was still standing in the station at Charleroi. We had been there 24 hours. I decided I must somehow get food, and without anyone molesting me I forced a way through the paling near the line, which was guarded by two German soldiers, who in the heat had fallen asleep, and ran across to a café. Directly the Belgian proprietor found I was not a German he gave me a loaf of bread, refusing payment, and told me I should find mineral water at a chemist up the street. He seemed utterly dumbfounded that I was an Englishwoman travelling on a German military train. I had just returned to the train with my provisions when it started, and I saw the boy who had hurried to fetch me eggs stand disconsolately by the palings as we rolled by. At every station, Landelies, Thuin, &c., we halted for ages. The congestion on the line must have been phenomenal. The officers on the platforms seemed surprised to see us, and asked us what we were doing; and when they heard we were "Red Cross" they gave us biscuits and chocolate.

"There is nothing else in the place," they said; "we have cleared out the eggs long ago, and the chickens are killed."

During these long halts English soldiers would have been smoking, laughing, and possibly ragging. These German soldiers got out of the train very quietly, were then marshalled together as if they were a choral union, and with a non-commissioned officer waving his arm like a baton they burst dolefully into one part-song after another. There had been a glorious sunset and now the moon was rising. This gloomy chanting seemed to me filled with the sorrow of nations. I thought of my suffering wounded now on their way to Germany as prisoners, of the dead lying on the battlefields. I had a strong suspicion that the whole scene was arranged to impress us. Surrounded by these foreign officers and their men, perfectly courteous and complacent, I felt more pitiably lonely than if I had been in the heart of a Canadian prairie.

It was a cold grey morning when we arrived at Erquelinnes a frontier town between France and Belgium. When the train started from Charleroi I had no idea at which point near Maubeuge we should be deposited. Frontiers and Customs are of no account in the march of armies. At Erquelinnes we saw a number of transport trains carrying broken-down auto-wagons on the trucks. Indeed, these damaged transports had passed us on two trains during the night.

I do not know the exact nationality of the stationmaster at Erquelinnes. He looked quite different from the other stationmasters we had seen and was one of the most obliging men I had met in the German occupation of Belgium. He gave me a cup of hot cocoa, but this did not bias me. He really was what men call "a decent chap." He told me that he expected down from Maubeuge thousands of French prisoners. The first batch had just arrived and he was entraining "Mon Général" and his staff, I concluded the Governor of Maubeuge.

Suddenly on the platform I saw about thirty British Tommies. They were prisoners. I might speak to them if the officer allowed me to. The officer was agreeable; so I had a few minutes' chat with them. They had all been slightly wounded in or near Maubeuge and had recovered. There was only one cavalryman amongst them, Corporal Merryweather, of the 4th Dragoon Guards. There were two Cameron Highlanders, and one man told me he came from Church Aston, near Newport in Shropshire, where I had lived. They were all fairly cheerful, and I gave them a few hints about keeping up their pluck. Of course the difficulty of understanding the English or German language for the two armies makes things most difficult for the prisoners, for if one does not understand German the sound of the language alone is unpleasant. The Englishman asked me if I would beg the German soldiers to open their ration tins as they had no knives. The German officer answered: —

"To please you, madam, it shall be done, but our men have hardly had bread to eat for three days."

The stationmaster came up and said he had got us a cart and a blind horse, and that two German soldiers should drive it for us to Maubeuge with our luggage and ambulance equipment.

"There are no motors," he said, "and the line has been blown up, so you ladies must walk."

I asked him how far it was and he said: —

"Little more than ten kilometres."

As one very nearly does that in a day's golfing, I thought it was a walk to attempt, and the nurses and doctor agreed with me. German soldiers had given my nurses coffee — a Prussian cook refused to sell it to us. I was about to give him a piece of my mind when the soldiers themselves inferred that he was a brute, so I left the matter alone. We were fairly hungry, but I had had the cocoa. My spirits had fallen to zero. It is impossible to describe the war-swept condition of Erquelinnes. On the top of the hill on a miserable looking dwelling I saw a Red Cross flag flying. I got permission to go there with one of the usual written passes.

As we went up the deserted, rubbish-strewn street a German soldier was playing a gramophone in a ruined house. The effect was ghastly. The Red Cross flag waved on a small convent which had originally sheltered 19 nuns. Two only were left; the rest had been sent away. Five French wounded lay here, and one old woman who had been shot through the leg. The condition of the wounded was very sad. The nuns were doing their best, but no doctor had visited them for days, for they were probably prisoners. The wounded had lain for a long time on the battlefield. Legs were not set, nor wounds properly dressed. One young fellow was very much cut about with shell. The doctor took a large piece of shell out of his leg, and maggots were in the wound. He was lying with the straw that was wrapped round his leg on the field, and he screamed when he was touched. His nerves had gone to pieces. It was pitiable. I longed for an ambulance to take them to hospital. I found they had been shelling Maubeuge from Erquelinnes for over 12 days. The inhabitants had all fled long ago and the Germans had looted the town. It was on September 8 at 6 in the evening that the forts of Maubeuge had surrendered.

It was on September 10 at 6 A.M. that we arrived at Erquelinnes. That walk to Maubeuge was a memorable one. The country is a wide-stretching plain, growing corn, turnips, &c. I should guess it was a rich agricultural district. Now it was utterly deserted, save for the German troops marching up the rough, dusty roads and the French prisoners marching down them. We passed between them all, and a rushing motor-car filled with swaggering German officers occasionally cast its dust upon us. After a time we cut across country to shorten our walk, but we were perpetually tripped up by barbed wire or hindered by the deserted trenches and the huge pit-like holes which had been made by the shells. A German officer passed with a detachment of infantry. He was evidently acting schoolmaster and taking out his little lot of soldiers to explain to them how the forts had fallen. He was rude to us, but we paid no heed. Presently we struck into the French prisoners again and continued our progress between them and the German guards. I spoke to the prisoners in French and told them that we had been nursing their wounded comrades at Namur. They then rushed forward with postcards and letters, asking us to let their relations know what had happened to them. Of course, we could only deal with a few. The Germans had told us that they had taken 40,000 prisoners. I should think that there were about 20,000, chiefly elderly reservists, "pères de famille," as they sadly told us. One man said, "We could have held on days and days in the forts, only they gave us the order to surrender." The German Guards called out to us good-humouredly: —

"What are you!"

"International," I replied, "for the sick and wounded."

"Ach, nein! Engländerin" (No! Englishwoman!), they said laughing amongst themselves.

They seemed much interested in us. Presently we came to a village. Every house was either ruined or deserted. In some houses the food was still on the table and the washing in the tub. What a frantic departure the inhabitants must have made; all around this village we saw dead cattle and horses swollen and stiff, killed by shell fire. There was a dreadful smell. I saw no human dead bodies, but numbers and numbers of long mounds, which were graves marked by empty shells and German helmets stuck on the top. Here and there were a few crosses. It was all heart-breaking, but still we walked, until we actually came to a farm that had not been destroyed. The owner sold us some eggs and gave us some coffee. She was a garrulous lady, and told us how she had got the right side of the Germans, and all her homeless neighbours sat round her piteously wondering why they had not been able to do so also. I christened that farm "La maison des mouches," the "house of flies." I had never seen so many flies in a house before. We went away with our eggs in an empty lyddite shell, and when we got to the next village we found the German soldiers had changed the blind horse and commandeered another horse, which promptly ran away, broke the traces, and upset the cart and all our luggage into the middle of the road. It took half an hour to quell that horse and get a new cart, but I must admit that the German soldiers did this, and on we went again. I took a photograph of a house which had been destroyed by shell fire. The whole front was blown away, only the bed stood unconcernedly in an upper room amid the débris.

When we had walked to within three miles of Maubeuge we met two squadrons of French Chasseurs. They were still riding their own horses, but they looked pretty miserable under a German escort. Then came a battery of field artillery. The officer asked me the way. I did not know it. How I hated that devilish German artillery; one never seemed able to escape from it — the fat black howitzers, like over-fed slugs, and the larger cannon, covered with wreaths and mottoes and their mouths protected by leather caps in the intervals of their hideous shouting. It was perfectly impossible to find out the history of the fall of Maubeuge with so many Germans about, but I did hear that the 17-inch siege cannon had been there for a long time, sunk in the backyard of a German gentleman's house who lived in the vicinity, and that they had been brought there as coal. The story sounds improbable.

The dreariest part of the day was meeting the poor people on the roads. They were going back with small bundles on their backs to their homes.

"Ma maison est-elle brulée, madame?" they would ask, and what *could* one reply as they passed on?

The Germans have a habit when they have conquered a place, burnt it partly and terrified it wholly, of plastering it with proclamations and surrounding it with guards and then saying, or rather coaxing, "Now go and be happy, my children, all is well; you have my permission, under certain stringent conditions of course, to fish in the rivers." I used to see frightened-looking individuals stealing forth to the banks of the Sombre or the Meuse, as the case might be, with fishing rods before I left Namur—strong is the passion even in war.

It was quite late in the evening when we reached Maubeuge. We had passed two forts on the way flying the German flag. These forts, however, only looked like raised hillocks of a peculiar construction. Buried in trees, the small town of Maubeuge is picturesque. A moat that surrounds it, the stone wall, and the fine gateway by which we entered over the bridge were intact, but in the streets war had played havoc. The only inn open had had many of its windows smashed by a shell which destroyed a great portion of the Red Cross Hospital opposite. It was evident that the Germans had deliberately shelled the town, and that may have been the reason why the forts were told to surrender. On September 11 there was no fighting round Maubeuge and no trace of the Allied Armies. They must have gone far into France. I remember hearing at Mons of the admiration of some German officers at the way in which our small English force had retired—"replié" was the word used. They said openly in the café within hearing of a Belgian gentleman who could understand German, that they had expected to take the whole force prisoners and thought the English had done a masterly stroke.

I determined, as Maubeuge was invested by the Germans, to report myself to the Commander, Major Abereron, at Headquarters. He asked me to bring in all the nurses and the doctor to his private room, and informed me that the French Red Cross were giving him a lot of trouble, that he had shot a doctor and even a nurse for being spies, and as he did not like to see a "highborn lady in an invidious position" he thought that we had better leave Maubeuge as soon as possible, or rather he regretted that he could not avail himself of our services!

He asked, "What, under the circumstances, do you wish to do?"

It was the first critical moment of difficulty that I had had so far with the German authorities. I had to call all my Scottish mother-wit to my aid.

"Our only object, mein Herr, is to nurse the wounded. Perhaps you will allow us to proceed into France, where we might find our own troops."

This amazing request on my part caused him to reflect. He was now joined by Baron W——, whose name I will not give as he had evidently known me before the war.

"You cannot go into France," said Abereron. "Have you any money on you?"

"I have sufficient," I replied.

"Then I will give you a pass," he said, "to enable you to go to England. If it is necessary to pay for services required you will do so."

I said, "I will try to go to Boulogne."

"No," he said, "not Boulogne. Boulogne is invested by the Germans. Baron W—— will get you an omnibus belonging to the hospital here. You must return it in three days. You will be accompanied by two members of the French Red Cross, who are accustomed to driving this motor, and I advise you to make your way to Ostend; you must give me your word of honour that if you fall in with British troops you will get out of the motor and not allow your English to capture it."

British troops. The very idea of them made me thrill. I had a vision of wrangling with Field-Marshal Sir John French on a Belgian roadside over my word of honour and this motor-car! I agreed, of course, to all the German's proposals. The position was difficult, and at all costs we must get away. The night we were forced to spend in the pothouse in Maubeuge was a very unpleasant one. The German officers objected to our having any rooms, and a German civilian doctor who had just arrived in the town was offensive in fluent English.

I said, "If you wish to abuse nine ladies, Sir, pray do so in German. It sounds better."

We got rooms at last, and I was fortunate in having one in which the windows had all been smashed by a shell, so there was plenty of air. One of the nurses slept on a mattress beside me. In the other room the nurses made ropes of towels and hung them over the window ledge in case of emergency! The doctor, with true British calm, sat in the courtyard writing his diary until a half-drunken German officer came and shook his fist at him, and said that if he did not go to the kitchen he would have his face off him. The doctor went to the kitchen. It is annoying how well a large number of the German officers speak French, and even English. I cannot help being ashamed of the fact that a large portion of our most intelligent and active soldiers and sailors do not speak any foreign language at all.

The omnibus appeared at 6 o'clock in the morning, and we left Maubeuge without any further restrictions, my only regret being that owing to exhaustion and the difficulty of the position I did not venture to visit the Red Cross hospitals which were full of French wounded. I left them a large quantity of our ambulance dressings, which unfortunately we had no room to take with us. We were soon bowling along a fine French road in the direction of Bavai. It was much cooler and rain was beginning to fall. We saw hardly any Germans on this road and the villages were not destroyed. All the people rushed out as we passed. I think they imagined we were German nurses, which was tiresome. At Bavai I asked in the Red Cross hospitals if there were any English, but they said they had all gone away as prisoners. We then went on to Valenciennes. Here the people crowded round our car. I had stopped to buy some food. They called out, "Has Maubeuge fallen? Has Maubeuge fallen?" They looked very miserable when I told them the news. A doctor came up and reported three English soldiers in the Valenciennes Hospital. I found Captain George Belville, of the 16th Lancers, there and two men of the South Lancashires. It was a good hospital and they were all doing well. Captain Belville had been shot in the right arm by a French soldier who had taken him for a German as he was stooping down to help a man on the ground. At a distance of about 400 yards German and English might easily be taken for each other. Of course, at close quarters they are totally unlike.

The first line of the German Army is impressive, brave, I should say, and fierce, and conveyed all the moral effect to Belgium that the Germans intended. After the first line the physique of the men is inferior. They seem to have no heart for the war, and would always be coming up to me to speak of their wives, their homes, and their work. They respected the Red Cross in those early days. They said they would far rather work than fight, but that Germany was winning so easily the war would not take long. They did not know why they were fighting, and brought forward most ridiculous reasons. I think they were told as many lies as possible to keep up their hopes.

Only a very few German troops were in Valenciennes on September 11. Except for the guards on the bridges one would have doubted German occupation. At Valenciennes I hesitated which road to take. My passport had been very successful so far, and my great desire was to go on to Lille, find the road to Boulogne, and chance it. Why did they say Boulogne was in the hands of the Germans? When we reached Tournai, which I visited to see if there were any English wounded, a priest whom I met on the road, and to whom I gave some of the post-cards which the French prisoners had begged us to get through to their relations, told me that they had just received notice of the passage of 40,000 German troops through Lille that day. This seemed a formidable number to encounter, so I made my greatest tactical mistake and turned north into Belgium, hoping to reach Ostend. A rumour had filtered through to Tournai that a number of English and Russian troops were in the north of Belgium and in possession of Antwerp, Ghent, and Malines. Once in Belgium, however, the German Guards on the roads began to get more frequent. We got past three patrols of Uhlans in safety. I used to stop the car 20 yards away from them and walk to meet them, holding out my passport. The third patrol searched my apron pockets for arms and then searched the motor till I began to wish that I had taken the French road. At Renaix we came to a full stop. We had run into a base of the German Army. A young officer got on to the car and took us to the Headquarters of the Staff at the inn. I told him that I was on my way to Ostend by Oudenarde and Bruges.

He repeated this to the Brigadier who was having luncheon with his officers, and my desire was greeted with a shout of laughter. I thought I had better go in and confront them all whilst they were eating and drinking. The Brigadier was perfectly civil.

"Die Frau Herzogin" was quite right — the shortest way to Ostend was by Oudenarde and Bruges — Abereron was a very good fellow — but how could he tell at Maubeuge the impossibility for an ambulance to pass from their lines into the British lines! No, no. I must go back to Brussels — no distance — only 30 miles, and get my commands from Feld-Marschal von der Goltz, Governor of Belgium, &c., and to make the way easy some officers would go in a motor before us and show us the way.

For the first time I felt powerless. Brussels was the one place I did not wish to return to. I knew how difficult it would be to get out of that city and how expensive to stay there. On many occasions obedience is a virtue; this was one of them. The Frenchmen with us, who had been rather enjoying the outing, grew pale. It was not my fault that the motor could not be returned to Maubeuge in three days, but that of Abereron's compatriots; so I washed my hands of all further responsibility. As I stepped back into the motor a German private suddenly ran out of the ranks and wrung my hand.

"Madame, Madame," he cried sympathetically, to the utter amazement of his comrades.

I have wondered since if he could have been a London waiter. At breakneck speed, swaying dangerously behind the German car, we followed on, once more returning to the centre of German occupation.

Marching
on Tanga

FRANCIS BRETT YOUNG

At this point, to my great unhappiness, I handed over my charge of the regiment. The officer who had been with them since they left Rhodesia overtook us, bringing with him orders for me to return to Nairobi. But now we were not only many hundred miles from Nairobi, but many days' journey from the railhead, and it seemed too great a pity that I should not see any of the fruits of our labours; so, like a bad soldier, I evaded my orders, asking that I might be retained with the brigade. The same evening, awaiting confirmation of my request, I was attached to the Combined Field Ambulance, and given charge of the Indian section, which was called B 120.

The change from regimental life was very abrupt. Henceforward I had to do with a number of African stretcher-bearers, Indian ward-orderlies and babu sub-assistant surgeons, Cape-boy muleteers, and a Boer conductor of transport. Nor could anything have been more different from the European conception of a Field Ambulance either in its constitution or its duties, for in time of action it might represent anything from a regimental aid-post to a casualty clearing station, or even take on the functions of a stationary hospital. The African stretcher-bearers, fifty of them, were untrained, and ready to disappear into the bush on the approach of danger. Only one European medical officer was allotted to each section; the only technical assistance on which he could count was that of two half-educated *babus*. But I was glad, at any rate, that I should still keep company with the brigade, and help to receive the sick and wounded of the regiment.

On the morning of the twenty-ninth we set out at daybreak from the camp between Old Lassiti and the river. In the dark we had quite missed the loveliness of that place, but now, in a faint light, and with many birds singing, we could see the lower slopes of the mountain crossed by a band of horizontal cloud from which little fleeces spilled over, and all the hillside below blue-black and washed with milky vapour, as are the flanks of the Old Red Sandstone hills in Wales.

I walked in front of the whole caravan, behind me the stretcher-bearers in ragged fours, led by their *Neapara* or headman, carrying a furled Red Cross flag. That morning they were very happy, talking and laughing together; and wondering what they were all thinking about, I listened, and found that they were all talking of places: of Kampala, of Nairobi, and of the camps of M'bu-yuni and Taveta. But most of all they spoke of distant places, and chiefly Kisumu, the capital of their own Kavirondo country. When all this wretched business is over, I thought, there will be great tales in Kisumu. But what intrigued me even more was to realise that these primitive people, who, only a few years ago, were walking in nakedness, were not only afflicted with the same nostalgia as myself, but found some relief from its twinges in thinking of places which they had loved and left, and in speaking of them too. For places, both strange and familiar places, had always meant more to me than anything else in life: the mere seeking of some new country—an unfamiliar village in a loved county, or even a new street in an old city, being something of an adventure. These stretcher-bearers, like myself, were out to see the world: they, like me, would carry home memories that they would treasure, a great hoard of sub-conscious wealth; and, perhaps, some day, in a village by the shores of the Nyanza, drowsy, and gorged with *m'hindi,* one of them would dream of this cool morning under Old Lassiti, just as I had dreamed the other night of Slapton Ley.

All through the Pangani trek I carried in my haversack one book, a thin paper copy of the *Oxford Book of Verse,* but what I read more often, in the little light that was left for reading, was a small-scale Bartholomew map of England, finely coloured with mountains and meadowland and seas, and there I would travel magical roads, crossing the Pennines or lazing through the blossomy vale of Evesham, or facing the salt breeze on the flat top of Mendip at will. In these rapt moments the whole campaign would seem to me nothing but a sort of penance by means of which I might attain to those 'blue, remembered hills.'

All that morning we were marching into the neck of the bottle, bent eastward by the sweep of the Pangani. At first the going was hard, over level spaces of short grass with driven sand between; but from this we passed to a kind of open slade where tall grasses bent and rippled in the wind like a mowing meadow at home. The lower air was full of dragonflies. We could hear the brittle note of their stretched wings above the soft tremor of grasses swaying slowly as if they were in love with the laziness of their own soft motion. Clinging to the heads of these grasses, and swaying as they swayed, were many beetles — brilliant creatures with wing-cases blue-black and barred with the crimson of the cinnabar moth. As we marched through the lane which we had trampled in those meadows they clung to their swaying grasses and took no heed of us though we had trodden their brothers to death in thousands. It was a wonderful day for them: the one day, perhaps, for which they had been created; and so, in a warm breeze blowing from the south, they swung their cinnabar bodies to the sun.

And from this, again, we passed to an upland, scattered with the bush, where the soil was like ochre, and an ochreous dust rose from our column and drifted away on the warm wind. It seemed as if we were too late again. There below us lay the valley through which the railway ran. There, with their rugged outlines shagged with forest, stood the South Pare Mountains. This was the point at which the enemy must make a serious stand, the point at which, if we had been moving fast enough and heaven knows we couldn't have moved faster — we might even cut him off. But the column moved on without stopping into the narrow bottle neck; which, surely, could never have happened if the enemy were there, and particularly since our heavier transport was following close behind, struggling now through the edge of the bush, and churning up the ochreous dust into the air.

We had never before been so near the Pare range. Very soft and summery it looked with its fair fantastic outlines against a blue sky. The whole of it was softened by dense patches of forest, except in one place where a slab of bare rock rose perpendicularly for several hundred feet. Watching these mountains, and enchanted by their beauty, I suddenly saw a little puff of smoke drifting away from the lower part of this sheer face.

'There's somebody there, at any rate,' I said to H— with whom I was walking. He shook his head. 'A bit of cloud,' he said, 'or perhaps a native's fire.'

We heard a distant boom.

'We're not too late after all. . . .'

'No . . . I suppose that's the bridge at Mikocheni.'

He had scarcely finished speaking when a great explosion on our right cut him short. Not many yards away a column of dust and black smoke shot up into the air.

'Good Lord . . . the blighters are having a plug at us.'

They had not gone after all.

It seemed that we had actually caught up with them, that we had moved too fast for their railway, and that they must now put up a rearguard action or leave their equipment behind.

Another shell and yet another screamed over our heads. This time their direction was perfect, and very soon they picked up the range as well. Four-point-one shells, high explosive: the *Königsberg's* legacy. Most of them were bursting well behind us, and we knew that our dust-raising transport must be getting it; but it was evident that the observer whose puffs of smoke I had seen from the cliff-side, must have had a good view of all our column, for the bush was fairly open and all the later units had their share of shelling.

With these things sailing over us, or sometimes bursting very near our track, we pushed on into a thicker patch of bush. It was now early afternoon, and we were ordered to halt and take what shade or cover we could find.

All that afternoon the four-inch boomed away; and once, for a short time, we heard the sharper explosion of our own mountain guns. We realised well enough that neither they, nor for that matter any of our artillery, could touch their naval guns, which can fire effectively at twelve thousand yards range; but we knew that the mountain gunners must be firing at something and that encouraged us.

All our ambulance lay scattered through the bush. Only the bearer subdivision of my section stood ready with their stretchers. Nor had they long to wait, for in a little while there came a call for stretchers, and I went out with the bearers to collect wounded. This was the first time that such work had fallen to my lot. One felt rather adventurous and small, moving out of the bush into a wide open space on which the mountain observation post looked down. It seemed, somehow, as if one were actually less protected from the bursting shells in the open than under the trees: which was ridiculous, for none of those thin branches could stay a flying fragment. We moved on at a steady pace over the rough grass. We could not have been walking there, along the edge of the Pare, on a more peerless day. The cool breeze of the afternoon swept all the grasses; the aromatic scent of the brushwood, thus diluted, suggested nothing more than bland summer weather.

At last we came to the first casualty, a sowar of the Indian Cavalry, but not, as it happened, one of their handsome, sinister Pathans. He was a Punjabi Musulman, one of that people which is the backbone of the Indian Army, and his name was Hasmali. Actually he had ridden past the face of the enemy's position, within range of Tanda station, and the shot in the abdomen which had laid him out had been fired while he was aiming at the engine driver of the last train. He thought that he had hit him too. Wounded, he galloped back, sprawling, a dead weight, on the horse's neck, until he reached the place where we found him. Now his dark eyes, of a brown that was hardly human, were full of pain, and more than pain, anxiety — as though he couldn't quite feel sure what would be the end of it. But I could . . . I was suddenly very sorry for the sowar Hasmali, and particularly when I saw his horse, a chestnut, most beautifully groomed, standing by with all its barbarous caparisons. Far more terrible to me than death was the sight of that apprehension in those brown eyes.

We carried him back over the same open space, breathing of summer. His horse followed meekly behind with long strides. We should not have taken the horse with us, but the beast wanted to come. Under an acacia thorn we hid the stretcher and gave him morphia, plenty of it, and dressed him. At first he was distressed, even more than by the pain of his wound, because we must uncover him. His native modesty was stronger even than his anxiety: but we gently persuaded him and the pain was too strong, and he yielded to us. In his agony he cried 'Aiai, aiai,' like any martyr in Greek tragedy. I think I shall remember the eyes of Hasmali, sowar of the 17th Cavalry, as long as I live.

It was nearly sundown when the order came for us to advance. Sheppard's Brigade had taken up a position in the loop of the Pangani, and the rest of us were going to encamp on the slightly higher ground which the enemy were still shelling. Our long column unwound itself from the tangles in which it had lain all afternoon, and as our dust rose the German gunners found us again.

To approach the new bivouac our transport must climb a steep and dusty hillside; and as we doubted if our cattle, already so fatigued, could drag the wagons through the dust, I stayed behind with half my bearers to put shoulders to the wheels. Every minute the sky was darkening. The four-inch shells were travelling overhead with a whisper which resembled that of silk tearing. I stood on the hillside waiting while the ammunition column stumbled past, the poor lank mules, the panting oxen. Apart from the gunfire that evening was extraordinarily quiet.

At the spot where I was waiting, a little thorn tree stood up against the orange sky, a straggling bush of many branches, from the ends of which the plaited nests of the bottle-bird hung like so many flagons of Chianti. In passing, one of our men had carelessly torn the bottom from one of them and all the flight of weavers had left the tree. But now, seeing that our column was endless, the owners of that broken home had returned, and were fluttering, from below, about the place where once their door had been. It seemed as if they couldn't believe the ruthless hurt that had been done them. I watched the sweet, bewildered fluttering of these small birds against the orange sunset. A native boy came up the path singing to himself. When he saw the unhappy weaver-birds he stopped his singing. He stood utterly still, his face uplifted under the branches, watching then. Then, very gently he put up his arm beneath the tired flutterers. I could see the whole picture, the native's thick lips parted in expectancy, and the wings of the homeless weaver-birds, in silhouette. Then one of the little things, tired with so much futile fluttering, dropped down gently to the perch of the boy's finger and rested there. This was the moment for which the bushman's instinct had been waiting.

Very softly he lowered his arm, until the bird was within reach of the other hand: but, as he made a swift movement to grasp it, it darted away. . . . In a second the delicate silhouette was broken.

There I waited until the last of our bullock carts had swayed past. By this time it was quite dark, and I hurried on to see where the rest of our column had got to. The stretcher-bearers of all three sections were nowhere to be seen: but the ambulance wagons, with their teams of eight mules, still plodded along in the rear of the ammunition carts. The enemy had now ceased firing: the trick of midnight bombardments by the map was one which they learned later. There seemed to be a definite track which the people in front of us were using, and so we marched on for a long way in the dark. As we went forward this track grew more narrow, the road more difficult to clear. But in the end we came to a deep nullah, at which the first of our ambulances stopped. The wheel base of the wagon was so long as to make it impossible to clear the channel which was as narrow as a trench. The Cape-boys lashed at their mules with long thongs, and the poor beasts, who could not move forward, plunged into the thorn at the side of the track, breaking the hood of the ambulance under which our patients were lying. Plainly we couldn't go forward. Plainly, too, we could not turn a team of eight mules in a track less than ten feet wide. Meanwhile, I supposed we were holding up the rest of the divisional transport. Either we must hack a way through the thorn — no easy matter in that pitchy night — or else we must stay where we were till daybreak. We wondered that we should ever have been expected to bring wheeled transport along such a road.

Then came a staff officer, who wanted to know where the hell we were all going to. I had hoped that he would have been able to tell me.

'God knows how anyone's going to get out of this mess,' he said.

'Isn't this the way to the brigade's camp?'

'No. . . . It's the way to the water. You can't go anywhere except into the Pangani down there. And a devil of a steep hill.'

'I'd better turn. . . ?'

'Turn? You can't turn. You'd better stay here until you're told to move. For God's sake don't go and make it worse.'

'Where is the camp then?'

'Oh, somewhere . . . anywhere on this blasted hill. They're all making little camps of their own.'

He rode off to find somebody else more worth cursing.

It was cheering in a way to know that we were no worse off than most of the others. As for the ammunition column which had led us into that blind alley, they were even more deeply mired than ourselves. And the real fun of the evening would begin when the transport animals of the division came down the blocked road to water.

I told the conductor to hold fast, deciding to beat about the hill until I found our lost stretcher-bearers. I had gathered that we were somewhere to the right of the place in which they had landed, and so I followed the old track backwards for a mile or so, hoping to find some traces of the point at which they had left it. But though this task might have been easy in the daytime, in that dense night it was nearly impossible. The track was so narrow, and the surrounding bush so thick that in many places I could not push my way on either side of the carts which blocked the way, and had perforce to climb over their tail-boards and walk along the pole between the sweating oxen. And when I had travelled a mile or more backwards I had still failed to find any branching of the road down which our bearers might have wandered. I therefore determined to trust to luck and a rough idea of the map, and cut across country in the direction where I supposed their camp to be.

In those days I knew little about bush, else I had realised how hopeless was my undertaking. In the darkness, even though the thorn was scattered with wide grassy lacunae, walking was difficult, and soon my knees were torn, for I could not see the brushwood that grew knee high and hindered my steps. I walked perhaps for an hour, but under those circumstances one does not measure time, and neither saw light nor heard the least sound. I steered by the Southern Cross and by the planet Jupiter which hung nearby. At last, with a suddenness which was curious, I heard the creaking of wheels. Somewhere not very far away transport was on the move, transport which had avoided the blind alley in which we had stuck. I was a long time finding it, but emerged, at last, upon a track over which many wheels had passed. I stooped in the darkness and felt the grasses to see in which direction they had been swept at the sides, and having settled this question, set off along the track until I overtook a tired string of bullocks. The drivers were Indians, and I could not find where they were going from them, but at last I came upon a corporal who assured me that this was the way to the camp, though which camp he could not say. And so I followed them to a dip in the land over which other transport animals, in front of them, were struggling. At the top of the rise many fires were burning. This I was told was the Fusiliers' camp. Nobody except the Fusiliers was there, but a little further on I should find General Headquarters. Sheppard's Brigade, and, probably, the rest of my unit lay some four miles away to southward. They were sitting on one side of the Pangani, the enemy on the other, and both were hard at work sniping. Nobody in this part of the world seemed inclined to help me.

I turned back along the same road. It seemed that I could do nothing better than rejoin my tangled transport. A mile or so down that dark track I came upon another train of struggling A.T. carts. They halted for a little rest.

'Who are you?' I said.

'Rhodesians.' And very surly Rhodesians.

'Thank the Lord. . . . Is Mr. B— there?'

And a moment later I heard B—'s homely Somerset voice with its reassuring 'burr.' 'Hullo, Doc!' it said. 'Is this anywhere near our camp?'

I told him that we were near General Headquarters and the Fusiliers, and that Sheppard's Brigade was supposed to be nearer the river, four miles or more away.

'The main thing is, have you any food?'

'No, this is the second line. Rations are with the first.'

They passed on, and in a little while I heard their creaking wheels no more. And then, strangely enough, taking a cross cut through the bush, I stumbled on H—, the commander of our British section, who had been wandering round in search of me and the lost transport, and in the process had lost himself. With some difficulty we managed to steer back to the place where I had left the column halted, only to find that it had vanished. There was no doubt about the place. Here was the trampled road among the thorns, the ruts of the wheels were there, and even the terrible nullah in which the ambulance had been broken.

'Well now,' I said, 'have you any idea where you came from?'

We hadn't, either of us; but somehow we managed to roll up in the dark about midnight. By this time we had quite forgotten about food. We slept as best we could without covering. It was hellishly cold. [. . .]

At dawn on the 6th June the whole force moved out of Buiko. We were almost sorry to leave this beautiful and pestilential spot, for our days of rest had been badly needed, and in a short time we had made ourselves very much at home. It seemed a pity to leave our trim *bandas* there untenanted, to say good-bye to the swaying reed-beds, to wake no more to the sound of weaver-birds chirruping in the thorn-tree against which our hut was built. No doubt it was well that we left all these things, for in a few days the plague of flies would have begun, and increased the dysentery with which, so far, we had not been seriously troubled.

At any rate the camp of the First Brigade was a good deal better than that of the divisional troops. It was no pleasant experience to pass their quarters in the early morning, when the dank air or the river suspended whatever odours there might be of mules unburied or refuse unconsumed. There must have been a great many dead animals about, for at times the stench was overpowering.

We breasted the little rise by Buiko Station, and passed through the garden of a bungalow where a white horse lay swollen with its legs stiff in the air; and then, through scanty bush we dropped towards the valley of the river. By this time we knew that we were going to cross the Pangani. Beneath a great baobab we halted. A crowd had gathered at the bridgehead, and it seemed likely that we should have to wait a long time for our turn.

Two bridges had been built. The upper of the two was a narrow foot-bridge carried on pontoons, its pathway strewn with rushes, and on either side screens of palm leaves so high that a mule or bullock could not see the water on its way over. A little below this, and depending for its stability on the same pontoons, ran a floating raft, which made a zigzag course, swinging over with the swift current on its beam. Over the foot-bridge trooped the infantry and their animals. The floating bridge carried the transport carts, which were run down the beach and dragged up on the further side by their drivers . . . hard work, since many of them were overladen for want of the bullocks which had died. Fifty yards below these bridges the sappers were busy on a third, which would be strong enough to transport the guns, the heavy wagons and even the armoured cars.

The morning was dull and oppressive, the Pare veiled in cloud; but a little later the sun struggled through, making a fine picture of that gathering by the river, shining on the halted files of the Kashmiris, the variously dappled cattle, picking out the red armlets of the water police, whose chief, the A.P.M., was condemned to swing backwards and forwards across the Pangani on that little raft for two whole days. And there the river raced under green shadows. Above her drooping acacias towered the misty Pare, for now she had turned her back for a space upon those mountains. The Kashmiris were talking lazily together in Gurkhali; the *drabis* were driving their bullocks to the bridge, and all the while the river sang its own swift song. Somewhere in the bush a hornbill called. In the foreground of our picture stood the Brigadier's car, and in it sat General Sheppard himself, reading a play of Shakespeare and well content. Indeed he had every reason to be pleased, for half the fighting men of the Brigade were on the other side already.

While we were waiting thus, happy, and a little thrilled to be on the road again, an officer rode down from the signal station at Buiko with the first news of the Battle of Jutland. We had nothing but Reuter's version of the Admiralty's first report and when we had read it our minds were filled with a torturing uncertainty which shadowed the whole of that day. For it seemed to us that we had suffered a heavy defeat in an utterly unexpected quarter. We had always taken it for granted that 'the Navy was all right,' even though it was in spite of their blockade, and because of the runners who had brought cargoes of munitions into German East, and put new life into the enemy, that we were still fighting in those outlandish climes. We didn't forget that much of their ammunition at Mikocheni had borne the stamp of 1915. If harm were done at home by those misleading words, a greater harm by far came to the spirits of those who were fighting far overseas, and waited many days for reassurance. And yet, in a way, the news was stimulating. It made us anxious to be done with this sideshow, to have it finished once and for all, so that we might help to get to the root of the whole tragedy, at home in Europe.

By nine o'clock we had crossed the river, and were skirting the margin of a vast swamp. All the sunny lower air swam with moisture: the ground was oozy and black. And yet no water was to be seen: only an infinite waste of brilliant reed-beds, standing up in the air so motionless that they made no whispering. When the sun began to beat through the moist air myriads of dragonflies, which had lain all night with folded wings and slender bodies stretched along the reeds, launched themselves into the air with brittle wings aquiver. Never in my life had I seen so many, nor such a show of bright ephemeral beauty. They hung over our path more like aeroplanes in their hesitant flight than any hovering birds. Again I was riding the mule Simba, and as I rode I cut at one of them with my switch of hippo hide, cut at it and hit it. It lay broken in the path, and in a moment, as it seemed, the bright dyes faded. I was riding by myself, quite alone; and as I dismounted I felt sick with shame at this flicker of the smouldering *bête humaine;* and though I told myself that this creature was only one of so many that would flash in the sun and perish; that all life in these savage wildernesses laboured beneath cruelties perpetual and without number: of beasts that prey with tooth and claw, of tendrils that stifle, stealing the sap of life, or by minute insistence splitting the seasoned wood, I could not be reconciled to my own ruthless cruelty. For here, where all things were cruel, from the crocodiles of the Pangani to our own armed invasion, it should have been my privilege to love things for their beauty and rejoice in their joy of life, rather than become an accomplice in the universal ill. I cursed the instinct of the collector which, I suppose, far more than that of the hunter, was at the root of my crime; and from this I turned back to the educative natural history of my schooldays, in which it was thought instructive to steal a bright butterfly from the live air to a bottle of cyanide, and to press a fragrant orchid between drab sheets of blotting-paper. And I thought, perhaps, when this war is over, and half the world has been sated with cruelty, we may learn how sweet a thing is life, and how beautiful mercy.

By midday the air of the swamp became intolerably hot. We moved into a more open plain, where raffia palms were growing, and a single grove of palm-trees which was marked on the map had been chosen as the furthest spot at which the division could concentrate. The heavier floating bridge was not yet ready, and the howitzers, the field artillery, and our own ambulance wagons had been sent back to the German bridge at Mikocheni, which was now in use. At 'Palms,' then, we halted, not, as one might imagine, in any shadowy oasis, but on the open plain, beneath a cruel sun.

Flag parties had marked out the area of the camp and the Baluchis were already at work on their trenches, when a message came through from the Intelligence Department, saying that natives reported the enemy to be advancing in force down both banks of the Pangani. At once the Brigade was ordered to fall in, to leave all transport except the first line behind, and to push on to the support of the 29th Punjabis who formed our advance-guard. This day, for the first time, I was left behind with my own section and the heavier baggage of all the others, to wait with the second line transport of the brigade.

I watched the long columns cross the open plain and disappear into the encircling bush, leaving us alone between the palms and the river. As we offered rather an obvious bait to any wandering patrol of the enemy we thought it well to retire a mile or so to the rear, where a great acacia stood up on the edge of the bush. Here, with a squadron of the 17th Cavalry for bodyguard, we settled for the night, feeling very much out of it, and wondering what was happening ahead. But although we listened eagerly for gunfire and held ourselves in readiness to advance at any moment, the evening was silent and unusually peaceful, with a pool of milky mist spilling over the tops of the Pare as the hot cliffs cooled, and eastward shafts of the low sun beating through copper clouds and washing vast stretches of the dry grass in amber light.

When we placed our camp under the big acacia we had not guessed that any village was near; but as soon as they saw that we were few, and not formidable, a group of villagers came out to speak with us. None of them were armed, except one small boy who carried a bow and cunningly fashioned arrows. With them were several women, so laden with watch-spring patterns of copper wire as to be unapproachable but coquettish withal. The old man was loud in complaint. He said that some of our troops, and from his description we recognised the Kashmiris, had driven away two of his sheep while they were grazing down by the swamp. We told him that if he applied at our camp he would be paid for the damage done. He shook his head, saying that he was afraid to enter such a great camp, and then, to show him that we were in earnest, we offered to pay him there and then, and handsomely, for any fruit or vegetables that he might bring us; but he swore that there were none in his village, that the Germans had stripped their mealie fields and plantain groves bare, and that as it was his people were starving. Certainly the natives who came with him were very thin, but I think they were more probably wasted by fever than by lack of food. With a certain melancholy civility, he bade us farewell, and when they had moved a little way from us, the others, who had kept silence throughout the interview, began to talk excitedly. They seemed to be upbraiding the old man for what he had said, though we could not imagine why.

I suppose it was quite likely that the Kashmiris had indeed driven away his sheep. The problem of feeding a Hindu regiment on active service is not easy, for strenuous work calls for a meat diet, and to them the slaughter of oxen is an impious act—so that the temptation to loot sheep or goats for food was great. And yet, on the whole, I do not suppose any invading army in the history of war has behaved better in this particular than the Indian troops of the East African force.

Riding on next morning at dawn, in a green way, by the river, we met a strange safari of a dozen ragged porters carrying burdens on their heads. I wondered to whom they belonged. Half a mile further on the owner himself came riding towards us. He looked tired and hollow-eyed, but he sat his horse with a most beautiful ease, carrying a second rifle and a bulky haversack. We stopped to talk.

His manner was rather quick and excited, not in the least what you would have expected from a man who has no nerves. Yes . . . he had been behind the Germans again. He'd been 'getting his own back' (in a faint Dutch accent) for that narrow shave at the rapids, by Njumba-ya-Mawe. He had been riding seven or eight miles ahead of us, in just such an open slade as that in which we were talking, and there, suddenly, he had spotted a German scouting party: a white man and seven askaris. 'But they never saw me,' he said . . .

'Must have been blind. So I slipped into the bush and let them pass, let them get about a hundred yards ahead of me. Then I came out, came on to the edge of the track and followed them. The fools never once looked behind. I moved up nearer. Quite an easy shot . . . I killed the white man and the askaris ran. Then I rode up and picked up his rifle and haversack and the rest of his kit. Here's the rifle . . . quite a good one. And here's a vacuum flask out of his haversack full of hot coffee. Would you like some?'

A nickel-plated flask with the word Thermofix embossed on it. And the coffee was excellent.

PART FOUR

POETRY

Australians passing along a duckboard track in the devastated Chateau Wood, a portion of the battlegrounds in the Ypres Salient, Belgium, October 29, 1917. From the Australian War Memorial, neg. E01220.

Introduction

Of the literary genres, poetry is the one most closely associated with the Great War. It seems that poetry—sometimes narrative in scope, sometimes lyrical—in its powerful concentration of metaphoric and symbolic language captures the essence of the war. On the home front, poetry was written by soldiers' sisters, wives, mothers, and lovers. It often expressed the profundity of longing, solitude, and bereavement. The soldiers' poetry often evoked feelings of patriotism at first, before slowly giving way to disillusionment and despair. The reader can gauge the changing attitudes toward the war by the erosion of Georgian and Edwardian sensibilities.

"I have a distaste," W. B. Yeats wrote in his introduction to the 1936 edition of *The Oxford Book of Modern Verse,* "for certain poems written in the midst of the great war. . . . I have rejected these poems . . . [for] passive suffering is not a theme for poetry. If war is necessary, or necessary in our time or place, it is best to forget its suffering as we do the discomfort of fever." Yeats excluded every single Great War poem but Herbert Read's "The End of a War," which ends with an apologia from Read: "It is not my business as a poet to condemn war. . . . Judgement may follow, but should never precede or become embroiled with the act of poetry."

Odd words these, strange to our more modern ears. A bit precious, too fastidious, they seem now, at the end of the century, to recall foolish denials of the obvious, like an eye averted from some painful but necessary sight. Such admonitions ring false, especially when viewed in the light of the poetry of Owen, Sassoon, Rosenberg, Gurney, and Sorley. Yeats seems content with espousing a form of repression that W. H. R. Rivers, physician to Owen, Sassoon and others, would find at the root of the symptoms of shell shock.

There were, throughout the war, poems that extolled the patriotic goals of the belligerents—poems that spoke of national destinies and chauvinistic enterprises. Many have passed into our collective memorializing of the war. Rupert Brooke's "The Soldier" opens with the famous line "If I shall die, think only this of me." No collection of poetry would dare omit John

McCrae's "In Flanders Fields," the last stanza of which calls for a seemingly endless generational reprise to the war. In Alan Seeger's poem, "Rendez-vous," there is even a certain romance at the thought of death's oblivion.

Though such themes continued throughout the war in the poetry practiced by thousands at home and at the front, for many the initial burst of bravado dissipated as the long years of steady attrition took their psychological toll. At home and in the field, the costly battles of the Somme and Verdun were reflected in poetry that has become to us the essential work of the Great War—poetry that is direct, critical, even brutal in its assertiveness.

Universally regarded as the preeminent war poet, Wilfred Owen writes of "the old lie" of patriotism that sends mere children off to battle. "What passing bells," he says "for these who die as cattle." Isaac Rosenberg contrasts the startlingly disparate nature of the France of the front lines to the France of ease and entertainment. His soldiers go about their ancient soldierly routines hunting for lice, collecting the fallen, and listening to birdsong at night as troops are inserted into the trenches. Sassoon particularizes soldiers sent out to continually repair the torn wire in no-man's-land, and he individualizes the suicides that occur when strain defeats self-control. He writes of official lies told to parents to ease their memories. Charles Hamilton Sorley admonishes the living about how the dead should be remembered. In more imagistic verse, Georg Trakl and Giuseppe Ungaretti write of night watches among the corpses, of regiments passing in the night enjoying a fleeting moment of camaraderie, of the grandchildren who will not be born.

In "Rouen," May Wedderburn Cannan shifts the focus to the French city where troops are marshaled and the wounded hospitalized. Margaret Postgate Cole and Eleanor Farjeon reflect on the loss of the men, of their absence from familial scenes. Charlotte Mew, writing about a war memorial in 1919, speaks of "passionate hands" leaving at the monument's foundation "violets, roses and laurel, with the small, sweet, twinkling country things."

All the poems provide a piece of the war. Patriotic, condemnatory, reflective, generalized apostrophes or particularized moments, the various natures of Great War poetry ensure its survival in the modern mind. Rivers and others knew that speaking out, no matter the fashion, was a way toward healing the war-damaged soul.

Poetry

Rupert Brooke

THE SOLDIER

> If I should die, think only this of me:
>   That there's some corner of a foreign field
> That is for ever England. There shall be
>   In that rich earth a richer dust concealed;
> A dust whom England bore, shaped, made aware,
>   Gave, once, her flowers to love, her ways to roam,
> A body of England's, breathing English air,
>   Washed by the rivers, blest by suns of home.
> And think, this heart, all evil shed away,
>   A pulse in the eternal mind, no less
>   Gives somewhere back the thoughts by England
>   given;
>   Her sights and sounds; dreams happy as her day;
>   And laughter, learnt of friends; and gentleness
>   In hearts at peace, under an English heaven.

May Wedderburn Cannan

ROUEN

> *26 April–25 May 1915*
> Early morning over Rouen, hopeful, high, courageous morning,
> And the laughter of adventure and the steepness of the stair,
> And the dawn across the river, and the wind across the bridges,
> And the empty littered station and the tired people there.

Can you recall those mornings and the hurry of awakening,
And the long-forgotten wonder if we should miss the way,
And the unfamiliar faces, and the coming of provisions,
And the freshness and the glory of the labour of the day?

Hot noontide over Rouen, and the sun upon the city,
Sun and dust unceasing, and the glare of cloudless skies,
And the voices of the Indians and the endless stream of soldiers,
And the clicking of the tatties, and the buzzing of the flies.

Can you recall those noontides and the reek of steam and coffee,
Heavy-laden noontides with the evening's peace to win,
And the little piles of Woodbines, and the sticky soda bottles,
And the crushes in the 'Parlour,' and the letters coming in?

Quiet night-time over Rouen, and the station full of soldiers,
All the youth and pride of England from the ends of all the earth;
And the rifles piled together, and the creaking of the sword-belts,
And the faces bent above them, and the gay, heart-breaking mirth.

Can I forget the passage from the cool white-bedded Aid Post
Past the long sun-blistered coaches of the khaki Red Cross train
To the truck train full of wounded, and the weariness and laughter,
And 'Good-bye, and thank you, Sister,' and the empty yards again?

Can you recall the parcels that we made them for the railroad,
Crammed and bulging parcels held together by their string,
And the voices of the sergeants who called the Drafts together,
And the agony and splendour when they stood to save the King?

Can you forget their passing, the cheering and the waving,
The little group of people at the doorway of the shed,
The sudden awful silence when the last train swung to darkness,
And the lonely desolation, and the mocking stars o'erhead?

Can you recall the midnights, and the footsteps of night watchers,
Men who came from darkness and went back to dark again,
And the shadows on the rail-lines and the all-inglorious labour,
And the promise of the daylight firing blue the window-pane?

Can you recall the passing through the kitchen door to morning,
Morning very still and solemn breaking slowly on the town,

And the early coastways engines that had met the ships at daybreak,
And the Drafts just out from England, and the day shift coming
    down?

Can you forget returning slowly, stumbling on the cobbles,
And the white-decked Red Cross barges dropping seawards for
    the tide,
And the search for English papers, and the blessed cool of water,
And the peace of half-closed shutters that shut out the world outside?

Can I forget the evenings and the sunsets on the island,
And the tall black ships at anchor far below our balcony,
And the distant call of bugles, and the white wine in the glasses,
And the long line of the street lamps, stretching Eastwards to the
    sea?

. . . When the world slips slow to darkness, when the office fire
    burns lower,
My heart goes out to Rouen, Rouen all the world away;
When other men remember I remember our Adventure
And the trains that go from Rouen at the ending of the day.

Margaret Postgate Cole

THE FALLING LEAVES
NOVEMBER, 1915

Today, as I rode by,
I saw the brown leaves dropping from their tree
In a still afternoon,
When no wind whirled them whistling to the sky,
But thickly, silently,
They fell, like snowflakes wiping out the noon;
And wandered slowly thence
For thinking of a gallant multitude
Which now all withering lay,
Slain by no wind of age or pestilence,
But in their beauty strewed
Like snowflakes falling on the Flemish clay.

Eleanor Farjeon

EASTER MONDAY
(IN MEMORIAM E.T.)

> In the last letter that I had from France
> You thanked me for the silver Easter egg
> Which I had hidden in the box of apples
> You liked to munch beyond all other fruit.
> You found the egg the Monday before Easter,
> And said, 'I will praise Easter Monday now —
> It was such a lovely morning.' Then you spoke
> Of the coming battle and said, 'This is the eve.
> Good-bye. And may I have a letter soon?'
>
> That Easter Monday was a day for praise,
> It was such a lovely morning. In our garden
> We sowed our earliest seeds, and in the orchard
> The apple-bud was ripe. It was the eve.
> There are three letters that you will not get.

Ivor Gurney

DE PROFUNDIS

> If only this fear would leave me I could dream of Crickley Hill
>   And a hundred thousand thoughts of home would visit my
>   heart in sleep;
> But here the peace is shattered all day by the devil's will,
>   And the guns bark night-long to spoil the velvet silence
>   deep.
>
> O who could think that once we drank in quiet inns and cool
>   And saw brown oxen trooping the dry sands to slake
> Their thirst at the river flowing, or plunged in a silver pool
>   To shake the sleepy drowse off before well awake?
>
> We are stale here, we are covered body and soul and mind
>   With mire of the trenches, close clinging and foul,
> We have left our old inheritance, our Paradise behind,
>   And clarity is lost to us and cleanness of soul.

O blow here, you dusk-airs and breaths of half-light,
　　And comfort despairs of your darlings that long
Night and day for sound of your bells, or a sight
　　Of your tree-bordered lanes, land of blossom and song.

Autumn will be here soon, but the road of coloured leaves
　　Is not for us, the up and down highway where go
Earth's pilgrims to wonder where Malvern upheaves
　　That blue-emerald splendour under great clouds of snow.

Some day we'll fill in trenches, level the land and turn
　　Once more joyful faces to the country where trees
Bear thickly for good drink, where strong sunsets burn
　　Huge bonfires of glory — O God, send us peace!

Hard it is for men of moors or fens to endure
　　Exile and hardship, or the northland grey-drear;
But we of the rich plain of sweet airs and pure,
　　Oh! Death would take so much from us, how should we not
　　　　fear?

YPRES–MINSTERWORTH
(TO F.W.H.)

　　Thick lie in Gloucester orchards now
　　　　Apples the Severn wind
　　With rough play tore from the tossing
　　　　Branches, and left behind
　　Leaves strewn on pastures, blown in hedges,
　　　　And by the roadway lined.

　　And I lie leagues on leagues afar
　　　　To think how that wind made
　　Great shootings in the wide chimney,
　　　　A noise of cannonade —
　　Of how the proud elms by the signpost
　　　　The tempest's will obeyed —

　　To think how in some German prison
　　　　A boy lies with whom
　　I might have taken joy full-hearted
　　　　Hearing the great boom

Of autumn, watching the fire, talking
  Of books in the half gloom.

O wind of Ypres and of Severn
  Riot there also, and tell
Of comrades safe returned, home-keeping
  Music and autumn smell.
Comfort blow him and friendly greeting,
  Hearten him, wish him well!

FIRST TIME IN

After the dread tales and red yarns of the Line
Anything might have come to us; but the divine
Afterglow brought us up to a Welsh colony
Hiding in sandbag ditches, whispering consolatory
Soft foreign things. Then we were taken in
To low huts candle-lit, shaded close by slitten
Oilsheets, and there the boys gave us kind welcome,
So that we looked out as from the edge of home,
Sang us Welsh things, and changed all former notions
To human, hopeful things. And the next day's guns
Nor any line-pangs ever quite could blot out
That strangely beautiful entry to war's rout;
Candles they gave us, precious and shared over-rations —
Ulysses found little more in his wanderings without doubt,
'David of the White Rock,' the 'Slumber Song' so soft, and that
Beautiful tune to which roguish words by Welsh pit boys
Are sung — but never more beautiful than there under the
  guns' noise.

MEMORY, LET ALL SLIP

Memory, let all slip save what is sweet
Of Ypres plains.
Keep only autumn sunlight and the fleet
Clouds after rains,

Blue sky and mellow distance softly blue;
These only hold
Lest I my pangèd grave must share with you.
Else dead. Else cold.

One would remember still
Meadows and low hill
Laventie was, as to the line and elm row
Growing through green strength wounded, as home elms grow.
Shimmer of summer there and blue autumn mists
Seen from trench-ditch winding in mazy twists.
The Australian gunners in close flowery hiding
Cunning found out at last, and smashed in the unspeakable lists.
And the guns in the smashed wood thumping and griding.

The letters written there, and received there,
Books, cakes, cigarettes in a parish of famine,
And leaks in rainy times with general all-damning.
The crater, and carrying of gas cylinders on two sticks
(Pain past comparison and far past right agony gone),
Strained hopelessly of heart and frame at first fix.

Café-au-lait in dug-outs on Tommies' cookers
Cursed minniewerfs, thirst in eighteen-hour summer.
The Australian miners clayed, and the being afraid
Before strafes, sultry August dusk time than death dumber —
And the cooler hush after the strafe, and the long night wait —
The relief of first dawn, the crawling out to look at it,
Wonder divine of dawn, man hesitating before Heaven's gate.
(Though not on Cooper's where music fire took at it.
Though not as at Framilode beauty where body did shake at it)
Yet the dawn with aeroplanes crawling high at Heaven's gate
Lovely aerial beetles of wonderful scintillate
Strangest interest, and puffs of soft purest white —
Seeking light, dispersing colouring for fancy's delight.
Of Machonachie, Paxton, Tickler and Gloucester's Stephens;
Fray Bentos, Spiller and Baker, odds and evens
Of trench food, but the everlasting clean craving
For bread, the pure thing, blessèd beyond saving.
Canteen disappointments, and the keen boy braving
Bullets or such for grouse roused surprisingly through
(Halfway) Stand-to.
And the shell nearly blunted my razor at shaving;
Tilleloy, Fauquissart, Neuve Chapelle, and mud like glue.
But Laventie, most of all, I think is to soldiers

The town itself with plane trees, and small-spa air;
And vin, rouge-blanc, chocolate, citron, grenadine:
One might buy in small delectable cafés there.
The broken church, and vegetable fields bare;
Neat French market-town look so clean,
And the clarity, amiability of North French air.

*

Like water flowing beneath the dark plough and high Heaven,
Music's delight to please the poet pack-marching there.

Thomas Hardy

CHANNEL FIRING

That night your great guns, unawares,
Shook all our coffins as we lay,
And broke the chancel window-squares,
We thought it was the Judgment-day

And sat upright. While drearisome
Arose the howl of wakened hounds:
The mouse let fall the altar-crumb,
The worms drew back into the mounds,

The glebe cow drooled. Till God called, 'No;
It's gunnery practice out at sea
Just as before you went below;
The world is as it used to be:

'All nations striving strong to make
Red war yet redder. Mad as hatters
They do no more for Christés sake
Than you who are helpless in such matters.

'That this is not the judgment-hour
For some of them's a blessed thing,
For if it were they'd have to scour
Hell's floor for so much threatening . . .

'Ha, ha. It will be warmer when
I blow the trumpet (if indeed
I ever do; for you are men,
And rest eternal sorely need).'

So down we lay again. 'I wonder,
Will the world ever saner be,'
Said one, 'than when He sent us under
in our indifferent century!'

And many a skeleton shook his head.
'Instead of preaching forty year,'
My neighbour Parson Thirdly said,
'I wish I had stuck to pipes and beer.'

Again the guns disturbed the hour,
Roaring their readiness to avenge,
As far inland as Stourton Tower,
And Camelot, and starlit Stonehenge.

Rudyard Kipling

GETHSEMANE (1914–1918)

The Garden called Gethsemane
    In Picardy it was,
And there the people came to see
    The English soldiers pass.

We used to pass — we used to pass
    Or halt, as it might be,
And ship our masks in case of gas
    Beyond Gethsemane.

The Garden called Gethsemane,
    It held a pretty lass,
But all the time she talked to me
    I prayed my cup might pass.
The officer sat on the chair,
    The men lay on the grass,

And all the time we halted there
  I prayed my cup might pass.

It didn't pass — it didn't pass —
  It didn't pass from me.
I drank it when we met the gas
  Beyond Gethsemane!

John McCrae

IN FLANDERS FIELDS

In Flanders fields the poppies blow
Between the crosses, row on row
  That mark our place; and in the sky
  The larks, still bravely singing, fly
Scarce heard amid the guns below.

We are the Dead. Short days ago
We lived, felt dawn, saw sunset glow,
  Loved and were loved, and now we lie
    In Flanders fields.

Take up our quarrel with the foe:
To you from failing hands we throw
  The torch; be yours to hold it high.
  If ye break faith with us who die
We shall not sleep, though poppies grow
    In Flanders fields.

Charlotte Mew

THE CENOTAPH
SEPTEMBER 1919

Not yet will those measureless fields be green again
Where only yesterday the wild sweet blood of wonderful youth was
    shed;
There is a grave whose earth must hold too long, too deep a stain,

Though for ever over it we may speak as proudly as we may tread.
But here, where the watchers by lonely hearths from the thrust of an
    inward sword have more slowly bled,
We shall build the Cenotaph: Victory, winged, with Peace, winged
    too, at the column's head.
And over the stairway, at the foot — oh! here, leave desolate,
    passionate hands to spread
Violets, roses, and laurel, with the small, sweet, twinkling country
    things
Speaking so wistfully of other Springs,
From the little gardens of little places where son or sweetheart was
    born and bred.
In splendid sleep, with a thousand brothers
               To lovers — to mothers
               Here, too, lies he:
Under the purple, the green, the red,
It is all young life: it must break some women's hearts to see
Such a brave, gay coverlet to such a bed!
Only, when all is done and said,
God is not mocked and neither are the dead.
For this will stand in our Market-place —
               Who'll sell, who'll buy
               (Will you or I
Lie each to each with the better grace)?
While looking into every busy whore's and huckster's face
As they drive their bargains, is the Face
Of God: and some young, piteous, murdered face.

Wilfred Owen

DULCE ET DECORUM EST

Bent double, like old beggars under sacks,
Knock-kneed, coughing like hags, we cursed through sludge,
Till on the haunting flares we turned our backs
And towards our distant rest began to trudge.
Men marched asleep. Many had lost their boots
But limped on, blood-shod. All went lame; all blind;
Drunk with fatigue; deaf even to the hoots
of tired, outstripped Five-Nines that dropped behind.

Gas! GAS! Quick, boys! — An ecstasy of fumbling,
Fitting the clumsy helmets just in time;
But someone still was yelling out and stumbling,
And flound'ring like a man in fire or lime . . .
Dim, through the misty panes and thick green light,
As under a green sea, I saw him drowning.

In all my dreams, before my helpless sight,
He plunges at me, guttering, choking, drowning.

If in some smothering dreams you too could pace
Behind the wagon that we flung him in,
And watch the white eyes writhing in his face,
His hanging face, like a devil's sick of sin;
If you could hear, at every jolt, the blood
Come gargling from the froth-corrupted lungs
Obscene as cancer, bitter as the cud
Of vile, incurable sores on innocent tongues, —
My friend, you would not tell with such high zest
To children ardent for some desperate glory,
The old Lie: Dulce et decorum est
Pro patria mori.

ANTHEM FOR DOOMED YOUTH

What passing-bells for these who die as cattle?
    — Only the monstrous anger of the guns.
    Only the stuttering rifles' rapid rattle
Can patter out their hasty orisons.
No mockeries now for them; no prayers nor bells;
    Nor any voice of mourning save the choirs, —
The shrill, demented choirs of wailing shells;
    And bugles calling for them from sad shires.

What candles may be held to speed them all?
    Not in the hands of boys but in their eyes
Shall shine the holy glimmers of goodbyes.
    The pallor of girls' brows shall be their pall;
Their flowers the tenderness of patient minds,
And each slow dusk a drawing-down of blinds.

GREATER LOVE

Red lips are not so red
    As the stained stones kissed by the English dead.
Kindness of wooed and wooer
Seems shame to their love pure.
O Love, your eyes lose lure
    When I behold eyes blinded in my stead!

Your slender attitude
    Trembles not exquisite like limbs knife-skewed,
Rolling and rolling there
Where God seems not to care;
Till the fierce love they bear
    Cramps them in death's extreme decrepitude.

Your voice sings not so soft, —
    Though even as wind murmuring through raftered loft, —
Your dear voice is not dear,
Gentle, and evening clear,
As theirs whom none now hear,
    Now earth has stopped their piteous mouths that coughed.

Heart, you were never hot
    Nor large, nor full like hearts made great with shot;
And though your hand be pale,
Paler are all which trail
Your cross through flame and hail:
    Weep, you may weep, for you may touch them not.

MENTAL CASES

Who are these? Why sit they here in twilight?
Wherefore rock they, purgatorial shadows,
Drooping tongues from jaws that slob their relish,
Baring teeth that leer like skulls' teeth wicked?
Stroke on stroke of pain, — but what slow panic,
Gouged these chasms round their fretted sockets?
Ever from their hair and through their hands' palms
Misery swelters. Surely we have perished
Sleeping, and walk hell; but who these hellish?

— These are men whose minds the Dead have ravished.
Memory fingers in their hair of murders,
Multitudinous murders they once witnessed.
Wading sloughs of flesh these helpless wander,
Treading blood from lungs that had loved laughter.
Always they must see these things and hear them,
Batter of guns and shatter of flying muscles,
Carnage incomparable, and human squander
Rucked too thick for these men's extrication.

Therefore still their eyeballs shrink tormented
Back into their brains, because on their sense
Sunlight seems a blood-smear; night comes blood-black;
Dawn breaks open like a wound that bleeds afresh.
— Thus their heads wear this hilarious, hideous,
Awful falseness of set-smiling corpses.
— Thus their hands are plucking at each other;
Picking at the rope-knouts of their scourging;
Snatching after us who smote them, brother,
Pawing us who dealt them war and madness.

SPRING OFFENSIVE

Halted against the shade of a last hill
They fed, and eased of pack-loads, were at ease;
And leaning on the nearest chest or knees
Carelessly slept.
        But many there stood still
To face the stark blank sky beyond the ridge,
Knowing their feet had come to the end of the world.
Marvelling they stood, and watched the long grass swirled
By the May breeze, murmurous with wasp and midge;
And though the summer oozed into their veins
Like an injected drug for their bodies' pains,
Sharp on their souls hung the imminent ridge of grass,
Fearfully flashed the sky's mysterious glass.

Hour after hour they ponder the warm field
And the far valley behind, where buttercups
Had blessed with gold their slow boots coming up;
When even the little brambles would not yield

But clutched and clung to them like sorrowing arms.
They breathe like trees unstirred.

Till like a cold gust thrills the little word
At which each body and its soul begird
And tighten them for battle. No alarms
Of bugles, no high flags, no clamorous haste, —
Only a lift and flare of eyes that faced
The sun, like a friend with whom their love is done.
O larger shone that smile against the sun, —
Mightier than his whose bounty these have spurned.

So, soon they topped the hill, and raced together
Over an open stretch of herb and heather
Exposed. And instantly the whole sky burned
With fury against them; earth set sudden cups
In thousands for their blood; and the green slope
Chasmed and deepened sheer to infinite space.

Of them who running on that last high place
Breasted the surf of bullets, or went up
On the hot blast and fury of hell's upsurge,
Or plunged and fell away past this world's verge,
Some say God caught them even before they fell.

But what say such as from existence' brink
Ventured but drave too swift to sink,
The few who rushed in the body to enter hell,
And there out-fiending all its fiends and flames
With superhuman inhumanities,
Long-famous glories, immemorial shames —
And crawling slowly back, have by degrees
Regained cool peaceful air in wonder —
Why speak not they of comrades that went under?

THE PARABLE OF THE OLD MAN AND THE YOUNG

So Abram rose, and clave the wood, and went,
And took the fire with him, and a knife.
And as they sojourned both of them together,
Isaac the first-born spake and said, My Father,
Behold the preparations, fire and iron,

But where the lamb, for this burnt-offering?
Then Abram bound the youth with belts and straps,
And builded parapets and trenches there,
And stretchèd forth the knife to slay his son.
When lo! An Angel called him out of heaven,
Saying, Lay not thy hand upon the lad,
Neither do anything to him, thy son.
Behold! Caught in a thicket by its horns,
A Ram. Offer the Ram of Pride instead.

But the old man would not so, but slew his son,
And half the seed of Europe, one by one.

Isaac Rosenberg

FROM FRANCE

The spirit drank the café lights;
All the hot life that glittered there,
And heard men say to women gay,
'Life is just so in France.'

The spirit dreams of café lights,
And golden faces and soft tones,
And hears men groan to broken men,
'This is not Life in France.'

Heaped stones and a charred signboard shows
With grass between and dead folk under,
And some birds sing, while the spirit takes wing.
And this is Life in France.

BREAK OF DAY IN THE TRENCHES

The darkness crumbles away.
It is the same old druid Time as ever,
Only a live thing leaps my hand,
A queer sardonic rat,
As I pull the parapet's poppy
To stick behind my ear.
Droll rat, they would shoot you if they knew

Your cosmopolitan sympathies.
Now you have touched this English hand
You will do the same to a German
Soon, no doubt, if it be your pleasure
To cross the sleeping green between.
It seems you inwardly grin as you pass
Strong eyes, fine limbs, haughty athletes,
Less chanced than you for life,
Bonds to the whims of murder,
Sprawled in the bowels of the earth,
The torn fields of France.
What do you see in our eyes
At the shrieking iron and flame
Hurled through still heavens?
What quaver — what heart aghast?
Poppies whose roots are in man's veins
Drop, and are ever dropping;
But mine in my ear is safe —
Just a little white with the dust.

LOUSE HUNTING

Nudes — stark and glistening.
Yelling in lurid glee. Grinning faces
And raging limbs
Whirl over the floor one fire.
For a shirt verminously busy
Yon soldier tore from his throat, with oaths
Godhead might shrink at, but not the lice.
And soon the shirt was aflare
Over the candle he'd lit while we lay.

Then we all sprang up and stript
To hunt the verminous brood.
Soon like a demons' pantomime
The place was raging.
See the silhouettes agape,
See the gibbering shadows
Mixed with the battled arms on the wall.
See gargantuan hooked fingers
Pluck in supreme flesh
To smutch supreme littleness.

See the merry limbs in hot Highland fling
Because some wizard vermin
Charmed from the quiet this revel
When our ears were half lulled
By the dark music
Blown from Sleep's trumpet.

RETURNING, WE HEAR THE LARKS

Sombre the night is.
And though we have our lives, we know
What sinister threat lurks there:

Dragging these anguished limbs, we only know
This poison-blasted track opens on our camp —
On a little safe sleep.

But hark! joy — joy — strange joy.
Lo! heights of night ringing with unseen larks.
Music showering our upturned list'ning faces.

Death could drop from the dark
As easily as song —
But song only dropped,
Like a blind man's dreams on the sand
By dangerous tides,
Like a girl's dark hair for she dreams no ruin lies there,
Or her kisses where a serpent hides.

DEAD MAN'S DUMP

The plunging limbers over the shattered track
Racketed with their rusty freight,
Stuck out like many crowns of thorns,
And the rusty stakes like sceptres old
To stay the flood of brutish men
Upon our brothers dear.

The wheels lurched over sprawled dead
But pained them not, though their bones crunched,

Their shut mouths made no moan,
They lie there huddled, friend and foeman,
Man born of man, and born of woman,
And shells go crying over them
From night till night and now.

Earth has waited for them
All the time of their growth
Fretting for their decay:
Now she has them at last!
In the strength of their strength
Suspended — stopped and held.

What fierce imaginings their dark souls lit
Earth! have they gone into you?
Somewhere they must have gone,
And flung on your hard back
Is their souls' sack,
Emptied of God-ancestralled essences.
Who hurled them out? Who hurled?

None saw their spirits' shadow shake the grass,
Or stood aside for the half used life to pass
Out of those doomed nostrils and the doomed mouth,
When the swift iron burning bee
Drained the wild honey of their youth.

What of us, who flung on the shrieking pyre,
Walk, our usual thoughts untouched,
Our lucky limbs as on ichor fed,
Immortal seeming ever?
Perhaps when the flames beat loud on us,
A fear may choke in our veins
And the startled blood may stop.

The air is loud with death,
The dark air spurts with fire
The explosions ceaseless are.
Timelessly now, some minutes past,
These dead strode time with vigorous life,
Till the shrapnel called 'an end!'

But not to all. In bleeding pangs
Some borne on stretchers dreamed of home,
Dear things, war-blotted from their hearts.

A man's brains splattered on
A stretcher-bearer's face;
His shook shoulders slipped their load,
But when they bent to look again
The drowning soul was sunk too deep
For human tenderness.

They left this dead with the older dead,
Stretched at the cross roads.
Burnt black by strange decay,
Their sinister faces lie
The lid over each eye,
The grass and coloured clay
More motion have than they,
Joined to the great sunk silences.

Here is one not long dead;
His dark hearing caught our far wheels,
And the choked soul stretched weak hands
To reach the living word the far wheels said,
The blood-dazed intelligence beating for light,
Crying through the suspense of the far torturing wheels
Swift for the end to break,
Or the wheels to break,
Cried as the tide of the world broke over his sight.

Will they come? Will they ever come?
Even as the mixed hoofs of the mules,
The quivering-bellied mules,
And the rushing wheels all mixed
With his tortured upturned sight,
So we crashed round the bend,
We heard his weak scream,
We heard his very last sound,
And our wheels grazed his dead face.

Siegfried Sassoon

WIRERS

'Pass it along, the wiring party's going out'—
And yawning sentries mumble, 'Wirers going out.'
Unravelling; twisting; hammering stakes with muffled thud,
They toil with stealthy haste and anger in their blood.

The Bosch sends up a flare. Black forms stand rigid there,
Stock-still like posts; then darkness, and the clumsy ghosts
Stride hither and thither, whispering, tripped by clutching snare
Of snags and tangles.
                    Ghastly dawn with vaporous coasts
Gleams desolate along the sky, night's misery ended.

Young Hughes was badly hit; I heard him carried away,
Moaning at every lurch; no doubt he'll die to-day.
But we can say the front-line wire's been safely mended.

HOW TO DIE

Dark clouds are smouldering into red
    While down the craters morning burns.
The dying soldier shifts his head
    To watch the glory that returns;
He lifts his fingers toward the skies
    Where holy brightness breaks in flame;
Radiance reflected in his eyes,
    And on his lips a whispered name.

You'd think, to hear some people talk,
    That lads go West with sobs and curses,
And sullen faces white as chalk,
    Hankering for wreaths and tombs and hearses.
But they've been taught the way to do it
    Like Christian soldiers; not with haste
And shuddering groans; but passing through it
    With due regard for decent taste.

LAMENTATIONS

I found him in the guard-room at the Base.
From the blind darkness I had heard his crying
And blundered in. With puzzled, patient face
A sergeant watched him; it was no good trying
To stop it; for he howled and beat his chest.
And, all because his brother had gone west,
Raved at the bleeding war; his rampant grief
Moaned, shouted, sobbed, and choked, while he was kneeling
Half-naked on the floor. In my belief
Such men have lost all patriotic feeling.

SUICIDE IN THE TRENCHES

I knew a simple soldier boy
Who grinned at life in empty joy,
Slept soundly through the lonesome dark,
And whistled early with the lark.

In winter trenches, cowed and glum,
With crumps and lice and lack of rum,
He put a bullet through his brain.
No one spoke of him again.

    .   .   .   .

You smug-faced crowds with kindling eye
Who cheer when soldier lads march by,
Sneak home and pray you'll never know
The hell where youth and laughter go.

THE ROAD

The road is thronged with women; soldiers pass
And halt, but never see them; yet they're here —
A patient crowd along the sodden grass,
Silent, worn out with waiting, sick with fear.
The road goes crawling up a long hillside,
All ruts and stones and sludge, and the emptied dregs
Of battle thrown in heaps. Here where they died
Are stretched big-bellied horses with stiff legs,
And dead men, bloody-fingered from the fight,
Stare up at caverned darkness winking white.

You in the bomb-scorched kilt, poor sprawling Jock,
You tottered here and fell, and stumbled on,
Half dazed for want of sleep. No dream would mock
Your reeling brain with comforts lost and gone.
You did not feel her arms about your knees,
Her blind caress, her lips upon your head.
Too tired for thoughts of home and love and ease,
The road would serve you well enough for bed.

THE HERO

'Jack fell as he'd have wished,' the Mother said,
And folded up the letter that she'd read.
'The Colonel writes so nicely.' Something broke
In the tired voice that quavered to a choke.
She half looked up. 'We mothers are so proud
Of our dead soldiers.' Then her face was bowed.

Quietly the Brother Officer went out.
He'd told the poor old dear some gallant lies
That she would nourish all her days, no doubt.
For while he coughed and mumbled, her weak eyes
Had shone with gentle triumph, brimmed with joy,
Because he'd been so brave, her glorious boy.

He thought how 'Jack,' cold-footed, useless swine,
Had panicked down the trench that night the mine
Went up at Wicked Corner; how he'd tried
To get sent home, and how, at last, he died,
Blown to small bits. And no one seemed to care
Except that lonely woman with white hair.

COUNTER-ATTACK

We'd gained our first objective hours before
While dawn broke like a face with blinking eyes,
Pallid, unshaved and thirsty, blind with smoke.
Things seemed all right at first. We held their line,
With bombers posted, Lewis guns well placed,
And clink of shovels deepening the shallow trench.
  The place was rotten with dead; green clumsy legs
  High-booted, sprawled and grovelled along the saps

And trunks, face downward, in the sucking mud,
Wallowed like trodden sand-bags loosely filled;
And naked sodden buttocks, mats of hair,
Bulged, clotted heads slept in the plastering slime.
And then the rain began, — the jolly old rain!

A yawning soldier knelt against the bank,
Staring across the morning blear with fog;
He wondered when the Allemands would get busy;
And then, of course, they started with five-nines
Traversing, sure as fate, and never a dud.
Mute in the clamour of shells he watched them burst
Spouting dark earth and wire with gusts from hell,
While posturing giants dissolved in drifts of smoke.
He crouched and flinched, dizzy with galloping fear,
Sick for escape, — loathing the strangled horror
And butchered, frantic gestures of the dead.

An officer came blundering down the trench:
'Stand-to and man the fire-step!' On he went . . .
Gasping and bawling, 'Fire-step . . . counter-attack!'
    Then the haze lifted. Bombing on the right
    Down the old sap: machine-guns on the left;
    And stumbling figures looming out in front.
    'O Christ, they're coming at us!' Bullets spat,
And he remembered his rifle . . . rapid fire . . .
And started blazing wildly . . . then a bang
Crumpled and spun him sideways, knocked him out
To grunt and wriggle: none heeded him; he choked
And fought the flapping veils of smothering gloom,
Lost in a blurred confusion of yells and groans . . .
Down, and down, and down, he sank and drowned,
Bleeding to death. The counter-attack had failed.

Alan Seeger

I HAVE A RENDEZVOUS WITH DEATH

I have a rendezvous with Death
At some disputed barricade,
When Spring comes back with rustling shade

And apple-blossoms fill the air —
I have a rendezvous with Death
When Spring brings back blue days and fair.

    It may be he shall take my hand
And lead me into his dark land
And close my eyes and quench my breath —
It may be I shall pass him still.
I have a rendezvous with Death
On some scarred slope of battered hill,
When Spring comes round again this year
And the first meadow-flowers appear.

    God knows 'twere better to be deep
Pillowed in silk and scented down,
Where Love throbs out in blissful sleep,
Pulse nigh to pulse, and breath to breath,
Where hushed awakenings are dear . . .
But I've a rendezvous with Death
At midnight in some flaming town,
When Spring trips north again this year,
And I to my pledged word am true,
I shall not fail that rendezvous.

Edith Sitwell

THE DANCERS
(DURING A GREAT BATTLE, 1916)

    The floors are slippery with blood:
The world gyrates too. God is good
That while His wind blows out the light
For those who hourly die for us —
We still can dance, each night.

    The music has grown numb with death —
But we will suck their dying breath,
The whispered name they breathed to chance,
To swell our music, make it loud
That we may dance, — may dance.

We are the dull blind carrion-fly
That dance and batten. Though God die
Mad from the horror of the light—
The light is mad, too, flecked with blood,—
We dance, we dance, each night.

Charles Hamilton Sorley

TWO SONNETS

I

Saints have adored the lofty soul of you.
Poets have whitened at your high renown.
We stand among the many millions who
Do hourly wait to pass your pathway down.
You, so familiar, once were strange: we tried
To live as of your presence unaware.
But now in every road on every side
We see your straight and steadfast signpost there.

I think it like that signpost in my land,
Hoary and tall, which pointed me to go
Upward, into the hills, on the right hand,
Where the mists swim and the winds shriek and blow,
A homeless land and friendless, but a land
I did not know and that I wished to know.

II

Such, such is Death: no triumph: no defeat:
Only an empty pail, a slate rubbed clean,
A merciful putting away of what has been.

And this we know: Death is not Life effete,
Life crushed, the broken pail. We who have seen
So marvellous things know well the end not yet.

Victor and vanquished are a-one in death:
Coward and brave: friend, foe. Ghosts do not say
'Come, what was your record when you drew breath?'
But a big blot has hid each yesterday
So poor, so manifestly incomplete.

And your bright Promise, withered long and sped,
Is touched, stirs, rises, opens and grows sweet
And blossoms and is you, when you are dead.

ALL THE HILLS AND VALES ALONG

All the hills and vales along
Earth is bursting into song,
And the singers are the chaps
    Who are going to die perhaps.
    O sing, marching men,
    Till the valleys ring again.
    Give your gladness to earth's keeping,
    So be glad, when you are sleeping.

Cast away regret and rue,
Think what you are marching to.
Little live, great pass.
Jesus Christ and Barabbas
Were found the same day.
This died, that went his way.
    So sing with joyful breath.
    For why, you are going to death.
    Teeming earth will surely store
    All the gladness that you pour.

Earth that never doubts nor fears,
Earth that knows of death, not tears,
Earth that bore with joyful ease
Hemlock for Socrates,
Earth that blossomed and was glad
'Neath the cross that Christ had,
Shall rejoice and blossom too
When the bullet reaches you.
    Wherefore, men marching
    On the road to death, sing!
    Pour your gladness on earth's head,
    So be merry so be dead.

From the hills and valleys earth
Shouts back the sound of mirth,

Tramp of feet and lilt of song
Ringing all the road along
All the music of their going,
Ringing swinging glad song-throwing,
Earth will echo still, when foot
Lies numb and voice mute.
    On marching men, on
    To the gates of death with song.
    Sow your gladness for earth's reaping,
    So you may be glad, though sleeping.
    Strew your gladness on earth's bed,
    So be merry, so be dead.

WHEN YOU SEE MILLIONS OF THE MOUTHLESS DEAD

When you see millions of the mouthless dead
Across your dreams in pale battalions go,
Say not soft things as other men have said,
That you'll remember. For you need not so.
Give them not praise. For, deaf, how should they know
It is not curses heaped on each gashed head?
Nor tears. Their blind eyes see not your tears flow.
Nor honour. It is easy to be dead.
Say only this, 'They are dead.' Then add thereto,
'Yet many a better one has died before.'
Then, scanning all the o'ercrowded mass, should you
Perceive one face that you loved heretofore,
It is a spook. None wears the face you knew.
Great death has made all his for evermore.

August Stramm

STORMTAKING

Frightful volleys resound off every angle
Shriek
Crack
Your life
Coming
At you
Gasping death

That skies shred.
Runaway dread butchers blind.
—*translated by Lucia Cordell Getsi*

BATTLEFIELD

Homeland softening, iron goes to sleep
Blood felts the seeping soil
Rusts run
Corpses slime
Absorption lusts for decomposing.
Murder's murder
Children's gazes
Blink.
—*translated by Lucia Cordell Getsi*

WOUNDS

Beneath the helmeted head earth bleeds
Stars fall
The universe gropes its way.
Showers bluster
Whirlwinds
Lonelinesses.
Fog
Weeping
Distance
Your gaze.
—*translated by Lucia Cordell Getsi*

IN THE FIRING

Deaths shuffle
Dying clatters
Solitary
Walls up
Solitude's
World deep towers.
—*translated by Lucia Cordell Getsi*

GRENADES

Knowing stops
Just a hunch floats and deludes
The deafening deadens dreadful woundings
Clapping tapping rooting shrieking
Keening cracking crackling creaking
Grinding thudding
The sky holds out
The stars sleet out
Time balms
Stubbornly worlds a space knocked senseless.
— translated by Lucia Cordell Getsi

WAR GRAVE

The bars supplicate like crossed arms
Script shies from the pale unknown
Flowers shameless
Dust timorous.
Spangle
Tears
Radiance
Forgotten.
— translated by Lucia Cordell Getsi

Georg Trakl

LAMENT

Sleep and death, the dark eagles
Sweep around this head all night long:
The icy wave of eternity
Would engulf the golden image
Of man. His purple body
Shatters on terrible reefs
And the dark voice spreads lamentation
Over the sea.
Sister of stormy sorrow,

Look, an anguished boat sinks
Beneath stars,
The silent visage of night.
                                        —translated by Lucia Cordell Getsi

IN THE EAST

Dark rage of the people—
Wild organs of winterstorm,
The purple wave of battle,
Of defoliated stars.

With shattered brows, silver arms
Night beckons dying soldiers.
In the shadow of autumn ash trees
Moan the ghosts of the slain.

A thorny wilderness girdles the city.
Down bleeding steps the moon hunts
The terrified women.
Wild wolves broke through the gate.
                                        —translated by Lucia Cordell Getsi

GRODEK
SECOND VERSION

At evening autumnal forests resound
With deadly weapons, the golden plains
And blue lakes, over them the sun
Rolls darkly away; the night enfolds
Dying warriors, the wild lament
Of their broken mouths.
Yet silently in the red cloud's
Willowground, temple of an angry god,
The spilled blood pools, lunar chill;
All streets decant in black decay.
Under golden branches of night and stars
The sister's shadow sways through the silent grove
To greet the ghosts of heroes, the bleeding heads;
And dark flutes of autumn sound softly in the reeds.
O more arrogant grief! you altars of bronze,

Today the hot flame of spirit is fed by a violent pain —
The unborn grandchildren.

— translated by Lucia Cordell Getsi

Giuseppe Ungaretti

WATCH
CIMA QUATTRO, DECEMBER 23, 1915

One whole night
thrust down beside
a slaughtered
comrade
his snarling
mouth
turned to the full moon
the bloating
of his hands
entering
my silence
I have written
letters full of love

Never have I held
so
fast to life

— translated by Allen Mandelbaum

BROTHERS
MARIANO, JULY 15, 1916

What is your regiment
brothers?

Word that trembles
in the night

Leaf just born

In the quivering air
involuntary rebellion

of man facing
his fragility

Brothers

— *translated by Allen Mandelbaum*

THE RIVERS
COTICI, AUGUST 16, 1916

I cling to this crippled tree
left alone in this ravine
that has the laziness
of a circus
before or after the performance
and watch
the quiet passage
of clouds across the moon

This morning I stretched out
in an urn of water
and like a relic
rested

The Isonzo as it flowed
polished me
like one of its stones

I lifted up
my flesh and bones
and made my way
across the water
like an acrobat

I squatted
near my war-
filthy gear
and like a bedouin
bent to share
the sun

This is the Isonzo
and here I have come

to know myself better
a pliant fiber
of the universe

My torment
is when
I do not feel I am
in harmony

But those hidden
hands
that knead me
give me
rare
felicity

I have gone over
the seasons
of my life

These are
my rivers

This is the Serchio
from whose waters have drawn
perhaps two thousand years
of my farming people
and my father and my mother

This is the Nile
that saw me
born and growing
burning with unknowing
on its broad plains

This is the Seine
and in its troubled flow
I was remingled and remade
and came to know myself

These are my rivers
counted in the Isonzo

This is my nostalgia
as it appears
in each river
now it is night
now my life seems to me
a corolla
of shadows

— translated by Allen Mandelbaum

PILGRIMAGE

VALLONCELLO DELL'ALBERO ISOLATO, AUGUST 16, 1916

In ambush
in these bowels
of rubble
hour on hour
I have dragged
my carcass
worn away by mud
like a sole
or like a seed
of hawthorn

Ungaretti
man of pain
you need but an illusion
to give you courage

Beyond
a searchlight
sets a sea
into the fog

— translated by Allen Mandelbaum

PART FIVE

Fiction

Men and pack mules rounding Idiot Corner, on Westhoek Ridge, moving up to the Front Line, Belgium, November 5, 1917. From the Australian War Memorial, neg. E01480.

Introduction

In *The Flower of Battle,* his engaging study of several lesser-known World War I novelists, Hugh Cecil categorizes the writers as those who found the war "unredeemed," "redeemed," or who became "the generation of the broken hearted." Early works often romanticized combat or focused on the patriotic duties of the citizenry. Though some of these works were critical of command decisions, the debunking of jingoism came more slowly until the outburst of bitterness and cynicism of the late 1920s. A decade after the war's end, the steady stream became a torrent of disenchanted works that lasted until the early 1940s. More recently, fictionalized accounts of the war have regained the public's attention, establishing a continuing interest in a conflict that damaged the twentieth century in its childhood.

Cecil says that more than four hundred British authors have written about the war. Naturally, this anthology includes only a sampling. Among those not included I would be remiss not to mention Henry Williamson's *A Chronicle of Ancient Sunlight* (completed in 1969). Williamson's fifteen-volume saga attempts to understand the war by placing it in the context of the times. There is also R. C. Sheriff's seminal play *Journey's End* (1929), which did much to form the public's perception of the war.

Another essential work, excerpted here, is Richard Aldington's *Death of a Hero.* Though smaller in scope than Williamson's study, Aldington's novel examines a certain segment of British society before and during the war through the young officer, Winterbourne.

From across the channel comes Henri Barbusse's *Under Fire.* Subtitled "The Story of a Squad," the novel's focus is the ordinary poilu, the French enlisted man. An early work on the war — appearing in 1917 — the novel depicts both the hardships and small pleasures of the common soldier. Barbusse harshly criticizes the shirkers and war profiteers who cared little for the murderous work at the front while wrapping themselves in the flag of glib nationalism.

Another Frenchman, Roland Dorgelès, also concentrates his attention on the recreation of the poilu's existence in and out of the trenches. In the passage included here, a new recruit sent to gather rations for his platoon encounters the scorn of an old soldier, a natural scrounger who realizes a greenhorn will return empty-handed, cheated unmercifully by the cunning of experienced soldiers.

In the selection from George Duhamel's *Civilization, 1914–1917*, the reader is taken away from the front-line and the back area billets to the hospital that holds the wounded Revaud. Though full of vignettes about combat, Duhamel's novel reminds the reader of the plight of millions who suffered the ordeals of treatment and therapy beyond the action of the front lines.

Published in 1978, Timothy Findley's *The Wars* illustrates the continuing interest in the Great War as a subject for literature. Findley focuses on a young Canadian officer, Robert Ross, whose admiration for horses leads him, at the novel's end, to an act of defiance that recognizes the value of life in a world where gruesome carnage is the rule. In this excerpt, the raw young officer discovers he is lost while ushering a herd of horses to the front.

Other recent fiction worth mentioning is Pat Barker's trilogy: *Regeneration, The Eye in the Door,* and *The Ghost Road.* Much of Barker's work is devoted to a fictionalized account based on historical fact: the treatment at Craiglockhart Hospital by W. H. R. Rivers of Wilfred Owen and Siegfried Sassoon for shell shock. Other books of interest are Sebastian Faulks's *Birdsong* and Susan Hill's *Strange Meeting.*

One of the true literary masterpieces of fiction was written by the Australian, Frederic Manning. In *The Middle Parts of Fortune,* the reader follows the life in the trenches of Bourne, a young officer. Through his eyes the reader experiences the terror of constant artillery fire and the fascinating camp life of the soldiers in billets.

In the selection from R. H. Mottram's *The Spanish Farm,* the reader is introduced to Madeleine and Jérôme Vanderlynden, owners of an ancient holding called "The Spanish Farm," as English troops arrive to encamp on their land. The interplay between the farmers and soldiers represents what must have been an almost uncounted number of such occasions as battle troops moved up and down the pavé roads to intrude on the lives of farmers and townspeople in Flanders and France.

"The Raid" is a complete short story by Herbert Read, also a notable poet of the war. We see the narrator as he prepares to carry out a trench raid in order to collect prisoners for interrogation. A cowardly fellow officer is pointed out and the raid itself described in vivid detail. Following this, the narrator reveals his confused and conflicted feelings toward a captured German. During the heat of action, the narrator would have easily killed the German; but, now, safe behind his own lines with a disarmed enemy, the soldier realizes their shared humanity.

Finally, there is an excerpt from the most famous of all Great War fiction, *All Quiet on the Western Front*. Published a decade after the war's end, it, like Aldington's *Death of a Hero,* is a bitter antiwar novel. Away from the war at a Soldier's Home, the narrator comes in close contact with Russian prisoners of war. Trading with them, listening to their melancholy songs, the narrator comes to both despise their animalistic survival qualities and admire their moments of nobility. As in "The Raid," the narrator's exposure to his enemy creates a baffling sense of doubt about the war.

The fictionalization of the war began early and continues still. The dilemmas combat raised are addressed in fiction through the personal reactions of the protagonists. Insights and responses are as varied as the writers' intellects. However, the early patriotic assessments from all sides — often glib and frequently uninformed — have not proven enduring. In contrast, the novels of the late 1920s indelibly etched in the modern mind a landscape of terror and despair. Yet these fictional soldiers perform their duties, they attend to their responsibilities. As ancient as warfare itself, the dreadful aspects of combat are mitigated by deep loyalties — if not to the abstractions of patriotism and nationalism, then devotion to one another, of poilu for poilu, and to one's own fragile sense of self.

The Death of a Hero

RICHARD ALDINGTON

After a few hours' sleep and a hasty meal, Evans and Winterbourne started for the Front line again. Evans was very much ashamed at having lost his way the night before, and the Major had strafed him for incompetence. Evans had not replied, as he might have done, that since the Major knew so well where they ought to have gone, he might have taken the trouble to lead them there.

It was about two on a sunny, cold afternoon. They skirted M— with its everlasting, maddening Zwiiing, CRASH! CLAAAANG! In the trenches on the edge of Hill 91 they met two walking wounded, unshaved, muddy to the waist. One had his head bandaged and was carrying his steel helmet; the other had his tunic half off, and his left hand and arm were bandaged in several places. They were talking with great gravity and earnestness, and hardly saw Evans and his runner. Winterbourne heard one of them say:

"I told that fuckin' new orfficer twice that some fucker'd get hit if he fuckin' well took us up that fuckin' trench."

"Ah," said the other, "foock 'im."

Evans and Winterbourne paused at the old Front line on the crest of the hill to take breath, and looked back. The blue sky was speckled all over with the little fleecy shrapnel bursts from Archies, pursuing three different enemy planes. The heavy shells fell reverberantly into M— at their feet. They looked over a broad, flat, grey-green plain, dotted with ruined villages, seamed with the long, irregular lines of trenches. The wavering broad ribbon of No Man's Land was clearly visible, blasted to the white chalk. They could see the flash of the heavies, and enemy shells bursting on cross-roads and round artillery emplacements. A Red Cross car of wounded bumping its way from the Advanced Dressing Station in M— was shelled all down the road by field artillery. They watched it eagerly, hoping it would escape. Once or twice it disappeared in the smoke of the shell-burst and they felt certain it was done for; but the car bumpingly reappeared, and finally vanished from sight in the direction of Rail Head.

"God! What a dirty trick! I'm glad they didn't get it," said Winterbourne, as they scrambled out of the trench.

"Ah, well," said Evans, "Red Cross cars have been used as camouflage before now."

They easily found the new Front line in the daylight. Directions in English had been hastily scrawled on the old German trench notices, and they wondered how on earth they could have missed the way the night before. The Front line was full of infantry: some on sentry duty, some sitting hunched up on the fire-steps; many lying in long, narrow holes like graves, scooped in the side of the trench. They found an officer, who took them along to show them where the new communication trench was wanted. Winterbourne, turning to answer a question from Evans, struck the butt of his rifle sharply against a sleeping man in one of the holes. The man did not stir.

"Your fellows are sleeping soundly," said Evans.

"Yes," said the officer tonelessly; "but he may be dead for all I know. Stretcher-bearers too tired to take down all the bodies. Some of 'em are dead, and some asleep. We have to go round and kick 'em to find which is which."

The new trench they were to dig had been roughly marked out, and ran from the old German front line to the lip of Congreve's Mine-crater, now used as an ammunition dump. A salvo of whizz-bangs greeted them as they went out to look at it.

"I don't altogether envy you this job," said the Infantry officer; "this is about the most unhealthy spot on Hill 91. The Boche shells it day and night. Your Colonel had a hell of a row about it with the Brigadier, but our fellows are too whacked to do any more digging."

Over came another little bunch of whizz-bangs, in corroboration — crash, crash-crash, crash. The grey-green, acrid smoke smelt foul.

"They're going to call it Nero Trench," he added, as they left him, "because the ground's so black with coal-dust and slag. Well, goodbye, best of luck. And, by the by, look out for gas."

The Nero Trench job was an intensified nightmare. The Germans had it "taped" with exactitude, and shelled it ruthlessly. Five minutes was the longest period that ever passed without salvoes of whizz-bangs. Evans and Winterbourne, Hume and his runner, walked continually up and down the line of men, who toiled hastily and nervously in the darkness to make themselves a little cover. When the shells came crashing near them, they crouched down on the ground. It was found after the first night that each man had simply dug a hole for himself instead of regularly excavating his three yards of trench. On some nights the shelling was so intense that Evans withdrew the men for a time to the shelter of a trench. They had several casualties.

And then the Germans began a steady, systematic gas bombardment of all the ruined villages in the advanced area. It began on the second night of the Nero Trench job. They had noticed on Hill 91 that a pretty heavy bombardment was proceeding from the German lines, and all the way down from M— they heard the shells continuously shrilling overhead. It puzzled them that they could not hear them exploding.

"Must be bombarding the back areas," said Evans. "Let's hope it gives 'em something to think about besides sending us up tons of silly papers."

But as they came nearer their village they could tell by the sound in the air that the shells must be falling close ahead of them. Soon they heard them falling with the customary ZWiiING, followed by a very unaccustomed soft PHUT.

"They can't all be duds," said Winterbourne.

A shell dropped short, just outside the parapet, with the same curious PHUT. Immediately a strange smell, rather like new-mown hay gone acrid, filled the air. They sniffed, and both men exclaimed simultaneously:

"Phosgene! Gas!"

They all fumblingly and hastily put on their gas-masks, and stumbled on blindly down the trench. Winterbourne and Evans scrambled out on to the road and got into the edge of the village. A rain of gas shells was falling on it and all round their billets—zwiing, zwiing, zwiing, zwiing, PHUT PHUT PHUT PHUT. Each took off his mask a second and gave one sniff—the air reeked with phosgene.

Evans and Winterbourne stood at the end of the trench to help out the groping, half-blinded men. As they filed by, grotesques with indiarubber faces, great, dead-looking goggles, and a long tube from their mouths to the box respirators, Winterbourne thought they looked like lost souls expiating some horrible sin in a new Inferno. The rolled gas-blankets were pulled down tightly over the cellar entrances, but the gas leaked through. Two men were gassed and taken off in stretchers, foaming rather horribly at the mouth.

The gas bombardment went on until dawn, and then ceased. Winterbourne fell asleep, with his gas-mask just off his face. Hitherto they had slept with the box respirator slung on a nail or piled with the other equipment; after the experience of this and the subsequent nights, they always slept with the respirator on their chests and the mask ready to slip on immediately.

The heavies began again soon after it was light. Winterbourne was awakened by one which crashed just outside his cellar. He lay on the floor for a long time listening to the ZWiiiING, CRASH, of the shells. He heard two ruined houses clatter to the ground under direct hits, and wondered if the cellars had held firm. They hadn't. But fortunately they happened to be unoc-cupied. Presently the German batteries switched off and began bombarding some artillery about five hundred yards to the left. Winterbourne profited by the lull to wash. He ran out of the cellar in his shirt-sleeves and gas-mask, with the canvas bucket in which he washed; and found that a shell had smashed the pump outside his billet. He knew there was another about three hundred yards to the right, although he had never been there.

It was another cold but sunny morning, with the inevitable white shrapnel bursts all over the sky. He was now so accustomed to them that he scarcely noticed their existence. Occasionally a very faint rattle of machine-gun fire came from the war in the air, of which he was nearly as ignorant as people in England of the war on land.

He took off his mask and sniffed. A fresh wind was blowing, and, al-though there was plenty of phosgene in the air, it was not in any deadly concentration. He decided to risk leaving the mask off. The ground was deeply delved with the conical holes made by the big shells thrown over, and pitted everywhere by the smaller holes of the gas shells. He found a dud, and examined it with interest. A brownish-looking shell, about the size of a five-nine.

The cottages were rather scattered, and unused as cellar-billets in this di-rection. The top storeys had gone from nearly all, but in several the ground floor was fairly intact. He looked into each as he passed. The wallpaper had long ago fallen and lay in mouldering heaps. The floors were covered with broken bricks, tiles, smashed beams, laths, and disintegrating plaster. Odd pieces of broken furniture, twisted iron beds, large rags which had once been clothes, and sheets, protruded from the mass. He poked about and found photographs, letters in faded ink on damp paper, broken toys, bits of smashed vases, a soiled satin wedding-gown with its veil and wreath of artificial orange-blossom. He stood, with his head bent, looking at this pa-thetic debris of ruined lives, and absentmindedly lit a cigarette, which he immediately threw away — it tasted of phosgene. "La Gloire," he murmured, "Deutschland über alles, God save the King."

The next cottage was less damaged than the others, and its rough wooden shutters were still on their hinges. Winterbourne peered through, and saw that the whole of the inside had been cleared of debris, and was stacked with quantities of wooden objects. He shaded his eyes more carefully, and saw they were ranks and ranks of wooden crosses. Those he could see had painted on them R.I.P.; then underneath was a blank space for the name; underneath was the name of one or other of the battalions in his division, and then the present month and year, with a blank space for the day. Excellent fore-thought, he reflected, as he filled his bucket and water-bottle. How well this War is organized!

About nine, Evans's servant told him to report immediately in fighting order. Wearily and sleepily he threw on his equipment, re-tied the string of his box respirator, and slung his rifle and bayonet over his left shoulder. He waited with the officers' servants, who gave him a piece of bread dipped in bacon grease to eat. Presently Evans came out and they started off.

"I've got to see an R.E. officer," said Evans, "about a new job on Hill 91. It's a bit further to the left of where we've been working, and it'll take us half an hour longer to get there."

Winterbourne seized the opportunity to put forward one or two ideas he had been thinking over:

"I hope you won't mind, sir, if I say something — it's not an official complaint at all, you understand, only what I've been personally thinking."

"Go ahead."

"Well, sir, I assume that the reason we are kept in billets instead of in the line is to give us more rest so that we come fresh to work. But here it doesn't work out that way, especially in the past fortnight; and it's likely to get worse instead of better. It seems to me that we should be much better off if we were in dug-outs in the reserve line. We have that long walk through the mud twice a day; we get all the shells meant for the transport and ration parties; we get an all-night strafing in the line; we're shelled all the way down; we come back to gassy billets, which are shelled with heavies twenty hours out of twenty-four. The cellars are no real protection against a direct hit. They're damper than dug-outs, and just as dark and ratty. There are far more whizz-bangs and light stuff in the line, but far fewer heavies; and if we had even fifteen-foot dug-outs, we'd get some sleep, instead of starting awake every ten minutes with a crump outside the cellar entrance. We're getting a lot of useless casualties, sir. I passed the cook-house as I came along, and the cook told me one of his mates had just gone down with gas from last night. And the S. M. looks as green as grass. Can't you get us put in the line, sir?"

Evans cogitated a moment or two:

"Yes, I think you're right. No, I can't get us moved. I haven't the authority. I wish I had. I'll ask the Major to put it before the Colonel. It's quite true what you say. In the past week we've had eight casualties in the line, and twelve here or going up and down. But with this show coming off I expect every trench and dugout will be packed."

Winterbourne felt enormously proud that Evans had not snubbed his suggestion. Evans went on, after a pause:

"By the way, Winterbourne, have you ever thought of taking a commission?"

"Why yes, sir; it was suggested by the Adjutant of my battalion in England. I believe my father wrote to him about it. He, my father, was very keen about it."

"Well, why don't you apply?"

It was now Winterbourne's turn to cogitate:

"I find it rather hard to explain, sir. For many reasons, which you might think far-fetched, I had and still have a feeling that I ought to spend the War in the ranks and in the line. I should prefer to be in the Infantry, but I think the Pioneers are quite near enough."

"They often come round for volunteers, you know. If you like, I'll put you down next time and the Major will recommend you to the Colonel."

"It's kind of you, sir. I'll think about it."

One night, two nights, three nights, four nights passed and still there was no big battle. And they were not moved. Every night they were shelled up the line, shelled in the line, shelled on the way back, and arrived in a hailstorm of gas shells. They had to wear their gas-masks for hours every day. And sleep became more and more difficult and precarious.

Winterbourne's intimacy with Evans and his own "education" put him in rather an ambiguous position. Evans trusted him more and more to do things which would normally have been done by an N.C.O. And Winterbourne's feeling of responsibility led him to take on and conscientiously carry out everything of the kind. One night there was supposed to be a gas-discharger attack by the British in retaliation for the heavy German gas bombardments. All the officers wanted to see it; and since it was staged for an hour before dawn, that meant either that one officer had to take the Company down or that the men had to be kept up two hours longer, exposed to artillery retaliation. Evans solved the problem. He sent for Winterbourne:

"Winterbourne, we want to stop and see the fun up here. Now, you can take the Company down, can't you? I'll tell Sergeant Perkins that you're in charge; but of course you'll give orders through him. Come back here and report after you get them back."

"Very good, sir."

There was no British gas attack, but the Germans put up what was then a considerable gas bombardment. They sent over approximately thirty thousand gas shells that night, most of them in and around the village where the Pioneers were billeted. The Company had to wear gas-masks over the last half-mile, and Winterbourne had a very anxious time getting them along. He had discovered a disused but quite deep trench running through the village almost to their billets, and he took the men along there instead of through the village street. It was little longer, but far safer. The shells were hailing round them, and Winterbourne didn't want any casualties. Sergeant Perkins and he managed to get men safely into billets. Winterbourne turned and said: "Well, goodnight, Sergeant; I must go up the line and report to Mr. Evans."

"You ain't going up agen, are you?"

"Yes, Mr. Evans told me to."

"'Struth! Well, I'd rather it was you than me."

Winterbourne fitted on his gas-mask, and groped his way out of the Sergeant's cellar. The night was muggy, a bit drizzly, windless and very dark—the ideal conditions for a gas bombardment. What little wind there was came from the German lines. He hesitated between taking the long muddy trench or the more open road; but since he was practically blinded in the darkness with his goggles, he decided to take the trench, for fear of losing his way. It was rather eerie, groping his way alone up the trench, with the legions of gas shells shrilling and phutting all around him. They fell with a terrific "flop" when they came within a few yards. He stumbled badly two or three times in holes they had made in the trench since he had come down. For nearly half a mile he had to go through the gas barrage, and it was slow work indeed, with the mud and the darkness and the groping and the tumbling. Interminable. He thought of nothing in the darkness but keeping his left hand on the side of the trench to guide him and holding his right hand raised in front to prevent his bumping into something.

At last he got clear of the falling gas shells, and ventured a peep outside his mask. One sniff showed him the air was deadly with phosgene. He groped on another two hundred yards and tried again. There was still a lot of gas, but he decided to risk it, and took off his mask. With the mask off he could see comparatively well, and travelled quite rapidly. About an hour before dawn he reported to Evans.

"There is a devil of a gas bombardment going on round the billets and for half a mile round, sir," said Winterbourne; "that's why I'm so late. The whole country reeks of gas."

Evans whistled.

"Whew! As a matter of fact, we've been drinking a bit in the dug-out with some Infantry officers, and one or two are a bit groggy in consequence."

"Better wait till dawn, then, sir. If you'll come up into the trench you'll hear the shells going over."

"Oh, I take your word for it. But the Major insists on going down at once. We've just heard that there isn't going to be a gas attack. You'll have to help me get them down."

"Very good, sir."

The Major was entirely sober; Evans was perfectly self-controlled; but the other four were all a little too merry. It was a perfect nightmare getting them through the gas barrage. They would insist there was no danger, that the gas was all a wash-out; and kept taking off their masks. They disregarded the

Major's peremptory orders, and Evans and Winterbourne had constantly to take off their own masks to argue with the subalterns and make them put on theirs. Winterbourne could feel the deadly phosgene at his lungs.

Just after dawn they reached the Officers' Mess cellar, fortunately without a casualty. Winterbourne felt horribly sick with the gas he had swallowed. The Major took off his gas-mask, and picked up a water-jug.

"Those confounded servants have forgotten to leave any water," exclaimed the Major angrily. "Winterbourne, take that tin jug and go and get some water from the cook-house."

"Very good, sir."

The shells were still pitilessly bailing down through the dawn. It was a hundred yards to the cook-house, and Winterbourne three times just escaped being directly hit by one of the ceaselessly falling shells. He returned to the Mess, and left the water.

"Thanks very much," said Evans; "you may go now, Winterbourne. Good-night."

"Goodnight, sir."

"Goodnight," said the Major; "thank you for getting that water, Winterbourne; I oughtn't to have sent you."

"Thank you, sir; goodnight, sir."

Outside the Major's and Evans's part of the cellar the other officers were sitting round a deal table by the light of a candle stuck in a bottle, which looked dim and ghastly. The place was practically gas-proof, with tightly-drawn blankets over every crevice.

"Win'erbourne," said one of them.

"Sir?"

"Run along to the Quar'master-Sergeant and bring us a bottle of whisky."

"Very good, sir."

Winterbourne climbed the cellar steps, lifted the outer gas-curtain rapidly, and stepped out. There was such a stench of phosgene that he snapped his mask on at once. The shells were falling thicker than ever. One hit the wall of the house, and Winterbourne felt bricks and dust drop on his steel helmet and shoulders. He shrank against what was left of the wall. Two hundred yards to the Q.M.S.'s billet. That meant nearly a quarter of a mile through that deadly storm — for a half-drunken man to get a few more whiskies. Winterbourne hesitated. It was disobeying orders if he didn't go. He turned resolutely and went to his own billet; nothing was ever said of this refusal to obey an officer's orders in the face of the enemy.

Winterbourne stood outside the entrance to his cellar, took off his steel helmet and folded down the top part of his gas-mask so that he could see, while still keeping the nose-clip on and the large rubber mouthpiece in his teeth.

The whitish morning light looked cold and misty, and the PHUT PHUT PHUT PHUT of the bursting gas shells continued with ruthless iteration. He watched them exploding; a little curling cloud of yellow gas rose from each shell-hole. The ground was pitted with these new shell-holes, and newly-broken bricks and debris lay about everywhere. A dead rat lay in a gas-shell hole just outside the entrance—so the War caught even the rats! There had been a young, slender ash-tree in what had once been the cottage garden. A heavy explosive had fallen just at its roots, splintered the slim stem, and dashed it prone with broken branches. The young leaves were still green, except on one side where they were curled and withered by gas. The grass, so tender a Spring green a week before, was yellow, sickly, and withered. As he turned to lift the gas blanket he heard the whizz and crash of the first heavy of the day bombardment. But the gas shells continued.

Inside the cellar was complete darkness. He took off his mask and fumbled his way down the broken stairs, trying not to wake the other runners. It was important to use only one match, because matches were scarce and precious. The air inside was foul and heavy, but only slightly tainted with phosgene. Winterbourne half-smiled as he thought how furiously he had contended for "fresh air" in huts and barrack-rooms, and how gladly he now welcomed any foul air which was not full of poison gas. He lighted his stub of candle, and slowly took off his equipment, replacing the box respirator immediately. His boots were thick with mud, his puttees and trousers torn with wire and stained with mud and grease. A bullet had torn a hole in his leather jerkin, and his steel helmet was marked by a long, deep dint, where it had been struck by a flying splinter of shell. He felt amazingly weary, and rather sick. He had known the fatigue of long walks and strenuous Rugby football matches and cross-country runs, but nothing like this continual, cumulative weariness. He moved with the slow, almost pottering movements of agricultural labourers and old men. The feeling of sickness became worse, and he wanted to vomit out the smell of gas which seemed to permeate him. He heaved over his empty canvas bucket until the water started to his eyes, but vomited nothing. He noticed how filthy his hands were.

He was just going to sit down on his blanket and pack, covered by the neatly-folded ground-sheet, when he saw a parcel and some letters for him lying on them. The other runners had brought them over for him. Decent of them. The parcel was from Elizabeth—how sweet of her to remember! And yes, she had sent all the things he had asked for and left out all the useless things people would send to the troops. He mustn't touch anything except the candles, though, until tomorrow, when the parcel would be carefully divided among everybody in the cellar. It was one of the good unwritten rules—all parcels strictly divided between each section, so that every one got something, even and especially the men who were too poor or too lonely to receive anything from England. Dear Elizabeth! how sweet of her to re-member!

He opened her envelope with hands which shook slightly with fatigue and the shock of explosions. Then he stopped, lighted a new candle from the stub of the old one, blew out the stub, and carefully put it away to give to one of the infantry. The letter was unexpectedly tender and charming. She had just been to Hampton Court to look at the flowers. The gardens were rather neglected, she said, and no flowers in the Long Border — the gardeners were at the War, and there was no money in England now for flowers. Did he remember how they had walked there in April five years ago? Yes, he remembered, and thought too with a pang of surprise that this was the first Spring he had ever spent without seeing a flower, not even a primrose. The little yellow coltsfoot he had liked so much were all dead with phosgene. Elizabeth went on:

"I saw Fanny last week. She looked more charming and delicate than ever — and such a marvellous hat! I hear she is *much* attached to a brilliant young scientist, a chemist, who does the most *peculiar* things. He mixes up all sorts of chemicals and then experiments with the fumes and kills dozens of poor little monkeys with them. Isn't it wicked? But Fanny says it's most *important* war work."

The sickness came on him again. He turned sideways and heaved silently, but could not vomit. He felt thirsty, and drank a little stale-tasting water from his water-bottle. Dear Elizabeth! how sweet of her to remember!

Fanny's letter was very rattling and gay. She had been there, she had done this, she had seen so-and-so. How was darling George getting along? She was so glad to see that there had been no fighting yet on the Western front. She added:

"I saw Elizabeth recently. She looked a little worried, but *very* sweet. She was with such a charming young man — a young American who ran away from Yale to join our Flying Corps."

The heavy shells outside were falling nearer and nearer. They came over in fours, each shell a little in front of the others — bracketing. Through the gas-curtain he heard the remains of a ruined house collapse across the street under a direct hit. Each crash made the cellar tremble slightly, and the candle flame jumped.

Well, it was nice of Fanny to write. Very nice. She was a thoroughly decent sort. He picked up the other envelopes. One came from Paris, and contained the *Bulletin des Ecrivains* — names of French writers and artists killed or wounded, and news of those in the armies. He was horrified to see how many of his friends in Paris had been killed. A passage had been marked in blue pencil — it contained the somewhat belated news that M. Georges Winterbourne, *le jeune peintre anglais,* was in camp in England.

Another letter, forwarded by Elizabeth, came from a London art-dealer. It said that an American had bought one of Winterbourne's sketches for five pounds, and that when he heard that Winterbourne was in the trenches he had insisted upon making it twenty-five pounds. The dealer therefore enclosed a cheque for twenty-two pounds ten, being twenty-five pounds less commission at ten per centum. Winterbourne thought it rather cheek to take commission on the money which was a gift; but still—Business As Usual. But how generous of the American! How amazingly kind! His pay was five francs a week, so the money was most welcome. He must write and thank . . .

The last letter was from Mr. Upjohn, from whom Winterbourne had not heard for over a year. Elizabeth, it appeared, had asked him to write and send news. Mr. Upjohn wrote a chatty letter. He himself had a job in Whitehall, "of national importance." Winterbourne rejoiced to think that Mr. Upjohn's importance was now recognized by the nation. Mr. Shobbe had been to France, had stayed in the line three weeks, and was now permanently at the base. Comrade Bobbe had come out very strong as a conscientious objector. He had been put in prison for six weeks. His friends had "got at" somebody influential, who had "got at" the secretary of somebody in authority, and Mr. Bobbe had been released as an agricultural worker. He was now "working" on a farm run by a philanthropic lady for conscientious objectors of the intellectual class. Mr. Waldo Tubbe had found his vocation in the Post Office Censorship Bureau, where he was very happy—if he could not force people to say what he wanted, he could at least prevent them from writing anything derogatory to his Adopted Empire. . . .

George laughed silently to himself. Amusing chap, Upjohn. He got out his jack-knife and scraped away the mud so that he could unlace his boots. Outside the shells crashed. One burst just behind the cellar. The roof seemed to give a jump, something seemed to smack Winterbourne on the top of the head, and the candle went out. He laboriously re-lit it. The other runners woke up.

"Anything up?"

"No, only a crump outside. I'm just getting into kip."

"Where've you been?"

"Up the line again, for the officers."

"Get back all right?"

"Yes, nobody hit. But there's a hell of a lot of gas about. Don't go out without putting on your gas-bag."

"Goodnight, old man."

"Goodnight, old boy."

Under Fire

The Dog

HENRI BARBUSSE

The weather was appalling. Water and wind attacked the passers-by; riddled, flooded, and upheaved the roads.

I was returning from fatigue to our quarters at the far end of the village. The landscape that morning showed dirty yellow through the solid rain, and the sky was dark as a slated roof. The downpour flogged the horse-trough as with birchen rods. Along the walls, human shapes went in shrinking files, stooping, abashed, splashing.

In spite of the rain and the cold and bitter wind, a crowd had gathered in front of the door of the barn where we were lodging. All close together and back to back, the men seemed from a distance like a great moving sponge. Those who could see, over shoulders and between heads, opened their eyes wide and said, "He has a nerve, the boy!" Then the inquisitive ones broke away, with red noses and streaming faces, into the downpour that lashed and the blast that bit, and letting the hands fall that they had upraised in surprise, they plunged them in their pockets.

In the centre, and running with rain, abode the cause of the gathering— Fouillade, bare to the waist and washing himself in abundant water. Thin as an insect, working his long slender arms in riotous frenzy, he soaped and splashed his head, neck, and chest, down to the upstanding gridirons of his sides. Over his funnel-shaped cheeks the brisk activity had spread a flaky beard like snow, and piled on the top of his head a greasy fleece that the rain was puncturing with little holes.

By way of a tub, the patient was using three mess-tins which he had filled with water—no one knew how—in a village where there was none; and as there was no clean spot anywhere to put anything down in that universal

412

streaming of earth and sky, he thrust his towel into the waistband of his trousers, while the soap went back into his pocket every time he used it.

They who still remained wondered at this heroic gesticulation in the face of adversity, and said again, as they wagged their heads, "It's a disease of cleanliness he's got."

"You know he's going to be carpeted, they say, for that affair of the shell-hole with Volpatte." And they mixed the two exploits together in a muddled way, that of the shell-hole, and the present, and looked on him as the hero of the moment, while he puffed, sniffled, grunted, spat, and tried to dry himself under the celestial shower-bath with rapid rubbing and as a measure of deception; then at last he resumed his clothes.

After his wash, Fouillade feels cold. He turns about and stands in the doorway of the barn that shelters us. The arctic blast discolours and disparages his long face, so hollow and sunburned; it draws tears from his eyes, and scatters them on the cheeks once scorched by the mistral; his nose, too, weeps increasingly.

Yielding to the ceaseless bite of the wind that grips his ears in spite of the muffler knotted round his head, and his calves in spite of the yellow puttees with which his cockerel legs are enwound, he re-enters the barn, but comes out of it again at once, rolling ferocious eyes, and muttering oaths with the accent one hears in that corner of the land, over six hundred miles from here, whence he was driven by war.

So he stands outside, erect, more truly excited than ever before in these northern scenes. And the wind comes and steals into him, and comes again roughly, shaking and maltreating his scarecrow's slight and fleshless figure.

Ye gods! It is almost uninhabitable, the barn they have assigned to us to live in during this period of rest. It is a collapsing refuge, gloomy and leaky, confined as a well. One half of it is under water—we see rats swimming in it—and the men are crowded in the other half. The walls, composed of laths stuck together with dried mud, are cracked, sunken, holed in all their circuit, and extensively broken through above. The night we got here—until the morning—we plugged as well as we could the openings within reach, by inserting leafy branches and hurdles. But the higher holes, and those in the roof, still gaped and always. When dawn hovers there, weakling and early, the wind for contrast rushes in and blows round every side with all its strength, and the squad endures the hustling of an everlasting draught.

When we are there, we remain upright in the ruined obscurity, groping, shivering, complaining.

Fouillade, who has come in once more, goaded by the cold, regrets his ablutions. He has pains in his loins and back. He wants something to do, but what?

Sit down? Impossible; it is too dirty inside there. The ground and the paving-stones are plastered with mud; the straw scattered for our sleeping is soaked through, by the water that comes through the holes and by the boots that wipe themselves with it. Besides, if you sit down, you freeze; and if you lie on the straw, you are troubled by the smell of manure, and sickened by the vapours of ammonia. Fouillade contents himself by looking at his place, and yawning wide enough to dislocate his long jaw, further lengthened by a goatee beard where you would see white hairs if the daylight were really daylight.

"The other pals and boys," said Marthereau, "they're no better off than we are. After breakfast I went to see a jail-bird of the 11th on the farm near the hospital. You've to clamber over a wall by a ladder that's too short—talk about a scissor-cut!" says Marthereau, who is short in the leg; "and when once you're in the hen-run and rabbit-hutch you're shoved and poked by everybody and a nuisance to 'em all. You don't know where to put your pasties down. I vamoosed from there, and sharp."

"For my part," says Cocon, "I wanted to go to the blacksmith's when we'd got quit of grubbing, to imbibe something hot, and pay for it. Yesterday he was selling coffee, but some bobbies called there this morning, so the good man's got the shakes, and he's locked his door."

Lamuse has tried to clean his rifle. But one cannot clean his rifle here, even if he squats on the ground near the door, nor even if he takes away the sodden tent-cloth, hard and icy, which hangs across the doorway like a stalactite; it is too dark. "And then, old chap, if you let a screw fall, you may as well hang yourself as try to find it, 'specially when your fists are frozen silly."

"As for me, I ought to be sewing some things, but—what cheer!"

One alternative remains—to stretch oneself on the straw, covering the head with handkerchief or towel to isolate it from the searching stench of fermenting straw, and sleep. Fouillade, master of his time to-day, being on neither guard nor fatigues, decides. He lights a taper to seek among his belongings, and unwinds the coils of his comforter, and we see his emaciated shape, sculptured in black relief, folding and refolding it.

"Potato fatigue, inside there, my little lambs!" a sonorous voice bellows at the door. The hooded shape from which it comes is Sergeant Henriot. He is a malignant sort of simpleton, and though all the while joking in clumsy sympathy he supervises the evacuation of quarters with a sharp eye for the evasive malingerer. Outside, on the streaming road in the perpetual rain, the second section is scattered, also summoned and driven to work by the adjutant. The two sections mingle together. We climb the street and the hillock of clayey soil where the travelling kitchen is smoking.

"Now then, my lads, get on with it; it isn't a long job when everybody sets to — Come — what have you got to grumble about, you? That does no good."

Twenty minutes later we return at a trot. As we grope about in the barn, we cannot touch anything but what is sodden and cold, and the sour smell of wet animals is added to the vapour of the liquid manure that our beds contain.

We gather again, standing, around the props that hold the barn up, and around the rills that fall vertically from the holes in the roof — faint columns which rest on vague bases of splashing water. "Here we are again!" we cry.

Two lumps in turn block the doorway, soaked with the rain that drains from them — Lamuse and Barque, who have been in quest of a brasier, and now return from the expedition empty-handed, sullen and vicious.

"Not a shadow of a fire-bucket, and what's more, no wood or coal either, not for a fortune." It is impossible to have any fire. "If I can't get any, no one can," says Barque, with a pride which a hundred exploits justify.

We stay motionless, or move slowly in the little space we have, aghast at so much misery. "Whose is the paper?"

"It's mine," says Bécuwe.

"What does it say? Ah, *zut,* one can't read in this darkness!"

"It says they've done everything necessary now for the soldiers, to keep them warm in the trenches. They've got all they want, and blankets and shirts and brasiers and fire-buckets and bucketsful of coal; and that it's like that in the first-line trenches."

"Ah, damnation!" growl some of the poor prisoners of the barn, and they shake their fists at the emptiness without and at the newspaper itself.

But Fouillade has lost interest in what they say. He has bent his long Don Quixote carcase down in the shadow, and outstretched the lean neck that looks as if it were braided with violin strings. There is something on the ground that attracts him.

It is Labri, the other squad's dog, an uncertain sort of mongrel sheep-dog, with a lopped tail, curled up on a tiny litter of straw-dust. Fouillade looks at Labri, and Labri at him. Bécuwe comes up and says, with the intonation of the Lille district, "He won't eat his food; the dog isn't well. Hey, Labri, what's the matter with you? There's your bread and meat; eat it up; it's good when it's in your bucket. He's poorly. One of these mornings we shall find him dead."

Labri is not happy. The soldier to whom he is entrusted is hard on him, and usually ill-treats him when he takes any notice of him at all. The animal is tied up all day. He is cold and ill and left to himself. He only exists. From time to time, when there is movement going on around him, he has hopes of going out, rises and stretches himself, and bestirs his tail to incipient demonstration. But he is disillusioned, and lies down again, gazing past his nearly full mess-tin.

He is weary, and disgusted with life. Even if he has escaped the bullet or bomb to which he is as much exposed as we, he will end by dying here. Fouillade puts his thin hand on the dog's head, and it gazes at him again. Their two glances are alike — the only difference is that one comes from above and the other from below.

Fouillade sits down also — the worse for him! — in a corner, his hands covered by the folds of his greatcoat, his long legs doubled up like a folding bed. He is dreaming, his eyes closed under their bluish lids; there is something that he sees again. It is one of those moments when the country from which he is divided assumes in the distance the charms of reality — the perfumes and colours of l'Hérault, the streets of Cette. He sees so plainly and so near that he hears the noise of the shallops in the Canal du Midi, and the unloading at the docks; and their call to him is distinctly clear.

Above the road where the scent of thyme and immortelles is so strong that it is almost a taste in the mouth, in the heart of the sunshine whose winging shafts stir the air into a warmed and scented breeze, on Mont St. Clair, blossoms and flourishes the home of his folks. Up there, one can see with the same glance where the Lake of Thau, which is green like glass, joins hands with the Mediterranean Sea, which is azure; and sometimes one can make out as well, in the depths of the indigo sky, the carven phantoms of the Pyrenees.

There was he born, there he grew up, happy and free. There he played, on the golden or ruddy ground; played — even — at soldiers. The eager joy of wielding a wooden sabre flushed the cheeks now sunken and seamed. He opens his eyes, looks about him, shakes his head, and falls upon regret for the days when glory and war to him were pure, lofty, and sunny things.

The man puts his hand over his eyes, to retain the vision within. Nowadays, it is different.

It was up there in the same place, later, that he came to know Clémence. She was just passing, the first time, sumptuous with sunshine, and so fair that the loose sheaf of straw she carried in her arms seemed to him nutbrown by contrast. The second time, she had a friend with her, and they both stopped to watch him. He heard them whispering, and turned towards them. Seeing themselves discovered, the two young women made off, with a sibilance of skirts, and giggles like the cry of a partridge.

And it was there, too, that he and she together set up their home. Over its front travels a vine, which he coddled under a straw hat, whatever the season. By the garden gate stands the rose-tree that he knows so well — it never used its thorns except to try to hold him back a little as he went by.

Will he return again to it all? Ah, he has looked too deeply into the profundity of the past not to see the future in appalling accuracy. He thinks of the regiment, decimated at each shift; of the big knocks and hard he has had and will have, of sickness, and of wear—

He gets up and snorts, as though to shake off what was and what will be. He is back in the middle of the gloom, and is frozen and swept by the wind, among the scattered and dejected men who blindly await the evening. He is back in the present, and he is shivering still.

Two paces of his long legs make him butt into a group that is talking— by way of diversion or consolation—of good cheer.

"At my place," says one, "they make enormous loaves, round ones, big as cart-wheels they are!" And the man amuses himself by opening his eyes wide, so that he can see the loaves of the homeland.

"Where I come from," interposes the poor Southerner, "holiday feasts last so long that the bread that's new at the beginning is stale at the end!"

"There's a jolly wine—it doesn't look much, that little wine where I come from; but if it hasn't fifteen degrees of alcohol it hasn't anything!"

Fouillade speaks then of a red wine which is almost violet, which stands dilution as well as if it had been brought into the world to that end.

"We've got the *jurançon* wine," said a Béarnais, "the real thing, not what they sell you for *jurançon,* which comes from Paris; indeed, I know one of the makers."

"If it comes to that," said Fouillade, "in our country we've got muscatels of every sort, all the colours of the rainbow, like patterns of silk stuff. You come home with me some time, and every day you shall taste a nonsuch, my boy."

"Sounds like a wedding feast," said the grateful soldier.

So it comes about that Fouillade is agitated by the vinous memories into which he has plunged, which recall to him as well the dear perfume of garlic on that far-off table. The vapours of the blue wine in big bottles, and the liqueur wines so delicately varied, mount to his head amid the sluggish and mournful storm that fills the barn.

Suddenly he calls to mind that there is settled in the village where they are quartered a tavern-keeper who is a native of Béziers, called Magnac. Magnac had said to him, "Come and see me, *mon camarade,* one of these mornings, and we'll drink some wine from down there, we will! I've several bottles of it, and you shall tell me what you think of it."

This sudden prospect dazzles Fouillade. Through all his length runs a thrill of delight, as though he had found the way of salvation. Drink the wine of the South—of his own particular South, even—drink much of it—it would be so good to see life rosy again, if only for a day! Ah yes, he wants wine; and he gets drunk in a dream.

But as he goes out he collides at the entry with Corporal Broyer, who is running down the street like a pedlar, and shouting at every opening, "Morning parade!"

The company assembles and forms in squares on the sticky mound where the travelling kitchen is sending soot into the rain. "I'll go and have a drink after parade," says Fouillade to himself.

And he listens listlessly, full of his plan, to the reading of the report. But carelessly as he listens, he hears the officer read, "It is absolutely forbidden to leave quarters before 5 P.M. and after 8 P.M.," and he hears the captain, without noticing the murmur that runs round the poilus, add this comment on the order: "This is Divisional Headquarters. However many there are of you, don't show yourselves. Keep under cover. If the General sees you in the street, he will have you put to fatigues at once. He must not see a single soldier. Stay where you are all day in your quarters. Do what you like as long as no one sees you — no one!"

We go back into the barn.

Two o'clock. It is three hours yet, and then it will be totally dark, before one may risk going outside without being punished.

Shall we sleep while waiting? Fouillade is sleepy no longer; the hope of wine has shaken him up. And then, if one sleeps in the day, he will not sleep at night. No! To lie with your eyes open is worse than a nightmare. The weather gets worse; wind and rain increase, without and within.

Then what? If one may not stand still, nor sit down, nor lie down, nor go for a stroll, nor work — what?

Deepening misery settles on the party of benumbed and tired soldiers. They suffer to the bone, nor know what to do with their bodies. "*Nom de Dieu,* we're badly off!" is the cry of the derelicts — a lamentation, an appeal for help.

Then by instinct they give themselves up to the only occupation possible to them in there — to walk up and down on the spot, and thus ward off anchylosis.

So they begin to walk quickly to and fro in the scanty place that three strides might compass; they turn about and cross and brush each other, bent forward, hands pocketed — tramp, tramp. These human beings whom the blast cuts even among their straw are like a crowd of the wretched wrecks of cities who await, under the lowering sky of winter, the opening of some charitable institution. But no door will open for *them* — unless it be four days hence, one evening at the end of the rest, to return to the trenches.

Alone in a corner, Cocon cowers. He is tormented by lice; but weakened by the cold and wet he has not the pluck to change his linen; and he sits there sullen, unmoving — and devoured.

As five o'clock draws near, in spite of all, Fouillade begins again to intoxicate himself with his dream of wine, and he waits, with its gleam in his soul. What time is it? — A quarter to five. — Five minutes to five. — Now!

He is outside in black night. With great splashing skips he makes his way towards the tavern of Magnac, the generous and communicative Biterrois. Only with great trouble does he find the door in the dark and the inky rain. By God, there is no light! Great God again, it is closed! The gleam of a match that his great lean hand covers like a lamp-shade shows him the fateful notice — "Out of Bounds." Magnac, guilty of some transgression, has been banished into gloom and idleness!

Fouillade turns his back on the tavern that has become the prison of its lonely keeper. He will not give up his dream. He will go somewhere else and have *vin ordinaire,* and pay for it, that's all. He puts his hand in his pocket to sound his purse; it is there. There ought to be thirty-seven sous in it, which will not run to the wine of Pérou, but—

But suddenly he starts, stops dead, and smites himself on the forehead. His long-drawn face is contracted in a frightful grimace, masked by the night. No, he no longer has thirty-seven sous, fool that he is! He has forgotten the tin of sardines that he bought the night before — so disgusting did he find the dark macaroni of the soldiers' mess — and the drinks he stood to the cobbler who put him some nails in his boots.

Misery! There could not be more than thirteen sous left!

To get as elevated as one ought, and to avenge himself on the life of the moment, he would certainly need — damnation! — a litre and a half. In this place, a litre of red ordinary costs twenty-one sous. It won't go.

His eyes wander around him in the darkness, looking for some one. Perhaps there is a pal somewhere who will lend him money, or stand him a litre.

But who — who? Not Bécuwe, he has only a *marraine,*[1] who sends him tobacco and note-paper every fortnight. Not Barque, who would not toe the line; nor Blaire, the miser — he wouldn't understand. Not Biquet, who seems to have something against him; nor Pépin, who himself begs, and never pays, even when he is host. Ah, if Volpatte were there! There is Mesnil André, but he is actually in debt to Fouillade on account of several drinks round. Corporal Bertrand? Following on a remark of Fouillade's, Bertrand told him to go to the devil, and now they look at each other sideways. Farfadet? Fouillade hardly speaks a word to him in the ordinary way. No, he feels that he cannot ask this of Farfadet. And then — a thousand thunders! — what is the use of seeking saviours in one's imagination? Where are they, all these people, at this hour?

Slowly he goes back towards the barn. Then mechanically he turns and goes forward again, with hesitating steps. He will try, all the same. Perhaps he can find convivial comrades. He approaches the central part of the village just when night has buried the earth.

The lighted doors and windows of the taverns shine again in the mud of the main street. There are taverns every twenty paces. One dimly sees the heavy spectres of soldiers, mostly in groups, descending the street. When a motor-car comes along, they draw aside to let it pass, dazzled by the head-lights, and bespattered by the liquid mud that the wheels hurl over the whole width of the road.

The taverns are full. Through the steamy windows one can see they are packed with compact clouds of helmeted men.

Fouillade goes into one or two, on chance. Once over the threshold, the dram-shop's tepid breath, the light, the smell and the hubbub, affect him with longing. This gathering at tables is at least a fragment of the past in the present.

He looks from table to table, and disturbs the groups as he goes up to scrutinise all the merrymakers in the room. Alas, he knows no one! Else-where, it is the same; he has no luck. In vain he has extended his neck and sent his desperate glances in search of a familiar head among the uniformed men who in clumps or couples drink and talk or in solitude write. He has the air of a cadger, and no one pays him heed.

Finding no soul to come to his relief, he decides to invest at least what he has in his pocket. He slips up to the counter. "A pint of wine — and good."

"White?"

"*Eh, oui.*"

"You, *mon garçon,* you're from the South," says the landlady, handing him a little full bottle and a glass, and gathering his twelve sous.

He places himself at the corner of a table already overcrowded by four drinkers who are united in a game of cards. He fills the glass to the brim and empties it, then fills it again.

"Hey, good health to you! Don't drink the tumbler!" yelps in his face a man who arrives in the dirty blue jumper of fatigues, and displays a heavy cross-bar of eyebrows across his pale face, a conical head, and half a pound's weight of ears. It is Harlingue, the armourer.

It is not very glorious to be seated alone before a pint in the presence of a comrade who gives signs of thirst. But Fouillade pretends not to under-stand the requirements of the gentleman who dallies in front of him with an engaging smile, and he hurriedly empties his glass. The other turns his back, not without grumbling that "they're not very generous, but on the contrary greedy, these Southerners."

Fouillade has put his chin on his fists, and looks unseeing at a corner of the room where the crowded poilus elbow, squeeze, and jostle each other to get by.

It was pretty good, that swig of white wine, but of what use are those few drops in the Sahara of Fouillade? The blues did not far recede, and now they return.

The Southerner rises and goes out, with his two glasses of wine in his stomach and one sou in his pocket. He plucks up courage to visit one more tavern, to plumb it with his eyes, and by way of excuse to mutter, as he leaves the place. "Curse him! He's never there, the animal."

Then he returns to the barn, which still—as always—whistles with wind and water. Fouillade lights his candle, and by the glimmer of the flame that struggles desperately to take wing and fly away, he sees Labri. He stoops low, with his light over the miserable dog—perhaps it will die first. Labri is sleeping, but feebly, for he opens an eye at once, and his tail moves.

The Southerner strokes him, and says to him in a low voice, "It can't be helped, it—" He will not say more to sadden him, but the dog signifies appreciation by jerking his head before closing his eyes again. Fouillade rises stiffly, by reason of his rusty joints, and makes for his couch. For only one thing more he is now hoping—to sleep, that the dismal day may die, that wasted day, like so many others that there will be to endure stoically and to overcome, before the last day arrives of the war or of his life.

Notes

1. French soldiers have extensively developed a system of corresponding with French women whom they do not know from Eve and whose acquaintance they usually make through newspaper advertisements. As typical of the latter I copy the following: "Officier artilleur, 30 ans, désire correspondence discrète avec jeune marraine, femme du monde. Ecrire," etc. The "lonely soldier" movement in this country is similar. — Tr.

Wooden Crosses

In the Sweat of Thy Brow

ROLAND DORGELÈS

With a great pile of packets in front of him like a pedlar's pack, the harassed quartermaster was calling out the post in the middle of a regular mob of soldiers, who were all plying their elbows and trampling on one another's feet. It was just at our door, between the communal washhouse — so tiny that there would hardly have been room for three washerwomen under its sloping shelter — and the notary's house, which wore a red scarf of virginia creeper crosswise on its front. We had clambered up on the stone seat and were listening attentively.

"Maurice Duclou, first section."

"Killed at Courcy," cried somebody.

"Are you sure?"

"Yes, his mates saw him fall in front of the church. . . . He'd caught a bullet. Now, . . . well, I wasn't there myself."

On the corner of the envelope the quartermaster wrote in pencil, *"Killed."*

"Edouard Marquette."

"He must be killed too," said a voice.

"You're a ninny!" protested another. "The night they said he was dropped he went on a water-party with me."

"Then," asked the quartermaster, "he would be in hospital? But we've not had his papers."

"My idea is that he was evacuated by another regiment."

"No, no, he was wounded; the Boches must have collared him."

"It's a great pity — it's always the ones that have seen nothing have most chat."

Everybody was talking at once in an uproar of opposing statements and insulting contradictions. The quartermaster, hard-pushed and in a hurry, brought them into agreement.

"I don't give a curse. I'll mark him off 'Missing.' André Brunet, thirteenth squad."

"Here for him."

The others were going on disputing in lowered tones; the men in the hindmost ranks were shouting to them to be quiet, and nobody could hear anything. Bréval listened through it all, anxiously listened, and when a name sounded like his, had it repeated.

"Isn't it for me, this time? Corporal Bréval? . . ."

But it was never for him, and turning his poor vexed face to us, he explained.

"She writes so badly that there might be nothing queer about it, eh?"

As the heap lessened his lips tightened. When the last one was called out, he went away, heart and hands empty alike. Just as he was going indoors he turned to us.

"By the way, Demachy, your turn on fatigue. You will take a bag and go to fetch the rations."

"What? The new chum going for rations! . . .You're making game of us."

And Sulphart, all indignant, left his particular group of pals to come up to the corporal.

"A lad that's just come, who fancies that carrots grow at the fruiterer's, that's the best you can find to send for the rations! Ah, you're up to tricks. . . . If every fool could swim you wouldn't need a boat to cross the Seine."

"If you want to go I'm not hindering you," replied Bréval calmly.

"Sure, I'll go," shouted Sulphart. "I'll go because I don't want the squad to get the same food as wooden horses, and because that lad looks to me as if he could choose a bit of beef about as well as I could say a Mass."

Demachy, who ever since he arrived had been overwhelmed by the cries, the noisy demands, and brutal gaities of the redhead, made an attempt to rehabilitate himself.

"I beg your pardon, I assure you that I shall know what to do very well. In barracks . . ."

He was going the wrong way about it. The mere words "active service" or "barracks" was enough to send Sulphart crazy, inasmuch as he had spent his three years in stubbornly defending the cause of right against vindictive Adjutants and officers of malevolent nature, who preferably sent good soldiers to sleep in the police station the night before leave. Anger choked him.

"Barracks! . . . He fancies he's still in barracks, the lark-skull! He's just come out of the depot and he would like to put it all over us again! . . .Well then, get on with it, go to the distribution, see the rations; they'll have a good laugh. The lads of the squad are always sure to be in a nice fix and no mistake. I don't care for myself, *I'll* manage all right."

And to show quite clearly that he was no longer one with a squad being led to the abyss by an incapable corporal, he sauntered off towards the church, whistling a little tune to himself.

The squads were being mustered when Gilbert came into the courtyard where the quartermaster had had unloaded, a few paces from the manure tank, the quarters of frozen meat which a man was now cutting up with an axe, potatoes, bully-beef, a burst sack from which trickled a thin stream of rice, and biscuits, which the youngsters were carrying off in their aprons to make pig's-meat with.

Stooping over the cask of wine, which they were tapping to make sure that it was properly full, those who were waiting their turn were arguing as to the number of bidons that would fall to each squad, and some of them were already clamoring that that wasn't their proper figure. Lentils were given out, sweet potatoes, coffee in the berry. Taken by surprise, Demachy remarked:

"But we have no coffee-mill?"

The others stared at him and laughed. Behind the group someone bellowed:

"You can go on enjoying yourselves! That's the lad they send to get the rations for a whole squad."

It was Sulphart, who had come out of curiosity, just to look on. Heavily embarrassed, his cap full of sugar, his pockets stuffed with coffee, his bag weighed down full of lentils, Gilbert was at his wit's end, with no notion where he could put his rice. As everybody was laughing round him, and the quartermaster shouting, "Come along, here's your lot; don't you want to have it to eat?" he lost his head and emptied it anywhere he could — into his bag along with the lentils. Then Sulphart burst out:

"Here, that's a bit too much! . . . You see the cookie's phiz if he'll like sorting out his rice and bugs! . . . Lord, what an army! And they talk about hoofing the Bosches out. What a joke! . . ."

Thoroughly furious, the new chum turned round, red all over.

"Look here, you shut up. All you had to do was to come here yourself."

Sulphart, without turning a hair, waited for the remainder of the distribution. He watched the corporal on duty throwing down great chunks of meat, some of an appetizing fresh redness, others thickly veined with tallow, on a muddied piece of tent canvas.

"We're going to draw lots for them," said the corporal.

"No!" protested several squads, "there will be some faking about it. . . . Share it out according to the number of men."

"There are fourteen of us in the second squad; I want that piece."

"And what about us, in the first . . . ?"

All stooping over the stall, hands stretched out, they were disputing in advance over the food, all shouting at once, under the impassive eye of the quartermaster.

"That will do with your howling," he said at last. "I'll distribute it. Third squad, . . . that piece. Fourth squad . . . Fifth squad . . ."

He had not time to finish, nor to point out the piece intended with the end of his stick. With a roar Sulphart hurled himself into the group.

"No!" he shouted, "I'm not having any. . . .You want us all in the squad to die of hunger. They're taking advantage of its being a lad that isn't up to snuff to do us in the eye."

The others hooted him, the quartermaster would fain have driven him away, but clean beyond all restraint, wildly waving his arms, he shouted louder than them all.

"I won't have that piece at all. . . . I'll tell the Captain, and I'll tell the Colonel too, if I have to. . . . It's always the same lot that get the best. . . . I want my proper share. . . . The fifth squad is the one with the most men in it. . . ."

"There are only eleven of you."

"That's a lie! . . .We'll make a complaint. . . That's nothing but bone!"

He was uttering cry upon cry, now shrill, now hoarse, now terrifying and now plaintive, thrusting one back and jostling others over. Those who had already been served were hugging their share to their hearts, as the mothers of Bethlehem must have held their babes on the night of Herod's slaughter. By good luck the quartermaster held out a chunk to him, taken at random, and at once he shut up completely, his calm recovered immediately, his anger all harmless and disarmed since he was served. He turned then to Demachy, while the distribution went on.

"You see," he said with a friendly air, "you've got the idea all right, but you don't give tongue enough. If you want to be better served than the others you've got to give tongue, even without knowing anything about anything: that's the only way to have your rights."

Gilbert Demachy listened without any answer, amused by this big brawler with his bristle beard; his attentive silence pleased Sulphart.

"Of course that blockhead of a Bréval never told you to fetch the bucket or the bottles for the pinard. What do you think you're going to carry it back in — in your boots? Good joy I thought something about it. There's a bucket, and I brought a can in case there might be brandy. . . . It's no matter, a corporal that doesn't go himself to the distribution; you only see that with the fifth. . . . He stayed behind once more writing to his old woman. . . . Blitherer!"

Sulphart did not deign to have any truck with the distribution of tins of bully-beef, a commodity for which he had nothing but contempt; but all the same he cried, "There's one short!" just to show that he was still on the spot.

"Now for the wine," said the quartermaster.

Sulphart dashed forward first of all, and as long as the distribution lasted he never raised his head; while a bucket was filling he groaned and moaned and uttered little cries of anguish, as if it was his heart's blood that was being run off.

"That'll do! . . . That'll do!" he cried. "It holds more than the proper measure. . . . Thief!"

But the others, who were accustomed to it all, endured the insults and kept the wine. His turn came at length, and he got his bucket filled up to the very brim, swearing that six new chums had turned up, that the corporal was going to lodge a complaint, that they had already been curtailed the day before, that the Captain. . . .

"Here, and bung off," said the exasperated quartermaster, pouring out a last quarter of a litre for him. "Lord, what a life!"

Highly pleased with himself, Sulphart went back like a conqueror, his bucket in one hand and his bag on his shoulder. They passed through the village, where the idle soldiers were roaming in quest of a pub, and on the way he tried to inculcate into the new chum the first principles of cunning and trickery essential for a soldier on campaign.

"Every man for himself, you know. I'd far rather drink other people's drink than have the others drinking mine. . . . It always is the modest folk that lose out."

Halting in a spot where nobody was passing, he dipped his drinking-cup in the bucket and offered it to Gilbert.

"Here," he said, "drink that, you've a right to it."

He had, in a word, drawn up in his own mind, and for his own sole personal guidance, a little treatise on the rights and duties of the soldier, in which it was fully and frankly conceded that the man on ration fatigue had a right to a cup of wine as a perquisite. He drank one too, since he was helping the man on duty, and started off again by so much the lighter. As they walked, he told Gilbert stories, talking in the same breath of his wife, who was a dressmaker; of the battle of Guise; the factory where he worked in Paris, and of Morache, the Adjutant, a re-enlisted man, our special horror. When they reached cantonments, he put down the bucket, taking oath that he had never so much as tasted the wine, and offering to prove it by letting anybody smell his breath; then he went to Demachy again, having taken a fancy to him.

"If I'd had the dibs like you," he said, "and had your education, I swear they wouldn't have seen me coming into the fire like this. I'd have put in for the officers' course, and I'd have gone and spent some months in camp, and then they'd have listed me sub-lieutenant in the middle of 1915. And by that the war'll be over. . . . What I say is, that you didn't know how to swim."

Civilization,
1914–1917

Revaud's Room

GEORGES DUHAMEL

Time did not hang heavy in Revaud's room. The rumbling of the war, the sound of the convoys marching past, the epileptic shocks of the cannonade, all the whistlings and pantings of the great machine of slaughter, reached his windows and shook them with an exhausted fury, as the ineffectual echoes of a tempest outside penetrate the depths of a crevasse. But this uproar fell as familiarly on the ear as the very pulse-beats of the wretched world, and time did not hang heavy in Revaud's room.

It was a long, straight chamber in which there were four beds and four men. Nevertheless, it was called "Revaud's room," for Revaud's personality completely filled it, as if it had been a coat cut to his measure. At the beginning of November there had been all sorts of villainous plots set on foot by Corporal Têtard to make Revaud change his room, and the plots succeeded. The poor man was hoisted to the upper floor, to a big dormitory of twenty beds, a splendid desert, with nothing intimate about it, ravaged by a hard and cruel light. In three days, by a sort of spontaneous decision of his soul and body, Revaud had wasted away in such an alarming fashion that it had been necessary to take him down in haste, behind his own door, to the back of his room, where the winter light came in filtered and full of a sort of indulgence.

That's how matters stood; when a man who was really seriously wounded, a very special case, was brought to the division, they would at once beg Mme. Baugan to take the matter up with Revaud. Revaud had to be coaxed a little, but he would always end by saying:

"All right, all right! Good heavens! I don't care! Put the fellow in my room, of course."

And Revaud's room was always full. In order to get there, it was not enough to have a mere broken collar-bone, or a smashed foot, or a little unimportant amputation of an arm. You must have "something strange and extraordinary the matter with you," a gap in the little intestine, for example, or a lesion of the spinal marrow, or you must be one of those cases where the "skull is crushed flat."

"In here," Revaud would say with pride, "in here we are all very rare cases."

There was Sandrap, a little man from the North, with a nose as round as a young apple, with beautiful, soft, light-gray eyes. He had been wounded three times and used to say every morning:

"They'd be struck all of a heap, those Boches, if they could see me now!"

There was Remusot, who had a great wound in his breast. It made a sound like "faouaou-raou-aou, faouaou-raouaou," and Revaud had said on the very first day:

"That's a queer noise you make! Do you do it with your mouth?"

The other had whispered in a toneless voice, "It's my breath trying to get through my ribs."

Finally there was Mery, whose spinal column had been broken by an explosive, and who "had no more feeling left in the whole lower half of his body than if it had not belonged to him."

All this little world of men lived on their backs, each in his place, in a general promiscuity of odor, noise, and sometimes thought. They knew one another by their voices rather than by sight, and Sandrap had been there a whole week before Revaud, seeing him pass on the stretcher close to his bed, on his way to be dressed, suddenly called out to him:

"Look here, Sandrap, you certainly have a funny sort of head! And you have a funny kind of hair, too!"

Mme. Baugan would arrive at eight o'clock, and she would at once begin to scold: "It smells bad here. Oh, oh! my poor Revaud!"

Revaud would evade the question.

"It's all right," he would say. "I've slept all right. I've nothing to complain of as far as that goes. I've slept all right."

Mme. Baugan would bustle about, getting fresh clothes and water; she would set about Revaud's toilet as if he were a child.

All at once, however, seized with shame and a sort of despair, the wounded man groaned:

"Madame Baugan, you mustn't be angry with me: I wasn't like this in civil life!"

Mme. Baugan began to laugh, and Revaud, without waiting, began to laugh too, for his whole face and his whole soul were made for laughter and he loved to laugh, even in the midst of the worst torment.

Having found that this reply pleased her, he brought it out often, and he would say to every one who came over to him, referring to his great misfortune, "I wasn't like that in civil life, you know."

The happiest phrases have only an hour's success. Revaud, who had brains, saw clearly that the moment was approaching when it would no longer do to affirm that "he had not been like that in civil life." It was then that he received the letter from his father. It arrived unexpectedly, one morning when he had just had his big old-fashioned French mustache cut, out of pure whim, after the American fashion. The whole hospital was sneaking past the corner of the door to have a peep at Revaud, who looked like some very sick foreign gentleman. He turned the letter over in his fingers, deformed by poverty and hard work, then he said with an air of uneasiness: "What are they after me now for, with that letter?"

Revaud was married; but as he had been six months without word from his wife, he had grown comfortably used to his isolation. He was in his own room, behind his own door, and he wasn't looking for a quarrel with any one. Why, then, should they send him a letter?

"What are they after me for now?" he repeated. And he held the letter out for Mme. Baugan to read to him.

It was a letter from Revaud's father. In ten lines of elaborate handwriting, full of thin strokes, heavy strokes, embellishments and flourishes, the old man announced that he was going to make him a visit at a near but unspecified date.

Once more Revaud found in laughter the ultimate object of his life. The whole day he played carelessly with the letter and cheerfully showed it to people, saying: "We're going to have a visit. My father's coming to see us."

Then he would add, confidentially: "My father's quite well off, you know, but he has had misfortunes. Just wait till you see my father; he has a whole bag full of tricks, that man has; and, besides, he wears a stiff collar."

Revaud ended by limiting all characterizations of his father's personality to this last statement: "My father! You wait and see: he wears a stiff collar."

The days passed, and Revaud spoke so often of his father that in the end he didn't know whether the visit had taken place or not. And so, by a special grace of heaven, Revaud never noticed that his father had not come to see him. Later, to signify this remarkable period, he would use words that sounded very big, and would say, "It was at the time of my father's visit."

Revaud was spoiled; he had no lack of cigarettes or company, and he would say with an air of satisfaction: "In this hospital I'm the *charculot*," by which he meant, the favorite little chick. Well, Revaud wasn't hard to please: it was enough for Tarrissant to appear between his crutches for the dying man to exclaim: "There's some one else coming to see me! I tell you I'm the *charculot* in here!"

Tarrissant had undergone the same operation as Revaud. It was a complicated affair which had taken place in the knee. Only, the operation had been very successful with Tarrissant and a good deal of a failure with Revaud; "for it all depends on the blood."

Even about the operation itself Revaud would have his joke: his knee had "dried up." He would look at Tarrissant, and, comparing himself with the convalescent, he would conclude without further comment:

"We are both of us dried up. Only, I'm a fool as well. And besides I've worked too much."

It was the only allusion that Revaud ever made to the disgrace of his marriage and to his life of hard work.

But then, really, why should one think of all those things? Hasn't a man trouble enough with a leg like that?

In the evening every one would make little preparations for the night, just like people who are getting ready for a journey. Remusot would receive an injection in his thigh and at once, bathed in sweat, he would enter a paradise where the fever displayed to him things that he was never willing to repeat to any one. Mery would have a big bowlful of his nightly concoction of herbs prepared for him, and placed where he could reach it by merely stretching out his hand. Sandrap would smoke his last cigarette, and Revaud would ask for his cushion. It was a little packet of cotton that was placed by his side. Only when he had it would Revaud consent to say: "That's all right, boys, you can go now." And after that, they would wander through a sleep as dense and terrible as a forest strewn with ambushes, each one steering his own way, as he pursued his dreams.

While their spirits were taking flight, their four bodies lay immovable, lighted by a small night-lamp. When a night watchman came, in his shuffling slippers, put his head in at the door, and heard the tormented breathings of these four, or surprised at times the wide-eyed, unseeing gaze of Remusot, he would think suddenly, as he watched these human relics cast up on a lee shore, of a shipwrecked raft, a raft drifting over the rolling ocean, with four human beings in distress.

The windows of the room continued to vibrate, as if in complaint, with the noise of the war. Sometimes, in the long night, the war would seem to pause, like a wood-cutter who stops to breathe between two blows of his axe.

Then they would awake, in this deep, deep silence, in a strange distress, and they would think of all that happens on the battle-field, of the hour when men no longer hear anything.

The winter dawn would appear, grudgingly, like a lazy, untidy slattern who gets up late. The attendants would come to wash the floors. They would blow out the dying night-lamp, smelling evilly out of its last remnant of oil. Then would come the toilet, and then all the pains and groans of the dressings.

At times, in the midst of the usual daily occupations, the door would open majestically and they would see a general enter, followed by the officers of his staff. He would stop short at the very threshold, half choked by some overpowering odor, then he would advance a little way into the room and ask who these men were. The doctor would whisper a few words in his ear, and the general would reply simply: "Ah! good! Very good!"

When he had gone out, Revaud would always remark, with an air of assurance: "That general never comes here without making me a visit. I know him very well."

After that there would be something to talk about the whole day.

A good many majors came, too, and some of them carried themselves very smartly. They would look at the charts tacked up on the walls, and say: "Well, well! They make a good showing in spite of it."

One day one of them was looking at Mery. He was a very great doctor who had a white beard, an immense waist-line, many crosses on his breast and the pink neck of a man who is always well fed. He had a kindly manner and an air of pity. In fact he said:

"Poor devil! Ah! But just suppose such a thing were to happen to me!"

But as a rule, nobody came, absolutely nobody, and the day, like the meat at meal-time, could be got through only by being cut up into an infinity of little morsels.

One day there was an event: Mery was carried off to be photographed by the X-ray. He reappeared, satisfied, saying, "That doesn't hurt, anyway!"

Another time they cut off Revaud's leg. He accepted it, murmuring:

"Well, at least I did my best to keep that leg! But such is life! Go ahead, my poor man!"

He had one more laugh yet; and no one ever has laughed or ever will laugh as Revaud laughed that day!

So they cut off his leg. The finest blood of France was shed once more. But this took place between four walls, in a little room as white as a dairy, and no one knew anything about it.

Revaud was put to bed again behind his door. He came to himself like a child and said:

"Yes, indeed! They certainly got me excited about that leg, and no joke!"

Revaud passed a fairly good night, and when Mme. Baugan entered the room the next morning, he said to her, in his usual way: "Quite well, Madame Baugan! I've slept all right!"

He said this, and then his head slipped to one side; he opened his mouth gradually, and he died without any more ado.

Mme. Baugan cried out: "Poor Revaud! Why, he's dead!"

She kissed his forehead and then at once she began to prepare him for burial; for the day's work is long and there is never any time to lose.

Mme. Baugan dressed Revaud, and she grumbled over it too, for it was not easy to put clothes on the corpse.

Sandrap, Mery, and Remusot said not one word. The rain trickled down the windows, which continued to tremble with the roar of the guns.

The Wars

TIMOTHY FINDLEY

Riding beside him was his batman, Bugler Willie Poole. Bugler was really an out-of-date rank and fairly meaningless but sometimes it was given to men whose age was suspect. In other wars they might have been drummer boys. Willie Poole was proud of his rank, however, because the fact was he actually played the bugle. 'Why,' Robert had asked, 'didn't you apply to play in the band?' 'Oh,' said Willie, 'if I was playing in the band I wouldn't be here.' He was that uncomplicated. He carried his bugle on a string across his back. Unlike Regis, Poole was not under-age — but he looked it. He was in fact nineteen like Robert but he didn't yet shave and his voice still wavered, not completely broken. He was covered with freckles and his hair was the colour of sand. He'd been assigned to Robert two days after Robert's arrival — his previous officer having been killed when he'd stepped outside one evening 'for a breath of air.' The breath of air had blown his head off.

'Do you remember any barns or houses along this road where we could bivouac?' Robert asked.

'No, sir,' said Poole. 'But I could ride ahead and see.'

'No,' said Robert. 'No one's riding ahead.' He turned in his saddle. 'I'm beginning to wonder if anyone's riding *behind*. Maybe we should stop and let the others catch us up.'

They reined in their horses.

Poole said, 'I have to get down, if that's all right.' Robert nodded.

Poole gave over his reins into Robert's hand and swung down onto the road. By the time he'd reached the edge of the ditch he'd already started to disappear. The air was foul with thick green fog. There was a smell that Robert could not decipher.

'What's that smell?' he said to Poole.

'Prob'ly chlorine,' Poole replied. His back was to Robert — with his coat elbowed out like wings. Robert could hear him urinating into the ditch.

'You mean you think there's a gas attack going on up front?' Robert had not yet had this experience. Poole had had it twice.

'No, sir. But the groun' is full of it here. There's some that says a handful of this clay could knock a person out.'

'I believe it,' said Robert. The smell was unnerving — as if some presence were lurking in the fog like a dragon in a story. Poole was quite correct; the ground was saturated with gas. Chlorine and phosgene were currently both in use. Mustard gas was still to come.

They were joined by the rider behind them with four horses. The horses were nervous and as soon as they were halted, they laid their ears back and started to skitter.

Robert did not get down himself, but he told the rider to dismount. He was nervous. He didn't know why. They waited.

Poole came back doing up his buttons. They stood there like that for fully five minutes — Robert on his horse, leaning forward to rest his stomach muscles, and the two men down in the road with the horses. The fog was full of noises. They were ill defined and had no perimeter. Distance had been swallowed whole.

'What if we've gone the wrong turning?' said Poole, whose innocence allowed him to make remarks like that — even to an officer.

Robert thought it was possible but didn't say so. He asked what the others thought the noises might be.

'Birds,' said Poole. The other man remained silent.

'I'd be very surprised if any birds had survived in this place,' said Robert.

Just as he said so, something flew out of the ditch.

The horses shied and one of them snorted. Robert stood in his stirrups trying to see what it was that had flown. More and more of whatever it was flew up after it. A whole flock of something. Ducks? He couldn't tell. It was odd — how they'd sat so still and silent till that moment.

'What can be keeping those blasted others?' he said.

'Orderly, maybe you'd best go back.'

'Yessir.'

'Poole and I will hold down here.'

The man got into his saddle.

'Give him your bugle, Poole.'

'Yessir.' Poole handed over the bugle from his back.

'Now — use it,' Robert said to the orderly. 'Keep on counting to fifty and every fifty give us a blast. Let me hear one now, just to see you know what you're doing.'

The man put the bugle to his lips and made a ragged noise with it. All at once the air was filled with shock waves of wings — sheet after sheet of them, rising off some marsh they could not see. The wind and the sound of their motion sent a shiver down Robert's back. Nothing could be seen except the shape of movement.

'All right. Go back,' Robert said. 'At a walk. And a blast at every fifty.'

'Yessir.'

The man turned his horse and was gone as he did so.

Robert muttered one to fifty. So did Poole.

There was a muffled shout from the trumpet.

'He's not very good at it,' said Poole.

'Well — he hasn't had your practice,' said Robert. 'Give him a week or so . . .'

They were both trying to joke. But they couldn't. There must be something terribly wrong and they knew it but neither one knew how to put it into words. The birds, being gone, had taken some mysterious presence with them. There was an awful sense of void — as if the world had emptied.

Robert leaned forward. Even Poole was beginning to disappear. He was cold. He had never been so cold. The fog was turning his greatcoat to mush. It was as if the rain had boiled and turned to steam — except that the steam was frigid. Robert tried to remember what it was like to bathe in hot water. He couldn't.

They waited.

The trumpet wailed and hooted further and further off in the green. The fog was full of light. Robert heard wings above them and around them. The birds were coming back. There was also the sound of lapping — of movement out in the field — and the sound reminded Robert of the early morning slap-slap-slap from the diving raft at Jackson's Point. Something floating in the water. All he could see was the shape of Poole and the heads and rumps of the horses — their lower parts obscured. The rain had stopped. An occasional chilly breeze blew through the fog — intimations of another world and other weather. These breezes carried the smells of smoke and ashes — bitter and acrid. The trumpet fell silent.

Poole led the horses back in Robert's direction. Warmth might be had by clustering. Neither man spoke. The horses didn't like being made to stand still. The wings had alarmed them.

'Name all the birds you can think of,' said Robert.

'Storks,' said Poole.

'I'm being serious,' said Robert.

'So'm I,' said Poole. 'I'm sorry, sir; but I just can't think of any birds but storks. I'm too damn cold . . .'

Starlings, Robert thought; they don't go away in winter. But these, whatever they are, are bigger than that. Ducks. They must be ducks. They're flying north and they need some place to rest so they've chosen these fields. That's what it is. They're resting.

The trumpet sounded. Close. Very close.

Poole was so startled he jumped.

'Ha . . . loooo!' Robert shouted. 'Good,' he said to Poole. 'They're here.' And then he shouted *ha . . . loooo!* again.

The trumpet replied.

Robert and the trumpet kept this up for six exchanges and after Robert's last haloo a voice came back from the fog.

'Don't move,' it said.

'All right,' said Robert. His voice thickened.

Poole stopped shivering. 'What can be wrong?' he whispered.

'We'll soon find out,' said Robert.

Each turned to watch where the voice had been. A man came floating through the fog. His collar was turned up. His hat was missing. This was not the man they had sent away. He was walking.

'Where's your horse?' Robert asked. 'Who are you?'

'Me,' said the voice.

'Who the hell is me?' Robert said.

'Me,' said the man. 'Levitt.'

Levitt was a new junior officer who'd joined the convoy at Bailleul that morning. He'd just come over from England.

'Where's the other chap?' said Robert. 'And why aren't you riding a horse? You shouldn't come up here without a horse.' He was angry. Levitt was supposed to be officer at the rear. This meant there was now no one of rank with the wagons and two of the wagons carried rum.

'I'm sorry,' said Levitt: 'but I had to come forward. The other chap was soaked to the skin. He and his horse . . .'

'What happened?' said Robert, cutting him off.

'They went through the dike, sir.'

'What dike?'

'*This* dike,' said Levitt.

Robert blinked. Levitt stared through the fog. Robert looked over his shoulder. Birds.

Levitt said: 'I can't tell how far, but somewhere back there you took the wrong turning and you've come out onto this dike and the dike is slowly collapsing.' Robert now perceived that Levitt himself was soaked to the skin. 'I didn't like the thought of sending one of the men,' Levitt went on, 'since there were all those horses and someone who knew what they were doing had to stay with them, so I came up myself. The corporal's in charge.'

'Thank you,' said Robert. Levitt's sense of detail was practical, if nothing else. 'All right,' Robert said. 'What's our situation?' He was trying not to shake — trying to sound like the C.O. — stiff and unmoved.

Levitt said there was a break in the dike and perhaps the break was a hundred to a hundred and fifty yards behind them. When the rider had gone through, the break was only about six feet across. When Levitt had come through it had widened to ten feet. By now, it might be fifteen or twenty.

Robert swallowed his alarm at having been so blind as to come out onto the dike in the first place. There would be lots of time to think about that. Now, the thing was how to get off. Three men and seven horses.

Levitt gave the bugle back to Poole and thanked him for it. 'I was glad of it out there,' he said; 'because it occurred to me — if any Germans were listening they wouldn't fire at a man with a bugle!' He laughed nervously. 'Anyone could be blowing a bugle.'

Poole said: 'You needn't worry about the Germans here, sir. They're a long ways off yet. At least as much as two miles or more.'

Levitt said: 'Oh.' He seemed somehow demoralized by this news. Perhaps he thought you weren't in the war unless the enemy could shoot you. In this he was much like everyone else who'd just arrived. You weren't a real soldier unless you were in jeopardy.

Robert was in the vanguard. He stayed on the horse, knowing the horse's footing would be surer, more sensitive than his own. His father had taught him always to trust the horse's judgement above his own when it came to path-finding.

The breeze had become a wind. The fog began to lift in places. The shape of the dike was perceptible — wide as a road; but the ditches weren't ditches at all. To the right there was a river, or canal and to the left there must be fields, though these were still unseen. The dike had in fact been often used as a road — and was rutted and torn by cartwheels.

One of the birds flew up and cut across Robert's path. The horse shied. Robert fought to control him. 'There, there, there,' he said. 'Soo, soo, soo.' The horse turned sideways — this side then the other. Any way but forward. Robert reined him in.

He crouched in the saddle: squinting. The horse would not go on.

'All right,' Robert said aloud. 'If you won't, then I must.'

He got down and soothed the horse by rubbing its muzzle. Then he left it standing there and struck out into the fog alone. Poole gave a shout and Robert shouted back that they should stay by his horse until he'd found the break. Once, looking over his shoulder he saw them all gathered there — the horses and Poole and Levitt and then the curtain was pulled again and they were gone.

He paused and listened. Surely he would hear something. A river-sound or a waterfall.

Faraway there was a booming noise.

Guns.

5.9s.

They should have been behind him, but these were in front and slightly to the right. How had he got so turned around?

He tested the ground with his heel. Still only mud and slush — the slush like glass that was splintered and mashed. The fog had begun to thicken again. It was full of shapes that waved their arms. Then Robert did hear something. Water. A smooth, deep sound like a sluiceway. The sound was his undoing. He stepped towards it expectantly. Suddenly, his right foot went down. All the way down to the knee through the earth.

Dear Jesus — he was going to drown. He went in all the way to his waist.

He fell back onto his shoulders. All he had to hold with was his elbows. These he ground into the clay like brakes. The slide took him forward so his legs were as much in front of him as below. Don't, he kept thinking; don't.

His hands were useless to him. If he was going to use them he would have to relax his elbows and he would only slip further in. He lay with his head back. The mud pressed down on his thighs. His neck was raw against his collar. He choked.

Many people die without a sound — because their brains are shouting and it seems they've called for help and they haven't. Robert kept thinking — why doesn't someone come? But no one did. He'd told them not to. The only sound he made was the *o* in don't and this got locked in his throat.

He pushed. He tried to force his pelvis forward and up. The muscles in his stomach made a knot. If he could only lift the weight. The mud spread wider over his thighs. It began to make a sucking noise at the back of his legs. The fog came down like a muffler over his face. One way or another — he would suffocate and drown. He began to push again and to lift — thrusting his pelvis upward harder and harder — faster and faster against the mud. His hat fell off. The wind and the fog were dabbling in his hair. The back of his head went all the way down and into the slush. In and out in and out in and out. With his buttocks clenched and his knees . . . He began to realize his knees were spreading wider and wider and his groin began to shudder. Warm. He was going to be saved. He was going to save himself. He sat up. His boots were still being held. But his thighs were free. He could see his knees. He began to pull at his legs with his hands. Nothing happened. Absolutely nothing. He leaned forward. He tried to pull at his breeches. His gloves were filled with mud and nothing would hold to them. He tore them off and locked his hands behind his right knee. Then he began to rock. His fingernails gouged his palms. He rocked from side to side and back to front.

His leg began to move. Then he locked his hands beneath his left knee and rocked from back to front again. Both legs slid further out till only the ankles were held and his knees touched his chin. He fell back all the way and lay on his side. He reached above his head and shoved his hands down hard through the mud until he could curl his fingers deep in the earth. He pulled himself forward with his legs like twisted ropes and then he gave a violent, sudden spasm and flopped face down in the slush. He was free. In a foot of water.

He could hear himself breathing. Whimpering. He closed his eyes. I don't want to drown, he thought. *Please don't drown.* He pushed himself up with his head hanging down.

His breathing died away.

He knelt with both hands fisted on his knees. He listened. Something was near him. He could feel it.

He opened his eyes and turned his head to one side.

Through the fog he saw a man like himself—in uniform and greatcoat—lying down on his side. His back was to Robert. He was moving—or trying to move. Certainly something about him was in motion. *Slap-slap-slap:* like the raft at Jackson's Point.

Robert rubbed his eyes.

At once they began to smart and in seconds they were burning. The chlorine in the mud. Robert was blinded. He began to feel in his pockets for a handkerchief. There were noises he could not identify. Movement. What? What was it? Had the man got up?

Robert desperately tried to see but his eyes wouldn't open. They were flooded with burning tears and his lids wouldn't lift. He caught a fleeting glimpse of something moving in the air.

A hand fell on his shoulder.

Robert yelled and grabbed at it. Bones and claws. It drew away. Robert shuddered. Birds.

Poole called: 'Sir? Lieutenant Ross?'

Robert said: 'It's all right.' Then he realized he hadn't even raised his voice, so he called out: 'It's all right. You can come forward now.' He tied the handkerchief around his eyes and sat back—waiting. Crows. They'd been crows all along—with wings as long as arms.

When Poole and Levitt reached him with the horses, Poole got Robert to his feet and Robert said to him: 'There's a man just there. He's dead I think.'

Poole said: 'Yes, sir.'

'Can we help?' said Robert. 'Should he be buried?'

'No,' said Poole. 'We'd best keep going.' He took Robert's arm.

From the gap, when Robert's eyes had cleared, he cast a single look back to where the man had been. He saw that the whole field was filled with floating shapes. The only sounds were the sounds of feeding and of wings.

And of rafts.

Robert went first—on horseback.

The gap in the dike had widened to almost thirty feet. The river washed through but by now the water levels were almost equal on both sides so the pull of the current was not too strong. Still, the horse had to swim for it. The breach was over nine feet deep. Robert took his boots out of the stirrups. He lay along the horse's neck and held onto its mane with one hand. In his other hand he held the lead line to three horses who came through the river behind him. He could feel the surge of the water against his legs as the horse's flank was turned by the current—but cold as it was, Robert was glad of it. The water was washing him free of the mud.

On the far side he could see that the men and the wagons and the rest of the convoy were drawn up near fires and he just kept thinking: warm, I'm going to be warm. The hardest part was not to swim himself—but to let the horse do the swimming. It was an odd sensation, being drawn through the water, almost submerged with his clothes flowing back and his knees pressed hard against the horse and the stirrups banging against his ankles. Pegasus. When he got to the other bank, Robert fell off the horse and the horse went suddenly up the incline without him. He was glad he'd had the sense to take his feet from the stirrups. Otherwise—he'd have been dragged. Several pairs of hands reached down and drew him to the top. The next thing he knew, he was naked and wrapped in a blanket and seated by a fire.

'Break out the rum,' he said.

Poole, who was also naked and wrapped in a blanket, played a tune on the bugle and everybody sang: *'We're here because we're here.'* They stayed all night in the middle of the road and sometime after they slept it snowed. In the morning, Robert did not look back towards the field where he'd nearly been drowned. The long meandering line of horses and wagons stretched ahead of him, black and sharp against the snow. When he gave the command to move, he rode up past them all with his eyes on the muddy road. Above them, the sky was breached by a wavering arm of wings. The crows were following.

The Middle Parts of Fortune

FREDERIC MANNING

The darkness was increasing rapidly, as the whole sky had threatened thunder. There was still some desultory shelling. When the relief had taken over from them, they set off to return to their original line as best they could. Bourne, who was beaten to the wide, gradually dropped behind, and in trying to keep the others in sight missed his footing and fell into a shell-hole. By the time he had picked himself up again the rest of the party had vanished; and, uncertain of his direction, he stumbled on alone. He neither hurried nor slackened his pace; he was light-headed, almost exalted, and driven only by the desire to find an end. Somewhere, eventually, he would sleep. He almost fell into the wrecked trench, and after a moment's hesitation turned left, caring little where it led him. The world seemed extraordinarily empty of men, though he knew the ground was alive with them. He was breathing with difficulty, his mouth and throat seemed to be cracking with dryness, and his water-bottle was empty. Coming to a dug-out, he groped his way down, feeling for the steps with his feet; a piece of Wilson canvas, hung across the passage but twisted aside, rasped his cheek; and a few steps lower his face was enveloped suddenly in the musty folds of a blanket. The dug-out was empty. For the moment he collapsed there, indifferent to everything. Then with shaking hands he felt for his cigarettes, and putting one between his lips struck a match. The light revealed a candle-end stuck by its own grease to the oval lid of a tobacco-tin, and he lit it; it was scarcely thicker than a shilling, but it would last his time. He would finish his cigarette, and then move on to find his company.

There was a kind of bank or seat excavated in the wall of the dug-out, and he noticed first the tattered remains of a blanket lying on it, and then, gleaming faintly in its folds a small metal disk reflecting the light. It was the cap on the cork of a water-bottle. Sprawling sideways he reached it, the feel of the bottle told him it was full, and uncorking it he put it to his lips and took a great gulp before discovering that he was swallowing neat whiskey. The fiery spirit almost choked him for the moment, in his surprise he even spat some of it out; then recovering, he drank again, discreetly but sufficiently, and was meditating a more prolonged appreciation when he heard men groping their way down the steps. He recorked the bottle, hid it quickly under the blanket, and removed himself to what might seem an innocent distance from temptation.

Three Scotsmen came in; they were almost as spent and broken as he was, that he knew by their uneven voices; but they put up a show of indifference, and were able to tell him that some of his mob were on the left, in a dug-out about fifty yards away. They, too, had lost their way, and asked him questions in their turn; but he could not help them, and they developed among themselves an incoherent debate, on the question of what was the best thing for them to do in the circumstances. Their dialect only allowed him to follow their arguments imperfectly, but under the talk it was easy enough to see the irresolution of weary men seeking in their difficulties some reasonable pretext for doing nothing. It touched his own conscience, and throwing away the butt of his cigarette he decided to go. The candle was flickering feebly on the verge of extinction, and presently the dug-out would be in darkness again. Prudence stifled in him an impulse to tell them of the whiskey; perhaps they would find it for themselves; it was a matter which might be left for providence or chance to decide. He was moving towards the stairs, when a voice, muffled by the blanket, came from outside.

'Who are down there?'

There was no mistaking the note of authority and Bourne answered promptly. There was a pause, and then the blanket was waved aside, and an officer entered. He was Mr Clinton, with whom Bourne had fired his course at Tregelly.

'Hullo, Bourne,' he began, and then seeing the other men he turned and questioned them in his soft kindly voice. His face had the greenish pallor of crude beeswax, his eyes were red and tired, his hands were as nervous as theirs, and his voice had the same note of over-excitement, but he listened to them without a sign of impatience.

'Well, I don't want to hurry you men off,' he said at last, 'but your battalion will be moving out before we do. The best thing you can do is to cut along to it. They're only about a hundred yards further down the trench. You don't want to straggle back to camp by yourselves; it doesn't look well either. So you had better get moving right away. What you really want is twelve hours solid sleep, and I am only telling you the shortest road to it.'

They accepted his view of the matter quietly, they were willing enough; but, like all tired men in similar conditions, they were glad to have their action determined for them; so they thanked him and wished him good-night, if not cheerfully, at least with the air of being reasonable men, who appreciated his kindliness. Bourne made as though to follow them out, but Mr Clinton stopped him.

'Wait a minute, Bourne, and we shall go together,' he said as the last Scotsman groped his way up the steeply pitched stairs. 'It is indecent to follow a kilted Highlander too closely out of a dug-out. Besides I left something here.'

He looked about him, went straight to the blanket, and took up the water-bottle. It must have seemed lighter than he expected, for he shook it a little suspiciously before uncorking it. He took a long steady drink and paused.

'I left this bottle full of whiskey,' he said, 'but those bloody Jocks must have smelt it. You know, Bourne, I don't go over with a skinful, as some of them do; but, by God, when I come back I want it. Here, take a pull yourself; you look as though you could do with one.'

Bourne took the bottle without any hesitation; his case was much the same. One had lived instantaneously during that timeless interval, for in the shock and violence of the attack, the perilous instant, on which he stood perched so precariously, was all that the half-stunned consciousness of man could grasp; and, if he lost his grip on it, he fell back among the grotesque terrors and nightmare creatures of his own mind. Afterwards, when the strain had been finally released, in the physical exhaustion which followed, there was a collapse, in which one's emotional nature was no longer under control.

'We're in the next dug-out, those who are left of us,' Mr Clinton continued. 'I am glad you came through all right, Bourne. You were in the last show, weren't you? It seems to me the old Hun has brought up a lot more stuff, and doesn't mean to shift, if he can help it. Anyway we should get a spell out of the line now. I don't believe there are more than a hundred of us left.'

A quickening in his speech showed that the whiskey was beginning to play on frayed nerves: it had steadied Bourne for the time being. The flame of the candle gave one leap and went out. Mr Clinton switched on his torch, and shoved the water-bottle into the pocket of his raincoat.

'Come on,' he said, making for the steps, 'you and I are two of the lucky ones, Bourne; we've come through without a scratch; and if our luck holds we'll keep moving out of one bloody misery into another, until we break, see, until we break.' Bourne felt a kind of suffocation in his throat: there was nothing weak or complaining in Mr Clinton's voice, it was full of angry soreness. He switched off the light as he came to the Wilson canvas.

'Don't talk so bloody wet,' Bourne said to him through the darkness. 'You'll never break.'

The officer gave no sign of having heard the sympathetic but indecorous rebuke. They moved along the battered trench silently. The sky flickered with the flash of guns, and an occasional star-shell flooded their path with light. As one fell slowly, Bourne saw a dead man in field grey propped up in a corner of a traverse; probably he had surrendered, wounded, and reached the trench only to die there. He looked indifferently at this piece of wreckage. The grey face was senseless and empty. As they turned the corner they were challenged by a sentry over the dug-out.

'Good night, Bourne,' said Mr Clinton quietly.

'Good night, sir,' said Bourne, saluting; and he exchanged a few words with the sentry.

'Wish to Christ they'd get a move on,' said the sentry, as Bourne turned to go down.

The dug-out was full of men, and all the drawn, pitiless faces turned to see who it was as he entered, and after that flicker of interest relapsed into apathy and stupor again. The air was thick with smoke and the reek of guttering candles. He saw Shem lift a hand to attract his attention, and he managed to squeeze in beside him. They didn't speak after each had asked the other if he were all right; some kind of oppression weighed on them all, they sat like men condemned to death.

'Wonder if they'll keep us up in support?' whispered Shem.

Probably that was the question they were all asking, as they sat there in their bitter resignation, with brooding enigmatic faces, hopeless, but undefeated; even the faces of boys seeming curiously old; and then it changed suddenly: there were quick hurried movements, belts were buckled, rifles taken up, and stooping, they crawled up into the air. Shem and Bourne were among the first out. They moved off at once. Shells travelled overhead; they heard one or two bump fairly close, but they saw nothing except the sides of the trench, whitish with chalk in places, and the steel helmet and lifting swaying shoulders of the man in front, or the frantic uplifted arms of shattered trees, and the sky with the clouds broken in places, through which opened the inaccessible peace of the stars. They seemed to hurry, as though the sense of escape filled them. The walls of the communication trench became gradually lower, the track sloping upward to the surface of the ground, and at last they emerged, the officer standing aside, to watch what was left of his men file out, and form up in two ranks before him. There was little light, but under the brims of the helmets one could see living eyes moving restlessly in blank faces. His face, too, was a blank from weariness, but he stood erect, an ash-stick under his arm, as the dun-coloured shadows shuffled into some sort of order. The words of command that came from him were no more than whispers, his voice was cracked and not quite under control, though there was still some harshness in it. Then they moved off in fours, away from the crest of the ridge, towards the place they called Happy Valley.

They had not far to go. As they were approaching the tents a crump dropped by the mule-lines, and that set them swaying a little, but not much. Captain Malet called them to attention a little later; and from the tents, camp-details, cooks, snobs, and a few unfit men, gathered in groups to watch them, with a sympathy genuine enough, but tactfully aloof; for there is a gulf between men just returned from action, and those who have not been in the show as unbridgeable as that between the sober and the drunk. Captain Malet halted his men by the orderly-room tent. There was even a pretence to dress ranks. Then he looked at them, and they at him for a few seconds which seemed long. They were only shadows in the darkness.

'Dismiss!'

His voice was still pitched low, but they turned almost with the precision of troops on the square, each rifle was struck smartly, the officer saluting; and then the will which bound them together dissolved, the enervated muscles relaxed, and they lurched off to their tents as silent and as dispirited as beaten men. One of the tailors took his pipe out of his mouth and spat on the ground.

'They can say what they bloody well like,' he said appreciatively, 'but we're a fuckin' fine mob.'

Once during the night Bourne started up in an access of inexplicable horror, and after a moment of bewildered recollection, turned over and tried to sleep again. He remembered nothing of the nightmare which had roused him, if it were a nightmare, but gradually his awakened sense felt a vague restlessness troubling equally the other men. He noticed it first in Shem, whose body, almost touching his own, gave a quick, convulsive jump, and continued twitching for a moment, while he muttered unintelligibly, and worked his lips as though he were trying to moisten them. The obscure disquiet passed fitfully from one to another, lips parted with the sound of a bubble bursting, teeth met grinding as the jaws worked, there were little whimperings which quickened into sobs, passed into long shuddering moans, or culminated in angry, half-articulate obscenities, and then relapsed, with fretful, uneasy movements and heavy breathing, into a more profound sleep. Even though Bourne tried to persuade himself that these convulsive agonies were merely reflex actions, part of an unconscious physical process, through which the disordered nerves sought to readjust themselves, or to perform belatedly some instinctive movement which an over-riding will had thwarted at its original inception, his own conscious mind now filled itself with the passions, of which the mutterings and twitchings heard in the darkness were only the unconscious mimicry. The senses certainly have, in some measure, an independent activity of their own, and remain vigilant even in the mind's eclipse. The darkness seemed to him to be filled with the shudderings of tormented flesh, as though something diabolically evil probed curiously to find a quick sensitive nerve and wring from it a reluctant cry of pain. At last, unable to ignore the sense of misery which filled him, he sat up and lit the inevitable cigarette. The formless terrors haunting their sleep took shape for him. His mind reached back into the past day, groping among obscure and broken memories, for it seemed to him now that for the greater part of the time he had been stunned and blinded, and that what he had seen, he had seen in sudden, vivid flashes, instantaneously: he felt again the tension of waiting, that became impatience, and then the immense effort to move, and the momentary relief which came with movement, the sense of unreality and dread which descended on one, and some restoration of balance as one saw other men moving forward in a way that seemed commonplace, mechanical, as though at some moment of ordinary routine; the restraint, and the haste that fought against it with every voice in one's being crying out to hurry. Hurry? One cannot hurry, alone, into nowhere, into nothing. Every impulse created immediately its own violent contradiction. The confusion and tumult in his own mind was inseparable from the senseless fury about him, each reinforcing the other. He saw great chunks of the German line blown up, as the artillery blasted a way for them; clouds of dust and smoke screened their advance, but the Hun searched for them scrupulously; the air was alive with the rush and flutter of wings; it was ripped by screaming shells, hissing like tons of molten metal plunging suddenly into water, there was the blast and concussion of their explosion, men smashed, obliterated in sudden eruptions of earth, rent and strewn in bloody fragments, shells that were like hell-cats humped and spitting, little sounds, unpleasantly close, like the plucking of tense strings, and something tangling at his feet, tearing at his trousers and puttees as he stumbled over it, and then a face suddenly, an inconceivably distorted face, which raved and sobbed at him as he fell with it into a shell-hole. He saw with astonishment the bare arse of a Scotsman who had gone into action wearing only a kilt-apron; and then they righted themselves and looked at each other, bewildered and humiliated. There followed a moment of perfect lucidity, while they took a breather; and he found himself, though unwounded, wondering with an insane prudence where the nearest dressing-station was. Other men came up; two more Gordons joined them, and then Mr Halliday, who flung himself on top of them and, keeping his head well down, called them a lot of bloody skulkers. He had a slight wound in the forearm. They made a rush forward again, the dust and smoke clearing a little, and they heard the elastic twang of Mills bombs as they reached an empty trench, very narrow where shelling had not wrecked or levelled it. Mr Halliday was hit again, in the knee, before they reached the trench, and Bourne felt something pluck the front of his tunic at the same time. They pulled Mr Halliday into the trench, and left him with one of the Gordons who had also been hit. Men were converging there, and he went forward with some of his own company again. From the moment he had thrown himself into the shell-hole with the Scotsman something had changed in him; the conflict and tumult of his mind had gone, his mind itself seemed to have gone, to have contracted and hardened within him; fear remained, an implacable and restless fear, but that, too, seemed to have been beaten and forged into a point of exquisite sensibility and to have become indistinguishable from hate. Only the instincts of the beast survived in him, every sense was alert and in that tension was some poignancy. He neither knew where he was, nor whither he was going, he could have no plan because he could foresee nothing, everything happening was inevitable and unexpected, he was an act in a whole chain of acts; and, though his movements had to conform to those of others, spontaneously, as part of some infinitely flexible plan, which he could not comprehend very clearly even in regard to its immediate object, he could rely on no one but himself. They worked round a point still held by machine-guns, through a rather intricate system of trenches linking up shell-craters. The trenches were little more than bolt-holes, through which the machine-gunners, after they had held up the advancing infantry as long as possible, might hope to escape to some other appointed position further back, and resume their work, thus gaining time for the troops behind to recover from the effect of the bombardment, and emerge from their hiding-places. They were singularly brave men, these Prussian machine-gunners, but the extreme of heroism, alike in foe or friend, is indistinguishable from despair. Bourne found himself playing again a game of his childhood, though not now among rocks from which reverberated heat quivered in wavy films, but in made fissures too chalky and unweathered for adequate concealment. One has not, perhaps, at thirty years the same zest in the game as one had at thirteen, but the sense of danger brought into play a latent experience which had become a kind of instinct with him, and he moved in those tortuous ways with the furtive cunning of a stoat or weasel. Stooping low at an angle in the trench he saw the next comparatively straight length empty, and when the man behind was close to him, ran forward still stooping. The advancing line, hung up at one point, inevitably tended to surround it, and it was suddenly abandoned by the few men holding it. Bourne, running, checked as a running Hun rounded the further angle precipitately, saw him stop, shrink back into a defensive posture, and fired without lifting the butt of his rifle quite level with his right breast. The man fell shot in the face, and someone screamed at Bourne to go on; the body choked the narrow angle, and when he put his foot on it squirmed or moved, making him check again, fortunately, as a bomb exploded a couple of yards round the corner. He turned, dismayed, on the man behind him, but behind the bomber he saw the grim bulk of Captain Malet, and his strangely exultant face; and Bourne, incapable of articulate speech, could only wave a hand to indicate the way he divined the Huns to have gone. Captain Malet swung himself above ground, and the men, following, overflowed the narrow channel of the trench; but the two waves, which had swept round the machine-gun post, were now on the point of meeting; men bunched together, and there were some casualties among them before they went to ground again. Captain Malet gave him a word in passing, and Bourne, looking at him with dull uncomprehending eyes, lagged a little to let others intervene between them. He had found himself immediately afterwards next to Company-Sergeant-Major Glasspool, who nodded to him swiftly and appreciatively; and then Bourne understood. He was doing the right thing. In that last rush he had gone on and got into the lead, somehow, for a brief moment; but he realized himself that he had only gone on because he had been unable to stand still. The sense of being one in a crowd did not give him the same confidence as at the start, the present stage seemed to call for a little more personal freedom. Presently, just because they were together, they would rush something in a hurry instead of stalking it. Two men of another regiment, who had presumably got lost, broke back momentarily demoralized, and Sergeant-Major Glasspool confronted them.

'Where the bloody hell do you reckon you're going?'

He rapped out the question with the staccato of a machine-gun; facing their hysterical disorder, he was the living embodiment of a threat.

'We were ordered back,' one said, shamefaced and fearful.

'Yes. You take your fuckin' orders from Fritz,' Glasspool, white-lipped and with heaving chest, shot sneeringly at them. They came to heel quietly enough, but all the rage and hatred in their hearts found an object in him, now. He forgot them as soon as he found them in hand.

'You're all right, chum,' whispered Bourne, to the one who had spoken. 'Get among your own mob again as soon as there's a chance.'

The man only looked at him stonily. In the next rush forward something struck Bourne's helmet, knocking it back over the nape of his neck so that the chin-strap tore his ears. For the moment he thought he had been knocked out, he had bitten his tongue, too, and his mouth was salt with blood. The blow left a deep dent in the helmet, just fracturing the steel. He was still dazed and shaken when they reached some building which he seemed to remember. They were near the railway station.

*　　*　　*　　*

He wished he could sleep, he was heavy with it; but his restless memory made sleep seem something to be resisted as too like death. He closed his eyes and had a vision of men advancing under a rain of shells. They had seemed so toy-like, so trivial and ineffective when opposed to that over-whelming wrath, and yet they had moved forward mechanically as though they were hypnotized or fascinated by some superior will. That had been one of Bourne's most vivid impressions in action, a man close to him moving forward with the jerky motion a clockwork toy has when it is running down; and it had been vivid to him because of the relief with which he had turned to it and away from the confusion and tumult of his own mind. It had seemed impossible to relate that petty, commonplace, unheroic figure, in ill-fitting khaki and a helmet like the barber's basin with which Don Quixote made shift on his adventures, to the moral and spiritual conflict, almost super-human in its agony, within him. Power is measured by the amount of resis-tance which it overcomes, and, in the last resort, the moral power of men was greater than any purely material force, which could be brought to bear on it. It took the chance of death, as one of the chances it was bound to take; though, paradoxically enough, the function of our moral nature consists solely in the assertion of one's own individual will against anything which may be opposed to it, and death, therefore, would imply its extinction in the particular and individual case. The true inwardness of tragedy lies in the fact that its failure is only apparent, and as in the case of the martyr also, the moral conscience of man has made its own deliberate choice, and asserted the freedom of its being. The sense of wasted effort is only true for meaner and more material natures. It took the more horrible chance of mutilation. But as far as Bourne himself, and probably also, since the moral impulse is not necessarily an intellectual act, as far as the majority of his comrades were concerned, its strength and its weakness were inseparably entangled in each other. Whether a man be killed by a rifle-bullet through the brain, or blown into fragments by a high-explosive shell, may seem a matter of indifference to the conscientious objector, or to any other equally well-placed observer, who in point of fact is probably right; but to the poor fool who is a candidate for posthumous honours, and necessarily takes a more directly interested view, it is a question of importance. He is, perhaps, the victim of an illusion, like all who, in the words of Paul, are fools for Christ's sake; but he has seen one man shot cleanly in his tracks and left face downwards, dead, and he has seen another torn into bloody tatters as by some invisible beast, and these experiences had nothing illusory about them: they were actual facts. Death, of course, like chastity, admits of no degree; a man is dead or not dead, and a man is just as dead by one means as by another; but it is infinitely more horrible and revolting to see a man shattered and eviscerated, than to see him shot. And one sees such things; and one suffers vicariously, with the inalienable sympathy of man for man. One forgets quickly. The mind is averted as well as the eyes. It reassures itself after that first despairing cry: 'It is I!'

'No, it is not I. I shall not be like that.'

And one moves on, leaving the mauled and bloody thing behind: gambling, in fact, on that implicit assurance each one of us has of his own immortality. One forgets, but he will remember again later, if only in his sleep.

After all, the dead are quiet. Nothing in the world is more still than a dead man. One sees men living, living, as it were, desperately, and then suddenly emptied of life. A man dies and stiffens into something like a wooden dummy, at which one glances for a second with a furtive curiosity. Suddenly he remembered the dead in Trones Wood, the unburied dead with whom one lived, he might say, cheek by jowl, Briton and Hun impartially confounded, festering, fly-blown corruption, the pasture of rats, blackening in the heat, swollen with distended bellies, or shrivelling away within their mouldering rags; and even when night covered them, one vented in the wind the stench of death. Out of one bloody misery into another, until we break. One must not break. He took in his breath suddenly in a shaken sob, and the mind relinquished its hopeless business. The warm smelly darkness of the tent seemed almost luxurious ease. He drowsed heavily; dreaming of womanly softness, sweetness; but their faces slipped away from him like the reflections in water when the wind shakes it, and his soul sank deeply and more deeply into the healing of oblivion.

The Spanish Farm

La Patrie Est En Danger

R. H. MOTTRAM

A farmer stood watching a battalion of infantry filing into his pasture. A queerer mixture of humanity could not have been imagined. The farmer wore a Dutch cap, spoke Flemish by preference, but could only write French. His farm was called Ferme l'Espagnole — The Spanish Farm — and stood on French soil. The soldiers were the usual English mixture — semi-skilled townsmen, a number of agricultural and other laborers, fewer still of seafaring and waterside folk, and a sprinkling of miners and shepherds, with one or two regulars.

The farmer, Mr. Vanderlynden, Jérôme, described in the communal records as a cultivator, sixty-five years of age, watching his rich grass being tramped to liquid mud under the heavy boots of the incoming files, and the shifting of foot-weary men as they halted in close column, platoon by platoon, made no protest. This was not merely because under the French law he was bound to submit to the needs of the troops, but also because, after twelve months' experience, he had discovered that there were compensations attached to the billeting and encampment of English. They paid so much per officer or man — not always accurately, but promptly always, and what would you more in war-time? The Spanish Farm was less than twenty kilometres from the Front, the actual trenches, whose ground-shaking gun-rumble was always to be heard, whose scouting aeroplanes were visible and audible all day, whose endless flicker of star-shells made green the eastern horizon all night. The realities of the situation were ever present to Mr. Jérôme Vanderlynden, who besides could remember a far worse war, that of 1870. Moreover, the first troops passing that way in the far-off days of 1914 had been French, and had wanted twice as much attention, and had never paid, had even threatened him when he suggested it.

*   *   *   *

Standing with his great, knotted, earthy fists hanging by his side, as the khaki stream poured and poured through the wide-set gate, he passed in review the innumerable units or detachments that had billeted in the Spanish Farm or encamped in its pastures. Uncritical, almost unreasoning, the old peasant was far from being able to define the difference he had felt when the first English arrived. He had heard tell of them, read of them in the paper, but was far from imagining what they might have been like, having no data to go on and no power of imagination. He had been coming in from getting up the last of the potato crop of 1914 when he had found flat-capped, mud-coloured horsemen at his gate. Sure that they were Germans (the Uhlans had been as near as Hazebrouck only a few weeks before), he hastily tied the old white horse in the tombereau, and had gone forward cap in hand. But his daughter Madeleine had already met the soldiers at the gate. A widower for many years, Jérôme Vanderlynden's house was kept by his youngest child, this Madeleine, now in her twentieth year. To say that he believed in her does not do justice to his feelings. She had been the baby of the family, had had a better education than he or his sons, at a convent in St. Omer; added to all this, plus her woman's prestige, was the fact that she inherited (from heaven knows where!) a masterful strain. What she said (and she was not lavish, of words) was attended to. Whether it were education, inspiration, or more probably an appreciation beyond the powers of her father, that told her that English cavalry officers would agree with her, it is certain that she started with those first squadrons of the Cavalry Division a sort of understanding that she would never have attempted with French troops. They paid her lib- erally and treated her respectfully, probably confusing her in their minds with English farmers' wives to whom they were in the habit of paying for hunt damage. They had money — officers and men wanted to supplement their rations and the horses' forage. Madeleine had eggs, coffee, soft bread, beer, fried potatoes, beans, oats. She could and did wash collars and shirts better than the average soldier servant. It took her some time to understand that every English officer required many gallons of water to wash in, at least once a day. But once she had grasped that too, she attended to it, at a small charge.

*   *   *   *

And now it was October, 1915; more troops than ever, especially infantry, were in the Commune, and an interpreter had warned Jérôme Vanderlynden that he would have a whole battalion in the farm. He made no remark, but Madeleine had asked several questions. More awake mentally than her father, it had not escaped her close reading of the paper that a new sort of English troops were coming to France. They were described indifferently as 'Territorials' and as 'New Army' or 'Kitchener's Army,' and neither Madeleine nor indeed the newspapers of the Departement du Nord knew of any difference between them and the Territoriaux of the French system. Madeleine put them down as second-line troops and stored the fact in her vigilant mind.

She came and stood beside her father, as the 10th Battalion, Easthampton-shire Regiment, broke up and moved off to its billets. Two of the sadly depleted companies went to adjacent farms, two remained on the premises. The officers — of whom only twelve survived the battle of Loos — were busy with non-coms., going through nominal rolls, lists of missing men or damaged equipment, trying to disentangle some sort of parade state and indent for replacements.

Madeleine did not bother about them. She said to her father: 'I am going to find the Quarta-mastere!'

She found him, standing amid his stores in the hop-press, and knew him by his gray hair and white-red-white ribbon. She had long ago inquired and found out that this rank in the English Army were chosen from among the old soldiers, and were quickest at getting to business. It had been explained to her that the white-red-white ribbon was for length of good conduct, and secretly tolerant of men's foibles as of a child's, she stored this fact also, for identification purposes.

In this instance, the Mess President having been killed, the old ranker, Lieutenant and Quartermaster John Adams, was acting Mess President, and doing nearly every other duty in the disorganization and readjustment that followed the tragic bungle of the New Army's first offensive.

He greeted her with his professional aplomb: 'Good day, Maddam, dinner for twelve officers; compris, douze!' He held up the fingers of both hands and then two fingers separately.

'All right!' returned Madeleine in English. 'Where are their rations?'

He replied, 'Ah, you're sharp!' and called to his storekeeper, 'Jermyn, officers' rations to Maddam and tell the mess cook!' He went on to bargain for other things — beds for the Colonel, the Adjutant and himself — and in the course of the argument Madeleine informed him that according to General Routine Orders there was to be no smoking in the barns and no unsanitary practices, that all gates must be kept closed, and no movables removed.

Handing him her price list, she withdrew to her long, coffin-shaped stove in the brick-floored kitchen.

*　　*　　*　　*

Dusk settled down on the Spanish Farm — autumn dusk — with swathed mists on the small, flat, chocolate-coloured fields, richest and best tilled in the world — now bare of crops. The brilliant colours of the last hop-leaves and of the regular rows of elms that bordered each pasture were hidden, but the tops of the trees towered above the mist-line into that wide blue vault that the old painters loved, nowhere wider than in the Flemish plain. The Spanish Farm stood on the almost imperceptible southern slope of the sandy ridge that divides in some degree the valley of the Yser from that of the Lys, whose flat meadows lay spread out, almost from Aire to the factory smoke of Armentières, at a slightly lower level to the south. Northward, behind the house, the ground rose very gradually in fertile field and elm-encircled pasture. Westward, black against the last glow of the sunset, two little 'planes droned their way from the aerodromes round St. Omer toward the eastern horizon, where the evening 'hate' was toned down by the distance to the low boom of 'heavies,' the sharper note of the field-guns, the whip-lash crack of rifles and machine-guns, and the flatter, squashed-out reports of mortars and grenades.

The house itself was a single-storied building of immensely thick walls of red brick — much as the settlers under Alva had left it three hundred years before — except for enlargement of windows and re-thatching — though the existing thatch was so old that wall-flowers tasselled its ridge from one octagonal, spoke-tiled chimney-stack to the other. Originally a simple block with a door in the middle, outbuildings had been added at each end, giving it the form of an unfinished quadrangle, the gap toward the south, enclosing the great steaming midden of golden dung. Completely surrounded by a deep, wide moat, access to it was only possible by a brick bridge on the southern side, guarded by a twenty-foot, extinguisher-roofed shot-tower, whose loop-holed bulk now served for tool-shed below and pigeon-loft above.

Further outbuildings stood outside the moat, a few to the north in the smaller pasture behind the house, but a long, broad range of cowshed, stable and hop-press stretched into the ten-acre 'home' or 'manor' pasture.

Never, since Alva last marched that way, had the old semi-fortress been so packed with humanity. Two companies, which even at their present weakness must have numbered over three hundred men, were getting rid of their arms and equipment and filing round to the north pasture where the cookers flared and smoked, the cooks, demoniac in their blackened faces and clothes, ladled out that standard compost that at any time before nine in the morning was denominated 'coffee,' at any hour before or after noon 'soup,' until the end of the day, when, as a last effort, it became 'tea.' Derisive shouts of 'Gyp-oh!' intended to convey that it was accepted for what it was — yesterday's bacon grease, hot water and dust from the floor of a lorry — greeted it, as it splashed into the tendered mess-tins of the jostling crowd.

*   *   *   *

Within the house, in the westward of the two principal rooms, Madeleine, with Berthe, most useful of the Belgian refugees about the place, had got her stove nearly red hot, and was silently, deftly handling her pots and dishes, while the mess cooks unpacked the enamelled plates and cups and carried them through to the other room, where the table was being set by the simple process of spreading sheets of newspapers upon it and arranging the drinking-cups, knives and forks thereon. Bread being cut, there only remained for 'Maddam,' as they called Madeleine, to say that all was ready, so that the brass shell-case in the passage could be used as a gong. The Colonel appeared, and the Adjutant, both regular soldiers, masking whatever they felt under professional passivity. There were no other senior officers; the only surviving Major was with a captainless outlying company. The two companies in the farm were commanded by Lieutenants. The junior officers were all Kitchener enlistments. Some of them had hoped to spend that night in Lille.

The conversation was not so brilliant as the meal. In many a worse billet, the Easthamptons looked back to their night at Spanish Farm. Every one was dog tired and bitterly depressed. The Colonel only sat the length of one cigarette. Adams took his food in his 'bunk.' The junior officers clattered up the narrow, candle-lit stair into the loft, where two of them had a bedstead and two others the floor. The Adjutant was left collating facts and figures, with the Doctor, who was going through his stores. To them came the runner from the guard-room (improvised in a tent at the brick-pillared gate of the pasture).

'Reinforcement officers, sir!'

There entered two rather bewildered young men who had passed during the previous forty-eight hours through every emotion from a desperate fear that the 'victory' of Loos would end the War without their firing a shot, to sheer annoyance at being dumped at a railhead and told to find a battalion in the dark. They had lost everything they had except what they carried on them, and were desperately hungry. The Adjutant surprised even himself at the cordial greeting he gave the two strangers — untried officers from a reserve battalion he had never seen. He knew nothing of their history or capabilities, but the sense of more people behind, coming to fill the gaps, warmed even the professional soldier's trained indifference. He got up and went to the door of the kitchen, calling for 'Maddam' and repeating 'Manjay' in a loud voice to indicate that further refreshment was required.

Madeleine had just finished, with Berthe, the washing and cleaning up of her cooking utensils, and was about to go to bed in her little single bedroom that looked out over the northern pasture. She was just as inclined to cook another meal as a person may be who has already worked eighteen hours and expects to rise at half-past five in the morning. Nor was there anything in the stare of the shorter, fair-haired new arrival, with his stolid silence, to encourage her. But the taller and darker of the two asked her in fair French if she could manage an omelet and some coffee. They regretted deranging her, but had the hunger of a wolf and had not eaten since the morning. Whether it was being addressed in her own tongue, or the fact that the young officer had hit on the things that lay next her hand and would not take five minutes, or whether it was something in the voice, Madeleine acquiesced politely, and set about providing what was asked.

The Adjutant stared. He was not accustomed to interpolations in foreign tongues in his orders. But this young officer was so obviously unconscious of offense, and the interference so opportune, that there was nothing to be said. He talked to the new-comers as they supped, and, apologizing for having to put them in the little ground-floor room with the orderly officer, retired to his own.

Silence and darkness fell upon the Spanish Farm, only broken by the steps of the sentries, the change of guard, and the dull mutter and star-shell flicker from the Line, and for some hours all those human beings that lay in and around the old house lost consciousness of their hopes, fears and wants.

*   *   *   *

English officers and men who billeted in the Spanish Farm (and practically the whole English Army must have passed through or near it at one time or another) to this day speak of it as one of the few places they can still distinguish in the blur of receding memories, one of the few spots of which they have nothing but good to tell. In part this may be easily explained. The old house was comparatively roomy, well kept, water-tight. There was less overcrowding, no leaking roof to drip on one's only dry shirt — and besides, though the regulations were more strictly observed here than anywhere, that fact gave almost an impression of home — order, cleanliness, respect ruled here yet a little — but perhaps there is another reason — perhaps houses so old and so continually handled by human beings have almost a personality of their own: perhaps the Spanish Farm that had sheltered Neapolitan mercenaries fighting the French, Spanish colonists fighting the Flemish, French fighting English or Dutch—and now English and Colonials fighting Germans—perhaps the old building bent and brooded over these last of its many occupants—perhaps knew a little better than other houses what men expected of it.

*   *   *   *

Madeleine thought no more of the War, and the population it had brought to the Spanish Farm, until half-past seven, when the mess-orderlies began to prepare breakfast. Obstinately refusing to allow anyone to touch her stove, she cooked that incomprehensible meal of oat-soup ('porridge' they called it!), and bacon and eggs, after which, she knew, they ate orange confiture. She, her father and the farmhands had long taken their lump of bread and bowl of coffee, standing. Her attention was divided between the hum of the separator in the dairy and her washing drying on the line, when she heard her father's voice calling: 'Madeleine leinsche!' ('Little Madeleine!') She called out that she was in the kitchen.

The old man came, moving more quickly than usual, voluble in Flemish, excited. The soldiers had moved out all the flax-straw lying in the long wooden drying-shed behind the house, on the pasture, and all the machines, reapers and binders, drills and rakes. Moreover, they had taken for firewood hop-poles that had been expressly forbidden.

Madeleine washed her hands at the sink, saying she would see about it. But she was saved the trouble. Her father went out into the yard, unable to keep still in his impatience, and she heard him in altercation with old Adams. They drifted into the mess-room. As she was drying her hands, there was a knock on the kitchen door, and she saw her father ushering in the dark young officer of the evening before. Her brow cleared. She had not the least doubt she could 'manage' the young man.

The young man surpassed expectations. Madeleine found it unnecessary to keep to her rather limited English. His French, while not correct, was expansive. He admitted her version of the farmer's rights under Billeting Law, but would not accept the sum, running into hundreds of francs, which Jérôme Vanderlynden, typical peasant at a bargain, asked for compensation. It appeared that the quiet-looking young man knew something of flax culture and more of agricultural machinery. He quoted within a very little the cost of restacking the flax, oiling the machinery, with the price of two burnt hop-poles. He offered forty francs.

Old Vanderlynden made his usual counter:

'What if I go to Brigade Headquarters about it?'

'Then you will get nothing at all. They are too busy and we move on to-day!'

The old man laughed and slapped his leg.

Madeleine, knowing by experience that the officer had been authorized to spend fifty francs (a sum which appealed to the English, being recognizable as a couple of sovereigns), began to respect him, took the money and signed the receipt.

Left alone, old Jérôme remarked that the young man was very well brought up. Madeleine was looking carefully through her pots and pans to see that nothing had disappeared into the big mess-box.

From the window she saw the battalion paraded, and watched them move off, as she passed hastily from room to room, counting things. Her father was round the outbuildings. The last to go was old Adams with the wagons. A great stillness fell on the old farm, the litter of papers, tins and ashes, and all the unmistakable atmosphere of a crowded place suddenly deserted.

The Raid

HERBERT READ

I. The Coward

It was early summer and the warm sun seemed to reanimate the desolate land. Before one of a group of huts a young subaltern was seated at a table. He was bareheaded and the sun played on the bright yellow strands of his hair. He played nervously with a match-stalk, splintering it with his finger-nails, scraping it aimlessly about the table. The sun played on the white bleached wood of the twirling match-stalk and on the dark blistered polish of the table. Nervous fingers rolled the hard stalk between soft plastic flesh. At times everything was very still. The dreamer wandered. The shreds of match-stalk seemed far away, brittle legs of birds, pattering on the hard brown table. The sun was buoyed in some kind of space, hard to conceive; where, too, the mind swayed in utter helplessness.

Why had all the horror suddenly become potent? Lieutenant P—— had been in France four months now, and all the time, in some degree, his life had been threatened. He had been sick, sick all the time—but the hunted life had each day sunk into renewing sleep; and day had succeeded day, and somehow the faith had been born that the days would pass in such a succession until the long terror was ended. But the present eventuality had made a difference. He had been selected to lead a raid, along with me, and a volunteer party of about thirty men. This sudden actualization of the diffused terror of our existence had made a difference to my friend. I could divine it as he sat there in his restless abstraction.

I was lying within the hut, beneath the corrugated vault of iron. My body was listless, my mind content. I saw P——, crumpled in his chair—his boots drawn under, his untidy puttees, his rounded shoulders and over-big flaxen

460

head. I saw men walking about the grassy plot in front of us, and in the sky, an easier reach for my recumbent eyes, a lark, a dot, a lark that was always singing in this region at the time of our stay there. The lark, and the men walking very near on an horizon, were more real to me than the vague wonder about my fate in the raid. I was afraid, but more interested in P——'s fear. I decided that he must in some way be imprisoned in his flesh — despite that mind, floating vacantly in the ether. He was an undersized but thick-set man of about twenty-three. He had a pale fleshy face and china-blue eyes, a coarse voice and a tendency to blush. He had been a teacher. He had a mother and a sweetheart, and he spent a lot of time writing letters. He never got free from his home thoughts; he was still bound in some sort of personal dependence to these ties. His mind, at any rate, was not free to lead its own existence, or to create the conditions of its existence. I think that is why he was a coward.

For he was a coward, in the only concise sense that can be given to that word. A coward is not merely a man who feels fear. We all experience fear; it is a physical reaction to the unknown extent of danger. But it is only cowardice when it becomes a mental reaction — when the mind, reacting to the flesh, submits to the instincts of the flesh.

As the time appointed for the raid drew nearer, P——'s manner began to change. We had always been thrown together a good deal: we were the only officers in the Company with tastes in common. But we were scarcely friends; there was something physical in his nature which repelled me. But now he began to make up to me more insistently. Presently the remainder of the battalion went into the trenches and we were left to rest and train for our enterprise. P—— then grew more confidential and spoke often of his home affairs. He seemed afraid to be out of my presence. He began to confess to me; to bemoan his fate; to picture the odds against us — the utter unlikelihood that we should ever come out of the business alive.

And then I asked him if he was afraid. He blushed and said: 'Yes, damnably.' He was obviously in an agony of mind, and then I began to have my own fear: that he would bitch the show and bring disgrace on us all. I put this to him. We had left camp and were on a visit to battalion headquarters, a mile or two behind the line. There was some sort of gun emplacement or old trench line into which we had climbed to look out over the sun-soaked plain: the larks were singing as always in the still clear sky. But P——'s face looked aqueous and blotchy. His eyes were uneasy, reflecting all his anguish. After a while I asked him to make a clean breast of it all to the Colonel. But I saw that he would never do that. He just hung his head and looked stupid.

When we reached the battalion I left P—— outside and went into the Colonel's shanty or dugout. I told about P——; deliberately. He was immediately taken off the raid and S——, an elderly subaltern who had already taken part in a previous raid, was asked to take his place. This he did with a bad grace.

P—— was killed in the end in a bombardment some months later. A night of confused darkness and sudden riot.

II. Fear

We greased our hands and faces and then blackened them with burnt cork so that they would not shine out in the dark night. We muffled our rifle slings and accoutrements so that no little noise should betray us. Then we made our way into the trenches to the point selected for our sally. A terrace such as is often found in French fields ran across No Man's Land, at right angles to the trenches. It led to an elbow in the enemy's line, and the concerted plan was that at midnight exactly the artillery and trench mortars should isolate this elbow with a barrage of fire, whilst we penetrated into the trenches and secured some of the enemy, dead or alive. We raiders were to creep along the guiding line of the bank in Indian file until within thirty yards or so of the enemy's position, then to creep round into a compact line facing the trench: this movement to be achieved by midnight. Then, immediately the barrage fell, we were to rush forward and do our best.

It was agreed that I should head the Indian file, and that S—— should bring up the rear. He was to prevent straggling and to see that the line swung round into position when I sent back the signal. The last thing we did before going out was to give each man a stiff dose of rum: then there were a few whispered farewells and a handshake or two. The night was moonless, but fair, and not quite pitch dark. You could distinguish a silhouette against the skyline. As soon as we passed our own wire entanglements we got down on our bellies and began to crawl. I had already explored the ground in two or three special night patrols, and had no difficulty in finding the bank and getting the right direction. I advanced a step at a time, the sergeant close behind me.

I feel that I ought not to neglect a single aspect of that slow advance to the enemy's line, for in those few minutes I experienced a prolonged state of consciousness during which I hung over a pit of fear, weighted down by a long and vivid anticipation of its nature, and now brought to the last tension by this silent agony of deliberate approach. Fear is more powerful in silence and loneliness, for then the mind is more open to the electric uprush of the animal. There is safety in action and unanimity and all the noisy riot of strife—until even that safety is beaten down by the pitiless continuance of physical shock, and then there is only safety in the mind again, if it rise like a holy ghost out of the raw stumps of the body.

I remember for a time feeling my heart unrulily beating in my breast, and a tight constriction at the throat. That was perhaps only excitement, or tense expectation of activity. It was not the shuddering grovelling impulse, the sudden jet of pus into the thrilling blood stream, that would sometimes, on the sudden near detonation of a shell, poison one's humanity. That, as I have said, is the only real kind of fear—the purely physical reaction. From that state a few men can recover because they have minds that can surmount a physical state: an imaginative sense of equilibrium. *Imaginative*—it was the men of imagination that were, if any, the men of courage. The men of mere brute strength, the footballers and school captains, found no way out of the inevitable physical reaction. Their bodies broke in fear because the wild energy of the instinct was impingeing on a brittle red wall of physical being. That was the feel of it, that was the reality. And P——? P—— was in another state of being. Because he had imagination he could visualize and thus anticipate this physical nature of fear. He could immerse himself in the imaginative embodiment of that animalistic impulse, and because he had no faith he had to succumb to that imaginative condition. Faith was the deepest reality we tested as we crawled for a few minutes along that bank—a few minutes that actually seemed an age. Faith was of many kinds. But essentially it was simply a level condition of the mind. It might be Christian—sometimes was, I observed. But more often it was just fatalistic, and by fatalism I mean a resolve to live in peace of mind, in possession of mind, despite any physical environment. Such was the faith, or philosophy, that belonged to a great body of men, and was held in very different degrees of intellectuality and passion. In some—they were the majority—it was a reversion to a primitive state of belief. Every bullet has its billet. What's the use of worryin'? But in others it was a subtler state of consciousness. The war seemed to annihilate all sense of individuality. The mass of it was so immense that oneself as a separate unit could not rationally exist. But there is a sense in which the death of individuality means the birth of personality. This truth is the basis of all sacrifice and martyrdom. A saint may die for his faith, but only because that faith is an expression of his personality. And so in the presence of danger, and in the immediate expectation of death, one can forget the body and its fears and exist wholly as a mind.

III. The Prisoner

We had gone perhaps three parts of our way, when we heard the sound of men working. Muffled coughs, thuds, indefinite clinks. I was nonplussed.

The explanation did not immediately occur to me. It hadn't time. I had a sudden sick fear that we must return, empty-handed shameful fools. I think this thought and image lasted the brief interval I had for reflection. For immediately the sergeant tugged my leg and crept close to my ear. He indicated somehow the right. I turned my head. Two figures loomed indistinctly in the dark. Approaching us. 'We must rush them,' I whispered. The sergeant said: 'Right; you give the tip.' The two figures, blundered nearer. I could see them hesitate across on the other side of the rim of a shell-hole. My heart had suddenly become calm. I was filled with a great exaltation. My body didn't exist, save as a wonderfully unconscious mechanism. I gave a great inhuman cry and dashed forward, barking with my Colt at the shadowy figures not ten yards away. One gave a wild bestial shriek and fell into the darkness. The other fired. We duelled, there in the dark. But I ran on, impelled by an unknown energy, the sergeant by my side. Just then the concerted moment arrived. A dark rainbow of shells hissed through the sky. The flash and detonation of heavy shells. The pale wavering rockets of the star-shells, they curved round us, fell among us. In that incessant theatrical light I saw my enemy dash into the shell-hole at his feet and fall down crying for mercy. I had my foot on his squirming body, sergeant his bayonet. It was an officer. I perceived that quickly, clearly. It was enough. I gave the order: 'Back to the lines.' We turned. The barrage was over now. Only a blind hiss of bullets from the German line. We walked back to the trenches. My men came chattering round, peering with black faces at the prisoner. Prodding him with their bayonets. Crying happily. Lusting to kill him. I tried to keep them off. The prisoner was talking to me, wildly excited. At last he found his French. I understood. He was so pleased! Explained that he was married and had children. He wanted to live. I tried to calm him. He was a professor of philology and lived at Spandau. I took away his revolver; the sergeant took his bright dagger. And thus we reached our own line. As the German hesitated on the parapet someone kicked him violently on the backside, so that he fell down. I cursed the fellow, but didn't stop to identify him. S—— was there, waiting for me, very much mystified by the turn of events, but jubilant at the sight of a prisoner. We made our way to the headquarters' dugout and descended with our charge.

IV. The Colonel

We blinked in the brilliant light of several candles. It was a square dugout with a fixed table served by benches from the walls. To get to the benches we had to crawl under the table. Our Colonel was a Welshman, temporarily attached from another regiment. When away from the trenches he was pleasant enough, though at bottom a weak and emotional nature. We did not trust him, for he was known to be a white-livered 'funk.' A bottle of whisky was by him on the table, as he sat facing the stairway. He had drunk a great deal, for he was highly nervous about the result of the raid, which would reflect on his reputation. He welcomed us effusively. I don't remember all the chatter and confusion in that confined space, but eventually some kind of order did emerge. D——, our signalling officer, who knew German, began to question the prisoner. The poor fellow was docile enough. He gave up his letters, papers and maps, but asked to keep a photograph of his wife, which we allowed. But a more disgusting scene followed. He had on his finger a signet-ring, perhaps rather a pretty one. The Colonel insisted on having it, and because it would not pass the knuckle, urged us to cut it off. The man was in a delirium and of course we disregarded him. But he made efforts to reach the prisoner himself and in the effort fell drunkenly over and rolled under the table. He lay stupidly there and fell to sleep. I watched the prisoner. He was terribly excited, but self-possessed. He was standing against the dark entrance, speaking forcefully and at length. D—— explained to us at intervals. He was passionately defending the German cause, arguing persuasively that we, the English, had been faithless to our common Teutonic stock. The future of Europe was with the Germanic nations; they alone had the energy, the fresh spirit, the nascent culture for the creation of a world polity.

V. The Way Down

S—— left at about two o'clock to report particulars to the Brigade Head-quarters, and at dawn I set out with the prisoner and the happy raiders. We had lost only one man, and there were no serious wounds. We filed down the communication trenches, leisurely enough, for we were tired. Our faces were still black with the charred cork. The sun rose up to greet us, and when finally we got out into the open country the day was warm and beneficent. The larks were singing again, as on my journey up with P——. But now the sky was pulsing with their shrill notes. On the way I talked to the prisoner, and once we rested for a while, sitting side by side on a fallen tree. He explained that when we first surprised them (he was a company officer with his orderly, visiting parties out at work on the battered wire entanglements) they had taken us for Senegalese troops, and his orderly's terror was perhaps largely due to this mistake. But we talked mostly of other things. I was eager to learn anything about their side — their state of mind, their public opinion, the possibility of revolution and an end of all this meaningless strife. Nietzsche was at that time still fresh in my awakening mind, and I stammered in broken enthusiasm about his books, but got no response. But he was too aware of his liberty, his safety, his bodily emancipation, to think of such things now. He was happy to be safe at last, but perhaps he was also a little chagrined. He was amazed at my youth and perhaps a little ashamed of being captured by what looked like a boyish prank. We strolled on again. I only recall his features with difficulty. He was fair and rather short. But I should not know him if I met him again.

When we reached the Brigade Headquarters I handed him over and stayed to watch him questioned. He stood at attention before a table in the open. And when this was done, he was given into the charge of a guard to be taken down to the Divisional camp. I last saw him standing at a distance from me, waiting to move. I gazed at him eagerly, tenderly, for I had conceived some sort of vicarious affection for this man. I had done my best to kill him a few hours before. I waved my hand as he left, but he only answered with a vague smile.

I then made for my battalion reserve and found a tent and a bed. I slept for more than twelve hours and in my sleep, perhaps from weariness, or because of some relaxation in my nerves, my heart seemed to stop and my blood to sweep round in a dark red whirlpool. In my dream I wondered if this was death. But when I awoke I was fresh and content. I was alive. There was light streaming in through the windows, and friendly voices.

All Quiet on the Western Front

ERICH MARIA REMARQUE

I already know the camp on the moors. It was here that Himmelstoss gave Tjaden his education. But now I know hardly anyone here; as ever, all is altered. There are only a few people that I have occasionally met before.

I go through the routine mechanically. In the evenings I generally go to the Soldiers' Home, where the newspapers are laid out, but which I do not read; still, there is a piano there that I am glad enough to play on. Two girls are in attendance, one of them is young.

The camp is surrounded with high barbed-wire fences. If we come back late from the Soldiers' Home we have to show passes. But those who are on good terms with the guard can get through, of course.

Between the junipers and the birch trees on the moor we practise company-drill each day. It is bearable if one expects nothing better. We advance at a run, fling ourselves down, and our panting breath moves the stalks of the grasses and the flowers of the heather to and fro. Looked at so closely one sees the fine sand is composed of millions of the tiniest pebbles as clear as if they had been made in a laboratory. It is strangely inviting to dig one's hand into it.

But most beautiful are the woods with their line of birch trees. Their colour changes with every minute. Now the stems gleam purest white, and between them, airy and silken, hangs the pastel green of the leaves; the next moment all changes to an opalescent blue, as the shivering breezes pass down from the heights and touch the green lightly away; and again in one place it deepens almost to black as a cloud passes over the sun. And this shadow moves like a ghost through the dim trunks and passes far out over the moor to the sky — then the birches stand out again like gay banners on white poles, with their red and gold patches of autumn-tinted leaves.

I often become so lost in the play of soft light and transparent shadow, that I almost fail to hear the commands. It is when one is alone that one begins to observe Nature and to love her. And here I have not much companionship, and do not even desire it. We are too little acquainted with one another to do more than joke a bit and play poker or nap in the evenings.

Alongside our camp is the big Russian prison camp. It is separated from us by a wire fence, but in spite of this the prisoners come across to us. They seem nervous and fearful, though most of them are big fellows with beards — they look like meek, scolded, St. Bernard dogs.

They slink about our camp and pick over the garbage tins. One can imagine what they find there. With us food is pretty scarce and none too good at that — turnips cut into six pieces and boiled in water, and unwashed carrot tops; — mouldy potatoes are tit-bits, and the chief luxury is a thin rice soup in which float little bits of beef-sinew, but these are cut up so small that they take a lot of finding.

Everything gets eaten, notwithstanding, and if ever anyone is so well off as not to want all his share, there are a dozen others standing by ready to relieve him of it. Only the dregs that the ladle cannot reach are tipped out and thrown into the garbage tins. Along with that sometimes go a few turnip peelings, mouldy bread crusts and all kinds of muck.

This thin, miserable, dirty garbage is the objective of the prisoners. They pick it out of the stinking tins greedily and go off with it under their blouses.

It is strange to see these enemies of ours so close up. They have faces that make one think — honest peasant faces, broad foreheads, broad noses, broad mouths, broad hands, and thick hair.

They ought to be put to threshing, reaping, and apple picking. They look just as kindly as our own peasants in Friesland.

It is distressing to watch their movements, to see them begging for something to eat. They are all rather feeble, for they only get enough nourishment to keep them from starving. Ourselves we have not had sufficient to eat for long enough. They have dysentery; furtively many of them display the blood-stained tails of their shirts. Their backs, their necks are bent, their knees sag, their heads droop as they stretch out their hands and beg in the few words of German that they know — beg with those soft, deep, musical voices, that are like warm stoves and cosy rooms at home.

Some men there are who give them a kick, so that they fall over; — but those are not many. The majority do nothing to them, just ignore them. Occasionally, when they are too grovelling, it makes a man mad and then he kicks them. If only they would not look at one so—What great misery can be in two such small spots, no bigger than a man's thumb—in their eyes!

They come over to the camp in the evenings and trade. They exchange whatever they possess for bread. Often they have fair success, because they have very good boots and ours are bad. The leather of their knee boots is wonderfully soft, like suede. The peasants among us who get tit-bits sent from home can afford to trade. The price of a pair of boots is about two or three loaves of army bread, or a loaf of bread and a small, tough ham sausage.

But most of the Russians have long since parted with whatever things they had. Now they wear only the most pitiful clothing, and try to exchange little carvings and objects that they have made out of shell fragments and copper driving bands. Of course, they don't get much for such things, though they may have taken immense pains with them—they go for a slice or two of bread. Our peasants are hard and cunning when they bargain. They hold the piece of bread or sausage right under the nose of the Russian till he grows pale with greed and his eyes bulge and then he will give anything for it. The peasants wrap up their booty with the utmost solemnity, and then get out their big pocket knives, and slowly and deliberately cut off a slice of bread for themselves from their supply and with every mouthful take a piece of the good, tough sausage and so reward themselves with a good feed. It is distressing to watch them take their afternoon meal thus; one would like to crack them over their thick pates. They rarely give anything away. How little we understand one another!

I am often on guard over the Russians. In the darkness one sees their forms move like sick storks, like great birds. They come close up to the wire fence and lean their faces against it; their fingers hook round the mesh. Often many stand side by side, and breathe the wind that comes down from the moors and the forest.

They rarely speak and then only a few words. They are more human and more brotherly towards one another, it seems to me, than we are. But perhaps that is merely because they feel themselves to be more unfortunate than us. Anyway the war is over so far as they are concerned. But to wait for dysentery is not much of a life either.

The Territorials who are in charge of them say that they were much more lively at first. They used to have intrigues among themselves, as always happens, and it would often come to blows and knives. But now they are quite apathetic, and listless.

They stand at the wire fence; sometimes one goes away and then another at once takes his place in the line. Most of them are silent; occasionally one begs a cigarette butt.

I see their dark forms, their beards move in the wind. I know nothing of them except that they are prisoners, and that is exactly what troubles me. Their life is obscure and guiltless; — if I could know more of them, what their names are, how they live, what they are waiting for, what are their burdens, then my emotion would have an object and might become sympathy. But as it is I perceive behind them only the suffering of the creature, the awful melancholy of life and the pitilessness of men.

A word of command has made these silent figures our enemies; a word of command might transform them into our friends. At some table a document is signed by some persons whom none of us knows, and then for years together that very crime on which formerly the world's condemnation and severest penalty fell, becomes our highest aim. But who can draw such a distinction when he looks at these quiet men with their childlike faces and apostles' beards. Any non-commissioned officer is more of an enemy to a recruit, any schoolmaster to a pupil than they are to us. And yet we would shoot at them again and they at us if they were free.

I am frightened: I dare think this way no more. This way lies the abyss. It is not now the time; but I will not lose these thoughts, I will keep them, shut them away until the war is ended. My heart beats fast: this is the aim, the great, the sole aim, that I have thought of in the trenches; that I have looked for as the only possibility of existence after this annihilation of all human feeling; this is a task that will make life afterward worthy of these hideous years.

I take out my cigarettes, break each one in half and give them to the Russians. They bow to me and then they light the cigarettes. Now red points glow in every face. They comfort me; it looks as though there were little windows in dark village cottages saying that behind them are rooms full of peace.

The days go by. On a foggy morning another of the Russians is buried; almost every day one of them dies. I am on guard during the burial. The prisoners sing a chorale, they sing in parts, and it sounds almost as if there were no voices, but an organ far away on the moor.

The burial is quickly over.

In the evening they stand again at the wire fence and the wind comes down to them from the beech woods. The stars are cold.

I now know a few of those who speak a little German. There is a musician amongst them, he says he used to be a violinist in Berlin. When he hears that I can play the piano he fetches his violin and plays. The others sit down and lean their backs against the fence. He stands up and plays, sometimes he has that absent expression which violinists get when they close their eyes; or again he sways the instrument to the rhythm and smiles across to me.

He plays mostly folk-songs and the others hum with him. They are like a country of dark hills that sing far down under the ground. The sound of the violin stands like a slender girl above it and is clear and alone. The voices cease and the violin continues alone. In the night it is so thin it sounds frozen; one must stand close up; it would be much better in a room; — out here it makes a man grow sad.

Because I have already had a long leave I get none on Sundays. So the last Sunday before I go back to the front my father and eldest sister come over to see me. All day we sit in the Soldiers' Home. Where else could we go, we don't want to stay in the camp. About midday we go for a walk on the moors.

The hours are a torture; we do not know what to talk about, so we speak of my mother's illness. It is now definitely cancer, she is already in the hospital and will be operated on shortly. The doctors hope she will recover, but we have never heard of cancer being cured.

"Where is she then?" I ask.

"In the Luisa Hospital," says my father.

"In which class?"

"Third. We must wait till we know what the operation costs. She wanted to be in the third herself. She said that then she would have some company. And besides it is cheaper."

"So she is lying there with all those people. If only she could sleep properly."

My father nods. His face is broken and full of furrows. My mother has always been sickly; and though she has only gone to the hospital when she has been compelled to, it has cost a great deal of money, and my father's life has been practically given up to it.

"If only I knew how much the operation costs," says he.

"Have you not asked?"

"Not directly, I cannot do that — the surgeon might take it amiss and that would not do, he must operate on Mother."

Yes, I think bitterly, that's how it is with us, and with all poor people. They don't dare to ask the price, but worry themselves dreadfully beforehand about it; but the others, for whom it is not important, they settle the price first as a matter of course. And the doctor does not take it amiss from them.

"And the dressings afterwards are so expensive," says my father.

"Doesn't the Invalid's Fund pay anything toward it, then?" I ask.

"Mother has been ill too long."

"Have you any money at all?"

He shakes his head: "No, but I can do some overtime."

I know. He will stand at his desk folding and pasting and cutting until twelve o'clock at night. At eight o'clock in the evening he will eat some of the miserable rubbish they get in exchange for their food tickets, then he will take a powder for his headache and work on.

In order to cheer him up a bit I tell him a few stories, soldiers' jokes, and the like, about generals and sergeant-majors.

Afterwards I accompany them both to the rail-way station. They give me a pot of jam and a bag of potato-cakes that my mother has made for me.

Then they go off and I return to the camp.

In the evening I spread the jam on the cakes and eat some. But I have no taste for them. So I go out to give them to the Russians. Then it occurs to me that my mother cooked them herself and that she was probably in pain as she stood before the hot stove. I put the bag back in my pack and take only two cakes to the Russians.

Appendix A

The Repression of War Experience[1]

W. H. R. RIVERS

I do not attempt to deal in this paper with the whole problem of the part taken by repression in the production and maintenance of the war-neuroses. Repression is so closely bound up with the pathology and treatment of these states that the full consideration of its rôle would amount to a complete study of neurosis in relation to the war.

It is necessary at the outset to consider an ambiguity in the use of the term "repression" as it is now used by writers on the pathology of the mind and nervous system. The term is currently used in two senses which should be carefully distinguished from one another. It is used for the *process* whereby a person endeavours to thrust out of his memory some part of his mental content, and it is also used for the *state* which ensues when, either through this process or by some other means, part of the mental content has become inaccessible to manifest consciousness. In the second sense the word is used for a state which corresponds closely with that known as dissociation,[2] but it is useful to distinguish mere inaccessibility to memory from the special kind of separation from the rest of the mental content which is denoted by the term dissociation. The state of inaccessibility may therefore be called "suppression" in distinction from the process of repression. In this paper I use "repression" for the active or voluntary process by which it is attempted to remove some part of the mental content out of the field of attention with the aim of making it inaccessible to memory and producing the state of suppression.

Using the word in this sense, repression is not in itself a pathological process, nor is it necessarily the cause of pathological states. On the contrary, it is a necessary element in education and in all social progress. It is not

473

repression in itself which is harmful, but repression under conditions in which it fails to adapt the individual to his environment.

It is in times of special stress that these failures of adaptation are especially liable to occur, and it is not difficult to see why disorders due to this lack of adaptation should be so frequent at the present time. There are few, if any, aspects of life in which repression plays so prominent and so necessary a part as in the preparation for war. The training of a soldier is designed to adapt him to act calmly and methodically in the presence of events naturally calculated to arouse disturbing emotions. His training should be such that the energy arising out of these emotions is partly damped by familiarity, partly diverted into other channels. The most important feature of the present war in its relation to the production of neurosis is that the training in repression normally spread over years has had to be carried out in short spaces of time, while those thus incompletely trained have had to face strains such as have never previously been known in the history of mankind. Small wonder that the failures of adaptation should have been so numerous and so severe.

I do not now propose to consider this primary mental problem of the part played by repression in original production of the war-neuroses. The process of repression does not cease when some shock or strain has removed the soldier from the scene of warfare, but it may take an active part in the maintenance of the neurosis. New symptoms often arise in hospital or at home which are not the immediate consequence of war experience, but are due to repression of painful memories and thoughts, or of unpleasant affective states arising out of reflection concerning this experience. It is with the repression of the hospital and of the home rather than with the repression of the trenches that I deal in this paper. I propose to illustrate by a few sample cases some of the effects which may be produced by repression and the line of action by which these effects may be remedied. I hope to show that many of the most trying and distressing symptoms from which the subjects of war-neurosis suffer are not the necessary result of the strain and shocks to which they have been exposed in warfare, but are due to the attempt to banish from the mind distressing memories of warfare or painful affective states which have come into being as the result of their war experience.

Everyone who has had to treat cases of war-neurosis, and especially that form of neurosis dependent on anxiety, must have been faced by the problem what advice to give concerning the attitude the patient should adopt towards his war experience. It is natural to thrust aside painful memories just as it is natural to avoid dangerous or horrible scenes in actuality. This natural tendency to banish the distressing or the horrible is especially pronounced in those whose powers of resistance have been lowered by the long-continued strains of trench life, the shock of shell explosion, or other catastrophe of warfare. Even if patients were left to themselves, most would naturally strive to forget distressing memories and thoughts. They are, however, very far from being left to themselves, the natural tendency to repress being in my experience almost universally fostered by their relatives and friends, as well as by their medical advisers. Even when patients have themselves realised the impossibility of forgetting their war experiences and have recognised the hopeless and enervating character of the treatment by repression, they are often induced to attempt the task in obedience to medical orders. The advice which has usually been given to my patients in other hospitals is that they should endeavour to banish all thoughts of war from their minds. In some cases conversation between patients, or with visitors, about the war is strictly forbidden, and the patients are instructed to lead their thoughts to other topics, to beautiful scenery and other aspects of experience.

To a certain extent this policy is perfectly sound. Nothing annoys a nervous patient more than the continual inquiries of his relatives and friends about his experiences at the Front, not only because it awakens painful memories, but also because of the obvious futility of most of the questions and the hopelessness of bringing the realities home to his hearers. Moreover, the assemblage together in a hospital of a number of men with little in common except their war experiences, naturally leads their conversation far too frequently to this topic, and even among those whose memories are not especially distressing, it tends to enhance the state for which the term "fed up" seems to be the universal designation.

It is, however, one thing that those who are suffering from the shocks and strains of warfare should dwell continually on their war experience or be subjected to importunate inquiries; it is quite another matter to attempt to banish such experience from their minds altogether. The cases I am about to record illustrate the evil influence of this latter course of action and the good effects which follow its cessation.

The first case is that of a young officer who was sent home from France on account of a wound received just as he was extricating himself from a mass of earth in which he had been buried. When he reached hospital in England he was nervous and suffered from disturbed sleep and loss of appetite. When his wound had healed he was sent home on leave, where his nervous symptoms became more pronounced so that at his next board his leave was extended. He was for a time an out-patient at a London hospital and was then sent to a convalescent home in the country. Here he continued to sleep badly, with disturbing dreams of warfare, and became very anxious about himself and his prospects of recovery. Thinking he might improve if he rejoined his battalion, he made so light of his condition at his next medical board that he was on the point of being returned to duty when special inquiries about his sleep led to his being sent to Craiglockhart War Hospital for further observation and treatment. On admission he reported that it always took him long to get to sleep at night and that when he succeeded he had vivid dreams of warfare. He could not sleep without a light in his room, because in the dark his attention was attracted by every sound. He had been advised by everyone he had consulted, whether medical or lay, that he ought to banish all unpleasant and disturbing thoughts from his mind. He had been occupying himself for every hour of the day in order to follow this advice and had succeeded in restraining his memories and anxieties during the day, but as soon as he went to bed they would crowd upon him and race through his mind hour after hour, so that every night he dreaded to go to bed.

When he had recounted his symptoms and told me about his method of dealing with his disturbing thoughts, I asked him to tell me candidly his own opinion concerning the possibility of keeping these obtrusive visitors from his mind. He said at once that it was obvious to him that memories such as those he had brought with him from the war could never be forgotten. Nevertheless, since he had been told by everyone that it was his duty to forget them, he had done his utmost in this direction. I then told the patient my own views concerning the nature and treatment of his state. I agreed with him that memories could not be expected to disappear from the mind and advised him no longer to try to banish them, but that he should see whether it was not possible to make them tolerable, if not pleasant, companions instead of evil influences which forced themselves upon his mind whenever the silence and inactivity of the night came round. The possibility of such a line of treatment had never previously occurred to him, but my plan seemed reasonable and he promised to give it a trial. We talked about his war experiences and his anxieties, and following this he had the best night he had had for five months. During the following week he had a good deal of difficulty in sleeping, but his sleeplessness no longer had the painful and distressing quality which had been previously given to it by the intrusion of painful thoughts of warfare. In so far as unpleasant thoughts came to him these were concerned with domestic anxieties rather than with the memories of war, and even these no longer gave rise to the dread which had previously troubled him. His general health improved; his power of sleeping gradually increased and he was able after a time to return to duty, not in the hope that this duty might help him to forget, but with some degree of confidence that he was really fit for it.

The case I have just narrated is a straightforward example of anxiety-neurosis which made no real progress as long as the patient tried to keep out of his mind the painful memories and anxieties which had been aroused in his mind by reflection on his past experience, his present state and the chance of his fitness for duty in the future. When in place of running away from these unpleasant thoughts he faced them boldly and allowed his mind to dwell upon them in the day, they no longer raced through his mind at night and disturbed his sleep by terrifying dreams of warfare.

The next case is that of an officer whose burial as the result of a shell-explosion had been followed by symptoms pointing to some degree of cerebral concussion. In spite of severe headache, vomiting and disorder of micturition, he remained on duty for more than two months. He then collapsed altogether after a very trying experience in which he had gone out to seek a fellow officer and had found his body blown into pieces with head and limbs lying separated from the trunk. From that time he had been haunted at night by the vision of his dead and mutilated friend. When he slept he had nightmares in which his friend appeared, sometimes as he had seen him mangled on the field, sometimes in the still more terrifying aspect of one whose limbs and features had been eaten away by leprosy. The mutilated or leprous officer of the dream would come nearer and nearer until the patient suddenly awoke pouring with sweat and in a state of the utmost terror. He dreaded to go to sleep, and spent each day looking forward in painful anticipation of the night. He had been advised to keep all thoughts of the war from his mind, but the experience which recurred so often at night was so insistent that he could not keep it wholly from his thoughts, much as he tried to do so. Nevertheless, there is no question but that he was striving by day to dispel memories only to bring them upon him with redoubled force and horror when he slept.

The problem before me in this case was to find some aspect of the painful experience which would allow the patient to dwell upon it in such a way as to relieve its horrible and terrifying character. The aspect to which I drew his attention was that the mangled state of the body of his friend was conclusive evidence that he had been killed outright, and had been spared the prolonged suffering which is too often the fate of those who sustain mortal wounds. He brightened at once, and said that this aspect of the case had never occurred to him, nor had it been suggested by any of those to whom he had previously related his story. He saw at once that this was an aspect of his experience upon which he could allow his thoughts to dwell. He said he would no longer attempt to banish thoughts and memories of his friend from his mind, but would think of the pain and suffering he had been spared. For several nights he had no dreams at all, and then came a night in which he dreamt that he went out into No Man's Land to seek his friend, and saw his mangled body just as in other dreams, but without the horror which had always previously been present. He knelt beside his friend to save for the relatives any objects of value which were upon the body, a pious duty he had fulfilled in the actual scene, and as he was taking off the Sam Browne belt he woke, with none of the horror and terror of the past, but weeping gently, feeling only grief for the loss of a friend. Some nights later he had another dream in which he met his friend, still mangled, but no longer terrifying. They talked together, and the patient told the history of his illness and how he was now able to speak to him in comfort and without horror or undue distress. Once only during his stay did he again experience horror in connection with any dream of his friend. During the few days following his discharge from hospital the dream recurred once or twice with some degree of its former terrifying quality, but in his last report to me he had only had one unpleasant dream with a different content, and was regaining his normal health and strength.

In the two cases I have described there can be little question that the most distressing symptoms were being produced or kept in activity by reason of repression. The cessation of the repression was followed by the disappearance of the most distressing symptoms, and great improvement in the general health. It is not always, however, that the line of treatment adopted in these cases is so successful. Sometimes the experience which a patient is striving to forget is so utterly horrible or disgusting, so wholly free from any redeeming feature which can be used as a means of readjusting the attention, that it is difficult or impossible to find an aspect which will make its contemplation endurable. Such a case is that of a young officer who was flung down by the explosion of a shell so that his face struck the distended abdomen of a German several days dead, the impact of his fall rupturing the swollen corpse. Before he lost consciousness the patient had clearly realised his situation, and knew that the substance which filled his mouth and produced the most horrible sensations of taste and smell was derived from the decomposed entrails of an enemy. When he came to himself he vomited profusely, and was much shaken, but "carried on" for several days, vomiting frequently, and haunted by persistent images of taste and smell.

When he came under my care, several months later, suffering from horrible dreams, in which the events I have narrated were faithfully reproduced, he was striving by every means in his power to keep the disgusting and painful memory from his mind. His only period of relief had occurred when he had gone into the country, far from all that could remind him of the war. This experience, combined with the horrible nature of his memory and images, not only made it difficult for him to discontinue the repression, but also made me hesitate to advise this measure with any confidence. During his stay in hospital the dream became less frequent and less terrible, but it still recurred, and it was thought best that he should leave the Army and seek the conditions which had previously given him relief.

A more frequent cause of failure or slight extent of improvement is met with in cases in which the repression has been allowed to continue for so long that it has become a habit. Such a case is that of an officer above the average age who, while looking at the destruction wrought by a shell explosion, lost consciousness, probably as the result of a shock caused by a second shell. He was so ill in France that he could tell little about his state there. When admitted to hospital in England he had lost power and sensation in his legs, and was suffering from severe headache, sleeplessness and terrifying dreams. He was treated by hypnotism and hypnotic drugs, and was advised neither to read the papers nor talk with anyone about the war. After being about two months in hospital be was given three months' leave. On going home he was so disturbed by remarks about the war that he left his relatives and buried himself in the heart of the country, where he saw no one, read no papers, and resolutely kept his mind from all thoughts of war. With the aid of aspirin and bromides he slept better and had less headache, but when at the end of his period of leave he appeared before a medical board and the President asked a question about the trenches he broke down completely and wept. He was given another two months' leave, and again repaired to the country to continue the treatment by isolation and repression. This went on until the order that all officers must be in hospital or on duty led to his being sent to an inland watering-place, where no inquiries were made about his anxieties or memories, but he was treated by baths, electricity and massage. He rapidly became worse; his sleep, which had improved, became as bad as ever, and he was transferred to Craiglockhart War Hospital. He was then very emaciated, with a constant expression of anxiety and dread. His legs were still weak, and he was able to take very little exercise or apply his mind for any time. His chief complaint was of sleeplessness and frequent dreams in which war scenes were reproduced, while all kinds of distressing thoughts connected with the war would crowd into his mind as he was trying to get to sleep.

He was advised to give up the practice of repression, to read the papers, talk occasionally about the war, and gradually accustom himself to thinking of, and hearing about, war experience. He did so, but in a half-hearted manner, being convinced that the ideal treatment was that he had so long followed. He was reluctant to admit that the success of a mode of treatment which led him to break down and weep when the war was mentioned was of a very superficial kind. Nevertheless, he improved distinctly and slept better. The reproduction of scenes of war in his dreams became less frequent, and were replaced by images the material of which was provided by scenes of home-life. He became able to read the papers without disturbance, but was loth to acknowledge that his improvement was connected with this ability to face thoughts of war, saying that he had been as well when following his own treatment by isolation, and he evidently believed that he would have recovered if he had not been taken from his retreat and sent into hospital. It soon became obvious that the patient would be of no further service in the Army, and he relinquished his commission.

I cite this case not so much as an example of failure, or relative failure, of the treatment by removal of repression, for it is probable that such relaxation of repression as occurred was a definite factor in his improvement. I cite it rather as an example of the state produced by long-continued repression and of the difficulties which arise when the repression has had such apparent success as to make the patient believe in it.

In the cases I have just narrated there was no evidence that the process of repression had produced a state either of suppression or dissociation. The memories of the painful experience were at hand ready to be recalled or even to obtrude themselves upon consciousness at any moment. A state in which repressed elements of the mental content find their expression in dreams may perhaps be regarded as the first step towards suppression or dissociation, but if so, it forms a very early stage of the process.

There is no question that some people are more liable to become the subjects of dissociation or splitting of consciousness than others. In some persons there is probably an innate tendency in this direction; in others the liability arises through some shock or illness; while other persons become especially susceptible as the result of having been hypnotised.

Not only do shock and illness produce a liability to suppression, but these factors may also act as its immediate precursors and exciting causes. How far the process of voluntary repression can produce this state is more doubtful. It is probable that it only has this effect in persons who are especially prone to the occurrence of suppression. The great frequency of the process of voluntary repression in cases of war-neurosis might be expected to provide us with definite evidence on this head and there is little doubt that such evidence is present. As an example I may cite the case of a young officer who had done well in France until he had been deprived of consciousness by a shell explosion. The next thing he remembered was being conducted by his servant towards the base, thoroughly broken down. On admission into hospital he suffered from fearful headaches and had hardly any sleep, and when he slept he had terrifying dreams of warfare. When he came under my care two months later his chief complaint was that whereas ordinarily he felt cheerful and keen on life, there would come upon him at times, with absolute suddenness, the most terrible depression, a state of a kind absolutely different from an ordinary fit of "the blues," having a quality which he could only describe as "something quite on its own."

For some time he had no attack and seemed as if he had not a care in the world. Ten days after admission he came to me pale and with a tense anxious expression which wholly altered his appearance. A few minutes earlier he had been writing a letter in his usual mood, when there descended upon him a state of deep depression and despair which seemed to have no reason. He had had a pleasant and not too tiring afternoon on some neighbouring hills, and there was nothing in the letter he was writing which could be supposed to have suggested anything painful or depressing. As we talked the depression cleared off and in about ten minutes he was nearly himself again. He had no further attack of depression for nine days, and then one afternoon, as he was standing looking idly from a window, there suddenly descended upon him the state of horrible dread. I happened to be away from the hospital and he had to fight it out alone. The attack was more severe than usual and lasted for several hours. It was so severe that he believed he would have shot himself if his revolver had been accessible. On my return to the hospital some hours after the onset of the attack he was better, but still looked pale and anxious. His state of reasonless dread had passed into one of depression and anxiety natural to one who recognises that he has been through an experience which has put his life in danger and is liable to recur.

The gusts of depression to which this patient was subject were of the kind which I was then inclined to ascribe to the hidden working of some forgotten yet active experience, and it seemed natural at first to think of some incident during the time which elapsed between the shell explosion which deprived him of consciousness and the moment when he came to himself walking back from the trenches. I considered whether this was not a case in which the lost memory might be recovered by means of hypnotism, but in the presence of the definite tendency to dissociation I did not like to employ this means of diagnosis, and less drastic methods of recovering any forgotten incident were without avail.

It occurred to me that the soldier who was accompanying the patient on his walk from the trenches might be able to supply a clue to some lost memory. While waiting for an answer to this inquiry I discovered that behind his apparent cheerfulness at ordinary times the patient was the subject of grave apprehensions about his fitness for further service in France, which he was not allowing himself to entertain owing to the idea that such thoughts were equivalent to cowardice, or might at any rate be so interpreted by others. It became evident that he had been practising a systematic process of repression of these thoughts and apprehensions, and the question arose whether this repression might not be the source of his attacks of depression rather than some forgotten experience. The patient had already become familiar with the idea that his gusts of depression might be due to the activity of some submerged experience and it was only necessary to consider whether we had not hitherto mistaken the repressed object. Disagreeable as was the situation in which he found himself, I advised him that it was one which it was best to face, and that it was of no avail to pretend that it did not exist. I pointed out that this procedure might produce some discomfort and unhappiness, but that it was far better to suffer so than continue in a course whereby painful thoughts were pushed into hidden recesses of his mind, only to accumulate such force as to make them well up and produce attacks of depression so severe as to put his life in danger from suicide. He agreed to face the situation and no longer to continue his attempt to banish his apprehensions. From this time he had only one transient attack of morbid depression following a minor surgical operation. He became less cheerful generally and his state acquired more closely the usual characters of anxiety-neurosis, and this was so persistent that he was finally passed by a medical board as unfit for military service.

In the cases I have recorded, the elements of the mental content which were the object of repression were chiefly distressing memories. In the case just quoted painful anticipations were prominent, and probably had a place among the objects of repression in other cases. Many other kinds of mental experience may be similarly repressed. Thus, after one of my patients had for long baffled all attempts to discover the source of his trouble, it finally appeared that he was attempting to banish from his mind feelings of shame due to his having broken down. Great improvement rapidly followed a line of action in which he faced this shame and thereby came to see how little cause there was for this emotion. In another case an officer had carried the repression of grief concerning the general loss of life and happiness through the war to the point of suppression, the suppressed emotion finding vent in attacks of weeping, which came on suddenly with no apparent cause. In this case the treatment was less successful, and I cite it only to illustrate the variety of experience which may become the object of repression.

I will conclude my record by a brief account of a case which is interesting in that it might well have occurred in civil practice. A young officer after more than two years' service had failed to get to France, in spite of his urgent desires in that direction. Repeated disappointments in this respect, combined with anxieties connected with his work, had led to the development of a state in which he suffered from troubled sleep, with attacks of somnambulism by night and "fainting fits" by day. Some time after he came under my care I found that, acting under the advice of every doctor he had met, he had been systematically thrusting all thought of his work out of his mind, with the result that when he went to bed battalion orders and other features of his work as an adjutant raced in endless succession through his mind and kept him from sleeping. I advised him to think of his work by day, even to plan what he would do when he returned to his military duties. The troublesome night-thoughts soon went; he rapidly improved and returned to duty. When last he wrote his hopes of general service had at last been realised.

In the cases recorded in this paper the patients had been repressing certain painful elements of their mental content. They had been deliberately practising what we must regard as a definite course of treatment, in nearly every case adopted on medical advice, in which they were either deliberately thrusting certain unpleasant memories or thoughts from their minds or were occupying every moment of the day in some activity in order that these thoughts might not come into the focus of attention. At the same time they were suffering from highly distressing symptoms which disappeared or altered in character when the process of repression ceased. Moreover, the symptoms by which they had been troubled were such as receive a natural, if not obvious, explanation as the result of the repression they had been practising. If unpleasant thoughts are voluntarily repressed during the day, it is natural that they should rise into activity when the control of the waking state is removed by sleep or is weakened in the state which precedes and follows sleep and occupies its intervals. If the painful thoughts have been kept from the attention throughout the day by means of occupation, it is again natural that they should come into activity when the silence and isolation of the night make occupation no longer possible. It seems as if the thoughts repressed by day assume a painful quality when they come to the surface at night far more intense than is ever attained if they are allowed to occupy the attention during the day. It is as if the process of repression keeps the painful memories or thoughts under a kind of pressure during the day, accumulating such energy by the time night comes that they race through the mind with abnormal speed and violence when the patient is wakeful, or take the most vivid and painful forms when expressed by the imagery of dreams.

When such distressing, if not terrible, symptoms disappear or alter in character as soon as repression ceases, it is natural to conclude that the two processes stand to one another in the relation of cause and effect, but so great is the complexity of the conditions with which we are dealing in the medicine of the mind that it is necessary to consider certain alternative explanations.

The disappearance or improvement of symptoms on the cessation of voluntary repression may be regarded as due to the action of one form of the principle of catharsis. This term is generally used for the agency which is operative when a suppressed or dissociated body of experience is brought to the surface so that it again becomes reintegrated with the ordinary personality. It is no great step from this to the mode of action recorded in this paper, in which experience on its way towards suppression has undergone a similar, though necessarily less extensive, process of reintegration.

There is, however, another form of catharsis which may have been operative in some of the cases I have described. It often happens in cases of war-neurosis, as in neurosis in general, that the sufferers do not suppress their painful thoughts, but brood over them constantly until their experience assumes vastly exaggerated and often distorted importance and significance. In such cases the greatest relief is afforded by the mere communication of these troubles to another. This form of catharsis may have been operative in relation to certain kinds of experience in some of my cases, and this complicates our estimation of the therapeutic value of the cessation of repression. I have, however, carefully chosen for record on this occasion cases in which the second form of catharsis, if present at all, formed an agency altogether subsidiary to that afforded by the cessation of repression.

Another complicating factor which may have entered into the therapeutic process in some of the cases is re-education. This certainly came into play in the case of the patient who had the terrifying dreams of his mangled friend. In his case the cessation of repression was accompanied by the direction of the attention of the patient to an aspect of his painful memories which he had hitherto completely ignored. The process by which his attention was thus directed to a neglected aspect of his experience introduced a factor which must be distinguished from the removal of repression itself. The two processes are intimately associated, for it was largely, if not altogether, the new view of his experience which made it possible for the patient to dwell upon his painful memories. In some of the other cases this factor of re-education undoubtedly played a part, not merely in making possible the cessation of repression, but also in helping the patient to adjust himself to the situation with which he was faced, thus contributing positively to the recovery or improvement which followed the cessation of repression.

A more difficult and more contentious problem arises when we consider how far the success which attended the cessation of repression may have been, wholly or in part, due to faith and suggestion. Here, as in every branch of therapeutics, whether it be treatment by drugs, diet, baths, electricity, persuasion, re-education or psychoanalysis, we come up against the difficulty raised by the pervasive and subtle influence of these agencies working behind the scenes. In the subject before us, as in every other kind of medical treatment, we have to consider whether the changes which occurred may have been due, not to the agency which lay on the surface and was the motive of the treatment, but at any rate, in part, to the influence, so difficult to exclude, of faith and suggestion. In my later work I have come to believe so thoroughly in the injurious action of repression, and have acquired so lively a faith in the efficacy of my mode of treatment, that this agency cannot be excluded as a factor in any success I may have. In my earlier work, however, I certainly had no such faith, and advised the discontinuance of repression with the utmost diffidence. Faith on the part of the patient may, however, be present even when the physician is diffident. It is of more importance that several of the patients had been under my care for some time without improvement until it was discovered that they were repressing painful experience. It was only when the repression ceased that improvement began.

Definite evidence against the influence of suggestion is provided by the case in which the dream of the mangled friend came to lose its horror, this state being replaced by the far more bearable emotion of grief. The change which followed the cessation of repression in this case could not have been suggested by me, for its possibility had not, so far as I am aware, entered my mind. So far as suggestions, witting or unwitting, were given, these would have had the form that the nightmares would cease altogether, and the change in the affective character of the dream, not having been anticipated by myself, can hardly have been communicated to the patient. It is, of course, possible that my own belief in the improvement which would follow the adoption of my advice acted in a general manner by bringing the agencies of faith and suggestion into action, but these agencies can hardly have produced the specific and definite form which the improvement took. In other of the cases I have recorded, faith and suggestion probably played some part, that of the officer with the sudden and overwhelming attacks of depression being especially open to the possibility of these influences.

Such complicating factors as I have just considered can no more be excluded in this than in any other branch of therapeutics, but I am confident that their part is small beside that due to stopping a course of action whereby patients were striving to carry out an impossible task. In some cases faith and suggestion, re-education and sharing troubles with another, undoubtedly form the chief agents in the removal or amendment of the symptoms of neurosis, but in the cases I have recorded there can be little doubt that they contributed only in a minor degree to the success which attended the giving up of repression.

Before I conclude, a few words must be said about an aspect of my subject to which I have not so far referred. When treating officers or men suffering from war-neurosis, we have not only to think of the restoration of the patient to health, we have also to consider the question of fitness for military service. It is necessary to consider briefly the relation of the prescription of repression to this aspect of military medical practice.

When I find that a soldier is definitely practising repression, I am accustomed to ask him what he thinks is likely to happen if one who has sedulously kept his mind from all thoughts of war, or from special memories of warfare, should be confronted with the reality, or even with such continual reminders of its existence as must inevitably accompany any form of military service at home. If, as often happens in the case of officers, the patient is keenly anxious to remain in the Army, the question at once brings home to him the futility of the course of action he has been pursuing. The deliberate and systematic repression of all thoughts and memories of war by a soldier can have but one result when he is again faced by the realities of warfare.

Several of the officers whose cases I have described or mentioned in this paper were enabled to return to some form of military duty with a degree of success very unlikely if they had persisted in the process of repression. In other cases, either because the repression had been so long continued or for some other reason, return to military duty was deemed inexpedient. Except in one of these cases, no other result could have been expected with any form of treatment. The exception to which I refer is that of the patient who had the sudden attacks of reasonless depression. This officer had a healthy appearance, and would have made light of his disabilities at a Medical Board. He would certainly have been returned to duty and sent to France. The result of my line of treatment was to produce a state of anxiety which led to his leaving the Army. This result, however, is far more satisfactory than that which would have followed his return to active service, for he would inevitably have broken down under the first stress of warfare, and might have produced some disaster by failure in a critical situation or lowered the morale of his unit by committing suicide.

In conclusion, I must again mention a point to which reference was made at the beginning of this paper. Because I advocate the facing of painful memories, and deprecate the ostrich-like policy of attempting to banish them from the mind, it must not be thought that I recommend the concentration of the thoughts on such memories. On the contrary, in my opinion it is just as harmful to dwell persistently upon painful memories or anticipations, and brood upon feelings of regret and shame, as to attempt to banish them wholly from the mind. It is necessary to be explicit on this matter when dealing with patients. In a recent case in which I neglected to do so, the absence of any improvement led me to inquire into the patient's method of following my advice, and I found that, thinking he could not have too much of a good thing, he had substituted for the system of repression he had followed before coming under my care, one in which he spent the whole day talking, reading, and thinking of war. He even spent the interval between dinner and going to bed in reading a book dealing with warfare. There are also some victims of neurosis, especially the very young, for whom the horrors of warfare seem to have a peculiar fascination, so that when the opportunity presents itself they cannot refrain from talking by the hour about war experiences, although they know quite well that it is bad for them to do so. Here, as in so many other aspects of the treatment of neurosis, we have to steer a middle course. Just as we prescribe moderation in exercise, moderation at work and play, moderation in eating, drinking, and smoking, so is moderation necessary in talking, reading, and thinking about war experience. Moreover, we must not be content merely to advise our patients to give up repression, we must help them by every means in our power to overcome the difficulties which are put in their way by enfeebled volition, and by the distortion of their experience due to its having for long been seen exclusively from some one point of view. It is only by a process of prolonged re-education that it becomes possible for the patient to give up the practice of repressing war experience.

Notes

1. Read at a meeting of the Section of Psychiatry, Royal Society of Medicine, December 4, 1917; published in the *Proceedings of the Royal Society of Medicine,* 1918, vol. xi. (Section of Psychiatry), pp. 1–17. See also *Lancet,* vol. 194 (1918), p. 173.
2. This term is used here in a wider sense than that adopted in this book.

Appendix B

Biographies

Richard Aldington (1892–1962) was an Imagist poet and was married to Hilda Doolittle (H. D.). He was also a novelist, biographer, and critic. He often wrote scathingly about the hypocrisy he saw in modern society.

Henri Barbusse (1873–1935) began his writing career as a Neo-symbolist poet, but is best known for his novels. After the war, Barbusse devoted himself and his writing to social causes. He embraced the peace movement and communism.

Marc Léopold Benjamin Bloch (1886–1944) was a French historian whose interdisciplinary approach to history revolutionized the twentieth century field of study. He served in the French infantry from 1914 to 1919 and was awarded the Croix de Guerre and the Legion of Honor for his bravery. His books include *The Royal Touch: Sacred Monarchy and Scrofula in England and France, French Rural History: An Essay on Its Basic Characteristics,* and *Feudal Society.* A member of the French Resistance during the Second World War, Bloch was captured and shot by the Nazis.

Charles Edmund Blunden (1896–1974) was an English poet, scholar, and critic. His works include *Poems, Pastorals: A Book of Verses,* and critical studies of Hardy, Hunt, Lamb, and Shelley.

Vera Brittain (1896–1970), an Englishwoman, was the author of twenty-nine books. In 1915 she gave up her studies at Oxford to serve as a nurse. Both her fiancé and brother were killed in the war.

Rupert Brooke (1887–1915) died of septicemia induced by sunstroke while in transit to Gallipoli. Handsome and talented, Brooke became a symbol of idealized youth slaughtered by the war. The author of *Poems,* he is best remembered for the sequence of sonnets *1914.* Brooke's war poems are patriotic, and it is interesting to speculate on what may have become of his talent had he arrived at and survived the failed Gallipoli campaign.

Horace Bruckshaw (1891–1917) studied to be an architect. He became a member of the local unit of the Territorials (B Company of the 4th King's Shropshire Light) and attended their training camps. Like so many others, Bruckshaw volunteered in 1914 at the outbreak of the war. He enlisted in the Plymouth Battalion of the Royal Marines Light Infantry. Oddly, Bruckshaw remained a private although he served for three years at Gallipoli, Salonika, and on the western front. He was killed in France during the Battle of Arleaux, which was known to the Royal Marines as the Capture of Gavrelle Windmill.

May Wedderburn Cannan (1893–1973) was a poet and novelist. She served in the Voluntary Aid Detachment and in the Intelligence Service during the war.

Guy Patterson Chapman (1889–1972) was an editor, biographer, and historian. He is the author of *The Dreyfuss Case: A Reassessment* and *The Third Republic of France: The First Phase.*

Alan Clark (1926–) was educated at Eton and Oxford and served in the Royal Air Force. His works include *The Fall of Crete* and *Barbarossa: The Russo-German Conflict, 1941–45.*

Margaret Postgate Cole (1893–1980) was the author of several books, some with her husband, D. H. Cole. Cole was politically active and engaged in questions of education.

Roland Dorgelès (1886–1973; pseudonym of Roland Lecavelé) was trained as an architect. He served at the front for four years and was seriously wounded. He wrote novels, criticism, and travel literature.

Georges Duhamel (1884–1966; pseudonym of Denis Thévenin) wrote poetry, plays, and literary criticism. He is best known for his novel cycles, *Vie et Aventures de Salavin* and *Chronique des Pasquier.* Duhamel was trained as a surgeon and served in the French medical corps.

Geoff Dyer (1958–) is the author of *Ways of Telling* and *The Colour of Memory.* His essays and reviews have appeared in numerous periodicals.

Eleanor Farjeon (1881–1965) was the author of children's stories whose audience included adults, as well.

Timothy Findley (1930–) was born in Toronto. A novelist and short-story writer, he is the author of *Famous Last Words, Not Wanted on the Voyage, The Last of the Crazy People,* and *Stones.*

Paul Fussell (1924–) was educated at Harvard. He served as an infantry officer in the U.S. Army in Europe during World War II. He is the author of several books, including *Wartime* and *The Great War and Modern Memory.*

Robert Graves (1895–1985) was a poet, classical scholar, and novelist. He is the author of *The White Goddess; I, Claudius; Claudius the God;* and *Collected Poems.* Seriously wounded during the Battle of the Somme, Graves wrote poetry as he recovered. A friend of Sassoon's, Graves intervened to save Sassoon's reputation after his public denouncement of the war. Graves's visit with Sassoon at the Craiglockhart Hospital is fictionalized in *Regeneration,* by Pat Barker.

Ivor Gurney (1890–1937) has often been labeled a "local" poet because of his evocation of his native Gloucestershire. However, Gurney, in his war poetry, came to write of the particularized soldier and his experience in ways quite unlike the works of Sassoon and Owen. Gurney was also a musician and composer. Mentally unbalanced from before the war, Gurney was placed in an asylum for the last fifteen years of his life.

Thomas Hardy (1840–1928) was one of England's greatest novelists and poets. He is the author of *Return of the Native, The Mayor of Casterbridge, Tess of the D'Urbervilles,* and *Jude the Obscure.*

Aubrey Herbert (1880–1923) was an Orientalist, linguist, and member of Parliament.

Alistair Horne (1925–), a historian, was educated at Cambridge. He served with the Royal Air Force during World War II, and, later, in the Coldstream Guards. *The Price of Glory* is part of a trilogy that also includes *The Fall of Paris* and *To Lose a Battle,* which combine to form a history of France from 1870 to 1940.

Ernst Jünger (1895–1998) was a novelist and essayist. As a young man, Jünger was a fervent militarist, but later became an advocate of peace and European union. During the Nazi period in Germany, Jünger served as a Captain, but he refused Hitler's courting. Jünger was wounded twenty times on the western front. His writings include *On the Marble Clifts, The Glass Bees,* and *Aladdin's Problem.*

Rudyard Kipling (1865–1936) was best known — through his short stories, novels, and poems — as a champion of British imperialism. He is the author of *Plain Tales from the Hills, Barrack-Room Ballads, Just So Stories, Kim,* and *The Jungle Book.* Kipling's attitude toward World War I changed when his son, John, was reported missing at the Battle of Loos in 1915, one of the earliest casualties (his son's grave remained unknown until 1992). Kipling undertook to write the story of his son's regiment in *The Irish Guards in the Great War: The First Battalion,* considered by many to be a masterpiece. Kipling was awarded the Nobel Prize for Literature in 1907. It is Kipling who provided the epitaph found on the countless graves of unidentified soldiers: "A Soldier of the Great War Known Unto God."

Cecil Lewis (1898–1997) joined the Royal Flying Corps at the age of 16 and a half and survived three tours of duty on the western front. After the war, he continued with his interest in aviation. Lewis was a founder of the British Broadcasting Corporation (BBC) and worked for the United Nations. He wrote for both the stage and screen. His autobiography is entitled *Never Look Back.*

Lyn Macdonald (1934–) resigned her position as a BBC producer in 1973 to devote herself to full-time research and writing on World War I. Her books include *1914: The First Months of Fighting, They Called It Passchendaele, The Roses of No Man's Land,* and *Somme.*

Frederic Manning (1887–1935), born in Australia, came to England and wrote poetry. He served in France and Ireland and left the army before the end of the war. *The Middle Parts of Fortune* was first issued in a private release by Peter Davies, and the author was listed only as Private 19022, Manning's serial number. An expurgated edition, *Her Privates We,* was later issued.

John McCrae (1872–1918), a Canadian, was an officer and medical doctor in France. He was the author of many poems and of several medical texts. "In Flanders Fields" is one of the most popular poems to come out of the war.

Charlotte Mew (1869–1928) was a poet of small but impressive work. Poor and in ill health, she was awarded a pension based on the support of Thomas Hardy, John Masefield, and Walter de la Mare.

Millicent, Duchess of Sutherland (1867–1955), was the eldest daughter of the fourth Earl of Rosslyn. She joined the French Red Cross and traveled to Belgium with an ambulance. She was awarded the Croix de Guerre and the Belgian Red Cross First Class. After the war she was involved in work that benefited the handicapped.

Alan Moorehead (1910–83), born in Australia, became a journalist and author. He was educated at Melbourne University. His books include *The White Nile, The Blue Nile,* and his memoirs, *A Late Education.*

R. H. Mottram (1883–1971) was a novelist, poet, biographer, and autobiographer. He went into the trenches in 1915 but was recalled because his fluency in French was a valuable asset for settling disputes between the military and French civilians over billeting. These events provided him with the material for his *Spanish Farm Trilogy, 1914–1918: The Spanish Farm; Sixty-Four, Ninety-Four;* and *The Crime at the Vanderlynden's.* This trilogy is considered one of the best literary works to come out of the war.

Wilfred Owen (1893–1918) was one of the most famous of the war poets. His poetry is full of the waste and savagery of war. Invalided to the famous Craiglockhart mental hospital near Edinburgh, he met Siegfried Sassoon there. Sassoon's commentary on Owen's poetry changed the poet's concept. Their relationship is described in Pat Barker's trilogy of the war. Returning to the front, Owen was killed a week before the Armistice. His family did not receive the news until the bells were ringing in celebration of the end of the war on November 11, 1918.

Max Plowman (1883–1941) first published his memoir under the pseudonym Mark VII (a designation of rifle cartridges). Plowman was the editor of *The Adelphi* for many years. He wrote poetry as well as *War and the Creative Impulse* and *The Faith Called Pacifism.*

Herbert Read (1893–1968) was a poet, literary critic, educator, and autobiographer. He is best known for his advocacy of modern art in Britain. He was knighted in 1953. When W. B. Yeats decided against including the World War I poetry of Owen and Rosenberg in the 1936 edition of *The Oxford Book of Modern Verse,* he did include Read's poem "The End of the War."

Erich Maria Remarque (1898–1970) was drafted into the German Army at the age of 18. His novel *All Quiet on the Western Front* was an immediate success that shocked the patriotic public. It has come to be the single most universally known work to emerge from the war. Remarque married film star Paulette Goddard and continued to write. His works were banned by the Nazis.

William Hulse Rivers Rivers (1864–1922) was an anthropologist and psychiatrist whose works were of importance in both disciplines. He is best known for *The Todas* and *The History of Melanesian Society*. Rivers did much to encourage psychoanalytic theory in Britain. While on the staff at Craiglockhart Hospital outside of Edinburgh during the war, Rivers treated Wilfred Owen and Siegfried Sassoon for shell shock, a battlefield condition ignored or dismissed by many. Rivers's treatment is best captured by Pat Barker in her World War I trilogy.

Isaac Rosenberg (1890–1918) was an artist trained at the Slade School of Art. His poetry writing began with his experiences in the trenches. Some have remarked that his "Break of Day in the Trenches" is the finest poem of the war.

Siegfried Sassoon (1886–1967) was a poet and novelist. Sassoon was wounded twice during the war. His antiwar poetry and public statement denouncing the war were explained by some as products of neurosis due to his wounding. For a time after he issued his statement, Sassoon was treated at Craiglockhart sanitorium by Dr. Rivers. While there, Sassoon met with his old friend Robert Graves and influenced another antiwar poet, Wilfred Owen. Sassoon published Owen's poetry after Owen was killed in combat. Sassoon's works include *Collected Poems, The Path to Peace,* and *Siegfried's Journey.*

Alan Seeger (1881–1916) was an American poet whose attitudes toward the war tied him more closely to Rupert Brooke than Wilfred Owen. Seeger died on July 4, 1916, during the Battle of the Somme. Seeger fought with the French Foreign Legion.

Edith Sitwell (1887–1964) was the sister of Sacheverell and Osbert. Known early for her stylistic devices, later, during World War II, her poetry gained recognition for its depth and concern for the human condition.

Charles Hamilton Sorley (1895–1915) died early in the war; however, he had already distanced himself in attitude from Rupert Brooke. He is considered by some to be the last of the Great War poets to be recognized for the power of his work. The poem "When you see millions of the mouthless dead" was found in his kit.

August Stramm (1874–1915) was a poet and dramatist. Stramm's work often took an extremely expressionistic form, and he is considered one of the most innovative poets of the war. He was killed on the Russian Front.

Herbert Sulzbach (1894–1985) volunteered for the army in 1914 and twice won the Iron Cross. His Jewish ancestry forced him to leave Nazi Germany. He was later interned on the Isle of Man. He was commissioned as a British officer in 1945. Much of his postwar life was spent promoting Anglo-German relations. In 1978 he won the Franco-German Paix L'Europe.

Georg Trakl (1887–1914) from an early date led a life of dissipation. He drank, drugged himself, and talked often of suicide. His first book of poems appeared in 1913. Trakl served as a medical orderly in the Austrian army. Put in charge of the wounded after the battle of Grodek, Trakl ran out of medicine and saw a soldier shoot himself. Trakl's poetry would influence Rilke. The poems were translated by Lucia Cordell Getsi.

Barbara Tuchman (1912–89), a historian, was awarded the Pulitzer Prize for history for *The Guns of August* and *Stillwell and the American Experience in China, 1911–1945*. She covered the Spanish Civil War for *The Nation* in 1937. She taught at the U.S. Naval War College and at Harvard.

Giuseppe Ungaretti (1888–1970) was an Italian poet whose poetry was very influential. He founded the Hermetic movement. His first volume of poetry was written on the battlefield. The poems were translated by Allen Mandelbaum.

Edward Campion Vaughan (1897–1931) served in the Royal Warwickshire Regiment. The manuscript of his diary arrived in the offices of Leo Cooper Publishers in 1981. It had lain neglected in a storage cupboard. Vaughan participated in some of the major battles on the western front. On November 4, 1918, he captured a bridge across the Sambre Canal and was awarded the Military Cross. Wilfred Owen was killed the same day trying to cross the same canal. Vaughan never wrote any other work.

Arthur Graeme West (1891–1917) came under the influence of C. E. M. Joad from their days at boarding school. Their relationship continued at Oxford. West was interested in poetry and in the writings of George Bernard Shaw and H. G. Wells. Joad, who came into possession of West's diary, reconstructed it purposely to paint a portrait of a young Englishman destroyed by the war before he actually died in combat. At the time of his editing, Joad was an atheist and pacifist. West was one of the first realistic poets of the war, and his diary is one of the earliest records of disillusionment.

Denis Winter (1940–) studied history at Pembroke College, Cambridge. He taught school for twenty years in London. *Death's Men: Soldiers of the Great War* is his first book. He is also the author of *Haig's Command: A Reassessment.*

Francis Brett Young (1884–1954) was a poet and novelist. He is the author of *The Dark Tower, My Brother Jonathan,* and *A Man About the House. Marching on Tanga: With General Smuts in East Africa* is considered by many to be one of the true literary gems to come out of World War I.

Appendix C

Further Suggested Works

Many of the works below provided factual information used in preparing this anthology.

Alverdes, Paul. *The Whistlers' Room*. New York: Covici, Friede, 1930.

Asprey, Robert B. *The First Battle of the Marne*. Philadelphia: J. B. Lippincott Co., 1962.

Beesly, Patrick. *Room 40: British Naval Intelligence, 1914–18*. New York: Harcourt, Brace, Jovanovich, 1982.

Bergonzi, Bernard. *Heroes' Twilight: A Study of the Literature of the Great War*. London: Macmillan, 1965.

Blunden, Edmund. *The Mind's Eye: Essays*. Freeport, N.Y.: Books for Libraries Press, 1967.

Bracco, Rosa Maria. *Merchants of Hope: British Middlebrow Writers and the First World War, 1919–1939*. Providence, R.I.: Berg, 1993.

Britten, Benjamin. *War Requiem, Opus 66*. London: Boosey and Hawkes, 1963.

Buchan, John. *Greenmantle*. Ware, England: Wordsworth Editions, 1994.

Buitenhuis, Peter. *The Great War of Words: British, American, and Canadian Propaganda and Fiction, 1914–1933*. Vancouver: University of British Columbia Press, 1987.

Carossa, Hans. *A Roumanian Diary*. Trans. Agnes Neill Scott. London: Martin Secker, 1929.

Carrington, Charles. *Soldier from the Wars Returning*. Aldershot, England: Gregg Revivals, 1991.

———. *A Subaltern's War*. New York: Arno Press, 1972.

Clark, Reverend Andrew. *Echoes of the Great War: The Diary of Reverend Andrew Clark, 1914–1919*. Oxford: Oxford University Press, 1985.

Cobb, Humphrey. *Paths of Glory*. New York: Viking Press, 1935.

Cobley, Evelyn. *Representing War: Form and Ideology in First World War Narratives*. Toronto: University of Toronto Press, 1993.

Cochrane, Peter. *Simpson and the Donkey: The Making of a Legend*. Melbourne: Melbourne University Press, 1992.

Cross, Tim, ed. *The Last Voices of World War I: An International Anthology of Writers, Poets, & Playwrights*. Iowa City: University of Iowa Press, 1988.

cummings, e. e. *The Enormous Room*. New York: Modern Library, 1934.

Davis, Richard Harding. *With the French in France & Salonika*. London: Duckworth and Co., 1916.

Dawn Patrol. Directed by Edmund Goulding. Fox, MGM, 1938.

De Houthulst, Willy Coppens. *Days on the Wing*. New York: Arno Press, 1980.

Douie, Charles. *The Weary Road: Recollections of a Subaltern of Infantry*. Stevenage, England: The Strong Oak Press, 1988.

Dunn, Captain J. C. *The War the Infantry Knew, 1914–1919*. London: Abacus, 1987.

Evelyn, Princess Blücher. *An English Wife in Berlin: A Private Memoir of Events, Politics, and Daily Life in Germany Throughout the War and the Social Revolution of 1918*. New York: E. P. Dutton and Co., 1920.

Farwell, Byron. *The Great War in Africa, 1914–1918*. New York: W. W. Norton, 1986.

Gallipoli. Directed by Peter Weir. Associated R & R Films, 1981.

Genno, Charles N., and Heinz Wetzel, eds. *The First World War in German Narrative Prose*. Toronto: University of Toronto Press, 1980.

Glover, Jon, and Jon Silkin, eds. *The Penguin Book of First World War Prose*. London: Viking, 1989.

Grand Illusion. Directed by Jean Renoir. Compagnie Jean Renoir, 1938.

Gray, Randal, ed. *Chronicle of the First World War*. 2 Vols. Oxford: Facts on File, 1990, 1991.

Graziano, Frank. *Georg Trakl: A Profile*. Durango, Colo.: Logbridge-Rhodes, 1983.

Guns of August. Created and produced by Nathan Kroll. Universal, 1965.

Harries, Meirion, and Susie Harries. *The Last Days of Innocence: America at War, 1917–1918*. New York: Random House, 1997.

Herwig, Holger H. *The First World War: Germany and Austria-Hungary, 1914–1918*. London: Arnold, 1997.

Holmes, Richard. *Army Battlefield Guide: Belgium and Northern France*. London: Her Majesty's Stationery Office, 1995.

Hopkirk, Peter. *Like Hidden Fire: The Plot to Bring Down the British Empire*. New York: Kodansha, 1994.

Ivelaw-Chapman, John. *The Riddles of Wipers: An Appreciation of the Trench Journal "The Wipers Times."* London: Leo Cooper, 1997.

Kipling, Rudyard. *The Irish Guards in the Great War: The First Battalion*. New York: Sarpedon, 1997.

Lawrence, T. E. *Selected Letters of T. E. Lawrence.* Ed. David Garnett. London: World Books, 1938.

Life and Nothing But [La Vie est Rien d'Autre]. Directed by Bertrand Travier. Orion, 1989.

The Lighthorsemen. Directed by Simon Wincer. Evergreen Entertainment, 1987.

MacFarlane, David. *Come from Away: Memory, War, and the Search for a Family's Past.* New York: Poseidon Press, 1991.

Mackenzie, Compton. *Gallipoli Memories.* London: Cassell and Co., 1929.

Mee, Charles L., Jr. *The End of Order: Versailles, 1919.* New York: E. P. Dutton, 1980.

Michelin Illustrated Guides to the Battlefields: Battlefields of the Marne. Milltown, N.J.: Michelin, 1919.

Michelin Illustrated Guides to the Battlefields: Rheims. Milltown, N.J.: Michelin, 1920.

Michelin Illustrated Guides to the Battlefields: Ypres. Milltown, N.J.: Michelin, 1920.

Onions, John. *English Fiction and Drama of the Great War, 1918–1939.* London: Macmillan, 1990.

O'Shea, Stephen. *Back to the Front: An Accidental Historian Walks the Trenches of World War I.* New York: Walker and Co., 1996.

Ouditt, Sharon. *Fighting Forces, Writing Women: Identity and Ideology in the First World War.* London: Routledge, 1994.

Laffin, John. *Panorama of the Western Front.* London: Grange Books, 1996.

Parfitt, George. *Fiction of the First World War: A Study.* London: Faber and Faber, 1988.

Paths of Glory. Directed by Stanley Kubrick. MGA/UA, 1957.

Pollard, A. F. *A Short History of the Great War.* New York: Harcourt, Brace and Howe, 1920.

Prior, Robin, and Trevor Wilson. *Passchendaele: The Untold Story.* New Haven: Yale University Press, 1996.

Sassoon, Siegfried. *Diaries, 1915–1918.* London: Faber and Faber, 1983.

Scott, Emmett J. *Scott's Official History of the American Negro in the World War.* New York: Arno Press, 1969.

Simkins, Peter. *Chronicles of the Great War: The Western Front, 1914–1918.* London: CLB, 1997.

Spears, Major-General Sir Edward. *Liaison 1914: A Narrative of the Great Retreat.* New York: Stein and Day, 1968.

Stallings, Laurence, ed. *The First World War: A Photographic History.* New York: Simon and Schuster, 1933.

Strachan, Hew, ed. *World War I: A History.* Oxford: Oxford University Press, 1998.

Stokesbury, James L. *A Short History of World War I.* New York: William Morrow and Co., 1981.

Swann, Thomas Burnett. *The Ungirt Runner: Charles Hamilton Sorley, Poet of World War I.* Hamden, Conn.: Archon Books, 1965.

Terraine, John. *Mons: The Retreat to Victory.* London: Leo Cooper, 1991.

Thomason, John W. *"Fix Bayonets!" and Other Stories.* New York: Charles Scribner's Sons, 1970.

Tuchman, Barbara W. *The Proud Tower: A Portrait of the World before the War, 1890–1914.* New York: Ballantine, 1996.

The Two Battles of the Marne: The Stories of Marshal Joffre, General Von Ludendorff, Marshal Foch, Crown Prince Wilhelm. New York: Cosmopolitan Book Corporation, 1927.

Webb, Barry. *Edmund Blunden: A Biography.* New Haven: Yale University Press, 1990.

The Wipers Times. London: Peter Davies, 1973.

York, Dorothea, ed. *Mud and Stars: An Anthology of World War Songs and Poems.* New York: Henry Holt and Co., 1931.

Ypres, 1914: An Official Account Published by Order of the German General Staff. Nashville: Battery Press, 1994.

Zweig, Arnold. *The Case of Sergeant Grischa.* Trans. Eric Sutton. New York: Viking Press, 1929.

Bibliography

Many of the books from which excerpts were taken also provided factual information used throughout this anthology; introductory material was often beneficial in this regard.

Aldington, Richard. *The Death of a Hero*. London: Chatto and Windus, 1929; reprint, London: Hogarth Press, 1984.

Barbusse, Henri. *Under Fire: The Story of a Squad*. Trans. William Fitzwater Wray. London: J. M. Dent, 1917.

Barker, Pat. *The Eye in the Door*. New York: Plume, 1995.

——. *The Ghost Road*. New York: Dutton, 1995.

——. *Regeneration*. New York: Plume, 1993.

Beaver, Patrick, ed. *The Wipers Times*. London: Peter Davies, 1973.

Bloch, Marc. *Memoirs of War, 1914–1915*. Trans. Carole Fink. Ithaca, N.Y., and London: Cornell University Press, 1980; reprint, New York: Cambridge University Press, 1991.

Blunden, Edmund. *Undertones of War*. London: Richard Cobden-Sanderson, 1928.

Brittain, Vera. *Testament of Youth: An Autobiographical Study of the Years 1900–1925*. New York: Macmillan, 1933.

Brooke, Rupert. "The Soldier." Faber and Faber, Ltd., n.d.

Brown, Malcolm. *The Imperial War Museum Book of The First World War*. Norman: University of Oklahoma Press, 1993.

Bruckshaw, Horace. *The Diaries of Private Horace Bruckshaw, 1915–1916*. Edited by Martin Middlebrook. London: Scolar Press, 1979.

Cannan, May Wedderburn. *In War Time*. Oxford: B. H. Blackwell, 1917.

Cecil, Hugh. *The Flower of Battle: British Writers of the First World War*. London: Secker and Warburg, 1995.

Cecil, Hugh, and Peter H. Liddle. *Facing Armageddon: The First World War Experienced*. London: Leo Cooper, 1996.

Chapman, Guy. *A Passionate Prodigality: Fragments of an Autobiography*. London: Ivor Nicholson and Watson, Ltd., 1933.

Clark, Alan. *The Donkeys*. London: Pimlico, 1996.

Cole, Margaret Postgate. *Poems*. London: George Allen and Unwin, Ltd., 1918.

Dorgelès, Roland. *Wooden Crosses*. New York: G. P. Putnam's Sons, 1921.

Duhamel, Georges. *Civilization, 1914–1917.* Trans. E. S. Brooks. New York: The Century Co., 1919.

Dyer, Geoff. *The Missing of the Somme.* London: Penguin, 1995.

Eksteins, Modris. *Rites of Spring: The Great War and the Birth of the Modern Age.* London: Black Swan, 1990.

Farjeon, Eleanor. *First and Second Love.* Oxford: Oxford University Press, 1959.

Faulks, Sebastian. *Birdsong.* New York: Vintage International, 1993.

Findley, Timothy. *The Wars.* Toronto: Clarke Irwin and Co., 1977; London: Penguin, 1978.

Fussell, Paul. *The Great War and Modern Memory.* New York: Oxford University Press, 1977.

Gilbert, Martin. *Atlas of World War I.* New York: Oxford University Press, 1994.

Graves, Robert. *Good-bye to All That.* New York: Doubleday, 1985.

Gurney, Ivor. *Collected Poems of Ivor Gurney.* Oxford: Oxford University Press, 1982.

Hardy, Thomas. "Channel Firing." In *The Complete Poems.* Ed. James Gibson. New York: Macmillan, 1976.

Hart, Captain B. H. Liddell. *The Real War: 1914–1918.* Boston: Little, Brown and Co., 1930.

Haythornthwaite, Philip J. *A Photohistory of World War One.* London: Arms and Armour Press, 1995.

———. *The World War One Source Book.* London: Arms and Armour Press, 1996.

Hemingway, Ernest. *A Farewell to Arms.* New York: Scribner's, 1957.

Herbert, Aubrey. *Mons, Anzac & Kut.* London: Edward Arnold, 1919.

Hill, Susan. *Strange Meeting.* Boston: David R. Godine, 1992.

Horne, Alistair. *The Price of Glory: Verdun 1916.* New York: St. Martin's Press, 1963.

Jünger, Ernst. *The Storm of Steel: From the Diary of a German Storm-Troop Officer on the Western Front.* Trans. Basil Creighton. New York: Howard Fertig, 1975.

Kipling, Rudyard. "Gethsemane." In *The Penguin Book of First World War Poetry.* Edited by Jon Silkin. London: Allen Lane/Penguin Books, Ltd., 1979.

Lewis, Cecil. *Sagittarius Rising.* New York: Harcourt, Brace and Co., 1936; reprint, Harrisburg, Pa.: Stackpole, 1963.

McCrae, John. "In Flanders Fields." In *The Penguin Book of First World War Poetry.* Edited by Jon Silkin. London: Allen Lane/Penguin Books, Ltd., 1979.

Macdonald, Lyn. *Somme.* London: Michael Joseph, 1983; reprint, London: Penguin, 1993.

Manning, Frederic. *The Middle Parts of Fortune.* New York: New American Library, 1979.

Marshall, S. L. A. *World War I.* Boston: Houghton Mifflin Co., 1987.

Mew, Charlotte. *Collected Poems.* London: Gerald Duckworth and Co., 1953.

Moorehead, Alan. *Gallipoli.* New York: Harper and Brothers, 1956; reprint, New York: Ballantine Books, 1996.

Mottram, R. H. *The Spanish Farm.* New York: The Dial Press, 1927.

Moynihan, Michael, ed. *A Place Called Armageddon: Letters from the Great War.* London: David and Charles, 1975.

Owen, Wilfred. *The Poems of Wilfred Owen.* Ed. Jon Stallworthy. London: Chatto and Windus, 1990.

Plowman, Max. *A Subaltern on the Somme in 1916.* New York: E. P. Dutton, 1928.

Read, Herbert. *Ambush.* New York: Haskell House Publishers, Ltd., 1974.

Reilly, Catherine W., ed. *Scars Upon My Heart: Women's Poetry and Verse of the First World War.* London: Virago Press, Ltd., 1981.

Remarque, Erich Maria. *All Quiet on the Western Front.* Trans. A. W. Wheen. Boston: Little, Brown and Co., 1929.

Rivers, W. H. R. *Instinct and Unconscious.* London: Cambridge University Press, 1922.

Rosenberg, Isaac. *The Collected Works of Isaac Rosenberg.* Ed. Ian Parsons. London: Chatto and Windus, 1979.

Sassoon, Siegfried. *Collected Poems of Siegfried Sassoon.* New York: E. P. Dutton, 1918.
———. *The Memoirs of George Sherston.* Harrisburg, Pa.: Stackpole Books, 1967.

Seeger, Alan. *Poems.* New York: Charles Scribner's Sons, 1917.

Sherriff, R. C. *Journey's End: A Play in Three Acts.* New York: Bretano's, 1929.

Silkin, Jon, ed. *The Penguin Book of First World War Poetry.* London: Allen Lane/Penguin Books, Ltd., 1979.

Sitwell, Edith. *Clown's Houses.* Oxford: B. H. Blackwell, 1918.

Sorley, Charles Hamilton. *The Collected Poems of Charles Hamilton Sorley.* Ed. Jean Moorcroft. London: Cecil Woolf, 1985.

Stramm, August. "Battlefield," "Grenades," "In the Firing," "Stormtaking," "War Grave," "Wounds." Trans. Lucia Cordell Getsi.

Sulzbach, Herbert. *With the German Guns: Four Years on the Western Front.* Trans. Richard Thonger. London: Leo Cooper, 1998.

Sutherland, Millicent, Duchess of. *Six Weeks at the War.* London: The Times, 1914.

Tapert, Annette, ed. *Despatches from the Heart: An Anthology of Letters from the Front During the First and Second World Wars.* London: Hamish Hamilton, 1984.

Taylor, A. J. P. *The First World War: An Illustrated History.* New York: Perigree Books, 1980.

Trakl, Georg. "Lament," "In the East," "Grodek." Trans. Lucia Cordell Getsi.

Tuchman, Barbara. *The Guns of August.* New York: Macmillan, 1962.

Ungaretti, Giuseppe. *Selected Poems of Giuseppe Ungaretti.* Trans. Allen Mandelbaum. Ithaca, N.Y.: Cornell University Press, 1975.

Vaughan, Edwin Campion. *Some Desperate Glory: The World War I Diary of a British Officer, 1917.* New York: Henry Holt and Co., 1981.

Wedd, A. F., trans. *German Students' War Letters.* Ed. Philipp Witkop. London: Methuen, 1929.

West, Arthur Graeme. *The Diary of a Dead Officer: Being the Posthumous Papers of Arthur Graeme West.* London: Imperial War Museum, 1991.

Williamson, Henry. *Chronicle of Ancient Sunlight.* London: Macdonald and Co., 1967.

Winter, Denis. *Death's Men: Soldiers of the Great War.* London: Allen Lane, 1978; London: Penguin, 1979.

Yeats, W. B., ed. *The Oxford Book of Modern Verse, 1892–1935.* New York: Oxford University Press, 1936.

Young, Francis Brett. *Marching on Tanga: With General Smuts in East Africa.* London: W. Collins Sons and Co., Ltd., 1917.